Representing the Cultural 'Other'

Japanese Anthropological Works on Korea

Representing the Cultural 'Other'
Japanese Anthropological Works on Korea

Chonnam National University Press
Gwangju 500-757
Republic of Korea

ISBN 978-89-6849-043-9 (93300)

First Printing: August 2013

Price: 20,000 won

CIP No. 2013015373

Representing the Cultural 'Other'

Japanese Anthropological Works on Korea

Edited by
Hyup Choi

Chonnam National University PRESS

■ Preface

Anthropology is often referred to as 'the study of other cultures.' Hence many foreign anthropologists have chosen Korea as their field of study. Among the foreign anthropologists who have studied Korea and Korean culture, Japanese anthropologists have been the dominant majority.

On account of geo-political reasons, Japan has a long history of studying the Korean peninsula. Most of the studies done before 1945 were carried out in connection with Japan's colonial expansion. To aid the colonial rule, the Japanese colonial government initiated various studies on Korean peninsula. At first, these were limited to studies on geography and natural resources, but were later expanded to include history, society, and culture. It is only in recent years that Korean anthropologists have shown some interests on these materials. The first visible sign of this interest was to be seen at the 34th annual meeting of The Korean Society for Cultural Anthropology held at KangWon National University during May 31 - June 1, 2002. At the meeting, a session was specifically assigned to examine the nature of socio-cultural studies done by Japanese anthropologists and folklorist during the Japanese occupation. The underlying assumption in this session was that the Japanese imperial power used anthropology for controlling and dominating Korea, then a colony of Imperial Japan.

Following the Second World War, the academic climate of Japan has changed. Since 1945, a new breed of anthropologists has been educated, and they have produced diverse and numerous anthropological studies concerning Korean culture and society. However, these numerous studies which have appeared since 1945 have never been the subject of systematic examination by Korean anthropologists, as most of such works were primarily circulated within Japanese academic circles. It is regrettable that no systematic attempt has been made to review and evaluate existing literature on Korean society and culture which was produced by the post-war generation of Japanese anthropology. Therefore, there is a critical need for research to examine these materials. The present book is a small step forward to deal with such research needs.

A group of anthropologists from Korea and Japan gathered during March 13-14, 2003 at Chonnam National University for a workshop entitled "Inter-cultural understanding through academic discipline of anthropology between Japan and Korea". This group exchanged ideas and opinions concerning the problem of cultural representation and the issues surrounding cultural understanding. After the workshop, some participants agreed to write a paper aiming at the examination and evaluation of Japanese anthropological studies on Korea. This volume contains the works of those anthropologists who kept their promises. The result includes five articles and an extensive bibliography of Japanese works on Korea.

Korean anthropologists, Hyup Choi and Kyung-soo Chun, focus their analysis on the colonial influence of Japan. As the disciplinary work of academicians should be considered as a part of socio-cultural products, the proper evaluation of the Japanese anthropological works during the colonial period inevitably invites consideration of colonial context. Kyung-soo Chun further deals with Japanese imperialism during the colonial era in relation with the discipline of ethnology - namely, anthropology in terms of methodology.

Three Japanese anthropologists, on the other hand, deal mainly with post-colonial Japanese anthropology of Korea. Abito Itoh's paper deals with Japanese anthropology in terms of theoretical and methodological orientations in studying Korean culture after World War II. Hiroshi Honda attempts a retrospective reading of *Chōsen nōson shakai tōsaki* (1944) written by Japanese sociologist Suzuki Eitarō so as to suggest other important research themes on the structure and composition of Korean local society. Honda's article presents a sort of reflexive point of view as a present-day Japanese ethnographer. Toshio Asakura's article is a comprehensive review of the books on Korea published after 1980 in Japan. He aims at identifying the aspects of Korean culture which have attracted a great deal of attention from Japanese intellectuals. Seiichi Matsumoto compiles a very extensive bibliography on Japanese publications concerning Korea in the fields of anthropology, ethnology, and folklore. Because of this comprehensive bibliography, this volume will serve as a good reference source book for those who are interested in any type of research concerning Japanese anthropological works on Korea.

This book is indebted to The Asia Research Fund as it provided financial assistance for the workshop held at Chonnam National University in 2003. Professors Mun-woong Lee and Kyung-gu Han who participated in the workshop also made indirect contributions through various discussions along the way. It is hoped that some of the theoretical and methodological issues raised by the authors in this volume will further stimulate more discussions among Korean and Japanese anthropologists, as it will certainly serve as a significant contribution to inter-cultural understanding through the academic discipline of anthropology between Japan and Korea.

June 3, 2013

Hyup Choi

■ Table of Contents

Japanese Colonial Context in the Early Making of Korean Anthropology

Hyup Choi
Chonnam National University

1. Introduction

Anthropology, from its beginning, has maintained the tradition of studying other culture. In doing so, anthropologists have long been considered their prime activity, specifically ethnography which has focused on structural depictions of culture, as an objective representation of other culture.

The issues surrounding cultural representation and/or misrepresentation have long been attracted various scholars' attention. Edward Said was one of the first notable scholars who added politico-economic dimension to the discussion by raising the issue of social construction of reality and entailed problem of representing others. In his seminal book *Orientalism* (1979), Said insisted that the East existed as the 'other' whose function was to define the West. According to him, the East is the construct of the Western ideas. His argument was powerful and convincing. Hence, many anthropologists have been concerned with the relationship of ethnographic representation to political and historical context. Especially, with the advent of postmodern anthropology, the construction of facts, history, and knowledge became a central issue. Postmodernists claim that all knowledge is relative, all voices are equal, therefore 'We' can only 'invent,' rather than more or less accurately come to know, the 'other.'

If Said and postmodern anthropologists are correct, representing Korean culture by foreign anthropologists entails objectifying Korea as the 'other.'

As a geographical field of interest, Korea has received very little attention by foreign anthropologists. However, there is one exception - Japanese. Japanese have accumulated large volume of research results on Korea since the beginning of the 20th century.

Japan has a long history of studying Korean peninsula. Most of the studies done before 1945 were carried out in connection with the Japanese colonial expansion in Korea. To aid the colonial rule, the Japanese colonial government initiated various studies on the Korean peninsula, at first, studies on geography and natural resources, and later on history, society, and culture.

The Japanese colonial empire was defeated in the Second World War, and the academic climate of Japan has changed. Since 1945, a new breed of anthropologists has been educated, and they have produced diverse and numerous anthropological studies concerning Korean culture and society. Considering the large amount of the works which has been accumulated by the succeeding generations of Japanese anthropologists, it is regrettable that no systematic attempt has been made to review and evaluate existing literature on Korean society and culture which was produced by Japanese anthropologists thus far.

A brief review of the relevant literature reveals that there are only several brief attempts to analyze and evaluate the studies on Korea carried out by the Japanese: Hyun-soo Park (1980, 1982), and Kyung-soo Chun (2002a, 2002b). Park who examined the colonial Japanese works on Korea concluded that Japanese imperialism, up until the end of World War II, mobilized ethnology (i.e., anthropology) and its methodology for governing the occupied Korea. Recently, Kyung-soo Chun wrote on the subject. In his paper (2002a) which was delivered at the 34th annual meeting of Korean Society for Cultural Anthropology, Chun examined the characteristics of the studies carried out by anthropologists at Keijo

Imperial University. Chun's another paper (2002b) also dealt with anthropological works of the colonial era: the title of his paper is "East Asian Multiculturalism and Imperialistic Centralization: Focusing on Japanese Ethnology in Histroy." Although these papers by Park and Chun are useful as they provide historical description of the Japanese activities during the colonial period, their focus of analysis is rather diffused and does not provide contextual explanation of the specified activities.

Considering the paucity of the studies which are concerned with the Japanese's works on Korea, there exists a certain research need to fill the gap. The purpose of this paper is to examine the nature and context of sociocultural studies done by the Japanese anthropologists and related personnels during the Japanese colonial era. The focus of my discussion will be limited to the situation before 1945, the year the Japanese colonial occupation ended.[1] Underlying assumption in this paper is that the Japanese imperial power used anthropology for controlling and dominating Korea, then a colony of Imperial Japan, and, such colonial circumstances provided a historical context within which Korean anthropology was born.

2. Anthropology and colonial encounter

Before we begin our discussion about how and when anthropology was introduced in Korea by Japanese, it is of utmost importance to consider the historical context in which such introduction was made: that of colonial invasion of Korea by Japanese. According to Asad, who pioneered study on the relationship between anthropology and colonialism, "imperial forces permitted anthropological studies to take place since the colonial power structure made the object of anthropological study accessible and safe - because of it sustained physical proximity between the observing European

1 Japanese works of post-colonial era will be examined by Professor Abito Itoh and Dr. Toshio Asakura, whose papers appear in this volume.

(*i.e., colonizer*)[2] and the living non-European (*i.e., colonized*) became a practical possibility"(1973: 19). Furthermore, Asad made another important point: "Anthropologists can claim to have contributed to the cultural heritage of the societies they study by a sympathetic recording of indigenous forms of life that would have been left to posterity. But they have also contributed, sometimes indirectly, towards maintaining the structure of power represented by the colonial system" (ibid., 17).[3] For this reason, looking through the eyes of the colonized, the word (anthropological) 'research' can be one of the dirtiest words in the indigenous world's vocabulary. Indeed, the way in which social studies under the banner of scientific research has been implicated in the worst excesses of imperialism remains a powerful remembered history for many of the world's colonized peoples. Thus, Linda Tuhiwai Smith, who is a leading theorist on decolonization of Maori, persuasively argued that anthropological (or scientific) researches "galls us that Western researchers and intellectuals can assume to know all that it is possible to know of us, on the basis of their brief encounters with some of us. It appalls us that the West can desire, extract and claim ownership of our ways of knowing, our imagery, the things we create and produce, and then simultaneously reject the people who created and developed those ideas and seek to deny them further opportunities to be creators of their own culture and own nations" (1999: 1). Then, it seems very clear, in any considerations regarding anthropological researches under colonial rule, "it is surely difficult to discuss it without understanding the complex ways in which the pursuit of knowledge is deeply embedded in the multiple layers of imperial and colonial practices" (ibid., 2). Korean experience during the late nineteenth and the early twentieth centuries provided

2 *Italics* by the present author.

3 Asad articulates what would later become a focal point in the discipline regarding the embedded structural relationship between anthropology and colonialism by situating this relationship within the power of worldwide political economy.

similar situation.

From the late nineteenth century, Japan sought to incorporate the Korean Peninsula into its expanding empire.[4] Japan, which had desired exclusive domination of the Korean peninsula, finally declared war on Russia in 1904, and dispatched two army divisions to Korea to occupy Seoul and other important locations as bases for their operations. Russo-Japanese war was ended in Japan's victory, thus, Japan was able to strengthen their military domination over Korean peninsula. In 1906, Japan set up a Bureau for the Governor-General in Seoul to manage not only Korea's diplomatic but internal affairs as well,[5] thereby extending the effects of the Japanese invasion to the police force and judiciary powers as well. In 1910, Japan finally took away Korea's, then, nominal sovereignty and turned Korea into a Japanese colony.

During the colonial period (1910-1945), Japan advertised as a national goal the assimilation of Koreans into the Japanese state. However, in reality, Japan's so called assimilation policy was in effect a policy designed to eradicate Korean culture by gradually replacing it with Japanese culture. It was, indeed, an attempt not merely to colonize but to Japanize Korea, and this could only be done by eliminating everything Korean (Caprio, 2009). Thus, for example, one of the first thing the Japanese Governor-General[6] ordered in 1910 was a nationwide search for books on Korean history and geography. The result of the search was that 200,000 to 300,000 books were confiscated and burned. Included in the proscription were

---

4 History records the period of Japanese occupation of Korean Peninsular as from 1910 to 1945. But that was the official history of Japanese rule in Korea. Actually, the Japanese government controlled everything in Korea since the Sino- Japanese War of 1894-95 (Vinacke, 1967: 143-144).

5 The first Governor-General was Ito Hirobumi, the mastermind and the archvillain behind the invasion.

6 The Governor-General was directly under the Japanese Emperor and exercised tremendous powers in the legislative, executive, and judiciary branches of government, and also possessed the authority of command over the army.

Korean history books, biographies of national heroes of earlier centuries, and Korean translations of foreign books relating to independence, the birth of the nation, revolution, etc. The colonial authority also prohibited public education related to the Korean language and Korean history. Then, in the later part of the 1930s, it became illegal to speak Korean in classrooms. Koreans were also forced to worship at Japanese Shinto shrines. Toward the end of colonial rule, in 1939, Koreans were even forced to change their names to Japanese names, and more than 80 percent of the Koreans complied with the name-change ordinance under the pressure.

In the mean time, Japanese authorities mobilized intellectuals so as to put serious amount of energy into activities justifying their colonial domination over Korea, working in every direction, international, domestic. Jimin Kim (2011) who examined the Japanese materials aimed at rationalizing their occupation of Korea vis a vis the international audience[7] concludes:

> Japan's English-language publications about Korea firstly intended to demonstrate to the world that Koreans were unfit to rule themselves and therefore could not participate as subjects in international terms, and that Japan had an inevitable burden of civilizing the country for the benefit of both countries.
>
> As there were almost no other English-language works about Korean history or society than publications by the Japanese government, Japan's English-language accounts about Korea were viewed as the most convincing

7 "To demonstrate that Japan was legitimately helping with the development and modernization of Korea, the Japanese government published English-language reports on the progress of Korea since the Japanese advance since the early 1900s. The most important English-language publication was *the Annual Reports on the Progress and Reforms in Korea*, which the Japanese authorities in Korea issued continuously from 1907 to until the end of colonial period. The obvious theme of the series was that Japan, a modern power, was improving Korea. The most striking aspect of the *Report* was that it — flaunted Japan's efforts in Korea as a wholly civilizing endeavor, a *mission civilisatrice*" (Kim, 2011: 33).

and trustworthy source of information about Korea. Based on Japan's publication about its rule in Korea, an editorial in an American journal, Nation, wrote that Japan was thoroughly developing Korea (p.33).

In addition, Japanese authority, from time to time, indirectly engaged in the process of historical distortion. One example would be that of engaging in the rewriting of Korean history. Historians employed at the Research Department of the Southern Manchurian Railroad Company were ordered, in effect, to distort Korean history. *The Historical Geography of Manchuria, Historical Geography of Korea,* and *Report of Geographical and Historical Research in Manchuria* are products of such historiography. In *The History of the Korean Peninsula* (1915), the Japanese limited the scope of Korean history to the peninsula, severing it from relations with the Asian continent.

Although we can enumerate endless list of such examples further, above mentioned circumstances would suffice to show the historical context in which anthropology was introduced in Korea.

3. Anthropology in Colonial Korea[8]

Anthropology, as a Western originated institution, was unknown discipline in Korea until the Japanese colonizer introduced it in the early 20th century. In nineteenth century, Japan was first to follow the steps of the Western modernization in East Asia. Meiji Japan was eager to learn and accept the Western science and scholarship, and a large number of Japanese scholars were sent to study in Europe and America. This naturally put Japan at the top of the list in East Asia, becoming a link

8 Parts of sections 3 and 4 were adopted from the author's paper which was presented at the International Symposium on "Locating Alternative Voices in Anthropology", held in Kolkata, India during November 19 through 23, 2011. The title of the paper was "Korean anthropology in historical perspective."

in the formation of any discipline, including anthropology in this region.

To facilitate the annexation process and colonial rule, anthropology was introduced and practiced in Korea by the Japanese colonizers during the early twentieth century, as it provided useful means of collecting necessary data for colonial rule. The most practical source-materials collected, even before the official annexation, were history/archaeological materials as well as informations which reveals socio-economic life conditions of Koreans. The Japanese colonial government used archaeology, a sub-division of anthropology, to claim Japan's ancient domination over Korean peninsula,[9] mobilized historians to distort Korean history, and carried out social survey to collect useful data for economic exploitation[10] and political domination. In sum, the Japanese colonialists

---

9 Japanese Imperialism intended to justify its colonialism by bringing out heteronomous features of Korea history. Thus, archaeological excavation projects, on Nakrang in northern part of Korea and Kaya in southern part of Korea, were given high priority by the Office of the Governor-General. It focused on the installation of Han Commandery in the north, and the archaeological proof of Mimana Nihonfu (任那日本府) in the south, which could be the foundation of its claim that Korea had been controlled by China and Japan since ancient times. Therefore, Pyongyang and Kimhae areas occupied the most important area in the historic spot investigation projects.

10 "Many Japanese settlers were interested in acquiring agricultural land in Korea even before Japanese land ownership was officially legalized in 1906. Governor-General Terauchi Masatake facilitated settlement through land reform. The Korean land ownership system was a complex system of absentee landlords, partial owner-tenants and cultivators with traditional (but no legal proof of) ownership. Terauchi's new Land Survey Bureau conducted cadastral surveys that reestablished ownership by basis of written proof (deeds, titles, and similar documents). Ownership was denied to those who could not provide such written documentation; these turned out to be mostly lower-class and partial owners who had only traditional verbal cultivator rights. This institutional change opened way for Japanese to own Korean farm land easily, i.e., enabling a huge amount of Korean land to be seized by the government and sold at subsidized costs to Japanese willing to settle in Korea as part of a larger effort at colonization. Japanese landlords included both individuals and corporations such as the Oriental Development Company. Many former Korean landowners as well as agricultural

used anthropology and other related disciplines not only to collect necessary data on Korean's life conditions but also to create a false image of the backward state of Korean society and culture, because it was an utmost necessity to find a logic that can justify their taking over of neighboring country. A sample of the works produced by the Japanese during the early period of colonial rule which might have some relevance with the matter mentioned above were as follows: *A Study on Korean Society* (1910) by Japanese Military Police Headquarters in Korea; *History of Korean Religions* (1911) by Aoyagi; *Folk Customs of Korea* (1914) by Imamura.

In terms of institutionalization of anthropology in Korea, establishment of Keijo University was the most significant event. The education Ordinance of May 1924 established Keijo Imperial University and its preparatory school in Seoul. However, duties of Keijo university were overseen by the Governor-General of the colonial government, unlike most of the imperial universities in Japan where the Ministry of Education was the overseeing entity. Another similar ordinance was applied to the imperial university in Taiwan. This clearly indicates that those universities established in the colonies of Taiwan and Korea were directly linked to the goals of colonial rule. Consequently, the Governor-General exercised great influences over the colonial universities since the instructors and faculty at these universities were registered as Governor-General's staff.

At Keijo Imperial University, an 〈Institute of Religious Studies and Sociology〉 was created in 1926, and a sociologist who had some anthropological training, named Akiba Takashi[11] was appointed to be

---

workers became tenant farmers, having lost their entitlements almost overnight" (http://en.wikipedia.org/wiki/Korea_under_Japan).

11 Akiba Takashi studied sociology at Tokyo Imperial University. Then he spent several years at the University of London under anthropology professor Perry. Completing his overseas training, he was appointed to Keijo Imperial University in Korea as an assistant professor. He was familiar with the methodology of social anthropology and set about laying the foundations for anthropological and

in charge of the religious studies. As the colonial expansion into the Continent Asia progressed, the <Manchuria and Mongolia Culture Research Society> was established in 1933 at the university. Such a move strongly suggest that, from Japanese point of view, Colonial Korea was widely seen as a bridge to the continent. To put it in a different words, colonial expansion and anthropological endeavors were closely linked to each other. Later Akiba was joined by a Physical anthropologist named Imamura Yutaka who served as a professor in the department of anatomy and also a trustee of the Japanese Anthropological Association. Another appointee was Akiba's own student Izumi Seiichi. Although institutional framework for anthropological research and training was established by creating university, it is worthy to note that, at Keijo university, the bulk of both professors and students were always Japanese. When the university opened in 1926, only five of 57 professors and 47 of 150 students were Korean. In 1941, only one of 140 professors and 216 of 611 students were Korean. The record shows that there was no Korean graduates majoring in anthropology from Keijo Imperial University.

Another important academic institutional creation was a government controlled organization for the research on Korean history. In 1922, the Japanese Governor-General established The Editorial Committee for Research on Korean History (朝鮮史編纂委員會). This Committee was renamed as The Korean History Compilation Committee (朝鮮史編修會) three years later. The committee was administered by the Governor-General of Korea and engaged in collecting of Korean historical materials and compilation of Korean history. The works of this committee, however, reflected a particular view of history designed to justify the colonial policy. The early activities of the Committee was devoted to validate Japanese colonization of Korea. Thus, for example, scholars affiliated with the Committee were eager to collect data which in effect confining Korean

---

folklore research in Korea.

history within the boundary of Korean peninsula. They claimed that Korean history had never rule over Manchuria: North Korean peninsula was the colony of China by Chinese Commanderies, whereas South Korean peninsula was the colony of Japan by Mimana Nihonfu (任那日本府). Today, some of the issues implanted by the Japanese colonizers concerning the East Asian history are still unresolved. One good example is the continued controversies surrounding the stone monument called Jumje-hyun shin-sabi (秥蟬縣神祠碑) found in Pyongyang. Korean archaeologist named Bogee Shon believes that the Japanese intentionally moved the stone monument which was originally located at Liaodong into Pyonyang, in order to demonstrate their theories that Chinese commanderies existed in Pyongyang (http://en.wikipedia.org/wiki/Korea_under_Japanese_rule, also see Sunjn Yi 2001).

Other notable activity which had some relevance to anthropology was numerous rural surveys. Needless to say, this activity was also motivated by colonial control. That is, the studies of villages during the Japanese colonial period had been conducted as part of the wider study of the colonial government's rural control policy (Lee, 2010). Lastly, although extremely few studies were done in the field of physical anthropology, it is proper to point out that, some Japanese scholars carried out physical anthropological study to prove racial differences amongst Asian ethnic groups.[12]

Although their purpose was not to preserve or to foster the development of Korean culture but, to a larger extent, to provide justification for their colonial policy, however, Japanese scholars had left a considerable amount of research results on various aspects of Korean culture during the period of their colonial engagement. According to Hyun-soo Park (1980) who

---

12 Hankook Daily News, Feb. 28, 2013: See the newspaper report on Girihara's (桐原眞一) study conducted in 1922. His research report appears in *New Tokyo Medical Journal* (東京醫事新誌), July, 1922 issue. Girihara classified Asian racial groups according to blood types, and ranked them in order.

reviewed Japanese studies on Korea during the colonial period, research activities of the colonial times can be divided into four stages. The four stages are as follows:

First stage (1868-1894): Just after Meiji Reform, Japanese government initiated information collecting activities in Korean peninsula by sending military agents and armed merchants. During this stage, large files of data were collected, and it was turn out to be useful for military operation later.

Second stage (1895-1905): This stage covers period between Sino-Japanese and Russo-Japanese Wars when in-land market-survey activities were strengthened. For these activities, more professionally trained survey organizations were mobilized so as to diversify area surveys in Korea as well as in China.

Third stage (1905-1919): Now, monopolistic domination over Korea by Japanese established, hence, the Japanese colonial government focused its information gathering activities on Korea's traditional legal-communal customs and institutions so as to utilize the data for colonial governance. The Governor-General's office acted as the control tower for the various researches.

Fourth stage (1919-1931): After a nationwide protest against the Japanese colonial rule that began on March 1, 1919, Japanese rule was relaxed somewhat, by easing some of its restrictive policies. In need of more sophisticated and effective control, the Japanese colonial government placed more emphasis on empirical fact finding surveys such as large-scale anthropological rural village surveys.

Fifth stage (1931-1945): As the colonial Japan began its expansion towards Manchuria and China, increased wartime mobilization made situation more tight and oppressive. Japanese government increasingly perceived Kore's independence as a threat. Koreans, the government proclaimed, were part of the Japanese empire, so their language, religion, and culture had to be the same as those of the Japanese. War time situation placed severe limits upon pure academic activities, thereby not allowing normal growth of anthropology as an objective scientific discipline.

4. Roots of Korean Anthropology

While numerous Japanese scholars were pursuing colonialist aims in research on Korean culture, some Korean scholars on the other hand began their own research in search of national identity and the meaning of traditional culture. In contrast to the Japanese who held what could be called a colonialist view of history, these Korean scholars held a nationalistic view. Many Korean intellectuals were drawn into folklore in their resistance to the colonial distortion of Korean national identity. In simple terms, they were eager to seek their cultural roots and identity through folklore studies. What they were seeking in their folklore studies included the proto-type, structure, and/or tradition of Korean culture. Most notable scholars in this regard during the colonial period were Song Sok-ha, Ch'oe Nam-son, Shin Chae-ho, Chong In-bo, Yi Neung-hwa, Son Jin-tae.[13] Especially, Song Sok ha and Son Jin-tae played major role in establishing the Korean Folklore Society (朝鮮民俗學會) in 1932, and the publication of the journal *Korean Folklore* (*Chosen Minsoku*, 朝鮮民俗) in 1933. Furthermore, some of these scholars even made use of anthropological theories such as evolutionism and diffusionism in order to suggest that Japanese culture originated from Korea (Kim, 2000: 60). To them, studying Korean folklore meant their way of responding to colonial distortion of Korean traditional culture.

---

13 These Korean scholars were concerned with religion and folklore in relation to national culture. The followings are their representative works which had deep anthropological significance. Yi Neung-hwa (1869-1943): *A General History of Korean Buddhism, A Study on Korean Shamanism, A History of Korean Taois* ; Son Jin-tae (1900-1950): *A Study on Korean National Culture* ; Song Sok-ha (1904-1948): *A Study on Korean Folk Culture.*

Today, many Korean anthropologists find Korean anthropology's root in the works and activities of the above mentioned folklore-oriented scholars (Han 1974, Moon 1999, Kim 2000). Although there exists differences in opinion concerning the history of Korean anthropology, all agree in that nationalistic folklore-oriented trend can be discernable as the most important element in the early making of Korean anthropology. Those Korean scholars maintained continuous interest in the traditional culture, thereby laying down foundations for the study of Korean 'culture' per se. If anthropology is easily defined as 'the study of culture', then, those were the first who devoted themselves for the study of Korean 'culture'.

After the liberation in 1945, Korea went through a series of turmoil: division of the country, Korean war, and economic hardship. Consequently, the whole nation had to mobilize for nation building during the 1950s. Social mood then was to reward knowledge production that served state goal of modernization and economic growth, and anthropology simply did not figure into those practical goals during the early post-war period. Therefore, introduction of modern anthropology at a societal level in Korea had to wait until 1960s. In the mean time, those folklore-oriented scholars who devoted themselves for the study of Korean culture continued their scholarly activities. More importantly, few members of the Korean Folklore Society (朝鮮民俗學會) which were established during the Japanese occupation, took initiative to form the first anthropological society, the Korean Society for Cultural Anthropology (韓國文化人類學會), in 1959. Im Soek-je, Lee Du-hyun, and Chang Ju-geun were the leading figures among the founding members, and all three were folklore-oriented scholars.

Entering into the 60s, a new era for Korean anthropology began, as the first anthropology department was established at Seoul National University in 1961. Creation of the anthropology department was a signal for departure from the folklore tradition in Korean anthropology. To put it in simple terms, Korean anthropology was entering into a new stage which opened door to Western influenced modern anthropology. In spite of this dramatic change, the striking characteristic of Korean anthropological history is that studies of Korean peoples themselves have, as before, predominated. A brief review on the studies conducted by Korean anthropologists since the mid 60s, when anthropology was systematically introduced through university system, reveals that overwhelming majority were concerned with Korean culture.[14] It was only after entering into the 90s, foreign area studies began to appear sporadically in Korean anthropological literature. But, still, the subjects of which most Korean anthropologists writes about are rather limited to Korean culture and society (Choi 1998). Indeed, old traditional forces lingers. When we compare Korean anthropology with that of Japanese or any other Western anthropology, Korean anthropology shows rather striking differences in this respect.

5. Concluding Remarks

Because of it's ties to the Western Enlightenment and colonial expansion, anthropology was framed in the West as 'the study of other cultures.' Thus, for example, Levi-Strauss once noted, "anthropology is the science of culture as seen from the outside", hence, if the natives were to study themselves, they were said to produce history or philology, not anthropology (Levi-Strauss 1966: 126). If Levi-Strauss is correct, then, considering its early tradition of studying themselves, Korean anthropology is, indeed, a different brand of anthropology, deviating from the Western tradition. Korean anthropology holds an unique position in the field of anthropology, having first developed with native scholars studying native culture, rather than with the past Western practice of studying the other (Choi 2011).

---

14 It is interesting to note that even the majority of those who went abroad for their advanced study during the 70s and 80s also chose Korea as their field of research.

This characteristic was, as pointed out earlier, related with the folklore-focused trend which was established during the Japanese occupation as means of responding to colonial distortion of Korean traditional culture. Even today, while Japanese anthropology was defined as the study of other cultures, Korean anthropology maintains the tradition of studying Korean culture strong, even though new generations of Korean anthropologists have expanded their interest into foreign area studies.

In retrospect, we find many changes in the study subjects of which anthropologists have dealt with on a world-wide scale. During the early 20th century, even Malinowski was worried about the disappearance of the cultural 'other' - primitives. Later, primitives have been gradually replaced by peasants of the world as major study subjects for anthropologists. We also witnessed American anthropologists, for example, returning home to find their cultural 'other' in their own society, in slums or in gay communities. Indeed, subjects, cultural other, and even the nature of ethnography are not fixed entity.[15] They can change through time as well. If then, Korean anthropology's tradition of studying their own culture may find a meaningful place in the world community of anthropology.

Now, as we have entered into a new era of Information Age, the discipline of anthropology faces a whole new sets of challenges. Therefore, this may be a high time for seeking 'alternate voices in anthropology.'[16] If we find some uniqueness in Korean anthropology, it is the point where we cultivate potentials so as to make contribution to Global Anthropology.

---

15 While *Tristes Tropiques* by Claude Levi-Strauss is called as "confessional" ethnography, Paul Rabinow's *Reflections on Fieldwork in Morocco* which deals with the matter of cultural translation can be labelled as "reflexive" ethnography. Many of Korean anthropologists' works can be called as "historical" ethnography.

16 Indian Anthropological Society held a symposium under the title of "Alternative Voices of Anthropology' in 2011. The purpose of the symposium was to question whether Global Anthropology should be a mere continuity of the Euro-American domination in the field, or be an attempt to accomodate local specificities of alternative voices.

Korea is one of the few nations with a long 'recorded' history. Furthermore, very dynamic nature of Korean society presents many kinds of different methodological challenges. Anthropologists working in Korea, as they were dealing with a complex society with extensive written records, often found themselves crossing over the boundaries of history and sociology. This rather complicated situation of Korean anthropology may prove to be a foundation providing basis for making unique contribution to the discipline anthropology. In the constantly changing world, Korean anthropology is now facing new challenges. One of the challenges will be how to transform the unique tradition that Korean anthropology has maintained, in accordance with the changing landscapes of anthropological inquiry. This is the reason why Korean anthropology should not be reduced to being a matter of collecting data to confirm Western theory.

■ References cited

Asad, Talal, ed., 1973, *Anthropology and the Colonial Encounter*. Ithaca, NY: Ithaca Press.

Caprio, Mark, E. 2009, *Japanese Assimilation Policies in Colonial Korea, 1910-1945*. Seattle: University of Washington Press.

Choi, Hyup, 1998, "Studying Korean culture and it's methodology." *The Academy Review of Korean Studies* 21:2:21-38.

__________, 2011, "Korean anthropology in historical perspective." Paper presented at the International Symposium on 〈Locating Alternative Voices in Anthropology〉 held in Kolkata, India during November 19 through 23.

Chun, Kyung-soo, 2002a, "Japanese anthropology of war and colonialism." Paper presented at 34th Annual Meeting of The Korea Society for Cultural Anthropology held at Chuncheon, during May 31 - June 1.

_______________, 2002b, "East Asian multiculturalism and imperialistic centralization: Focusing on Japanese Ethnology in History." Paper presented at 2002 Busan Asian Games International Conference held at Busan during Sept. 25-26.

Han, Sang-bok, 1974, "Reflection and orientation of Korean cultural anthropology: The field of social anthropology". *Korean Cultural Anthropology* 6: 213-217.

Kim, Kwang-Ok, 2000, "History, power, culture, and anthropology in Korea: Toward a new paradigm for Korean studies." *Korea Journal* vol. 40 (Spring): 54-100.

Kim, Jimin, 2011, *Representing the Invisible: The American Perceptions of Colonial Korea (1910-1945)*. Doctoral dissertation, Columbia University.

Lee, Yong-ki, 2010, "The Study of Korean villages during the Japanese colonial period and colonial modernity." *International Journal of Korean History* Vol.15 No.2: 35-67.

Levi-Strauss, Claude, 1966, "Anthropology: Its achievements and future." *Current Anthropology* 7: 124-27.

Moon, Okpyo, 1999, "Korean anthropology: A search for new paradigms." *The Review of Korean Studies* 2: 113-137.

Park, Hyun-soo, 1980, "Socio-cultural survey of the Japanese colonial government in Korea." *Korean Cultural Anthropology* 12: 71-92.

____________, 1982, "Village studies during the Japanese occupation." *Anthropological Studies* 2: 36-59.

Said, Edward, 1979, *Orientalism: Western Concepts of the Orient*. London: Penguin Books.

Smith, Linda Tuhiwai, 1999, *Decolonizing Methodologies: Research and Indigenous Peoples*. London: Zed Books.

Vinacke, Harold M., 1967, *A History of the Far East in Modern Times*. London: George Allen & Unwin Ltd.

Yi, Sunjin, 2001, *A Research about the Tombs of Nangnang around Pyongyang*. Seoul: Jungsim.

Anthropology of Colonialism and War under Imperial Japan

Kyung-soo Chun
Seoul National University

I. Introduction: Why?

It is necessary to explore the reasons for studying the history of a discipline, and particularly in anthropology, the relationship between "colonialism and anthropology" and its development into an independent subfield. The evolution of a unified discipline calls for more than just research into the separate work conducted by scholars; it demands analysis of the historical context that informed such work. This approach reveals not only a theoretical perspective of how scholars adhered to traditions and developed their scholarship, but also the underlying politics of that scholarship.

I consider myself lucky to be living and working in a time when facts (history) and what is thought about those facts (memory) can be discussed with relative freedom. What we now call historical background was experienced by past scholars as forced silence, fabrication, and suppression of knowledge, making scholarship inseparable from politics. These scholars first suffered under oppression and then were made to suffer again as they subsequently became objects of suspicion. The only way to restore their reputations is to clarify facts by mobilizing history and memory. I believe this responsibility falls on us.

Researchers who delve into these complexities face the problems of comparison as well as issues external to scholarship. It seems nearly impossible to do scholarship that takes truth and justice as its ultimate goals and remains untouched by jingoism or a crude patriotism. In 1919, Franz Boas wrote a scathing account of the scholars who had worked with the U.S. Intelligence Service during World War I (Boas 1919). As a result, Boas and his followers were charged with "un-American" conduct by the American Anthropological Association and were divested of any public office in the federal government (Gould 1989: 256-257). By standing strong in the face of this anger, Boas earned himself the title of "father" of American anthropology, and in the United States a strict code of ethics for anthropologists was subsequently formed under the aegis of the American Anthropological Association.

Research in this area must not ignore the perspectives of scholars. What was the perspective, under what conditions was it formed, how deeply did it penetrate research - these questions require rigorous analysis. This calls for consideration of not only an etic, but also an emic perspective. If we begin with a preconceived standard divided between "good" and "evil", however, research on the relationship between colonialism and scholarship will inevitably lose most of its value.

For example, I would caution against the following kind of argument: "We can call Professor Kanaseki Takeo (1897-1983) of Taihoku Imperial University, Professor Akiba Takashi (1888-1954) of Keijo Imperial University, and Professor Omachi Tokuzo (1900-1970) of Manchuria Imperial University···scholars engaged in colonial research at 'imperial' universities established in the colonies" (Kawamura 1996: 7). Here, Kawamura points to individual researchers, and by qualifying their achievements as "colonial research", he ends up undervaluing the system of colonial rule. A better approach would be to first evaluate the system and show what relevance it had to colonial rule before turning to individual researchers and their level of complicity. If a detailed critical analysis and prior understanding of the system are neglected, virtually all scholars of that time could be accused of complicity with colonial rule.

I further argue against the logic that "regarding the academic surveys conducted by the Government-General as identical to the work of commercial enterprises is problematic" (Kurosawa 1973: 513). This assumes that the Government-General's direction of academic surveys was a given. It is important to point out that there was a standardized understanding of academic surveys in government-affiliated projects, but not in joint government-university projects. The assumption that academic research must always be independent of government brings up historical ambiguities.

In the research conducted so far on the relationship between colonialism and scholarship (including anthropology), evaluation of the scholars who were involved in that relationship tends to rely too heavily on "primordialism." Because they were involved in academic research that furthered the interests of colonial rule, they were inevitably labeled "bad." Researchers interested in this question have concentrated on gathering materials to provide evidence for this categorization, and to do so they relied on a considerable amount of decontextualized sources. While these critiques were largely valid, my point is that they entail problems of procedure. I argue that these criticisms were developed without rigorous research. I thus firmly oppose such arguments, for three reasons.

First, critical evaluations of colonial research tend to be overrun with navel-gazers, who are trapped in reflection for its own sake, although people are guilty of this to different degrees. The past is implicated in imperialism, and because that past is "bad", reflection on it is laid aside and nothing further is mentioned. Later scholars, influenced by their predecessors who refused to talk about this past, are consequently deprived of the very chance to think about these issues for themselves. Thus nonproductive issues in academia are passed on by these navel-gazers. Reflection for the sake of reflection can lead to the concealment of facts. Reflection on the past under the accurate judgment of whether or not something is a fact can be productively applied to the future, but reflection that sidesteps this procedure runs the risk of concealing facts of the past. Thus, it obscures the future. Contemporary Japanese scholars, heirs of the tradition of their predecessors, are thus in a valuable position to critique and amend the misinterpretations of their predecessors.

The second reason concerns the sentimentalists. By this I mean those who take a paternalistic perspective mixing emotion into analysis, as they magnify and denounce problems of the past in order to vindicate its political victims. This paternalist introduction of emotion obstructs the delicate question of whether something constitutes a fact, increasing the possibility of historical misinterpretations. The result is that it does not allow anyone to shed the shackles of their ongoing victimhood, as the past victims of politics are made into the future victims of history. This ties victims of Orientalism to yet another kind of Orientalism.

Third, there are what I call the one-track minds. Like the view that sees everything in the psychiatric ward as identical, this perspective reduces all interests to a single issue and obsessively delves into that issue to the exclusion of everything else. Phenomena have the power to move things. Adherence to criticism for the sake of navel-gazing, criticism for the sake of sentiment, and criticism with blinders on all miss the original point, which is analysis of phenomena. I cannot stress enough that the genre of "anthropology and colonialism" and analysis of the researchers involved in colonial anthropology must question these three critical perspectives.

II. Balancing Perspectives: How?

An anthropological perspective of colonialism and its attendant problems is quite different from the perspectives taken in history or sociology. By adhering to the marginal position advocated by anthropology, anthropologists place themselves between the colonizers and the colonized (Memmi 1973). If they do not take one side or the other, and fail to choose a perspective that recognizes the places were both sides meet, namely colonialism and its products, anthropological research into colonialism will fail to even establish a basic framework.

Taking a critical eye to anthropological research conducted during colonialism will inevitably become increasingly sensitive. This research, whether the products of collaborators with colonial power or tools used by colonial power, was where colonial rulers met the objects of their rule. Like historians and sociologists, anthropologists cannot view their subjects from a seemingly safe distance, and so anthropological discussion of colonialism will be fraught with more tension than other perspectives.

Most discussions of Japanese colonialism up to now have borrowed heavily from the framework of "anthropology and colonialism" (van Bremen & Shimizu Akitoshi 1999) put forward by Talal Asad (1973) and directly applied it to the Japanese context. In this paper, I challenge the perspectives that take the process and results of this research as their starting point. The issues of colonialism debated in Western academic circles do not necessarily apply to Japanese colonialism and do not proceed along the same track. A different issue found in Japanese colonialism is that of war.[1] Colonial issues brought up in Western anthropology do not directly tie into the issue of war, while Japanese colonialism in its later stages evolved into war. If we do not see Japanese imperialism, moving from colonialism to war, as wholly different from the Western case, we risk gravely misunderstanding not only the meaning of Japanese colonialism, but also its consequences.

The work of Nakao Katsumi (1997), which has shed light on the

1 My point here is that anthropology has a structurally different problem by seeing colonialism as a separate yet equal issue to all discussion of colonialism and the issue of war. The issue of war within the framework of colonialism is not accepted as a part of the debate. This is not to say that critical discussion of the relationship between war and anthropology is non-existent. Nakao (1999) and Shimizu (1999) mention this point, but these discussions are limited in that they are situated war within the framework of colonialism.

Ethnological Research Institute in Tokyo and the ethnologist Oka Masao, is significant in this respect. His effort to verify things that cannot be separated and things that can is meaningful not only as a substantive evaluation of the relationship between anthropology and colonialism, but also as a recovery of pieces of history that have been lost. Although I actively support the position taken by Nakao, we must distinguish between the qualitatively distinct issues of colonialism and war.

The claim that in the West, colonialism's connection with anthropology was focused on the side of colonial rule demands a separate perspective for the issue of anthropology's connection to war. To view Japanese anthropology solely through the lens of colonialism is to lose the considerable parts that have to be uncovered within the framework of war. At the same time, it excludes discussion of Japanese anthropology as it related to war. Applying a Western framework of the anthropology of colonialism to the Japanese colonial context thus brings up problems of perspective.

Yet another problem in the discussion of colonialism involves the possibility of bringing together ethics and science. If we begin by asking what kind of organizations participated in the colonial project or calling certain individuals "those bastards", we become accomplices in the destruction of truth. In the debate over anthropology and colonialism the difficult-yet important-thing is how far is it possible to distance ourselves from the views of the moralizers. In starting with the question of hegemony, meaning power and resistance, discussion soon falls into simplistic dichotomy of "power" as bad and "resistance" as good. Pursuing this sort of argument, despite its ethical possibilities, is inadequate from the standpoint of science. It is important to point out that questions of ethics give up half way on the "how" and "why" questions that are so critical to science. The basis for the discussion of the relationship between colonialism and anthropology is twofold. First, we must resist the temptations of a moral values judgment and second, we must ask ourselves how a process based on empirical evidence can be guaranteed.

Individual researchers, as members of an organization (a good example being the Ethnological Research Institute established during the Pacific War, which was called the "Greater East Asia War" by the Japanese), undoubtedly worked toward the goals of those organizations. This is a case of "research in support of policy" conducted by individual researchers who were participating in "research supported by policy." However, the attempt to distinguish between research supported by policy and research in support of policy in the work begun, pursued, and concluded by individual researchers is the responsibility of the next generation of scholars. If we begin by asking how strict the distinction should be, yet not trying to make that distinction, we are left with nothing to evaluate or pursue. In so doing, the discussion of the relationship between anthropology and colonialism becomes meaningless, and discussion that does not undergo that process risks creating the work and confusion of the moralizers.

We are then able to move on to the next stage of evaluating the actual work of an individual researcher. This may have been research in support of policy, or research supported by policy in which the outcome of the research did not directly support that policy, and even research that directly countered policy aims. A single researcher does not show a consistent subjectivity, and in cases when the produced results were twisted by the demands of policy, we can see that researcher as having a "fractured subjectivity" (Thomas 1994: 60).[2] Thomas persuasively argues that this is a typical pattern in the union of anthropology and colonialism; if a particular researcher were to only produce research that supported

2 Some arguments tried to conceal militarism, as in the following example. "I think that the duty of Southern Resource Development was the natural burden of our compatriots in the most culturally advanced nation···Taiwan, which China used to call the a nation without Buddhism, thirty years later has civilized its ignorant natives, and in so doing we have glorified peace, and instead of dreaming of militarism, we advocate making equal opportunities for mankind" (Matsukura 1926: 149-150). This must be distinguished from the "fractured subjectivity."

policy, she/he would justifiably be excluded from subjects of academic discourse.

Even in research supported by policy, the creation of knowledge in the pursuit of truth and justice (the justice mentioned by Weber is his "scholarship as vocation"), which is the evaluation of pure fact and phenomena without supporting policy, is meaningful. The example of Dr. Kano Tadao, who worked in the Philippines, Borneo, and Taiwan as "full-time non-regular staff" or an "army inspector" under the auspices of the military government during the "Greater East Asia War", can be viewed from this perspective. Therefore, researchers in colonial Taiwan are now regarded very highly for their field research and scholarship (Hsu Mok-ju 1993). In Kano's case, he did not welcome the responsibilities imposed on him as an "inspector"[3] in the army. Whatever the titles or responsibilities, however, many researchers did not resent the help such work gave them in collecting research materials.

At the end of Izumi Seiichi's reports, he had no choice but to make indirect mention that his work was supported by policy. It is easy to read his personal distress and his own position as a victim of the system. Recognizing the very human pain of being unavoidably placed in such a position is both a right and duty for researchers today. There are two reasons for seeing this process as meaningful. First, reading the pain between the lines when it is not directly expressed ultimately points us toward issues of justice. Second, those who had no choice but to accept their lot as an extremely indirect, yet painful, alternative, were also clearly

---

3 Inspectors, as civilians engaged in the military government in occupied territories, were appointed as non-regular staff in the army or navy. They worked outside the government offices, and during the Greater East Asia War, they were posted to the occupied territories in southeast Asia, Oceania, and Taiwan. Inspectors and chief inspectors were sent by Imperial order to improve the position of personnel necessary for military government. As of January 1943, this applied to 292 chief inspectors and 2,429 inspectors from the army and 38 chief inspectors and 1,115 inspectors from the navy.

victims of the system.

Researchers with a fractured subjectivity were victims of the system, and like Kano, labored to produce research irrespective of policy support. Those researchers who got lost in their complicity with the system were also its victims. Of course, granting the recognition or position of "victim" does not acquit the scholarship of researchers who directly or indirectly cooperated with the war effort. Under imperial Japanese militarism, the fact that Japanese anthropologists did not produce research or arguments that challenged the collective or any particular person is an issue of culture. The anthropology (and ethnology) that developed in Japan, with its strong tradition favoring the collective, reflects this tradition. This issue can be analyzed apart from the often discussed cultural dynamism of Japanese society.

This paper aims to shed light on the anthropological work accomplished in Japan's colonies of Taiwan and Korea during the imperial era from a comparative perspective. I also want to provoke discussion of how, and to what degree, Japanese colonial anthropology was connected to colonialism. The era I focus on is the so-called "Fifteen Year War" (Eguchi 1991), referring to the period between the invasion of Manchuria in 1931 and the end of World War II in 1945. It was during this period that Japanese imperialism spread throughout Asia and the Pacific in an ongoing series of wars. In this discussion, I will focus on the following issues.

First, I will compare the foundation and nature of the two imperial universities in colonial Taiwan and Korea as they related to anthropological work. Second, I will examine the major groups of researchers who were centered around the anthropology-related classes and departments that were instituted at each imperial university, analyzing their main work from a comparative perspective. Here, I focus on the academic societies, research groups, and professional publications in which they were involved. Third, I look at the concrete facts of how, and to what degree, the two schools of anthropology[4] were involved in mobilization for military attacks as Japan's war reached its peak.

III. Imperial Universities in the Colonies

According to the Shimonoseki Treaty concluded after the 1894 Sino-Japanese War, Taiwan was ceded to Japan in 1895 and became a Japanese colony. Although there was fierce resistance by the Taiwanese in their hopes to establish a "Democratic Republic of Taiwan", it was quelled in the face of repressive military power and Taiwan remained under Japanese domination for the next fifty years. Japanese administration of Taiwan had two aspects: harsh exploitation and a policy of civilizing the Taiwanese (Mabuchi 1987: 212-213). The existence of indigenous Taiwanese quickly became a subject of interest for Japanese anthropologists, such as early researchers Ino Kanori and Torii Ryuzo. Because of "education of the ignorant tribes···, a guideline resting on 'Pacification(Dowahshugi)' raised the banner of 'Universal Brotherhood (Itsidozin)' "(Okawa 1987: 214-215), it was not until much later, in 1928, that university education for the children of Japanese settlers in Taiwan was made possible with the establishment of Taihoku Imperial University in Taipei.

Although colonial rule began later in Korea, the necessity of a university was recognized there first. As a result, a preparatory course for Keijo Imperial University was established in 1924, and the main program of the university was officially opened in 1926. Taihoku Imperial University, like other imperial universities in Japan itself, did not have preparatory courses and was instead connected to a high school specially designed for entrance into the main program of the university. The question remains why these preparatory courses, which existed only in Hokkaido Imperial

---

4 So far the term "Taihoku anthropology" does not exist, but the term "Keijo anthropology" has already appeared in the recollections of Japanese researchers (Committee for a Compilation for the Fifty-Year Anniversary of the Founding of Keijo Imperial University 197.

University (at that time Hokkaido was an internal colony in Japan), were exceptionally used for Keijo Imperial University.

Unlike most of the imperial universities in Japan, those established in the colonies of Taiwan and Korea were directly linked to the goals of colonial rule. According to the imperial university ordinance, duties were to be overseen by the Governor-General instead of the Ministry of Education. The imperial universities in the colonies were thus placed under the control of the Governor-General, who held absolute authority for colonial rule. The instructors and faculty at these universities were registered as Government-General staff. The recollections of these scholars demonstrate the place of the university and scholarship, supporting the claim that "if there was a general atmosphere of the deplorable custom of making much of government and little of the people, then the Government-General always made much of officials and little of scholarship" (Miyamoto, Segawa, Mabuchi 1987: 178).[5]

The question of how scholarship, research, and education- the raison d'etre of a university- functioned in the imperial universities of Japan's colonies can be clearly seen in a range of events that unfolded in Keijo Imperial University under the name of science and scholarship. I will focus on those related to anthropological work.

At the time, the Ministry of Education of imperial Japan paid great attention to the naming of the university. The story behind the name

5 The following is further testimony to the dominance of government institutions. "Assistants were government officials appointed by the generals, and as Government-General staff, they wore the same uniform as the naval officers. My first salary was 60 yen. The colonial bonus was six percent for military-appointed government officials and five percent for other high officials. Accordingly, I got 96 yen a month, with the addition of a 20 yen housing allowance. I had graduated in history from Keio University, but the regular salary for graduates of Tokyo Imperial University in the government was 75 yen with a 25 yen housing allowance. There was a big difference, and we just took it for granted" (Miyamoto 1982b: 34).

"Keijo Imperial University" goes like this. In the early 1920s, the Korean Government-General was in a difficult position due to heated discussion among Koreans over the establishment of a university for Koreans. Stressing the necessity of a university for the education of the children of Japanese residing in the colony, it pushed forward the establishment of an imperial university in the colony. At first the name "Chosen Imperial University" was brought up, but the imperial Ministry of Justice that from the legal point of view it could be taken to mean a university of the "Chosen empire", and in the end the proposal to call it "Keijo Imperial University" was accepted. Extending this to colonial Taiwan, from the outset there would have been no consideration of naming Taihoku Imperial University, established in 1928, "Taiwan Imperial University." The imperial universities established in the colonies were connected to the issue of colonial rule, and even their naming was a sensitive point.

There were also subtle differences in the names of faculties. Although there was a Faculty of Law and Humanities at Keijo Imperial University, at Taihoku Imperial University there was Faculty of Humanities and Government. While it seems that there should have been a Faculty of Law at Taihoku Imperial University, as there was at Keijo Imperial University, there was likely a similar reason behind the use of the name Faculty of Humanities and Government. The different names reflected the circumstances of each place. It can be argued that there is a meaningful difference in the emphasis of "law" in Korea and "government" in Taiwan. "Taiwan, originally without sovereign rulers, faced problems in the method of rule. With no education in constitutional government, the biggest task was educating the indigenous people and inculcating an awareness of constitutional government" (Furuno 1991: 232). In Taiwan, the form of rule prior to law was the issue at hand, and those issues were reflected in the assigning of names to faculties during the foundation of the imperial university.

At Keijo Imperial University, an "Institute of Religious Studies and

Sociology" was created in 1926, and at Taihoku Imperial University, an "Institute of Ethnography.Ethnology" was created in 1928. The former referred to a institute physically joining religious studies and sociology, as shown in the insertion of "and" between "religious studies" and "sociology." When Keijo Imperial University opened its doors, the scholar of religion Okamatsu Chijo was appointed as professor and the sociologist Akiba Takashi as assistant professor to the department. Because there was at first a greater emphasis on studies of religion, a religious scholar was made full professor and reference to religion was placed first in the department title. It is important to note that the sociologist who was selected for the department had experience working in the field of shamanism. This reflects the extent to which the issue of religion was seen as critical in the rule of colonial Korea.

Akiba, who had been trained in sociology (of course, sociology at the time incorporated the traditions of anthropology and folklore) at Tokyo Imperial University, was appointed to the imperial university in Korea as an assistant professor following a period of foreign study in England and Europe. He had absorbed the methodology of social anthropology and set about laying the foundations for anthropological and folklore research in Korea. The combination of religious studies and sociology can be clearly seen in his main focus of research, Korean shamanic customs. On the other hand, his ongoing interest in sociology (in the narrow sense) also appears in the acceptance of Suzuki Eitaro, a graduate of Tokyo Imperial University in sociology and rural sociology, as assistant professor in the institute of religious studies and sociology. This reflects the recognition that the reality of colonial Korea also called for a rural sociologist.

Today, the stereotype that "sociology is for studying civilized societies and anthropology (ethnology) is for studying uncivilized societies" is still in currency in some areas. The fact that both universities had a department of psychology further demonstrates the purpose of the imperial universities as a contribution to the aims of colonial rule. The abbreviations of "sociology institute" at Keijo Imperial University and "ethnography institute" at Taihoku Imperial University appear in records of the time. In references to "reports and surveys relating to indigenous tribes by the ethnography institute at Taihoku University" (Kurosawa 1973: 506) and "thanks to Professor Utsushikawa and Mr. Miyamoto Nobuto for permitting photography of the artifacts in the ethnography institute" (Okada 1936: 116), reference to the institute of ethnography.ethnology as the ethnography institute is clear.[6]

1. Keijo Imperial University

On June 2, 1933 there was a celebration marking the establishment of the Manchuria and Mongolia Culture Research Society, headed by president of the university, Yamada. At the lecture meeting (held on January 17, 1933) and the foundation celebration there were lectures on "Observations of the Hunchun and Jiandao Regions" by Sugihara Tokuyuki (professor of medicine) and on the ethnicity and culture of ancient Manchuria by Toriyama Kiichi (dean of the Faculty of Law and Humanities). A series of lectures on Manchurian history by Inaba Iwayoshi, a Korean Government-General criminal investigator, was held on June 6, 8, 10, 13, and 15 (*Ch'ŏnggu-hakch'ong* 13: 188). The start of activities following the formation of the society was connected to the Manchurian Incident in 1931 and subsequent events opening up the continent to Japanese control. Colonial Korea was widely seen as a bridge to the continent, and in the minds of many scholars, Keijo Imperial University had the responsibility to play a suitable role.

---

6 The abbreviations of sociology department at Keijo Imperial University and ethnography department at Taihoku Imperial University were commonly used. "Thanks go to Professor Utsushikawa and Mr. Miyamoto Nobuto for permission to use the artifacts of the ethnography department (italics mine)" (Okada 1936: 116).

Manchukuo was established in 1932, and following the annexation of Jehol (Chengde) in April 1933 and the invasions of Huabei and Inner Mongolia, a military government was established in Mongolia between April 1935 and February 1936. The Inner Mongolian Army was created in August 1936. On July 7, 1937 the Lugouqiao (Marco Polo Bridge) Incident set off the Sino-Japanese War, and the Japanese Kwantung Army set up a puppet regime in the occupied territories. The Chainan Autonomous Government (top advisor Kanai Shoji) was created in Zhangjiakou on September 4 1937, the Jinbook

Autonomous Government in Taidong on October 15, and the Allied Mongolian Autonomous Government in Huhohaote on October 27. On November 22 the Mongolian Union Committee was established to cover the three autonomous governments, with a Japanese (Kanai) appointed as top advisor. On September 1, 1939 the Japanese Kwantung Army abolished the three governments and instead inaugurated the Allied Mongolia Autonomous Government as a single government to rule the Mongolian-Manchurian region. At a commemorative ceremony on September 2, 1940 marking the one-year anniversary of the formation of a single government, Kanai emphasized that "politically, both the Construction of a New Order in East Asia and the One Manchuria and Mongolia Regional Circle have important roles to play" (Mongolian News Service 1941: 11).

The expansion of the Manchuria and Mongolia Culture Research Society into the Continental Culture Research Society is a clear indication of the expansion of Japan's sphere of interest. This means that as "Keijo Imperial University is located on the Korean peninsula, which is a stepping stone for the empire onto the continent and can be used for the march to northern Mongolia and Manchuria" (Odaka 1939: 3), the interest and areas that were assigned to the university expanded from Manchuria and Mongolia further into the continent. The Continental Culture Research Society organized the Keijo Imperial University Manchuria-Mongolia

Academic Survey Team between late July and early September 1938 and conducted comprehensive surveys of Beijing, Zhangjiakou, Weixian, Wutaishan, Xuanhua, Dehua, Linxi, and Chifeng. The work done by the survey team reflected the character of Keijo Imperial University itself.

The activities of the university in 1937, during the Sino-Japanese War, establish that it was working toward direct support of the war effort. According to the president of Keijo Imperial University (also appointed as director of the Continental Culture Research Society): "In achieving the goals of a holy war [meaning the Japanese-led war during WWII] in this meeting, we need to research the Japanese mind, spirit, and culture, but the purpose behind the lectures in this university is the recognition that we also need to acquire all modes of knowledge of the continent and further our understanding of the temperament and customs of the continent's native people. From its very beginning, Keijo Imperial University has had such an interest in researching the continent, organizing the conference on Manchurian-Mongolian culture immediately following the Manchurian Incident and leading research survey expeditions. With the Sino-Japanese War, our society's organization has been restructured and research on continental culture will push forward beyond Manchuria and Mongolia, investigating many fields-history, geography, industry, economy-and publishing the results and holding lectures" (Hayami 1940: 4). Such remarks are indicative of the general opinion among professors at the university.[7] The research society, represented by the president of

7 "At the end of March 1938, Professor Takenaka and Izumi went to Zhangjiakou as part of an advance contingent. They contacted both the headquarters of the army division stationed there and the XX Autonomous Government and received directions on the possibility and administrative aspects of a trip··· They applied to the Department of Cultural Works in the Foreign Office for support to cover the cost of the trip and requested further supported from financial circles in Keijo. His Excellency Minami Jiro of the Korean Government-General gave 1000 yen, and the Department of Foreign Affairs of the Government-General provided 500 yen, and the Chosŏn Bank, Chosŏn Industrial Bank, and Mr. Kobayashi each

gave 1000 yen, and the Eastern Colonization Corp gave 500 yen. The Continental Culture Research Society at Keijo Imperial University provided a loan. The Department of Cultural Works in the Foreign Office decided on a deposit of 3000 yen, and the Osaka Mainichi News Service gave support of 1000 yen··· The Chosŏn Government-General Railway Authority, the Manchurian Railway Authority, and the Southern Manchurian Railway Corp through their kindness provided free transportation of staff and materials···. On June 7 President Hayami of Keijo Imperial University, Mr. Aibara, head of the Education Bureau in the Chosŏn Government-General, and Colonel Iwazaki attended the inauguration of the expedition team. Mr. Izumi, who is part of the economic team in the administration office, mountain climbing team and academic survey team, plays a central role in this expedition··· The headquarters of the Chosen Army expressed their good wishes and support of the plan··· The supplies were consigned to Zhangjiakou on July 7, and on July 9 Izumi and Hattori left from Keijo with the advance contingent and headed for Zhangjiakou. The detachment visited the Government-General and the Korean Army Headquarters on July 14, announcing their departure to the South Chosŏn Governor-General, Mr. Ono the Commissioner of State Affairs, and Mr. Koisi the Commander of the Korean Army. They paid homage at the Royal Shrine and prayed for the success of the expedition. The group left Keijo on July 21, and the main detachment and advance contingent arrived in Zhangjiakou on July 14. They made a tour of OO camp and XX camp, the Army Special Service Agency, Mengjiang United Autonomous Government Committee, and the XX Autonomous Government and received instructions, seeking permission to travel to Inner Mongolia with the Army Special Service Agency and the Mengjiang United Autonomous Government Committee. ···A support team was given special duties by the XX camp and joined the expedition··· On July 26 all members of the expedition team listened to an explanation of the military, political, and economic importance and specificities of the Mongolian region, attended a welcoming ceremony sponsored by the Mengjiang United Autonomous Government Committee and the XX Autonomous Government on the outskirts of Zhangjiakou, and on July 28 gave a luncheon party in the same place. At a lecture sponsored by the Mengjiang United Autonomous Government Committee, this writer gave a lecture on statism and Commander Suzuki lectured on continental expansion route··· On the night of July 28, some of the expedition members received an invitation to a party from the camp Chief of Staff. On July 29 we left Zhangjiakou and returned again on August 17. It lasted twenty days··· On October 15 we gave a report lecture sponsored by the Continental Culture Research Society in the auditorium at Keijo Imperial University. In the meeting room of the Faculty of Law and Humanities we exhibited about fifty photographs and a few hundred artifacts. The Governor-General attended the exhibition" (Odaka 1939: 4-14).

the university, was deeply involved in research sensitive to the current state of affairs and announced that "the Keijo Imperial University Continental Culture Research Society, reflecting the needs of today's affairs, will host three weekly lectures on continental culture between September 9 and November 8, 1939" (Hayami 1940: 1).

"National policy and principle are the two wheels of the car, ⋯ and the political and economic administration of the continent must first depend upon the dispassionate and carefully collected knowledge of the continent's customs and culture. In a word, where the flag of the military goes, so too must go the flag of science. As the front line in the march to the continent, the question of how military installations, political administration, academic research, and scientific surveys can integrate each other is now to be answered through our direct experience. It is our role as the advance guard point in the continental culture war" (Odaka 1939: 15-16). The writer of this passage was at the time a professor at Keijo Imperial University, and later became a professor at Tokyo University after World War II. He introduced Izumi (who studied under Akiba Takashi and became a professor of anthropology at Tokyo University after the war) to the Pacific Federation and recommended the appointment of Izumi as a member of the resource survey team sent to New Guinea during the war. It is not difficult to read the nature and reality of the military-academic complex in this metaphor of a "flag of science" following the "flag of the military."

Academic work accomplished in the university sphere of Keijo Imperial University to a large extent exhibited the typical features of a bureaucratic-military-academic complex. Collaboration between bureaucratic offices headed by the Department of Cultural Activities in the Ministry of Foreign Affairs and military authorities headed by the Army Headquarters in the colony of Korea, and groups of scholars in Keijo Imperial University defined how academic surveys were conducted. The argument for seeing Keijo Imperial University as "a cultural device for colonialism" (Chŏng

Kyu-yŏng 1999: 21) is an accurate one.

2. Taihoku Imperial University

As the hunger for learning increased among residents in Taiwan, a university was created to educate the children of Japanese settlers living in Taiwan and provide a convenient base for academic research of the southern regions, including southeast Asia, Oceania, and Taiwan (Taiwanese Society for Education 1939: 955). The Taiwan Government-General, in order to secure teaching staff for the school, made a public announcement of the "dispatch of twenty people as overseas researchers in 1926" (Taiwanese Society for Education 1939: 955). They generally concluded from twenty-two to twenty-four months of overseas study and as soon as they arrived back in Taiwan they were hired on as professors for Taihoku Imperial University.

The opening of Taihoku Imperial University was officially announced on March 17, 1928. It initially began with two faculties- humanities and government, and science and agriculture- but was increased to include a Faculty of Medicine in 1936. The Faculty of Humanities and Government consisted of philosophy, history, literature, and government studies. Of the twenty-five courses offered in the faculty, there was one on "ethnography and ethnology." There were five students from Japan itself in the history department (Taiwan Government-General 1939: 192-194), with one in philosophy, ten in literature, and fifty-three in government studies, resulting in a total of sixty-nine students in the entire faculty. The school was operated as course-centered more than department-centered (Taihoku Imperial University Lecture Imperial Order No. 33). "Of the courses created within the Faculty of Humanities and Government···the most promising ones researching Taiwan and exhibiting its local culture are South Seas history, and ethnography.ethnology" (Taiwanese Society for Education 1939: 956-957). There was also a prescribed number of assistants: one each for government studies, literature, psychology, and ethnography/ ethnology. This suggests a very different treatment accorded to the ethnography institute: the assignment of assistants to this department was considered equivalent to the natural sciences for lab work (Miyamoto 1985c: 43).

There is one salient point in comparing the two imperial universities. At Keijo Imperial University, academic survey work conducted under the auspices of the university as a whole was frequent and directed toward the continent, while at Taihoku Imperial University most academic work was pursued within the confines of individual departments. Research conducted by a university, in today's parlance, can be referred to as "within the educational system", but reports suggest that this work can only be seen "as an individual event." Moreover, because this work involved a high level of participation by bureaucratic offices and the Army Bureau, it begs the question of how academic the process and results were. It is highly significant that the aims of this academic survey work were clearly to establish an advance guard point in the invasion of the continent. On the other hand, the department-centered work of Taihoku Imperial University was relatively more academic at that time.

Despite the risk of simplification in analyzing the work done at these two universities, both rooted in Japanese imperialism, we can see differences in form and organization of survey work between Taihoku Imperial University's department-centered activities and Keijo Imperial University's university-centered ones. Both universities reflected the specific features of their respective areas, and it is clear that the one was given a role as an advance base in the incursions into the southern regions, and the other in the march toward the continent.

The anthropologists of Taihoku Imperial University working under the auspices of their department, produced work of higher academic value than the professors of Keijo Imperial University, who were members of research teams under the direction of the university itself. A good illustration is a comparison between the *The Formosan Native Tribes: A Genealogical and Classificatory Study* (1935) by Utsushikawa Nenozo (with Miyamoto and Mabuchi), a member of the ethnography institute at Taihoku Imperial University, and the "Research on Chosen Shamanic Customs" (1937) coauthored by Akamatsu and Akiba of Keijo Imperial University's Institute of Religious Studies and Sociology. In data collection methods, relationships with informants, and the analysis and organization of data, Utsushikawa's work is incomparably superior. His work was the result of a protracted residence, while the work of Akamatsu and Akiba was based on short verification visits. It is worth remarking that with differences in the form and organization of their work, some points that show qualitative differences also left similar tracks behind them.

Today, the archives on the conditions at Taihoku Imperial University and work done by the ethnography institute housed in National Taiwan University are comparatively well organized. They were able to leave behind good records of the colonial era because following Japan's defeat in the war, the Japanese professors at the university had already been there for three to four years and were able to smoothly transfer the system to Chinese hands. At Keijo Imperial University, on the other hand, all channels were cut off. As the Japanese professors seem to have beat a hasty retreat back to Japan, they were unable to hand over the system to Koreans and many university documents were scattered or destroyed. With the loss of these documents, the task of analyzing the conditions of Keijo Imperial University is considerably more difficult than for Taihoku Imperial University.

After Keijo Imperial University closed its doors with the end of the war, it continued on at the same location and with the same infrastructure as Kyŏngsŏng University for a year. Only the Chinese characters denoting "imperial" were omitted. From August 1946 Kyŏngsŏng University became Seoul National University, under the jurisdiction of the American military government in Korea. There is no way to know whether documents relating to Keijo Imperial University and Kyŏngsŏng University were purposefully concealed during this process, or whether they were lost during the Korean War that broke out in 1950.

IV. Classrooms and Academic Societies: Making Schools of Anthropology

The "Institute of Religious Studies and Sociology" (abbreviated as sociology institute) at Keijo Imperial University and the Institute of Ethnography.Ethnology (abbreviated as ethnography institute) at Taihoku Imperial University differed in their organization, management, and aims, but with their common situation in a Japanese colony, they shared many similarities as well. In both universities, lectures and research on anthropology (physical anthropology) took place in the anatomy department of the Faculty of Medicine. Related specialists maintained close relationships with anthropology-related departments and were able to work together cooperatively and productively. This point deserves some emphasis. On the basis of the network of relations between these professionals, it becomes possible to discuss and compare the scope of academic schools of thought. Below, I aim to establish a basis for discussing the so-called school of Taihoku anthropology and the school of Keijo anthropology.

Aspects of academic work are pursued through departments (or laboratories) and academic societies, and the academic achievements of anthropologists working in colonial Taiwan and Korea progressed to the point that they formed separate schools of anthropology. Indeed, anthropology flowered in the imperial universities of the two colonies.

1. School of Taihoku Anthropology

In Taihoku Imperial University, complex issues of misunderstanding, or unwillingness to understand, the naming of departments distorts not only the essential issues related to the major roles in establishing departments, but also certain aspects of the history of Japanese anthropology itself. Instead of placing an "and" between the two words "ethnography" and "ethnology" in the title, a point (".") was put right between them instead, strongly implying that the two were not seen as separate. This leads one to think that at the very least, the phrase does not physically combine the two separate disciplines of ethnography and ethnology. This was likely meant to do away with the misunderstandings that could arise from the absence of a point between "ethnography" and "ethnology", and incorrectly calling the discipline "ethnography-ethnology" (*tozokujinshugaku*). With the point, this was neatly avoided.

There was only one full professor at the apex of the institute to give it a hierarchical organization. The name of the department was not an expression of problems external to the discipline, but rather reflected internal problems. At that time, some groups called the discipline "ethnography" (*tozokugaku*), while others preferred the common translation of "ethnology" (*jinshugaku*), and so a phrase incorporated both terms into the departmental name was decided on. It could also have been a term respecting the names of disciplines that were referred to differently at different times in the history of Japanese anthropology.

A failure to properly consider the meaning of this "." will result in unnecessary misunderstanding. For example, the reference that "for generations it was curiously called 'ethnography-ethnology' "(Kurata 1992) brings up a "curious" comment on the department name. In fact, its name was not "ethnography-ethnology" but "ethnography.ethnology" Ignoring the meaning of the point between "ethnography" and "ethnology" is indeed to make the curious term "ethnography-ethnology."

Immediately upon his return to Japan from the United States, Utsushikawa began to use the terms ethnography and ethnology in conjunction, such as his use of the term "ethnographic or ethnological relationship" (Utsushikawa 1919: 234). "In a Japanese dictionary from the Taisho period, the term ethnography is defined as 'the study of the native customs and practices of various regions.' The first person to use this term was Dr. Torii···. The term ethnology was widely in use at the time and meant anthropology. During the Meiji and Taisho periods it was used in a wide sense to refer to the combined study of physical and cultural aspects of anthropology. Professor Utsushikawa had studied anthropology at Harvard, and as physical measurement was a part of the course of study there, he learned of it as the basis of ethnology" (Miyamoto 1983b: 32). Compared with the point that "the terms consistently used by Torii were 'ethnology' and 'ethnography' " (Shimizu 1995: 12-13), Utsushikawa intended to continue on with the concepts that had been used from early on in Japanese anthropology, and it can be argued that he made an effort to realize this spirit in naming the department as the "Institute of Ethnography.Ethnology" at Taihoku Imperial University where he was appointed as professor.

From its inception, the character of the department was closely connected to colonial rule. This point is revealed in Utsushikawa's opinions on "ethnology" expressed during his twenty-two month trip to study abroad in Europe in 1926. "There is no country possessing colonies that does not have a department of ethnology in its premier university. In the United States, in England (Australia and South Africa), in Germany, in the Netherlands, in Belgium, in Italy- all have departments related to ethnology. The appearance of a department championing the colonies at the University of Paris is only natural" (Utsushikawa 1927: 149-150). Utsushikawa was clearly expressing a critical understanding of colonial policy and applied anthropology, and had given great thought to the realities of colonial rule in creating the name "Institute of Ethnography.Ethnology."

Utsushikawa later continued to freely use the term "ethnography. ethnology" Such references include "my teacher Dr. Dixon··· the greatest ethnographer.ethnologist···" (*Nanpo Tozoku* volume 3 issue 3, p.88, July

1935), "Dr. Dixon, ethnographer.ethnologist and professor of anthropology at Harvard University in the United States···" (Utsushikawa 1935b: 156), "his specialization is ethnography or ethnology" (Utsushikawa 1935b: 161). It is striking that he used Malinowski's (1922) articulation of the difference between ethnography and ethnology, and it should be pointed out that at the time Utsushikawa paid close attention to developments in Western anthropology in Europe and the United States. In a journal publishing the results of an international meeting of the International Association of Anthropology and Ethnology, he explained that *tozokugaku* is ethnography, *minjokugaku=jinshugaku* is ethnology, and *jinruigaku* is anthropology (Utsushikawa 1939).

As discussed above, to Utsushikawa "ethnography.ethnology" included the meaning of ethnography and ethnology in a single term, and so it can also be understood to mean anthropology. At that time, the term ethnology was used in Japan to refer to anthropology, and as the placement of "ethnography" in front of "ethnology" combined the hitherto commonly used term "customs" (*tozoku*) with what was now technically being called "ethnography" (*tozokugaku*), this can be interpreted part of the effort to indigenize an imported discipline. Before Utsushikawa had begun work in this field, the word and concept of "customs" (*tozoku*) was already in wide usage in Japan, and so this was an attempt to utilize this popular meaning.

There is also a historical context to the use of "ethnography.ethnology." In Japan, the words "customs" and "ethnography" had been used since the late nineteenth century to refer to ethnology (*minjokugaku*), and during his travels in the West, Utsushikawa himself had used the term "*tozokugaku*" (ethnography) to apply to ethnology. Later, adding on "ethnology" (*jinshugaku*), because the English term "anthropology" was usually translated as "*jinshugaku*" (ethnology) in Japanese, Utsushikawa, who had been educated in American anthropology, was unable to abandon "anthropology" and so added on the term "*jinshugaku*." In other words, it can be suggested that Utsushikawa was thinking in terms of a combination of the European ethnology (*minjokugaku*) and the American anthropology (*jinruigaku*), resulting in the creation of a department named ethnography.ethnology.

The English name given to the department, "Institute of Ethnology", was explained as being for exchanges with foreign departments, but this does not give the reason behind the choice of "ethnology" or explain what meaning was attached to it. Utsushikawa was educated in anthropology in the United States during the latter half of the 1910s. At that time in the United States, the term "ethnology" most commonly referred to research on native North Americans. Of course, in Europe ethnology was used in a similar sense to refer to social anthropology. Research on the indigenous people of Taiwan was the purpose behind the Institute of Ethnography.Ethnology, and actually department members (Miyamoto and Mabuchi), beginning with Utsushikawa, proceeded with this research as the biggest project of the department and published their results as a book titled *The Formosan Native Tribes: A Genealogical and Classificatory Study*.

Mabuchi Toichi (Mabuchi 1947) explained the use of the term "ethnography.ethnology" for the department as a reflection of the Government-General's avoidance of the term "ethnology" (*minjokugaku*) because of its connotations of "nation" (*minjoku*) and thus the Taiwanese nationalist movement. This is very likely a retrospective interpretation as he later on took the political situation of the time into account. Using "*minjokugaku*" to refer to a discipline was common practice in Japan, but the word "*minjoku*", as it related to the Taiwanese nationalist movement, was avoided by the Government-General and the term "Institute of Ethnography.Ethnology" and "customs of the southern regions" (*nanpotozoku*) seems to have won out. In areas where the word *tozoku* was used, subsequent replacement in favor of *minjoku* can be explained this way. From the years prior to the Pacific War, there was discussion in Japan on liberation of the nations in Asia from Western rule, so the word "*minjoku*" received a flood of popularity. Then, following resistance to the journal title *Nanpo Dozoku* (Ethnographic Journal of Southeast Asia, Oceania and Taiwan), the title was changed to *Nanpo Minzoku* (Mabuchi 1973: 2).

Utsushikawa, who was "the first to do joint fieldwork just when Japanese cultural anthropology was taking its first steps" (Yamazaki 1992: 102) with his surveys in Lanyu (southern Taiwan) in 1929 (at the time Utsushikawa was 34 years old, Miyamoto was 28, Kano was 22, and Mabuchi was 21, Yamazaki 1992: 103), produced "the first anthropological results in Japanese anthropology" (Mabuchi 1987: 237) in the fieldwork for his *The Formosan Native Tribes* (1935). This research was academically influenced by Taihoku Imperial University and the ethnography institute and played a colossal role in the history of Japanese anthropology. Above this book's title was added the headnote "a project commemorating the former Government-General of Formosa, Kamiyama", and was given an English title. In the preface Shidehara, the president of Taihoku Imperial University, wrote that "Professor Utsushikawa Nenozo did most of the research··· assisted by Mr. Miyamoto and Mr. Mabuchi, a non-regular staff member" (pp.1-2). The influence of this work is still felt today, and has been judged as "an extraordinarily detailed and important piece of work" (Hsu Mok-ju 1993: 145). It is therefore necessary to examine in depth the contributions of the ethnography institute in its connection to Utsushikawa, Miyamoto, and Mabuchi, and the people who surrounded it.

Utsushikawa Nenozo (1884-1947) established the foundations for Japanese anthropology's research areas, including southern China, Southeast Asia, and the South Pacific. Born in Fukushima prefecture, at the age of thirteen he went to the United States for study. While studying anthropology at the University of Chicago, it is recorded that he was admitted to the Tokyo Anthropological Society. He ("N. Utsurikawa") gave an address in January 1914 at M. D. Hall, at the University of

Chicago. By 1918 he was studying under Professor Roland Burrage Dixon and wrote his Ph.D. dissertation on Indonesian culture, conducting his fieldwork in Southeast Asia and the East Indies on a scholarship from Harvard. He did not follow the ideas of the American school of cultural history, proposing instead the importance of analytic investigation of design (Utsurikawa 1921). After his return to Japan, his lectures on anthropology in the history department of Keio University "were once a week···and Omori's excavations of shell mounds began with Professor Utsushikawa, and were attended by students, graduates, and members of the history department. A human bone came out of part of the shell mound, and Professor Utsushikawa and Dr. Koganei were called for" (Miyamoto 1982a: 37).[8]

His career was as follows. In 1919 he served at Keio University as a non-regular lecturer in the Faculty of Literature (offering a course on ethnology in the history department),[9] in 1921 he was professor at Tokyo Economic College (covering English as well and using the *Origin of Species* as a text). In 1922 he worked as a non-regular staff member conducting a range of surveys for the Taiwan Government- General, and in 1925 he sat on the board of trustees for the Tokyo Anthropological Society. In 1926 he was appointed as professor to Taipei High School and went to study in England, France, the Netherlands, Germany, and

8 Dr. Koganei studied comparative anatomy in Germany and lectured on anatomy at Tokyo Imperial University. He was influenced by Tsuboi, a great figure in Japanese anthropology.

9 A course in ethnography.ethnology was created at Taihoku Imperial University, and Utsushikawa seems to have moved there close to when the courses on anthropology at Keio University were expanded. "Up to now there were anthropology courses offered at Keio University, but this time they have invited Mr. Oyama, to anthropology and Mr. Harada and Mr. Takahashi to archaeology. Ethnology, as before, is in the charge of Yanagita Kunio" (Journal of Anthropology 43(7): 323, July 1928). Utsushikawa's participation in the Southern Discussion Society (formed in 1922) led by Yanagita Kunio seems related to the fact that he was lecturing in the Department of History at Keio University.

India for twenty-two months as an overseas researcher for the Taiwan Government-General. He returned on March 3 1928, and was appointed as a professor to Taihoku Imperial University, to conduct courses on ethnography.ethnology in the Faculty of Humanities and Government. In 1929 he worked as a non-regular staff member in the Taiwan Government-General's museum, and in 1934 he sat on the board of trustees for the International Association of Anthropology and Ethnology and served as a secretary in the Japanese Ethnological Association. In 1936 he was presented with an award by the Imperial Academy in Japan for his work *The Formosan Native Tribes* and served as a trustee for the Archaeological Society. In 1937 he was sent to Europe (on duty for the Taiwan Government-General) and held a seat on the discussion committee of the International Association of Anthropology and Ethnology. In 1938 he served as a councilor for Taihoku Imperial University. In 1940 he was appointed dean of the Faculty of Humanities and Government, and in 1941 went on trips to Southern China and Indochina. In 1943 he became director of the Southeast Asia, Oceania and Taiwan Humanities Research Institute and went to Celebes and Java. In 1944 he became a member of Academy of Science in Japan and in 1945 he retired and remained on until November 1945 as a member of the reconstruction group for National Taipei University. He returned to Japan in December. He died on February 9, 1947 at the age of 62.

The connection between Professor Utsushikawa and the Taiwan Government-General was first formed in 1922 when Shidehara (at the time a Ph.D. in history and seated in the House of Lords)[10] had sat

---

10 Shidehara's penname meant "Lives on Spring Hill", and his attainments in traditional Korean painting were considerable. When he began advising on politics for the Great Han Empire (pre-colonial Korea) on August 22 1904 (year 37 of the Meiji period), he directed educational reform as a member of an institute of higher learning. In November 1905 an agreement to establish a Residency-General was reached, and it was installed on February 1 1906. Ito Hirobumi was appointed as the first Resident-General and Shidehara resigned and returned

on the committee that created the plans for the university. On an early trip to Taiwan he recognized the need for creating a department related to anthropology and selected Professor Utsushikawa (Miyamoto 1983b: 33 & 1985c: 43). He later gave a number of speeches at the regular meetings of the Southeast Asia, Oceania and Taiwan Ethnographic Society led by Utsushikawa.

The writings of Utsushikawa on his trip to Europe, where he was sent as a foreign researcher by the Taiwan Government-General, are illuminating. The first dispatches were sent home from Shanghai on April 9, 1926 under the title "The Correspondence of Utsushikawa Nenozo." He first wrote "[April] 5, 6:00 pm: Arrived in Shanghai from Kobe aboard the French packet Borurucca" (*Jinruikaku Jatssi* Journal of Anthropology 41(5): 295). The letter arriving on June 15 had been sent from London. "I sojourned two or three days in Paris and arrived in London on the evening of May 18. Attended a lecture hosted by the Anthropological Society here by the Dutchman Van Vuureu, who was giving a talk and showing pictures on funerary customs of the Toraja tribe on Celebes Island" (*Jinruikaku Jatssi* Journal of Anthropology 41(7): 335, 1926). "Visited Professor Haddon at Cambridge University and received an invitation to dinner. Talked about the Pacific Meetings. Met the young Buxton of Oxford, and Professor Seligman of the University of London was indisposed due to an illness. Written in London, July 10" (*Jinruikaku Jatssi* Journal of Anthropology 41(9): 470, 1926).

In his letter dated January 5 from Paris, he wrote, "The meeting of the Pacific Academic Society has concluded with great success, and I traveled for a month and a half through Scotland, Ireland, and Wales. I arrived in Paris at the beginning of November, and met people connected to the Ethnography/Ethnology Research Institute at the Sorbonne" (*Jinruikaku Jatssi* Journal of Anthropology 42(1): 45, 1927). There is

---

to Japan. He has left behind a large number of works on Korean history.

also part of a letter sent on August 26, 1927, while he was waiting for a boat in Helsinki. In his letter from Helsinki dated September 6, he wrote "after traveling for a long time in the southern regions, spending some time in the Netherlands and staying a short while in Belgium, I have finally come north. From Uppsala in Sweden I move on to Russia's Leningrad" (Utsushikawa 1927b). His final letter, dated January 20, 1927, was sent from Smyrna, Georgia, in which he states "having left Europe behind by way of the Balkans, I came to Smyrna through Turkey" (*Jinruikaku Jatssi* Journal of Anthropology 43(3), 1928).[11]

Professor Utsushikawa's two-year trip can be called an anthropologist's quick take on Europe. He reviewed in detail the state of anthropological research at the major universities of Europe and collected relevant materials.

11 The following excerpt was omitted from Utsushikawa's publication list written by Mabuchi Toichi. "An Introduction to the Major Universities of France and England: Professor Seligman, who lectures in ethnography and ethnology at the London School of Economics and Political Science at the University of London gives a course called "General Ethnography and Ethnology", Dr. Malinowski teaches "Social Anthropology", "Melanesian Culture", "Primitive Psychology", and "Comparative Linguistics." Mr. Chase of the British Museum gives a course on "Primitive Technology", and Mr. Iathis assists. Also, Professor Westermark in the sociology department gives courses on family and Professor Hobhouse lectures on social psychology. Mr. Berry teaches cultural anthropology at London University College. At Oxford, physical anthropology and cultural anthropology are separate, with the former subdivided into comparative anatomy and fossil man and ethnological physiology. Most of these courses are led by Dr Buxton. The subfields in cultural anthropology include archaeology, ethnography/ ethnology, social anthropology, and technology and are largely led by Dr. Marrett, while Mr. Baruphoa from the Pitt-Rivers Museum of Ethnography handles courses on technology··· At Cambridge Dr. Haddon lectures on "General Anthropology", "Social Anthropology", and "Primitive Technology, and is with an anthropology committee also at Cambridge, it is associated with archaeology, linguistics, psychology, geology, and architecture. There is a museum of archaeology, ethnography and ethnology at London University College, displaying many artifacts from the South Pacific. Other than that, at Wales University there is a course in geography and anthropology, ···and in the Department of Geography at the University of Edinburgh in Scotland there is a course titled "Economic Ethnography" (Utsushikawa 1927: 147-150).

While investigating research trends he also attended the meetings of various international academic societies. A considerable amount of time must have been spent in travel.

From 1928, when Taihoku Imperial University opened, Professor Utsushikawa gave almost annual courses on the introduction to ethnography.ethnology along with training and practice in ethnography. ethnology. His texts for the latter course included Frazer's *The Golden Bough*, Rosalind Moss's *Life after Death in Oceania*, Edward Westermark's *Early Belief and Social Influence*, and Duley's *The Peoples of Asia*. The introductory and training courses had titles such as The Ethnography of the South Pacific and Southeast Asia, The Ethnography of the South Pacific (Micronesia and Indonesia), and The Ethnography of Indonesia. The introductory courses were generally based on physical anthropology and European prehistory in the first semester, and the social structure of Australian aboriginals and the material culture of Micronesia in the second. The "seminar" courses were conversation-oriented, and consisted of giving an outline of the text in turns, followed by the professor's explanations or comments. Conducting the class in this manner clearly shows the influence of an American graduate education.[12]

---

12 The following is a list of courses and their reading materials offered by Professor Utsushikawa.

1928: Introduction to Ethnography and Ethnology (2), Training and Practice in Ethnography and Ethnology (1), Frazer's The Golden Bough

1929: Introduction to Ethnography and Ethnology (2), Training and Practice in Ethnography and Ethnology (1), Frazer's The Golden Bough

1930: Introduction to Ethnography and Ethnology (2), Ethnography of the South Pacific and Southeast Asia (1)

1931: Introduction to Ethnography and Ethnology (2), Ethnography of the Pacific (Micronesia, Indonesia) (2)

1932: Introduction to Ethnography and Ethnology (2), Ethnography of Indonesia (2)

1933: Introduction to Ethnography and Ethnology (2) Reading and Practice in Ethnography and Ethnology (2), Rosalind Moss's Life after Death in Oceania

1934: Introduction to Ethnography and Ethnology (2)

Utsushikawa was a member of the Society for the Survey of Historical Relics, Scenic Areas, Nature, and Memorial Objects, run under the auspices of the Government-General (Taiwan Government-General 1936: 156). Traveling to the Netherlands, he compiled a list of about "25,000 pages" of documents related to Taiwan housed in the National Archives in the Hague (Utsushikawa 1938: 4). It is necessary to mention the variations in the spelling of Utsushikwa's name, and why there were such discrepancies in how his name appeared on each document is a question to be considered. In 1934 Utsushikawa's name appeared in English as "Utsurikawa" (Taihoku Imperial University, Faculty of Humanities and Government, Department of History Annual Research Report 2, 1935), but in a Government-General document on staff, his name was recorded as "Utsushikawa."

Miyamoto Nobuto (1901-1989), during his period as a student at Keio University, attended courses taught by Yanagita Kunio and Utsushikawa. He graduated from the Department of Asian History in 1928, and was called on by Utsushikawa to take a position as assistant professor in the ethnography institute in the Department of History, in the Faculty

---

1935: Introduction to Ethnography and Ethnology (2), Reading and Practice in Ethnography and Ethnology (2), Westermark's Early Belief and Social Influence
1936: : Introduction to Ethnography and Ethnology (2), Reading and Practice in Ethnography and Ethnology (2), Duley's The Peoples of Asia
1937: Introduction to Ethnography.Ethnology (2), Reading and Practice in Ethnography.Ethnology
1938: Introduction to Ethnography.Ethnology (2), Special Topics in Ethnography. Ethnology (2)
1940: Introduction to Ethnography.Ethnology (2)
1941: Introduction to Ethnography.Ethnology (2)
(See Taihoku Imperial University, Faculty of Humanities and Government, Department of History, Annual Report 1: 451-455, 1934). (Taihoku Imperial University, Faculty of Humanities and Government, Department of History, Annual Report 2: 421, 1935). There is no record of titles for courses after 1942. The university had already been pulled into the war, so courses were discontinued and professors were mobilized in research institutes and committees to help prepare for war.

of Humanities and Government at Taihoku Imperial University. In early July 1928 he followed Professor Utsushikawa on a field survey trip to Taruko, located in northeastern Taiwan. Miyamoto, who was a strong field researcher, led many field surveys for the history department. At the request of the Government-General, in 1935 Miyamoto accompanied Utsushikawa on a trip to Xiamen University to help preserve the university museum and library's collections. As a civilian employee, he went to Kwantung in 1937, then under the occupation of the Japanese army, and spent a year heading cultural operations there. At the height of the war, Miyamoto temporarily took a position in the Government-General's Bureau of Culture and Education to help with a policy countering the "Ancestral Shrine Movement" of the Taiwanese natives and was appointed as an investigator to cope with the problem of ancestral shrines (Miyamoto 1985: 47).[13]

Appointed to a naval investigation agency in 1943, he was assigned to conduct religious surveys in Java as a military staff member in mid November that year (*Nanpo Minjoku* 7(1.2): 133). After Japan's defeat in the war, Taihoku Imperial University was renamed National Taiwan University under the Republic of China, and Miyamoto stayed in Taiwan

---

13 "The later period of Japanese rule, … in particular after the outbreak of the Greater East Asia War, these tendencies became stronger. In homeland Japan the National Spirit Enhancement Movement gained steam, while in Taiwan the Yellow Chrysanthemum Movement reached its peak. Linked to this, a movement to abolish ancestral shrines in the villages of Taiwan has risen. …The idols of the abolished shrines were collected in one place and burned, and we have gathered the idols from some villages in the specimen room at Taihoku Imperial University…. The state of things has become serious, and there is criticism of this within Japan, and as the criticism of Taiwan intellectuals increases, by direction of the Government-General there was a conference on religious problems. The Governor-General consulted with president Shidehara of the university and Shidehara reached an agreement with Professor Utsushikawa. At that time, I was lecturing in the same department and was moved by the Government-General's Bureau of Culture and Education to deal with the problem of the ancestral shrines" (Miyamoto 1988: 3-4).

as a professor to hand over the duties to Chinese hands. After completion of the transfer in 1948 Miyamoto returned to Japan and in 1949 he was hired on as a professor at Tokai University, where he was head of cultural anthropology until 1972 (Mabuchi 1997). Miyamoto began to strengthen the position of the ethnography institute by organizing the university's references and folklore materials, and has left behind a wide body of research in archaeology, physical anthropology, and cultural anthropology.

Mabuchi Toichi (1909-1988) was born in the city of Hirado in Nagasaki prefecture, and after graduating from Kumamoto High School, entered Tokyo Imperial University's school of economics in 1928. Five months later, in May, he transferred to the history department of the newly opened Taihoku Imperial University. The atmosphere of the school of economics at Tokyo University was dominated by Marxist interpretations of economics, and Mabuchi, who had been interested in this since his days in high school, visited Utsushikawa's house in Taipei that May and also received some training from the ethnography institute. From that year on, he participated in surveys of the indigenous Taiwanese, and in 1930 wrote his dissertation for the history department on "unilateral and bilateral descent in ancient China" (Taihoku Imperial University, Faculty of Humanities and Government, Department of History Annual Report 1: 460, 1934), and appears to have become "the first and last student of the Institute of Ethnography.Ethnology" (Yamazaki 1992: 100).

From March of 1931 until 1932, he led surveys as a non-regular staff member of the Government-General, contributing his results to the enormous compilation *The Formosan Native Tribe*.[14] In the register of staff in the history department published in June 1935, Mabuchi is listed as an adjunct professor, but his name is absent from the staff register published in September of 1936.[15] In January 1937 he became a non-regular

---

14 Mabuchi worked in the field for 425 days, Miyamoto for 129 days, and Utsushikawa for 88 days. See Utsushikawa's preface to A Study of the Genealogy of Formosan Native Tribes.

staff member of the Department for Compilation of the Dictionary of Indonesian Customs and Terminology in the Imperial Academy in Japan, and in October of that year he became a researcher for the subsidiary Institute of Ethnology attached to the Japanese Ethnological Association. Furuno Kiyoshi and Mabuchi Toichi, non-regular staff members of the Imperial Academy, began surveys of the native tribes in central, south, and eastern Taiwan on March 10, 1938. Furuno returned on April 9 and Mabuchi on April 15 (*Nanpo Dozoku*, Ethnographic Journal of Southeast Asia, Oceania and Taiwan 4(4): 36). In October 1940 Mabuchi started work at the Department of East Asian Economic Surveys on the Southern Manchurian Railroad, and in June 1943 he was brought by Utsushikawa back to his alma mater Taihoku Imperial University to become a staff member of the Southeast Asia, Oceania and Taiwan Culture Institute and an assistant professor. In December that year he was appointed as a naval non-ranking non-regular staff member and was sent to Celebes (Makasaru, today Kalimantan) and Java.

The conclusion that "without Professor Mabuchi, ethnological research on southeast Asia would not have been what it is today in Japan" (Obayashi 1988: 329) is highly fitting. As the Pacific War was coming to a head, specialists on the southern regions of Asia were asked to write a wide range of papers. Terms like the so-called "Greater East Asian Co-prosperity Sphere" or the "Southern Regions Sphere" were part of the rhetoric created with imperial Japan's invasions. The word "nation" (*minjoku*) gained prominence, and together with the phrase "Greater East Asian Nation",

---

15 Mabuchi is still listed as an adjunct professor on the history department staff register published in June 1935. He is prescribed as a Taihoku Imperial University adjunct professor (starting January 1939), and placed in the Faculty of Letters, with no rank. Only in special cases was an allowance paid out. Adjunct professors required a bachelor's degree or acknowledgement of significant ability, and could be appointed at the recommendation of the dean of the faculty (Taiwan Government-General 1936: 31). At that time adjunct professors received fifty yen in salary per month.

scholars manufactured a new national collectivity centered around Japan. There was no small number of studies twisting this logic (Hasebe 1944). Mabuchi was extremely careful and circumspect in his use of this sort of rhetoric, but being appointed as an assistant professor to the Southeast Asia, Oceania and Taiwan Culture Institute and being obliged to fulfill his duties to the navy, he was unable to fully avoid the overall structure of the war. In this we can read the perspective and concerns of a an intellectual caught in the fractured subjectivity between war and scholarship.

For example, Mabuchi used the phrase "the scope of the so-called Southern Regions Sphere" in one of his articles (Mabuchi 1943: 158). In his use of this term, we can read at least a purposeful indirectness. He wedged "so-called" before the iron clamps of the word "Southern Regions Sphere." This is not direct evidence of his intentions, but it must be noted that except for Mabuchi, no other writer in this almanac put "so-called" in front of "Southern Regions Sphere." In addition, after the title "Societies of the Southern Regions Sphere" there is added in parentheses "Societies of the Native People of the Southern Regions." Perhaps the title originally received by Mabuchi was "Societies of the Southern Regions Sphere", which he resubmitted as "Societies of the Native People of the Southern Regions." It is likely that the final title was a compromise between Mabuchi's desire to avoid the phrase Southern Regions Sphere and the goals of the other side.

The phrases that appear in Furuno's paper "Religions of the Southern Regions Sphere", which mentioned the same Almanac of the Southern Regions Sphere, were at odds with Mabuchi's view. Furuno's assertion of a "requirement to Japanize the few million in the Greater East Asian Co-prosperity Sphere" and Mabuchi's expressions are the antithesis of each other. Regardless of the high quality of the work itself, even if Furuno had not used such sentences as cited above, the insertion of such phrases is indicative of his political stance.

Ethnography.ethnology was the first course listed in the history department. In a department independent of the government bureaucracy, it was normal to have professors, assistant professors, and assistants, but in an office or institute that was not a department, there were only professors and assistant professors. However, the building used by the ethnography institute extended into the area used for several other classes, and the course was research-oriented. Given these considerations, it is not difficult to guess parts of Japan's policy toward the southern regions of Asia. Ethnography.ethnology was not placed within a major department; instead it was a common required course, and students of the history department were required to take it. However, it was not a requirement of the major. For example, in universities of the colony, students in the Faculty of Humanities and Government all took the Introduction to Ethnography.Ethnology (Miyamoto 1983b: 34 & 1985c).

In 1934, the ethnography institute had Utsushikawa as professor, Miyamoto as assistant professor, and Mabuchi as adjunct lecturer after his graduation (Taihoku Imperial University, Faculty of Humanities and Government, Department of History Annual Report 1: 461, 1934). It was formed around students from the history department, and published essays related to ethnography in a historical readings group that held presentations and discussions on items of research. For example, the second meeting on June 7, 1930: the period of wearing mourning among the native tribes of Formosa, Mabuchi; the eighth meeting on May 9, 1931: Tales of Porisha, Miyamoto; the twenty-fifth meeting on February 18, 1933: burial methods among tribes other than the Paiwan and Ami, Mabuchi (Taihoku Imperial University, Faculty of Humanities and Government, Department of History Annual Report 1: 457-459).

As material-gathering trips were frequent, the increase in the size of the collection demanded a separate specimen room. Construction started in September 1933. The facility was completed and organized in April 1934, and in commemoration of the university's foundation day, it was opened on May 17. The large exhibition room was devoted to artifacts from Taiwan's indigenous people, and archaeological artifacts were arranged in a smaller room (Taihoku Imperial University, Faculty of Humanities and Government, Department of History Annual Report 2: 422, 1935). Together with ethnological and ethnographical research, collection of ethnographic materials on indigenous Taiwanese was seen as the most urgent task at hand. Effort was poured into the collection of such materials, so in March 1936 the institute purchased 137 types of ethnographic artifacts relating to indigenous culture, totaling about three hundred items, originally owned by Mr. Ino Kanori. Mr Kanori was the first fieldworker in Taiwan and was active during the late nineteenth and early twentieth centuries. Later the collection acquired 1905 types of artifacts, totaling about 2500 items, from the indigenous tribes, gathered by the ethnography institute's expeditions. These were added to artifacts from the Papua tribe of New Guinea and the Illongot tribe in the Philippines, as well as from excavations in southern China. These items were displayed in the same room, created as the Ethnographic Specimen Room. With the completion of the northern wing of the research center in the middle of the building, it is clear that a high degree of consideration was given to ethnographic research at Taihoku Imperial University.

In 1936, the eighth anniversary of the founding of Taihoku Imperial University, materials related to the history department were put on display in the Exhibition Rooms 3 and 4 as part of the Faculty of Humanities and Government Exhibition (May 17 and 18), with Room 4 focusing on display of ethnographic artifacts. The following categories of items were included in the display. 1) European Paleolithic artifacts (ethnography course display), 2) Taiwanese Stone Age artifacts (same as above), 3) ethnographic materials from indigenous Taiwanese tribes (same as above), and 4) ethnographic materials from other tribes neighboring Taiwan (same as above). In one portion of Exhibition Room 3 were "references on Japanese occupied territories of indigenous peoples" (ethnography course display). The exhibitions display items were thus displayed according to each course (*Nanpo Dozoku*, Ethnographic Journal of Southeast Asia, Oceania and Taiwan 4(1): 62-63, 1936), and the main force behind the exhibition was the ethnography institute. These materials allow us to infer the relative importance of the institute within Taihoku Imperial University.

The research activities of the ethnography institute pursued anthropology in the broad sense. Surveys were done on sites in northern Taiwan, where pottery and bones as well as gold-work items were excavated. For about a week in the middle of October 1936, Professor Utsushikawa, accompanied by Miyamoto, went on a fieldwork trip. They attempted to record indigenous language and music, and this work was meaningful not only in preserving authentic linguistic and music forms, but also in starting a collaboration with the linguistics institute in making vinyl records as resources for phonetics and music theory. The results were produced in nine records with eighteen plates (Taihoku Imperial University, Faculty of Humanities and Government, Department of History Annual Report 4: 581, 1937).

"Because the anthropology department at Tokyo Imperial University mainly focused on natural anthropology, the Ethnography and Ethnology Research Institute was Japan's premier department in cultural and social anthropology…. Such great minds as the sociologist Okada Yuzuru, the anatomist Kanaseki Takeo, the linguists Ogawa Toru and Asai Keirin, the agricultural economist Okuda, not to mention the archaeologist Kokubu Naoichi, all had a relationship with the institute, and Furuno, on research trips from Japan, also came to visit it" (Yamaji 1999: 74). The ethnography institute exceeded the shadow cast by Taihoku Imperial University, built with the purpose of administration of southern China and the southern regions of Asia. The site of the systematic pursuit of sociocultural anthropology, which had not taken hold in Japan, was Utsushikawa's ethnography institute, and its influence could be felt even after the war.[16]

16 The Department of Anthropology at Tokyo Imperial University was created in

The Southeast Asia, Oceania and Taiwan Ethnographic Society, established in 1929 after the creation of the ethnography. institute, modeled its organization after the institute, and from 1931 began the publication of the journal *Nanpo Dozuku*. The English title of the journal was *The Ethnographic Journal of Southeast Asia, Oceania, and Taiwan*. In the choice of this English title by the Society, which was headed by Utsushikawa, we can to reconfirm the meaning of "*tozokugaku*" as "ethnography." The Society held forty meetings in the nine years between December 1929 and November 1938[17] and appears to have played a crucial role in fostering

---

the Faculty of Science and pursued research in archaeology and ethnology. In a dictionary published by Sandhodo Publishing Co. in 1928, the term "ethnology" was explained as meaning ethnology and ethnography. The first person to use the term "cultural anthropology" was Nishimura Shinji, and the term first appeared in a Taisho era book titled Cultural Anthropology (Miyamoto 1983b: 33).

17 Regular meeting of the Southeast Asia, Oceania and Taiwan Ethnographic Society

1st meeting, December 2 1929: Observations on the Pantsua title of Asian ethnicities, Utsushikawa Nenozo (Monkey Festival), Abe Akiyoshi

2nd meeting, January 27 1930: On Paiwan, Miyahara Atsushi

3rd meeting, February 27: Katamigo, Shidehara

4th meeting, March 31: On Wanyoon, Ozaki

5th meeting, April 30: Sites on XXXXXX, Miyamoto Nobuto; Sumatra and Brazil, Abe Fumio

6th meeting, Mary 26: South Pacific Customs on Celebes, Miyoshi

7th meeting, July 1: Travels in Timor, Hayasaka Ichiro

8th meeting, October 23: XXX Yami tribe and Bataan Islands, Utsushikawa

9th meeting, November 29: On Shaishatu tribe, Fujizaki Sainosuke

10th meeting, December 22: Religions of the islanders, Masuka Fukutaro

11th meeting, February 2 1931

12th meeting, March 16: Movement of Rituals among the Kabaran tribe

13th meeting, April 13: Native People of Celebes Island and Taiwan, Miyoshi

14th meeting, June 1: Writing of the Miao tribe, Maejima Shinji

15th meeting, September 5: Social Meaning of Age Classifications, Okada Ken

16th meeting, November 5: The History of Native Taiwan XXX, Yamanaka

17th meeting, December 21: Custom Shure Appearing in Native Language, Ogawa Naoyoshi

18th meeting, March 4 1932: On XXX and XXX, Rikimaru Jien

19th meeting, June 1: Origins of the word of Potato, Ando Seiji

the school of Taiwan anthropology.

At one point, the Society admitted thirty-eight new members en masse, including colonial officials in charge of indigenous tribes and even police officers from local areas *(Nanpo Dozoku, Ethnographic Journal of Southeast Asia, Oceania, and Taiwan* July issue, 1935, pp.89-90). Before Taihoku Imperial University's ethnography institute was established, this seemed

---

20th meeting, October 9: Origin and Spread of Livestock, Yamane
21st meeting, December 24: On XX, Kuwata Rokuro
22nd meeting, February 16 1933: On Gold and Silver in XXX, Obada Jun
23rd meeting, October 7: Beliefs of Taiwan's Primitive jar, Miyamoto
24th meeting, November 29: Travels in the Southern Lands and South Pacific, Higashionno
25th meeting, January 20 1934: A Trend in Religious Ethnology, Furuno
26th meeting, March 17: The Five-Year Festival of the Paiwan tribe, Miyamoto
27th meeting, June 7: Stories of the Yarut, Hirata
28th meeting, September 14: Research on the Physiology of Naisen people, Japanese, and Native Tribes of Taiwan, Mori
29th meeting, December 8: Travels in Okinawa, Suto
30th meeting, June 15 1935: XXX Rikimaru, On Place Names and Administrative Regions in Taiwan, Mizukoshi Koichi
31st meeting, June 22: The Mountains and Sea of XXX, Miyoshi
32nd meeting, February 20, 1936: Later Moona.Rudao, Mizukoshi
33rd meeting, June 6: On the XXX of Taiwan, Ozaki; On the Character and Jar of the Paiwan tribe, Miyahara
34th meeting, January 23 1937: Report on Surveys of the Sanpares Nigritos tribe, Asai; Development of the Concept of Private Ownership in Primitive Society, Utsushikawa
35th meeting, May 14: The Interim Taiwan Survey Society, Osato Takehachiro, Hotta Shinen
36th meeting, September 25: Travels in Europe, Utsushikawa (together with Taipei Anthropological Society)
37th meeting, November 17: Music of Okinawa, Higa Moriaki
38th meeting, February 16 1938: XXX of Taiwan's Native Tribes and Ethnicities of the Southern Regions, Utsushikawa; Prospecting for Stone Age XXX, Agai
39th meeting, March 19: Displaying XXXX Artifacts, Film on Ethiopia
40th meeting, November 19: Pastaidze in Shaisat tribe (using film an records), Utsuhikawa, Miyamoto

to have been the chance to concentrate the research staff and accumulated materials on the indigenous people of Taiwan in the school of Taipei anthropology. The publication of *Nanpo Dozoku* began in 1931 and its academic significance and influence can be understood in the context of the publication in Tokyo of the anthropological research periodicals *Minjoku* (Ethnos) in 1925, *Minzokugaku* (Folklore) in 1929, and *Dorumen (*Dolmens*)* in 1932. With the breakout of war between Japan and China in 1937, from 1938 *The Ethnographic Journal of Southeast Asia, Oceania, and Taiwan* became a "quarterly publication" that produced only one issue per year. It ceased publication with volume 7 number 1 in 1944, at the peak of the Pacific War.

A board member of the Southeast Asia, Oceania and Taiwan Ethnographic Society, Utsushikawa served as the society's secretary in 1940 and became president in 1941. The eleven board members included Kanaseki Takeo and Miyamoto, with four secretaries and a nine-member publication committee, with Okada Ken, and Miyamoto holding additional posts as publication committee director, secretary, and member respectively. The society was an expanded organization. Later, following the transfer of Okada Yuzuru to Tokyo Teacher's College and Sudou Toshikazu to the First High School, Hisano Yoshitaka, Mabuchi Toichi, and Himeoka Isao joined the society as board members (*NanpoMinjoku* 7(1.2): 134). Details on the official trips taken by the president and board members is of interest.

Professor Utsushikawa, Mr. Hisano and Mabuchi, all of whom were "full-time non-regular staff" or "naval inspectors", were charged with establishing a surveys department in Makasaru Research Institute, and on November 19, 1943 Utsushikawa went to Makasaru (today Kalimantan) in Indonesia. After making inspection tours of Celebes, Java, and Bali to gather data, he returned on January 14, 1944. Mabuchi went to Makasaru on December 25, 1943 and Hisano went on January 5, 1944. Miyamoto, appointed as an army inspector, had proceeded to his post in the middle of the previous November to carry out surveys on the religions of Java (*NanpoMinjoku* 7(1.2): 133). As a naval inspector, Obata Jun, also a director of the Society, was commissioned by the Department of Special Services in the Hainan Island Navy to carry out a compilation of the island history, and completed a report following field surveys. It was published with the authorization of the Department of Special Services in the Hainan Island Navy (*NanpoMinjoku* 7(1.2): 134).

A look at the work undertaken by the scholars associated with the ethnography institute reveals a few clear trends. "In the actions of Taihoku Imperial University's Institute of Ethnography.Ethnology, Okada and Furuno began surveys of the indigenous Taiwanese tribes and Okada authored 'The Family in Primitive Society' (1942) and Furuno wrote 'The Ritual Life of Native Tribes' (1945), attempting an analysis of the social structure of each of Taiwan's indigenous tribes. Okada and Furuno were both heavily influenced by Radcliffe-Brown in the functionalist school of British social anthropology, and their work later became the cornerstone for functionalist anthropology in Japan" (Mabuchi 1987: 237).

In the midst of this, a person who formed a close relationship with the ethnography institute and the group composed of Utsushikawa, Miyamoto, and Mabuchi was Kano Tadao. He "was accepted into Taihoku Imperial University in 1925 and, having an interest in entomology and other fields in the biological sciences as well as research in cultural anthropology on the indigenous tribes of Taiwan, he participated in a research trip led by the ethnography institute in the spring of 1929, doing his own surveys on insect and bird life and collecting specimens of small animals. That spring he collected samples of birds, insects, and small animals. Kano stuffed several of the birds he collected on this trip" (Yamazaki 1992: 102; Miyamoto, Segawa, Mabuchi 1987: 31). After that, he was accepted into and graduated from the Department of Geology in the Faculty of Science at Tokyo Imperial University, and as a non-regular staff member for the Taiwan Government-General and the police department, conducted cultural-historical research in Taiwan and Southeast Asia for a monthly salary of seventy yen (Taiwan Government-General 1936: 146-148). He also worked as a non-regular staff member for the Japanese Colonization Federation (Yamazaki 1992: 244). His last research paper was completed in June 1943, and between July 1943 and March 1944 he threw himself into ethnological research in the Philippines (Kano 1944: 569). In 1945, at the age of thirty-eight, he disappeared while doing surveys in Borneo (Yamazaki 1992: 320) as an official army inspector and he is still on the list of those missing in action.

Kano and those like him were guided by their field materials and devoted everything to their work. Although their dispatch into the field was driven by political and military motives, they remained true to their research based on academic interests. In pursuing his data, Kano was an inexhaustible field worker who went to any lengths in any conditions to collect materials. In his reports and research articles, he only referred to the data he himself had collected and analyzed, without succumbing to political rhetoric. Regardless of war or military considerations, if there were data at a site or scholarly materials could be collected, he went-even to war zones. It is now acknowledged that "in their impact on the development of cultural anthropology in Taiwan, the discoveries of Kano Tadao remain a permanent contribution" (Hsu Mok-ju 1993: 145). He also produced skilled sketches. His diaries and a small number of his field notes are stored with the work of Izumi Seiichi in the library of the National Museum of Ethnology in Osaka. The question remains of how Kano's personal belongings came to be in Izumi's charge.

A scholar active in anthropology in Taiwan, Kanaseki Takeo published perhaps the greatest amount of work outside Utsushikawa's institute. Originally an assistant professor at Kyoto Imperial University, Kanaseki was appointed as a professor in the Taiwan Government-General's vocational college. He had orders to pursue research in anatomy and anthropology and on September 16 1934, on his way to study abroad in the West, he passed through Taiwan (*Dorumen* 3(10): 77). When the Faculty of Medicine was established in Taihoku Imperial University in 1936, he was invited to serve as professor for the second lecture in anatomy (Yamazaki 1992: 229). Together with the opening of the Faculty of Medicine, Professor Mori and assistant professor Miyauchi of Tokyo Imperial University, and Kanaseki Takeo of Kyoto Imperial University were all expected to do anthropology in Taiwan within the Department of Anatomy in the Faculty of Medicine (*The Ethnographic Journal of Southeast Asia, Oceania, and Taiwan* 4(1): 63, 1936). Professor Kanaseki had given lectures on anthropology at Kyoto Imperial University,[18] and after leaving for his new post at Taihoku Imperial University "gave special lectures on 'physical anthropology' in the office of ethnography" (Sung Ban-hun 1983: 49).

In 1942, on a commission from the Japanese navy, he conducted anthropological surveys in Hainan Island and at night excavated skeletons from indigenous burial sites, returning with them to Taiwan aboard a naval plane (Nez Manashi 1983: 36). He was invested in the German-style racialism that sprung from Nazi ideology and advocated policies based on eugenics (Kanaseki Takeo 1941). The second edition of the journal he directed, *Minjoku Taiwan* (Customs of Taiwan), declaring that "for the building of a Greater East Asia, a strong sense of duty is being awakened, even in the homeland, and all of us editors once again resolve to exert ourselves to the utmost" (*Minjoku Taiwan*, no. 20, February 1943, p.48) in editorial note of the issue, increased the support for the Greater East Asia Co-Prosperity Sphere.

With the use of the keyword "Greater East Asia" in this move, the influence of Yanagita Kunio, who carried the banner of folklore high, cannot be ruled out. In October 1943, a round-table meeting that set

18 "[Kanakane sensei] was appointed to Taipei Imperial University in 1936, so the class 'Introduction to Anthropology' he taught at Kyoto University was no longer offered" (Kakuta 1983: 72).

forth the direction of *Minjoku Taiwan* was held in Yanagita Kunio's house in Tokyo. The meeting was titled "Round-table for Building a Greater East Asian Folklore and Commissioning *Minjoku Taiwan* for Mr. Yanagita Kunio" (time: afternoon of October 17; venue: the house of Yanagita Kunio in Tokyo) (*Minjoku Taiwan* 30: 2-15). The participants included Yanagita Kunio, Hashiura Yasuo (editor of *Minkan Densho*, Transmission of Folklore), Okada Yuzuru (professor at Tokyo Teacher's College), Nakamura Tetsu (professor at Taihoku Imperial University), and Kanaseki Takeo (professor at Taihoku Imperial University). A selection of the issues raised at this round-table is as follows. "Yanagita: A Greater East Asian folklore society reciprocally [cooperating]··· with the goal of a folklore for the Greater East Asia Co-Prosperity Sphere···[establishing] common topics between the various ethnicities within the Greater East Asia Co-Prosperity Sphere, with the participation of such figures as Korea's Mr. Akiba and Manchuria's Mr. Omachi." "Kanaseki: a congress in Tokyo once a year···" (*Minjoku Taiwan* 30: 2-15). With the opening of a folklore conference under the auspices of a commemorative conference for Yanakita Kunio Sensei, the need for even more cooperation and unity hereafter among the ethnicities of the Greater East Asia Co-Prosperity Sphere was felt keenly and "proposal for international joint research subjects" (1944) was put forward with three topics: "foreigners, ancestors, and marriage ethics" (*Minjoku Taiwan* 30: 25). Such topics were presented in the round-table discussion that was recorded in the thirtieth issue of *Minjoku Taiwan*.

Minjoku Taiwan, centered around Kanaseki Takeo, "collected and recorded folkloric data from Taiwan and its outlying regions", and "is not limited solely to folklore and folk customs, but is widely interested in, for example, indigenous history, geography, and natural features" (from an editorial in the first edition of *Minjoku Taiwan*).[19] The editor/publisher

19 This folklore was the folklore of the Folklore Society established by Yanagita,

of this journal was Matsuji Tamotsu, while actual responsibility for it lay with Kanaseki Takeo, who wrote not only the first edition but also most of the opening pages of each issue. As the writer of the content in the first issue, Chin Sou-hyoung (Taihoku Imperial University's ethnography institute), and the photographer Matsuyama Keizo (also Taihoku Imperial University's ethnography institute) were also included. Thus it is evident that they maintained a close relationship with the ethnography institute. *Minjoku Taiwan* first came out in July 1941 and began the publication of articles to "introduce and research customs and culture."

Minjoku Taiwan operated a "Fieldwork Meeting." For example, the seventh "Fieldwork Meeting" was held on February 14 in the Taipei Community Center, with Yang Un-pyung delivering a lecture titled "Assorted Old Tales." The cost of attending the meeting was fifty chŏn (*Minjoku Taiwan* twentieth edition, p.48). Kanaseki Takeo was also involved in a wide range of other activities. In May 1936 he established Taihoku Imperial University's Anthropology Discussion Group, built around the university's Department of Anatomy which had opened the previous month, and from May 1937 held regular monthly meetings.[20]

---

and is the study of the of traditional folk customs and their transmission. The members of the committee were "Aizu Yaichi, Akiba Takashi, Ariga Kizaemon, Inami, Ishida Miniosuke, Utsushikawa, Uno, Oka Masao, Origuchi Nobuo, Kindaichi Kyosuke, Koizumi Tetsu, Kon Wajiro, Nakayama Taro, Nishida Naojiro, Hayakawa Kotaro, Matsumura Takeo, Matsumoto Nobuhiro, and Miyamoto Seisuke." A list of members was compiled in the 1930s and included Ishida Mikinosuke, Uno, Origuchi Nobuo, Kindaichi Kyosuke, Koizumi Tetsu, Matsumura Takeo, Matsumoto Nobuhiro (members in capital), Akiba Takashi, Utsushikawa, and Nishida Naojiro (regional members). The members distinguished as members in capital and "regional" should be noted.

20 Regular meetings of Taihoku Imperial University's Anthropology Discussion Group:

1st meeting, May 27 1937: On the Craniums of Taiwan Savage, Kanakane Takeo; A Regional Glimpse of Caucacus, Tomita Masaji

2nd meeting, June 26: Linguistics and Anthropology, Asai

Led by Kanaseki Takeo, the Department of Anatomy collected and researched materials related to physical anthropology, and produced considerable results. Their work covered Taiwan and Okinawa and fanned out across the South Pacific. Anthropological surveys of Okinawa Prefecture and the Yonaguni Islands were conducted by Miyauchi Eizo and Wata Kaku of Taihoku Imperial University's Department of Anatomy. They began in Jilung and, accompanied by four students, arrived in Okinawa Prefecture and the Yonaguni Islands. They took anatomical measurements of one hundred men and one hundred women, making casts of their hands and feet and gathering much other ethnographic material (*Ethnographic Journal of Southeast Asia, Oceania, and Taiwan* 4(4):68, 1938). Research in physical anthropology on the indigenous groups of Taiwan was also directed by Kanaseki Takeo (*Ethnographic Journal of Southeast Asia, Oceania, and Taiwan* 4(4):68, 1938). Putting together the work of the Taipei anthropologists, it was pursued as anthropology in the broad sense of the term, while divided into specialties, so rather than being active in each separate discipline, wherever possible the adjacent disciplines cooperated and produced joint work

As the Pacific War came to a head, those involved in Taiwan anthropology took employment in large numbers as inspectors or

---

3rd meeting, September 25: Travels in Europe, Utsushikawa

4th meeting, October 25: Excavation sites in Kaoshung, Miyamoto Nobuto

5th meeting, December 18: Distribution of Blood Types and Kin Relations among the Taiyaru, Maruyama

6th meeting, January 29 1938: Ancient Man in East Asia, Kanakane Takeo

7th meeting, February 15: The Research on the Native Tribes of Taiwan, Segawa Kokichi (Ethnographic Journal of Southeast Asia, Oceania, and Taiwan 4(4): 35-36, 1938).

9th meeting, September 23: Held in small conference room in the Taihoku Construction Hall from 7:30 pm; Thoughts on Micronesia, Suzuki Masao; Customs and Physiology of Yonaguni Islanders, Kanenaga Hiroshi, Waka Kaku, and Miyauchi Etsuzo (Ethnographic Journal of Southeast Asia, Oceania, and Taiwan 5(1.2): 71, 1938).

non-regular staff in military groups in order to carry out research that would assist in the war effort. They were active in collecting material from all regions of Southeast Asia, Oceania, and Taiwan. This critical time is often still understood as a clear example of anthropological work enlisted by the army. The idea that "by challenging head-on the Government-General's perspective of 'ownerless primitives,' Utsushikawa and his colleagues separated themselves from the strategies of colonialism" (Yamaji 1999: 86) in some ways fails to capture the entire system of colonial rule. To undervalue the fact that Utsushikawa was also given duties by the Government-General and the navy and carried out research in occupied territories is to regard him as someone who was caught up in emulating heroism. Utsushikawa left no traces of confronting the Government-General and the colonial rule it exercised.

From 1935 on the presentations of research at the regular meetings of the Southeast Asia, Oceania and Taiwan Ethnographic Society started to decline, and from 1939 even the meetings themselves seem to have been discontinued. After 1939 Professor Utsushikawa's university lectures grew less frequent and from 1942 there is no record of any lectures at all. If we accept this as a fact of the times, the atmosphere following the Sino-Japanese War and surrounding the Pacific War can be taken as indirect evidence of the large amount of other work for professors of imperial universities outside of the universities themselves. This explains the process in which anthropologists were recreated as civilians involved in the military.

2. Keijo School of Anthropology

The term "Keijo school of anthropology" was coined by Japanese alumni of Keijo Imperial University after they had returned to Japan and organized an alumni club. This provides a strong basis for seeing the anthropological researchers of the university within a single scholarly current. The Keijo school of anthropology can be broadly classified as the research and publication in physical anthropology led by Akiba Takashi, an assistant professor in sociology within the "Institute of Religious Studies and Sociology" in the Faculty of Law and Humanities, his student Izumi Seiichi, and Imamura Yutaka, who worked in the Department of Anatomy in the Faculty of Medicine. Their cooperation and experience in researching together provides the basis for calling them a "school" of anthropology.

Akiba Takashi's career and activities can be summarized as follows. The Institute of Religious Studies and Sociology was headed by Professor Akamatsu Chijo. Akamatsu Chijo, a native of Yamaguchi, had studied religion at Tokyo Imperial University. Before his appointment to Keijo Imperial University, he wrote several essays on the anthropology of religion and the concept of "mana", the first one published in March 1926. He developed an interest in shamanism in colonial Korea and conducted joint research with the sociologist Akiba.

Akiba, as an overseas researcher at Keijo Imperial University, received an official order to study in Europe. He left in 1924. His foreign study lasted for twenty-two months. The work he produced and the influences he absorbed during this time require some attention. Akiba's London address was 227 Valley Road, Streatham, London, SW16. A letter he sent back to the Japanese Sociological Association on June 29 1925, which was published in the association's newsletter (17: 100-101), stated: "I spend my days at the University of London and the British Museum. During the upcoming summer vacation, Professor Westermark is planning to rest and research in Morocco, Professor Hobbhouse in France, Dr. Malinowski in Italy, and Dr. Ginsburg in the countryside. Myself, I go to Mr. Perry's research office in University College. Westermark, at the advanced age of sixty-three, stands an imposing at the height of 180 cm and over the past twenty years has established twenty research sites in Morocco. Each year he has spent the summer in Africa and the winter in Finland for research and lecturing. Most years Dr. Malinowski publishes a steady stream of papers on the eastern regions of New Guinea, working so hard that it has adversely affected his health. …The theories of the Continental scholars are based on the work of these thinkers… working hard at writing painstaking, rigorous monographs."

Generally, Akiba spent his time in Perry's research office in the University College at the University of London. Academically, Perry leaned toward diffusionism. Although Akiba was not directly instructed in the scholarship of Westermark and Malinowski, he showed great interest in the ethnographic monographs that were influenced by their work. However, the first paper Akiba published after leaving Europe, in 1928 ("Polyandry in Feminine Country" *Shakaikaku Jatssi* Journal of Sociology 51: 1-26) seems not to have been heavily influenced by the new Malinowskian academic trends. A further paper published in 1928 and two more articles on the "intensive method" appearing in *Shakakaku Jatssi* (Journal of Sociology) in 1929 show a vastly different slant. Akiba's papers written prior to 1924, the year he left Europe, show no essential difference in their content over the course of his studies.

During his time in Europe, Akiba "saw more than thirty museums on ethnography or ethnology" (Akiba 1927a: 123). Perhaps the greatest portion of his time during his two years there was spent visiting museums and this experience was trimmed into a series of stories on the "museum circuit" (Akiba 1927a, 1927b). This experience later led him to establish a "Korean Folk Reference Room" at Keijo Imperial University, which can be seen as the motive behind turning it into an "exhibition room" (museum). The greatest factor in pushing his interests more in the direction of anthropology and folklore than sociology was is fondness for museums.

Akiba returned to Japan from England on November 2, 1926. On November 29, he delivered an address to the Tokyo Sociological Society's twenty-fourth meeting titled "Marriage Customs in Bretagne", and on December 23 of the same year he gave a paper titled "On Wife's House" at a meeting of the Japanese Sociological Association at Tokyo University. The title of another paper he was scheduled to present at the Japanese Sociological Association's fourth conference on November 3 1928 was "Research Method in Sociology", but he actually gave one called "On the Intensive Method." At the same conference, Suzuki Eitarou (instructor at Kifu Agricultural High School) gave a paper titled "Sociological Research Method in Rural Communities."

A paper Akiba (1928a) wrote on the marriage custom in which the groom carries a wooden goose to the bride's house and sets it on a table, is not based on in-depth research. In Korea's thirteen provinces, he hurried through only a sample of seventeen spots while collecting data. The evidence of his methods of data collection is tacked on at the very end of his essay. He further cites old references. Akiba reminisced that "I give my good wishes for surveying the marriage customs of Korea alone for a year and my thanks to the students who surveyed the customs of their hometowns during their summer vacations. I am indebted to the talents of Mr. Kato Kankaku as a field worker. I am grateful for Mr. Kato's efforts in surveying Pyŏngnam Sŏhŭng" (Akiba 1928a: 86).[21]

Through 1928 and 1929, after his appointment to Keijo Imperial University, Akiba's academic inclinations were not centered on his studies in Europe, but rather on the opportunities he had at the university to put into practice the bits and pieces he had picked up along the way. This was the confirmation and realization of the goal inherent in the

21 Kato Kankaku was a graduate of Aichi University. In 1933 attended lectures in anthropology and archaeology at Tokyo Imperial University. In 1935, with the completion of his course requirements, he went to study in Russia as a non-regular staff member for the anthropological society of his university, and in 1941 he traveled all through the Korean peninsula on anthropological and archaeological research. As a non-regular staff member for the Korea Government-General Bureau of Education Department of Text Book Compilation and Dongguk-Yeonsang, he worked at the civic memorial. His address was in the civil memorial in Chung-gu, Keijo.

construction of an imperial university in colonial Korea. In his appointment to Keijo Imperial University in 1926, an accidental reading of Imamura Tomoe's *Report on the Folk Customs of Korea* belatedly recalled him to the work of Malinowski. Imamura was a high ranking colonial officer at that time. This seems to have been what brought Akiba to write his paper of 1929. He took hold of a new academic direction, which was precisely the fieldwork he had witnessed from London, convincing him of what it was to write a monograph. The contents of the letter he had sent to the Sociological Association in 1925 were directly reproduced in his 1929 paper (which he finished writing on November 2, 1928). His reasons, or some of them, for editing and publishing the third volume of *Journal of Korean Folklore* (1941) commemorating the seventieth birthday of Imamura Tomoe can be found here.

The two papers Akiba published in 1928 and 1929, both of which focused on Western reference materials that were unable to escape the amateurism of an nineteenth-century evolutionary stratification, were totally devoid of the nuances that come from fieldwork. There are a few clues to the background of the paper. Akiba's position in the journal published on July 1, 1928 was stated as "professor of Keijo University;" the final date of the draft, "Showa 3.5.16" may have indicated the date on which the draft was completed; the details of "Keijo Daily Newspaper" appearing in footnote 26; and the inclusion in the postscript of the words "after my homecoming I met with Professor Shiratori at the Toyo Library, whose first words were about reference materials in England. Before going to Europe, this task had been the teaching I received from him." These suggest that the paper was the revised version of a paper he had written before his trip to Europe, supplemented with the materials he had collected while he was there. Given that Akiba's subsequent publications were based on fieldwork, the trends shown in his work done as he was being appointed to Keijo Imperial University can be understood as his experience of great change. His paper included in a 1929 compilation called *Religious Studies* shows traces of the same inclinations, and falls into the same category into his previously published piece that appeared in a 1928 volume of the *Shakaikaku Jatssi* (Journal of Sociology). In no way can it be read as a result of influences that had to have been absorbed by Akiba during his study abroad.

Akiba's paper on the "intensive method" that was published in *Shakaikaku Jatssi* (Journal of Sociology) in 1929 "argues for the 'intensive method' as a single method of specific research on actual society" (Akiba 1929b: 10). However, a closer analysis of the substance of this paper shows that Akiba was looking at only the superficial aspects of this method. He made no mention of functionalism, which was the ideological underpinning of the intensive method at that time.

The results of his research based on the "intensive method" he mentioned in his 1929 *Shakaikaku Jatssi* article, regardless of qualitative depth, began to appear in 1931. The subject of this work was almost always shamanism. This is undoubtedly related to the interests of the religious studies scholar Akamatsu Chijo (cf. Akamatsu 1929, 1935). Akiba's paper published in *Religious Studies (New Edition)* in 1932 supports the conclusion that it was a part of the work done with Akamatsu that was supported by research funding from the Imperial Academy of Japan. "For the last three years I have visited sixty villages scattered along the railroad, and gone into the homes of three hundred shamans, especially female shamans" (Akiba 1933a: 116). The paper appearing in the April 1933 issue of *Dorumen* was finished in Keijo (Seoul) on February 18 1933, and evinces no relation to his work done between 1930 and 1932. After his appointment to Keijo Imperial University, most of his time was spent in his work. His method was fieldwork, and this fieldwork was that which he had learned in England. However, it must be pointed out that the level of this fieldwork was fairly superficial.

Akiba's research on colonial Korea was funded by the Imperial Academy of Japan and his work in Manchuria by the Department of

Cultural Activities in the Ministry of Foreign Affairs. The turning point seems to have been in 1932 and 1933. This was likely an adaptation to changes in the international political climate, such as the military invasion of Manchuria and the creation of Manchukuo, in an atmosphere of the transition from "colonialism" to "war." To a significant degree, the subject of this research could not be free from compromise with preparatory stages of natural resource surveys for the invasion. In September 1936, in the middle of the Manchurian and Mongolian Ethnological Investigation Trip, conducted with the support of the Department of Cultural Activities, he used questionnaires to survey Mongolian students at the Xing'an Military Academy and to collect data on the influence of Han Chinese culture on Mongolians. The government agencies that cooperated to make this work possible were military. Accordingly, Akiba's acknowledgements added at the end of his reports thanked to the Special Task Forces Agency of the regional Army and the staff and students of the Xing'an Military Academy. The Xing'an Military Academy, which was under the direct jurisdiction of the Manchurian Military Government, was a military organization installed with the aim of creating Mongolian military elites. In March 1937, he used questionnaires at the Southern Manchurian Middle High School, surveying the social status of the occupations of 276 Manchurian students (Akiba 1938).

To collect data from the frontier regions in Manchuria, Akiba conducted his field investigation based on the work done by Jochelson, Sternberg, and Shirokogoroff, as well as the data and survey reports of the Manchukuo Department of Security. This research must be seen in its connection to the pacification work that was part of Japanese military operations on the front line. He wrote: "The fall of 1935… I saw an Orochon village, …large villages grouped together from eight places in the back country of the Xing'an Mountains for the purposes of pacification work" (Akiba 1944: 348). In addition, Akiba wrote that "my guide to the Xing'an Mountains, Mr. Yoshioka Yoshihito, was a brave young man who was also at that time concentrating on pacification of the Orochon tribe" (Akiba 1944: 349). This is evidence that the boundaries between anthropological research and pacification work were undifferentiated. Akiba also recorded that "in 1936, Mr. Izumi Seiichi, who was in my research office, went into the Xing'an Mountains alone" (Akiba 1944: 348), showing that his student Izumi had also been mobilized into this work.

During his residence in Keijo (Seoul), Akiba associated with the Korean folklorists Song Sŏk-ha, Son Chin-t'ae, and Yi Nŭng-hwa, and took visitors from Japan on research trips among the many islands of Korea's south coast. As reference to "my friend Song Sŏk-ha" (Akiba 1933b: 9) suggests, Akiba clearly saw Song Sŏk-ha as his friend. Akiba said that both also coauthored a book on the Korean mask dances, showing the extent to which Akiba valued Song Sŏk-ha's scholarship. They overcame an age difference of sixteen years and the status difference between an imperial university professor and a young colonial subject, and their meeting both stripped away masks and drew Akiba into helping establish the Korean Folklore Society. Akiba, whose eyes turned toward continental China from 1933 on, continued these interests as he threw himself into research on shamanism there.

In the summer of 1936, associates at the Attic Museum (Miyamoto Seitarou, Ogawa Toru, and Murakami Kiyofumi) dispatched from Tokyo traveled to Imja-do, Su-do, Nakwŏl-do, Hŏsa-do, Taei-do, and Jŭng-do, islands in Chŏllanam-do province in the southwest of Korea, for a three-day trip to explore folk customs. Their records of the trip show that Akiba accompanied them. The area they covered was in Muan-gun county, stretching from the port of Mokp'o northwest to the sea (Shibusawa Keizo 1939).

Akiba, who was nominally a professor of the sociology department, actually did his research in the field of social anthropology, and invited more sociological researchers to be members of the department. By bringing in Suzuki Eitaro, who majored in rural sociology, it appears that Akiba was attempting to fill the department with members better suited to its title. However, we cannot claim that Suzuki's work had nothing whatsoever to do with anthropology. For example, a paper by Suzuki on house spirits (*yashiki-kami*) in Japanese rural villages (Suzuki 1935) and another one on John Embree's monograph on the social anthropology of Japanese villages (Suzuki 1940a) were both published in the journal *Minjokukaku Kenkyu* (Studies in Ethnology).

With the new construction of the main administrative building at Keijo Imperial University, the Korean Ethnographic Reference Exhibition Room was created in two rooms of the former administration office and displayed about a thousand artifacts, such as axes, earthenware, and utensils, from the art and artifacts collected by Professors Oda, Imanishi, and Akiba (Museum Research 1932: 7 volume 5 no. 1). "The sociology institute at Keijo Imperial University, since it was founded in 1926, has put effort into the collection of folk artifacts under the direction of Akiba, up to 1700 in total. Fifty of these items were displayed on May 2 last year [1934] at the celebration for the tenth anniversary of the founding of Keijo Imperial University. Included were mostly things related to Korean folk customs, with a few Mongolian-Manchurian and Eskimo items" (*Shakaikakuto*, Sociologists, volume 8 no. 7, July 1934). The Eskimo material had been brought from the Korean folk collection at the Danish Museum through the cooperation of Oka Masao. Akiba received an official order to be the director of the Keijo Imperial University Exhibition Hall in May 1942" (Shimamoto 1955: 315). This suggests that Akiba was in fact in charge of the exhibition hall, which was the university's museum.[22]

22 The responsibilities for "participation" began with bureaucrats in the Meiji government, and the details of this hall were identical to the legislature, with authority for establishing the political system and instituting the legal system. However this position was monopolized by Satsuma, Choshu, Tosa, and Higo, who had come out of each region, and was abolished at the time of the reform of government organization in 1869. Instead, a position titled "councilor was created. Why a position called Sanyo appeared at Kyŏngsŏng Imperial University

Izumi Seiichi (1915-1970) was Akiba's only student in the university's sociology department.[23] Following a climbing accident on Halla-san mountain on Cheju-do islands during his student days, Izumi transferred from the Korean language department to sociology in 1936. He borrowed a copy of Malinowski's *Argonauts of the Western Pacific* from Akiba, and for Akiba "in only ten years [following his appointment to the university], his first student appeared" (Izumi Kimiko 1972: 32-33). Izumi graduated in 1938 with a thesis on Cheju-do island while working as Akiba's personal assistant in the sociology research office. In July of that year, he also participated a research trip to Inner Mongolia and Manchuria. In December he enlisted in the Asahikawa 7th Division of the Japanese Army and was posted to Harbin. In the summer of 1941 he was assigned to the General Staff Office and made confidential monthly preparations in the strategic plans for a landing in Allied-held territories in southeast Asia and Oceania (Izumi Kimiko 1972: 74). He returned to Keijo in January, 1942. There were no assistant positions available in the Faculty of Humanities, so on the recommendation of Prof. Odaka, who was an international law specialist as well as the dean of the Faculty of Science and Engineering (and the head of a mountaineering club), he officially gained a position as an assistant. An ex-soldier in the

---

remains unknown.

23 Title of Akiba's classes:

1927: Introduction and Practice in Sociology (reference research on the family)
1928: Overview of Sociology, Folklore and Sociology, Primitive Sociology
1933: Studies in Chosŏn Folklore (two hours per week)
1934: Introduction to Sociology, Special Topics in Sociology (Primitive Society), Practice in Sociology (Sorokin's Contemporary Sociological Theories)
1935: Chosŏn Customs
1936: Introduction to Sociology, Primitive Society (Special Course), Practice in Sociology

There were very few students being brought up by Akiba through these classes. Moritani (assistant professor) gave courses on Social Policy and East Asian social economy. At the time, all classes in archaeology were handled by Fujita Ryosaku.

university, Izumi was put in charge of upholding regulations in the Department of Student Affairs in the main administrative building, and directed the emergency response during air raid alarms (Izumi Kimiko 1972: 78).

The draft of Korean students began, and study became impossible in the university. Izumi discussed the situation with Professor Odaka Asao and they sent a letter to the Pacific Federation. There was a position in the Army Department of Special Inspection, and the work involved conducting surveys among the Dayak of Borneo. At the time there was an uprising among the Dayak, which brought with it the possibility of death during research. Izumi turned down the position as a military special inspector and in the fall of 1942 was once again contacted by the Pacific Federation to participate in large-scale natural resource surveys in western New Guinea. The leader of the trip was a lieutenant-general in the Navy, and the assistant leader was Professor Tayama Rizaburo of Tohoku Imperial University. Geologists from universities and museums formed the core of the expedition and were accompanied by zoologists, botanists, and agriculturists. The group was divided into six teams. Izumi was in charge of administering affairs and anthropological surveys (Izumi Kimikio 1972: 82). The expedition left on January 18, 1943 and included 100 scholars and more than 800 members in total. The contract was to last for ten months, but Izumi received a telegram stating that his father had passed away. Oon August 19 he moved to Palau and from there returned home (Fujimoto Hideo 1994: 172). Izumi, who was listed on the New Guinea Resource Survey Expedition third team's register as the one in charge of transportation, was formally designated as a non-regular staff member of the Office of Southeast Asia and Oceania Affairs in the Navy Department, and carried into effect the resource survey report (dated November 20) for the 4th branch office of the Navy Department's Office of Southeast Asia and Oceania Affairs. Izumi was in charge of and reported on ethno-geography (Satake Gisuke 1963: 106). He also directed the academic survey team and his work according to plan was regarded as exceptional (Hatae Nobuhiro 1968: xii).

Holding a position as an assistant in the Faculty of Science and Engineering at Keijo Imperial University, Izumi conducted surveys of the Orochon in December 1943, and in June 1944 traveled through Inner Mongolia on the third Inner Mongolia and Manchuria academic survey trip. "When the Continental Natural Sciences Research Institute was established in June 1945, [he] moved from the office of student affairs to the institute as an assistant professor" (Izumi Kimiko 1972: 105-107). The director of the institute was Professor Imamura Yutaka, a physical anthropologist at Keijo Imperial University. As an assistant professor for the Continental Natural Sciences Research Institute, Izumi was collecting data in China's Hubei region when the war ended. The Japanese Friendship Association in Keijo was reorganized as the Overseas Japanese Salvage Association for the war, with Professor Imamura Yutaka as director and Izumi as head of accounting in the hospital department (Izumi Kimiko 1972: 111). Leaders of the First Salvage Hospital Train were Professors Imamura Yutaka and Suzuki Kiyoshi, and Izumi was recovered to Japan on December 18 (Izumi Kimiko 1972: 105-107). In April 1949, he became an assistant professor at Meiji University, and in 1950 went on a field investigation trip to Tsushima Island. In November 1951, he became a professor at Tokyo University and founded the department of cultural anthropology in its Eastern Culture Research Institute. Working for UNESCO, in September 1952 he was sent to Brazil and in June 1954, he again went to work in Brazil, this time for the Japanese Ministry of Foreign Affairs.

On the recommendation of Yawata Ichiro, Izumi Seiichi joined the Tokyo Anthropological Society in December 1938 (*Jinruikaku Jatssi* Journal of Anthropology 53(7): 364), and at the 525th meeting of the society on March 11 1939, he read a paper titled "Observations of Folk Customs in Inner Mongolia" with Tada Fumio (a geographer). The substance of the paper was based on data he had gathered in the summer of 1938 while he was on Keijo Imperial University's Inner Mongolia and Manchuria Academic Expedition. Izumi was indeed a product of Keijo Imperial University. His father had also held various positions as professor (in international law) at the same university, and he saw the university in its heyday as a student and then as an assistant professor. In his days as a student there he was very involved in the Mountaineering Club and was also prominent in the university's literature club.

None of Izumi's documents make mention of Song Sŏk-ha or Son Chin-t'ae, who were both active in folkloric and anthropological circles in colonial Korea. Akiba Takashi (born in 1888) not only wrote of the two scholars, but also played an important role with them in the Korean Folklore Society and edited the final issue (no. 3, 1940) of the journal *Chosen Minsoku* (Korean Folklore). Akiba referred to Song and Son as his "scholar-friends" and "friends", and coauthored a book on Korean mask dances with Song. Akiba, as a professor of Keijo Imperial University, had close relationships with Korean folklorists, but the fact remains that his student Izumi did not maintain such relationships and was immersed in research on the continent. Looking at the big picture, this corresponds to the general goals in the establishment of the university in the first place. Colonial Korea was meant to be a stepping stone in the advance into the continent, and the evidence of this in academic fields as well is the scholarly link and legacy between Akiba and Izumi.

What I want to emphasize in this section is the non-existence of a relationship between Izumi Seiichi and Korean scholars (Song Sŏk-ha and Son Chin-t'ae). Two possible explanations come into play here. First, the absence of material showing a relationship between Izumi and the Korean Folklore Society at the height of his career is most likely because in the mid and late 1930s, the society had nearly ceased functioning. Second, Korean scholars were only involved in research on Korean culture. However, most of Izumi's work did not focus on Korean subjects. While he did leave behind some research on Cheju-do, it must be remembered that Cheju-do presented a Korea outside Korea, and therefore to Izumi, who had grown up on the mainland, it was an "other" culture in the tradition of social anthropology.

Population census figures for July 1945 are included in a box of Izumi Seiichi's papers, now stored in the archives of the National Museum of Ethnology in Japan. These are fresh data on the population censuses in rural villages in the Ordos and Hubei regions in China, and as yet have not been analyzed, written up, or presented. Immediately following his return to Keijo on August 16, Izumi was organizing the material he had brought with him from the field. Izumi's situation in the tensions he faced between August 18, 1945 and September 1, can easily be imagined (Saguchi 1976).[24] In this midst of this vortex, on August 23 Izumi was

24 Saguchi was dispatched as a member of the Mengjiang team in July 1945, and "with the end of the war on August 15 five members of the team—Ono Shinobu, Sugiua Kenichi, Tokunaga Yasumoto, and Saguchi Toro—stuck together and escaped Dandong, and we took refuge in Keijo on August 17" (Saguchi 1976: 33). "On the afternoon of August 18 we went to the imperial university and met with Mr. Izumi Seiichi, who offered accommodation… Student Public Security Team(Keijo University) entered the main administrative building and people who were normally allowed entrance had difficulty…. There were no police anywhere …" (Saguchi 1976: 41). "On August 19, we went to the main administrative building of the university and talked with Mr. Izumi, and had an interview with the president and received his advice" (Saguchi 1976: 42). "On August 20, we went to Keijo University and met Mr. Izumi" (Saguchi 1976: 43). "On August 21, we met Mr. Izumi and with Dr. Imamura Yutaka drank some brandy Mr. Izumi had brought back from Beijing. Later, we went to Dr. Imamura's residence and talked with assistant professor Suzuki about the Mengjiang Survey Team. Dr. Imamura has published much of the scholarly work done by Japanese during the Greater East Asia War, and as a cultural movement in many countries, emphasized the need for this work. On August 22 at the main administrative building, we talked of many other things with Mr. Izumi. He suggested opening the Continental Sciences Research Institute, Ethnology Research Institute, and the Anthropological Ethnological Discussion Society. On August 23, we drank with Dr. Imamura, and discussed the problems of departing on board a boat with the intercession of Mr. Izumi" (Saguchi 1976: 44).

in the process of analyzing the material he had brought back from China. Facing the end of the war, colonial liberation, social disorder, and personal danger, he remained true to his research and sat quietly analyzing his data. This is the surest picture of Izumi as a scholar.

Izumi's nickname－"The Originator of Andes Studies in Japan" (Onuki Yasuo 1988)－remains a problem. I see it as a generational issue - younger scholars nickname their seniors. However, this image leaves room for considerable misinterpretation of Izumi's academic path. Izumi intended to research Andes archaeology, and putting this thought into practice began as an accident. The question of whether there is a logical reason behind the accident might rest on an exaggerated analogy. He met a Peruvian businessman of Japanese ancestry, who clearly supported Izumi's work in the beginning. Izumi had never studied archaeology, and there is no official record of his attending an archaeological excavation during his coursework. The point of whether he did archaeology in a totally different region and discipline in the Japanese academic climate that valued such "get up and go", despite the fact that there can be no productive conclusion, requires careful consideration.

The person who directed physical anthropology at Keijo Imperial University was Imamura Yutaka, professor in the department of anatomy

---

"On August 25, from 3:00 in the afternoon an Anthropological Ethnological Discussion meeting was held under the auspices of the Keijo University Continental Sciences Research Institute. Ono, Sugiura, and Saguchi attended and introduced their work and careers. Altogether there were twenty people. We went home and many of us got together for drinks. Mr. Sugiura got drunk and broke some glasses" (Saguchi 1976: 45). "On the night of August 27, we were invited to Mr. Izumi's house for brandy. The three of us met－Dr. Imamura, Mr. Asahi, and Mr. Sakai…on the 28th we bought a mal of rice for 120 yen" (Saguchi 1976: 46). Here, there is no mention of Izumi's promotion to assistant professor. Accordingly, we must use some indirect sources that place his first day as an assistant professor on June 5. "On August 29 we went to the university and met Mr. Izumi. We went to the exhibition hall and looked at the artifacts from Korea and New Guinea" (Saguchi 1976: 47). "On September 1 we went to Mr. Izumi's house" (Saguchi 1976: 49). Preparing for departure for Japan.

and also a trustee of the Japanese Anthropological Association. He wrote that when leading data collection trips in various areas around the major military camps and outposts in Xing'an and the south, "through your good will, I have gained great expediency in my measurements··· To Lieutenant General Kodama, Major General Kajii, Colonels Matsumoro, Teada, Kawasaki, Shimonaga, Major Izumi, Harada, Yoshietsu, and Fujimaki army surgeon, and all of you, I express my gratitude and thanks" (Imamura Yutaka 1934: 726). At that time, the collection of data in physical anthropology was not just measurements of the body, and collecting bones and physical remains would have been nearly impossible without the assistance of the army. This would have been particularly the case in combat zones.

In connection with the Manchurian-Mongolian Culture Research Society at Keijo Imperial University, in the summer of 1935 he spent a month in the north doing physical anthropology surveys on ethnic groups including Manchurians, Sains, Daruhu, Orochon, Orok, and Shibei. In the summer of 1941 he also led a month-long survey trip in the villages of Manchuria. In August 1942, he carried out field work in the far eastern corner of Manchukuo, and in summer of 1943 he conducted further surveys of the Daruhu and Manchurians in the downstream regions of the Black river. He ventured to the Ordos region across the Yalu River in the summer of 1944 as leader of a twenty-person survey team that included colleagues from the Faculty of Law and Humanities and the Faculty of Science and Engineering at Keijo Imperial University. In areas which were combat zones, he conducted surveys of Koreans who had been born in the border regions between Korea and Manchuria. All the survey reports on the physical anthropology of the Hurjeon minority that had been published in 1942 (Horiuchi, Masaki, Miyamoto 1942; Suzuki and Hirano 1942) were also the result of work led by Imamura Yutaka.

3. A Comparison of the Two Schools

Akiba, who had traveled to Europe as Keijo Imperial University's overseas researcher, sent letters describing his experiences to the Japanese Sociological Association. And interestingly enough, Taihoku Imperial University's Utsushikawa, who two years later traveled to Europe under the same conditions, sent news to the Tokyo Anthropological Society. When we think of the discipline of anthropology, the question of which side was more active in their duty could be comparatively interpreted. The goals behind Utsushikawa and Akiba's trips to study in Europe can be outlined in three ways. First, the trips were teacher guarantees for the imperial universities. Second, they functioned as a kind of rite of passage integrating scholars into the practice of colonialism. From the late nineteenth century, it is correct to understand such trips has a rite of passage in learning leadership at the Japanese Ministry of Education. Third, unlike Akiba, Utsushikawa was already acknowledged as a major scholar. To Akiba, the study abroad was about learning leadership, but to Utsushikawa it was a matter of learning European anthropology as opposed to the American style. For Japanese imperialism, European social anthropology was more necessary than American cultural anthropology. This raises the issue of anthropology's relationship to colonialism (cf. Asad 1973).

The nature of the scholarship developed by the two scholars at their respective imperial universities overlaps in some areas, but also each had their different orientations. Accordingly, from the very beginning Taihoku Imperial University's ethnography institute and Keijo Imperial University's sociology institute maintained quite different characteristics, and the two professors made obvious the regional demarcation of roles within Japanese academic circles. It is also interesting to note that their students further solidified each professor's orientation.

"The imperial university newly built [in 1928] in Taipei created new courses in ethnology and ethnography in the Faculty of Humanities and Government, and in the middle of March Mr. Utsushikawa Nenozo, returning home from study abroad in Europe, was appointed as a professor to the university and will teach classes. Until now, there has been only one class in anthropology at Tokyo Imperial University, and now with the creation of a similar class in anthropology at Taihoku Imperial University, it is a great boon to Japanese anthropology" (*Jinruikaku Jatssi*, Journal of Anthropology 43(7): 323, July 1928). There is a meaningful difference with the classes in social anthropology that were already being offered by the Institute of Religious Studies and Sociology in Keijo Imperial University in 1926. The ethnography institute in Taihoku Imperial University covered a single field (whether ethnology or anthropology) in terms of content, but in the case of Keijo Imperial University the separate fields of religious studies and sociology were put into one research office. Of course, the main area covered by sociology was largely social anthropology thanks to the presence of Akiba, but actually Akamatsu and Akiba shared a common interest in research on shamanism.

Utsushikawa, who followed the tradition of the American school of cultural history, met the British and European tradition of social anthropology and the anthropology practiced at Taihoku Imperial University was anthropology in the broad sense - including of course cultural anthropology as well as physical anthropology and archaeology. At Keijo Imperial University, Akiba, who had studied sociology at Tokyo Imperial University, came into contact with social anthropology through his study in England, and pursued anthropology in the narrow sense - meaning social anthropology (which includes folklore). At Keijo Imperial University, the professors in his department - the "Institute of Religious Studies and Sociology - were Akamatsu, with Akiba as an assistant professor. Under the course structure it appears that independent courses in anthropology could not be offered. Of course, this does not mean that sociology classes were given independently either. It is likely that this only became possible after Akiba had been promoted to full professor. Of course the department supported lectures, professors, and research in social anthropology and anthropology. Accordingly, the creation of the "course in ethnography.ethnology" at Taihoku Imperial University can be seen as the only such case as in all Japanese territory at that time.

Comparing the undergraduate theses of Utsushikawa's student Mabuchi and Akiba's student Izumi, the former focused his research on kinship, a cornerstone topic in anthropology, while the latter wrote an ethnography of a village. Mabuchi gathered his data through reference materials on his topic, and Izumi used data collected through field work. The anthropological styles of these two pure "domestic products" starting from their theses are radically different, but it is clear that the basis of their work, with clear topics and regional focuses, was Japanese anthropology, which had its roots in traditional anthropology itself. It must not be forgotten that the process in which these two men grew to become the foundation of Japanese anthropology began in the imperial universities of the colonies.

The scholarly compilations that directed the academic world also reflected the specific characteristics of each region. It is useful to make a comparison between the *Nanpo Tojoku* (Ethnographic Journal of Southeast Asia, Oceania, and Taiwan) and *Minjoku Taiwan* (Folklore in Taiwan), both published in colonial Taiwan, and *Chosen Minjoku* (Korean Folklore), published in colonial Korea. *Chosen Minjoku* was managed by Koreans, with the participation of Japanese scholars, and later came under the control of Japanese. This activity left very little impact. *Ethnographic Journal of Southeast Asia, Oceania, and Taiwan* (later renamed the *Ethnological Journal of Southeast Asia, Oceania, and Taiwan*) and *Minjoku Taiwan* were managed by Japanese scholars centered around the university, with some portions attended to by Taiwanese. Both produced an abundance of scholarship, and their influence is still felt today.

"First edition of *Minjoku Taiwan*: Published by the Taipei branch office of a Japanese publishing company located in Tokyo, and edited by Okada Ken, Kanaseki Takeo, Hwang Tu-lie, Suto Toshikazu, Jin Sue-hyung, and Manzoji Ryu. …Until further notice we are aiming for a monthly edition of 32 pages…and we are publishing the first edition" (*Minjokukaku Kenkyu*, Studies in Ethnology, December 1941, pp.436-437). The goal of a monthly publication was a high aim. This reflects the level of research and writing that was going on, and accordingly we can recognize *Minjoku Taiwan* as having very open inclinations. Jin Sue-hyung seems to have held an unofficial position in the ethnography institute at Taihoku Imperial University. Jin Sue-hyung and Hwang Tu-lie, both native Taiwanese researchers, assisted Kanaseki Takeo, and their participation in the first issue and further publication of the journal offers an interesting comparison with colonial Korea. Korean researchers (Song Sŏk-ha and Son Chin-t'ae) formed the center of operations and Japanese researchers (Akiba Takashi and Imamura Tomeo) participated from the outside. After publication of the first edition of *Chosen Minjoku* in 1933, they took over management and shut down publication. Unlike the *Minjoku Taiwan* in Taiwan, publication of *Chosen Minjoku* was kept under a tight rein and writing was subject to restriction by the colonial government. Although beginning with a quarterly publication target, only three issues were published in seven years. While the publisher of the first issue was the Korean Song Sŏk-ha, by the third and final issue (published in 1940) that had changed to Akiba Takashi (Chun Kyung-soo 1999).

In comparing the contexts of *Minjoku Taiwan*, which started publication in 1941, and *Chosen Minjoku*, which had already been shut down by 1940, several points can be made. The Manchurian Incident and the Sino-Japanese War (1937) and the start of the Pacific War in 1941 had already occurred, and the Japanese empire was entirely drawn into the vortex of war. However, the highly academic journal *Minjoku Taiwan* began publication in Taiwan in 1941 and actively produced scholarship throughout the war. This was true not only for anthropology but for many other disciplines as well. Further, the scope of its activity in anthropology actually expanded and deepened during the war. In colonial Korea, however, by 1940 almost all academic activity had been forced to shut down. Both the Korean Folklore Society and the Chindan Society had been dissolved. Again, this applied not just to anthropology, and the systematic shutting down of all academic activity must be interpreted as a structural issue.

V. Paramilitary Anthropology during the "Greater East Asia War"

The colonies' imperial universities were already controlled by the university presidents, and as we have seen with the research institutes operated within these universities (for example, the Manchuria-Mongolia Culture Research Institute and the Continental Culture Research Institute at Keijo Imperial University), they could not be separated from the invasions being carried out by the Japanese army. In particular, at the time of the Manchurian Incident and the Sino-Japanese War, it is clear that academic work on the continent was in close relation to military exercises. The colonies' imperial universities played a fundamental role in the process.

"In August 1932, the Ministry of Education was aiming for a moral integration of all citizens toward a wartime structure and created the National Culture Research Institute" (Yanagita Kunio Institute 1988: 879). Manchukuo was founded in 1933 and in October of the same year, with the cooperation of the Department of Cultural Works in the Ministry of Foreign Affairs and the Japanese Kwantung Army High Command, the Manchurian Japanese Culture Federation was founded. With the announcement of the order to establish Kenkoku Daikaku (another imperial university in Manchuria) in August 1937, after the Lugouqiao (Marco Polo Bridge) Incident and the start of the Sino-Japanese War, Kenkoku University was opened with the value of "harmony among the five nations [Han Chinese, Manchu, Mongolian, Tibetan, and Uighur]" (Kawamura

Minato 1996: 202-203). The Manchurian version of the "Japan-Korea One Ancestry" propaganda came into play. In November 1938, the Greater East Asia Construction of a New Order was announced, which was an attempt to rule Asia with the same concept behind the Greater East Asia Co-Prosperity Sphere.

"The National Mobilization Law came into effect and many staff at Taihoku Imperial University received their call-up papers and were drafted into the army. At that time the Japanese Army was invading Fukien in mainland China. The library and museum at Fukien University were taken over and because all the materials there were scattered and lost, the Taiwan Government-General issued an order to the university authorities to deal with the situation. After consulting with the university authorities, Professors Utsushikawa and Kanda Zenichiro, a professor of Chinese literature who could read classical Chinese, and myself were dispatched" (Miyamoto Nobuto 1985b: 42). This is another face of the military-academic complex. The army went first, and in the process of seizing territory, the universities were sent by the government to clean up the mess the army had made.

The Manchurian Ethnological Society was established under the auspices of the Manchurian Japanese Culture Federation in 1942 (Kawamura Minato 1996: 203). This was the product of an expanding interest in the continent, the starting point of which was Manchuria. The limited natural resources and labor in imperial Japan were all concentrated on the continent, and the academic climate in colonial Korea turned stagnant. This process tallied with the Japanese plans to invade continental Asia. The Korean peninsula, as a stepping stone to China, was one stage in the entire plan. After the Sino-Japanese War, Korea's role as a base for the advance to the continent was largely transferred to Manchukuo.

The Sino-Japanese war intensified and Taiwan became a base for the southern advance. The traditions of Chinese culture were negated in Taiwan, and the Taiwan Government-General pushed forward a policy of violence, such as the burning of ancestors' memorial tablets, in order to strengthen the "Taiwanese Conversion into Japanese" (Kominka) movement. The Government-General also created an interim intelligence bureau, employing people to oversee public opinion polls among the Taiwanese, the "Kominka" Movement and the "Enlightenment Movement." Utsushikawa, dean of the Faculty of Humanities and Government, decided to send me to the interim intelligence bureau, and Professor Kanaseki agreed with him" (Kawahira 1983: 54). The year was 1941.

In December 1941 the Japanese Navy attacked Pearl Harbor. War was declared on December 8 and almost immediately, on December 12, the war was named the "Greater East Asia War"(Yanakita Kunio Institute 1988: 865), and in January 1942 suddenly began the southern advance (Nelson 1980: 204). The National Moral Mobilization Movement (1937) and the Patriot Movement (1940) were an attempt to organize national education to unite the government and the people for the militarization project. There were specific programs that specialists had to implement, and in the big picture of the invasion and war, the task that fell to anthropology was "in May 1942, to create a Ethnological Research Institute within the Greater East Asian Federation and [to carry out] the culture and education policy report through cultural surveys of the many tribes in the Greater East Asia Co-Prosperity Sphere, …to appoint the head and executive secretary of the committee to establish [the research institute], and in 1943 to inaugurate the institute with an official proclamation" (Yanagita Kunio Institute 1988: 891).

Ethnologists established the Ethnological Research Institute to do work for the military authorities. The Japanese Ethnological Society was reformed into an auxiliary organ and its scholarship was made to contribute to the ethnic policies of the Greater East Asia Co-Prosperity Sphere, and later the role of a "war criminal" discipline was given to ethnology (Ishida 1970: 17). The framework of the military-academic complex was at first a system in which scholars followed where the army led, but later on in Japanese ethnology, where academics became subordinate to the military, it became a part of the military. Nakao writes: "The very establishment of the Ethnological Research Institute incorporates the issue of ethnologists' complicity in the war effort, and until now the history of these academic societies has been described in ambiguous and uncertain terms. I think the subject was a taboo in Japanese ethnology. The research institute included many important anthropologists who would go on to build the foundations of Japanese anthropology after the war, in particular Oka Masao and Furuno Kiyoto, both of whom had deep connections with the military" (Nakao 1999: 21). I do fully agree.

"Hainan Island was taken by the Japanese military, and in Taihoku Imperial University there was a plan to send a survey team there. For the most part, this seems to have been an order from the authorities. Ten members made up the team, including Professor Kanaseki. The aim was most likely to explore the resources of the undeveloped island. The boat was a military transport ship. At the time, the area's public security was maintained by the navy's land forces, and we were put up in naval barracks, and we ate with the soldiers. …The headquarters sent a truck and followed the military guards with a machine gun mounted on the roof above the driver's seat, pointed straight ahead" (Miyamoto Nobuto 1983: 43-44). Keijo Imperial University formed the Manchurian Mongolian research team, but it was exactly the same situation. Accordingly, these activities were not carried out independently within the university, and it is not difficult to see both survey trips as following orders by institutions that jointly covered both colonial Taiwan and Korea. They would have been difficult without the support, cooperation, and attendance of the military. The survey teams were dressed in uniforms similar to the military's, and although their equipment differed, they were ready for combat. Here we see the typical face of the military-academic complex.

Japanese militarists, who intended to reach their goal of bringing scholarship into the war effort by establishing the Ethnological Research

Institute, had established the "Total War Research Institute" and prepared to mobilize anthropologists - even before the Greater East Asia War had begun. "The Total War Research Institute aimed to 'command education and training of researchers and managers for a total national war,' and lasted from September 20 1940 until March 31 1945. The institute, in addition to comprehensive research for the war effort, recruited research students from the civil service, the military, and civilian organizations, providing education on a total war…. The texts used at the institute included *Studies in Ethnology* (1941) and *Ethnological Research Facilities of the Empire* (1941). Compared with the *Studies in Ethnology*, an official document presented at the creation of the Ethnological Research Institute on January 16 1943, that which was written by the Total War Research Institute remains quite simplistic" (Nakao 1999: 21-22).

Preparations for "total war" involved the creation of a range of auxiliary agencies and organizations that took on the appearance of academic organizations directed by the government, and scholars were mobilized en masse for this work. For example, the Dr. Shidehara, a literature specialist and former president of Taihoku Imperial University, Professor Uno from Tokyo Imperial University, and Miyoshi from the Endowment for Research on South Seas Economy all lectured in the 'course on the new founding of southeast Asia and Oceania,' sponsored by the Southeast Asia and Oceania Research Society and supported by the Cabinet Information Board (*Nanpo Josei*, Southern Situations no. 69, July 1942), and on November 2 1942, as a training office for the personnel necessary to rebuild southeast Asia and Oceania, the government decided to establish the Konan Training Center and announced the mobilization for the organization in the Official Gazette. The director was Shidehara, and in the official trainers were Ando Enshu, Kurihara Minoru, Katsura Teijiro, and the director was Chiyo (*Nanpo Josei*, Southern Situations no.75 p.46, January 1 1943). Even the archaeologist Egami Namio was mobilized to collect information needed for military intelligence. Reports were published on the ongoing ethnic problems in Manchuria (as printed matter published by the Ethnological Research Institute, the front cover was stamped "secret" in black and "top secret" in red).

The navy's civil administration authorities conducted surveys on items necessary for rule and development and prepared to establish a basic policy for the rebuilding of southeast Asia and Oceania. In order to ensure academic progress on these regions, the "Makasaru Comprehensive Science Research Institute" was set up in Makasaru City (now Ujungbandang in Kalimantan, Indonesia) as a comprehensive science institution that would mobilize sufficient personnel and material resources in the area and contribute to the war effort. The institute integrated a number of laboratories in the area, and aimed to conduct integrated research on southeast Asia and Oceania quickly and in close cooperation with other research institutes in the Greater East Asia region (*Nanpo Josei*, Southern Situations, no. 81 p.38, July 1943). The institute celebrated its opening on July 7 1943, marking the anniversary of the start of the Sino-Japanese War, and brought together a scholarly team under the director Dr. Sonobe (professor emeritus at Tokyo Imperial University and the director of the Navy Department of Special Inspection), …establishing a charge toward science and technology" (*Nanpo Josei*, Southern Situations 81: 36, July 1943; *Nanpo Josei*, Southern Situations 82: 33, August 1943).

Together with the establishment of a large-scale research facility, a range of research institutes were also set up in the imperial universities to support the war effort, and Taihoku Imperial University and Keijo Imperial University were no exception. A Southeast Asia and Oceania Resources and Science Research Institute was established in the Faculty of Agricultural Science at Taihoku Imperial University on May 1 1942 (Furuno Naoya 1991: 247). On March 5 1942, an Imperial order for establishment of a Southeast Asia and Oceania Humanities Research Institute together with the Resources and Science Research Institute was presented for deliberation at a regular meeting of the Cabinet council held at the official residence of the Prime Minister (*Nanpo Josei*, Southern Situations 78: 44, April 1943; *Minjoku Taiwan*, 20th edition, p.48). This format was later applied to Keijo Imperial University in June 1945 with the establishment of the Continental Resources and Science Research Institute.

The Southeast Asia and Oceania Humanities Research Institute was established in Taihoku Imperial University by Imperial order on March 15 1943. It was divided into two departments, the second of which mainly focused on culture and ethnological surveys. Utsushikawa Nenozo was appointed director of the institute. Other full-time staff included Professors Hisano Yoshitaka and Obata Kiyokane, assistant professors Mabuchi Toichi and Kagawa Hideo, and the remaining fourteen part-time staffs were recruited from the Faculty of Humanities and Government. Together with the Southern Regions Ethnographic Society, it was proclaimed to contribute to the future of ethnology in southeast Asia, Oceania, and Taiwan (*Nanpo Minjoku* 7(1.2): 133). Japanese ethnology (anthropology) and anthropologists were increasingly drawn into the war zone. "Army surveys heading for Borneo …necessarily supported the invasion. Izumi's abandonment of his trip in Borneo was based on this reason" (Yamazaki 1992: 245). From the perspective of anthropology or ethnology, "practical ethnology… an 'ethnology as the science of cultural change', is related to legitimate ethnology as it is commonly understood" (Koyama 1944: 46) and was the result of an evolving synergy.

The "Continental Resources and Science Research Institute Order", established in Keijo Imperial University in June 1945, records the following. "With new resources required during wartime, a research institute has been established. …From now on institute staff will utilize each government organization and university faculty. The mission of the research institute is the basic research for the rapid development and advanced utilization of resources for a strong, self-sufficient sphere linking Korea, Manchuria, Mongolia, and the north. …The director was given a term of three years and members terms of two years. Members who proved inadequate were dismissed. Showa 20.6.5" (Imamura Yutaka 1945: 4).

An interesting issue emerging from the bulletins of the institute is its mobilization of university professors for war preparations, and those professors were all assigned to basic research in extracting the resources needed for the war effort. The appointment of the director, Imamura Yutaka (a physical anthropologist), in pursuing research in physical anthropology focusing on the fighting power of Koreans, demonstrates again the connection between war and anthropology. In joining the Japanese colonies to war, anthropology, (or military anthropology) in the military-academic complex was a prominent theme.

VI. From Colonialism to War: The Evolution of Practical Ethnology

As the fifteen years of war started, Japan's colonies were mobilized for war, and anthropologists experienced an about-face in their work as they left their surveys necessary for colonial administration and were dispatched to conduct research for the war effort and control of occupied territories, in preparation for total war. The official titles of anthropologists sent out into the field changed from professor or researcher to full-time non-regular staff or inspector. The written appointments moving them from one life to another were no longer issued by the Government-General or the Ministry of Education but were elevated to the Cabinet and the High Command. Anthropologists (although the Japanese ones) responded to this government move with the term "practical ethnology."

Like the assertion by a Pacific researcher that "practical ethnology is a powerful tool for colonial rule" (Sugiura 1941: 179), the sociologist Koyama, who claimed that "practical ethnology··· an 'ethnology as the science of cultural change', is related to legitimate ethnology as it is commonly understood" (Koyama 1944: 46), published a book on labor resources for the war effort. The idea of publishing *Practical Ethnology* in the southern regions migrated north. Imamura Yutaka, pursuing research in physical anthropology on the fighting power of Koreans, was unable to escape the framework linking anthropology to war. This clearly shows the evolution from colony to war. This transition in the identity of Japanese anthropology also emerges in the research career of Kano Tadao, who produced some of the best in-depth anthropology of his time. His change from being a non-regular staff member of the Police Bureau in the Taiwan Government-General to an army inspector epitomizes the main current in Japanese anthropology at the time.

Anthropologists were mobilized for the war and became civilians attached to the army under the official titles of army inspector (in Borneo) or naval non-regular staff (in New Guinea). Their duties were carried out according to the elaborate military tactics of the Army and Navy Departments, and inspectors assisting the military government in occupied territories performed work necessary for military operations. "Inspectors for the Military Government of the Southern Occupied Territories are like military engineers, …actually inspectors are the engineers of the Great Japanese Empire. Inspectors face physical harm, in enemy territory they are always risking the threat of attack, and need great courage in order to rule other nations that have abandoned their hostility…. Inspectors are brought into the High Command and given administrative posts, …and as military engineers for the Great Japanese Empire, they are assigned to the direct rebuilding of the southern regions. They are called army inspectors and navy inspectors" (Incognito 1943: 5).

"Kano's trip to north Borneo was due to a request from the Army Department for ethnological surveys of the area. …Hijikata (an inspector for the Army), who had been in charge of such surveys in formerly British-held territories before Kano, was diagnosed with a gastric ulcer and was evacuated back to Japan through Singapore and Hong Kong aboard a hospital ship. He left instructions for Kano to continue his work. Hijikata was admitted to Tennoji Red Cross hospital in Osaka on March

17. …The ethnology team of the Borneo garrison's North Borneo Survey Division contacted Izumi Seiichi through the Pacific Federation and Professor Odaka of Keijo Imperial University, and instated Izumi, who had been discharged from the army, with the title of army inspector" (Yamazaki 1992: 242). However, Izumi refused the post. It was Kano who ended up taking it.

"The commander of the survey staff was officially announced on March 22, 1944. He was recorded as 'full-time non-regular army staff' and put in charge. This was announced by the Cabinet. In the event of dispatch as an inspector, the commander was listed as an 'official army inspector.' …In actuality, full-time non-regular staff and inspectors were not qualitatively different. Kano, being in a head position, was something of an anomaly for receiving the status of commander third class equivalent to the colonel on his official record. His status as a commander third class was for the thorough completion of the surveys" (Yamazaki 1992: 245-246).

The meaning given to colonial Korea, the stepping stone to the continent, and Taiwan, the stepping stone to southeast Asia and Oceania, was put into practice through the expansion and promulgation of the concept of the Greater East Asia Co-prosperity Sphere. The imperial universities, created in order to put the empire's goals into practice, established and operated research institutes that met the goals of the Co-Prosperity Sphere, and directed and supported the researchers who carried out the research to realize those goals. To reach these goals in Japan itself, anthropologists were mobilized and ethnological research institutes were put into operation. The Ethnological Research Institute in Japan (established in January 1943), the Southeast Asia, Oceania, and Taiwan Resources and Science Research Institute and the Southeast Asia, Oceania, and Taiwan Humanities Research Institute in Taiwan (established 1943), and the Continental Resources and Science Research Institute in Korea (established in June 1945) were all pursuing a single goal-building the Greater East Asia Co-Prosperity Sphere and supporting the war effort in their respective regions. It must be recognized that the researchers' activities in these organizations were collaborating with the war system.

"With the start of the Greater East Asia War, millions of our countrymen went out through all of east Asia and made contact with other nationalities, and we once again keenly feel the need for ethnological research…. It's not a pastime or the hobby of busybodies, but rather a genuine issue. Scholars, soldiers, statesmen, and civilians all face the many problems that have deep roots in custom. …Even if customs were to be ignored under the Emergency Military Government…and the state of affairs were to return to normal, the importance of customs would become clear. …We can safely say that Taiwan has been made into a base for ethnological research in the southern regions" (Utsushikawa 1943: 1). In Utsushikawa's preface to an issue of *Minjoku Taiwan*, he predicted that if the war fever climaxed and military administration expanded, interest in anthropology or folklore would decrease.

It appears that Utsushikawa gave little thought to the place of anthropology in war. His prediction missed its mark: he became the director of a research institute complicit in the war effort and was sent to Makasaru to carry out his duties. His student Miyamoto Nobuto did the work of an inspector and Mabuchi Toichi received an order sending him to the Southeast Asia and Oceania Humanities Research Institute as an assistant professor, overseeing institute work for the war effort. There were no exceptions. This was one aspect of the collectivism prevalent in Japanese society; all seem to have participated equally in the building of a paramilitary anthropology for war.

"From August 1943 or so, research team members sent to western New Guinea (now Irian Jaya) to conduct surveys for the Administration Office of Southern Region of the Navy began to come under attack. After the combat at Guadalcanal, the American counterattack was strengthened and surveys were ceased that year" (Yamazaki 1002: 220).

Although it is an obvious point, these academic surveys were suspended because the Japanese military was forced out of the survey areas. Like the sacrifices suffered by the military in the war zone, scholars mobilized as civilians in the army became victims of the war. Of the four full-time staff members at the Southeast Asia and Oceania Humanities Research Institute, two were killed and one was unable to return from Celebes and Java. The institute was nearly shut down in the chaos of the war's end. The lack of information on what happened to Kano Tadao is still a sensitive issue in Japanese anthropological circle.

"Around 1942, after the start of the war between Japan and America, war in the South Pacific became imminent and the 20th division was pulled out of Korea to supplement the Japanese army in the South Pacific, a fleet of five-ton and eight-ton navy vessels was formed in Pusan and sent to Wewak in New Guinea in January 1943" (Furuno 1990: 221-222). It was no coincidence that the High Command's decision to send the 20th division of the Chosen Army in colonial Korea to New Guinea and to dispatch of Izumi Seiichi on the Naval Resources Survey team to New Guinea occurred at the at the same time. All such moves were tactics of the High Command based on war conditions.

In the preface of a translation of Oswald Menghin's world history of the Stone Age, Oka Masao (1898-1982) of Japan's Ethnological Research Institute who had asserted "Imperial year 2603" and "a self-reliant Asia under a holy war" (Oka: 1943) and Izumi Seiichi of Keijo Imperial University participated in a round-table meeting sponsored by the "Manchurian" Ethnological Society (established in May 1942). They presented a report titled "A Comparison of Lifestyles and Conditions of the Natives of New Guinea and the Orochon Tribe" (Kawamura 1996: 207). Imanishi Kinji, an authority in the Kyoto school of anthropologists, posed for a photograph with military officials before his departure on an expedition to Xing'an in 1942, and in April 1944 he was appointed as the director of the Northwest Research Institute, a branch office of the Ethnological Research Institute, and left for his post in Zhangjiakou in Inner Mongolia. The link between anthropology and the High Command can be found in the Ethnological Research Institute and its leading figure, Oka Masao. Oka Masao was also the axis around which Japanese anthropology at that time was mobilized for the military operations of the High Command. This is the real face of the so-called "practical ethnology."

VII. Conclusion: The Legacy of the Defeated

The discipline of anthropology originated in the West, and this naturally put Japan at the top of the list in East Asia, becoming a link in the formation of the discipline in this region. When we consider that it is the nature of anthropology to focus on the particularity of culture, rather than universality, the development of anthropology through the process of imitation must necessarily have its limits. The habit of trying to reproduce the academic structure and perspective in the West can also be found in the anthropological debate on colonialism. As a result, instead of searching for "originality", it paves the way for "rent."

The introduction of Western anthropology's debate over colonialism into Japanese anthropology has not been an issue. However, the application of it to anthropology in Japan has forcibly limited the understanding of Japanese anthropology during imperial eras, which was formed around the dual axes of colonialism and war, from only the perspective of colonialism. Although claiming to discuss the same subject, the question of what perspective is being applied and on what concepts it is based has meant that the process and results of interpreting Japanese history is different.

Following Japan's defeat in the war, the ethnological research put out in the Japanese Ethnological Society, of which Oka Masao had been president, was solidified by its editor Ishida Eiichiro in 1948. An editorial committee was formed in 1949, and with Ishida "those taking part in editing are Izumi Seiichi, Mabuchi Toichi, and Miyamoto Nobuto. Mr. Miyamoto and Mr. Mabuchi are at Taihoku Imperial University, and Mr. Izumi is at Keijo Imperial University. They are rare ethnologists in Japan, having accumulated decades of experience in field research throughout East Asia - from Manchuria and Mongolia in the north to Indonesia and New Guinea in the south" (Ishida 1949: 83). The organization of the editorial committee around people trained in ethnology at the imperial universities of the colonies demonstrates the extent to which ethnographic pursuits in the colonies later became the central basis for the Japanese Ethnological Society. From 1950, Miyamoto Nobuto was replaced in the editorial committee by Sugiura Kenichi, a specialist in Micronesia. The committee was thus triangulated around three people, each of whom had been trained in one of Japan's three major colonial regions.

Japanese anthropology shares an indissoluble bond with colonialism. "Izumi was active on the continent based in Korea, Mabuchi in southeast Asia based in Taiwan, and Sugiura in Micronesia" (Shimizu 1998). All three had lengthy careers following the imperatives of imperialism in the colonies. Japanese anthropology, collaborating with the war in the colonial period, had no choice but to accept defeat at the end of the war. Anthropology and war were in collusion. The organization of the journal *Minjokukaku Kenkyu* (Studies in Ethnology) reflected this climate materially and symbolically.

In Taiwan there has been some criticism of anthropological work done during the colonial period, but many elements of it were passed on. In post-1945 Korea, there was no move whatsoever to preserve any of the perspectives on anthropological work from the colonial period. It was not a matter at all; until now there has been no mention of the issue. Everything associated with the colonial period stands unquestioned or has been completely erased. Discussion of the issue has become taboo.

After the war, Japanese anthropologists working in Taiwan were able to discuss their recollections and reflections on the past through a range of channels. In Korea, however, this was impossible, and anthropologists who had worked there seemed to have made a pledge not to speak. Scholars who returned from Taiwan had opportunities to talk about their work, but those coming home from Korea remained consistently silent. They have by now passed away. Things spoken of have remained spoken of to the end, and silence has remained silence.

In contemporary Japanese anthropology, work on colonial Korea and the advance into the continent has been left behind, unlike work on Taiwan, southeast Asia, and southern China, largely because of political changes, but if look at the internal dynamics of the discipline itself, it seems also related to an opposition between reflection and silence. By reflecting, it became possible to escape the legacy of defeat, but remaining silent, this was impossible. The problem is that of past versus present. The past is history, but thinking about history is memory existing in the present. Silence tries to imprison memory, but an imprisoned memory merely focuses its energy in another direction. The energy of an imprisoned memory operates by misinterpretation. This is reflected in international politics, and is also at work within the discipline of anthropology.

Curses and condemnation demanding repentance and reflection are only emotional war. This sort of simplifying dichotomy cannot nourish a consciousness or reinterpretation of history. It works only as a poison. The dead cannot speak. However, a glossalia through shamans is possible. History without lies is divided up into pieces through silence, but work of connecting the scattered pieces into a single narrative continues in the memories we all carry. The question of how well the narrative is formed rests on the capacity of memory. Although the dead cannot speak, those who die still silent can borrow the lips of a shaman to tell their story. The living can make their memory for them. It is not a denunciation of having died without telling this story, but the efforts of the living built on the testimonies of the dead join together to be reformed into memory. I see this as ethnographic work relevant for scholarship.

Akiba Takashi, who "died in a newly built storeroom known as 'Blue Hill Lodge'" (Shimamoto 1955: 303), erected Korean guardian poles of the Spirit General in front of his research office at Aichi University, built a small Korean-style Buddhist hermitage in his home, after salvaging his experiences in colonial Korea tried to recreate them at his office and at home. His memory of the past was still alive, but what was his reason for remaining silent? He meant to store romance and memory, but the reality of things confined him in silence.

As the invasion was reaching its peak in 1931 with the Manchurian Incident and the Sino-Japanese War in 1937, Izumi and Mabuchi were entering anthropology as researchers under their teachers, and with the outbreak of the Pacific War in 1941 they were given the chance to practice their craft as independent scholars. Both were trained in the field of anthropology at the high peak of colonialism and both again worked as specialists during the war time. For the decades they worked as researchers in anthropology, they were unable to avoid the war. The connection between the war and the many opportunities they had to do anthropological fieldwork must be recognized, and the connection between war and concerns over the academic perspectives mobilized for the war effort. In-depth analysis, understanding, and critique of this point is a responsibility for the next generation of anthropologists and in the process also offers the opportunity to build a new anthropology. The issues directly connected to the identity of Japanese anthropology and the indigenization of anthropology (an imported discipline) can be discovered here.

One comparison necessarily calls for further comparison. Comparison is unending work. A not inconsiderable number of anthropologists worked for the Office of Strategic Services, America's wartime secret services agency. One product of this work was Ruth Benedict's research on Japan, *The Chrysanthemum and the Sword*. Later on, directly critical work on scholars who had been active in intelligence during the war remained rare in both the American Anthropological Association and U.S. anthropology in general. In the late 1960s, critique of American anthropologists who had worked southeast Asia, originating in Thailand and Vietnam, ultimately resulted in the expulsion of those who had cooperated with intelligence agencies, and one ended up committing suicide. In 1971 the Mead Committee in the American Anthropological Association was set up to deal with the Camelot Project in relation to Thailand. To put it concisely, the result was a differentiation between the Second World War and the Vietnam War. Evaluating the participation of anthropologists in war differs with time, demanding different judgments.

Before passing moral judgments on anthropologists involved in Japan's wars of invasion, we face the task of rigorous analysis. Whatever the form reflecting its time, the status of war criminals (cf. Ishida Eiichiro's warning) is given to anthropologists who participated in the war, and we require justice in accordance with the details and extent of the war crime. In this process, we can create a set of ethical guidelines for ourselves and future anthropologists.

■ References cited

(Korean)

全京秀, 1999,『韓國人類學 百年』, 서울: 일지사.

鄭圭永, 1999, "콜로니얼리즘과 학문의 정치학: 15년 전쟁 하 경성제국대학의 대륙연구",『教育史學研究』9: 21-36.

(Japanese)

赤松智城, 1926, "古代文化民族からマナの觀念に就いて",『民族』1(3-6).

________, 1929, "北方民族の巫術の起源に就いて",『宗教研究』新6(3): 79-88 & 同 6(5): 95-104.

________, 1935, "滿洲旗人の家祭",『民族學研究』1935年 第2號: 1-9.

赤松智城・泉 靖一, 1938, "赫哲族調査報告",『民族學研究』第4號: 12-33.

秋葉 隆, 1927, "博物館巡禮",『民族』2(6): 123-128.

_______, 1928a, "博物館巡禮",『民族』3(6).

_______, 1928b, "奠雁考: 朝鮮婚姻風俗の一研究",『民族』3(6): 63-86.

_______, 1928c, "女國の多夫婚姻に就いて",『社會學雜誌』51: 1-26.

_______, 1929a, "女人國の神聖婚姻",『宗教研究』新6(2): 1-14.

_______, 1929b, " 'Intenstive Method'に就いて",『社會學雜誌』57: 1-11.

_______, 1931, "朝鮮の巫稱に就いて",『青丘學叢』3: 192-194.

_______, 1932a, "書評: 日本神話の研究(松本信廣 著)",『青丘學叢』10: 154.

_______, 1932b, "踴る巫と踴らない巫: 朝鮮における巫の一分類",『宗教研究』新9(3):27-41.

_______, 1933a, "巫女の家",『ドルメン』1933年 4月號: 116-118.

_______, 1933b, "假面を祀",『ドルメン』1933年 1月號. 9-11.

_______, 1934, "滿洲薩滿教の家祭",『宗教研究』新11(1): 112-128.

_______, 1935a, "薩瑪の巫祭と大仙の巫術: 滿洲巫俗踏查報告",『民族學研究』1935年 第2號: 15-35.

_______, 1935b, "滿洲シャーマン見學メモ",『ドルメン』4(2): 52-57.

_______, 1936, "オロチョン・シャーマニズム: 大興安嶺東北部オロチョン族踏查報告(2)",『民族學究』1936年 第4號: 30-42.

_______, 1937, "蒙古人と漢文化: 文化傳播の一統計",『青丘學叢』27: 1-30.

_______, 1938, "滿洲青年の職業意識",『社會學』5(秋季號): 288-290. (日本社會學會年報).

_______, 1939, "多島海巡航記",『朝鮮多島海旅行覺書』アチック・ミューゼアム編. 東京: アチック・ミューゼアム. pp.1-7.

_______, 1944, "オロチョン族の社會と文化",『社會學研究』1: 342-355.

_______, 1949, "巫と火: 朝鮮シャーマニズムにおける聖火の行事",『民族學研究』14(1): 13-16.

鈴木榮太郎, 1929, "農村社會學研究法",『社會學雜誌』58: 1-23.

_________, 1935, "屋敷神考",『民族學研究』第2號: 72-87.

_________, 1940a, "社會人類學上の研究としてのエンブリー氏の'スエ村'と日本農村社會學",『民族學研究』第4號: 47-67.

_________, 1940b, "美國農村社會學の事", 社會學 7: 370-373.(日本社會學會年報).

中生勝美, 1997, "民族研究所の組織と活動: 戰爭中の日本民族學",『民族學研究』62(1): 47-65.

________, 1999, "地域研究と植民地主義人類學",『地域研究論集』2(1): 19-36.

古野直也, 1991,『臺灣軍司令部 1895-1945』, 東京: 國書刊行會.

古野淸人, 1943, "南方圈の宗教",『南方年鑑』(昭和18年版). 東京: 南方年鑑刊行會.

匿名, 1939, "沿革", 創立三十年記念論文集, 臺灣總督府博物館編. 臺北: 臺灣博物館協會. pp.3-7.

匿名, 1943, "占領地司政官",『南方情勢』75: 5.

岡 正雄(譯), 1943, メンギーン著『石器時代の世界史(上)』東京: 聖紀書房.

馬淵東一, 1942, "インドネシア農耕民と土地",『南方亞細亞の民族と社會』, 滿鐵東亞經濟調查局 <新亞細亞>編輯部. 東京: 大和書店. pp.135-151.

________, 1943, "南方圈の社會",『南方年鑑』(昭和18年版) 東京: 南方年鑑刊行會. pp.155-182.

________, 1947, "移川先生の追憶",『民族學硏究』12(2):

________, 1973, "<南方土俗>景印本刊行에 寄"『南方土俗(南方民族)』影印本. 臺北: 東方文化書局景印. pp.2-8.

馬淵 悟, 1987a, "臺灣と歷史: 解說", 宮本延人, 瀨川孝吉, 馬淵東一,『臺灣の民族と文化』東京: 六興出版. pp.207-213.

_______, 1987b, "臺灣の人類學史: 解說", 宮本延人, 瀨川孝吉, 馬淵東一,『臺灣の民族と文化』東京: 六興出版. pp.236-239.

_______, 1997, "宮本延人",『臺灣原住民研究』2.

大川正彦, 1987, "植民地政策: 解說", 宮本延人, 瀨川孝吉, 馬淵東一,『臺灣の民族と文化』東京: 六興出版. pp.214-218.

黑澤隆朝, 1973,『臺灣高砂族の音樂』東京: 雄山閣.

移川子之藏, 1919, "比律賓北呂宋 イフガオ族に就いて",『人類學雜誌』34(7): 221-234.

__________, 1919. 2, "南海蠻夷小論" 1919年 2月. travelling around the coastal lines of Thai and Cambodia for 9 pages. "廣い人類學の見地から南海の人種について極めて包括的に敍述する". focusing on the classification of the physical anthropology.

__________, 1927a, "歐洲人類學雜記",『人類學雜誌』42(4): 146-154.

__________, 1927b, "北歐の旅",『民族』3(1): 96.

__________, 1930, "臺灣東部阿眉族の稱呼パンジャに關する二三の考察",『民俗學』2卷 3號: 149-159.

__________, 1934, “Patuを繞く太平洋文化交涉年代と臺灣發見の類似石器”, 『臺北帝大史學科研究年報』 第1輯.

__________, 1935a, “ローランド・ディクソン教授の逝去”, 『南方土俗』 1935年 7月號, p.88.

__________, 1935b, “故ローランド・バレッジ・ディクソン教授, Prof. Roland Burrage Dixon (1873-1934)”, 『民族學研究』 1935年 7月 pp.156-163.

__________, 1938, “和蘭ハーグ國立文書館所藏臺灣關係文書目錄”, 『臺北帝國大學文政學部史學科研究年報』 5: 1-76. 1937年 發行.

__________, 1939a, “姓名としての高砂族個人・家族・氏族名”, 『創立三十年記念論文集』, 臺灣總督府博物館編. 臺北: 臺灣博物館協會. pp.323-336.

__________, 1939b, “國際人類學・民族學學術會議と想出”, 『民族學研究』 5(2): 118-124.

__________, 1942, “南洋の民族移動”, 『南方亞細亞の民族と社會』 滿鐵東亞經濟調査局 〈新亞細亞〉 編輯部. 東京: 大和書店. pp.11-36. introducing the Western books.

__________, 1943a, “民俗硏究の現實性”, 『民俗臺灣』 20: 1.

__________, 1943b, “南方民族の社會”, 『西南太平洋』, 每日新聞社 編. 東京: 每日新聞社. pp.n16-31.

宮本延人, 1948, “戰後の臺灣民族學界を省”, 『民族學研究』 13(4): 425-428.

________, 1982a, “私の臺灣紀(1)”, 『松前文庫』 30:

________, 1982b, “私の臺灣紀(2): 土俗學人種學研究室의 建設”, 『松前文庫』 31:

________, 1983a, “私の臺灣紀(3)”, 『松前文庫』 32:

________, 1983b, “私の臺灣紀(5)”, 『松前文庫』 34: 33.

________, 1983c, “金關丈夫教授と私”, 『エトノス』 21: 41-45.

________, 1985a, 『臺灣の原住民族: 回想. 私の民族學調査』 東京: 六興出版.

________, 1985b, “私の臺灣紀(13)”, 『松前文庫』 42:

________, 1985c, “私の臺灣紀(14)”, 『松前文庫』 43:

________, 1985d, 『臺灣の原住民族: 回想・私の民族學調査』 東京: 六興出版.

________, 1988, 『日本統治時代臺灣における寺廟整理問題』 奈良: 天理敎道友社.

宮本延人・瀨川孝吉・馬淵東一, 1987, 『臺灣の民族と文化』 東京: 六興出版.

川平朝申, 1983, “追憶 金關丈夫博士”, 『エトノス』 21: 53-55.

倉田 勇, 1992, “馬淵東一”, 『社會人類學年報』 18: 149-168.

岡田 謙, 1936, “原始社會における社會關係”, 『臺北帝國大學文政學部哲學科研究年報』第3輯.
杉浦健一, 1941, “民族學と南洋群島統治”,『大南洋: 文化と農業』太平洋協會 編. 東京: 河出書房. pp.173-218.
清水昭俊, 1995, “民族學と文化人類學: 學會の改稱問題”,『民博通信』70: 8-27.
神田喜一郎・移川子之藏, 1938, “厦門大學文化陳列所 支那明器の保管”,『博物館研究』11(10): 63.
臺灣總督府, 1936, 臺灣總督府及所屬官署 職員錄. 臺北: 臺灣時報發行所.
__________, 1939,『臺灣事情』(昭和14年版). 臺北: 臺灣總督府.
臺灣教育會, 1939a,『臺灣教育沿革誌』. 臺北: 青史社.
__________, 1939b,『臺灣教育』. 臺北: 臺灣教育會.
大林太良, 1988, “馬淵東一教授を悼む”,『民族學研究』53(3): 329-330.
鹿野忠雄, 1944, “紅頭嶼ヤミ族と飛魚, 附 比律賓バタン諸島의 飛魚漁”, 平野義太郎 編,『太平洋圈(民族과 文化 上卷)』東京: 河出書房. pp.503-573.
山崎柄根, 1992,『鹿野忠雄』東京: 平凡社.
山路勝彦, 1999, “‘梁山泊’の人類學, それとも?: 臺北帝國大學土俗人種學研究室”,『關西學院大學社會 學部紀要』83: 73-89.
金關丈夫, 1941, “皇民化と人種の問題”,『臺灣時報』23(1): 24-29.
ネズ マサシ, 1983, “〈ドルメン〉”,『エトノス』21: 34-37.
中村 哲, 1983, “金關丈夫先生像”,『エトノス』21: 39-40.
宋文薫, 1983, “金關丈夫先生”,『エトノス』21: 49-51.
佐口 透, 1976, “1945年滿鮮紀行: 終戰前後の日本海域”,『日本海文化』3: 33-51.
角田文衛, 1983, “金關丈夫先生”,『エトノス』21: 72-73.
松倉鐵藏, 1926,『臺灣博物館の手引』. 臺北: 臺灣總督府博物館.
尾崎秀眞, 1939, “總督府博物館の思出”,『創立三十年記念論文集』臺灣總督府博物館編. 臺北: 臺灣博物館協會. pp.373-375.
尾高朝雄, 1939, “京城帝國大學蒙疆學術探險隊の成立と探險旅行の經過”,『蒙疆の自然と文化: 京城帝國大學蒙疆學術探險隊報告書』京城帝國大學大陸文化研究會 編. 東京: 古今書院. pp.3-17.
________, 1940, “國家の目的と大陸經營”,『大陸文化研究』京城帝國大學大陸文化研究會 編. 東京: 岩波書店. pp.1-37.
速水 滉, 1940, “序言”,『大陸文化研究』京城帝國大學大陸文化研究會 編. 東京: 岩波書店. pp.1-5.
今村 豊, 1934, “內蒙古人計測旅行雜記”,『ドルメン』3(10): 725-729.

_______, 1935a, “珍本 雞林醫事”, 『ドルメン』 4(1): 58-60.
_______, 1935b, “朝鮮石器時代人”, 『ドルメン』 4(6): 188-192.
_______, 1945, “設立趣旨”, 『大陸資源科學研究所要覽(昭和20年)』. 京城: 大陸資源科學研究所.
堀井五十雄・正木正明・宮本 潔, 1942, “赫哲族調査報告”, 『人類學雜誌』 57(9): 377-385.
鈴木 誠・平野伍吉, 1942, “赫哲調查報告”, 『人類學雜誌』 57(4): 147-154.
長谷部言人, 1944, “人種”, 『大東亞民族誌』 東亞經濟懇談會 編. 東京: 鱒 書房. pp.37-85.
川村 湊, 1996, 『‘大東亞民俗學’の虛實』 東京: 講談社.
大貫良夫, 1988, “泉 靖一: 日本アンデス學の創始者”, 『文化人類學群像: 日本編』 綾部恒雄編. 京都: アカデミア出版會. pp.411-432.
島本彦次郎, 1955, “秋葉隆博士の生涯と業績”, 『朝鮮學報』 9: 303-322.
岩崎繼生, 1933, “朝鮮民俗學界の展望”, 『ドルメン』 1933年 4月號. pp.12-115.
涉澤敬三, 1939, “小序”, 『朝鮮多島海旅行覺書』 アチック・ミューゼアム編. 東京: アチック・ミューゼ アム. pp.1-3.
佐竹義輔, 1963, 『西イリアン記』 東京: 廣川書店.
波多江信廣, 1968, 『西イリアンの思い出』 東京: 川島書店.
泉 貴美子, 1972, 『泉靖一と共に』 東京: 芙蓉書房.
京城帝國大學創立五十周年記念誌編纂委員會, 1974, 『紺碧遙かに - 京城帝國大學創立五十周年記念誌』 東京: 耕文社.
藤本英夫, 1994, 『泉 靖一傳』 東京: 平凡社.
柳田國男研究會, 1988, 『柳田國男傳』 東京: 三一書房.
石田英一郎, 1949, “編輯後記”, 『民族學研究』 14(2): 83.
_________, 1970, “民族學から文化人類學へ”, 『石田英一郎全集』 第四卷. 東京: 筑摩書房. pp.14-20.
小山榮三, 1944, 『南方建設과 民族人口政策』 東京: 大日本出版株式會社.
臺北帝國大學文政學部史學科 研究年報 1: 451-457, 1934年 發行.
臺北帝國大學文政學部史學科 研究年報 2: 421 & 423-424, 1935年 發行.
臺北帝國大學文政學部史學科 研究年報 3: 382, 1936年 發行.
臺北帝國大學文政學部史學科 研究年報 4: 581-582, 1937年 發行.
『南方土俗』 4卷4號 pp.36-37. 1938년.
『南方土俗』 5卷 1.2號: 71.

江口圭一, 1991, 『十五年戰爭小史』 青木書店.

江上波夫, 1943, 『滿洲國の諸民族概況と目下重要な民族問題』 東京: 和光社.

蒙疆新聞社, 1941, 『蒙疆年鑑』.

南方硏究會, 『南方情勢』 69號(1942년 7월), 『南方情勢』 75號(1943年 1月), 『南方情勢』 81號(1943年 7月), 『南方情勢』 82號(1943年 8月). 南方情勢社.

『社會學徒』 8卷 7號, 1934年 7月號, 社會學徒社 發行.

許木柱, 1993, "臺灣民族學硏究的回顧與展望", 『民族學報』(國立政治大學) 20: 143-150.

(English)

Asad, Talal, 1973, *Anthropology and the Colonial Encounter*. London: Ithaca.

Boas, Franz, 1919, "Scientists as Spies", *Nation* (Dec.) 12, 1919.

Gould, Stephen Jay, 1989, *Wonderful Life: The Burgess Shale and the Nature of History*. New York: W.W.Norton.

Malinowski, Bronislaw, 1922(1961), *Argonauts of the Western Pacific*. New York: E.P.Dutton.

Memmi, Albert, 1967, *The Colonizer and the Colonized*. Boston: Beacon Press.

Nakao, Katsumi, 1999, "Japanese Colonial Policy and Anthropology in Manchuria", *Anthropology and Colonialism in Asia and Oceania*. ed. by Janvan Bremen & Shimizu Akitoshi. Surrey: Curzon. pp.245-265.

Nelson, Hank, 1980, "TAIM BILONG PAIT: The Impact of The Second World War on Papua New Guinea", *Southeast Asia Under Japanese Occupation*. ed. by Alfred W. McCoy. New Haven: Yale University Southeast Asia Studies. pp.204-220.

Shimizu Akitoshi, 1999, "Colonialism and the Development of Modern Anthropology in Japan", *Anthropology and Colonialism in Asia and Oceania*. ed. by Janvan Bremen & Shimizu Akitoshi. Surrey: Curzon. pp.115-171.

Thomas, Nicholas, 1994, *Colonialism's Culture: Anthropology, Travel and Government*. Princeton, N.J.: Princeton University Press.

Utsurikawa, Nenozo, 1921, "Demon Design on the Bornean Shield: A Hermeneutic Possiblity", *American Anthropologist* 23: 138-148.

van Bremen, Jan & Shimizu Akitoshi, 1999, *Anthropology and Colonialism in Asia and Oceania*. Surrey: Curzon.

Japanese mode of Anthropological study on Korea

Abito Itoh
University of Tokyo

1. Introduction

In this paper I discuss the Japanese way of anthropologically studying Korean society and culture through a historical review of the development of Japanese intellectual traditions as a basic framework for understanding the behavior and performance of Japanese researchers, and also examine the conditions of their on-site surveys and their related conduct in the field.

Needless to say, all processes of academic work and even its very organization are themselves socio-cultural constructs in each given context. Further-more, all scholars anthropologists included are enmeshed to varying degrees of awareness in such institutionalized settings, as the people they study are embedded in their own institutions.

We also share a common recognition as members of the world-wide circle of anthropology that all studies are made in the inter-subjective contexts of a partnership between the researchers and the researched. We find a variety of intellectual traditions even among Western societies and their specific culture-bound historical development. I recollect that I once participated in a rather polemical symposium entitled National approaches to Japanese studies", organized by Joseph Kleiner at the Germany Center for Japanese Studies (Deutche Institut fur Japanstudien der Philipp-Franz-von-Siebold-Stiftung). The event was held in Tokyo

1989, and it attracted numerous participants from many different countries who represented an equally great variety of unique interests and approaches (Befu & Kleiner 1992). In my presentation, I tried to differentiate between two types of approaches found among Korean anthropologists working in Japanese studies: theory-oriented agendas among the 'elite-course' students trained in American Universities, and description-oriented perspectives among the 'non-elite' students trained in Japan (Ito 1992). Since then, I have also become conscious of native features ingrained in the body of Japanese anthropological research to compare with those of Korean scholars who are always brimming witty suggestions for identifying what is 'Japanese'.

2. Anthropological Studies in Japanese Contexts

Under the concepts of 'anthropological studies' in my title above, I mean not only cultural or social anthropology in a narrow sense, but also the traditional field of Japanese folk-life-studies, known as Nihon-minzokugaku (日本民俗學) and also ethnology (民族學). Complexedly embedded in Japan's historical and social context, these three intellectual fields could together be said to have moulded the comprehensive body of Japanese-styled anthropological research despite the lack of a shared cognition among some members in each group. It is actually not easy to generalize about the specific definition of anthropology among contemporary Japanese scholars because of the wide range of differences between their socio-cultural, intellectual, and more concretely their formal educational backgrounds. I find a fairly wide variety of cognitive impressions regarding the nature of anthropology even among my colleagues in the Department of Cultural Anthropology at Tokyo University, most of whom were trained within the Department. It is also understood that all researchers in Japan today have been influenced either directly or indirectly by Western anthropology, to varying degrees. But the influences are different for each individual, and we find diversity of standards about how a given piece of research should be judged as anthropological in its nature or content. However, I nonetheless believe that there is a need to understand this very nature of anthropology as it exists in Japan as a good example among many other possible of the complexity of Japanese historical process experienced by its society. I also suggest that it is not only urgent for Japanese anthropologists, but also very helpful for other anthropologists studying Japanese society, to understand such socio-cultural aspects of native features in Japanese anthropology. This is true essentially if one is to make full use of Japanese native texts written for Japanese readers.

First, I deal with the development of the folk-life-study known as 'Minzoku-gaku', typically characterized as the primary indigenous intellectual tradition. In their specific interests, its practitioners have inherited two different intellectual backgrounds, traceable to the Edo Period, which later became integrated into the national trend to recognize native cultural traditions amidst frantic nation-building since the dawn of the Meiji Era. Along the way, these were elaborated and modified until they eventually formed into the codified, academic movements of Kyodokenkyu (鄉土硏究) or Minzokugaku (民俗學). One intellectually inherited tradition that had an influence on all of this was an inherent curiosity about the interest of, and ways of thinking among, ordinary Japanese people in their daily lives not only on the part of people researched but also among researchers. Talking and writing about everyday life has long been important to the Japanese in general. Already in the eighteenth and nineteenth centuries, for example, official ethnographic accounts and local village records describing real conditions in different localities were being compiled in large numbers, and even when this was done under the direction of the area han-government, the actual field surveys and recording were often entrusted to local intellectuals. Many such ethnographic accounts and local records were also written purely on the initiative of individual intellectuals and other circles of interested people, which existed in almost every region, and were maintained hereditarily, from one generation to the next. They maintained volumes of hand-written periodical journals recording their everyday lives over several generations. During the Edo period there was a high rate of literacy even among commoners especially in comparison with other countries and even in rural villages there were people with intellectual interests who left records of local life that were simply based on their own experiences and observations for posterity. In the practical fields of farming, fishing and forestry, these have been preserved in the well-known form of voluminous agricultural writings (nosho 農書), and it should also be stressed that in the fields of local history and folk-life studies there were native researchers in most places who were not mere informants but maintained close contacts with specialists. Among those born into prestigious families or experienced farming households (tokunouka 篤農家), there were some who were expected to consider the practice of such popular scholarship in order to make a contribution to local society and understand the significance of recording their observations and experiences. They appear to have been aware that, while rural life under-went gradual change due to constant exposure to external influences on the one hand, there also existed distinctive local traditions that did not easily change on the other. Furthermore, in some regions and especially in Meiji Period, these social traditions, such as describing one's own life, were preserved more by local folk-life scholars with greater comparative perspectives. While engaged in gathering the wealth of unique folk knowledge in each region, they also formed local folk-life-study associations and even published their own journals. Such local associations have been integrated into the nation-wide Society for Folk-life-Study (Nihon Minzoku Gakkai 日本民俗學會), but are still sustained by regional intellectuals with special enthusiasm. Moreover, although they have been criticized for having been lacking in theoretical frameworks based on logical analyses of their subject matter, they nonetheless possessed effective, descriptive framework based on lon-term visions born of the accumulation of practical experience that covered all aspects of local society and culture even when compared with professionally-trained scholars outstanding in social scientific research. Their scholarship may have been lacking in systematic logic, but it was pluralistic, holistic, experiential and practice-oriented, much like the indigenous knowledge of local farmers that is now receiving more cognition and forcing a reevaluation of official development paradigms for marginalized societies. In addition, it shows evidence of a stance that would seek to understand society and culture in the context of continual and sustainable change.

These native traditions of social research and recording were to be seen in folk-life-studies as well, as developed into academic associations with the support of intellectual leaders like Yanagida Kunio (柳田國男), Origuchi Shinobu (折口信夫) or Shibusawa Keizou (澁澤敬三) in official sectors during the course of nation-building since Meiji Era. They are also behind the fact that people other than those who have obtained university degrees and attained special status are also able to become researchers of high fame in local communities. Formerly, many local writers compiled detailed ethnography of rural life with the support of Shibusawa Keizou's Atic-Museum. A fine example is a valuable record of farming life by a farmer, Yoshida Saburo (吉田三郎), who lived at the foot of Mt. Samukaze (or Kampu 寒風山) on Oga (南鹿) Penninsula in Akita Prefecture (Yoshida 1938). There are also the records that were written by school students from their own research as well, under the guidance of Takeuchi Toshimi (竹内利室), an assistant elementary school teacher (Takeuchi 1934). The compilation of such detailed records by area inhabitants in the 1930s probably has few parallels anywhere else in the world. Even today it is by no meams easy to differentiate clearly between research done by specialists and nonspecialists in folk-life-studies. It is also worth noting that because of the promotion and strong popular awareness of national culture since the Meiji Era, the interests of local researchers in specific places have, through continual comparison with other regions, deepened their perceptions of their own regional traditions within the nation of Japan as a whole.

In view of this intellectual background, it is clear that it would by no means be sound to confine the anthropological works in Japan to research by specialists. Nor would it be prudent to neglect the work of locals and dilettants. Even though such works may be overtly subjective or lacking in anthropological refinement or systematic discussion, they are the results of self-perceptions based on the authors' own participation with a full native intuition that could be of prime importance. This is all the more so in a society such as that of Japan, which attaches greater importance to pluralistic, inclusive, and experiential ideas and feelings than to systematic and logical thought and frameworks. Moreover, introducing these perceptions and descriptions based on the native interests of the Japanese themselves as student of Japanese culture will probably prove of greater interest to non-Japanese researchers.

Another tradition of in the evolutionary background of Japanese folk-life studies was the national-learning movement (kokugaku 國學), initiated in Edo Period. The goal of national-learning was to clarify indigenous and distinctive features of Japanese culture as opposed to cultural traits originating on the continent aspects of Han Chinese Great Tradition, which had excerted a powerful conforming influence upon peripheral societies, and also to establish the cultural and spiritual identity of the Japanese people. In particular, a focus was placed on Japan's own spirituality and aesthetic sensibility, differing from logical and systematic cognitive frameworks found in Buddhism, Confucianism, and other facets of Han-Chinese learning introduced from mainland East Asia, and also those of Western learning (yougaku 洋學) brought in through the port city of Nagasaki. Teachers and proponents of kokugaku placed emphasis on classical literature, such as the Kojiki (『古事記』), Nihon Shoki (『日本書紀』),

and Manyoushu (『萬葉集』), and they upheld Shinto and folk beliefs as bases for the expression of their native, 'pure' state.

For the most part, intellectuals involved in Kokugaku-oriented studies belonged to the urban merchant class and the rural establishment in Edo Period. On the other hand, government administrators and the ruling class supported orthodox, Chinese-learning, and especially neo-Confucianism (shushigaku 朱子學), which had been introduced via Korean intellectuals and texts based on the Korean editions. This continental philosophical tradition became the dominant ideology among the ruling class, and was the ethical basis for the administration of official feud schools (han-ko 藩校) managed by the local feudal lords. In the course of the nation-wide modernization movement since Meiji Reform, the Kokugaku tradition became more directly combined with nationalistic Shintoism, or Shinto Revivalism, promoted by the Meiji government and organized as a new basis for re-establishing the spiritual identity of the Japanese, many of whom felt that something essential had been lost in the very midst of that Western-influenced rush to embrace and adopt modernity.

Those involved in the kokugaku movement concentrated on the native folk-culture tradition perceived to have been in danger of extinction and became especially interested in folk beliefs as ethnographical evidences of a Japanese native mode of identification with the natural surroundings. Therefore, nationally-organized intellectuals in folk-life studies were especially interested in the description of indigenous rural life in individual local settings and they sought out a national model of Japanese culture through comparison and generalization.

By way of contrast, the growth of ethnology has roughly coincided with Japan's overseas expansion and, underpinned by an interest directed primarily at foreign peoples and cultures, it has developed in close conjunction with archaeology, linguistics and the study of ancient East Asian history. In this respect it contrasts with folk-life studies, which embody characteristics of national learning and are concerned with the study of only the Japanese people. Practitioners and students of ethnological studies expanded their research fields to include other parts of East Asia, northern China, Mongolia, Korea and Taiwan, southeast Asia and the southern islands, including Micronesia and parts of Melanesia, under the influence of Japan's military expansion.

Initially, folk-life studies and ethnology complemented one another and there were close exchanges between them, both of which shared a native approach based on detailed description and comparison, but once Japanese ethnology came under the influence of the academic traditions of Austria and Germany and then general Western anthropology, the gap between their respective interests broadened as related exchanges declined. Today each has its own separate academic associations. This ideological divide exists despite their homonymous nomenclature; the Japanese-language terms for these two traditions (folk-life study and ethnology) are pronounced exactly the same differentiated only by the substitution of one Chinese ideogram for another. Interestingly, however, once war-time political taboos relating to the study of Japanese ethnicity were lifted, these native ethnologists began to cultivate an interest in the origin of Japan's ethnic culture, and they have produced a large body of relevant research.

On the other hand, anthropology research in the narrow sense of the term had been pursued on a small scale prior to World War II by a limited number of Western-trained students of ethnology and religion, but it was only after the war that cultural anthropology was introduced in earnest to the university curriculum, and this was guided by American scholarship sponsored by the Allied Occupation Policy. During the early postwar era, when researchers were unable to engage in overseas fieldwork, interest in the homeland grew among native ethnologists influenced by cultural anthropology, and theories on the kinship system and plurality in the social structure of Japanese society, for example, attracted considerable attention. Intensive, anthropologically-informed field methods were introduced to native studies of Japanese society, and investigators took into account prewar data and findings that were closely related to questions concerning the cultural identity of Japanese people.

Above, I have presented a brief review of the historical development of three different intellectual traditions that have been, and still are, major components of Japanese anthropological studies. Folk-life-studies, ethnology and cultural anthropology, these can be said to represented triple-layered identity of the Japanese, running parallel with corresponding levels of cognitive reality for a people that has lived in the archipelago for centuries but also has been exposed to different "great-traditions" and world system. Some scholars in folk-life-studied are becoming increasingly conscious of anthropological perspectives and the integration of them with traits of the indigenous intellectual tradition. Also, among the anthroplogically-oriented scholars a growing interest in the applied fields concerning common social issues and a greater consciousness of native traits within their own anthropological traditions is detectable.

As I indicated above, we are now in a position to better recognize the bipolar orientations of native and global, more openly acknowledged in Japan in anthropological studies than in any other field. Still, in spite of the influences of American anthropology in formal higher education, and the internalization of this among anthropologically-oriented scholars, it is not easy to assess the extent to which Japanese scholars have adopted the strong emphasis on theory found in Western anthropology. In fact, especially in comparison with Korean or Taiwanese researchers, I find that some native approaches are still quite consistent among contemporary anthropological scholars in Japan, characterized by a general emphasis on description of concrete cases derived through close observations, and much generalizing from the accumuration of detailed case studies. As I have already suggested, it must be recognized that these pervasive features within Japanese scholarly traditions are embedded in the indigenous mindset, inseparably from the general way of thinking, based on folk knowledge and daily practice-oriented behavior among ordinary Japanese people.

More concretely, the Japanese tend to be very conscious of keeping close relations with their surroundings in composing their own lives. All such things surrounding them are situated in the continuous realm of human life and work and are indispensable vehicles for self-representation and inter-communicating. Reality is never assumed in any ideological framework, systematically constructed by abstract concepts, but rather in the tangible surroundings or situations of ordinary life as identifying themselves. The Japanese even tend to try to assume a spiritual continuity between tangible things or physical surroundings and human life, and are attracted by observing and describing such corporeal spheres. Although such philosophies of recognition and identification among people in 'non-human' surroundings have usually been regarded as 'primitive' by 'civilized' people, it is quite remarkable that such outlooks are still unconsciously shared among all category of elites in contemporary Japan according to my observations.

3. Japanese Field Researches in Korea

It seems to me that such shared cognitive orientations among Japanese intellectuals have been also quite naturally applied in the study of other societies. Especially in the case of research on Korea, I find some adaptive and advantageous conditions for Japanese scholars to apply their own style. The geographical proximity of the two nations has been a factor of no small importance, for reaching field sites in Korea from Japan does not take long at all. It is no major trip, and the cost is often lower than that of traveling within Japan's borders. In contrast to conducting field research in other more distant countries, scholars unable to obtain funding can still manage to engage in survey at their own expense.

Additionally, there has never been any need to obtain special permission to move freely in the field, and it is possible to get a good feeling for conditions at the site of study in advance, so good comparative research can be conducted efficiently over short periods of time, even during regular breaks in the academic work schedule. A series of brief periods of field work extending over a long time span can lead to excellent results through the accumulation of many layers of case studies in the long run.

The volumc of informations available on Korean studies is also overwhelming when compared to that on China or Southeast Asia. This is due to the long history of social and cultural exchanges between Japan and Korea, a shared basic understanding of Buddhism and Confucianism as the great tradition of Han-Chinese origin, and the experiences of colonial process and Korean immigrants in Japan. Also, since there is a much business and tourism between the two countries today, one can obtain abundant non-academic informations on Korea, in addition to journalism. It is also much easier for Japanese to learn Korean than any other foreign languages because of the similarities in their syntax.

Another point to be made is that the fixed division between researcher and researched does not seem to be valid for Japanese investigators of Korean culture, and the situations must be the same for Korean researchers in Japan. Koreans also tend to be very interested in Japanese ways of life, and they often observe us carefully and ask many questions about Japanese people, reveling in comparisons they can make between the two. Korean people regard the Japanese as members of the same East Asian society, and assume that Japanese behave in fundamentally similar ways to themselves. Japanese will be expected to conform to Confucian norms, the common basis for behavior. Furthermore, since Japanese anthropologists might be accepted as potential partners, we cannot so easily be allowed to stay in our rooms alone drinking coffee like some American anthropologists I once witnessed in the field. Partly because Japanese scholars are very interested in the practice-oriented way of research familiar to the everyday lives of informants, and also because it is often difficult for Japanese anthropologists to differentiate between academic works from their life-styles, they might not fit the stereotype of the dignified academic authority as their Korean counterparts may more easily do.

4. Concluding Remarks

In general, due to these geographical and socio-cultural advantages, Korean studies by Japanese scholars have been characterized by the accumulation of a great mass of data through the maintenance of a rich interchange with informants over many years. Also, areas of interests and themes of research are rather highly specialized and focus on some specific issues or objects with which each anthropologist can be identified. A typical criticism voiced by anthropologists abroad is that the particular interests of many Japanese anthropologists are not necessarily in anthropological issues in the global sense, but rather constitute very practical matters or address concrete tangible objectives of observation, which rather fit to the reality for Japanese people.

In sum, the most basic form of Japanese anthropological Korean studies is characterized by a primary emphasis on a native mode of practice-oriented approaches to native realities, which they share with a most of Japanese researchers.

■ References

Harumi Befu & Josef Kleiner eds., 1992, *Othernesses of Japan: Historical and Cultural Influences on Japanese Studies in Ten Countries*. Monographien aus dem Deutchen Institute für Japanstudien der Philipp-Franz-von-Siebold-Stiftung.

Ito Abito, 1992, "The Style and Background of Japanese Studies in Korea", in Harumi Befu & Josef Kleiner eds., *Othernesses of Japan: Historical and Cultural Influences on Japanese Studies in Ten Countries*. Monographien aus dem Deutchen Institute für Japan-studien der Philipp-Franz-von-Siebold-Stiftung, pp.319-326.

Takeuchi Toshimi ed., 1934, *Shougakusei ga-shirabetaru Kami-Ina Kawashima-mura Kyoudoshi* (Ethnography of kami-Ina Kawashima Village Researched by Elementary School Pupils). Tokyo: Atic-Museum, Vol.2

__________________, 1936, *Shougakusei ga-shirabetaru Kami-Ina Kawashima-mura Kyoudoshi. Zoku-hen* (Ethnography of kami-Ina Kawashima Village Researched by Elementary School Pupils, Additional Issue). Tokyo: Atic-Museum, Vol.7.

Yoshida Saburo, 1938, *Oga-Samukaze-Sanroku Noumin Nichiroku* (A Daily Records by a Villager at the Foot of Mt.Samukaze). Tokyo: Atic-Museum, Vol.16.

The Genealogy of Ethnographic Surveys on Korea:
A Retrospective Examination of Suzuki Eitarō's *Chōsen Nōson Shakai Tōsaki*

Hiroshi Honda
University of Tokyo

1. Introduction

The aim of this paper is to genealogically investigate the tradition of ethnographic surveys on Korean society through a retrospective reading of *Chōsen nōson shakai tōsaki* (1944) written by Japanese sociologist Suzuki Eitarō. By genealogically I mean a method that sheds light on marginal memories repressed or concealed under the orthodox history (cf. Choi 1997, pp.361-362; Janelli & Yim 1998). The concept of the Korean "natural village" (*shizen-son* in Japanese) espoused by Suzuki has implicitly and explicitly shaped the post-liberation rural sociology of Korea and also anthropological surveys of Korean peasant society. For example, there is the idea of the *chayŏn-burak* (*chayŏn* means natural and *burak* means village in Korean), suggested by postcolonial Korean rural sociologists as a revisionist alternative to *shizen-son*, but based on more or less on the same social unit. Furthermore, a basic element for research in the anthropological fieldwork of Korean peasant society after the 1960's was a traditional *tong* or *ri*, precisely what Suzuki had considered a Korean natural village. Although his natural village theory defined the orthodox history of Korean peasant studies since the liberation, there still remain some fully unexamined phenomena among those described by Suzuki in his brief field surveys in colonial Korean peasant villages, on which he also never got the chance to follow up. Here I focus on these phenomena, which have been hidden beneath the dominant natural village theory, and suggest other important research themes on the structure and composition of Korean local society.

The remainder of this paper is as follows. First, I review major trends in ethnographic surveys on Korean peasant society prior to Suzuki's research. Next, I sketch his academic life as a founder of Japanese rural sociology, and also outline his field trips to rural Korea. The main portion of the rest of the paper is dedicated to an examination of *Chōsen Nōson Shakai Tōsaki*, published as a travel piece on his second field trip to Korea, which lasted from the eighth to the 22nd of March 1943. I present an alternative reading of the document that does necessarily converge with the concept of a natural village, and offer a hypothetical perspective to deconstruct the concept of the Korean natural village in terms of social stratification, mobility and networks extending beyond the boundaries of a traditional village.

2. Ethnographic Surveys on Korean Peasant Villages Before Suzuki

Arguably, the first academic research on Korean peasant villages was *Buraku Chōsa* (Research on Traditional Villages) sponsored by the Chōsen Sōtokufu Chūsūin (Advisory Council of the Governor-general of Korea) as a part of *Kyūkan Chōsa* (Research on Traditional Customs). In the course of the shift of Japan's colonial policy after the March First Movement (1919), the Council changed its research principles and divided the entire *Kyūkan Chōsa* into four sections: *Minji Kansyū* (Customs in Civil Affairs), *Shōji Kansyū* (Customs in Commercial Affairs), *Seido* (Administrative Institutions) and *Fūzoku* (Manners and Customs). *Buraku Chōsa* was devised as a supplementary project to *Fūzoku Chōsa*, headed by Odauchi Michitoshi, professor of geography at Waseda University. It was intended to contribute to the colonial policy by investigating the origins and development of traditional villages as well as by examining economic and social conditions among their residents (Chōsen Sōtokufu Chūsūin 1938, pp.133-134). According to the first volume of *Chōsen Buraku Chōsa Yosatsu Hōkoku* (the Preliminary Report of the Research on Korean Traditional Villages), the project was carried out according to the following plan:

Duration	Objectives
One month	Selecting and investigating three traditional villages different in terms of natural features, industries, and life styles, which thus could contribute to a comparison between the northern and southern halves of the Korean Peninsula
	Making a master plan of the research on traditional villages in Kyŏngsŏng and seeking responses from each provincial office on the main agenda of the plan
Three months	A general survey on rural life in each province and preliminary surveys of the thirteen villages selected

Furthermore, from 1923 Chūsūin planned to investigate eight points in collaboration with Chōsaka (the Research Office of the Governor-general of Korea). These were: 1) the history of a traditional village, 2) social institutions of a traditional village, 3) social conditions of a traditional village, 4) economical conditions of a traditional village, 5) manners and customs, 6) the physical structure of a peasant house, 7) natural boundaries, and 8) the state of industry. However, the project was postponed due to rearrangement of the colonial administration caused by the Great Kanto Earthquake.

The first volume of *Chōsen Buraku Chōsa Yosatsu Hōkoku* has two chapters. The first, *Buraku Chōsa*, is divided into three sections: 1) The Significance of *Buraku Chōsa*, 2) Methodology of *Buraku Chōsa*, and 3) The Plan of *Buraku Chōsa*. The second chapter, Examinations of

Traditional Villages, has three sections: 1) General Features of Traditional Villages, 2) Characteristics of Traditional Villages, and 3) Conclusions. Here, I give special mention to three among the six sections. First, in the second part of Chapter One, Odauchi describes his research from start to finish. This is mainly based on field journals from his 1921 October, December trip, and it makes for a good comparison with Suzuki's *Tōsaki*. Odauchi covered all provinces of the Korean Peninsula, and as he moved southward from North Pyŏng-an Province his focus shifted from subjects such as commerce, religions (especially Christianity and new faiths), people engaged in slash-and-burn cultivation, and Chinese merchants to themes such as *yangban* (local gentry), class consciousness, rice cultivation, lineage villages, relationships between landlords, local managers and tenants, Confucianism, historic spots, and fishing. In the section on general features of villages, after having touched on the lives of wandering slash-and-burn cultivators, he describes the spatial arrangement of a peasant settlement, various kinds of *kye* (rotating-credit associations and other associations with specific purposes) which he regards to be indispensable for the economic and social existence of villages, *ture* (task groups for agricultural work), marketplaces where daily necessities are traded, the structure and arrangement of peasant houses, and the size of villages. Some of the customs listed here, communal rituals of a village, various kinds of groups organized within its territory and *ture*, for example, are also central components of Suzuki's natural village, described below. Regarding spatial arrangements, he shows much interest in villages where the same clan members live en masse, - *dōzoku buraku* according to Zenshō Eisuke. Writes Odauchi, "In this kind of traditional village, residents tend to be bound by traditional, conservative conventions. However, autonomous control has been established historically. Activities such as rituals, labor and recreation are carried out communally. Housewives cultivate good relations with one another, while they generally have few chances for social contacts in the rest of the country. Various kinds of *kye* associations are also organized". It is interesting to note that Odauchi describes an excellent example of a Korean village community of this type. He has also allotted many pages to typical examples such as Hahoe-dong of North Kyŏngsang Province and Sangsin-ri of North Chŏlla Province in the section on characteristics of the sixteen traditional villages he visited.

From the 1920 s into the 1930 s, two part-time employees of the governor-general carried out research projects related to my focus. In this capacity, Zenshō Eisuke surveyed the living conditions of rural Koreans from 1923 to 1935. He wrote more than 20 extensive reports, including three volumes of *Chōsen no Shūraku* (Korean Settlements) published from 1933 to 1935. Murayama Chijun, employed by the governor-general from 1919 to 1941, surveyed Korean social affairs, folk beliefs and rituals. Among his reports, *Burakusai* (Village Rituals) is best for comparative examination here. First, I look at Zenshō s *Chōsen no Shūraku*. The contents of the three volumes are:

> Vol. 1 (general survey): origins, terminology, typology, size, altitude and institutions of settlements, peasant villages, mountain villages, fishing villages, capitals and towns
> Vol. 2 (characteristics of settlements – especially descriptions of standard, relatively distinctive villages other than *dōzoku buraku*): immigrant villages, model villages (for the Rural Revitalization Campaign), idiosyncratic villages, hot-spring villages and mining villages
> Vol. 3 (*dōzoku buraku*): history of clans, history of *dōzoku buraku*, essential qualities of *dōzoku buraku*, spatial distribution of *dōzoku buraku*, *dōzoku buraku* and Confucian powers, idiosyncratic *dōzoku buraku*

Among the various types of Korean villages, Zenshō regards *dōzoku buraku* as especially important – allotting to their study the largest portion of his report. He writes, This effectively contributes to further clarifying the quintessential concept of the Korean village. In addition, in order to build our basic knowledge on Korean history, administration, self-government, social organization, culture, thoughts, and people s lives, I strongly feel that it is necessary to thoroughly investigate the history of *dōzoku buraku* to define its essence and explore its influence (Zenshō 1935, p.2). Therefore, he has adopted the same perspective as Odauchi in the sense that both sought a model example of Korean villages among *dōzoku buraku*. On the other hand, he has failed to define *buraku* (a traditional village) in terms of their social organization and communality. It was all that he could do to follow up on the history of local administrative institutions.

Concerning the definition of *buraku*, Murayama treads the same basic path as Zenshō. In his report on village communal rituals he grants the lion's share to a description of rituals and related customs, including an overview of rituals, commonly worshipped divinities, ritual processes, the dates of rituals, costs, and the relationships between rituals and village meetings. How, then, has he grasped the *buraku* concept? In the beginning of the report he writes, "On the whole, the *buraku* people who worship (a particular divinity) form a small group that co-resides, relying on bonds mediated by the locality. It is generally smaller than the lowest administrative unit, and so therefore may be regarded as a ritual body constituting the smallest unit within *buraku*. Accordingly, while one administrative *buraku* generally contains a few ritual bodies, it might have just one or possibly several or more than ten" (Murayama 1937, p.1). Therefore, Murayama's *buraku* is the smallest administrative unit. This is typically known as *shin-dōri* (a modern administrative village). Following Murayama s definition, a *burakusai* (a village communal ritual) can be considered a ritual that people forming the smallest unit within a *buraku* engage in cooperatively.

Here an extra note on Korean traditional and modern administrative villages is warranted. In pre-modern Korea, the lowest and smallest administrative unit in peasant society was called *tong* (*dō* in Japanese) or *ri* (*ri* in Japanese). It was probably comprised of one settlement or possibly a few, distinguished from one another by the proximity of residences. In the 1910's, the governor-general of Korea enforced a rearrangement of administrative divisions. As a result, many of the former villages were consolidated into single modern administrative villages. As Suzuki has indicated, however, a social unit based on the traditional administrative village continued to function as a substantial social unit, even after the rearrangement. This unit seems to have been called *burak* (*buraku* in Japanese), the term having been imported from Japan. In fact, even the Japanese colonizers sometimes utilized this unit in their rule over Korea. From 1932 on, the governor-general Ugaki Kazushige carried out the Rural Revitalization Campaign (*Nōson shinkō undō*). The unit of focus for revitalization projects, such as *kōsei shidō buraku* (a village selected to be put under the official guidance for the revitalization) or *mohan buraku* (a model village), was not necessarily a modern administrative village, but often was a social unit corresponding to a traditional village. A notification entitled *Nōka Keizai Kōsei Sidō Keikaku Yōkō* (Principles of Revitalization and Guidance of Peasants Economy), issued by the inspector general of political affairs in 1933 says, (*kōsei*) *shidō buraku* need not be a division such as *ri* or *dō* (a modern administrative village). It should be appointed among villages or settlements constituted by a group of about 30 to 40 households (Kim Ik-han 1996, pp.182-183).

As discussed below, Suzuki started his field research on Korean peasant villages soon after his arrival at Keijō Imperial University. During a two-day field trip in July 1922, he had already formed the impression that a Korean natural village was a former *tong* or *ri* - a traditional administrative village, and he continued to uphold this position throughout his career, concentrating on the improvement of his Korean natural village theory and the comparative study of it and the Japanese natural village. On the other hand, variation in Korean villages as described by Odauchi or Zenshō had appears to have been ignored. In the following sections I outline the theoretical limitations of Suzuki s natural village theory and seek a new perspective on Korean peasant society.

3. Suzuki s Career and his Research on Korean Peasant Society

Suzuki Eitarō was born on September 17th, 1894 in Gōnoura Town, Iki County, Nagasaki Prefecture. After graduating from the First Public High School he entered the college of literature at Tokyo Imperial University, originally majoring in sociology but changing to ethics shortly before graduating in March 1922. Akiba Takashi, who later invited him to Keijō Imperial University, entered the senior course at Tokyo Imperial University in April 1920, majored in sociology, and graduated a year before Suzuki. Suzuki entered the graduate school at Kyōto Imperial University where he studied sociological methodology under Yoneda Shōtarō, and his first teaching post was at Gifu High School of Agriculture and Forestry – currently the college of agriculture at Gifu University. From that point, he enthusiastically engaged in field research on Japanese peasant society, which resulted in the publication of *Nōson Shakai Chōsahō* (Survey Methodology for Peasant Villages) in 1932 and *Nōson Shakaigakushi* (The History of Rural Sociology) the following year. Finally, in 1940, he compiled the fruits of many years of study into *Nihon Nōson Shaiaigaku Genri* (Principles of Japanese Rural Sociology), published by Jichōsha. Exactly two years later he left for Korea.

Suzuki was appointed to Associate Professor of Sociology at the college of law and literature, Keijō Imperial University, in April 1942. Ishikawa Taizō, an undergraduate student in sociology who had entered the university in 1940, reflected on this appointment:

> The course of sociology at Keijō (Imperial) University was established by Professor Akiba (Takashi). Among the graduates was Izumi Seiichi, who later made a name for himself in the field of cultural anthropology at the

University of Tokyo and gained an unparalleled reputation through his extensive field surveys. (Members of) the department of sociology also engaged in research and expeditions not only all over Korea but also as far as Manchuria and Mongolia, and therefore became very well known in folklore. As for the institution of sociology, however, it could have been characterized as an idiosyncratic division, so the need for a professor who majored in general sociology was keenly felt in order to complete and reinforce its academic competence. It was in response to this demand that Professor Suzuki (Eitarō) arrived at Keijō (Imperial) University (Ishikawa 1973, p.3).

Although Suzuki s stay in Korea, which ended in November 1945 with his return to Japan as a repatriate from the former colony, did not last long, he went on a field trip at least four times under the war regime and published one book and four essays in result. The table below outlines the four main field trips and the resulting publications.

	Date	Duration	Sites	Related publications
1st	July 1942	Two days	Tonsan-dong and Fuji Nōson in the suburbs of Kunsan City, North Chŏlla Province*	*Chŏsen Nōson Shakai Bekkenki* (1943)
2nd	March 1943	15 days	Wŏnju County of Kangwŏng Province; Chech ŏn County of North Ch ungch ŏng Province; Yŏngju and Sangju Counties of North Kyŏngsang Province	*Chōsen Nōson Shakai Tōsaki* (1944), *Chōsen no Nōson Shakai Shūdan ni Tsuite* (1943), *Chōsen no Sonraku* (1943)
3rd	February 1944	Approx. one week	Sinjŏn-dong, Posŏng County of South Chŏlla Province	*Konan Nōson Chōsa Yachō Nukigaki* (1944)
4th	May 1944	Unknown	Myŏngchŏn-dong, Myŏngchŏn County of North Hamgyŏng Province; Taech on, Sunch ŏn County of P yŏng-an Province	

* This field trip was planned as part of an inter-disciplinary research project on peasants life in and around Fuji Nōson sponsored by the Keijō Imperial University branch of the Union for Total War.

Tōsaki - the only book ever published on his research in Korea - is a record of his second field trip, which also spawned two articles. One of them, Chōsen no Nōson Shakai Shūdan ni Tsuite (On Peasant Social Groups in Korea), he himself considered to be the most systematic research report on Korean peasant villages that (he) wrote during the years of (his) stay in Korea. He also added, "When I published it, I felt that I had completed more than half of my task to organize the systematic knowledge of Korean rural sociology." In my view, this second trip had defined the core of his sociological understanding of Korean peasant villages. My next task is to investigate the exact kind of phenomena in which he was interested, what in particular he actually surveyed in the field, and how he developed his theory out of the data he gleaned.

4. Reading Tōsaki

Chōsen Nōson Shakai Tōsaki was published by Ōsakayagō Shoten in May 1944. It has a three-page preface and the main text covers 245 pages. Two thousand copies of the first edition were printed. It was to be contained in the fifth volume of his collected writings (Suzuki 1973) together with five other articles, one of which had appeared in 1963, and other unpublished drafts and field notes on Korean peasant society, but in this second edition of *Tōsaki* the editors intentionally rewrote a number of passages (cf. Hattori 1974). Therefore, I use the first edition here for investigation.

4-1. Contents and Styles of Description

The contents and number of pages of each chapter are as follows:

1. Introduction: aims and methods of the research trip: 3pp.
2. Wŏnju Town: 10pp.
3. A Shrine for Confucian Sages and Intellectuals: 13pp.

4. Konhyŏn-dong Buraku: inter-marriage zone etc.: 27pp.
5. Visit to Wŏlun-dong Buraku: 6pp.
6. The Clan Organization of Hansan Yi: 12pp.
7. Private Records: 3pp.
8. Social Groups in Konhyŏn-dong: 23pp.
9. From Kangwŏng Province to North Ch ungch ŏng Province: 6pp.
10. *Hyangsajurye* (local ceremony of archery and drinking): 13pp.
11. A Record of the Stay in Kuryong-ri: 7pp.
12. Origin Stories of the Ŭihŭng Pak Clan: 7pp.
13. Clan Organization and Funerary Customs: 9pp.
14. Miscellaneous Memoranda: 9pp.
15. A Social Analysis of Kuryong-ri: 30pp.
16. From Kuryong-ri to Sunhŭng: 7pp.
17. Sosu Private Academy and the Altar to Prince Kŭmsŏng-kun: 10pp.
18. Tongho-ri Buraku: 15pp.
19. From Sunhŭng to Sangju: 6pp.
20. Narratives Collected in Sangju: 4pp.
21. A Record of the Last Two Days: 4pp.

As witnessed in the above list, different types of texts - journal entries, transcriptions of field notes, monographic descriptions of the field sites and analyses of data on particular themes are artlessly intermingled. The flow of the description, however, roughly follows the temporal sequence of events, which enables the reader of the text to experience vicariously the process of Suzuki's fieldwork, selecting key informants at every field site, collecting data through interviews and observations, and analyzing them.

Suzuki's aim is explained in the preface. In his view, family, clan organization and village ("social frames" in his words) comprise the basic framework of Korean social structure, and in order to understand the structure of Korean society one needs to comprehend these social frames in their original form, unblemished by modern culture. Therefore, it is best to visit a comparatively rural district that is relatively free of modern idiosyncrasies and carefully investigate first-hand. For that reason, explains Suzuki, he chose that particular field trip, and for him the book represents an accurate report of the research. In addition, he intended it to be an introductory explanation of Korean life and culture through its presentations of individual, private affairs. Furthermore, he wanted it to serve as a good example of field research for students who were also to carry out field studies that might contribute directly to the establishment of the New Order (Japanese imperialism) in East Asia.

This aim of the research is again explained in the first chapter. Suzuki writes, "I am trying some case studies in order to investigate the basic structural organization in Koreans' lives" (p.1). In the chapter, however, the following three points are primary.

(1) Conditions of the function of leadership in general social life by Confucian intellectuals
(2) Clan organizations of the *yangban* (local gentry)
(3) The social integration of the former counties

Suzuki's second trip lasted for 15days, from the eighth to the 22nd of March. I have reconstructed in detail the time schedule from Suzuki's daily memoranda in *Tōsaki*. He was 48 years old, and not in the best of health. Furthermore, he had to eat Korean food and stay at traditional inns from time to time, which seems to have bored him. But even under such conditions he was busy from early morning to late at night conducting interviews, making observations, and associating with people in the field or checking and supplementing his field notes. He visited four towns and four peasant villages including Wŏnju Town, Konhyŏn-ri, Wŏlun-dong, Chech ŏn Town, Yŏngju Town, Tongho-ri and Sangju Town. All the four villages were inhabited by *yangban* family members. He made relatively long stays in Konhyŏn-ri and in Kuryong-ri, spending 4 days in each. Many pages of *Tōsaki* are dedicated to these. Sections describing social groups and organizations in Kuryong-ri are also contained in his essay, Chōsen no Sonraku (A Korean Village) (Suzuki 1943c).

4-2. Monographs of Villages and His Conceptualization of a Korean Natural Village

What did Suzuki mean by natural village? First, let us take a brief look at his own definition from the second chapter of *Nihon Nōson Shakaigaku Genri.*

> A village is a social unit based on the assemblage of people linked by belonging to the same locality. There, other diverse social relations also directly connected them. They share their own system of social ideals that organizes all domains of their social life. If we regard local society simply as an assemblage based on spatial proximity (of residences), the village in this sense would be an entity that clearly transcends it. There also exist organizations mediated by many other social bonds, and their own social ideals in principle control them in all aspects of their social life, based on face-to-face interactions. Many groups within its boundaries are also regulated by this so-called unifying general will. This sort of social unity is what I call a village, and thus could be referred to as a natural village (Suzuki 1940, p.36).

In other words, a natural village to Suzuki is a social unit based on locality, within the boundaries of which groups and social relations are accumulated and which is controlled and regulated by a system of social ideals, or "the spirit (*seishin*) of natural village." As mentioned above, Suzuki had already gotten the impression that a Korean natural village was a traditional administrative village through his first expedition. Tunsan-buraku (93 households), his first field site in Korea, was one of the six *buraku* units of Ŏŭn-ri, a modern administrative village of

233 households. It was again divided into two settlements, traditional Tunsan-dong and also Shingi-ch"on, which had been originally settled by immigrants more than ten years earlier and was inhabited by 12 households. Suzuki has regarded the traditional village, that is, traditional Tunsan-dong, as a basic village community. In support of this, he listed several facts. Among them are "the fact that it organizes a ritual group to worship a shrine for the mountain god communally, the fact that it has a village-based association as an institution of self-government, the fact that it sponsors cooperative voluntary operations and village festivities, the fact that it organizes *ture* as an action group for communal labor and the fact that it has common property" (Suzuki 1943a, pp.52-53).

In writing this report, Suzuki also devised a plan for research on the social structure of Tunsan-dong for the sociological research team of the Keijō Imperial University branch of the Union for Total War. The contents of the plan, entitled Plan for Research on the Social Organization of Tunsan-dong, Mainly on Historical Changes in Activities of Various Kinds of Groups and Their Districts' are as follows (Suzuki 1943a, p.71):

(1) Administrative Local Groups
(2) On Rituals for the Village God
(3) Kye Groups
(4) Neighbors' Associations
(5) Economic Groups
(6) Groups Established by the Administration
(7) Lineage Groups
(8) Village Meetings, Customs of Communal Labor, Organizations for Punishment and Commendation and Communal Worship
(9) Zones of Inter-Marriage and Zones of Commercial Transactions
(10) Customs in the Treatments of Newcomers

These generally correspond to the components of the Japanese natural village described in *Nohon Nōson Syakaigaku Genri*. The first, fourth, fifth and sixth items in the list above are very similar to four of the types of social groups for Japanese peasant villages in the latter. The second item can correspond to the *Ujiko* group (an association for worshipping a village shrine) or *Danto* group (a group of adherents to a Buddhist temple) listed as two of the types of Japanese peasant social groups. The third should correspond to *Kōchū* groups (rotating credit and other associations), and the seventh to consanguineous groups, both in the same list. Furthermore, the eighth and tenth must be related to the unity and social consciousness of the natural village, while the ninth is related to zones of common interest, all of which are taken up in the latter book as well.

All of the four villages Suzuki visited in his second expedition were ones where *yangban* family members inhabited en masse (*dōzoku buraku* in Zenshō s terminology). This is evidenced in the following listing of the composition of each village in terms of clan membership and former, traditional status.

(1) Konhyŏn-ri

a) Until 30 years ago

Yangban: Hansan Yi (about 20 households), Kwak (2), Chinju Yu (7 or 8) and Chŏnju Yi (7 or 8)

Sangmin (commoners): not specified

Nuja (slaves): Kimhae Kim (5 households), Wŏnju Ŏm (2) and Chang (5 or 6)

b) At present

Hansan Yi (26 households, only 20 of which are called *yangban*, while other 6 households are treated better than commoners), Wŏnju Wŏn (2 households), Chang (5 or 6), Yu (7 or 8, which are called *yangban*), Chŏnju Yi (7 or 8, which are called *yangban*), Ch ŏngsong Sim (5 or 6, which are called *yangban*), Ŏm (4) and Wŏn (3)

(2) Wŏlun-dong (33 households)

Yŏnan Kim (10 households; *yangban*)*, Chŏnju Yi (4; *yangban*?) and *sangmin* households – there had also been many Kim slaves until 30 years ago.

* There are 30 more households of Yŏnan Kim family in other settlements of the same modern administrative village and more in other villages of the same district.

(3) Chŏktŏk-ri (41 households) of Big Kuryong-ri

Ŭihŭng Pak (7 households; *yangban*)*, Milyang Pak (8; *yangban*), Munhwa Yu (5; *yangban*) and *sangmin* households

* A total of 60 households exist in Big Kuryong-ri.

(4) Tongho-ri (underlined families are classified as *yangban*; the others are *sangmin* households)

Ŭisŏng Kim (9 households), Chinsŏng Yi (5), Pup yŏng Yi (2), Kimhae Kim (2), Milyang Pak (2), Yech ŏn Yim (2), P ungsan Yu (1), Kyŏngju Ch oi (1), Chinju Kang (3), P yŏngsan Sin (1), Pongsŏng Kŭm (2), Wŏn (1), Kwangsan Kim (2), Namyang Hong (2), Sŏnsŏng Kim (3), Sunhŭng An (2) and Wŏlsŏng Yi (1)

For investigating the process of the development of Suzuki s Korean natural village theory, Chapter Fifteen of *Tōsaki*, on the social organizations of Kuryong-ri, is one of the best examples. It consists of 12 sections: 1) general conditions of the village, 2) administrative social divisions, 3) village rituals, 4) village associations and associations for promotion of private education, 5) *ture, p'umasi* (labor exchange) and *homissise* (festivities after weeding in paddy fields), 6) joint prayers, 7) neighborhood relations, 8) family lines and social stratification within the village, 9) *hyangyak* (local pact for mutual help and control), 10) ways of making living and marketplace, 11) folk beliefs and 12) tug of war and Korean folk wrestling (pp.149-178). Except for the last two sections on folk customs and beliefs, each is related to one of the first, second, third, fourth, fifth, and ninth items of the research plan for Tunsan-dong. The eighth and ninth sections, however, are items that did not appear in the former research plan. Regarding the definition of a Korean natural village, it should be noted that Middle Kuryong-ri, one of the five traditional villages that constitute Big Kuryong-ri, was considered a natural village in the second section:

> Middle Kuryong-ri is called *tong* in its real sense, which could be looked upon as forming a natural village that has functioned as an administrative unit for hundreds of years. It also forms a religious association jointly worshipping the same *sŏnghwang-dang* (shrine for the local guardian gods). In addition, it is equipped with a set of village associations (p.152).

Communal rituals among villagers and *kye* associations based on the traditional village are described in the following two sections, and both of these should be indispensable components of the Korean natural village. From the fifth to eighth sections, Suzuki shows concrete examples of social groups and relations accumulated within the boundary of this "natural village."

It could be said that the discovery of a natural village in Korean peasant society that also supports the Japanese natural village theory and the accepted typology of groups and relations observed there would be the point of completion for Suzuki's Korean natural village theory. In the essay entitled Chōsen no Nōson Syakai Syūdan-ni Tsuite (On Social Groups in Korean Peasant Villages), he classifies Korean peasant social groups into ten categories and explicates them one by one. There, nine out of the ten categories are almost the same as categories he has used to classify Japanese peasant groups, with only "class groups" excluded from the original list. Another indicates groups for self-defense, a new category for accommodating Korean examples. In the conclusion, however, he suggests that although a Korean natural village is better equipped with group organizations than a Japanese natural village, it is hard to say that the former was better integrated in terms of emotional harmony or a sense of unity, and he sates that "in order to understand the (Korean) natural village in its totality, we need to investigate further questions on zones of common interest and social differentiation other than the subject of peasant social groups" (Suzuki 1943b, No.12, p.15). These points, I believe, could make it possible to re-read *Tōsaki* in a manner that would not necessarily amount merely to the substantiation or reification of a natural village. In this light, I re-examine below a Korean natural village in terms of status, social stratification and mobility, returning again to Suzuki s original description in *Tōsaki*.

4-3. Status, Social Stratification and Zones of Common Interest

First, let us consider Suzuki s understanding of status and social stratification in pre-modern Korean society. He uses the term *kaikyū* (class) to designate status or social strata, which he considers to be the same, determined by one of the three factors: that is, privilege, skill or wealth (Suzuki 1940, pp.564-569). As far as we can see from this comment in *Nihon Nōson Shakaigaku Genri*, there appears to be no discrimination in Suzuki's terminology between status as prescribed in terms of legal or customary privilege or honor and social prestige, on the one hand, and economic classes defined in terms of wealth or relations of production on the other. In regard to the types of *kaikyū* in pre-modern Korea, Suzuki classifies residents in traditional villages into at least three classes: *yangban* (aristocrats or local gentry), *sangmin* (commoners) and *nubi* (slaves) (Suzuki 1944, pp.32-33; p.40; p.75; pp.91-92). This is reminiscent of the four-status theory introduced by Imamura Tomo and others into Japanese literature, and which was also adopted by Shikata Hiroshi in discussing the distribution ratio of households by status in the Chosŏn Period (Imamura 1919, pp.17-41; Shikata 1938). Here, the four levels are *yangban*, *chung-in*, *sangmin* and *chŏnmin* (slaves and others who engage in despised professions). *Chung-in*, however, could be excluded from the case of status stratification in rural society; the term indicated members of family lines whose hereditary professions are technical officials' such as medical doctors, astrologers and translators in the court, and accordingly those who belonged to this class mainly lived near Changgyo Bridge and Sup'yogyo Bridge in the center of the capital (Tanaka 1920, p.60). It was highly probable that Suzuki adopted the four-status classification that must have prevailed among Japanese intellectuals in Korea, and which might have been originally supported by Koreans in and around Keijō (Seoul) at that time (cf. Yoshida 1998).

Among members of each of the three classes, or *kaikyū*, in rural society then, many of the slaves - especially those who had belonged to *yangban* households - had supposedly moved to regions other than their native places after the emancipation at the end of the Chosŏn Period. The following passages from *Tōsaki* are relevant.

> People of *yangban* status never engaged in agricultural labor before. People of *nongja* class did most of that work. There were also a considerable number of *nongja* people in my household, but I permitted them to change their professions and residence after I became the head because it was not morally good to restrict them. However, some of them have remained. For some, *nongja* status was a hereditary one. In the case of *nongja* families, not only men but also women worked out in the fields (pp.32-33: the testimony of Yi Chunggu, about 50 years old, the most senior descendent of Hansan Yi in Konhyŏn-ri).

> There were many *nuja* people whose surname was Kim until 30 years ago. Here, the rest of the residents were mainly of *yangban* status. All who engaged in agricultural work were people of *noja* status (p.57: the testimony of Kim Yunyŏn in Wŏlun-dong).

All the surnames listed above (about 20 households of Hansan Yi, 2 households of Kwak, 7 or 8 households of Chinju Yu and 7 or 8 households of Chŏnju Yi) are of *yangban* status. Some of the others were *sangmin* and *nuja*. There were 12 to 13 households of *nuja* status (p.75: the testimony of Yi Kapgye and a member of Chŏnju Yi clan in Konhyŏn-ri).

> There were people of *nuja* status here before, but none of them remain now. None of the people of the former *nuja* status lives in his original residence, but has moved out to another region (p.167: the testimony of Pak Yongnim, 71 years old, in Kuryong-ri).
>
> Slaves belonged to specific households, but they have all emigrated out (p.227: the testimony of Kim Kyŏngnim, about 70 years old, in Tongho-ri).

The surnames and the number of *nuja* households 30 years before Suzuki's visit (in the 1910's) have been indicated in the previous section. *Nongja* or *nuja*, mentioned by the informants above, meant slaves who were formerly owned by a specific household and denied the freedom to change their professions or to move out.

As we could read from the passages above, many of the former slaves had already emigrated to other regions when Suzuki visited these villages and reported that "the head of the family (Yi Chunggu of Hansan Yi) was not inclined to talk about *noja*" (p.33). It seems to have been difficult for him to learn much from his informants even about the remaining former slaves, and this was probably because Suzuki simply used the term *yangban* or *sangmin* in most of the passages describing the former status stratification comparatively. For example, he compares *yangban* with *sangmin* in terms of a zone of inter-marriage (pp.33-44), the treatment of newcomers (pp.94-95), marriage customs (pp.50-51), status stratification among clan members and kinship organization (p.62; p.222). As the four-status classification proliferated amid changing conditions in rural society, the categories of *yangban* and *sangmin* have become polarized in a dichotomous relationship, as can be evidenced in Suzuki's concept.

It therefore came to be a prescriptive force in the way that traditions associated with former social status were viewed by researchers and also be Korean people as well. The division of traditional villages into *panch'on* (those inhabited mainly by men of *yangban* status) and *minch'on* (those inhabited by people categorized as *sangmin*), often echoed by Korean villagers today, is a typical example.

On the other hand, as a trained researcher Suzuki also identified conditions in the field that could not be framed by the simple dichotomy or classification into the three status levels. First, regarding the economic base of *yangban*, he saw pre-modern *yangban* people as landowners who relied on the labor of slaves or *mŏsŭm* (farm laborers employed on one-year contracts). In his own words: People of *yangban* status never engaged in agricultural work before. People of the *nongja* class did most of the agricultural labor (p.32). Similarly, he also wrote: There were about 15 households of *yangban* people who never engaged in agricultural labor 40 to 50 years ago. Households of *yangban* used to hire about three laborers on one-year contract before" (p.227). He also reports that men of *yangban* status would indulge in poetry and scholarship without earning any income (p.91). On the other hand, the poor could engage in agricultural labor alone as tenants or farm laborers even among *yangban* residents. The following passages illustrate this, and also suggest that the economic division deepened under colonial rule.

> Even though he is a member of a *yangban* family, a poor man would have become a tenant farmer. They were completely different from *nongja* in terms of status, however. *Nongja* were slaves, while the tenants were only in contractual relations with their landlords (p.33).

> According to the district headman, nearly all of the farmland is owned by this household (that is, the most senior household of the Hansan Yi family) and all of the villagers are now tenants of the clan. Needless to say, there are many households belonging to the Hansan Yi family among the tenants (p.33).

Poor men of *yangban* status used to engage in farming even in old days (pp.91-92).

Here (in Big Kuryong-dong) the residents specialize in farming, so they tend to look down on occupations other than that. (...) Men of *yangban* status could engage in farming, but they never engaged in other occupations (p.172).

Men of *yangban* status who were not rich could engage in farming (p.227).

Suzuki also recorded evidence supporting the contention that family lines of *yangban* had been ranked according to various factors, their relative status within the respective clan as well as in the *yangban* community based on the scale of a traditional county:

The Hansan Yi family in Konhyŏn-ri is a high-ranked *sajok* (a term indicating, in this context, the higher half of *yangban* status engaged mainly in scholarship) group among *yangban* and its reputation is well known in the county. The primary *hyangjok* (the lower half of *yangban* status sometimes engaged in menial obligations) groups among *yangban* in Wŏnju County are Kimhae Kim and Hwengsŏng Ko and they are scattered across every corner of the county. In Konhyŏn-ri, however, a Hansan Yi family that ranks highly as *sajok* accounts for two thirds of the village population. In that sense, Konhyŏn is a famous example of a *dōzoku-buraku* in the county (p.29: the testimony of An Yunok in Wŏnju Town).

Even among the family lines with surnames and clan seats in common (indicating that they belong to the same patri-clan), some are of *yangban* status and others are of *sangmin*, and there exists differentiation according to class or social status among the men of *yangban*. If a distinguished figure appears, his descendents will become influential as well. Consequently, if a man had many ancestors who had ascended to high ranks and positions as bureaucrats, he would naturally achieve a high social position as well. In such a case, a new branch of clan would be formed to distinguish his

> own line from the others of the same clan. While clan organization in Korea is based on grouping of agnatic kin, the organization of agnatic kin is secured by the notion that one's social position is determined hereditarily (p.62: the testimony of Yi Chunggu).
>
> In general, different branches of the same clan could be different in terms of class. Even among members of the same clan, some might be of *yangban* status and others of *sangmin*. And among the men of *yangban* there are individuals of different rank. A man could not even marry a woman of a different rank from his own. Although it is difficult to accurately grade them now, the hierarchy of *yangban* ranks definitely existed before (p.222: the testimony of Kim Kyŏngnim).

For the last two decades, historical surveys on Korean local society in the late Chosŏn period have shown that families of high bureaucrats and Confucian scholars had settled in rural areas and formed a social stratum that played an important role in the administration of their respective counties as well as in indoctrinating peoples there with Confucian morals. Their social standing was called *sajok* in the literature, and they formed exclusive communities within the general scope of the former counties. Economically, they were landlords who also farmed some themselves, a sort of Korean version of landed gentry. The term *yangban*, which had originally meant bureaucrats in the court, came to be used as an honorific term for *sajok* families or branches of a clan by the end of Chosŏn Period. What Suzuki called *yangban* in *Tōsaki* was a group of descendents of *sajok* families or a social status endowed to it. His field data listed above shows a meticulous stratification among *sajok* in the late Chosŏn period. Suzuki regarded as typical of *yangban* those family lines that had established localized cores in one or a few peasant villages (*dōzoku buraku* in Zenshō s terminology), thus forming a local lineage called *chongjung* or *munjung*. For example, regarding clans in Tongho-ri he reports, Only the families of the Ŭisŏng Kim clan form *munjung* (in this village). In general, an ordinary *yangban* family of less than 10 households would not be considered *munjung*. Although a group of the smaller number of high-ranked *yangban* households could be called *munjung*, the one and only *yangban* clan that could be called *munjung* in this village is that of the Ŭisŏng Kim family (p.219). Households of the Ŭisŏng Kim family in this village were among the descendants of a mother and a son who had moved to Sunhŭng County five generations earlier. Eighteen households of the descendants, including 9 households in Tongho-ri, formed the Sunhŭng branch. They played a leading role in the activities of Confucian intellectuals as well as in the management of the public Confucian academy and private schools in Sunhŭng County (pp.218-222). These examples point to the fact that the Ŭisŏng Kim family was not only a dominant family group in Tongho-ri but was also one of the most highly ranked among nearly 40 *munjung* groups that formed the core of the Confucian community in Sunhŭng County. On the other hand, there were more than 10 peripheral *yangban* families in Tongho-ri alone that could not take active roles in Confucian life, thus never forming *munjung* as has been shown in the last section. Similarly in the example of Konhyŏn-ri, five or six households of the Chŏngsong Sim clan that had not lived there 30 years earlier - having immigrated more recently - were accorded *yangban* status. On the other hand, six households of the Hansan Yi clan were said to have received better treatment than *sangmin* even though they were not classified as *yangban*. In Wŏlun-dong, four households of the Chŏnju Yi clan were supposed to have been of *yangban* status but were not actually specified as such. In the case of Chŏktŏk-ri of Big Kuryong-dong, eight *yangbang* households of Milyang Pak lived there in addition to Ŭihŭng Pak and Munhwa Yu households, which were counted as dominant among the *yangban* families in Chechŏn County. All of these peripheral *yangban* families must have occupied marginal positions in each county's *yangban* community, and thus could be regarded as minor *yangban* families.

In regard to the reinforcement of patrilineal kinship organizations, the example of a Ŭihŭng Pak family group in Kuryong-ri should be noted. They formed an association (*chonggye*) owning a joint property based on the ritual group for worshipping their founding ancestor and his son and grandson. Suzuki reports, They have reorganized the association recently and established a general assembly, a young men's association and a housewives' association within it. These serve in domestic education as well as in fostering mutual friendship" (p.128). He further reports, "Officials of the *chonggye* association are the president (Mr. Pak Yongnim), the vice-president, the director-general and the secretaries. It has been less than three years since this kind of steering body was established. Before that, it was not equipped with any sort of permanent organization, but only had an institution that met irregularly. When necessary, the most senior family and the president of the association arranged a meeting, calling the whole clan" (p.129). This example shows that the reorganization and reinforcement of patrilineal kin groups was still underway during the colonial period even among the major *yangban* families.

Then was there any room for minor *yangban* families or those who were not of local *yangban* to challenge the status or social prestige formerly monopolized by *sajok* family members? The organization of *munjung* associations and reinforcement of clan associations could be a social function of major *yangban* kin groups, enabling them to assert their social prestige as *yangban*. In other words, the mutual acknowledgement of *yangban* status as well as the ranking of *yangban* kin groups in the scope of a former county relied partly on the formation of a patrilineal kinship organization. This is also the case with what Suenari characterized as "yangbanization", the process in which minor *yangban* families try to assure their status as *yangban* and to attain a higher rank by practicing ideal behaviors as *yangban* (Suenari 1987). Concerning non-*yangban* people, however, he never discussed the possibility that a man or a group of non-*yangban* (perhaps including those of *sangmin* status in the same former county as well as recent immigrants of *yangban* status) would attain *yangban* status by reinforcing their kin organizations or associating with local *yangban* company, and neither did Suzuki. On the other hand, ambiguity in the boundary around *yurim* (a company of Confucian intellectuals) indicated by Suzuki might point to latent vacillation of *yangban* status.

In the third chapter, on *munmyo* (shrines for Confucian sages attached to a Confucian academy) and *yurim*, Suzuki refers to the definition of *yurim*. After a passage indicating that the worshipping body of *munmyo* came to be borne by the county governor and *yurim* after students and clerks vacated a local Confucian academy, he discusses the blurring of boundaries between groups.

> These days, the definition of *yurim* has become quite ambiguous. In addition, profits from the property of a county Confucian academy cannot be spared for the expense of its rituals alone. This causes various kinds of problems. But anyway, even now, *munmyo* is virtually run by *yurim* company of a former county. The principal (of the academy) is elected from among the company and takes the heaviest responsibility. The company also elects his assistants (*changŭi*) by mutual vote every three or four years. The principal also nominates some members of *yurim* as ritual officiants and butlers every time a *munmyo* ceremony is performed. But the boundary of the *yurim* company is the current topic…. In order to cope with the current changes, a new type of association named *Yudohoe* (an association for the practice of Confucian ways) has been established. But it seems difficult to expect it to vitalize an overaged organization of local *yurim* so that it may preserve its traditional style (pp.19-21).

The following two passages prove that *yurim* membership was not necessarily acknowledged according to definite and objective criteria but rather approved by the company on the basis of a subjective, mutual understanding even before the current state of ambiguity. Nevertheless, or perhaps because of that, it could maintain a definite boundary.

> To be a member of the *yurim* society is to obtain a sort of social power, but there is no clear-cut criteria for admittance. Membership, I suppose, is decided solely on the basis of vague opinions among the company (pp.20-21).
>
> All clerks who were in charge of the property of local Confucian academies in the county offices I visited this time were of one accord in admitting that the boundary of *yurim* society in its strict sense was not clear. They added, however, that men who had been regarded as *yurim* within each village seemed to have been universally assessable. I suppose it was probably true (p.22).

The *yurim* company was not necessarily a solidly institutionalized society, as the president of the *chonggye* association said: "The *yurim* society had no particular ceremony for initiation" (p.21).

According to the testimonies of the aged intellectuals Suzuki interviewed, the basic requirements for one to be admitted *yurim* in the old days were literacy in classical Chinese, an academic career as a student of a public or private academy, sophisticated manners, not being involved in despised professions (i.e. commercial business) and descent from *yangban* ancestors (especially from celebrated scholars or successful candidates of the higher civil-service examination). Some indicated that those who had failed in the higher civil-service examination or who were not appointed as bureaucrats also acted as *yurim*. In other words, the core of *yurim* before was comprised of descendents of *yangban* families educated in classical Chinese and Confucianism who possessed good manners in terms of Confucian morality. The typical figure was one who had studied for the civil-service examination. On the other hand, the *yurim* company of Suzuki's time had already started to become an amorphous entity, at least in some counties. Quoting Pak Yongnim, he reports: "It could be said that *yurim* these days is a company of men from the middle class or above who know classical Chinese. Some have graduated from elementary schools alone. *Yangban* status is not required for admittance" (p.21). This means that *yangban* families had no more monopolized social prestige represented in *yurim* figures at that time. Suzuki's examples point to the fact that *yangban* as a social category or a group had survived even after the abolition of the pre-modern status system and the consequent deprivation of legal as well as customary privileges attached to the former status. If it is true, then social prestige as *yurim* must have been one of the important bases for recognition as *yangban*, together with membership of the county-level *yangban* community and the organization of patrilineal kin groups. Suzuki's trained eyes have never missed this ambiguous phenomenon, which could have been easily overlooked by other foreigners. His field surveys in colonial Korea could be highly evaluated in this sense alone.

Finally, I discuss the concept of *sangmin* and its implications. Suzuki interviewed three household heads of *sangmin* status in Konhyŏn-ri, and concluded provisionally that a zone of inter-marriage is generally smaller in the case of *sangmin* than in that of *yangban* (p.40). The problem with this is that none of the three households interviewed had been in the village for many generations. In the case of Kim Kyehak, his father had relocated from Yangp ŏng County in Kyonggi Province. So Pongjun left his native home in Iksan County of North Chŏlla Province 62 years earlier at the age of 14 and, after wandering from one place to another and living from hand to mouth, he finally settled in Konhyŏn-ri. In the instance of Ŏm Sŏksŏng, his great-grandfather had immigrated from Yŏngwŏl County of Kangwŏn Province, but the generational distance from the original settler was never greater than that in *yangban* families such as the Hansan Yi group of the same village. All of them possessed rather shallow knowledge on each genealogy and two of them didn't even know how many generations had passed since the time of their respective founding ancestors (pp.33-40). This shows that although the *sangmin* category was presented as a concept to counter that of *yangban*, the former did not necessarily constitute a substantial entity on par with the latter. The term *sangmin* at that time seems to have pointed to the residual, generic set of people that were not of *yangban* status. Rather, the former slave category could be regarded as having been a more solid entity in the sense that they had settled in local society and that their status had been defined hereditarily.

5. Conclusions

In analyzing a mass of historical documents preserved by the Pak family of Taejŏ-ri in Yech ŏn County of North Kyŏngsang Province, Yi Yŏnghun, a Korean historian, has concluded that it is difficult to define a pre-modern administrative village as a community:

> If we removed these lines of networks and circles of associations, what would be left for the lowest administrative unit called Taejŏ-ri? The remainder is just a spatial arrangement of the villagers residences on the one hand, and the cultivated fields and the mountains and the forests surrounding them on the other. We cannot find a community integrated into a corporate body as an entity to which members endowed with relatively equal qualifications share a strong sense of belonging. It would be misleading to define Taejŏ-ri in the 19th century as a community that indicates an historical entity and I suppose that it was also a case with a great number of other villages (at that time). It was simply a relationship in which a lot of networks and associations whose boundaries and cores were different from one another had overlapped. (Yi Yŏnghun 2001, p.282).

If this were true, Suzuki's assumption that a Korean natural village or a village community, if it existed, would be a traditional, administrative village could be ill founded. Although he presented village-based associations and joint worship of local guardian divinities as evidence that his natural villages 'such as Tunsan-dong or Middle Kuryong-ri' were in fact such, these institutions could not be necessarily permanent nor universal in my view (cf. Honda 2002). Here, I do not insist that no local social units in colonial Korea were founded on community-like social relations, but I do disagree with Suzuki's universalized claim that a traditional administrative village in colonial Korea was a perpetual community. All of the four villages he visited in his second field trip were *dōzoku buraku* mainly inhabited by *yangban* households. This suggests that if he found any community-like atmosphere there it might have been based on, or at least reinforced by, agnatic kin relations. Fellow villagers of *sangmin* status, or former slaves, could have been linked to this community by economic relations with *yangban* landlords or through status-based relations with a former master. In this case, a community found in *yangban dōzoku buraku* would have been an entity in which a core of *yangban* households is attended by their satellite households of tenants or former slaves. The model I have shown here is no more than a hypothesis, but it leads to the question of whether a village mainly inhabited by *sangmin* households in colonial Korea could have been regarded as a natural village. Unless high mobility among *sangmin* people shown in the end of the last section were an idiosyncratic feature confined to Konhyŏn-ri, to find a device which could regenerate the social integration of a natural village, if it existed, would be the next task.

In this report, I have attempted a genealogical investigation of Suzuki Eitarō s *Chōsen Nōson Shakai Tōsaki*. My method has been retrospective as well in the sense that I, as a student of anthropology of Korea trained in a Japanese community of Koreanists, have re-examined the very foundation of our field of study. In conclusion, I emphasize that a natural village in Korea was and is never an *a priori* entity. Our task will be to investigate social and cultural interactions among agents in local society, as well as to explore the historical contexts of groups, relations and institutions that were presupposed as components of the Korean natural village.

■ References

Choi, Chungmoo. 1997. "The Discourse of Decolonization and Popular Memory", In Tanie E. Barlow (ed.), *Formation of Colonial Modernity in East Asia*. pp.349-372, Durham & London: Duke University Press.

Chōsen sōtokufu chūsūin. 1938. *Chōsen Kyūkan Seido Chōsa Gaiyo* [Outline of the Research Projects on Korean Traditional Customs and Institutions]. Keijō: Chōsen Sōtokufu.

Hattori, Tamio. 1974. *Suzuki Eitarō Chosakusyū Vol. 5 Chōsen Nōson Shakai no Kenkyū Kankō no motsu Mondaiten ni tsuite* (On Problems of the Publication of the Fifth Volume of Collected Works of Suzuki Eitarō). In *Mirai* No.89, pp.48-56, Miraisha.

Honda, Hiroshi. 2002. "Kankoku no Chiiki Shakai ni okeru Chiensei to Kyōdōsei" (Localized Community in Korean Rural Society), In Itō Abito & Han Kyŏnggu (eds.), *Kannichi Shakai Soshiki no Hikaku* [Comparative Study on Social Organizations of Korea and Japan]. pp.243-273, Tokyo: Keio Gijuku Daigaku Shuppankai.

Imamura, Tomo. 1975[1919]. *Chōsen Fūzokushū* [Collected Essays on Korean Manners and Customs] (reprint of the third edition). Tokyo: Kokusho Kankōkai.

Ishikawa, Taizō. 1973. "Suzuki Sensei to Keijō" (Professor Suzuki and Keijō), In *Geppō* (Monthly Newsletter) *Suzuki Eitarō Chosakushū* (Collected Works of Suzuki Eitarō) No.6, pp.3-5, Tokyo: Miraisha.

Janelli, Roger L. & Dawnhee Yim. 1998. "The Genealogy of Making Harmony among Co-Workers of a South Korean Conglomerate", In Mutsuhiko Shima & Roger L. Janelli (eds.), *The Anthropology of Korea: East Asian Perspective*. pp.171-190, Osaka: National Museum of Ethnology.

Kim, Ik-han. 1996. *Shokuminchiki Chōsen ni okeru Chihou Shihai Taisei no Kōchiku Katei to Nōson Shakai Hendō* (Process of the Construction of

Local Administration System and Rural Social Change in Colonial Korea). Unpublished Ph. D. dissertation, Graduate School of Humanities and Sociology, The University of Tokyo.

Murayama, Chijun. 1937. *Burakusai* (Village Rituals). Keijō: Chōsen Sōtokufu.

Odauchi, Michitoshi. 1923. *Chōsen Buraku Chōsa Yosatsu Hōkoku Vol. 1* (The Preliminary Report on the Research of Korean Traditional Villages). Keijō: Chōsen Sōtokufu.

Shikata, Hiroshi. 1976[1938]. Richō Jinkō ni kansuru Mibun Kaikyū betsu teki Kōsatsu (Study on the Population in Yi Dynasty in terms of Status and Class Differentiation). Reprinted and contained in the second volume of *Chōsen Shakai Keizaishi Kenkyū* (Study on Social and Economic History of Korea). Tokyo: Kokusho Kankōkai.

Suenari, Michio. 1987. "Kankoku Shakai no Yangban ka" (Yangbanization in Korean Society), In Abito Itō, Teruo Sekimoto & Takeo Funabiki (eds.), *Gendai no Shakaijinruigaku 1 Shinzoku to Kazoku no Kōzō* (Current Social Anthropology 1: Structure of Kinship and Family). Tokyo: Tokyo Daigaku Shuppankai.

Suzuki, Eitarō. 1940. *Nihon Nōson Shakaigaku Genri* (Principles of Japanese Rural Sociology). Tokyo: Jichōsha.

__________. 1943a. "Chōsen Nōson Shakai Bekkenki" (A Record of a Brief Look at Korean Rural Society), In *Minzokugaku Kenkyū* (Journal of Japanese Society of Ethnology) 9, pp.47-73.

__________. 1943b. "Chōsen no Nōson Shakai Shūdan ni tsuite" (On Social Groups of Korean Peasant Villages), In *Chōsa Geppō* (Monthly Research Report) (Chōsen Sōtokufu) Vol. 14, No. 9. pp.1-23; No. 11, pp.1-19; No. 12, pp.1-15.

__________. 1943c. "Chōsen no Sonraku" (A Korean Village), In *Tōa Shakai Kenkyū* (Study on East Asian Societies) Vol. 1, pp.286-318, Tokyo: Seikatsusha.

__________. 1944. *Chōsen Nōson Shakai Tōsaki*. Tokyo: Ōsakayagō Shoten.

__________. 1963. "Chōsen no Kei to Pumashi" (*Kye* and *P umasi* in Korea), In *Minzokugauku Kenkyū* (Journal of Japanese Society of Ethnology) Vol. 27, No.3, pp.552-558.

____________. 1973. *Suzuki Eitarō Chosakushū Vol. 5: Chōsen Nōson Shakai no Kenkyū* (Collected Works of Suzuki Eitarō vol. 5: Study on Korean Rural Society). Tokyo: Miraisha.

Tanaka, Tokutarō. 1921. "Chōsen no Shakai Kaikyū" (Korean Social Classes), In *Chōsen* (Korea) March 1921, pp.53-63, Keijō: Chōsen Sōtokufu.

Yi, Yŏnghun. 2001. "18·19 Segi Taejŏri-ŭi Sinbun Kusŏng-gwa Chach i Chilsŏ" (Status Composition and Self-governmental Order in Taejŏri Village in the 18th and 19th Century), In An Pyŏngjik & Yi Yŏnghun (eds.), *Matchil-ŭi Nongmin-dŭl* (Peasants in Matchil Village). pp.245-299, Seoul: Iljogak.

Yoshida, Mitsuo. 1998. "Chōsen no Mibun to Shakai Shūdan" (Status and Social Groups in Chosŏn Period), In *Sekai Rekishi* (World History) (Iwanami Kōza (Iwanami Lectures) Vol. 13, pp.215-234, Tokyo: Iwanami Shoten.

Zenshō, Eisuke. 1933a. *Chōsen no Shūraku Vol. 1* (Korean Settlements). Keijō: Chōsen Sōtokufu.

____________. 1933b. *Chōsen no Shūraku Vol. 2.* Keijō: Chōsen Sōtokufu.

____________. 1935. *Chōsen no Shūraku Vol. 3.* Keijō: Chōsen Sōtokufu.

Korean Society as seen from the Japanese Perspective:

A Thorough Analysis of Books Published in Japan

Toshio Asakura
National Museum of Ethnology, Japan

Introduction

This study aims to identify characteristics of contemporary attention toward Korean culture in Japanese society, through a content analysis of books published in Japan. The data for analysis consist of approximately 600 nonfiction hardcovers and paperbacks which are either books on Korean culture written by Japanese, Korean or ethnic Korean authors, or counterparts on Japanese culture written by Korean authors. Although the sample comes from a non-random personal collection of the researcher, it covers almost all the books of this type published after 1980. By sorting and analyzing the sample by author, title, and year of publication, the study seeks to examine what aspects of Korean culture have been most represented in Japanese society and how such trend has changed over time. While providing a general picture of public attention toward Korean culture in Japanese society, the researcher intends to examine reflexively how anthropologists should respond to such popular interest.

I. Analysis by author

(1) Japanese authors

Japanese authors have written about Korean people and culture from many different angles, based on their varied standpoints: journalist, scholar, diplomat, businessman, international student, entertainer, and so forth. It is thereby assumed that each author presents Korea differently, depending on his/her viewpoint, or the subjects level and circumstances in terms of how he/she relates to Korea. Focusing primarily on those who have published several books, this section of the paper reviews what types of Japanese authors have published what kinds of books on Korea.

a. Journalists

As an employee of Kyodo News Service, Kuroda Katsuhiro studied Korean at Yonsei University in Korea from 1978 to 1979. From 1980, he spent approximately 4 years in Seoul as a correspondent and head of the Seoul branch for Kyodo News Service. Since 1989, he has been residing in Seoul, keeping a close watch on Korean society as head of the Sankei Press Seoul branch. He has published more than 20 books on Korean society, starting from *Kankoku Shakai wo Mitsumete · Nite Hinarumono* (Watching over Korean Society: Looks the Same but is Different, 1983). Some of his other books are *Seoul Gentaiken - Kankoku no Seikatsu wo Tanoshimu Ki* (Original Experience of Seoul: Record of Enjoying Seoul Life, 1985), *Kankokujin no Hasso* (The Koreans' Conception, 1986), *Seoul Retsuretsu* (Seoul Enthusiasm, 1993), *Kankokujin no Rekishikan* (Koreans' Historical Views, 1999), *Nikkan Taihen - Naze "Kakobanare" Dekinainoka* (Japan-Korea Relations out of Control: Why Not "Leaving the Past behind"?, 2001), and *Nikkan Shinko* (New Speculations on Japan-Korea Relations, 2002).

Shigemura Toshimitsu of the Mainichi Press moved to Korea in 1975 to study in graduate school at Koryo University. From 1980, he stayed in Seoul as a correspondent for 5 years. He has published several books including *Kankoku ga Wakaru Saishin Sourugo Joho* (Understanding Korea through the Latest Vocabulary Information from Seoul, 1988) and *Kankoku hodo Taisetsu na Kuni ha Nai* (There is No Country as Important as Korea, 1998).

b-1. Stayers in the 1960's-70's Korea

When the present writer started to have interest in Korea in the late 1970's, Cho Shokichi's *Souru Yugakuki - Watashi no Chosengo Shojiten* (Journal of Studying in Seoul: My Small Korean Dictionary, 1978) was the only book available to learn about Korean life. In this book, the author uses a sharp sense of language to vividly express his life experiences in Seoul, where he studied from November 1968 to March 1970. Later, he published the second volume titled *Fudangi no Chosengo - Watashi no Chosengo Shojiten 2* (The Korean Language of Everyday Wear: My Small Korean Dictionary II, 1988), which included what he wrote for magazines between 1984 and 1987. Cho Shokichi, a major in Korean modern literature, died young in 1988 at the age of 47. *Chosen · Kotoba · Ningen* (Korea, Language, and Human, 1989) is a posthumous collection of his essays and commentaries. He was a pioneer of fieldwork in Korea, opening the door for the next generation.

b-2. Stayers in Korea around 1980

Korean society observed a series of political disturbances at the turn of the year 1980, namely President Park Chung Hee's assassination in 1979 and students' protest for democracy, followed by the Gwangju uprising in 1980. Correspondingly, attention to Korea among the Japanese at this time revolved primarily around politics, particularly democracy movement. In the midst of such trend, Sekikawa Natsuo's *Seoul no Renshu Mondai - Ibunka he no Toshi Noto* (Exercise of Seoul: Transparent Notebook for 2 Different Culture, 1984) brought fresh sensation to Japanese readers by reporting Koreans' lived experiences set in the early 1980's Seoul. The present writer, who studied in Korea around the same time, found the book significantly reflecting his experiences and views on the Korean society. Following this book, Sekikawa published another unique reportage titled *Kaikyo wo Koeta Homuran - Sokoku to Iu Na no Ibunka* (Home Run Going over the Straits: Different Culture in the Name of the Mother Country, 1984). Based on interviews with "Korean Japanese" baseball players who played in the Korean professional baseball league, this book informed Japanese readers about ethnic Koreans living in Japan and Korean society in a whole new way.

Similarly, Takizawa Hideki's *Souru Sanka - Aru Kankoku Ryugakuki* (Admiration Songs for Seoul: A Record of Studying in South Korea, 1984) featured the social reality of the 1980's Seoul through a detailed description of people's everyday lives. Takizawa wrote this book based on his one-year stay in Korea from 1982 as a visiting scholar at Seoul National University. This one-year stay was not actually his first time being in Seoul, but it was said to be influential enough to have renewed his understanding about Korea. Specialized in Japanese modern economic history and Korean societal ethics, he later wrote several scholarly books like *Kankoku Shakai no Tenkan* (The transformation of Korean Society, 1988), *Kankoku no Keizai Hatten to Shakai Kozo* (The Economic Development and Social Structure of Korea, 1992), and *Ajia no naka no Kankoku Shakai* (Korean Society within Asia, 2000). At the same time, he has also published *Kankoku he no Samazamana Tabi* (Various Journeys to Korea, 1992), an essay that traces along the footprints of his interests in Korea.

Nozaki Mitsuhiko visited Korea for the first time in 1975. After that, he studied in Seoul for two years and completed his master's work in Korean literature at Dongguk University. From the standpoint of a Korean literary major, he became interested in feng shui, the native history of the Lee Dynasty. Based on these interests, he has written such books as *Kankoku no Fusuishitachi* (Feng Shui Practitioners in Korea, 1994), *Chosen no Monogatari* (The Story of Korea, 1998), and *Koria no Fushigi Sekai - Chosen Bunkashi 27wa* (Korea's Wonder Land: 27 Stories of Korean Cultural History, 2003).

Furuta Hiroshi spent six years in South Korea from July 1980 mainly as a Japanese language teacher. After studying Korean-language teaching methods in graduate school at Seoul National University, he taught Japanese at universities such as Yonsei Universiy and Hanyang University. He wrote two books based on what he saw and heard while he was in Korea. One is *Kanashisa ni Warau Kankokujin - Nihongo Kyoshi no Wajin Kankokuden* (Smiling Koreans in Sorrow: Biography of a Japanese Language Teacher in Korea, 1986), and the other is *Souru no Jyushatachi - Kankokujin no Seishin Fudo* (Confucian in Seoul: Koreans' Mental Climate, 1988). Subsequently, Furuta, who has specialized in history of East Asian thoughts, has published *Chosen Minzoku wo Yomitoku* (Reading into the Koreans, 1995) and *Higashi Ajia no Shiso Fukei* (Scenes of East Asian Thoughts, 1998) etc.

Among many researchers in Korean studies who stayed in Korea around 1980, including the present writer, relatively well-known to the general public would be Yomota Inuhiko and Kawamura Minato.

Yomota stayed in Seoul for one year from 1979 as a visiting scholar at Konkuk University. In 1986, six years after his return to Japan, he started writing *Wareraga 〈Tasha〉 Naru Kankoku* (Korea where We Become "Others", 1987). According to Yomota, the most shared images on Korea among the Japanese at the time of 1979 were poverty, political conspiracy, and grudges against Japan. However, once Seoul was selected as a host city for the Olympics after rivalry with Nagoya, "Korea boom" hit Japan. This accounts for the arrival of Japan's so-called "Japan-Korea New Age." According to the author, this book shows, reviewing these situations, a dimension of Korea that was experienced by a Japanese who was a foreign teacher and great fan of movies.

Yomota stayed in Seoul again from August to December 2000 as a visiting researcher at the Institute for Japanese Studies, Chung-Ang University. In *Souru no Fuukei - Kioku to Henbo* (Landscape of Seoul: Memory and Transfiguration, 2001), he examines how Seoul has changed since he stayed in the city last time 21 years ago. Here, he does so in relation to such factors as the city's conditions, transformation of traditional customs, recollections of the Gwangju uprising and comfort women, and the city's reactions toward President Kim Dae-Jung's Nobel prize winning. In the meantime, he retouched on what he wrote for a NHK TV lecture course textbook for the year 2002, and it became his third book on Korea titled *Daisukina Kankoku* (My Favorite Korea, 2003).

In *Watashi no Pusan* (My Pusan, 1986), Kawamura Minato relates his stories of teaching Japanese and Japanese literature at Dong-A University, Pusan from 1982 to 1986. Also, Kawamura has published a couple of books on Seoul. Although he has never settled in the city, he says Seoul has been a place for him to meet a variety of people and literary work since his first visit to the city in the mid 1970's. *Souru no Yushu* (The Melancholy of Seoul, 1988) and *Souru Toshi Monogatari - Rekishi.Bungaku.Fukei* (Seoul City Stories: History, Literature, and Landscape, 2000) are his recollection of such encounters in Seoul as a literary critic. Furthermore, in *Kiisen - "Mono Iu Hana" no Bunkashi* (Kiseng: Cultural Description of "Talking Flowers", 2001), he endeavors to examine self-portrait images of Japanese men through an exploration of the peculiar culture of kiseng, which was shaped by distortion of colonialism, sexuality, and gender.

b-3. Stayers in Korea after the Seoul Olympics

In 1988, the Olympics took place in Seoul. Democratization was declared by President Roh Tae-Woo in the previous year, and the Korean society had become a mass consumption society as a result of achieving high economic growth.

Ogura Kizo, who left for Korea in 1988, published *Toky・Souru Monogatari・Bijinesuman ga Kataru Sugao no Kankoku* (Tokyo/Seoul Story: Real Face of Korea in the Eyes of Businessmen, 1991) with Song

He-Min. Ogura completed a doctorate program in philosophy at Seoul National University in 1995, and he has been trying to address themes concerning Koreas society, culture and people from a Korean philosophical perspective. Some of his books are *Kankoku ha Ikko no Tetsugaku de Aru - 〈Ri〉 to 〈Ki〉 no Shakai Shisutemu* (Korea is a Philosophy: Social System of Logic and Energy, 1998), *Kankokujin no Shikumi - 〈Ri〉 to 〈Ki〉 de Yomitoku Bunka to Shakai* (Mechanism of Koreans: Reading Culture and Society through Logic and Energy, 2001), and *Kankoku, Hikisakareru Kosumosu* (Korea: Cosmos Torn Apart, 2001).

Kohari Susumu went to Seoul in November 1991 and returned to Japan in 1997 with a master s degree from Sogang University and a doctorate degree from Seoul National University. He has published *Kankoku Wocchingu* (Watching Korea, 1995), *Seikimatsu Kankoku wo Yomitoku* (Reading into Korea at the End of the Century), *Kankoku to Kankokujin* (Korea and Its People, 1999), keeping his eyes on contemporary Korean society.

Mizuno Shunpei (Nohira Toshimi) went to Korea upon graduation from Tenri University in 1990. He completed his masters work in 1993 and his Ph.D. work in 1995 at Chonnam National University. At present, he is a lecturer in Japanese and Japanese literature at Chonnam National University but is also popular on TV in Korea. He has examined Koreans views on Japan through analysis of publications in Korea. These books include *Kankoku Hannichi Shosetsu no Kakikata* (How to Write Korean Anti-Japan Novels, 1996), *Kannichi Senso Boppatsu? Kankoku Kettai Hon no Sekai* (Outbrake of Korea-Japan War? World of Korean Strange Books, with Okita Shoji, 2001), *Nihonjin ha Bikkuri! Kankokujin no Nihon Gishi* (Surprise for the Japanese! Koreans False History of Japan, 2002). Recently, he published two books which report on the latest Korean trend: *Kankoku no Wakamono wo Shiritai* (Wanting to Know about Young People in Korea, 2003) and *Nazedaka Kankoku de Ichiban Yumeina Nihonjin-Watashi ga TV de Ninkimono ni Natta Fuka～i Riyu* (Somehow,

I am the Most Well-known Japanese in Korea; Profound Reasons Why I Became Popular on TV, 2003).

b-4. Women

Kamiya Niji graduated from International Christian University (ICU) in 1983. When she was an undergraduate student at ICU, she went to Yonsei University as an exchange student. Through her trips to Korean rural villages, she learned about the modern historical footprints of Japanese colonial period and came to question about the historical significance of the past 100 years for Japanese people. Since then, she has continued her journey into Korean history and culture. She published *Kankoku Chikai Mukashi no Tabi* (Korea: a Journey to the Recent Past, 1994), *Kankoku no Chiisana Mura de* (In a Korean Small Village, 1997), and *Kankoku Rekishi Manpo* (Ramble through Korean History, 2003).

Toda Ikuko stayed in Korea for her study from 1983 to 1987. Since her return to Japan, she has introduced Seoul to Japanese readers particularly from the everyday context of life. She published *Fudangi no Souru Annai* (Seoul Guide in Casual Wear, 1988) and *Chorumuni - Kankoku no Wakamonotachi* (Cheolmeuni: Young People in Korea, 1988), and she has also been engaged in translation work.

Kawamura Ako, the wife of Kawamura Minato, has reported on the situation of Korea from her viewpoint as a housewife. Based on her family life in Pusan, she wrote *Tonari no Kuni no Onnatachi - Gendai Kankoku Shomin Jijo* (Women of the Neighboring Country: The Lives of Ordinary People in Contemporary Korea, 1987) and *Kankoku Dauntaun Monogatari* (Korean Downtown Story, 1988).

Manabe Yuko published *Kyanpasu ni Miru Ibunka - Kankoku Gurashi no Sobyou* (Different Culture Seen on Campus: Rough Sketch of Korean Life, 1996) based on her experience of working as a Japanese language teacher at a Korean university. After she stayed in Korea from 1987 to 1988, she taught Japanese at Keimyung University for 2 years from 1991. She applied a sociological perspective to write *Yorusa no Tanjo - Kankoku Minshu Undo niokeru Han no Rikigaku* (Appearance of "Yolsa" - Minjung Movements and Han Korean Ethos, 1997) and *Koshu Jiken de Yomu Gendai Kankoku* (Reading Contemporary Korea through the Kwangju Uprising, 2000)

In addition to those already mentioned above, there are a considerable number of books on Korea by female writers. The list of these books includes Onoda Misako's *Wanda Rando Souru* (Wonderland Seoul, 1981), Kamo Yoshiko's *Souru, Kankokugo Sekai heno Tabi - Watashi no 80 Nendai* (Seoul, Journey to the Korean Language World: My 80's, 2001), Tsutsui Makiko's *Souru no Choppari - Watashi no Ryugakuki* (Choppali in Seoul: My Memoirs of Studying Abroad, 1991), Kurihara Yoko's *Mama.Boi no Kankoku・Feminisuto Yugakuki* (Mama Boys Korea: Feminist Recollection of Studying in Korea, 1995), Watanabe Mayumi's *Kankoku no Obachan ha Erai!* (Korean Aunties are Great!, 1999), and Nishimura, Keiko's *Keiko.Kankoku Funtoki* (Keikos Record of Challenges in Korea, 2002).

Some background information about these female writers is as follows. Onoda stayed in Seoul for three years from 1977 as a wife of a correspondent. Kamo went to Korea in 1982 and became a Japanese language teacher. Tsutsui went to Seoul to study in 1987, and Kurihara spent a year as a visiting researcher at Wonkwang University from 1994. Watanabe moved to Seoul as a wife of a newspaper correspondent in 1994 and spent two years in Seoul with her husband and children. Nishimura moved to Seoul in 1998 for business.

c. Writers (authorship)/entertainers

Komuro Naoki, who has been writing since 1980s, published three paperbacks that responds to the Japanese public interest in Koreas democratization and economic development. The titles of the paperbacks are *Kankoku no Higeki* (South Koreas Tragedy, 1985), *Kankoku no Noroi*

(South Korea's Curse, 1986), *Kankoku no Hokai* (South Koreas Corruption, 1988).

Toyota Aritsune, whose publication record covers a wide range of genres from a history novel to a social critique, has also published a series of Korea-related paperbacks. They are *Kankoku no Chosen · Nihonjin ga Shiranai Keizai Kyuseicho no Himitsu* (Koreas Challenge: Secrets of Rapid Economic Growth that Japanese Dont Know, 1978), *Nihonjin to Kankokujin, Koko ga Ochigai · Daremo Kakenakatta Rinkokujin no Ishiki to Kodo* (Here is How Different the Japanese and the Koreans are: Our Neighbors Consciousness and Behavior which Anyone Has Never Been Able to Tell You About, 1985), *Iikagen ni Shiro Kankoku · Nihon wo Shittoshi Sagesumu Shin no Riyu* (Thats More than Enough!: Real Reasons for Koreas Jealousy and Contempt for Japan, 1994), *Kankoku he Ikari to Kanashimi* (Dear Korea, Anger and Sorrow, 1996), *Ima Kankokujin ha Nani wo Kangaeteiruka* (What are Koreans Thinking Now, 2002) etc. These series of books correspond to the state of Japan-Korea relations of the time, capturing such moments and stages as economic growth, anti-Japan/Korea-phobia, and the World Cup.

Ko Shintaro, known as a cartoonist and TV and Radio commentator, has published *Omoshiroi Kankokujin · Tomodachi dakara Kokomade Ieru* (Interesting Koreans: What Cannot Be Said without Friendship, 1994), *Motto Omoshiroi Kankokujin - Ai ga Arukara Kokomade Ieru* (More Interesting Koreans: What Cannot Be Said without Love, 1995). *Dare mo Iwanakatta Kankokujin no Honne no Uragawa* (What Nobody told You about the Other Side of Koreans' Real Intention, 2002).

Kuroda Fukumi is an actress who is known as the most knowledgeable person about Korea in the entertainment industry. After her first visit to Korea, she acquired the Korean language skill by self-study. In 1988, when Korea received significant media attention on the eve of the Seoul Olympics, her knowledge about and interest in Korea led her to act as reporter and receive interviews from the press. *Souru Mai Haato* (Seoul

My Heart, 1988) described the tie she had developed with Korea through these experiences. Thereafter, she has published essays of this type one after another while actively involving with a range of cultural events concerning Korea. For example, *Souru no Tatsujiin* (Master in Seoul, 1994), *Souru Mai Haato 2* (Seoul My Heart 2, 1999), *Souru Mai Deizu* (Seoul My Days, 2002), and *Tonari no Kankokujin Keiko to Taisaku* (Our Korean Neighbors: Trend and Strategy, 2003).

d. Diplomats

Okazaki Hisahiko(pen name: Nagasaka Satoru)'s *Tonari no Kuni de Kangaetakoto* (What I Thought in the Neighboring Country, 1977) is based on his recollection of working as a diplomat between 1973 and 1976 at an Japanese embassy in Seoul. He has a feeling that both citizens of Japan and Korea are the "victims of intellectual blank" that emerged as a result of the 36 year colonial era and the following 30 years of post-war period.

Machida Mitsugu's *Souru no Nihon Taishikan kara* (From a Japanese Embassy in Seoul, 1999) is a journal of a diplomat who worked at several Japanese embassies in Korea over the course of his career. Machida joined the Ministry of Foreign Affairs right after he received a degree in Korean Studies from Tenri University in 1958. During his 40 year's career in foreign service, he spent 25 years in Korea starting from a position as Vice-Consul in Pusan from 1965, Counsellor at the embassy in Seoul from 1982, Head Officer in Cheju Island from 1990, Consul General in Pusan from 1993, and finally Chairman of Culture and Official Report from 1996.

Michigami Hisashi, the author of *Nihon Gaikokan, Kankoku Funtoki* (A Japanese Diplomat, Record of His Challenges in Korea, 2001), studied in graduate school at Seoul National University between 1984 and 1986 as an elite diplomat and was appointed to work in the embassy in Seoul in 1998. Through debates with many South Koreans, the book explores the new image of Korea and the difference of historical views between Korea and Japan.

e. Others

In recent years, many books are published by authors of the younger generation. Toomori Kei, free-lance writer and illustrator, is one of them. He started off as a chief editor of a small theme paper on contemporary Korea. Since this paper turned out to be successful, he has been committed to writing about Korea. His publications include *Ekisentorikku.Souru · Genki na Rojiura.Meiso suru Shinsedai* (Eccentric Seoul: Lively Back Alley and the Wandering New Generation, 1997), *Chotto Matte! Kankoku · Funarena Senshinkoku no Tomadoi* (Wait a minute! Korea: Bewilderment of the Inexperienced Advanced Country, 1998), *Gurutto Souru · Chikatetsu de Meguru Ima. Mukashi* (Going Around Seoul: Traveling by Subway to the Present and the Past, 2000).

(2) Koreans

a. Lee O-Young

Lee O-Young's *Chijimi Shiko no Nihonjin* (The Compact Culture: The Japanese Tradition of Smaller is Better, 1982) appears to be the most well-known work among Korean's books on the Japanese. Before this book, Lee O-Young's writing had been introduced to Japanese readers through *Han no Bunkaron · Kankokujin no Kokoro no Soko ni Arumono* (Examining Culture through Han: What Koreans Have at the Bottom of Their Mind, 1978) and its enlarged edition, *Kankokujin no Kokoro* (The Mind of the Koreans, 1982). In South Korea, Lee O-Young is a highly recognized author, publishing a number of novels, drama scripts, and movie scenarios. One of the most important works is *Kankoku to Kankokujin* (Korea and the Koreans), which analyzes Koreas heritage of spiritual culture through methodological application of contemporary literary criticism. He has successively held the posts of editorial writer of the news paper, university professor, and Director General of Agency for Cultural Affairs. *Furoshiki Bunka no Posuto Modan ·Nihon.Kankoku no Bunbutsu kara Mirai wo Yomu* (Post Modernism of Wrapping-Cloth Culture: Reading the Future from Japanese and Korean Culture, 1989) and *Kaeru ha Naze Furuike ni Tobikondaka ·Haiku.to Nihonjin no Hasso* (Why did the Frog Jump into the Pond?: "Haiku" and Japanese Peoples Ideas, 1993) have been introduced to Japan.

b. Kim Yong-Woon

Born in Tokyo and educated at Waseda University, Kim Yong-Woon returned to Korea in 1947. He continued his study in the U.S.A. and Canada and went back to Korea again in 1969. Although his major is in mathematics, he has constantly written 9 about Korean and Japanese cultures from a comparative perspective. Part of his extensive publication record includes *Kankokujin to Nihonjin - Soutai Bunka no Purizumu* (Koreans and the Japanese: Prism of Opposite Cultures, 1983), *Sakoku no Han Paradaimu - Nikkan Bunka no Ishitsusei* (Generic Paradigm of Isolation: Otherness in Japanese and Korean Cultures, 1984), *Nikkan Minzoku no Genkei - Onaji Tane kara Chigatta Hana ga Saku* (Ethnic Prototype of the Japanese and Koreans: Different Flowers from the Same Seed, 1986), and *"Kashiko Gata" Nihonjin to "Kachiki Gata" Kankokujin* ("Brainy" Japanese and "Strong-minded" Koreans, 1994).

c. I Gyu-Te

I Gyu-Te, who has his own serial column in the Chosun Ilbo, is known as one of the most popular and fertile columnists in South Korea. Some of his work have been translated into Japanese, and *Kankokujin no Ishiki Kozo* (Structure of Consciousness among Koreans, 1977), *Kankokujin no Kokoro no Kozo - Kurashi to Minzoku ni Saguru* (Koreans's Mind Structure: Seeking in Livelihood and Folk Customs, 1986), and

Kankokujin no Jyoucho Kozo (Koreans' Emotional Structure, 1995) are available in Japan.

(3) Koreans in Japan

a. Yoon Hak-Jun

Yoon Hak-Jun came to Japan in 1953. Using "Yangban" as a keyword, he analyzes the modernization of his mother country. Some of his books are *Ondoru Yawa - Gendai Yanban Ko* (Ondol Night Tales: Contemporary Reflections on Yangban, 1983), *Rekishi Mamireno Kankoku - Gendai Yanban Kiko* (Korea Covered by History: Contemporary Accounts of Yangban, 1993), and *Kankoku Yangan Sodoki* (Korea Yangban Commotion Record, 2000).

b. Kim Yang-Ki

Kim Yang-Ki was born in Tokyo 1933. His interests cover a wide range of fields of study including Eastern theatre play, comparative culture, and comparative folklore. His Korea-related work can be categorized into three types. The first type has its focus on culture and people as in *Chosen no Geino* (Korean Entertainment Art, 1981), *Hanguru no Sekai* (The World of Hangul, 1984), *Kankoku Kamengeki no Sekai* (The World of Korean Mask Play, 1987), and *Kankokujin no Makkana Honto* (Koreans' Obvious Truth, 2000). Secondly, there are books that look at Japanese and Korean cultures comparatively. *Kimuchi to Oshinko* (Kimchi and Oshinko, 1978), *Nomen no youna Nihonjin* (Japanese like No Mask, 1981), and *Nihon no Bunka Kankoku no Fushu* (Japanese Culture and Korean Customs: Comparative Cultural Theory, 1999) fall into this category. Finally, the last type is related to resident Koreans in Japan. His books of this type include *Kankokujin ka Nihonjinka Ima koso Zainichi Doho Bunka no Sozo wo* (Koreans or Japanese: It's Time to Create Original Culture for Koreans in Japan, 1986) and *Ima Nihon to Kankoku wo Kangaeru -*

Dosureba Shin no "Kyosei" ga Dekirunoka? (Thinking Japan-Korea Relations Now: How Can We Achieve Real "Harmony"?, 1992).

c. Chung Dae-Kyun

Born in Iwate prefecture in 1948, Chung Dae-Kyun has conducted studies on Japan-Korea relations and ethnicity focusing on collective images that come across between ethnic/national groups. While *Kankoku no Imeiji* (The Image of Korea, 1995) examined how the image of Korea has changed in post-war Japan, in *Irubon no Imeiji* (The Image of Japan, 1998), he reversely dealt with Koreans' views on Japan. There is also a book titled *Zainichi Kankokujin no Shuen* (The End of Resident Koreans in Japan, 2001), in which he presents his views on what Koreans residing in Japan can do to survive in Japanese society.

d. O Son-Fa

O Son-Fa, who moved to Japan in 1983, is the most fertile Korean writer in Japan of all. Her first book was *Sukaato no Kaze* (The Wind of a Skirt, 1990), reportage about women from Korea who intend to stay permanently in Japan. Since the publication of this book, she has published more than 30 books including *Zoku Sukaato no Kaze* (The Wind of a Skirt, Sequel Version, 1991), *Shin Sukaato no Kaze* (The Wind of a Skirt, New Version, 1992), *Watashi ha Ikanishite ⟨Nihon Shinto⟩ to Nattaka* (How I Became a "Believer in Japan", 1999), and *Umi no Kanata no Kuni he - Nihon wo Mezasu Kankoku.Chejyudo no Onnatachi* (Toward the Country in the Other Side of Sea: Women of Korea/Cheju Island Aiming for Japan, 2002). Her subjects are not limited to Koreans and Japan-Korea comparison. Many of her books actually deal with Japan such as *Nihonjin wo Bokensuru - Aimaisa no Misuterii* (Exploring in the Japanese: The Mystery of Ambiguity, 1997), *Nihon ga Kirai na Nihonjin he* (To Japanese who don't Like Japan, 1998), and *Nihonteki Seishin no Kanosei - Kono Kuni ha Shizundamamadeha*

Owaranai (The Potentiality of Japanese Spirit: This Counrty won't End at the Bottom, 2002).

e. Kyo Nobuko

Kyo Nobuko was born in Kanagawa in 1961. She debuted as a non-fiction writer in 1961 with *Goku Futsuu no Zainichi Kankokujin* (Just an Ordinary Korean Living in Japan, 1987). She spent two years in South Korea and wrote *Watashi no Ekkyo Ressun: Kankoku Hen* (My Lesson for Border-Crossing: Korea Version, 1993) and *Nikkan Ongaku Noto - 〈Ekkyo〉 Suru Tabibito no Uta wo Otte* (Notebook for Japan-Korea Music: Tracing "Border-crossing" Travelers' Songs, 1998). In these books, "border-crossing" is used as a keyword to capture music and pop culture in Japan and Korea. In search for the footsteps of those who left the Korean penisula, she later traveled through former Manchuria, Russian Far East, and Central Asia to record the "memories of lives in foreign lands."

f. Kang Hi-Bong

Born in Tokyo in 1954, Kang Hi-Bong used a Japanese name of Ko Tateo to publish *Shirarezaru Nikkan Sakkaa Gekitoshi* (Japan-Korea Soccer: Revealing an Unknown History of Fierce Fighting, 1998). Later, by his Korean name, he has published *Kankoku Furusato Kaido wo Yuku* (Going on a Korean Country Road, 2000), *Konnani Sugoinoka! Kankoku no Choheisei* (What an Astonishment! Conscription System in Korea, 2000), and *Souru Chudoku - Kankoku ni Hamatta Nihonjintachi* (Seoul Poisoning: Japanese who are Crazy about Korea, 2002). In addition, based on his energetic search works, he has written articles for many journals in relation to the topics of Korean history, culture and sports.

II. Titles (Contents)

(1) Dualistic titles

Most of the book titles concerning Japan-Korea cultural comparison use the binary terms to symbolize the cultures of Japan and Korea in a dualistic manner. For instance, Kim Yang-Ki's *Kimuchi to Oshinko* (Korean Pickles and Japanese Pickles, 1978) and *Ondoru to Tatami* (Korean Floor Heating and Japanese Floor Mat, 1990), Chi Myong-Kwan's *Chogori to Yoroi* (Korean Dress and Japanese Armor, 1988), Han Jun Sok's *Bun no Bunka to Bu no Bunka* (Culture of Literary and Culture of Military, 1989), Kim Yong-Woon's *"Kashiko-gata" Nihonjin to "Kachiki-gata" Kankokujin* ("Brainy" Japanese and "Strong-minded" Koreans, 1994), O Son-Fa's *Wasabi to Togarashi* (Japanese Horse Radish and Korean Chili Pepper, 1995) and *Joui no Kankoku Kaikoku no Nihon* (Korea as a Closed Society and Japan as an Open Society, 1996), Watanabe Shoichi and O Son-Fa's *Nihon no Kyoman Kankoku no Goman* (Japan's Overconfidence and Korea's Arrogance, 1993) and *Kankoku no Gekijo Nihon no Mujo* (Korea's Hot-headedness, Japan's Cold-heartedness, 1996), Wang Su-Young's *Kado ga Tatsu Kankokujin Maruku Osameru Nihonjin* (Offensive Koreans and Inoffensive Japanese, 2000), Sin Yoon Sik's *Gorioshi no Kankokujin Kireigoto no Nihonjin - Zainichi Kankyo no Me de Mita Bunkaron* (Pushy Koreans and White-washy Japanese: Note on Culture through the Eyes of a Korean in Japan, 1999), and Kato Hideaki's *"Han" no Kankokujin "Kashikomaru" Nihonjin* ("Frustrated" Koreans and "Scared" Japanese, 1988).

(2) Models based on cultural "shiko"(orientation)

After Lee O-Young's *"Chijimi" Shiko no Nihonjin* (The Compact Culture: The Japanese Tradition of "Smaller is Better"), published in 1982, drew people's attention, several books of the similar title followed. Park

Joon-Hee published *"Kakudai Shiko" no Nihonjin* (A Passion to be the Greater: An Analytical Observation on Japanese Personality) in 1986, and Joo Kwan-Joong wrote *"Kiri Shiko" no Nihonjin - Kankokujin ga Mita Chosho to Tansho* ("The Japanese Preference of Cutting: It Strength and Weakness from the Perspective of a Korean, 1988).

Park Joon Hee, university professor in education, developed his model of Japanese personality and culture based on the three major classics on the Japanese: "shame culture" from *The Chrysanthemum and the Sword: Patterns of Japanese Culture* by Ruth Benedict, Doi Takeo's *"Amae" no Kozo* (The Anatomy of Dependence), and Lee O-Young's *"Chijimi" Shiko no Nihonjin* (The Compact Culture: The Japanese Tradition of "smaller is Better"). According to his conclusion, "Amae (dependence)" is the "twisted version of the passion to be the greater" that is seen only under the limited setting of the Japanese social life, and the "compact culture" is nothing but the "suppressed form of the passion to be the greater" that is demonstrated through the limited context of the Japanese spiritual life. Moreover, "shame" is defined as a crucial weapon to reinforce this mechanism, particularly in regards to strengthening group solidarity as significant part of the Japanese social life.

Joo Kwan-Joong, professor in politics and philosophy, made an interpretation of Japanese personality and culture using the term "cut" as a keyword. Showing various Japanese life scenes where the word "cut" is used, he points out that the Japanese tradition of using the sword, embedded in the mentality of Japanese, has created the Japanese "cutting" culture.

(3) Korea-phobia and Anti-Japan

Every time whatever political problems arise between Japan and Korea, be it politicians' comments, issues of history textbooks or comfort women, attention concentrates on a hateful relationship between Koreans and Japanese.

There are many publication titles which include the words "Kenkan (Korea-phobia)" and "Hannichi (Anti-Japan)", including *Nihonjin to Kankokujin - Hannichi Kenkan 50nen no Hate* (Japanese and Koreans: After 50 years of Anti-Japan and Korea-Phobia, 1995) edited by Journal SAPIO, Takasaki Soji's *"Hannichi Kanjo" Kankoku.Chosenjin to Nihonjin* ("Anti-Japan Sentiment": Koreans and Japanese, 1993), Kuroda Katsuhiro's *Kankoku.Hannichi Shokogun* (Korea, Anti-Japan Syndromc, 1995), *Kenkan Hannichi no Kozo* (The Structure of Korea-phobia and Anti-Japan, 1997) by Mochizuki Mikio and Im Yeong-Chun, O Son-Fa's *"Hannichi" wo Suteru Kankoku* (South Korea Discarding "Anti-Japan", 2000) and *"Hannichi Kankoku" ni Mirai ha Nai* (No Future for Korea of "Anti-Japan", 2001).

In addition, there are a good number of books whose titles used the words "kirai (dislike)"and "suki (like)." For example, Shigemura Toshimitsu's *Kankokujin ha Honto ni Nihonjin ga Kiraika* (Do Koreans Really Hate Japanese?, 1987), Sakuwa Toru's *Nihonjin (Kankokujin) ha Sukidaga Nihon (Kankoku) ha Kirai - Nikkan no Gakusei Ishiki Chosa* (I like Japanese (Koreans) but don't like Japan (Korea): Attitude Survey of Japanese and Korean Students, 1998), Sugano Tomoko's *Suki ni Natteha Ikenai Kuni - Kankoku J-POP Sedai ga Mita Nihon* (Never Been Allowed to Like the Country: Japan from the Perspective of the Korean J-POP Generation, 2000), and Yamada Yukari's *Irubon ha Sukidesuka?: Kankoku Shinsedai kara no Messeiji* (Do You Like Japan?: A Message from the Korean New Generation, 2002).

(4) "Ugly" Koreans and Japanese

Minikui Kankokujin - Wareware ha "Nittei Shihai" wo Sakebisugiru (Ugly Koreans: We Argue Over "Japanese Imperial Rule" Too Much, 1993) received attention as a best-seller written by a Korean journalist named Pak Tae Heok. However, the Korean press reported that this "book of self-reflection" was a trumped-up work compiled by a Japanese critic called Kato Hideaki, who used data provided by his Korean cooperator. People argued over whether a person named Pak Tae-Heok really exists and who the real author of this book is. In response to this, Pak Tae-Heok and Kato Hideaki published *Minikui Kankokujin - Rekishi Kenshohen* (Ugly Koreans - Chapter of Historical Verification, 1995), proving that Pak Tae-Heok do exist.

In this commotion, Kim Yong Woon published a book titled *Minikui Nihonjin - "Kenkan" tai "Hannichi" wo Koete* (Ugly Japanese - Going beyond "Korea-phobia" vs. "Anti-Japan", 1994) while Im Yeong-Chun raised objections to the content of *Minikui Kankokujin* (Ugly Koreans) in *Minikui Kankokujin ga Minikui Nihonjin ni Kotaeru* (From Ugly Korean to Ugly Japanese, 1995).

(5) A controversy over "There is no Japan"

In 1993, a Koreas popular female newscaster from KBS, Chun Yu -Ok's book titled *'Nihon ha Nai'* (There is No Japan) sold more than one million copies creating a sensation in Korea. In the following year of 1994, this book was also published in Japan under the new title of *Kanashii Nihonjin* (Miserable Japanese). Chun Yu -Ok further published *'Nihon ha Nai 2'* (There is No Japan 2, 1995), and it was also translated into Japanese as *Zoku. Kanashii Nihonjin* (Sad Japanese, Sequel Version, 1995) and *Shin. Kanashii Nihonjin* (Sad Japanese, New Version, 1996).

On the other hand, Seo Hyun-Seop, diplomat, published a book titled *'Nihon ha Aru'* (There is Japan), and this book has been introduced into Japan as *Nihon no Soko Jikara* (Japans Strength in Reserve, 1995). Seo Hyun-Seop's *Nihonjin to Erosu・Kankoku Gaikokan no Nihonjinron* (Japanese and Eros: a Korean Diplomats View on Japanese, 1998), a best-seller with the sales record of over 150,000 copies, has been also translated into Japanese.

In Yu Je-Sun's *Gehinna Nihonjin* (Vulgar Japanese, 1994), Chun Yu-Ok's *Nihon ha Nai* (There is No Japan) has been criticized for stealing more than half of the information Yu Je-Sun collected.

Furthermore, a talk between Kato Hideaki, who is regarded as the real author of *Minikui Kankokujin* (Ugly Koreans) and Chun Yu -Ok appeared in *Minikui Nihonjin vs. Kanashii Nihonjin* (Ugly Japanese vs. Sad Japanese, 1995), edited by Kato Hideaki, Chun Yu-Ok, Obayashi Takashi, and Choi Seo Myeon.

(6) South Korean Syndrome

The South Korean syndrome is a term that used to be frequently used. For example, this word was used to describe the situation where a bridge or a building that looks well-constructed falls down due to the superficial incomplete work. It refers to Koreans negative customs and practices, and the term was used to seek the solution for such problems. Books dealing with the Korean syndrome include Yanagi Tomonao's *Kankokubyo Shindan - Senshinkoku he no Takai Hadoru* (Diagnosis of the Korean Syndrome: High Hurdle for an Advanced Country, 1993) and Momose Tadashi's best-seller, *Kankoku ga Shindemo Nihon ni Oitsukenai 18 no Riyu* (18 Reasons why Korea will never Catch up with Japan, 2001). Also, Ito Jyunko's *Byo to shiteno Kankoku Nashonarizumu* (South Korean Nationalism as a Disease, 2001) examines the Korean syndrome in relation to Korea's nationalism. The author, who has stayed more than 10 years in Seoul, reveals the ambivalent nature of the nationalism through many real episodes. There is also a phrase of "All about the 'South Korean syndrome' related by a Korean" on the book cover of *Ido no naka no Kankokujin* (The Koreans in the Well, 1999), which was written by a well-known journalist in Korea.

(7) Self-deprecating or self-reflexive views on Korea by Korean authors

In 1997, A severe economic crisis hit Korea, forcing the country to appeal for IMF assistance. The prevailing content of the books published at this time was a self-deprecating or self-reflexive view on Korea by a Korean author. For example, Kim Ji-Ryong's *Watashi ha Kankokujin. Demo Nihon Bunka ga Sukida!* (I am Korean, but I like Japanese Culture!, 1998), Cho Seong-Kwan's *Naze Kankoku ha Dame nanoka* (Why is Korea Useless?, 1998), I Jong-Hak's *Kankokujin no Watashi ga Kankoku wo Kirai ni Natta 48 no Riyu* (The 48 Reasons Why I Came to Hate Korea, 1998), and I Don-Fun's *Kankoku ha Nihon wo Minarae* (Korea Must learn from Japan, 2000). The authors of these books are typically from the younger generation.

(8) Mirrors

Some books have expressed the relationship between Japan and Korea using the word "mirror." For example, *Kankoku to iu Kagami - Sengo Sedi no Mita Rinkoku* (A Mirror Called Korea: The Neighbor through the Eyes of the Post-war Generation, 1986) edited by Kawamura Minato and Chung Dae-Kyun, Matsuno Yutaka's *Sugao no Kankokujin - Nihonjin wo Utsushidasu Kagami* (The Real Face of the Koreans: A Mirror that Projects the Japanese, 1998), O Son-Fa's *Shin Skaato no Kaze - Nikkan Aawase Kagami no Sekai* (The Wind of a Skirt, New Version; the Japan-Korea World, Mirrors Set against Each Other, 1992), and *Kagami no nakano Nihon to Kankoku* (Japan and Korea in the Mirror, 2000).

Also, the word parallelism found in the title of Chung Dae Kyung's *Nikkan no Pararerisumu - Atarashii Nagameai ha Kano ka* (The Parallelism between Japan and Korea: the Possibility of Creating New Views on Each Other, 1992) is considered to have a meaning similar to the word mirror.

(9) "Associating" rather than "learning"

Overall, encyclopedias often use the word "learn" in their titles such as *Chosen wo Shiru Jiten* (Encyclopedia of leaning about Korea, 1986) by Ito Abito, Omura Masuo, Kajimura Hideki, Takeda Yukio, *Kankoku · Chosen wo Shirutame no 55 Sho* (The 55 Chapters to Learn about Korea) by Inoue Hideo and Chung Cho-Mi, Asakura Toshio's *Kankoku wo Shiru Q & A 115* (115 Qs & As to Learn about Korea, 2000), Ishizaka Koichi and Tateno Akira's *Gendai Kankoku wo Shirutame no 55 Sho* (The 55 Chapters to Learn about Contemporary Korea, 2000), Cho Hi-Chol's *Gendai Kankoku wo Shiru Kiiwaado 77* (The 77 Key-words to Learn about Contemporary Korea, 2002), and Kim Yong Gwon's *Hayawakari Kankoku wo Shiru Jiten* (Quick Reference for Learning about Korea, 2002).

However, the word "associate" is more frequently used than "learn" for the titles of many general books, and Kusano Jun's *Chotto Shiritai Kankoku* (Wanting to Learn a Little Bit about Korea, 1985) seems to be the only book that uses the word "learn." Those books that use "associate" in their titles include Kim Yang-Ki's *Wakai Kankokujin to Tsukiau Ho* (How to Associate with Young Koreans, 1987), Watanabe Mamoru's *Nihonjin Girai no Kankokujin to Tsukiau Hoho* (How to Associate with Koreans who don't like Japanese, 1996), Pyeong Jin -Il & Voice 9000's *Kankokujin to Jyouzu ni Tsukiau Ho* (How to Associate with Koreans Well, 1997), Osaki Masaru's *Kankokujin to Tsukiau Ho* (The Way of Associating with Koreans, 1998). Moreover, Nakamura Kinya's *Kankokujin ga Migatte ni Mieru Riyu* (The Reasons Why Koreans Look Selfish, 1996) seems to have its title as a result of associating with Koreans.

(10) Change

After the 1980's, Korean society have dramatically changed politically, economically, and culturally. Moreover, the speed of the change was surprisingly fast. It is often said that 1 year for Seoul is equivalent to 3 years or 5 years for Japan.

In the domain of scholarly books, Shima Mutsuhiko and Asakura Toshio edited *Henbosuru Kankoku Shakai - 1970～80 Nendai no Jinruigaku Chosa no Genba kara* (Changing Korean Society: From the Field of Anthropological Research in the 1970's ～ 80's, 2000) from the perspective of anthropology while Kobayashi Takayuki published *Henbosuru Gendai Kankoku Shakai* (Changing Contemporary Korean Society, 2000) from a sociological point of view.

Whereas, in terms of popular books, less attention has been paid to this society change, and there are only two books found: Kim Kyeung-Hun's *Kankoku ga Kawaru - Shin Sedai no Seikatsu to Iken* (Korea is Going to Change: The Lives and Views of the New Generation, 1995) and Momose Tadashi's *Kankoku ha Kawatta, Nihon ha Dosuru* (Korea has Changed. What would Japan do?, 2000).

(11) From Seoul to Cheju-do and Chin-do

The place name used most frequently in the title of the book is Seoul without any doubt. For example, Yoshioka Tadao's *Souru Rapusodi* (Seoul Rhapsody, 1985), Kuroda Katsuhiro's *Souru Hatsu Korega Kankoku da* (From Seoul: This is Korea, 1985) and *Souru no Yushu* (Seouls Melancholy, 1988), Yomota Inuhiko's *Annyon.Souru: Kankou Nichijo Zakka Jiten* (Hello Seoul: Dictionary of Koreas Daily Goods 1986), Furuta Hiroshi's *Souru no Jyushatachi* (Confucian in Seoul, 1988), Kuroda Fukumi's *Souru no Tatsujin* (Master in Seoul, 1994), and Okada Osamu's *Souru no Kaze* (The Wind of Seoul, 1994).

However, in recent years, there has been an increased use of Cheju-do or Chin-do in the title, replacing Seoul. These examples are Togawa Akio's *Harukanari Saishuto* (Distant Cheju-do, 1999), Kang Hi-Bongs

Saishuto (Cheju-do, 2003), Ito Abito's *Kankoku Chin-do no Minzoku Kiko* (Account of Folklore from Chin-do, Korea, 1999), *Ono Masami's Kankoku no Katsumi-kun to Chindo no Keiko-san* (Katsumi in Korea and Keiko in Chin-do, 2001).

(12) Individual themes

a. Linguistic culture

There are books that are not merely language textbooks but are designed to look at culture through language. These books are Watanabe Kyuron and Suzuki Takao's *Chosengo no Susume* (Invitation to the Korean Language, 1981), Watanabe Kyuron's *Hajimete no Chosengo- Rinkoku wo Shirutameni* (For Beginners in Korean: for the Purpose of Learning about the Neighboring Country, 1983), *Kankoku Gengo Fukei - Yuragu Bunka · Kawaru Shakai* (South Korean Linguistic Landscape: Swinging Culture and Changing Society, 1996), Kim Yang-Ki's *Hanguru no Sekai* (The World of Hangul, 1984), Ogura Kizo's *Kankokugo Hajime no Ippo* (The First Step of Learning Korean, 2000), and *Ono Toshiakis Nihongo to Kankokugo* (Japanese and Korean, 2002).

b. Food culture

Seoul hosted Asian Games in 1986 and the Olympics in 1988. Around this time, Korean food started gaining popularity in Japan, accelerated by the domestic fad for ethnic and spicy foods. Many books on Korean food culture were published during this period. For example, Onoda Misako's *Kankoku no Shokutaku Arakaruto* (A La Cart Menus from the Korean Dining Table, 1985), Morieda Takashi and Asakura Toshio's *Shoku ha Kankoku ni Ari* (Food Starts from Korea, 1986), Maki Hiroshi's *Kankoku Meisai Monogatari* (Stories of Korean Vegetables, 1987), Hayashi Hiroaki's *Yakiniku Bunka to Sashimi Bunka* (Barbeque Culture and Raw Fish Culture, 1987), Ienaga Yasumitsu and Ro U-Hyon's *Kimuchi Bunka to Fudo* (Kimchi Culture and Climate, 1987), Ryu Sang-H'is *Tabete Shiru Kankoku* (Learning about South Korea through Food, 1988), and *Kankoku no Shoku* (Food in South Korea, 1988) by Hwa He-Seon and Ishige Naomichi.

Books on Korean food have been continuously published. Immediately before and after Japan co-hosted the FIFA World Cup tournament with Korea in 2002, the following books were published: Chong Dae-Sung's *Yakiniku ha Sukidesuka?* (Do You Like Korean Barbecue?, 2001), *Yoku Wakaru Yakiniku · Kankoku Ryori no Rekishi* (The Easy History of Korean Dishes and Barbecue, 2003), Kurota Masahiro's *Kankoku wo Taberu · Shoku kara Mita Kankokujin* (Eating Korea: Koreans Seen from the Food, 2001), Sasaki Michio's *Kankoku no Shoku Bunka* (The Food Culture of Korea, 2002). Furthermore, some of the Korean-language academic books on Korean food culture have been translated into Japanese. They are Yun Seo-Seok's *Kankoku no Shoku Bunkashi* (The Food History of Korea, 1995), Lee Seong-Woo's *Kankoku Ryori Bunkashi* (The History of Korean Culinary Culture, 1999), and Kang In-Hee's *Kankoku Shoku Seikatsushi* (The History of Korean Food Life, 2000).

c. Entertainment

Over the last few years, with the growing interest in Korean pop culture among Japanese, the following books have been published. They are Ichinohashi Kaiko's *Noreban he Iko - Korian Poppusu no Genzai* (Lets Go Singing: The Current Status of Korean Pops, 1996), *Kankoku Karuchaa Nabigeetaa* (Korean Cultural Navigator, 1998), Tashiro Chikayo's *Kankoku Entaateimento Zanmai* (All You can Enjoy about Korean Entertainment, 2000), *Kankoku Entaateimento Zanmai 2* (All You can Enjoy about Korean Entertainment 2, 2001) and *Kankoku ha Doramachikku- Entaateimento de Miru Kankoku Sutairu* (Dramatic Korea: a Korean Style through Entertainment, 2003).

d. Others

There are also books on Korean railroads such as Takagi Kunio's *Kankoku Zenshi Zensen* (The Complete Guide to South Korean Railroads, 1993) and Nakajima Hiroshi and Yamada Toshihide's *Kankoku no Tetsudo* (Railroads in Korea, 1997).

The other type of recent books is military-related. Some of the examples are Kang Hi Bong's *Konnani Sugoinoka! Kankoku no Choheisei* (What an Astonishment! Conscription System in Korea, 2000), Lee Sung-Chan's *Omaera Guntai Shitteruka!?* (Do You Guys Know an Army!?, 2002) and Zoku Omaera Guntai Shitteruka!? (Do You Guys Know an Army!?, Sequel Version 2003), and Kwon Chun-O's *Ashita kata ha Heishi* (Will be a Soldier Tomorrow, 2003).

(13) International Marriage

Hirai Hisashi's *Souru Taryong* (The Seoul Chanting, 1993) and *Nikkan Kosodate Senso* (The Japan-Korea Child-Rearing Battle, 1995) are essays written by a Japanese correspondent, who has been married to a Korean woman. The author stayed in Seoul for one year as a student from the end of 1983 and as a correspondent of the Kyodo News Service from 1989 to 1992. Toda Ikuko, married to a Korean photographer, wrote *Souru Saranhe -Nikkan Kekkon Monogatari* (I love Seoul: A Story of Japan-Korea Marriage, 1994). In addition, Yamasaki Shin has written *Chima · Chogori no Kuni kara* (From the Country of Korean Ethnic Dress, 1999) based on his experience of getting married to a Korean woman. Shinohara Tsukasa's *Tsuma wo Metoraba Kankokujin* (Nothing Better than a Korean Wife, 1999) and Hidaka Hiroshi's *Bibinba Kazoku - Soredemo Tsuma ha Kankokujin* (The Mixed Family: Even though My Wife Remains Korean, 2000) also revolve around the experiences and stories of Japanese-Korean couples and families.

(14) Korea experienced by ethnic Koreans in Japan

Sagisawa Megumu's *Kimi ha Kono Kuni wo Sukika* (Do You Like this Country?, 1997) is a story of a third-generation Korean resident of Japan, Masami, who decided to leave for Korea to study. With a fresh sensitivity, Sagisawa portrays Masami's youthful days that take place in two cities, Tokyo and Seoul, separating herself from the image of ethnic Koreans seen in the writings of the older generation such as Lee Yang Ji, who stayed in Korea in the 1980's.

Such ethnic Koreans of the new generation have published their views on Korea based on their own experiences. For example, Jin Won-Song's self-searching essay *Souru no Hodo nite - Hi Nihon Taiken to shite no Kankoku Seikatsu* (On a Pavement in Seoul: Korean Life as a Non-Japanese Experience, 1994) raises a question of ethnic identity based on the second-generation author's experiences living in Korea for 4 years. A 2.5 generation ethnic Korean, Lee Jun-Mi has written *Watashi ga Kankoku he Itta Riyu* (The Reason Why I went to Korea, 1998).

III. Year of publication

The year of publication listed with each book mentioned in the sections for the title and the author has supposedly provided some idea about the publication trend by year. Thus, this section chronologically reviews the circumstances and backgrounds of the Korea-related publication industry by every five years from around 1980.

(1) Around 1980

Kankoku kara no Tsuushin (Message from Korea) is a serial column that had been published in the journal Sekai (The World) since the volume of May 1973. The columns of the journal were also published as a series of *Iwanami Shinsho* (the Iwanami Paperback Series). The book became a best-seller, but the popularity gradually wore off after the peak of 1974 and 1975. Although the journal column continued up till the volume of March 1988, the publication of the Iwanami paperbacks was stopped by the 4th book of the series in 1980. With an increased number of international students and travellers, the image of South Korea provided by *Kankoku kara no Tsuushin* (Message from Korea) has increasingly become subject to contestation around 1980.

The channel for the introduction of Koreas scholarship and culture was initially through the *Kan* (The Han) journal published by the institute of Korean Studies. The *Kan* (The Han) journal started in 1972 and ended with its 100th volume in 1980. In 1979, the Korean Cultural Service, Embassy of the Republic Korea started publishing a new journal *Gekkan Kankoku Bunka* (Monthly Korean Culture), and it was distributed more widely than before.

(2) Around 1985

Around this time, with Cho Yong-Pil's *Pusan-ko Ni Kaere* (Come Back to the Port of Pusan) becoming a huge hit, Prime Minister Nakasone Yasuhiro visited President Chon Du-Hwan in Seoul, and President Chon Du-Hwan visited Emperor Hirohito in Tokyo. People often used the phrase Japan-Korea New Age to describe such situation.

In 1984, Nippon Hoso Kyokai (Japan Broadcasting Corporation)'s Hangul language course has started, and Gekkan Kiso Hanguru (Monthly Hangul Basics) started in 1985. Many Korean language books were also published in paperback form. Kuroda Masahiro's *Hanguru ha Muzukashikunai* (Hangul is not difficult, 1985) and *Hanguru ha Omoshiroi* (Hangul is interesting, 1986), for example.

Moreover, a lot of popular magazines featured Korea one after another such as *Chosen.Kankoku wo Shiru Hon* (Book of Learning about Korea, 1984) edited by Bessatsu Takarajima and *Kankoku Shin Hakken* (New

Discovery of Korea, 1985) by Bessatsu Taiyo. A popular magazine *Heibon Panchi* also featured two special articles about Korea in January 1985, titled *Kakkoii Kankoku* (Stylish Korea) and *Issatsu Marugoto Kininaru Kuni no Daitokushu* (Special Issue on the Attractive Country).

(3) Around 1990

In 1988, the Olympic was held in Seoul. The Seoul Olympics brought a number of publications about Korea to Japan, and this trend continued after the Olympics. A magazine *Bessatsu Takarajima* featured *Atarashii Kankoku wo Shiru Hon* (Book of Learning about New Korea, 1987) and *Atarashii Souru wo Aruku Hon* (Book of Walking into Renewed Seoul, 1988).

Around the same time, the International Cultural Society of Korea, which had issued a monthly magazine *Ajia Koron* (Asia Public Opinion) since 1972, started publishing an English-language quarterly culture magazine *KOREANA* from fall 1987 and its Japanese-language sister magazine *Koriana* from spring 1988. This happened based on their observation that "with Korea's rising status in the international arena, the interest in Korean culture has been rising as well." Additionally, the publisher of this magazine was changed to the Korean Foundation from the volume 17 (the issue of Spring 1992).

(4) Around 1995

Since 1994, Nishina Kenichi and Tateno Akira's *Shin Kankoku Dokuhon* (New South Korea: A Reader) series have been published by a Japanese publisher, Shakai Hyoron Sha. The publisher had printed 2 books under the *Kankoku VIEWS* (Korea VIEWS) series, which is a Japanese-language edition of a Korean monthly journal *Sahoe P'yongnon* (Social Review). *Sahoe P'yongnon* (Social Review)'s merger with another Korean monthly magazine called *Kil* (Street) created the opportunity to compile *Shin Kankoku Dokuhon* (New Korea: A Reader), an introductory reader series consisting of translated materials from a variety of Korean publications. Around this time, books on Japan by Korean writers started to come out. These books include Kim Young-Myung's *Wakaki Kankokujin Gakusha ga Mita "Taikoku Nihon"* ("Big Country Japan" through the Eyes of a Young Korean Scholar, 1994), Han Su-San's *Tonari no Nihonjin* (A Japanese Neighbor, 1995), and Kim Hyun-Ku's *Kim Kyojyu no Nihon Dangi - Kankokujin no Mit Nihon no Kyozo to Jitsuzo* (Professor Kim's Lecture on Japan: Japan's Illusion and Reality Seen from a Korean, 1997).

(5) Around 2000

As the 21st century begins, South Korean popular novels and movie scripts have been translated and become available in Japan over a little time interval.

In the meantime, since 1999, the Japan-Korea Cultural Foundation has produced a translation series of first-rate Korean scholarly books on the history, society, and culture of Korea, and the series has been published by Hosei University Press.

In 2002, a new type of textbooks on Korea has been published one after another, including *Kawamura Minatos Chi no Koryaku Shiso Dokuhon Kankoku* (Capture of Wisdom, Intellectual Reader, South Korea), Furuta Hiroshi and Ogura Kizo's *Kankokugaku no Subete* (All about South Korea), Kim Yong-Gwon's *Hayawakari Kankoku wo Shiru Jiten* (Quick Reference for Learning about Korea) and *Kino Hyoron 33 Tokushu Anata no Shiriai Kankoku no Subete* (Kino Review 33, Special Issue: All about Korea that You Want to Know).

The trend of the mid 1990s, an increase of books on Japan by Korean authors, has continued into the 2000s. For example, Kim Sung-Kyu's *Mo Hitotsu no Nihon* (Another Japan, 1998), Cha Dong-Jin's

Nihon.Kankoku.Chugoku Ima Nanji? · Wakaki Kankokujin Bijinesuman no Omoi (Japan, Korea, and China What Time is It Now?: Thoughts of a Korean Young Businessman, 2000), Woo Su-Keum's *Tatakareru Kakugo de Kaita Kankokujin Woo-kun kara Nihon heno Chokugen* (Expecting to be Bashed: A Korean, Woos Candid Opinion for Japan, 2000) and *Kankokujin Woo-kun no Nikkan no Kabe tte Nandaro* (A Korean, Woo's Question, What's "the Wall between Japan and Korea"?, 2003).

Some of the books have been published by young female writers. An Ree, one of the Koreans who studied overseas at private expense after Korea's liberalization of overseas trips in 1989, wrote *Tokyo Korian Jyunjo Nikki* (Diary of a Naive Korean Girl in Tokyo, 1999). Kim Sang-Mi published *Kankoku N Sedai Hakusho* (South Korean N-Generation Report, 2002).

Furthermore, Kim Wan-Sop's *Shinnichiha no Tameno Benmei* (Excuse for the Pro-Japan, 2002) and Lee U-Jong's *Manga Kim Jong-Il* (Comic Kim Jong-Il, 2003) are translated versions of the original books that are abandoned in Korea.

IV. Anthropology and folklore

Since this volume includes a rather comprehensive bibliography that focuses on academic books on anthropology and folklore, this section limits itself to reviewing general books and providing an overview of the publication concerning the fields of anthropology and folklore.

(1) Before 1980

Korean-language books on the Koreans were translated into Japanese. For example, Yoon Taek-Lim's *Kankokujin- Sono Ishiki Kozo* (The Koreans: The Structure of Their Consciousness, 1975), Choi Jae Seok's *Kankokujin no Shakaiteki Seikaku* (The Social Character of the Koreans, 1977), Kim Yeol-Gyu's *Kankokujin no Shinri* (The Mentality of the Koreans, 1978).

For the domain of anthropology, attention concentrates on the topics of shamanism, family and kinship. For shamanism, the following books were published: Ryu Tong-Shik's *Chosen no Shamanisumu* (The Shamanism of Korea, 1976), Seo Jeong-Beom's *Kankoku no Shamanisumu* (The Shamanism of South Korea, 1980), Choe Kil-Sung's *Chosen no Matsuri to Zazoku* (Korean Festivals and Shamanistic Customs, 1980). In regards to family and kinship, Nakae Chie's *Kankoku Noson no Kazoku to Saigi* (Family and Ancestor Rituals in a Korean Rural Village, 1973), Lee Kwang-Kyu's *Kankoku Kazoku no Kozo Bunseki* (A Structural Analysis of Korean Family, 1978), Choi Jae-Seok's *Kankoku Noson Shakai Kenkyu* (A Study of Korean Rural Society, 1979), Kim Taik-Kyu's *Kankoku Dozoku Sonraku no Kenkyu -Yanban no Bunka to Seikatsu* (A Study of the Clan Villages: The Culture and Life of Yangbang, 1981).

Folklore texts were printed in such books as Im Tong-Gwon's *Chosen no Minzoku* (The Folklore of Korea, 1969), *Kankoku Minzokugaku Gaisetsu* (An Introduction to Korean Folklore, 1969) edited by Lee Du-Hyun, Chang Chu-Gun, and Lee Kwang-Kyu, and Chang Chu-Gun's *Kankoku no Kyodo Shinko* (Korean Native Beliefs, 1982).

(2) After 1980

Into the 1980's, less books were translated into Japanese as most of the Japanese researchers in Korean studies have acquired the Korean language skill by this time.

On the other hand, textbooks on Korea were published. Some of the examples are Ito Abito's *Motto Shiritai Kankoku* (Captivating Korea, 1985), *Motto Shiritai Kankoku Dai 2 Han* (Captivating Korea 2, 1997) and *Ajia Dokuhon Kankoku* (Asia Reader: Korea, 1996), Choe Kil-Sung's *Kankoku Minzoku he no Shotai* (Invitation to Korean Folklore), and

Honda Hiroshi's *Kaigai Hito Zukuri Handbook Kankoku* (Handbook for Overseas Networking: Korea).

Additionally, there are Kim Yang-Ki's *Yonde Tabisuru Sekai no Rekishi to Bunka Kankoku* (Reading for Traveling, World History and Culture: Korea, 1993) and Tsuruzono Yutaka's *Shin Ajia Seikatsu Bunka Dokuhon Kankoku - Kasasagi to Tora no Kuni de* (New Asian Life Culture Reader, Korea: In a Country of Tiger and Magpie, 1999).

In 1999, the Association for the Study of Korean Culture and Society was formed, and the association's publication *Kankoku Chosen no Bunka to Shakai* (Korean Culture and Society) Vol.1 was published in 2000.

(3) General books

Although still relatively small in number, some anthropologists and folklorists have published books for the general public. For example, Takeda Akira's *Ki no Kari - Kankoku no Hito to Ie* (Chevron: Korean People and Houses, 1983), Shima Mutsuhiko's *Kankoku Noson Jijo -"Jyu" no Kuni ni Ikiru Hitobito no Seikatsushi* (Korean Rural Living: Ethnography of Those Who Live in the Country of "Confucianism", 1985), Asakura Toshio's *Nihon no Yakiniku Kankoku no Sashimi* (Korean Barbecue in Japan, Japanese Sashimi in Korea, 1994), Tsunami Takashi's *Hanguru to Togarashi - Okinawahatsu. Higashi Ajia Ittari Kitari no Bunkaron* (Hangul and Chili Pepper: Cultural Commentary on the Go, from Okinawa to East Asia, 1999).

Concluding Observations

This paper has provided a general overview of books on Korean culture and society in Japan, particularly focusing on the ones published after 1980. Even though it is difficult to say the result of this analysis directly reflects the contemporary attention toward Korean culture in Japanese society, it seems useful to some extent for understanding the general trend and change.

That is to say, a quantitative increase in and a wide variety of interests. Until the 1980s, despite the geographical proximity, Japan and Korea both lacked an understanding of each others' culture and society. However, the more freely people have started to travel between the countries, the easier it has become to learn about each other. In the meantime, increased attention has brought increased demand for information, resulting in mass production of publications for general readers. In addition, TV and the internet have enabled people to have access to the latest information on various topics without any effort.

However, the other side of the coin is the possibility of getting overwhelmed or distracted by information overflow. Under these circumstances, it seems critically important to reconsider what a mutually favorable relationship would be with the neighboring country.

Recent years have seen a publication of paperbacks dealing with a range of topics from food, clothing, shelter, language to manners, which are considered to be basic to a interactive relationship between the citizens of Japan and Korea. Some of these books are *"Kankokujin" Soko ga Shiritai Dokkiri Zatsugaku* (Surprising Trivia You Ever Wanted to Know about "Koreans", 2000) by Hyper Press, *Nihonjin to Kankokujin Naruhodo Jiten* (Nod-getting Cyclopedia of "Japanese" and "Koreans", 2002) by Korean Works, Oshima Yuji's *Dareka ni Tsui Shaberitakunaru Nikkan Naruhodo Zatsugaku no Hon* (Book of Japan-Korea-Related Trivia that You Can't Keep Just to Yourself, 2002), *Tenku Kikaku's Korian Sutairu* (Korean Style, 2002) edited by Sagisawa Megumu etc. Yet, this kind of "trivia" belongs to a field in which anthropologists should be working on. In this sense, it is fair to say that the contribution of anthropological research has not reached over to the general public.

Modern-day academics can no longer do their research without considering the question of societal contribution and benefits. Needless to say, anthropologists who have researched on Korean society and culture are expected to make more effort to communicate their research outcome to the general public. By so doing, anthropologists need to contest their own roles in society, asking themselves, "What is the role of an anthropologist?"

Regarding author names, both Korean and Japanese names are listed in the Asian customary order with last name first, without separating last and first names either by a comma or upper-case letters.

In this paper, for the sake of convenience, the name "Korea" is used to refer to the Republic of Korea, or South Korea.

APPENDIX I

Bibliography: Japanese Studies on Korea

(English translation)

Compiled by Seiichi Matsumoto

Toyo University of Japan

Akada, Mitsuo. 1975. "Korean Graveyards and Ancestor Worship Rites", in Koichi, Mori, ed., *Graveyards: A study of Japanese Ancient Culture*. (197-217), Kyoto: Sekai-shiso-sha.

Akamatsu, Chijo and Akiba, Takashi. 1937. *A Study of Korean Shamanism*. Osaka: Osaka-ya-go-shoten.

Akiba, Takashi. 1932. "The Belief of Snake Spirits in Jeju Island: An Attempt of Chagui Culture", *Seikyu-gakuso* 7: 100-110.

Akiba, Takashi. 1949. "Shamanism and Fire: Sacred fire rites in Choson Shamanism", *Minzokugaku-kenkyu* 14(1): 13-16.

Akiba, Takashi. 1950. *A Field Research of Choson Shamanism*. Tanba: Yotoku-sha.

Akiba, Takashi. 1954. *Chosen-minzokushi*. Tokyo: Rokusan-shoin.

Amino, Husako. 1997. "Korean-shaman's Religious World: From a Research of Jindo Island in South Jeolla Province", *The Japanese Journal of Ethnology* 62(3): 273-293.

Amino, Husako. 1997. "Korean-shaman's Sense of Deity Focusing on Deity of Smallpox", *Tokyo-toritsu-daigaku-jimbun-gakuho* 280: 43-66.

Amino, Husako. 1998. "A Memorandum about a View of Life of Shamans: From a Field Note of Jindo in South Jeolla Province", *Tokyo-toritsu-daigaku-jimbun-gakuho* 290: 139-155.

Amino, Husako. 1998. "Client and Regular Shaman", in Ogo Kin'ichi, Kaji Akira, Sasaki Kokan, Higa Masao, Miyamoto Masaru eds., *Society and Symbols:*

Anthropological Approach. (A Commemorative Collection of Papers in Honor of Prof. Muratake Seiichi's 70th Birthday), Tokyo: Iwata-shoten.

Amino, Husako. 1999. "A Memorandum on Visits to Religious Workers in Jeju Island: From a Field Research of Kimnyung", *Genbun-ken* 75, Senshu University.

Amino, Husako. 1999. "Patronage as an 'Alien'", in Mio Yuko and Honda Hiroshi eds., *Cultural Multi-Centeredness in East Asia.* Institute of Asia-Africa Language and Cultural Studies, Tokyo University of Foreign Languages.

An, Byeong-Kon. 1993. "Current Situation of Studies of Traditional Family in Korea", *Shakaigaku-hyoron* 44(1): 46-53.

An, Byeong-Kon. 1995. "An Attempt of Typicalization of Separated Lineal Family in Korean Traditional Family-in Comparison with Potential Lineal Family in Japanese Ie", *Kansai-gakuin-daigaku-shakai-gakubu-kiyo* 72: 153-163.

Ando, Kunihiro. 1989. "Hypocaust and Floor: Structure of Korean Houses", *Kikan-minzokugaku* 49: 59-71.

Aono, Masaaki. 1990. "The Position of the Policy of Reorganization of Farm Villages during the Colonial Period: A Study Based on the Period of Movement for Promotion of Villages", *Chosen-gakuho* 136.

Aono, Masaaki. 1991. "Nucleus Figures in Choson Village: A Case Study of Gyeonggi Yeoju-gun", *Chosen-gakuho* 141.

Aono, Masaaki. 1995. "The Choson Governor-General Office's Religion Policy: Focusing on the 1930's", *Seiwa-daigaku-ronshu-jimbun-gakukei* 23.

Aono, Masaaki. 1996. "The Choson Governor-General Office's Policy on Shinto Shrines: Focusing on the 1930's", *Chosen-gakuho* 160.

Aono, Masaaki. 1996. "The Kingdom of Heaven on Earth of Chondokyo in Modern Choson", *Seiwa-daigaku-ronshu-jimbun-gakukei* 24.

Aono, Masaaki. 1997. "The Choson Governor-General Office's Policy on Shamanism", *Seiwa-daigaku-ronshu-jimbun-gakukei* 25.

Aono, Masaaki. 1999. "Construction of New Capital City of Gumgangdo in Modern Choson", *Seiwa-daigaku-ronshu-jimbun-gakukei* 27.

Aono, Masaaki. 2001. *Popular Religion of Villages in Choson: Focusing on Chondokyo and Gumgangdaedo under the Colonial Rule.* Shakai-hyoron-sha.

Aoyagi, Kiyotaka. 1973. "Structure of Household and House of Village A in Daechon-myeon, Gwangsan-gun, South Jeolla Province: Interim Report", *Asia-bunka-kenkyu* 7: 51-60.

Aoyagi, Yuko. 1989. "The Position of Women and a Movement for Revision of Family Law in Modern Korea", *Joseigaku-nenpo* 10: 42-46.

Aruga, Kizaemon. 1973. "Suzuki Eitaro's Choson Studies", *Mirai* 83: 2-11.

Asakawa, Shigeo & Sakata, Shohei. 1997. "Hypocaust and Dome Houses: Residences of Koreans in Cataract Village, Heilongjiang Province", *Kikan-minzokugaku* 81.

Asakura, Toshio. 1981. "A Preliminary Report of Investigation of Dochodo Island in South Jeolla Province(1): Focused on Marriage", *Meiji-daigaku-daigakuin-kiyo* 18: 78-87.

Asakura, Toshio. 1982. "A Preliminary Report of Investigation of Dochodo Island in South Jeolla Province (2): About Funeral", *Meiji-daigaku-daigakuin-kiyo* 19: 49-61.

Asakura, Toshio. 1983. "A Preliminary Report of Investigation of Dochodo Island in South Jeolla Province (3): About Gye (fraternity)", *Meiji-daigaku-daigakuin-kiyo* 20: 17-31.

Asakura, Toshio. 1983. "Families of a Village in Dochodo Island, South Jeolla Province", *Social Anthropology* 9: 153-166.

Asakura, Toshio. 1984. "A Preliminary Report of Investigation of Dochodo Island in South Jeolla Province (4): An Aspect of Rural Communities seen in 'Chib-an' election", *Meiji-daigaku-daigakuin-kiyo* 21: 19-31.

Asakura, Toshio. 1985. "Social Character of A Korean Village: Focusing on Gye (fraternity)", *Chosen-shi-kenkyu-kai-kaiho* 81: 11-14.

Asakura, Toshio. 1986. *Food is in Korea*. (Morieda Takashi and Asakura Toshio), Tokyo: Kobun-do.

Asakura, Toshio. 1987. "Current Situation of Korean Folklore", *Minzokugaku-hyoron* 27: 11-20.

Asakura, Toshio. 1987. "Thought of Korean Society: A Memorandum about Locality", *Field* 2: 41-50.

Asakura, Toshio. 1988. "Modern Korean Society and Women: Focusing on Networks of Housewives in Collective Housing Area in Seoul",

Minpaku-tsushin 42: 63-67.

Asakura, Toshio. 1989. "Ancestral Tablet Worship of Korea", in Watanabe Yoshio ed., *Races and Culture around China Sea 3: A Rite of Ancestral Worship.* (121-143), Tokyo: Gaifu-sha.

Asakura, Toshio. 1989. "Change of Korean Rite of Ancestral Worship: Focusing on Residents in Urban Apartments", *Kokuritsu-minzokugaku-hakubutsukan-chosa-hokoku-sho* 13(4): 741-786.

Asakura, Toshio. 1989. "Korean Rite of Ancestral Worship and Social Organization", in Watanabe Yoshio ed., *Races and Culture around China Sea 3: A Rite of Ancestral Worship.* (41-64), Tokyo: Gaifu-sha.

Asakura, Toshio. 1990. "A Research on Korean Geomancy: Reflection and Prospect", in Takeda Akira ed., *Progress and Questions of Folklore.* (331-357), Tokyo: Kokusho-kanko-kai.

Asakura, Toshio. 1990. "Locality of Korean Society", in Sugiyama Koichi and Sakurai Tetsuo eds., *Cultural Anthropology of Korean Society*. Tokyo: Kobun-do.

Asakura, Toshio. 1992. "Annual Cyclic Rites in Modern Korean Society", *Gekkan-shinika* 3(4): 62-67.

Asakura, Toshio. 1992. "Current Situation and Prospect of Studies on Traditional Culture in Modern Korean Society", *Kokuritsu-minzokugaku-hakubutsukan-chosa-hokoku* 17(4): 809-850.

Asakura, Toshio. 1992. "Moving Korean", *Field* 2: 41-50.

Asakura, Toshio. 1994. "Japanese Roast Meat and Korean Raw Fish: When 'nized' with Food Culture", *Ningen-sensho* 178 Tokyo: Noson-gyoson-bunka-kyokai.

Asakura, Toshio. 1994. "Koran Family and Child Rearing", *Education and Medicine* 42(7).

Asakura, Toshio. 1998. "Aspects of Yangbanization", in Mutsuhiko, Shima and Roger L. Janelli, eds., *The Anthropology of Korea: East Asian Perspectives* (Senri Ethnological Studies 49: 191-211). Osaka: Kokuritsu-minzokugaku-hakubutsukan.

Asakura, Toshio. 1998. "A memorandum about Korean Drinking Culture", in Ishige Naomichi ed., *Treatises Cultural History of Liquor and Drinking.*

Tokyo: Heibon-sha.

Asakura, Toshio. 1998. "Changing Villages in Islands: Family Life and Its Change in Villages of Southwestern Island Area in the 1980's", in Shima Mutsuhiko and Asakura Toshio eds., *Changing Korean Society: From the Field of Research of Anthropology.* (147-184), Tokyo: Daiichi-shobo.

Asakura, Toshio. 1998. "Japanized Korean Food: Focusing on Roast Meat", in Ishige Naomichi ed., *Japanese Food Culture.* Aji-no-moto-shoku-no-bunka-center.

Asakura, Toshio. 1998. *Changing Korean Society.* (Shima Mutsuhiko and Asakura Toshio eds.), Tokyo: Daiichi-shobo (Academic series new Asia : 26).

Asakura, Toshio. 1999. "A Participation Report of Korean Cultural Anthropology Society", *Minpaku-tsushin* 83: 88-93.

Asakura, Toshio. 1999. "Korea's Medicine and Food Coming From the Same Source (Special Issue: A Desire for Eternal Youth and Immortality)", *Asia-yugaku* 2.

Asakura, Toshio. 2000. "Symbols of Korean Culture in Japan", *Kokuritsu-minzokugaku-hakubutsukan-chosa-hokoku-sho* 14.

Asakura, Toshio. 2000. "Japanese Food in Korea (Special Issue 'Japanese Food Over the Border')", *Vesta* 39.

Asakura, Toshio. 2000. "Japanese Food in Korea", *Vesta* 37, Aji-no-moto-shoku-no-bunka-center.

Asakura, Toshio. 2000. "Let's Know about Korea Q&A 115", *Kikan-minzokugaku* 24(2) 92.

Asakura, Toshio. 2000. "Yangban's Eating Habits: in Search for Research Methods", *Seikyu-gakujutsu-ronshu* 16, Kankoku-bunka-kenkyu-shinko-zaidan.

Asakura, Toshio. 2000. *Let's Know about Korea Q&A115.* Suita: Senri-bunka-zaidan.

Asakura, Toshio ed. 2000. *Symbols of Korean Culture in Japan.* Suita: Kokuritsu-minzokugaku-hakubutsukan.

Asakura, Toshio. 2001. Asakura Toshio, O Seonhwa and Miyatsuka Toshio, "From Smokeless Roaster to A Charcoal Fire, There is no slump in Korean Barbecue Business", *Shokun* 33(2).

Asakura, Toshio. 2002. "Asking to Mr. Toshio Asakura about Life in Seoul:

An Exhibition of Seoul Style in 2002(Making Up Seoul Style in 2002)", *Kikan-minzokugaku* 26(2): 100.

Asakura, Toshio. 2002. "Social History of Korean Markets", in Jeong Seungmo, et al., *Korean Science and Culture: 11*. Hosei-daigaku-shuppan-kyoku.

Asakura, Toshio. 2002. *Seoul Style in 2002*. Asakura Toshio, Sato Koji et al. Senri-bunka-zaidan.

Asakura, Toshio. 2003. "Korea: Settlement Style of Great Chinese Tradition Based on Chinese Characters (Special Issue 'Wise Remarks and Famous Phrase Related to Food: Tradition and Creation')", *Vesta* (49).

Asakura, Toshio and Okada,. 1999. "Dialogue: Change of Food Culture(1)", *Shoku-seikatsu-kenkyu* 20(2): 21-29.

Asakura, Toshio and Okada,. 1999. "Dialogue: Change of Food Culture(2)", *Shoku-seikatsu-kenkyu* 20(3): 19-25.

Asanuma, Masashi. 1995. "The Structure of Korean Rite of Ancestral Worship: Focusing on the Rite of Ancestral Worship of Chaegoujeon", *Kodai-bunka-kenkyu* 55.

Asaoka, Koji. 1991. "Korean Traditional Technique: Smith Forging and Products", *A Research on Korean Traditional Culture: For the Comparison with Okinawa* 89-116, Naha: Okinawa-kenritsu-geijutsu-daigaku-ryu-kan-densho-bunka-chosa-dan.

Cheong, Tae-Seong. 1977. *Korean Sitology*. Tokyo: Kodan-sha.

Cheong, Tae-Seong. 1979. *Korean Foodways: Thinking about Relationship with Japan*. Tokyo: Shibata-shoten.

Cheong, Tae-Seong. 1981. *How to Cook Korean Dishes*. (Jeon Jinsik, Cheong Tae-Seong), Noson-gyoson-bunka-kyokai.

Cheong, Tae-Seong. 1982. *Korean Cookbook*. Heibon-sha, (Toyo-bunko : 416).

Cheong, Tae-Seong. 1983. *Gurel Cookbook*. (Jeon Jinsik, Cheong Tae-Seong), Shibata-shoten.

Cheong, Tae-Seong. 1984. *Food of Korea*. Tokyo: Tsukiji-shokan.

Cheong, Tae-Seong. 1985. "Spice as Korean Culture Traits", in Ishige Naomichi ed., *Essays Eating Culture of Far East Asia*. Heibon-sha.

Cheong, Tae-Seong. 1985. *The Complete Collection of Korean Cookbooks 1*. (Jeon Jinsik, Cheong Tae-Seong) Shibata-shoten.

Cheong, Tae-Seong. 1985. *The Complete Collection of Korean Cookbooks 3.* (Jeon Jinsik, Cheong Tae-Seong) Shibata-shoten.

Cheong, Tae-Seong. 1985. *The Complete Collection of Korean Cookbooks 4.* (Jeon Jinsik, Cheong Tae-Seong) Shibata-shoten.

Cheong, Tae-Seong. 1986. *The Complete Collection of Korean Cookbooks 2.* (Jeon Jinsik, Cheong Tae-Seong) Shibata-shoten.

Cheong, Tae-Seong. 1986. *The Complete Collection of Korean Cookbooks 5.* (Jeon Jinsik, Cheong Tae-Seong) Shibata-shoten.

Cheong, Tae-Seong. 1986. *The Complete Collection of Korean Cookbooks 6.* (Jeon Jinsik, Cheong Tae-Seong) Shibata-shoten.

Cheong, Tae-Seong. 1987. *Liquor of Korea.* Tokyo: Tsukiji-shokan.

Cheong, Tae-Seong. 1992. *Japan and Korea in the Food Culture.* Tokyo: Kodan-sha.

Cheong, Tae-Seong. 1992. *Society and Culture in East Asia.* Publishing Division of Essays in Celebration of the 20th Anniversary: Osaka University of Economics and Law Press.

Cheong, Tae-Seong. 1995. *An Introduction to Food Culture.* (Ishige Naomichi, Cheong Tae-Seong) Kodan-sha.

Cheong, Tae-Seong. 1998. "Invigoration of Korean People", *Forward 21.* 2(8)

Cheong, Tae-Seong. 1998. "Liquor Culture of Korean Peninsula", "About SUSUKORI", in Ishige Naomichi ed., *Essays Cultural History of Liquor.* Heibon-sha.

Cheong, Tae-Seong. 1998. "People and Liquor", *Forward 21.* 2(10).

Cheong, Tae-Seong. 1998. *An Introduction to Korean Home Cooking.* (Kin Nichirei, Cheong Tae-Seong) Noson-gyoson-bunka-kyokai.

Cheong, Tae-Seong. 1998. *Food and Liquor of Korean Peninsula: Ethnic Tradition Which Was Formed By Confucian Culture* (Chukoshinsho1443). Tokyo: Chuo-koron Co.

Cheong, Tae-Seong. 1999. *Cultural History of Choson Dishes.* (Lee Seonguwo), Heibon-sha.

Cheong, Tae-Seong. 1999. Sawa Maiko, Hibi Yoshiko and Cheong Tae-Seong, "Comparative Study of Food Culture in Japan and Korean Peninsula: 1 ; Japanese Young People's Taste in Kimchi (Feature on Korean Studies)",

Ningen-kenkyu 7.

Cheong, Tae-Seong. 2000. "A Study of Favorite Food of Choson People Based on the Records of Choson Tsushinshi (The Visit of the Korean Emissarry)(1)", (Cheong Tae-Seong, Hibi Yoshiko), *History of Life Culture* 37.

Cheong, Tae-Seong. 2000. "Food Thought of Korean Peninsula: Food Culture Produced From Confucian Ethics", in Fukui Katsuyoshi, Akimichi Tomoya, Tanaka Koji eds., (Lecture Humanity and Environment 6) *Question About Food Ethics: The Harmony of Body and Environment*. Showa-do.

Cheong, Tae-Seong. 2001. "A Comparative Study of Food Culture of Japan and Korea(2) Young People's Taste for Hot Taste: A Case of Japan and Korea" (Hibi Yoshiko, Sawa Maiko, Cheong, Tae-Seong, et al,) *Human Culture* 9.

Cheong, Tae-Seong. 2001. "A Study of Favorite Food of Choson People Based on the Records of Choson Tsushinshi (The Visit of the Korean Emissarry)(2)", (Sawa Maiko, Hibi Yoshiko, Cheong, Tae-Seong), *History of Life Culture* (40).

Cheong, Tae-Seong. 2001. "Confectioneries of Korean Peninsula and Its Traits (Special Issue Foreign Food Culture and Japanese confections", *Japanese Confectioneries* (8).

Cheong, Tae-Seong. 2001. "Interview with Mr. Cheong Tae-Seong: Will Kimchi Fix in Japanese Food Culture? (Special Issue Fermented Hot-Taste Culture)", *Science of Food* 279.

Cheong, Tae-Seong. 2001. "Will Kimchi Fix in Japanese Food Culture? Vol. 2 Interview with Mr. Cheong Tae-Seong (Special Issue Fermented Hot-Taste Culture)", *Science of Food* 280.

Cheong, Tae-Seong. 2001. *Do You Like Korean Barbecue?* Shincho-sha, (ShinCho-sensho).

Cheong, Tae-Seong. 2002. "Japanese Food Culture and 'Zainichi' Koreans (Special Issue 'Zainichi' Koreans in History: Thinking About the Meaning of 'Zainichi' Koreans From the Perspective of Past, Present, and Future of East Asia) -(Life Environment of 'Zainichi' Koreans)", *Kan* 11.

Cheong, Tae-Seong. 2002. "The Way to Make Makkolli (Korean Traditional

Raw Rice Wine) and Its Culture", *Japan Brewage Association Journal* 97(4).

Cheong, Tae-Seong. 2002. *Healthy Kimchi.* Shoden-sha.

Cho, Kyeundal. 1994. "Legitimacy and Heresy in Donghak", in Mizoguchi Yuzo, Hamashita Takeshi, Hiraishi Naoaki, Miyajima Hiroshi eds., *History From Outside* (Thinking in Asia 3), 55-98, Tokyo: Tokyo-daigaku-shuppan-kyoku.

Choe, Kil-Sung. 1973. "The Process of Divine Skill in Korean Shamanism", *The Japanese Journal of Ethnology* 38(2): 108-119.

Choe, Kil-Sung. 1976. "A Rite of Departed Souls and A View of Soul in Korean Shamanism: An Analysis into the Structure of the Myth of Princess Bari", *Chosen-gakuho* 78.

Choe, Kil-Sung. 1976. "A Rite of Departed Souls in Korean Shamanism", *Kikan-jinruigaku* 7(3): 54-74.

Choe, Kil-Sung. 1977. "Kinship and Marital Relationship in the Group of Korean Shamans: Focusing on Regular Shamans in the East Coast", *Institute of Oriental Culture, University of Tokyo Bulletin* 71: 263-295.

Choe, Kil-Sung. 1977. tr., Lee Doo-hyun, Jang Ju-Keun, Lee Kwan-Kyu, *An Introduction of Korean Folklore.* Tokyo: Gakusei-sha.

Choe, Kil-Sung. 1978. "Actions of Korean Regular Shamans, An Analysis into the Group", *The Japanese Journal of Ethnology* 42(4).

Choe, Kil-Sung. 1980. "A Cultural Anthropological Study on Korean Barbecue of Korean in Japan", *Annual Report of Social Anthropology* Vol. 6(1980), Tokyo Metropolitan University Social Anthropology Society, Tokyo: Kobun-do.

Choe, Kil-Sung. 1980. *Festivals and Shamanism of Korea.* Tokyo: Daiichi-shobo.

Choe, Kil-Sung. 1984. "Wedding Ceremony After Death", *Minwa-no-techo* (Japan Folktale Club) 22: 125-127.

Choe, Kil-Sung. 1984. (Fukudome Noriaki tr.,) *Korean Shamans*. Kokubun-sha.

Choe, Kil-Sung. 1984. *Korean Shamanism: Social Anthropological Studies*. Tokyo: Kobun-do.

Choe, Kil-Sung. 1987. "A Thought on Deity Onari of Okinawa", *Japan Folklore* 169.

Choe, Kil-Sung. 1988. "Reflection and Prospect of Folk Studies of Japan in Korea", *Japan Folklore* 175.

Choe, Kil-Sung. 1989. (Book Review) "Umesao Tadao, Moriya Takeshi eds., Festivals are Deities' Performance: Japan and East Asia Relating to Entertainment", *Minzokugaku-kenkyu* 54(1).

Choe, Kil-Sung. 1989. "A Anthropological Studies of Japan in Korea (Special Issue: Japan Seen From Outside [including comments, Q&F])", *The Japanese Journal of Ethnology* 54(3).

Choe, Kil-Sung. 1990. "A Thought on Market at Sea", in Takeda Akira ed., *Progress and Challenges of Folklore* 459-476, Tokyo: Kokushokankokai.

Choe, Kil-Sung. 1990. "Trend of Studies of Japanese Culture in Korea", *Kikan-koreana* 3(3).

Choe, Kil-Sung. 1991. "Geomun Island: Southern Island Colonized Under the Japanese Rule", *Quaterly Nature and Culture* 34.

Choe, Kil-Sung. 1991. "Village Festival of Korea", Uematsu Akashi ed., *Folk Customs and Rites around China Sea 2 Rites of Deity*. (27-37), Tokyo: Gaifu-sha.

Choe, Kil-Sung. 1992. "Acceptance of Japanese Culture and Conflicts in Korea", *Shiso* 817: 167-176.

Choe, Kil-Sung. 1992. "The Relations Between Christianity and Shamanism in Korea", *Korean and Japanese Culture: Homogeneousness and Heterogeneousness; Forum: Korean Culture and Japanese Culture*; '92 Cultural Agent of Korea in Japan, (40-43), Tokyo: Korean Cultural Center.

Choe, Kil-Sung. 1992. No Seonghwan, Choe Kil-sung (Comment), The Myth of Nation Concession and Ethics of Regality 〔including Commentary: Studies of Japanese Culture in Korea〕 (Kojiki Getting Out of Myth 〈Special Issue〉) *Gendai-shiso* 20(4).

Choe, Kil-Sung. 1992. tr. By Shigematsu Mayumi, *Ancestor Worship of Korea*. Ochanomizu-shobo.

Choe, Kil-Sung. 1993. "Yanagita Kunio and Korea", in Ueda Masaaki ed., *Religious Rites and Traditions of Deities*. Doho-sha Publishing.

Choe, Kil-Sung. 1993. "A Rite of Departed Souls of Korean Shamanism", in Matsuzaki Kenzou ed., *Marriage of Departed Souls of East Asia* (293-317),

Tokyo: Iwata-shoten.

Choe, Kil-Sung. 1993. "Change of Korean Shamanism: Home Again of Shamanism", *Shunju* 345.

Choe, Kil-Sung. 1993. "Korea's Religion and the Social System", in Kim Yang-Gi supervised, *Korea* (124-135: 146-155), Tokyo: Shincho-sha.

Choe, Kil-Sung. 1993. "Noro(Female Shaman) of Okinawa and Regular Shaman of Korea", *Nicchu-bunka-kenkyu* 5: 46-54.

Choe, Kil-Sung. 1993. "The Meaning of Drinking of Liquor and Tea in Korean Society", *Bulletin of the Folklore Society of Japan* 195: 98-109.

Choe, Kil-Sung. 1993. "Transformation of Culture by Colonization", in Kim Yang-Gi supervised, *Korea* (305-315), Tokyo: Shincho-sha.

Choe, Kil-Sung. 1994. "An Introduction of Folk Journal of Geomun Island", *Japanese Colonization and Transformation of Culture: Korea, Geomun Island.* (83-104), Tokyo: Ochanomizu-shobo.

Choe, Kil-Sung. 1994. "Cultural Anthropology of 'Dabang'(Korean Coffee House)", *Kokusai-kenkyu* (Kokusai-chiiki-kenkyu-jo, Chubu University) 10: 199-213.

Choe, Kil-Sung. 1994. "Folklore and Anthropology Under the Japanese Rule", *Japanese Colonization and Transformation of Culture: Korea, Geomun Island* 3: 32, Tokyo: Ochanomizu-shobo.

Choe, Kil-Sung. 1994. "Modernization and Religion for Korean Women", in Miyake Hitoshi, Suzuki Masataka eds., *Shamanism and Folk Customs of East Asia.* (182-196), Tokyo: Keiso-shobo.

Choe, Kil-Sung. 1994. "Universality of Korean Christianity and Racial Traits for Zainichi Koreans", *Kokusai-kenkyu* 10, Kokusai-chiiki-kenkyu-jo, Chubu University.

Choe, Kil-Sung. 1994. "Women in Korean Shamanism", in Miyake Hitoshi, Suzuki Masataka eds., *Shamanism and Folk Customs of East Asia.* Tokyo: Keisoshobo.

Choe, Kil-Sung. 1994. *Japanese Colonization and Transformation of Culture: Korea, Geomun Island.* Tokyo: Ochanomizu-shobo.

Choe, Kil-Sung. 1994. Manabe Yuko trans., *Anthropology of 'Han'.* Tokyo: Hirakawa-shuppan-sha.

Choe, Kil-Sung. 1995. "Korean Belief Scourge", *Asia's View of Soul*. (35-62), Yuzankaku.

Choe, Kil-Sung. 1995. "Transformation of Japanese Culture and Conflicts (Priority Areas Studies 'Information-Oriented Society and Humanity' The Year of 1991 The 5th Symposium 'Transformation of Culture and the Present') (Section 3 Information Culture Network of Asia)", *Report, The Bulletin of the Institute of Socio-Information and Communication Studies*. The University of Tokyo 48.

Choe, Kil-Sung. 1996. "Ancestor Worship of Korea: Mortuary Tablet as a Spirit-dwelling Object and Shamanism", in Umehara Takeshi, Nakanishi Susumu eds., *Depths of Japan Relating to Soul*. (35-50), Tokyo: Kadokawa Shoten Publishing Co. Ltd.

Choe, Kil-Sung. 1996. "Calendar of East Asia", *Aurora* (kansai for um21) 2: 122-129.

Choe, Kil-Sung. 1996. "Discussion: Cultural Area around East China Sea (Special Issue: Comparative Culture of East China Sea)", Suwa Haruo, Kawamura Minato, Choe Kil-sung et al. *Nicchu-bunka-kenkyu* 9.

Choe, Kil-Sung. 1996. "Prostitution in Modern Korean Society", *Nicchu-bunka-kenkyu* 9: 84-94, Bensey-sha.

Choe, Kil-Sung. 1996. "Rice Cakes in Rice Farming of Korea", *Asia's Rice Farming and Japan*. (138-162), Yuzankaku.

Choe, Kil-Sung. 1996. "Vietnam and Korea", *Nicchu-bunka-kenkyu* 2 (China's Chang Jiang Culture and Japan, Vietnam). (55-65), Bensey-sha.

Choe, Kil-Sung. 1996. *Invitation to Korean Folk Customs*. Tokyo: Fukyo-sha.

Choe, Kil-Sung. 1997. "Invasion and Friction of Culture Between Japan and Korea", in Aoki Tamotsu et al. eds., *Coexistence of Different Cultures*. (Iwanami Lecture Cultural Anthropology 8, pp.85-104), Tokyo: Iwanami Shoten.

Choe, Kil-Sung. 1997. "Korea's Nationalism and Religion", Nakano Tsuyoshi et als. Eds., *Religion and Nationalism*. Sekai-shiso-sha.

Choe, Kil-Sung. 1997. "Korean Confucianism, and Mourning and Death in Shamanism", Komoto Mitsugi, Yagi Toru eds., *Series Comparison of Family(9) Family and Rites of Departed Soul*. Tokyo: Waseda University

Press.

Choe, Kil-Sung. 1997. "Saemaul Movement and Village Development Movement", *Bulletin of the National Museum of Japanese History* 70: 161-183.

Choe, Kil-Sung. 1998. "Belief in Malevolent Spirits", Shima, Mutsuhiko and Roger L. Janelli eds., *The Anthropology of Korea: East Asian Perspectives* (Senri Ethnological Studies 49, 95-107), Osaka: National Museum of Ethnology.

Choe, Kil-Sung. 1998. "Korean Feeling on Chastity", Suwa Haruo ed., *Sex of Asia*. Bensey Publishing.

Choe, Kil-Sung. 1998. "Discrimination in Marriage and Ethnic Identity for Zainichi Koreans", *The Theory of Modern Japanese Culture*. Tokyo: Iwanami Shoten.

Choe, Kil-Sung. 1998. "Folk Cultural Interchange Between Japan and Korea Seen From Korea", *Research on folk music: Journal of the Society for Japanese Folk Music*. 28-30, Society for Japanese Folk Music.

Choe, Kil-Sung. 1998. "Festivals and Nationalism in Korean Society", *Deities of East Asia and Festivals*. (213-257), Yuzankaku.

Choe, Kil-Sung. 1998. "Korea: Colony and Image of Japan", *Information-Oriented Society and Culture*. Tokyo: University of Tokyo Press.

Choe, Kil-Sung. 1998. "Marriage with the Han People and Ethnic Identity for Korean People in China", *Hikaku-kazoku* 13, Hikaku-kazoku-shi-gakkai.

Choe, Kil-Sung. 1998. "The Korean War and Change of Korean Society", in Shima Mutsuhiko, Asakura Toshio eds., *Changing Korean Society: From the Field of Research of Anthropology in the 1970's～80's*. (305-332), Tokyo: Daiichi-shobo.

Choe, Kil-Sung. 1998. "Traditional View of Value and Modernization in Confucian Cultural Area", in Aoki Tamotsu, Saeki Keishi eds., *What Is the Asian Value?* TBS Britannica, (129-143).

Choe, Kil-Sung. 1999. "A View of Chastity of Korean People", in Suwa Haruo ed., *Sex of Asia*. Tokyo: Bensey Publishing Inc.

Choe, Kil-Sung. 1999. "Anthropological Study of Korean Names", in Ueno Kazuo, Mori Kenji eds., *Name and Society: Family History of Naming*. Tokyo: Waseda University Press.

Choe, Kil-Sung. 1999. "Destruction of Buildings of Government General of Choson and Geomantic Nationalism", *Bulletin of the Folklore Society of Japan*. 218.

Choe, Kil-Sung. 1999. "Discrimination in Marriage and Ethnic Identity for Zainichi Koreans", in Aoki Tamotsu et al. ed., *The Theory of Modern Japanese Culture(11) Love and Difficulties*. Tokyo: Iwanami Shoten.

Choe, Kil-Sung. 1999. "Korea: Colony and Image of Japan", in Aoki Tamotsu, Kajiwara Kageaki eds., *The Culture of Information-Oriented Society(1) Information and Image of Asia*. Tokyo: University of Tokyo Press.

Choe, Kil-Sung. 1999. "The Existence of Zainichi Koreans: Rites of Ancestor Worship of Confucianism and Identity", *Lecture: Japan Folklore* 10, Yuzankaku.

Choe, Kil-Sung. 2000. "The Era of Japanese Empire and Korean Folklore", Nakao Katsumi ed., *Perspective of Colonial Anthropology*. Tokyo: Fukyo-sha.

Choe, Kil-Sung. 2000. "Fa Lun Gong and Breakdown of Superstition in China", *Aurora* 19, Meeting for Thinking of Kansai in 21C.

Choe, Kil-Sung. 2000. "Introduction: A Comparative Study of East Asian Cultures", Choe Kil-sung, Hinata Kazumasa eds., *Myth, Religion, Shamanism: An Attempt of Comparison Between Japanese and Korean Culture*. Fukyo-sha.

Choe, Kil-Sung. 2000. "The Partition of the Korean Peninsula and Tourism to Hostile Each Other", *Socio-cultural Studies of Asia, Societies and Cultures of Asia*. Graduate School for International Development and Cooperation, Hiroshima University.

Choe, Kil-Sung. 2001. "Geomancer, Shamanism, Christianity in Seoul (Special Issue: Coexistence of History of 600 Years and Future)", *Asia Yugaku* (34).

Choe, Kil-Sung. 2001. "Sexual Assault and Prostitution of the UN Forces During the Korean War", *Asian Social Culture Studies* (2).

Choe, Kil-Sung. 2001. "The Belief of the King of Ships (Special Issue: Ocean Culture of Korea", *Gekkan-kanku-bunka* 261.

Choe, Kil-Sung. 2002. "New Year's Day of Korea (Special Issue: New Year's Day of Asia)", *Asia Yugaku* (46).

Choe, Kil-Sung. 2002. *Cultural Anthropology of 'Pro-Japanese' and 'Anti-Japanese'*. Akashi-shoten, (Akashi Library 40).

Choi, Baek. 1979. "Five Family Control in Korea", *The Japanese Journal of Ethnology* 44(2): 160-167.

Choi, Baek. 1987. "Ancestor Worship and Social System of Korea: A Case Study of Uiseong Kim in Cheonjeon-dong, Andong-gun", *Annual Report of Asian-Africa Cultural Research Institute*. Toyo University, 22: 58-82.

Choi, Chang-Cho. 1997. Kim Jaeho, Shibuya Shizuaki trans. *Geomantic Thought of Korea*. Jinbun-shoin.

Choi, In-Hak. 1976. *A Study of Korean Old Stories*. Tokyo: Kobun-do.

Choi, In-Hak. 1977. *Collections of Korean Legends*. Tokyo: NHK Publishing Association.

Choi, In-Tag. 1989. "Double Grave System and Rites for the Dead: A Case Study of Sugashima of Toba-shi (Special Issue: Japan Seen From Outside [including comments and Q&F])", *The Japanese Journal of Ethnology* 54(3).

Choi, In-Tag. 1996. Choi In-Tag, Ishikawa Hiroyuki, Mori Masafumi, "How Can We Talk About Amami and Okinawa? (Special Issue: Focusing on Ryukyu Studies)", *The Japanese Journal of Ethnology* 61(3).

Choi, In-Tag. 1998. Umeda Hiroyuki, Matsubara Takatoshi eds., "Traditional Society", *Handbook of Korea: Language and Culture*. Toho-shoten.

Choi, In-Tag. 1999. *A Research Note of Fishing Village of Korea: Change of Religious Ceremonies*. Miyazaki Public University School of Humanities Bulletin (6)1.

Choi, In-Tag. 2002. *Ryukyu-Asian Ethnic Customs and History*. Commemorative Treatise Publication, Yoju-shorin, 2002.7.

Choi, Jae-Yool. 1988. "About Gye (Fraternity) of Korea", *Annual Report of Asia-Africa Cultural Research Institute*. Toyo University, 23: 181-190.

Choi, Jai-Seok. 1953. "A Range of Relatives in Korean Villages", *The Japanese Journal of Ethnology* 27(3): 541-551.

Choi, Jang-Jib. 1997. *Political Change in Modern Korea: Historical Conditions for Modernization and Democracy*. Bokutaku-sha.

Choi, Jong-Min. 1994. "People Engaged in Korean Classical Music", *Koreana*

7(3).

Choi, Yun. 1992. "A Research Study of Poor Families in Small Towns of Korea", *Ryukoku-daigaku-shakaigaku-ronshu*.

Chung, Daekyun. 1978. "Social Relations in the Korean Community of Ikegami-cho (1)", *Chosen-kenkyu* 185.

Chung, Daekyun. 1979. "A Theory of Foreign Residents (1)" (Chung Daekyun: Wetherall, William), *Chosen-kenkyu* 196.

Chung, Daekyun. 1979. "Problems concerning Zainichi Koreans at the Crossroads (1) Is it Fleeing to Freedom? New Viewpoint of the Theory of Zainichi Koreans 〈Special Issue〉", *Chosen-kenkyu* 189.

Chung, Daekyun. 1979. "Social Relations in the Korean Community of Ikegami-cho (2)", *Chosen-kenkyu* 186.

Chung, Daekyun. 1980. "A Theory of Foreign Residents (2)", (Chung Daekyun: Wetherall, William), *Chosen-kenkyu* 202.

Chung, Daekyun. 1981. "Custody Experience of Japanese American (contribution)" (Don Nakanishi : Chung Daekyun), *Shiso-no-kagaku* Vol. 6. 126.

Chung, Daekyun. 1984. "Temptation and Repulsion toward Japan: An Analysis into Interests in Japan of Korean Students of the department of Japanese", *Kaigai-jijo* 32(2).

Chung, Daekyun. 1985. " 'Japanese Culture' in South Korea under the Military Administration", *Kaigai-jijo* 33(2).

Chung, Daekyun. 1985. "Busan News Reported by Two People (1) Pictures of Busan", *Gendai-korea* 251.

Chung, Daekyun. 1985. "Busan News Reported by Two People (2) A Labyrinth Called Korea", *Gendai-korea* 255.

Chung, Daekyun. 1985. "Busan News Reported by Two People (4) Ancestors' Home", *Gendai-korea* 257.

Chung, Daekyun. 1986. "Zainichi Koreans, Assimilation or Dissimilation?", *Gendai-korea* 263.

Chung, Daekyun. 1986. *A Mirror Named Korea*. (Kawamura Minato and Chung Daekyun), Toyo-shoin.

Chung, Daekyun. 1987. "A Homeland of Close View (Imagination of Overseas Japanese: From North America)", *Shiso-no-kagaku* Vol. 7. 93.

Chung, Daekyun. 1987. "Ancestors' Home: Experiences in Korea of Zainichi Koreans", *Kaigai-jijo* 35(2).

Chung, Daekyun. 1988. "Driving Away the Korea Theory of Culturism", *Chuo-koron* 103(11).

Chung, Daekyun. 1989. "The Unfortunate Connection: Theories of Japanese and Korean National Identity", *Chuo-koron* 104(5).

Chung, Daekyun. 1990. "A Myth of Zainichi Koreans", *Shokun* 22(10).

Chung, Daekyun. 1991. "When Will Anti-Japanism in Korea Change?", *Chuo-koron* 106(2).

Chung, Daekyun. 1991. "Why Is Japanese Culture Put Under Taboo in Korea?", *Shokun* 23(5).

Chung, Daekyun. 1992. "Los Angels Riot: Korean Report(Focus and Issue)", *Gendai-korea* 322.

Chung, Daekyun. 1992. *Parallelism of Japan and Korea*. Sanko-sha.

Chung, Daekyun. 1993. "The Character of Korea's Nationalism", *Shiso* 823.

Chung, Daekyun. 1994. "The Structure of Anti-Japanism in Korean Society: Background of Both-Sided Response to Japanese Culture", *Sekai-shuho* 75(13).

Chung, Daekyun. 1995. "Progressive Japanese Who Make Korea Miserable (Postwar Verification 5: Asia's Experience of Japan 〈Special Issue〉)", *Shiso-no-kagaku* Vol. 8. 33.

Chung, Daekyun. 1995. *Image of Korea*. Chuo-koron Co. Chuko-shinsho.

Chung, Daekyun. 1996. "Ethnic Fatigue of Zainichi Koreans: Minor Opinions of Nationality Clauses", *Chuo-koron* 111(10).

Chung, Daekyun. 1997. "About Anti-Japanism in Korea", Kurihara Akito ed., *Lecture: Sociology of Discrimination (3) The Structure of Discrimination in Modern World*. Kobun-do.

Chung, Daekyun. 1997. "Three-Men Openhearted Discussion by Intellectual Koreans: Foolish Anti-Japan Feelings in Korea" (Choe Kilsung, O Seonhwa, Chung Daekyun), *Seiron* 295.

Chung, Daekyun. 1997. "Why Don't They Claim Nationality of Japan? (Special Issue: Nationality of Zainichi Koreans)", (Chung Daekyun, Nishioka Tsutomu), *Gendai-korea* 375.

Chung, Daekyun. 1998. "An Openhearted Talk Between Taiwanese and Korean: The Hearts of Zainichi Koreans, The Hearts of Coexistence", (Kin Birei, Chung Daekyun), *Seiron* 306.

Chung, Daekyun. 1998. "Territory of Japanese Manners: The Method and the Process of Acceptance of Japanese Culture in Korea", Igarashi Akio ed., *Changing Asia and Japan: Japanese Popular Culture Which Infiltrates into Asia*. Senri-shobo.

Chung, Daekyun. 1998. *Image of Japan*. Chuo-koron Co. (Chuko-shinsho).

Chung, Daekyun. 2000. "Japanese society is pluralized and activated because Japan chooses the path of the 'Korean-Japanese' (SIMULATION REPORT: From post-baby boomers to Korean-Japanese: People from new Nippon who gain power", *SAPIO* 12(20) (261).

Chung, Daekyun. 2000. "A Talk: Korean Beauty and Japanese Beauty: When They Understand Each Other's Difference, The Relationship Which Irritate Each Other Will Be (Special Issue: Changing Asia, Unchanged Japan)", (Chung Daekyun, O Sunhwa), *Voice* 271.

Chung, Daekyun. 2000. "Quit Korean, Be Japanese: About the Border Which Zainichi Koreans Can't Stand", *Seiron* 336.

Chung, Daekyun. 2001. "Korea: The Past Which Cannot Be Let Alone Between Japan and Korea", *Sekai-shuho* 82(26) 4006.

Chung, Daekyun. 2001. "The End of Zainichi Koreans", *Bungei-shunju* (Bunshun-shinsho).

Chung, Daekyun. 2001. "The Franchise of Foreign Permanent Residents: Are Zainichi Koreans the Privileged Classes? (If You Are in Confusion, Evil Laws will Be Passed Openly.)", *Shokun* 33(4).

Chung, Daekyun. 2002. "Japan and South Korea at crossroad in terms of policy. From a history policy to an actual policy", *Shokun* 34(1).

Chung, Daekyun. 2002. "Changing Image of Zainichi Koreans (Special Issue Zainichi Koreans in History: Thinking About the Meaning of Zainichi Koreans From the Perspective of Past, Present, and Future of East Asia-Views about Zainichi Koreans", *Kan* 11.

Chung, Daekyun. 2002. "The Misfortune of Korea's Nationalism", *Shogaku-kan* (Shogaku-kan-bunko).

Chung, Daekyun. 2003. "Debate: Is It Possible to Share Understanding of History Between Japan and Korea?", (Fujioka Nobukatsu, Chung Daekyun, Katsuoka Kanji), *Shokun* 35(1).

Chung, Ki-Hwan. 1993. "Decrease of population of Farmhouses and Change of the Structure of Family", *Sonraku-shakai-kenkyu* 80.

Chung, Seung-Mo. 1994. "Seoul Markets", *Koreana* 7(3).

Chung, Chin-Sung. 1991. "A Comparative Study of Family Structure of Korea and Japan: Focusing on the Relationship between Stalling Progress of Nuclear Family and Women's Labor in Japan", *Social Science Studies* 42(4): 121-144.

De Vos, George A. and Sofue, Takao ed. 1984. *Religion and Family in East Asia* (Senri Ethnological Studies 11). Osaka: Kokuritsu-minzokugaku-hakubutsukan.

De Vos, George A. and Sofue, Takao ed. 1986. *Religion and Family in East Asia*. Berkeley, Los Angels and London: University of California Press.

Deguchi, Akiko. 1987. "Old Raft Ship of Jeju Island", *Kikan-minzokugaku* 42: 72-79.

Deguchi, Akiko. 1987. "Old Raft Ships in the East Coast of Korea", *Minpaku-tsushin* 35: 39-48.

Deguchi, Akiko. 1987. "Classification of Development Styles of Dugout Canoe and Regional Types: Focusing on Japan and Neighboring Regions", *Study Report of Kokuritsu-minzokugaku-hakubutsukan* 12(2): 449-497.

Deguchi, Akiko. 1996. "Conventional Structural Ship of Korea", *Seikyu-gakujutsu-ronshu* 9: 97-142.

Ejima, Shusaku. 1976. "A Problem of Analysis into Family Structure of Korean Village: Focusing on the Issue of Using the Concept of Dozoku", *Hiroshima Shudo University Treatises 〈Humanities〉* 16(2): 87-112.

Ejima, Shusaku and Maruyama, Koichi. 1976. "Emigration and Social Structure: A Case Study of Kumyang-ri", in Noguchi Takashi ed., *Emigration and Cultural Change: A Case Study of Hapcheon of Korea*. (149-234), Tokyo: Japan Science Shinko-kai.

Emori, Itsuo. 1982. "Historical Change of the Ceremony of Marriage and Folk Customs: in Contrast With Korea", *Chiba-shigaku* 1: 93-117.

Emori, Itsuo. 1982. "Introduction", in Emori Itsuo, Choe Yonggi eds., *A Study of the Institution of the Same Blood of Yangban.* (1-37), Tokyo: Daiichi-shobo.

Emori, Itsuo. 1982. "Marriage Customs", in Emori Itsuo, Choe Yonggi eds., *A Study of the Institution of the Same Blood of Yangban.* (206-232), Tokyo: Daiichi-shobo.

Emori, Itsuo. 1982. "The Structure of Yangban Rule and Historical Change", in Emori Itsuo, Choe Yonggi eds., *A Study of the Institution of the Same Blood of Yangban.* (118-148), Tokyo: Daiichi-shobo.

Emori, Itsuo and Choe, Yonggi, eds. 1982. *A Study of the Institution of the Same Blood of Yangban.* Tokyo: Daiichi-shobo.

Endo, Koichi. 1997. "Basic Trend of Social Works in Colony: An Introduction to Studies of Administration of Government-General of Choson (Meiji 43-Showa16)", *Meiji-gakuin-ronso* 592.

Fijita, Akiyoshi. 2001. "Interchange Between Korean Peninsula and Neighboring Regions Seen From Islands", Fujita Akiyoshi, Lee Seonae, Kawahara Norifumi, *Seikyu-gakujutsu-ronshu.* 19.

Fuchigami, Kyoko. 1991. "Faith Healing in Korean Christianity: Christianity in Modern Society of Shamanism", *Keio University Graduate School of Sociology Bulletin* 31: 1-8.

Fuchigami, Kyoko. 1992. "Faith Healing in Korean Christianity: The Christian Church in Korea and Shamanism", *Bulletin of Nanzan Institute for Religion & Culture.* 16:33-59.

Fuchigami, Kyoko. 1993. "Ethnic History and Folk Religion Viewed From Prayer House: Frontier of Korean Christianity", *Shukyo-kenkyu* 296: 105-130.

Fuchigami, Kyoko. 1994. "Korean Christianity and Shamanism: Prayer House and Korean Church Relating to Cure by Divine Intervention", in Miyake Hitoshi, Suzuki Masataka eds., *Shamanism and Folk Customs of East Asia.* (232-253), Tokyo: Keiso-shobo.

Fuchigami, Kyoko. 1996. "Tangun and God in Modern Korea", *Shukyo-kenkyu* 307: 287-288.

Fuchigami, Kyoko. 1997. "Memorial Service for Miscarried Baby of Korean Buddhism", *Peace and Religion* 16: 98-103.

Fuchigami, Kyoko. 1997. "Soul of Miscarried Baby of Korea: The Belief in Mary of Modern Korea", *Shukyo-kenkyu* 311: 294-295.

Fuchigami, Kyoko. 1999. "Female Shaman of Lamentation: Impulse of Ceremony in Korean Folk Religion", in Miyake Hitoshi ed., *The Horizon of Folk Religion*. (275-286), Tokyo: Shunju-sha.

Fujii, Takashi. 1975. "Yanagita Kunio's Senses of Asia", *Asia-keizai* 16(3): 68-77.

Fukudome, Noriaki. 1984. "Korean Shamanism", (Choe Kilsung), *Shukyo-kenkyu* 58(2): 246-250.

Fukudome, Noriaki. 1986. Rites of Ancestor Worship in S-dong of Korean East Coast", *Nishi-nihon-shukyo-gaku-zasshi* 8: 105-117.

Fukudome, Noriaki. 1987. "Korean Family Ceremonies and Ancestors", *San'in Minzoku* 49: 1-9.

Fukudome, Noriaki. 1991. "Korean Shamanism and Ceremony of Cure", *Kyoiku-to-igaku* 39(4).

Fukuoka, Yasunori and Kim, Myeong-Soo. 1997. *Life and Senses of Zainichi Korean Youth*. Tokyo-daigaku-shuppan-kai.

Furuno, Kiyoto. 1976. "Korea From the Perspective of Religious Anthropology", *Chosen-gakuho* 79: 1-11.

Fuse, Tetsuji. 1973. "Book Review 〈*Structure of Villages and Kinship System*〉", *Mirai* 81: 60-64.

Gamo, Masao. 1966. "Social Anthropology: Its Completion and Development in Japan", in Nihon-minzoku-gakkai ed., *Reflection and Prospect of Japanese Ethnology*. (27-49), Tokyo: Shibusawa Foundation of Ethnological Studies (Minzokugaku-shinko-kai).

Gibo, Eijiro. 1986. "Korean Tug of War: A Case Study of Naeryo-ri, Buan-eup, North Jeolla Province", *Okinawa Folk Studies* 6.

Goda, Hiroko. 1998. "Kinship and Concept of Genealogy Seen in Sillabongi: Based on King Galmun and Rank Status System", Ogo Kinichi, Kaji Akira, Sasaki Kokan, Higa Masao, Miyamoto Masaru eds., *Society and Symbols: Anthropological Approach, A Commemorative Collection of Papers in Honor of Prof. Murafu Seiichi's 70th birthday*. Iwata-shoten.

Goda, Hiroko. 1998. Kinship of the Koryo Dynasty Era and Formation of Concept of Genealogy: A Thought on Kindred and One's Own Group", *Himeji*

Human Studies 1(1).

Gotoda, Yuko. 1994. "Full Gospel Church in Seoul: Rapid Development in the 1970's and Its Background", *Hokuriku Gakuin College Bulletin* 26: 201-217.

Gotoda, Yuko. 1995. "A People and Senses of Culture in English Textbooks of Korean Junior High School", *Hokuriku Gakuin College Bulletin* 27: 195-210.

Hagiwara, Hidesaburo. 1978. "Korean Shamanism", *Kikan-minzokugaku* 4: 110-113.

Hagiwara, Hidesaburo and Choi, In-Hak. 1974. *Korean Shamanism*. Tokyo: Daiichi-houki Publishing.

Hamamoto, Mariko. 1996. "Zainichi Koreans: Identity of Zainichi Koreans", in Aoki Tamotsu et al. eds., *Iwanami Lecture Cultural Anthropology 7 Ethnography on Moving*. Iwanami-shoten.

Han, Jingxu. 1994. "Big Holidays of Korean People: A Case Study of S-Province of Jilin Province, China", *The Japanese Journal of Ethnology* 59(2): 161-169.

Han, Jingxu. 1995. "Ethnicity of Choson People in China: A Case Study of Third Generations", *The Japanese Journal of Ethnology* 60(3): 249-259.

Han, Jingxu. 1997. "Village Life of Choson People in China: A Research Report of Seonghwa Village in Jilin Province", *Study Report of Kokuritsu-minzokugaku-hakubutsukan* 21(3).

Han, Jingxu. 1999. "Women Crossing the Border- interview with 2 North Korean Women", *Seinan University International Culture Treatises* 14(1).

Han, Jingxu. 2000. "Data: North Korea Report", S*einan University International Treatises* 14(2).

Han, Jingxu. 2000. "House of Choson People in China", *Seinan University International Culture Treatises* 15(1).

Han, Jingxu. 2001. "The Theory of China's Policy on Races", *Seinan University International Culture Treatises* 15(2).

Han, Jingxu. 2001. *Korean Chinese: Choson People*. Chugoku-shoten.

Han, Myung-Hee. 1994. "Particularity of Korean Classical Music: Its Root and Classification", *Koreana* 7(3).

Han, Seung-Mi. 2000. "Modern Consumption: Globalization, Japanization, and Politics of Korea Relating to Cultural Identity", *The Journal of Pacific Asia, Asia Pacific Research Society* 6.

Han, Tong-Kwi ed. 1973. *Ceremonial Occasion of Korea: Now and the Past From the Perspective of Folklore*. Tokyo: Kokusho-kanko-kai.

Harajiri, Hideki. 1986. "Ethnicity of Zainichi Koreans: A Case Study of A-District of Chikuho", *The Japanese Journal of Ethnology* 51(3): 275-289.

Harajiri, Hideki. 1989. *Life of Zainichi Koreans*. Tokyo: Kobun-do.

Harajiri, Hideki. 1993. "Data on Emigration Policy under the Rule of President Pak and the Trend of Its Research", *Research and Studies* 24(1).

Harajiri, Hideki. 1996. "Cultural Anthropological and Sociological Basic Studies for the Practice of Education of International Cultural Understanding in Itan-shi, Hyogo Province", Harajiri Hideki, Kuraishi Ichiro, Kim Myeongmi, *Study Promotion Treatises* 32.

Harajiri, Hideki. 1996. *Countries of Peninsula and Archipelago*. Harajiri Hideki, Rokutanda Yutaka, Shinkan-sha.

Harajiri, Hideki. 1997. "Children of Ikuno", *Hormon Culture* 7.

Harajiri, Hideki. 1997. *Daily Life of Zainichi Koreans: Anthropological Approach*. Akashi-shoten.

Harajiri, Hideki. 1998. "(Book Review) '*Life and Senses of Zainichi Korean Youth*' by Fukuoka Yasunori, Kim Myeongsu", *Korean Minority Studies* (1).

Harajiri, Hideki. 1998. "Local Community and School Education: A Comparison of Korean Towns in Japan and America", Ebuchi Kazuhiro ed., *A Study of Transculturalism*. Akashi-shoten.

Harajiri, Hideki. 1998. "Network Community of People in Jeju Island (Special Issue: The World of Jeju Island)", *Geography* 43(5).

Harajiri, Hideki. 1998. "The Present and the Past of Jeju Island (Special Issue: The World of Jeju Island)", *Geography* 43(5).

Harajiri, Hideki. 1998. *Koreans as 'Zainichi'*. Kodan-sha, (Kodan-sha Gendai-shinsho).

Harajiri, Hideki. 2000. "A Comparative Study of Korean Towns: New Theory of Ethnicity", Igarashi Takeshi ed., *Multiracial System of America: Creation of 'Nation'.* Tokyo-daigaku-shuppan-kyoku.

Harajiri, Hideki. 2000. "The Paternal Line, Shared Territorial Bonding: The Process of Reconstruction of Race", Yoshihara Kazuo, Suzuki Masataka, Suenari Michio eds., *Reconstruction of Blood Ties: Priority of the Paternal Line and the Union of the Same Surname in East Asia*. Fukyo-sha.

Harajiri, Hideki. 2000. "Truth and Falsehood of Zainichi Koreans in Postwar Japan: Korean Laborers Depicted on Asahi Daily (Special Issue: Critique of Governor Ishihara)", *Sekai* (680).

Harajiri, Hideki. 2000. *Ethnography of Korean Towns: Hawaii, L.A., Ikuno*. Tokyo: Chikuma-shobo.

Hattori, Shiro. 1948. "Relationships Among Japanese, Ryukyu Language, Korean, and Altaic", *The Japanese Journal of Ethnology* 13(2): 109-131.

Hattori, Tamio. 1973. "(Book Review) *'Studies of Choson Village'* by Suzuki Etaro", *Asia-keizai* 14(10): 92-96.

Hattori, Tamio. 1974. "Problems Concerning the Publication of 'Studies of Choson Village', 'The Collection of Suzuki Etaro's Works V", *Mirai* 89: 48-56.

Hattori, Tamio. 1975. "The Theory of Comparative History of the Concept of Consanguinity in Japan and Korea: Focusing on Adopted Children and Inheritance", *Asia-keizai*, 16(2): 60-72.

Hattori, Tamio. 1976. "A View of Korean and Japanese Family: Concerning '*Studies of Korean Rural Society*' by Choi Jai-Seok", *Asia-keizai* 17(3): 77-83.

Hattori, Tamio. 1976. "(Book review) Lee Kwang-Kyu, *An Analysis into the Structure of Korean Family* (1975)", *Asia-keizai* 17(10).

Hattori, Tamio. 1977. "(Book Review) '*An Analysis into the Structure of Korean Family*'(1975) by Lee Kwang-Kyu", *The Japanese Journal of Ethnology* 41(4): 395-397.

Hattori, Tamio. 1978. Hattori Tamio, Uyama Hiroshi, "Management Senses of Korean Jaebeol Owners: Findings Report (Special Issue: The Current Situation of Korean Economy)", *Asia-keizai* 19(7).

Hattori, Tamio. 1978. tr., Lee Kwang-Kyu, *An Analysis into Family Structure of Korea.* Kokushokankokai Co. Ltd.

Hattori, Tamio. 1979. "(Book Review) '*Studies of the Ruling Class of Choson*'(1977) by Kim Yeongmo", *Asia-keizai* 20(8): 114-116.

Hattori, Tamio. 1979. "What Is Korean Style Management? - in Comparison With Japanese Management (The Latest Korean Report for Japanese Companies)", *Chuo-koron Management Issues* 18(6).

Hattori, Tamio. 1980. "(Book Review) *'A Comparative Study of Industrial Technology of Japan, China, and Korea: An Approach From the Perspective of the Comparative Theory of Technology'* by Moritani Masanori", *Asia-keizai* 21(10): 116-121.

Hattori, Tamio. 1980. "How Far has Korea Come?: The Living Standard in the 1970's", *Korea Review* 22(217): 11-24.

Hattori, Tamio. 1980. "Marital Relations of Noble Yangban in the Late Choson Era: Formation and the Meaning of Sub-Lineage Union", *Asia-keizai* 21(6): 22-56.

Hattori, Tamio. 1982. "About the Possession of Stocks by Korean Jaebeols", *The Social Science: Bulletin of the Institute for the study of Humanities and Social Sciences, Doshisha University* 30: 122-169.

Hattori, Tamio. 1982. "Formation of Business Elite in Korea", *The Monthly Journal of the Japan Institute of Labour* 24(2): 77-90.

Hattori, Tamio. 1982. "Management Environment of Korea: Its Features and Challenges", *International Economy* 19(9): 96-99.

Hattori, Tamio. 1983. "Ah! Yangban's Senses: After Reading *'Folk Tale of Hypocaust'* by Yun Hakjun", *Chosen-kenkyu* 230: 40-45.

Hattori, Tamio. 1984. "(Book Review) *'Managemental Characteristics of Korean Companies'* by O Jongseok", *Asia-keizai* 25(1): 103-105.

Hattori, Tamio. 1984. "Korean Companies: What Is the Differences From Japan? (Including Data) Three-cornered Talk by Toba Kin'ichiro, Hattori Tamio and Tamaki Motoi", *Gendai-korea* 241.

Hattori, Tamio. 1984. "Ownership and Management of Modern Korean Companies: Focusing on Jaebeol Conglomerates", *Asia-keizai* 25(5/6): 132-150.

Hattori, Tamio. 1984. "Stockholders Structure of Listed Companies in Korea: 1981-1982", *Asia-keizai* 25(7): 70-80.

Hattori, Tamio. 1985. "The Role of Jaebeols in Korea's Economic Development (including Comments) (Challenges of Modern International Economy:

International Finance and Open Markets [The 43rd All-Japan Conventions of the Japan Society of International Economics]) (Free Theme)", *International Economy* 36.

Hattori, Tamio. 1985. "Politics and Economy", in Ito Abito ed., *Let's Know About Korea More.* (233-260), Tokyo: Kobun-do.

Hattori, Tamio. 1986. Sakurai Hiroshi, Hattori Tamio, "The Republic of Korea (Developing Region Studies in Japan 1978~85, Region Part 〔Including Documents List〕) (East Asia)", *Asia-keizai* 27(9-10).

Hattori, Tamio. 1987. Hattori Tamio, Takuki Masayuki, *Research Data on Korean Political Elite* (Asian Studies Documentation Series Vol. 52), Institute for Oriental Culture, University of Tokyo.

Hattori, Tamio. 1987. *Structure of Development* (Asian Industrialization Series 2). Institute of Developing Economies.

Hattori, Tamio. 1988. *Management Development of Korea.* Bunshin-do.

Hattori, Tamio. 1991. "An Attempt of the Theory of Network (Ⅰ): Human Relationship and Power in the Choson Dynasty Era", *Asia-keizai* 32(6): 59-82.

Hattori, Tamio. 1991. "An Attempt of the Theory of Network (Ⅱ): Marital Relation of Andong-Kims in the late Choson Dynasty Era Vol. 1", *Asia-keizai* 32(9): 64-92.

Hattori, Tamio. 1991. "An Attempt of the Theory of Network (Ⅲ): Marital Relation of Andong-Kims in the late Choson Dynasty Era Vol. 1", *Asia-keizai* 32(10): 45-103.

Hattori, Tamio. 1992. "Jaebeol of East Asia Now (1) Korea: The Limitation of the Family Rule which Realized Rapid Growth: Change Into Highly Developed Country and A Shift in Generations", *Sekai-shuho* 73(31).

Hattori, Tamio. 1992. *Korea: Network and Political Culture.* Tokyo: University of Tokyo Press.

Hattori, Tamio. 1993. "An Aspect of Choson Society: An Approach From Human Relationship (Special Issue: Continuity and Conversion in Choson's Modern History)", *Chosen-shi-kenkyu-kai-ronbun-shu* 31.

Hattori, Tamio. 1994. "Possession and Management of Korean Jaebeol -The 2nd Essay", *The Journal of Tokyo Keizei University* 188.

Hattori, Tamio. 1995. "30 Years of Economic Ties Between Japan and Korea Vol. 1 (Special Issue: The Current Situation of Japan-Korea Relationship)", *Gendai-korea* 357.

Hattori, Tamio. 1996. Hattori Tamio, Sato Yukihito, *The Mechanism of Development in Korean and Taiwan.* (Kenkyu-sosho: No.464), Institute of Developing Economies.

Hattori, Tamio. 1999. "Dissolution of Jaebeols and Continuation of Management: Experience of Dissolution of Zaibatsu in Japan", *Hyoron: Shakai-kagaku* 59.

Hattori, Tamio. 2000. "Economic Development and the Union of the Same Surname: Focusing on Korean Society", in Yoshihara Kazuo, Suzuki Masataka, Suenari Michio eds., *Reconstruction of Blood Ties: Priority of the Paternal Line and the Union of the Same Surname in East Asia.* Fukyo-sha.

Hattori, Tamio. 2001. "Problems Concerning the Social Development of South Korea", *Doshisha Review of Sociology* (5).

Hattori, Tamio. 2001. "Formation and Transformation of Japanese and Korean Conglomerate Groups (An Institutional Approach to Korea's Economic Crisis: A Comparative Study of Development of Conglomerates of Japan and Korea)", *NIRA Policy Research* 14(9).

Hattori, Tamio. 2001. Matsumoto Koji, Hattori Tamio, *Dissection of Korean Economy.* Bunshin-do.

Hattori, Tamio. 2001. Meaning and Challenges of Korean Society Studies (Special Issue: Japan Seen From Modern Asia)", *Sociological Review of Kobe University* 18.

Hattori, Tamio. 2002. Hattori Tamio, Funazu Tsuruyo, Torii Takashi, *Formation and Features of Asian Middle Classes* (Kenkyu-sosho: No.521). Institute of Developing Economies, Japan External Trade Organization.

Hattori, Tamio and Omichi, Yasunori. 1985. *Korean Companies: People and Management.* Tokyo: Nihon Keizai Shimbun.

Hattori, Tamio and Uyama, Hiroshi. 1978. "Management Senses of Owners of Korean Jaebeols: Findings Report", *Asia-keizai* 19(7): 69-81.

Hattori, Tamio ed. 1987. *Korea's Industrialization: Composition of Development.*

Tokyo: Asia-keizai Publishing.

Hayashi, Fumiki. 1994. "Change of Korean Folk Events", *Gendai-Korea* 339: 2-3.

Hayashi, Fumiki. 1997. "Family in Korean Circus: Structure and Strategy of Moving Groups", *Doshisha Review of Sociology*, 1st Issue. (51-65), Doshisha University Sociology Society.

Hayashi, Fumiki. 1998. "Development Process of Korean Circus - in the Stream of Moving Entertainments Groups", *Kikan-minzokugaku* 83: 104-109.

Hayashi, Fumiki. 1999. "A Brief History of Studies on Korean Markets", in Asakura Toshio ed., Murayama Chijun, *A Study of Korean Market.* (235-252), Tokyo: Kokusho-kanko-kai.

Hayashi, Fumiki. 1999. "Bibliography of Studies on Korean Markets", in Asakura Toshio ed., Murayama Chijun, *A Study of Korean Market.* (253-273), Tokyo: Kokusho-kanko-kai.

Hayashi, Fumiki. 1999. "Life Strategy of Peddlers in Korea and Its Change", (Institute for the Culture of Travel), *Study Report of Institute for the Culture of Travel* 8: 127-138.

Hayashi, Fumiki. 2000. "Trip and the Life of Trip", *Mahora* 24: 40-41, Institute for the Culture of Travel.

Hayashi, Fumiki. 2002. "(Conference report): Impressions of 〈Joint International Conference for the Commemoration of the 100th Anniversary of Korean Immigration to the United States〉", *The Japanese Journal of Ethnology.* 67(2).

Hayashi, Fumiki. 2002. "*Social History of Markets* by Jeong Seongmo et al.", *Studies and Culture of Korea.* Hosei-daigaku-shuppan-kyoku.

Heo, Kwang-Mo. 2000. "The Lower Classes in Pre-war Kyoto and an Inflow of Choson People", *Korean-Minority Studies* 4.

Hidemura, Kenji. 1987. "A Memorandum about Fictive Kinship of Korea", *Common Culture* 10: 55-67, (Seijo University Graduate School of Japanese Common Culture Student Council).

Hidemura, Kenji. 1990. "Christianity and Traditional Culture in Korean Society", *Shakaigaku-Journal* 28(2): 147-170.

Hidemura, Kenji. 1992. "Church and Women: An Aspect of Korean Christianity",

Meisei University Studies Bulletin 28: 13-20.

Hidemura, Kenji. 1994. "Shamanism in Christianity", *Korean Culture,* (Aug.) 8-12.

Hidemura, Kenji. 1995. "Christianity in Modern Korean Society", in Tanabe Shigeharu ed., *Rebirth of Religions in East Asia: Politics of Religious Experiences.* Kyoto: Kyoto University Press.

Hidemura, Kenji. 1995. "The Present of Korean Christianity and Its Understanding", *Annual Report of Social Anthropology* 21: 79-100.

Hidemura, Kenji. 1996. "Christianity of Korea: Focusing on the Period up to 1945", in Harajiri Hideki, Rokutanda Yutaka eds., *Countries of Peninsula and Archipelago.* (131-156), Tokyo: Shinkan-sha.

Hidemura, Kenji. 1998. "Between Confucianism and Shamanism: Christianity in Korean Society (Report of Workshop in 1998) (Workshop (2) The Acceptance of Christianity in East Asia", *Religion and Society.* (Extra Number) 1998.

Hidemura, Kenji. 1998. "People Who Do not Tell They Are 'Yangban': Research on Fishing Village in Korean East Coast in the middle of 1980's", in Shima Mutsuhiko, Asakura Toshio eds., *Changing Korean Society: From the Field of Research of Anthropology in the 1970's~80's.* (185-222), Tokyo: Daiichi-shobo.

Hidemura, Kenji. 1998. "Social Change and Christianity in Modern South Korean Society" in Shima, Mutsuhiko and Roger L. Janelli, eds., *The Anthropology of Korea: East Asian Perspectives* (Senri Ethnological Studies 49), (111-127), Osaka: Kokuritsu-minzokugaku-hakubutsukan.

Hidemura, Kenji. 1999. "From Accepted Christianity to Missionizing Christianity: Concerning the Development of Korean Christianity", *Chosen Bunka-kenkyu* 6.

Hidemura, Kenji. 1999. "Ministers and Church: Originality of Korean Christianity", Mio Yuko, Honda Hiroshi eds., *Multi-Centrality of Culture in East Asia.* Research Institute for Languages and Cultures of Asia and Africa, Tokyo University of Foreign Studies.

Hidemura, Kenji. 2000. "Korean Society and Culture", "Religious Culture in Korea", in Yoshida Mitsuo ed., *History and Society of Korea.* The Society for the Promotion of the Open University.

Hidemura, Kenji. 2000. "Special Issue 2, Seoul with Historical Scent", Kuwano Eiji, Tsukiashi Tatsuhiko, Hidemura Kenji et al., *Gekkan-shinika* 13(7) (Serial number 149).

Hidemura, Kenji. 2001. "Walking in Korea (1) In the Village Toward East Sea", *Asia Yugaku* (24).

Higa, Masao. 1991. "Clans of Korea and Okinawa: An Introduction to Comparative Studies", Naha: Okinawa-kenritsu-geijutsu-daigaku-ryu-kan-densho-bunka-chosa-dan, *A Study of Korean Traditional Culture: A Comparative Study with Okinawa*, 51-58.

Higa, Masao. 1996. "Comparative Theory of Folk Customs of Social Structure of Regions Around China Sea: Structure and Formation of Clans of Korea and Okinawa", *Nicchu-bunka-kenkyu* 9.

Higaki, Ko. 1984. "Ancestor Worship of Japan and Korea", *Esoteric Culture* 145: 1-33.

Higaki, Ko. 1984. "Confucian Feature of Hupo-ri and Ancestor Worship of Japan and Korea", Joint Research Group on Fishing Communities of Japan and Korea, *Japan-Korea Joint Research Report Vol. 2: Hupo-ri, Pyeonghae-up, North Gyeongsang Province in Korea.* (159-189), Kobe: Joint Seminar of Fishing Community of Japan and Korea Office.

Higaki, Ko. 1986. "A Study of Ancestor Worship in Jangjwa-ri, Wando-up, Wando-gun in South Jeolla Province", *Japan-Korea Joint Research Report Vol. 4 : Wando-gun in South Jeolla Province of Korea.* (163-185), Kobe: Joint Seminar of Fishing Community of Japan and Korea Office.

Higuchi, Atsushi. 1990. Higuchi Atsushi, Nam Bujin and Kim Miyeong, "Korean Village and Old Tale", *Monthly Report of Senshu University Research Institute for Social Science* 318.

Higuchi, Atsushi. 2001. "Issues surrounding 〈A Study of a Tale of Brothers Throwing Gold〉", *Senshu Humanities Treatises* 69.

Higuchi, Setsuo. 1986. "The City System of Korea and Change of Seoul", *Geography* 31(12): 18-25.

Hinata, Kazumasa. 1992. "'Niga-byaku-do (Redeeming Road to the Pure Land Between the River and the Fire)' and Korean Shamanism Rites: By the Medium of Mukaekou, Jodo Garden, and Noh Song 'Pontoon Bridge'",

Meiji University Research Institute for the Humanities Bulletin 32.

Hinata, Kazumasa. 1993. " 'Niga-byaku-do (Redeeming Road to the Pure Land Between the River and the Fire)' and Korean Shamanism Rites 2", *Meiji University Research Institute for the Humanities Bulletin* 34.

Hinata, Kazumasa. 1994. " 'Niga-byaku-do (Redeeming Road to the Pure Land Between the River and the Fire)' and Korean Shamanism of Rites of Departed Soul in Korea", *Japanese Scientific Monthly* 47(12).

Hioki, Koichiro. 1983. "Cultural Differences of Organizational Behavior: An Attempt of Comparison of Japan and Korea", (Hioki Koichiro, O Jongseok), *Organizational Science* 17(1): 37-47.

Hiraki, Makoto. 1982. " 'Samganghaengsildo Vol. 2' and Edification (Photo print 'Samganghaengsildo Vol. 2')", (Hiraki Makoto Bibliographical Comment). *Chosen-gakuho* 105.

Hiraki, Makoto. 1986. "Korea Mission History of Tenrism in the Meiji Era", *Chosen-gakuho* 119-120.

Hiraki, Makoto. 1986. "The Belief in the Deity of Heaven in Korea: Concerning the Translational Term for Oyagami, Kami", *Tenri University Journal* 151.

Hiraki, Makoto. 1987. *A Study of Social Cultural History of Choson*. Tokyo: Kokushokankokai Co. Ltd.

Hiraki, Makoto. 1990. "Senses of Divine Chastisement Concerning Drought and Society during Jungjong and Myeongjong era of Choson", *Chosen-gakuho* 134.

Hiraki, Makoto. 1991. "About Regalia in Korean Peninsula: Focusing on Choson Dynasty", Matsubara Masatake ed., *The Position of Regality*. Tokyo: Kobun-do.

Hiraki, Makoto. 1991. "The Regalia in the Choson History: Focusing on Choson Dynasty Era", *Chosen-gakuho* 138.

Hiraki, Makoto. 1995. "The Rite of Wongudan in the Late Choson Era (1)", *Chosen-gakuho* 157.

Hiraki, Makoto. 1998. "Development of Hangeul Culture in the Cultural Area of Chinese Characters", *Gaikokugo-kyoiku* (Tenri University). 24.

Hiraki, Makoto. 1999. "An Aspect of Confucian Education in Country Villages of Choson: About Hyangeumju-uirye and Hyangsa-uirye", *Tenri University Journal* 50(2) 190.

Hiraki, Makoto. 1999. "A Bibliographical Introduction of 'Hyangeumju-yeui-jeol'"(Photo print 'Hyangeumju-yeui-jeol')" *Chosen-gakuho* 172.

Hiraki, Makoto. 1999. tr., "Kim Ingeol, Social Change in the Late Choson Era and Studies of Social History of Country Villages", *Chosen-gakuho* 170.

Hiraki, Makoto. 2000. "The Rite of Wongudan in the Late Choson Era (2): Renaming From 'Wongudan' to 'Namdan'", *Chosen-gakuho* (176-177).

Hiraki, Makoto. 2001. *Study of the History of Korean Society and Culture 2*. Aun-sha.

Hirasawa, Yutaka. 1984. "A Comparative Study of Characters of Fisheries Cooperative Association of Japan and Korea", *Japan-Korea Joint Research Report Vol. 2: Hupo-ri, Pyeonghae-up, North Gyeongsang Province in Korea.* (141-158), Kobe: Joint Seminar of Fishing Community of Japan and Korea Office.

Hirasawa, Yutaka. 1986. "Use of Fishing Grounds for Laver and Brown Seaweed in Wando-gun", *Japan-Korea Joint Research Report Vol. 4 : Wando-gun in South Jeolla Province of Korea.* (37-42), Kobe: Joint Seminar of Fishing Community of Japan and Korea Office.

Hirata, Junji. 1984. "The Movement of Social Folk Customs of Korean Fishing Villages: A Case Study of Keumeum 3-ri, Pyonghae-myeon, Uljing-gun, North Gyeongsang Province", *Japan-Korea Joint Research Report Vol. 2: Hupo-ri, Pyeonghae-up, North Gyeongsang Province in Korea.* (208-231), Kobe: Joint Seminar of Fishing Community of Japan and Korea Office.

Hirata, Junji. 1986. "The Movement of Social Folk Customs of Korean Fishing Villages: A Case Study of Jangjwa-ri, Wando-up, Wando-gun in South Jeolla Province", *Japan-Korea Joint Research Report Vol. 4 : Wando-gun in South Jeolla Province of Korea.* (208-224), Kobe: Joint Seminar of Fishing Community of Japan and Korea Office.

Honda, Hiroshi. 1989. "Economic Development of Villages and the Position of Women: A Comparative Study of Japan and Korea (Special Issue: Japan Seen From Outside [including comments and answers])", Moon

Okpyo, Honda Hiroshi trans. *The Japanese Journal of Ethnology* 54(3).

Honda, Hiroshi. 1993. "Cherishing Memory of Ancestors by the Medium of Graves: A Case Study of a Village in the Southeastern Korea", *The Japanese Journal of Ethnology* 58(2), 142-169.

Honda, Hiroshi. 1994. "Formation and Development of Gaengjeong-Confucianism: Aboriginal Religious Movements of Korea and Creation of Racial Culture", *The Journal of the Department of Liberal Arts* 27: 1-22, The University of Tokyo.

Honda, Hiroshi. 1994. "The Current Situation of the Theory of Korean Family: A Case Study of a Remote Mountain Village in Namwon-gun of South Jeolla Province", *Chosen-gakuho* 152: 109-166.

Honda, Hiroshi. 1995. "Whose is the Folk Art?: An Aspect of Folk Inheritance in Modern Korean Folk Village", *Chosen Bunka-kenkyu* 2: 141-172.

Honda, Hiroshi. 1996. "(Book Review): *'Asian Reader: Korea'* by Ito Abito", *The Japanese Journal of Ethnology* 61(2): 340-341.

Honda, Hiroshi. 1996. "(Book Review): *An Invitation to Korean Folk Customs,* by Choi Kil-sung", *The Japanese Journal of Ethnology* 61(2): 342.

Honda, Hiroshi. 1996. "The Current Situation of Folk Culture in Namwon Province: A Case Study of Two Folk Culture Festivals", *Seikyu-gakujutsu-ronshu* 8: 116-130.

Honda, Hiroshi. 1996. "Trend of Moving of People Between Japan and Korea and Characters of Korean Newcomers", *Seikyu-gakujutsu-ronshu* 8: 246-283.

Honda, Hiroshi. 1998. "The End of Small Farming Community and the Current Situation of Korean Villages: Fieldwork of Namwon(1989～)", in Shima Mutsuhiko, Asakura Toshio eds., *Changing Korean Society: From the Field of Research of Anthropology in the 1970's～80's.* (261-304), Tokyo: Daiichi-shobo.

Honda, Hiroshi. 1999. "Practice and Evaluation of Confucian Norms: A Case Study of Awarding of Confucian Schools in Namwon of the Southwestern Korea", Mio Yuko, Honda Hiroshi eds., *Multi-Centrality of Culture in East Asia.* Research Institute for Languages and Cultures of Asia and Africa, Tokyo University of Foreign Studies.

Honda, Hiroshi. 1999. Hyangsin Group and Cultural Tradition in Korean Local Eup: Trend of Urbanization and Local Authority in Namwon-up during the Colonial Period", *Asia-africa-gengo-bunka-kenkyu* 58.

Honda, Hiroshi. 1999. (Mio Yuko, Honda Hiroshi eds.,) *Multi-Centrality of Culture in East Asia.* Research Institute for Languages and Cultures of Asia and Africa, Tokyo University of Foreign Studies.

Honda, Hiroshi. 2001. Mio Yuko, Honda Hiroshi eds., *Multi-Centrality of Culture in Eas tAsia.* Fukyo-sha, (Asian Study Report Series No.3).

Honda, Hiroshi. 2002. "(Book Review), *Yangban: A Cultural Anthropological Study of Changing Korean Society*, by Okada Hiroki", *The Japanese Journal of Ethnology* 67(3).

Honda, Hiroshi. 2003. "Korean Villages and Towns (Special Issue: The Depths of Korea)", *Chiri* 48(3) 571.

Honda, Yasuji. 1978. "Korean Festivals and Deity's Place", *Entertainment* 20(8): 31-33.

Honda, Yasuji. 1982. "Korean Entertainment", *Asia Review* 11(2): 60-75.

Hong, Hyeon-Su. 1994. " 'Distinction Between Men and Women' in the Current Public Textbooks of Korea: Change in Honorific Expressions in Conjugal Conversation", *Annual Report* 8: 63-77, The Institute for Women's Studies at Ochanomizu University.

Hong, Hyeon-Su. 1996. " 'Distinction Between Men and Women' in Textbooks of Korean Elementary Schools", *Ningen-bunka-kenkyu-nenpo* 19: 178-187, Ochanomizu University.

Hong, Hyeon-Su. 2001. "Family Situation Surrounding Youth: Focusing on Educational Favor and Relations Between Mother and Child: (Special Issue: The Situations of Korean Youth)", *Gekkan: kankoku-bunka* 263.

Hori, Ichiro. 1970. "The Religion Situation of Korea", *Mirai* 50: 2-10.

Hwan, Lucy. 1999. "Dramatic Parts of Shaman Kut by Moo-dang", Suzuki Masataka, Nomura Shinichi eds., *A Study of Masks and Shamanism: Japan and Korea.* Daiichi-shobo.

Hwang, Eun-Cha. 1995. "The Trend of Women's Studies in Korea", *Asia-josei-kenkyu* 4: 83-87.

Hwang, Hye-Seong and Ishige, Naomichi. 1988. *Korean Food.* Tokyo: Heibon-sha.

Hwang, P'ae-Kang. 1991. *Korean Myth and Legend.* Tokyo: Toho-shoten.

Hyon, Yong-Chun. 1972. "Shamanism of Jeju Island: Complex Belief Seen through Ceremonial Forms", *The Japanese Journal of Ethnology* 36(4): 269-279.

Hyon, Yong-Chun. 1975. "Sinbang of Jeju Island", *Etonos* 3.

Hyon, Yong-Chun. 1977. "The Ritual of Mourning of Jeju Island: A Case Study of K Village", *The Japanese Journal of Ethnology* 42(3): 249-266.

Hyon, Yong-Chun. 1985. *A Study of Shamanism of Jeju Island.* Tokyo: Daiichi-shobo.

Hyon, Yong-Chun. 1990. "The Function of the Myth of Shaman Song in Jeju Island", in Abe, Ito, Ogiwara eds., *The World of Ethnic Peoples Vol. 1: Ethnography of Ceremonies and Traditions.* (563-533), Tokyo: Shogakukan.

Hyon, Yong-Chun. 1991. "Deities and Festivals of Jeju Island", *Shizen-to-Bunka* 34.

Ichikawa, Shigeru. 2001. "Change of the Myth of Tamra (Symposium Report Historical Studies and Myths)", *Shiteki* 23.

Ide, Koki. 2000. "A Study of Identity of Korean Japanese: From Stories about Origins", *Bulletin of the Graduate School, Toyo University Graduate program of Sociology* 37.

Iida, Takafumi. 1986. "An Introduction to Choson Temples in Ikoma Mountainous District", *Annual Bulletin on Economics and Social Science. Toyama-daigaku-nihonkai-keizai-kenkyujo*, 12.

Iida, Takafumi. 1989. "Several Forms of Temples of Buddhism and Folk Religion in the Zainichi Korean Communities", *Annual Bulletin on Economics and Social Science, Toyama-daigaku-nihonkai-keizai-kenkyujo.* 15.

Iida, Takafumi. 1994. "Opening Ceremonies of a Zainichi Korean Shamanic Temple and Social Network", *Toyama University Economic Treatises* 39(3).

Iida, Takafumi. 2000. "Religious Tradition and Development of Christianity: From the Perspective of Comparison Between Korea and Japan", in Kobayashi Takayuki ed., *Changing Modern Korean Society.* Sekai-shiso-sha.

Iida, Takafumi. 2002. "Cultural Creation and Traditions of Zainichi Koreans" (Special Issue Overseas Compatriots and Their Culture), *Gekkan:*

kankoku-bunka 274.

Iida, Takafumi. 2002. "Religions of Zainichi Koreans: The Process of Cultural Creation" (Special Issue: Zainichi Koreans in History: Thinking About the Meaning of Zainichi Koreans From the Perspective of Past, Present, and Future of East Asia)(Life Environment of Zainichi Koreans), *Kan: History, Environment, Civilization.* 11.

Iida, Takafumi. 2002. *Religions and Festivals of Zainichi Koreans*. Sekai-shiso-sha.

Ijichi, Noriko. 1997. "Living History, Selected Word: The Filed work in Jeju Island and Osaka", *Jinbun-Ronso* (Graduate School of Literature and Human Sciences, Osaka City University) 25: 29-44.

Ijichi, Noriko. 2000. "Life Practice Essay in Daily Life: From the Experiences in Modern Korea and Jeju Island", in Kobayashi Takayuki ed., *Changing Modern Korean Society.* (188-211), Kyoto: Sekaishisosha.

Im, Tong-Kwon. 1990. "Folk Customs of Distribution", Takeda Akira ed., *Development and Challenges of Folklore.* Tokyo: Kokushokankokai Co. Ltd.

Im, Tong-Kwon. 1994. "Village Festivals of Korea and Traditional Thought", *Koreana* 7(1).

Imamura, Minoru. 1998. "Events of New Year's Day of Kangwon Province of Korea Seen from Tottori Province, Japan", *Studies of the culture in North-East Asia* (Tottori Women's College) 7: 29-51.

Imamura, Minoru. 1998. "Marriage System in Kangwon Province of Korea", *Studies of the culture in North-East Asia* (Tottori Women's College) 8: 45-69.

Inaba, Tsugio. 1982. "Confucian Influences Seen in the Names of Korean Places", *The World of Geographical Names: Chiri* (Extra Edition), 162-163.

Inaba, Tsugio. 1998. "The History of Relations Between Japan-Korea and Japan-North Korea From the Perspective of Korea and North Korea: An Analysis into History Textbooks of High Schools", Ebuchi Kazuhiro ed., *A Study of Trans-culturalism.* Tokyo: Akashi-shoten.

Inaduki, Tadasi. 1997. "Local Community and Racial Relation: The Intention of Union or Separation Between Japanese and Zainichi Koreans", Okuda Michihiro ed., (Urban Sociology Studies Library 7) *Sociology of Urban*

Ethnicity: The Meaning of Race, Culture, and Coexistence. Kyoto: Minerva-shobo.

Inafuku, Mikiko. 1991. "About Maturing Process of Korean Shamanic Workers", *A Study of Korean Traditional Culture: From the Perspective of Comparison with Okinawa.* (23-34), Naha: Okinawa-kenritsu-geijutsu-daigaku-ryu-kan-densho-bunka-chosa-dan.

Ishige, Naomichi and Ruddle, Kenneth. 1987. "(Asian Markets) Korean Fair 'Jangsi'", *Kikan-minzokugaku* 39: 102-113.

Ishige, Naomichi ed. 1981. *Food Culture of East Asia.* Tokyo: Heibon-sha.

Itagaki, Ryuta. 1999. "Literacy Investigation in the Colonial Choson", *Studies for Languages and Cultures of Asia and Africa, Tokyo University of Foreign Studies* 58.

Itagaki, Ryuta. 2000. "Bureaucracy and Villages in the Movement for Village Development: Focusing on Documentalism", *Chosen-gakuho* 175.

Itagaki, Ryuta. 2000. Im Jihyeon, Itagaki Ryuta trans., "Opinions About Korean Nationalism and Power: Questions of Comparative History (Special Issue: Post-Cold-War and East Asia)", *Modern Thought* 28(7).

Itagaki, Ryuta. 2001. Kim Seongrye : Itagaki Ryuta trans. "Politics of National Violence and Sex: Focusing on Jeju 4.3 Genocide (Special Issue: The Memory of Racial Panic and Emigration)", *TRACES* 2.

Itagaki, Ryuta. 2001. Kwon Hyeokbeom : Itagaki Ryuta trans., "Globalization and the Perception of America: Beyond American Hegemony and Racism (Postwar East Asia and the Existence of America: Thinking About the Post Colonial Situation in East Asia)", *Modern Thought* 29(9) (Extra Edition).

Itagaki, Ryuta. 2001. Moon Busik : Itagaki Ryuta trans., " 'Gwangju' After 20 Years: Historical Memory and Human Memory (Postwar East Asia and the Existence of America: Thinking About the Post Colonial Situation in East Asia)", *Modern Thought* 29(9) (Extra Edition).

Itagaki, Ryuta. 2002. "Ordinary Schools and Local Communities During the Colonial Period: Focusing on a School in Sangju, North Gyeongsang Province", *Chosen-shi-kenkyu-kai-ronbun-shu* (40).

Itaya, Toru. 1984. "Entertaining Feature of Korean Shamanism: A Case Study of the East Coast Area" Geinou-shi-kenkyu 86: 1-41.

Ito, Abito.(Itoh, Abito) 1973. "An Aspect of Korean Farming Community: A Case Study of Jindo in South Jeolla Province", in Nakane Chie ed., *Family and Rites of Korean Village.* University of Tokyo Press.

Ito, Abito. 1973. "An Aspect of Korean Farming Community: A Case Study of Jindo in South Jeolla Province", *Toyo-bunka* 53: 147-159.

Ito, Abito. 1977. "A Comment on 'Priest Structure of Memorial Service for the Dead in Korea' by Sato Nobuyuki", *Kikan-jinruigaku* 8(1): 141-142.

Ito, Abito. 1977. "An Analysis into Chinhan-sai Seen Through Gye System: A Study of Village Structure of Jindo in South Jeolla Province", *The Japanese Journal of Ethnology* 41(4): 281-299.

Ito, Abito. 1977. "Gye in the Korean Farming Community: A Case Study of the Village in Jindo, South Jeolla Province", *The Memoirs of the Institute for Oriental Culture, University of Tokyo* 71: 167-230.

Ito, Abito. 1977. tr. With Shima, *Social Characters of Korean People.* by Choi Jai-Seok, Gakusei-sha.

Ito, Abito. 1978. "Japanese Festivals and Urbanization", *Asian Review* 7(9): 120-122.

Ito, Abito. 1979. tr. With Shima, *Studies of Korean Farming Community.* by Choi Jai-Seok, Gakusei-sha.

Ito, Abito. 1980. "Tradition of Yangban and the Lower Classes: Cultural Anthropological Studies of Korean Society", *Chuo-koron* 95(4): 312-319.

Ito, Abito. 1980. "Yangban Family Seen Through Change of a Head Family", *Gekkan-kankoku-bunka* 2(9): 27-31.

Ito, Abito. 1981. tr. With Shima, *A Study of a Korean Village of the Same Clan.* by Kim Taek-Kyu, Gakusei-sha.

Ito, Abito. 1982. "Jar and Housewife: The Territory of Women in Korean Village", *Kikan-minzokugaku* 24: 26-35.

Ito, Abito. 1982. "Korean Peninsula", in Sofue Takao, Hoshino Hirokazu eds., *Anthropology for Social Studies Vol. 1.* (134-159), Tokyo: Tokyo Horei Publishing Co. Ltd.

Ito, Abito. 1983. "Jar for Ancestor Spirits: Social Implication of Household in Rural Korea", *East Asian Cultural Studies* 22(1-4): 187-204.

Ito, Abito. 1983. "Social Background of Confucian Rites: A Case Study of a Village in Jindo, South Jeolla Province", in Ebuchi Kazuhiro, Ito Abito eds., *Ceremonies and Symbols: Cultural Anthropological Study.* (415-442), Fukuoka: Kyusyu University Press.

Ito, Abito. 1984. "Modernization and Tradition of Korea Reconsidered", in Kokugakuin-daigaku-nihon-bunka-kenkyu-jo ed., *Rediscovery of Asian Culture: Toward Comparative National Literature.* (112-119), Tokyo: Kobun-do.

Ito, Abito. 1985. "Food and Culture", *Food.* University of Tokyo Press (Tokyo University Open Lecture 41).

Ito, Abito. 1985. "Seoul and Korean Cities: A Huge Capital and the Growth of Local Cities", *Weekly Asahi Hyakka, 483* (World Geography 77 China, East Asia: Korea) 177-181.

Ito, Abito. 1985. ed., *Let's Know More About Korea.* Tokyo: Kobun-do.

Ito, Abito. 1986. "Korean Peninsula", in Japanese Society of Ethnology ed., *Japanese Ethnology 1964-1983.* (186-188), Tokyo: Kobun-do.

Ito, Abito. 1986. "Legitimacy and Aboriginality: Choson Folk Culture and an Aspect of Syncretism in Modern Korea", *Cultural Anthropology* 3: 131-147, Kyoto: Academia-shoten.

Ito, Abito. 1986. "Women in the Korean Traditional Society", in Institute for Research on Christian Culture, University of the Sacred Heart Tokyo ed., *Women and Civilization.* (134-158), Tokyo: Shunju-sha.

Ito, Abito. 1986. (Ito Abito, Omura Masuo, Kajimura Hideki and Takeda Yukio Supervised.,) *A Dictionary About Choson.* Tokyo: Heibon-sha.

Ito, Abito. 1987. "Group and Non-Group in Korean Kinship Organization", in Ito, Sekimoto, Funabiki eds., *Modern Social Anthropology 1: Relatives and Social Structure.* (163-186), Tokyo: University of Tokyo Press.

Ito, Abito. 1987. "Kim Taek-Kyu, Jang Ju-Keun, Lee Kwang-Kyu, Lee Doo-Hyun", *Cultural Anthropology Dictionary.* Tokyo: Kobun-do.

Ito, Abito. 1987. "The Korea Theory From the Perspective of Cultural Anthropology: Human Relations of Korea", *Gendai-Korea* 275.

Ito, Abito. 1987. "Yosakoi Matsuri, A Comparative Study of Chinese and Korean Festivals (Urban Festivals: An Urban Anthropological Study

<Symposium>)", *Kikan-jinruigaku* 18(3).

Ito, Abito. 1989. Ito et al., *Ancient Japan and Korea, 9: Shamanism and Korean culture.* Tokyo: Gakusei-sha.

Ito, Abito. 1990. "Ancestors and the Perception of History in Korea", in Abe, Ito, Ogiwara eds., *The World of Ethnic Peoples Vol. 2, Unity and Movement of Society.* (196-217), Tokyo: Shogakukan.

Ito, Abito. 1991. "Religion and Social Integration in Korea", in Umesao, T., Hardacre, H. & Nakamaki, H. eds. *Senri Ethnological Studies 29.* (87-95), Osaka: National Museum of Ethnology.

Ito, Abito. 1991. "Choson Genealogy", in *Japanese Family Names Lineage Conspectus* (History Reader Special Edition), (448-451), Tokyo: Shin-Jinbutsuoraisha Co. Ltd.

Ito, Abito. 1991. "Korean Kinship System and the Perception of History", *Shiso* 808: 139-151.

Ito, Abito. 1992. "Family Guardian Deity", *Seikyu* 15: 92-99.

Ito, Abito. 1992. "Fishing Boat", Tanikawa Kenichi ed., *Fishing-Boat People: Fishing Boat and Itoman* (Data Collection of Japanese Folk Culture Vol. 3), San'ichi-shobo.

Ito, Abito. 1992. "Village Schoolhouse", *Seikyu* 14: 117-123.

Ito, Abito. 1992. "Style and Approach of Japanese Studies in Korea", in Befu, Harumi and Joseph Kreiner eds., *Othernesses of Japan: Historical and Cultural Influences on Japan Studies in Ten Countries.* (319-326), Philipp: Franz-von-Siebold: Stiftung Deutsches Institute fu'r Japanstudien.

Ito, Abito. 1992. The Perception of History in Korea and Japan", in Chian, Jiao ed., *Home Bound: The Study of East Asian Societies* (Symposium in Honor of Professor Fei Hsiao-tung's 80th Birthday). (167-177), Hong Kong: University of Hong Kong Press.

Ito, Abito. 1993. "Coordination and Brokerage: Leadership in Community Development in Rural Korea.", International Conference on Korean Studies in East Asian Anthropology 1992. National Museum of Ethnology.

Ito, Abito. 1993. (Book Review) "*Countries and Society of East Asia(4) Korea: Network and Political Culture* by Hattori Tamio", *Asia-keizai* 34(10).

Ito, Abito. 1993. "Folk Belief of Jindo: Concerning Mountains", *Seikyu* 16: 98-105.

Ito, Abito. 1993. "Folk Belief of Jindo: Maegwi and Method", *Seikyu* 17: 88-93.

Ito, Abito. 1993. "Messianism in Modern Times", *Modern Times and Toynbee* 82: 6-9.

Ito, Abito. 1993. "Pilgrimage and Ancestors in Korea", *Sinika* 9: 26-27.

Ito, Abito. 1993. "Religions and Social Integration in Choson", in Umesao Tadao, Nakamaki Hirochika eds., *Comparative Studies of Civilization of Religion.* (191-216), Tokyo: Shunju-sha.

Ito, Abito. 1993. "Society and Confucianism of East Asia: Prospect of Korean Ethnography", in Mizoguchi Yuzo, Hamashita Takeshi, Hiraishi Naoaki, Miyajima Hiroshi eds., *Mixing Asia,(Thinking in Asia), 1.* (53-76), Tokyo: University of Tokyo Press.

Ito, Abito. 1993. *Community Development and Cultural Tradition in Korea.* East Asian Regional Conference 1993. Japan Society for International Development.

Ito, Abito. 1994. "Earthenware in Villages of Jindo", *Seikyu* 19: 140-147.

Ito, Abito. 1994. "Sutra-Chanting Person", *Seikyu* 20: 98-108.

Ito, Abito. 1994. "Tradition of Taoism in Korean Folk Belief", *Chosen-bunka-kenkyu* 1: 179-191.

Ito, Abito. 1995. "Events of New Year's Day in Jindo", *Seikyu* 21: 84-91.

Ito, Abito. 1995. "Geomancy", *Seikyu* 22: 92-99.

Ito, Abito. 1995. "Gye (1) Public Gye of Village", *Seikyu* 23: 102-109.

Ito, Abito. 1995. "Gye (2) Voluntary Gye", *Seikyu* 24: 150-157.

Ito, Abito. 1995. "Jip and Family", *Korean Culture* 17: 19-24.

Ito, Abito. 1995. "Prospect of Choson Studies From the Perspective of Cultural Anthropology", *Chosen-gakuho* 156: 1-12.

Ito, Abito. 1995. "Roots of Modern Korean Culture", *Creo* Vol. 1, 42-47.

Ito, Abito. 1995. "Use of Earthenware in Korean Village", in Yoshida Shuji ed., *Anthropology of Life Technique.* (168-184), Tokyo: Heibon-sha.

Ito, Abito. 1996. "Folk Customs of Choson and Modern Life", *History and Culture of Choson.* Tokyo: The Society for the Promotion of The University of the Air.

Ito, Abito. 1996. "Korea, Choson", in Josef Kreiner ed., *Japanese Ethnology.*

(238-251), Tokyo: Shin-yo-sha.

Ito, Abito. 1996. "Korean Mountains and Culture", *Korean Culture* (Special Issue: Korean Mountains and Culture) (1996.7): 2-7.

Ito, Abito. 1996. "Korean Religions and Folk Belief", *History and Culture of Korea.* Tokyo: The Society for the Promotion of The University of the Air.

Ito, Abito. 1996. "Saemaul Movement and Folk Culture", *Seikyu* (Seikyu-bunka-sha) 24: 128-135.

Ito, Abito. 1996. *Asian Reader: Korea.* Tokyo: Kawade Shobo Shinsha Publishers.

Ito, Abito. 1997. "Centricity and Peripherality in the Space Perception of Korea", in Suenari Michio ed., *Current Situation of East Asia: An Attempt of Anthropological Studies.* (55-73), Tokyo: Fukyo-sha.

Ito, Abito. 1997. ed., *Let's Know More About Korea 1.* Second Edition, Kobun-do.

Ito, Abito. 1998. "Coordination and Brokerage: Leadership in Community Development in Rural Korea", in Shima, Mutsuhiko and Roger L. Janelli, eds., *The Anthropology of Korea: East Asian Perspectives* (Senri Ethnological Studies 49), (157-170), Osaka: National Museum of Ethnology.

Ito, Abito. 1998. "Farming Life in Jindo and Its Change", in Shima Mutsuhiko, Asakura Toshio eds., *Changing Korean Society: From the Field of Research of Anthropology in the 1970's~80's.* (39-86), Tokyo: Daiichi-shobo.

Ito, Abito. 1999. "History and the Current Situation of Korean Religious Culture", *Voyages into History, Literature and Thought* 30: 83-89.

Ito, Abito. 1999. "Lecture Record 'Korean Development and Korean Limitations: Its Culture and Social Background'", *Japan-Korea Economic Association Report.* 326.

Ito, Abito. 1999. *Travelogue of Folk Customs of Korean Jindo Island.* Tokyo: Seikyu-bunka-sha.

Ito, Abito. 2000. "Cultural Anthropology (2): Current Situation and Prospect of Choson and Korean Studies (Prospect of Eastern Studies in 21st Century)", *Toho-gaku* 100.

Ito, Abito. 2000. "Principle of Patrilineal Blood Relationship and Modern Connection: Concerning Korean Society", Yoshihara Kazuo, Suzuki

Masataka, Suenari Michio eds., *Reconstruction of Blood Relation: Paternal Origin and Union of the Same Surname in East Asia.* Fukyo-sha.

Ito, Abito. 2000. ed., *A Dictionary About Choson.* (New Revision Supplement), Heibon-sha.

Ito, Abito. 2002. (Ito Abito, Han Gyeonggu eds.,) *A Comparative Study of Korean and Japanese Social Organization.* Keio University Press (Japan-Korea Joint Library : 5).

Ito, Abito. 2003. "Interchange Between Japan and Korea Seen in Ssigim-kut (Special Issue: Interchange Between Japan and Korea in Asia) (Joint Works of Japan and Korea, Solution of Common Issues)", *Kokusai-koryu* 25(2).

Ito, Kaichi. 1980. "International Comparative Cultural Studies Based on the Differences of Senses 2: A Comparative Study Between Japan and Korea", *Bulletin of Tokyo Gakugei University. Section 2, Humanities* 31: 15-25.

Ito, Yoshihide. 2000. "A Comparative Study of Japanese and Korean Festivals: Izaiho, Kangneung-Tano Festival, Eunsan-Byeolsin Festival", Choe Gilseong, Hinata Kazumasa eds., *Myth, Religion, Shamanism: An Attempt of Comparison of Japanese and Korean Culture.* Fukyo-sha.

Iwamoto, Michiya. 1993. "A Comparative Study of Japanese and Korean Symbolic Systems Concerning 'Double Suicide of Parent and Child: An Folk Analysis into Suicidal Cases as Mythological Stories", *Bulletin of the National Museum of Japanese History* 54: 73-144.

Iwamoto, Michiya. 1997. "Symbolism of Capital Castle and Rites of Regalia: A Case Study of Choson", *Bulletin of the National Museum of Japanese History* 74: 135-148.

Izumi, Seiichi. 1965. "Korean Sentimental Journey", *Nippon* 9(1).

Izumi, Seiichi. 1966. "Korean Studies in Korea", *Tosho* 198 (Feb.): 32-36.

Izumi, Seiichi. 1966. *Jeju Island.* Tokyo: The Institute of Oriental Culture, The University of Tokyo.

Izumi, Seiichi. 1968. "The World of Korean Shamanism: Focusing on Korean Shamanism", *Sekai* 267: 224-231.

Izumi, Seiichi. 1969. "A Study of Shamanic Origin", *Toyo-bunka* 46, 47: 55-74.

Izumi, Seiichi. 1970. "A Commentary on 'A Form of Ancient Ceremonies and Myths' Written by Jang Ju-Keun", *Bungaku* 38(11): 159.

Izumi, Seiichi. 1970. "A Study of Teikoku University in the Colonial Period", *Chuo-koron* (Jan.).

Izumi, Seiichi. 1970. "Korean Shamanism", *Chosen-gakuho* 56: 1-12.

Izumi, Seiichi. 1970. "Talk with Kim Seokbeom: Home Town Jeju Island", *Sekai* 293: 245-256.

Izumi, Seiichi. 1970. *Man in the Culture.* Tokyo: Bungei-shunju-sha.

Izumi, Seiichi. 1971. *Mountains in the Distance.* Tokyo: Shincho-sha.

Izumi, Seiichi. 1971. *Works of Izumi Seiichi 6* What is Required to Cultural Anthropology, 397, Tokyo: Yomiuri-shinbun.

Izumi, Seiichi. 1972. *Works of Izumi Seiichi 1* A Record of Fieldwork(1), Tokyo: Yomiuri-shinbun.

Izumi, Seiichi. 1972. *Works of Izumi Seiichi 5* Cultural Anthropology, Journey of Speculation, 385, Tokyo: Yomiuri-shinbun.

Izumi, Seiichi. 1972. *Works of Izumi Seiichi 7* Eyes of Cultural Anthropology, 465, Tokyo: Yomiuri-shinbun.

Jang, Ju-Keun. 1973. *Folk Belief of Korea: Shamanism and Shamanic Songs.* Tokyo: Kinka-sha.

Jang, Ju-Keun. 1982. *Local Belief of Korea.* Matsumoto Seiichi Trans. Tokyo: Daiichi-shobo.

Jeon, Kyoung-Uk. 1999. "Related Aspects of Korean Masque and Ceremonies", Suzuki Masataka, Nomura Shinichi, eds., *A Study of Masks and Shamanism: Japan and Korea.* Daiichi-shobo.

Jeong, A-Young. 2000. *Racial Relations of Choson Race in China.* Japanese Association for Asian Studies.

Jeong, Yoon-Suk. 2000. "Japanese Culture and Korean Youths Crossing the Border: Things Seen in the Culture of Korean Youths: From the Perspective of Japanization of Korean Youth Culture", *Graduate School Treatises 2,* Chukyo University Graduate School of Social Science.

Ji, Young-Im. 2001. "(Book Review) 'Choe Kil-sung, Hinata Kazumasa eds., *Myth, Religion, Shamanism: An Attempt of Comparison of Korean and Japanese Culture.* '2000, Fukyo-sha", *Journal of International Cooperation* 7(2).

Ji, Young-Im. 2002. "Formation of National Cemetery in Modern Korea: Focusing on the Objects of Burial", *The Journal of social and cultural studies on Asia* (3).

Jin, Dae-Chul. 1996. "Cultural Change of Ritual for Ancestor Worship of Zainichi Koreans: A Case Study of Ideal Rites and Modern Rites", *The Japanese Journal of Ethnology* 60(4).

Jin, Dae-Chul. 1999. "Recurrence to Traditional Culture: Revival of Traditional Masque and Regeneration of Masque as Movement of Popular Culture Vol. 1", *Treatises of Chukyo University Graduate School of Social Science* 1.

Jin, Dae-Chul. 2000. "Recurrence to Traditional Culture for 50 Years in Postwar Korea: Revival of Traditional Masque and Regeneration of Masque as Movement of Popular Culture Vol. 2", *Treatises of Chukyo University Graduate School of Social Science* 2.

Jodo, Takuya. 1992. *Forcible Recruitment and Drafting of Korean People.* Tokyo: Shakai-hyoron-sha.

Joo, Nam-Chull. 1994. "Traditional Houses of Seoul", *Koreana* 7(3).

Kabumoto, Chizuru. 1996. "The Way to Die of Modern Korean People: Focusing on Hospice Movement", *East Asian Area Studies* 3: 47-60.

Kabumoto, Chizuru. 1997. "A Comparative Study of Social Welfare of Buddhism in Japan and Korea Vol. 1: Focusing on the Social Welfare of Korean Jogyejong", *Annual Report of Japanese Buddhism Society of Social Welfare* 27: 85-105.

Kabumoto, Chizuru. 1998. "A Comparative Study of Social Welfare of Buddhism in Japan and Korea Vol. 3: Concerning Real Lives of Visitors of Buddhist Welfare Facilities for Elderly", *Annual Report of Japanese Buddhism Society of Social Welfare* 29: 79-105.

Kabumoto, Chizuru. 1998. "Fiction and Reality of Korean Welfare Society", in Nishina Kenichi, Tateno Akira, eds., *New Korean Reader 8 Welfare of Korea: Hope and Reality.* (123-133), Shakai-hyoron-sha.

Kabumoto, Chizuru. 1998. "Korea's Policy of Welfare for Elderly: The Period Until 1980", *Annual Report of Research Institute for Social Works* 34: 1-17.

Kabumoto, Chizuru. 1999. "Hospice Movement of Korea", *NHK Social Welfare*

Seminar 12, (Feb.) 140-145.

Kabumoto, Chizuru. 1999. "Reality and Direction of Korean Social Welfare System", *Gekkan-fukushi* (Apr.) 38-41.

Kabumoto, Chizuru. 2000. (trans) "Current Situation and Problems of Korean Social Workers", Lee Yeongbun, *The Journal of Social Sciences and Humanities* 310: 55-86.

Kabumoto, Chizuru. 2000. (trans) "Overseas Specialist System: Korea", in Soeda Akemi,, Furukawa Kojun, eds., *For Being Social Worker, Mental Health Worker, Care Manager.* (140-143), Seshin-shobo.

Kabumoto, Chizuru. 2000. "Formative Process of Pension Program for the Aged and Elderly Aid System in Korea", *The Journal of Social Sciences and Humanities* 310: 25-53.

Kabumoto, Chizuru. 2000. "Guarantee of Old Age", in Ishizaka Koichi, Tateno Akira eds., *55 Chapters for Understanding Modern Korea.* (68-71), Akashi-shoten.

Kabumoto, Chizuru. 2000. "Hospice Movement of Korea", in Carl Becker ed., *Thought of Care for Life and Death.* (184-204), Hozokan.

Kabumoto, Chizuru. 2000. "Life History of Users of a Nursing Home", in Soeda Yoshiya, Tarukawa Noriko eds., *Modern Society and Family Policy.* (163-193), Minerva-shobo.

Kabumoto, Chizuru. 2000. "Rites of Ancestor Worship and a View of Life and Death", in Ishizaka Koichi, Tateno Akira eds., *55 Chapters for Understanding Modern Korea.* (146-149), Akashi-shoten.

Kabumoto, Chizuru. 2000. "Social Insurance System", in Ishizaka Koichi, Tateno Akira eds., *55 Chapters for Understanding Modern Korea.* (64-67), Akashi-shoten.

Kabumoto, Chizuru. 2000. "The Entry into Society of Handicapped People", in Ishizaka Koichi, Tateno Akira eds., *55 Chapters for Understanding Modern Korea.* (72-75), Akashi-shoten.

Kabumoto, Chizuru. 2000. "Unemployment, Poverty, Hunger: Rediscovery of Undernourished Children in Korea", *Boshi-kenkyu* 20: 61-80.

Kamata, Shigeo. 1980. ed., *Temple and History of Choson Buddhism.* Tokyo: Daihorin-kaku.

Kamata, Shigeo. 1991. *Lecture 5: Acceptance of Buddhism and Change* (Korea Edition), Tokyo: Kosei Publishing Co.

Kameyama, Keiichi. 1977. "A Comparative Study of Japanese and Korean Fishing Folk Customs", *Bulletin of the Folklore Society of Japan* 109: 1-17.

Kameyama, Keiichi. 1978. "Belief of Korean Fishermen: Focusing on Deity for Whom People Enshrine in Ships", *Historical Treatises in Honor of Mr. Namae Yoshio's 60th Birthday.* pp.289-308.

Kameyama, Keiichi. 1983. "About the Character of Deity Whose Rites Are Performed on Fishing Boats in Korea: A Comparative Study with Japan", *Shicho* 14: 69-80.

Kameyama, Keiichi. 1984. "From the Investigation of Fishing Folk Customs of Korea", *Minzokugaku-hyoron* 24: 72-83.

Kameyama, Keiichi. 1985. "Locality of Deity Whose Rites Are Performed on Fishing Boats", *Toho Gakuen College Bulletin* 4: 37-68.

Kameyama, Keiichi. 1986. *Folk Study of Fishing Culture.* Tokyo: Kobun-do.

Kameyama, Keiichi. 1991. "A Comparative Study of Japanese and Korean Deity Whose Rites Are Performed on Ships", *Kikan-shizen-to-bunka* 34.

Kameyama, Keiichi. 1991. "An Attempt of Comparison of Fishermen's Faith", *A Research on Korean Traditional Culture-in Comparison with Okinawa.* Naha: Okinawa-kenritsu-geijutsu-daigaku-ryu-kan-densho-bunka-chosa-dan.

Kamiya, Niji. 1997. *In a Small Village in Korea: Memory of Near Past.* Gaifu-sha.

Kanai, Tenbi. 1972. "Byeolsin-Festival in the Suburbs of Buyeo (Eunsan): Korean Onbashira-Festival", *Kikan-jinruigaku* 3(3): 118-132.

Kanda, Yoriko. 1994. "Shamanic Rites and Confucian Rites of Jeju Island: Men and Women of the Island of Three Manys", in Miyake Hitoshi, Suzuki Masataka eds., *Shamanism and Folk Customs of East Asia.* (197-231), Tokyo: Keiso-shobo.

Kanda, Yoriko. 1994. "Shamanic Rites and Women of Jeju Island", *Center for Women's Studies Journal,* Toyoko Gakuen Women's Junior College 19(1).

Kanda, Yoriko. 1994. "Shamans and Women of Jeju Island", *Gekkan-kankoku-bunka* 719.

Kaneko, Erika. 1963. "Korean Interview", *The Japanese Journal of Ethnology*

27(3): 605-606.

Kang, Myoung-Gu. 1997. "Formation of Labor Culture in Korea-insight and Incorporation of Class Conditions", in Kurihara Akira ed., *Lecture: Sociology of Discrimination (3) Discriminative Structure of the Modern World.* Tokyo: Kobun-do.

Kang, Sin-Hang. 1991. "Regality and Invention of the Korean Script", *Chosen-gakuho* 138: 19-44.

Kasamoto(Miyajima), Mika. 1998. Miyajima Mika, "Ethnic Transnational Actors in East Asia: Focusing upon Transnational Activities of Ethnic Chinese and Ethnic Koreans (Review of International Actors)", *International relations* 119.

Kasamoto(Miyajima), Mika. 1998. Miyajima, Mika "Transnational Education and Scientific Interchange of Choson People Living in Yanbian" Journal of the Japan Sea Rim Studies (4).

Kasamoto(Miyajima), Mika. 2001. Kasamoto Mika "Unification Studies of a Korean Researcher in Yanbian: Focusing on 'Development of the South-North Relations and the Role of Ethnic Koreans in China' and 'Cooperative Relations With Choson People in China and Unification of North and South' Written by Bang Suok", *The Bulletin of the Graduate School of Social Sciences of Waseda University* (Special issue).

Katayama, Takahiro. 1985. "Relativity of Gender: A Cultural Anthropological Study of Korean Confucianism", *Bulletin of the Research Institute of Comparative Education and Culture* 36: 21-40.

Katayama, Takahiro. 1985. "Social Change of Korea and Development of Family Culture: Focusing on the Period after the Second World War", in *An Integrated Comparative Study of Changing Process of Educational Policy in Postwar Asian Countries and Its Social Cultural Basis,* (19-26), Kyushu University Faculty of Education.

Katayama, Takahiro. 1990. "Women and Confucianism in Korea", in Sugiyama Koichi and Sakurai Tetsuo eds., *Kankoku-shakai-no-bunka-jinruigaku.* (159-172), Tokyo: Kobun-do.

Kato, Koichi. 1993. "Farmhouses of Shonai Region of Tohoku District and Farmhouses of North Jeolla Province: A Comparative Study of Management

Risk of Modern Family", *Journal of rural studies* 29: 43-76.

Kato, Kyuzo. 1979. "An Excursive Memorandum on the Dangun Myth", *Japanese Scientific Monthly* 32(7): 32-36.

Kato, Kyuzo. 1991. "Acculturation of Korean People in Central Asia", in Hatanaka Sachiko and Harayama Akira eds., *History and Society of Northeast Asia*. Nagoya: The University of Nagoya Press.

Kato, Takashi. 1985. "Singing and Dancing Shaman", *Kikan-minzokugaku* 9(4).

Kato, Takashi. 1987. "Deities of Grandmothers: An Experience Report of Tano Festival in Kangneung", *Kikan-minzokugaku* 39: 6-26.

Kato, Takashi. 1987. "The 'Kut' of Cow Play: Reviving Festivals of Cow-Play", *Kikan-minzokugaku* 11(4).

Kato, Takashi. 1989. "Festival of Grandma in Yongdeung", *Kikan-minzokugaku* 13(1).

Kato, Takashi. 1990. Kato Takashi et al. *Furniture Decoration of Korea* (Asian Folk Pictures Series). Hirakawa-shuppan-sha.

Kato, Takashi. 1990. *Manshin, Female Shamans: Korean Shamanism*. Tokyo: Hirakawa-shuppan-sha.

Kato, Takashi. 1993. *Feast with Shaman Deities: Korean Shamanic Festivals*. Tokyo: Hirakawa-shuppan-sha.

Kato, Yasushi. 1979. "A Structural Analysis of Two Myths of Jeju Island", *The Japanese Journal of Ethnology* 44(1): 83-90.

Katsuki, Yoichiro. 1996. "Traditional Ships of North Gyeongsang Province of Korea", *Mingu-monthly* 29(3): 6340-6342.

Katsuki, Yoichiro. 1997. "Traditional Ships and Fishery of Brown Seaweed in Rabuk of North Gyeongsang Province: A Research Note of Korean Fishery (1)", *Rekishi-to-minzoku* 14.

Kawa, Kaoru. 1998. "Doyu-kai in the Colonial Choson: A Study of Nationalism During the Colonial Period", *Chosen-shi-kenkyu-kai-ronbun-shu* 36.

Kawa, Kaoru. 2001. "About the Sound Record of Yuhobunko Owned by Gakushuin University Research Institute for Oriental Cultures Gakushuin University", *Archivist* (52).

Kawa, Kaoru. 2001. "Korean Women Under All-Out War (Special Issue: 'Empire', Women in a Colony)", *Rekishi-hyoron* (612).

Kawagoe, Michiko. 2000. "Experiences of Zainichi Koreans: Concerning Called Names and Experiences", *Korean Minority Studies* 4.

Kawahara, Norihumi. 2001. Fujita Akiyoshi - Lee Seonae, Kawahara Norifumi, "Interchange Between Korean Peninsula and Other Areas Seen From Islands: Focusing on Jeju Island", *Seikyu-gakujutsu-ronshu* 19.

Kawakami, Shinji. 1996. "Curer in Korean People in Yanbian of China", *Journal of Religious Studies* 307: 291-292.

Kawakami, Shinji. 1997. "Relations Between Korean Medium Bosal (Bodhisattva) and Ancestors: A Comparative Study of Seoul and Jindo Island in South Jeolla Province", *Kokugakuin-daigaku-kiyo* 35: 31-35.

Kawakami, Shinji. 1997. "Shamanism and Buddhism in Korea: Focusing on Practitioners Called Bosal (Bodhisattva)", *Journal of Religious Studies* 311: 293-294.

Kawakami, Shinji. 1998. "A Study of Shamanic Rites in Modern Korean Society: A Case Study of Jindo in South Jeolla Province", *Journal of Regional Development Studies* (1).

Kawakami, Shinji. 1998. "Ancestors as Objectives of Shamanic Rites in Korea: A Case Study of Jindo in South Jeolla Province", *Komazawa-shukyogaku-kenkyu-kai-shukyogaku-ronshu* 20: 81-96.

Kawakami, Shinji. 1999. "A Study of Classification of Korean Descending Divine Shamans From the Perspective of Descending Divine Spirits: Focusing on Workers Called Bodhisattva or Fortune-Teller", Mio Yuko, Honda Hiroshi eds., *Cultural Multi-Centricity in East Asia.* Research Institute for Languages and Cultures of Asia and Africa, Tokyo University of Foreign Studies.

Kawakami, Shinji. 2002. "A Study of Korean Practitioners in Yanbian: Focusing on the Relation to Korean Shamanism", *Shukyo-gaku-ronshu* 21.

Kawamori, Hiroshi. 1991. "Tales Concerning Visitors: From the Perspective of Comparison of Japan and Korea", *Bulletin of the National Museum of Japanese History* 35.

Kawamori, Hiroshi. 1993. "A Typical Analysis into Stories of Marriage of Different Species: From the Perspective of Comparison of Japan and Korea", *Bulletin of the National Museum of Japanese History* 50: 385-406.

Kawamori, Hiroshi. 1994. "Classification System of Korean Oral Tales: From the Perspective of Comparative Studies", *Bulletin of the Folklore Society of Japan* 199.

Kawamori, Hiroshi. 1996. "Geomancy as Comparative View: Concerning Burial of the Dead in East Asia (Mourning Rites and the Concept of Death-Mourning Rites and the Concept of Death of Neighboring Countries)", *Bulletin of the National Museum of Japanese History* 68: 187-201.

Kawamori, Hiroshi. 2000. *Structure of Japanese Old Stories and Narrators.* Osaka University Press.

Kawamura, Minato. 1984. "'Jinogwi Kut (Exorcism)' of Ulsan", *Gunzo* 39(11): 268-272.

Kawamura, Minato. 1986. (With Chung Daekyun), *Mirror Named Korea: Korea From the Perspective of Postwar Generation.* Tokyo: Toyo-shoin.

Kawamura, Minato. 1986. "Narrator of Soul, Hwang Seokyeong", *Gunzou* 41(4).

Kawamura, Minato. 1986. *My Busan.* Nagoya: Fubaisha.

Kawamura, Minato. 1988. Amino Yoshihiko and Kawamura Minato, *Social History of Archipelago and Peninsula: Searching New View of History* (Conversation with 'the Present' 8). Tokyo: Sakuhin-sha.

Kawamura, Minato. 1989. *Mirror Named Asia.* Shichosha.

Kawamura, Minato. 1992. *Traveler of Mother Asia.* Jimbun-shoin.

Kawamura, Minato. 1993. "Discrimination, Geomancy, the Cosmic Dual Forces: Nakagami Kenji and Seoul (Special Issue: Nakagami Kenji)", *Eureka* 25(3).

Kawamura, Minato. 1994. "Why Were 'Seopyeon-jae' So Popular?: An Aspect of Korean Culture", *Gendai-shi-techo* (Pocket Diary of Modern Poet) 37(9).

Kawamura, Minato. 1994. Suwa Haruo and Kawamura Minato, *Folk Customs and Entertainment of Asian Rice Farmers.* Tokyo: Yuzankaku Inc.

Kawamura, Minato. 1995. *Japanese Across the Sea.* Tokyo: Seido-sha.

Kawamura, Minato. 1995. Suwa Haruo and Kawamura Minato, *Asian View of Soul.* Tokyo: Yuzankaku Inc.

Kawamura, Minato. 1995. Suwa Haruo and Kawamura Minato, *Folk Customs and Entertainment of Asian People in Mountains and Seas.* Tokyo: Yuzankaku Inc.

Kawamura, Minato. 1996. "Empire of Composition: An Aspect of Cultural Imperialism by Modern Japan", Sakai Naoki, ed., *Deconstruction of Nationality.* Tokyo: Kashiwashobo Publishing Co. Ltd.

Kawamura, Minato. 1996. Suwa Haruo and Kawamura Minato, *Asian Rice Farming Culture and Japan.* Tokyo: Yuzankaku Inc.

Kawamura, Minato. 1996. Suwa Haruo, Kawamura Minato and Choe Kil-sung, et al., "Discussion: East China Sea Rim Cultural Area (Special Issue: Comparative Cultures of the Rim of East China Sea)", *Nicchu-bunka-kenkyu* 9.

Kawamura, Minato. 1996. *Truth and Falsehood of 'Folklore of Great East Asia'.* Tokyo: Kodansha Ltd.

Kawamura, Minato. 1997. Suwa Haruo and Kawamura Minato, *Visiting Deities.* Tokyo: Yuzankaku Inc.

Kawamura, Minato. 1998. "School Excursion of Post Colonialism: Oe Shinobu 'Trip to Japanese Colonies'", *Nami* 32(7).

Kawamura, Minato. 1999. "Iconography of Kisaeng", Suwa Haruo, ed., *Asian Sex.* Tokyo: Bensey Publishing Inc.

Kawamura, Minato. 1999. "Sakaguchi Ango's Ancient History and Korean Peninsula (Sakaguchi Ango and Japanese Culture)", *Kokubungaku-kaishaku-to-kanshou* (Exposition and Appreciation of National Literature 9, 64) (Extra Issue).

Kawamura, Minato. 1999. *Your Home is the Place Where You Were Born: The Theory of Literature of Zainichi Koreans.* Tokyo: Heibonsha Ltd.

Kawamura, Minato. 2000. "Walking as a Shaman: Encounter with a Korean Shaman (Special Issue: Scenery with a Medium)", *Tohoku-gaku* 2.

Kawamura, Minato. 2000. *Great Japanese Empire in Writings.* Tokyo: Iwanami Shoten.

Kawamura, Minato. 2000. *Seoul City Story.* Tokyo: Heibonsha Ltd.

Kawamura, Minato. 2001. "Destructive Force of 'Sonants': Japanese Seen From Korean (Special Issue: The Frontiers of Language)", *Kokubungaku: Kaishaku-to-kyozai-no-kenkyu* (A Study of Exposition and Materials of

National Literature) 46(12) 675.

Kawamura, Minato. 2001. *Kisaeng.* Tokyo: Sakuhinsha.

Kawamura, Minato. 2002. "Seoul: From Geomantic City to Future City (Special Issue: A Theater of Civilization, Capital: Its Change and Future) (World Capitals)", *Civil Engineering Consultant* 214, Tokyo: Japan Civil Engineering Consultants Association.

Kawamura, Minato. 2002. *Korea.* (Thought Reader6), Tokyo: Sakuhinsha.

Kawase, Takaya. 1996. "View of Nation and View of Modern Civilization: About Racial Representatives of Cheondokyo", *Annual Review of Religious Studies* 14.

Kawase, Takaya. 1998. "A Report on the 6th Interchange Symposium of Japanese and Korean Religious Researchers: Race and Religion in Modern East Asia: Concerning a Sense of Duty", *Annual Review of Religious Studies* 16.

Kawase, Takaya. 1998. "Tonghak and Its Teachings", *Journal of Religious Studies* 72(3).

Kawase, Takaya. 2001. (Book Review) "'Birth of Patriot: Dynamics of Han in Korean Popular Movements' Manabe Yuko", *Religion and Society* (7).

Kawase, Takaya. 2001. "Japanese Christianity and Colonial Mission in the Colonial Choson", *Shiso-shi-kenkyu* (1).

Kawase, Takaya. 2002. "Japanese Buddhism and Religious Policy in the Colonial Choson: Focusingon the Jodo Shin Sect", *Transactions of the Institute for Japanese Culture and Classics* 89.

Kawashima, Fujiya. 1976. "Movement of a Clan and Its Character Seen in the Case of Munhwa-Yu", *Chosen-gakuho* 70: 43-74.

Kayanuma, Noriko. 1999. "Destination of Star Festival: A Comparative Study of Big Dipper Belief in Japan and Korea", *Sakushin Gakuin University Women's College Bulletin* (23).

Kayanuma, Noriko. 2000. "Talking about Asia: Searching for Polestar Belief: A Comparative Study of Big Dipper Belief in Japan and Korea (2)", *Asia Yugaku* (18).

Kayanuma, Noriko. 2000. "Talking about Asia: Searching for Polestar Belief: A Comparative Study of Big Dipper Belief in Japan and Korea", *Asia*

Yugaku (13).

Kigana, Setsuko. 1990. "Localization of Roman Catholicism in Korea: A Case Study of Roman Catholicism in Hoengseong, Hoengseong-gun, Gangwon Province", *Jomin-bunka* 13: 1-10.

Kim, Byoung-Chul. 1996. "Reconsideration of People Living in Boat Household: Focusing on an Analysis into Negotiation with Lands of Races Living on Ships", *The Japanese Journal of Ethnology* 61(1).

Kim, Byoung-Chul. 1997. "Japan and 'Ship as House'", *Interdisciplinary Cultural Studies, The University of Tokyo* (2).

Kim, Byoung-Chul. 1999. *People Living in Boat Household of Japan: Fishers Living in Boats at Toyoshima Island.* The Fuji Xerox Setsutaro Kobayashi Memorial Fund.

Kim, Byoung-Chul. 2000. "Imperialism and Movement of Fishermen: Historical Anthropological Study of Appearance in Choson Sea of Fishermen in Toshima, Hiroshima Province (1)", *Journal of International Relations, Asia University* 9(1-2).

Kim, Byoung-Chul. 2000. "Imperialism and Movement of Fishermen: Historical Anthropological Study of Appearance in Choson Sea of Fishermen in Toshima, Hiroshima Province (2)", *Journal of International Relations, Asia University* 10(1).

Kim, Byoung-Chul. 2000. "Physical Technique of Fishermen: Combination of Traditioal Technique and the Latest Technology", *The Japanese Journal of Ethnology* 65(2).

Kim, Byoung-Chul. 2001. "A Historical Anthropological Study of Appearance of Modern Shipping Life (1)", *Journal of the Institute for Asian Studies* (28).

Kim, Byoung-Chul. 2001. "Modern Nation and Fishermen", *Journal of International Relations, Asia University* 11(1).

Kim, Ch'eol. 1865. Korea's Population and Economy. Tokyo: Iwanami-shoten.

Kim, Eung-Yeo. 1977. "Farming Family and Spontaneous Interest Groups in Korea", *Annals of Family Studies* 3: 43-54.

Kim, Eun-Mi and Motomura, Hiroshi. 1992. "A Study of Married People's Attitude Toward Women's Work in Korea: Concerning Attributive Factors and

Family Directivity", *Annals of Family Studies* 17: 27-40.

Kim, Hak-Hyoun. 1999. "Zainichi Koreans in the Path of 'Coexistence'", Miyamoto Masaru, Shimizu Yoshimi eds., *Lecture of Cultural Anthropology: Thinking about Culture and Policy.* Yachiyo-shuppan.

Kim, Hwan. 2000. *Korean Almanac.* Akashi-shoten.

Kim, Ik-Ki, Park Kyeong-Suk and Kojima, Hiroshi. 1998. "Geographical Network of Aged Parents in Modern Korea and Japan", *Journal of Population Problems* 54(4): 63-84.

Kim, Joon-Hwa. 1997. "Reconstruction of Ethnic Culture of Korean People in China: Focusing on a Case of 'Rite of Ancestor Worship' and 'Wedding Ceremony'", *Bulletin of the Research Institute of Comparative Education and Culture, Kyushu University* (49):39-47.

Kim, Joon-Hwa. 1998. "A Study of Identity of Zainichi Koreans: A Study of Methodological Shift to 'Research on the Actual Condition' and 'the Theory of Relations'", Ebuchi Kazuhiro ed., *Transculturalism Studies.* Akashi-shoten.

Kim, Ki-Ho. 1997. "Problems and Prospect of Preservation of Cities in Korea: A Case Study of Korean-Style House Preservation District, Kahoe-dong", *The Journal of the Tokyo Institute for Municipal Research* 88(11).

Kim, Mi-Ran. 1993. "Expansion of Women's Higher Education and Culture in Korea: Academic Background for Women and 'Wise Mother and Good Wife'", *Bulletin of the Faculty of Education, The University of Tokyo* 33: 55-66.

Kim, Mi-Suk. 1991. "Labor of Married Women and Women's Labor Policy in Korea: Focusing on Mother Protective Policy and Nursery Policy in the 1980's", *Shakaigaku-journal Studies* 47(2): 285-304.

Kim, Mi-Young. 1991. "Housewives' Rights of Korea: Focusing on 'Living Room Transfer' in Andong Province", in *A Study of Korean Traditional Culture: From the Perspective of Comparison with Okinawa.* (59-74), Naha: Okinawa-kenritsu-geijutsu-daigaku-ryu-kan-densho-bunka-chosa-dan.

Kim, Mi-Young. 1993. "Neighborhood From the Perspective of Mutual Aid in Marriage: A Case Study of Seonchang, South Gyeongsang Province, Korea", *The Japanese Journal of Ethnology* 57(4): 437-455.

Kim, Mi-Young. 1993. "Paternal Relatives in Seonchang, South Gyeongsang Province, Korea", *Hakusan-jinruigaku* 2.

Kim, Mi-Young. 1998. "A Study on 'Thought of Particular Male Babies' in Contemporary Korean Society", Shimizu Hiroaki, Haga Masaaki and Matsumoto Seiichi eds., *Anthropology of Sex and Age: Treatises in Honor of Prof. Takahashi Toichi's 70th Birthday.* Tokyo: Iwata-shoin.

Kim, Myoung-Mi. 1996. Harajiri Hideki, Kuraishi Ichiro, Kim Myeongmi, "A Cultural Anthropological and Social Basic Study for Practice of Cultural Understanding Education in Itami-shi, Hyogo Province", *Research Aid Treatises* 32.

Kim, Myoung-Mi. 1998. (Book Review), "Lee Cheong-yak, 'House of Hearts for Third Generation of Zainichi Koreans'", Korean Minority Studies (1).

Kim, Myoung-Mi. 1999. (Book Review), "Ryang, Sonia. North Koreans in Japan: Language, Ideology, and Identity", *Korean Minority Studies* (2).

Kim, Myoung-Mi. 2000. "Reconsideration of Ethnicity Theory in Japan: Focusing on Boundary Theory", *The Japanese Journal of Ethnology* 65(1).

Kim, Myoung-Mi. 2002. (Book Review), "Harajiri Hideki 'Ethnography of Korean Towns: Hawaii, LA, Ikuno'", *The Japanese Journal of Ethnology* 67(2).

Kim, P'a-Mang. 1994. "Tea Ceremony as Invitatory Manners", *Nomura Art Gallery Research Bulletin* 3: 12-28.

Kim, Pong-Chin. 1994. "Tributary System and Formation of Modern Choson", in Mizoguchi Yuzo, Hamashita Takeshi, Hiraishi Naoaki, Miyajima Hiroshi, eds., *Society and Nation.*(Thinking in Asia 4) (213-238), Tokyo: Tokyo- daigaku-shuppan-kai.

Kim, Sang-Bo. 1998. "Ceremonial Feast in East Asia: A Comparative Study", Ishige Naomichi ed., *Treatises: Cultural History of Liquor and Drinking.* Heibon-sha.

Kim, Sang-Kyu. 1993. "Concepts of Kinship Group in East Asia", *Shakaigaku-zasshi* (Kobe University Sociology Seminar).

Kim, Taek-Kyu. 1963. "Activity Condition of Korean Society for Cultural Anthropology", *The Japanese Journal of Ethnology* 27(4): 664-665.

Kim, Taek-Kyu. 1990. "Kinship System in East Asia: A Comparative Study of Continuance and Change From the Perspective of Idea and Reality of Kinship System", *Chosen-gakuho* 134: 1-46.

Kim, Taek-Kyu. 2000. *Cultural Comparative Theory of Japanese and Korean Folk Customs.* Kyushu-daigaku-shuppan-kai.

Kim, Tae-Kon. 1990. Sakakura Masayasu trnas. "Meaning of New Year Festival", in Takeda Akira, ed., *Progress and Problems of Folklore.* (441-457), Tokyo: Kokusho-kanko-kai.

Kim, Tae-Kon. 1991. "Concept of Deity and World View in Korea", in Uematsu Akashi, ed., *Folk Customs and Rites of China Sea Rim Area 2 Rites of Deitie.,* (423-441), Tokyo: Gaifu-sha.

Kim, Tae-Kon. 1994. Fuchigami Kyoko trans. "Symbolic Meaning of Concept of Deity and Rites in Korean Shamanism", Miyake Hitoshi, Suzuki Masataka eds., *Shamanism and Folk Customs of East Asia.* Tokyo: Keiso-shobo.

Kim, Tae-Kon, Chi, Ch'un-Sang and Hyon, Yong-Chun. 1977. *Calling Souls: Korean Shaman.* Tokyo: Kokusho-kanko-kai.

Kim, Tae-Young. 1999. Identity, *Beyond Policy: Ethnicity of Zainichi Koreans.* Sekai-shiso-sha.

Kim, Yang-Gi. 1991. "Shamanism Rites and Music", Fujii Tomoaki ed., *Ethnic Music Series 5* (Rites and Music, Folk Belief Edition), Tokyo: Tokyo-shoseki.

Kim, Yang-Gi. 1999. *Japanese Culture, Korean Customs.* Akashi-shoten.

Kimura, Kan. 2000. *Korean Nationalism and Senses of 'Small Country'.* Minerva-shobo.

Kishi, Shodo. 1999. "A Study of Living Culture in a Village near the Basin of the Nakdong River of Korea Vol. 1: About the Funeral Institution and Inheritance", *Gifu-joshi-daigaku-kiyo* (28).

Kishi, Shodo. 2000. "A Study of Living Culture in a Village near the Basin of the Nakdong River of Korea Vol. 2: A Survey of Farmers' Opinions Toward the Succession of Farming Households in Each Area", *Gifu-joshi-daigaku-kiyo* (29).

Kishi, Shodo. 2001. "A Study of Living Culture in a Village near the Basin of the Nakdong River of Korea Vol. 3: A Survey of Farmers' Opinions Toward the Succession of Farming Households in Each Area", *Gifu-joshi-*

daigaku-kiyo (30).

Kishi, Shodo. 2002. A Study of Living Culture in a Village near the Basin of the Nakdong River of Korea Vol. 4: A Survey of Opinions of Farmers at Waegwan Toward the Succession of Farming Households", *Gifu-joshi-daigaku-kiyo* (31).

Kishibe, Kumi. 1976. "Wisdom of Choson Folktale", *Korea Review* 18(173): 42-46.

Kitami, Toshio. 1986. "Woman Diver of Jeju Island", Ito Abito, Ohmura Masuo, Kajimura Hideki, Takeda Yukio eds., *A Dictionary About Korea.* Tokyo: Heibon-sha.

Ko, Kwang-Min. 1991. "Belief District and Administrative District in Some Areas of Jeju Island", in *A Study of Korean Traditional Culture: From the Perspective of Comparison with Okinawa.* (35-46), Naha: Okinawa-kenritsu-geijutsu-daigaku-ryu-kan-densho-bunka-chosa-dan.

Ko, Sa-Myoung. 1998. " 'Meaning of Life' and Ever Since", Study Society for Zainichi Koreans ed., *Korean Minority Studies(1).* Shinkan-sha.

Ko, Sun-Hwi. 1997. "From Jeju Island to Yokohama: An Attempt of Settlement in Japan in the 1980's" Okuda Michihiro ed., Urban Sociology Studies Library(7) Sociology of Urban Ethnicity: Asking about the Meaning of Ethnic People, Culture and Coexistence, Kyoto: Minerva-shobo.

Ko, Yon-Ui. 1998. *Existence of Race: Zainichi Koreans as Third World.* Shakai-hyoron-sha.

Kobayashi, Kazumi. 1999. "Method and Process of Social Survey of All Households in a Korean Village: A Record of Survey of a Village in the Suburb of Daegu", Memoirs of Osaka Kyoiku University. 2, *Social science and home science* 48(1), pp.27～49.

Kobayashi, Kazumi. 1999. *Basic Structure and Change in Korean Rural Community: Results of Survey of Households in a Village in the Suburb of Daegu.* (A4 Edition, 92p.).

Kobayashi, Kazumi. 2000. "Educational Problems and Migration in Korean Villages: A Case Study of a Village in the Suburb of Daegu", Memoirs of Osaka Kyoiku University. 2, *Social science and home science* Vol. 2, 48: 2, (pp.75-88).

Kobayashi, Kazumi. 2000. "Migration and Working Structure in a Village in the Suburb of Korean Cities: A Result of Survey of Households in B-ri of Daegu", *A Comparative Study of Japanese and Korean Village Structure.* (International Research Report for Research Fund of Ministry of Education, Culture, Sports, Science and Technology 1997-1999), pp.61-75(Japanese), pp.111～125(Korean).

Kobayashi, Kazumi. 2000. tr., Lee Changgi, "Korean Houses and Villages", *A Comparative Study of Japanese and Korean Village Structure,* (International Research Report for Research Fund of Ministry of Education, Culture, Sports, Science and Technology 1997-1999), pp.17～31.

Kobayashi, Kazumi. 2000. tr., Lee Changgi, "Structural Principle of Korean Family Group: Focusing on Formative Factors", Kobe University Research Group of Sociology, *Journal of Sociology* No.17, pp.102～116.

Kobayashi, Kazumi. 2001. "School Migration of Youths in Villages near the Suburb of Daegu: A Case Study of S Village in Daegu of Korea", *Japanese Village Community Studies* No.8, pp.12～23.

Kobayashi, Takayuki. 2000. ed., *Changing Modern Korean Society.* Kyoto: Sekai-shiso-sha.

Kobayashi, Yuriko. 1987. *Korean Family.* Tokyo: Japan Research Institute.

Kodama, Toshihiko. 1991. "About Change of Laws Related to Trade Union in Korea Vol. 1", *Treatises of Chiba University of Commerce* 29(2).

Kodama, Toshihiko. 1991. "About Change of Laws Related to Trade Union in Korea Vol. 2", *Treatises of Chiba University of Commerce* 29(3).

Kodama, Toshihiko. 1991. "Concerning the Revision of Korean Family Law", *Jurist* 988: 80-82.

Kodama, Toshihiko. 1993. Aso Miyuki, Kodama Toshihiko, "A Comparative Study of Relations Between Companies in Japan and Korea: Japanese-Style Corporate Group and Korean-Style Corporate Group", *Treatises of Chiba University of Commerce* 31(1).

Kodama, Toshihiko. 1995. *Korean Industrialization and Corporate Group.* Gakubun-sha.

Koguma, Eiji. 1996. "Colored Colonial Empire: Exclusion of Japanese Emigrants and Choson Ruling Theory around 1920's", Sakai Naoki ed., *Deconstruction of Nationality.* Kashiwa-shobo.

Koguma, Eiji. 1998. "Japanese Born in Korea: Korean Member of the House of Representatives Park Chungeum", Study Society for Zainichi Koreans ed., *Korean Minority Studies(1).* Shinkan-sha.

Koguma, Eiji. 1998. *Boundary of Japanese, Okinawa, Ainu, Taiwan, Korea; From Colonial Rule to Movement of Return.* Shinyo-sha.

Kono, Michihiro. 1991. ed., World Geography Seminar 1 New Revision, *East Asia.* Tokyo: Taimeido.

Kozawa, Yasunori. 1984. "A Report of Comparative Research of Japanese and Korean Coastal Fishing Village", *Japan-Korea Joint Research Report, No.2,* Joint Research Group for Fishing Community of Japan and Korea.

Kozawa, Yasunori. 1996. "Words of Folk Belief of Higashiiwami: Sketch of Oral Traditional Culture Sketch", *Annual Journal of the Asia-Africa Cultural Research Institute* No.30.

Kozawa, Yasunori. 1997. "Japan as Reflected in the Readers' Letters of Korean News Papers", *Annual Journal of the Asia-Africa Cultural Research Institute* No.31.

Kozawa, Yasunori. 1998. "Korean Sayings and Popular Belief on Sex", Shimizu Hiroaki, Haga Masaaki, Matsumoto Seiichi eds., *Anthropology of Sex and Age.* Iwata-shoin.

Kozawa, Yasunori. 1998. "Korean Taboo: A Case Study of East Coast", *Annual Journal of the Asia-Africa Cultural Research Institute* No.32.

Kozawa, Yasunori. 1998. With Usami Takanori, "Jukbyeon Youth Meeting and Sirum Circle", *Annual Journal of the Asia-Africa Cultural Research Institute* No.32.

Kozawa, Yasunori. 1999. "Dispute about the Name of Japanese Emperor in Korean Media", *Annual Journal of the Asia-Africa Cultural Research Institute* No.33.

Kozawa, Yasunori. 2000. "Korea Seen From Dispute about the Combination of Hanguel and Chinese Characters", *Annual Journal of the Asia-Africa Cultural Research Institute* No.34.

Kumagai, Osamu. 1972. "Tug of War as a Farming Rite in Korean Peninsula", *Chosen-gakuho* 64: 1-13.

Kumagai, Osamu. 1975. "Dong-jae: Its Essence and Character", *Chosen-gakuho* 74: 97-110.

Kumagai, Osamu. 1975. "Fire Festival in Korean Peninsula: Character and Change", *Kikan-dolmen* 7.

Kumagai, Osamu. 1978. "Legend of Floting Island in Korean Peninsula", *Chosen-gakuho* 87: 101-111.

Kumagai, Osamu. 1979. "Rites and Convention Concerning Red Beans in Korean Peninsula", *Chosen-gakuho* 92: 1-15.

Kumagai, Osamu. 1980. "Ho-beob-ryong in 'Samguk-yusa'", in Editing Committee for Treatises in Honor of Dr. Kokubu Naoichi's 70th Birthday, ed., *Japanese Ethnic Culture and Its Vicinities: Treatises in Honor of Dr. Kokubu Naoichi's 70th Birthday.* (History, Race Part), (519-532), Shimonoseki: Shin-nippon-kyoiku-tosho.

Kumagai, Osamu. 1981. "Pogwa (Gourd) in Korean Peninsula", *Chosen-gakuho* 101: 29-38.

Kumagai, Osamu. 1984. *Folk Customs and Rites in East Asia.* Tokyo: Yuzankaku.

Kumakura, Isao. 1976. "An Introduction to History of Green Tea: Japan and Korea", *Fuzoku* 14(3): 1-19.

Kumekawa, Emiko. 1975. "Folk Costume of Korea 1", *Musashino Women's University Bulletin* 10: 109-123.

Kuramochi, Kazuo. 1993. "A Positive Study of Migration and Change of Family Structure in Korean Villages in the late 1980's: A Case Study of Four Villages in South Chungcheong Province", *Journal of Asian Studies* 39(3): 1-34.

Kurata, Masahiko. 2000. "Racial Coexistence in Asia and Zainichi Koreans", Hashiuchi Takeshi et al. eds., *Prospect of Coexistence Society of Multi-Culture.* Nippon Hyoron-sha.

Kurita, Eiji. 1991. "Shinto Shrines in Korea During the Colonial Period", *Journal of West Japan Religious Science* 13.

Kurokawa, Kozo. 1979. "Comments on 'A Comparative Study of Folk tale of Northeast Asia' (Usuda Jingoro, Choe Inhak ed.)", *Kokugakuin-zasshi* 80(4): 55-58.

Kusano, Taeko. 1984. "Thought of Attraction of Korean Traditional Music",

Gendai-Korea 242: 48-56.

Kusano, Taeko. 1984. *Arirang: Thought of Attraction of Korean Traditional Music.* Tokyo: Hakusuisha.

Kusano, Taeko. 1986. "Arirang, Music, Musical Rule, Instruments, Kayageum, Songs, Korean Fiddle, Korean Harp, National Classical Music, Sanjo, Changgu, Daegeum, Taryeong, Doraji, Dance, Balsam, Folk Songs", Ito Abito, Ohmura Masuo, Kajimura Hideki, Takeda Yukio eds., *A Dictionary About Korea.* Tokyo: Heibon-sha.

Lee, Byoung-Nam. 1998. "A Study of Shamanism in Ancient Korea: Focusing on Sodo Belief", Ogo Kinichi ed., *Asian World: Focusing on Its Structure and Original Meaning Vol. 1.* Yachiyo-shuppan.

Lee, Chang-Gi. 2000. "Structural Principle of Korean Family Group", *Journal of Sociology* 17.

Lee, Cyung-Ja. 2000. "Korean Eating Manners" Akino Koji, Obata So eds., *Asian Food Culture.* Kenpakusha.

Lee, Doo-Hyun. 1981. "Korean Outdoor Masque" *Kikan-minzokugaku* 15: 104-113.

Lee, Doo-Hyun. 1990. *Choson Entertainment History.* Tokyo: Tokyo-daigaku-shuppan-kai.

Lee, Doo-Hyun. 2000. "Praying for Iron of Kangsin Shaman: An Introduction to Comparative Studies of Northeast Asian Shamanism and Korean Shamanism", Choe Kil-sung, Hinata Kazumasa eds., *Myth, Religion, Shamanism: An Attempt of Comparison of Japanese and Korean Culture.* Fukyo-sha.

Lee, Ho-San. 1999. "Korean Shamanism: A Study of Documentaries", *Asia-bunka-kenkyu* 6, (International Asian Society).

Lee, Hui-Yeong. 1966. "An Essay on the Succession of Successive Queen, Bin in the Koryo Dynasty: An Examination of a Phenomenon in Formative Process of the Institution of Non-Marriage of the Same Surname", *The Japanese Journal of Ethnology* 31(1): 28-37.

Lee, In-Ja. 1994. "Grave Story (Special Issue: What Do Women Long For in Religio): Religious Senses in Life", *Shiso-no-kagaku* Vol. 8, 20.

Lee, In-Ja. 1996. "Duality of Identical Expression of Emigrants in Another Culture: Focusing on Grave of Zainichi Koreans", *The Japanese Journal of Ethnology* 61(3).

Lee, In-Ja. 1999. "Emigrating Life, Returning Death: A Case Study of Returning Home of a Dead Body of a Zainichi Korean From Jeju Island", Shintani Takanori ed., Lecture: Man and Environment(9), *Environment after Death.* Showado.

Lee, Jin-Young. 1993. "A Preliminary Study of Social Cultural Meaning of Kinship Vocabulary of Okinawa", *The Japanese Journal of Ethnology* 58(1).

Lee, Jin-Young. 1993. "Watanabe Yoshio, Challenges of Folk Informative Theory-informative Anthropology of Okinawa", *The Japanese Journal of Ethnology* 57(4).

Lee, Jin-Young. 2000. "Geneology and Historical Senses of Vietnam and Korea", Research Society for Social Culture of Vietnam ed., *Society and Culture of Vietnam (2),* Fukyo-sha.

Lee, Kwang-Kyu. 1982. "Aged People Problems in Korea", *The Japanese Journal of Ethnology* 46(4): 410-421.

Lee, Kwang-Kyu. 1986. "Aspects of Change of Farming Family in Korea", *Community Journal* 76: 29-53.

Lee, Kyeong-Sin. 1992. "Health and Nutritive Condition of Korean Youths Seen From School Lunch Service", *Science of Health* 34(21).

Lee, Kyeong-Won. 1997. *A Comparative Study of Current Situation of Sex Role Assignment in Japan and Korea : A Case Study of Chuncheon of Korea and Nara of Japan.*

Lee, Man-Kap. 1971. "Change of Korean Postwar Family", *Sociology Review* 85: 82-90.

Lee, Peom-Chik. 1991. "Regality and O-chal in the Choson Dynasty", (Asai Yoshizumi trans.) *Chosen-gakuho* 138: 45-52.

Lee, Sang-Ho. 1997. "Korean Traditional Small Eel Fishing Vol. 2", *Gekkan-mingu* 29-11.

Lee, Sang-Ki. 1991. "40 Years of Korea: Japan Relations (1945-1985): Cultural Change of Korean Society", *Kikan-koreana* 4(3).

Lee, Seung-hyun. 2000. "(Book Review) 'Research Society for Korean Religion ed., Lecture of Korean History of Religious Culture'", *Tokyo University Annual Report of Religious Science.* 18.

Lee, Sun-E. 1996. Lee Sanggo, Lee Seonae trans. "Korean Traditional Small Eel Fishery (1)", *Gekkan-mingu* 29(7).

Lee, Sun-E. 1996. Lee Sanggo, Lee Seonae trans. "Korean Traditional Small Eel Fishery (2)", *Gekkan-mingu* 29(8).

Lee, Sun-E. 1997. Lee Sanggo, Lee Seonae trans. "Korean Traditional Small Eel Fishery Vol. 2", *Gekkan-mingu* 29(11).

Lee, Sun-E. 1998. "Learning of Traditional Dyeing Technique: in Search for Traditional Dyeing Technique (8) Dyeing of Astringent Persimmon of Jeju Island", *Journal of Textiles Consumption Science* 39(1).

Lee, Sun-E. 1999. "Korean Delivery Culture", *Miyazaki Public University, Department of Humanities Bulletin* 7(1).

Lee, Sun-E. 1999. "Monograph of Procreation, Delivery, and Child Rearing: Babies in Another Culture(5) Current Situation of Korean Delivery Culture", *Prenatal Care* 18(10) 229.

Lee, Sun-E. 2000. "A Case Study of Use of Resources of Shores with Many Rocks and Food Culture(1) Focusing on Hyuganada", *Miyazaki Public University Department of Humanities Bulletin* 8(1).

Lee, Sun-E. 2001. "Life of Fishermen: Focusing on the Lives of Woman Divers(Special Issue: Korean Ocean Culture)", *Gekkan-kankoku-bunka* 261.

Lee, Sun-E. 2001. "Strategy for Use of Unusual Resources: A Case Study of Clam Go Stones of Hyuganada", *Miyazaki Public University Department of Humanities Bulletin* 9(1).

Lee, Sun-E. 2001. Fujita Akiyoshi, Lee Seonae, Kawahara Norifumi, "Interchange Between Korean Peninsula and Other Regions Seen From Islands: Focusing on Jeju Island", *Seikyu-gakujutsu-ronshu* 19.

Lee, Sun-E. 2001. *Women Diver of Jeju Island Crossing Sea.* Akashi-shoten.

Lee, Sun-E. 2002. "A Case Study of Use of Resources of Shores with Many Rocks Around South Coast of Hyuganada: A Comparative Study with Ulsan", *Japan Studies* 25.

Lee, Sung-Woo. 1998. "Korean Food Culture", Ishige Naomichi, Yoshida Shuji eds., *Lecture: Food Culture(1) Human Food Culture*. Ajinomoto Food Culture Center.

Lee, Sung-Woo. 1999. Cheong Tae-Seong, Sasaki Naoko trans. *Cultural History of Korean Food.* Heibon-sha.

Lee, Wol-Sun. 1986. "Current Situation and Prospect of Korean Women: Concerning 'Women White Paper'", *Sociology of Human Science, Psychological Studies* (Student Association of Kansai Univerisity Graduate School of Sociology) 26: 59-74.

Lee, Young-Joo. 2001. "Pure Blood lineage of Imperial Family From the Perspective of Marriage Rule: Family Lineage and Blood lineage in Modern Japan", *Journal of Japanese Folklore* 225.

Lee, Young-Sook. 1998. "Racial Discrimination and Education: Stereotype and Medium", Saeki Yutaka ed., *Iwanamikoza Modern Education: Crisis and Reformation(5) Education of Coexistence.* Iwanami-shoten.

Mabuchi, Kazuo. 1982. "Geographical Names of Korean Peninsula", *The World of Geographical Names: Geography.* (Extra Edition), 160-161.

Makino, Nobuo. 1998. "Korea's Women's University in the Cataclysm: Trend and Current Situation", *Human Studies* 34: 57-68.

Makino, Tatsumi. 1973. "Focusing on Natural Village of Korea", *Collection of Suzuki Eitaro's Works V, A Study of Korean Village.* (499-526), Tokyo: Mirai-sha.

Manabe, Yuko. 1990. "Social Relations Concerning Korean Shamans: The Theory of Han of Living in Urban Society", *Hikaku-minzokugaku-kenkyu* 1.

Manabe, Yuko. 1990. (Manabe Yuko, Ogasawara Shin), "Function of Shamanic Rites for the Unity of Communities: A Case Study of Big Haul Festival of Sorae Port of Korea", *Sociology* 35(2).

Manabe, Yuko. 1991. "Death in Korean Shamanism: Concerning 'Han'", *Hikaku-minzokugaku* 3: 193-201.

Manabe, Yuko. 1994. "Birth of Patriot: Concerning View of Life and Death in Korean Movement Group", *Sociology* 39(2): 19-36.

Manabe, Yuko. 1994. "Shamanic Thought and Popular Movements", *Gekkan-kankoku-bunka* 16(8): 13-18.

Manabe, Yuko. 1994. tr., Choe Kil-sung, *Anthropology of Han.* Hirakawa-shuppan-sha.

Manabe, Yuko. 1996. "Change of Traditional Society Accompanied with

Reclamation Projects: Chang-ri, Buseok-myeon, Seosan-gun, South Chungcheong Province", *Seikyu-gakujutsu-ronshu* 8: 149-161.

Manabe, Yuko. 1996. "Formation of Myth of Martyr in Korean Popular Movements: Concerning the Life and the Death of Jeon Taeil", *Religion and Society* 2: 46-67.

Manabe, Yuko. 1996. "Gwangju in Korean Popluar Movements(2): The Present of Democratic Holy Land, Gwangju" Gekkan-hyakka, 409: 12-15.

Manabe, Yuko. 1996. "Gwangju in Korean Popular Movements (1)", *Gekkan-hyakka* 408: 8-11.

Manabe, Yuko. 1996. *Different Cultures Seen in Campus: Sketch of Life in Korea.* Tokyo: Hirakawa-shuppan-sha.

Manabe, Yuko. 1997. " 'Play' and 'Sincerity' of Anti-Japanese Culture in Korea", *Three-Colored Flag* 595: 24-29.

Manabe, Yuko. 1997. "Gwangju in Korean Popular Movements (3): People Who Gather in Gwangju", *Gekkan-hyakka* 411: 10-13.

Manabe, Yuko. 1997. "Gwangju in Korean Popular Movements (4): Between Poplular World and Ideology", *Gekkan-hyakka* 417: 17-20.

Manabe, Yuko. 1997. *Birth of Patriot: Dynamics of 'Han' in Korean Popular Movements.* Tokyo: Hirakawa-shuppan-sha.

Manabe, Yuko. 1998. "Ideology of Korean Popular Movements From the Perspective of Simmel Religious Sociology: Focusing on Formation and Development of Popular Theology", *Journal of Simmel Studies Society* 4: 10-17.

Manabe, Yuko. 2000. "Why Do Japanese Scholars Study Korean Shamanism?: From Self-Examination to Post Modern Folklore (The 25th Anniversary Special Issue 25 Years of Region Studies: New Generation of Region Studie)", *Tsukuba University Region Studies* 18: 141-155.

Manabe, Yuko. 2000. *Modern Korea Seen From Gwangu Event.* Tokyo: Heibon-sha.

Manabe, Yuko. 2001. "Pilgrimage of Modern Korea and Ethnicism: After the Gwangju Event in 1980 (Life, Aging, Death: Japanese View of Life: View From Inside, View From Outside)", *Kokuritsu-rekishi-minzoku-hakubutsukan-kenkyu-hokoku* 91.

Manabe, Yuko. 2001. Iwai Hiroshi, Kashio Naoki, Manabe Yuko et al., "A Report of Symposium 2000 'Criticalness of Religion and Study Perspective of Confusing Modern Religions'", *Religion and Society* (7).

Maruyama, Koichi. 1978. "Sociality of Residence: A Preliminary Research Report of Korean Houses", *Kyusyu Journal of Anthropology* 6: 49-55.

Maruyama, Koichi. 1979. "A Memorandum about Conservatism and Reformism of Korean Confucianism: Focusing on an Analysis of Kinship Structure", *Hirodai-Asia-kenkyu* 1: 25-37.

Maruyama, Koichi. 1979. "Social Expansion of Sex: The Case of Korea", in Ayabe Tsuneo, ed., *Man's Life: A Cultural Anthropological Study.* (95-98), Kyoto: Academia-shuppan-kai.

Maruyama, Koichi. 1980. "Formation of National Identity in Korean Society", *Bulletin of the Research Institute of Comparative Education and Culture* 31: 65-80.

Maruyama, Koichi. 1982. "Centripetalism and Centrifugalism of Remote Island Culture: National Identity Based on the Case of Geomun Island in Korea", in Gondo Yoshio ed., *A Comparative Study of Education of National Identity in Developing Countries' Identity Education.*(A General Report(A) for Scientific Study Fund of 1981) (26-31).

Maruyama, Koichi. 1982. "Cultural Durability and Changing Process of Culture in Japanese and Korean Immigrants Community", in Ayabe Tsuneo ed., *A Study of American Ethnic Culture.* (201-248), Tokyo: Kobun-do.

Maruyama, Koichi. 1982. "Lifelong Separation with Children in Confucian Society", *Education and Medicine* 30(3): 45-51.

Maruyama, Koichi. 1982. "Peripheral of Culture: A Case Study of Geomun Island, South Jeolla Province, Korea", *Bulletin of the Research Institute of Comparative Education and Culture* 33: 39-54.

Maruyama, Koichi. 1983. "Development of Inside and Outside in Korean Society", in Ebuchi Kazuhiro, Ito Abito eds., *Ries and Symbol: A Cultural Anthropological Study.* (443-466), Fukuoka: Kyushu-daigaku-shuppan-kai.

Maruyama, Koichi. 1983. "Minority in the City: Postwar Life and Culture of Zainichi Koreans", in Hiroshima City ed., *New History of Hiroshima Urban Ethnic Culture.* (301-390), Hiroshima: Hiroshima City.

Maruyama, Koichi. 1985. "Centrifugalism and Centripetalism of Central Culture in Education: A Case Study of Geomun Island, South Jeolla Province, Korea", in Hironaka Kazuhiko ed., *A Comparative Study of Changing Process of Educational Policy in Postwar Asian Countries and Its Social Cultural Base.* (37-52).

Maruyama, Koichi. 1985. "Cultural Pluralism and Meritocracy in Education Vol. 2, A Case of Korean American", *Bulletin of the Research Institute of Comparative Education and Culture* 36: 1-19.

Maruyama, Koichi. 1986. "Durability of Marginal Culture: A Case Study of Korean Insular Community", *Bulletin of the Research Institute of Comparative Education and Culture* 37: 15-23.

Maruyama, Koichi. 1987. "A Study of Development of Confucianism in Korean Remote Island Society", *Bulletin of the Research Institute of Comparative Education and Culture* 38: 35-46.

Maruyama, Koichi. 1990. "An Aspect of Remote Island Studies: A Case Study of Geomun Island", in Sugiyama Koichi, Sakurai Tetsuo eds., *Cultural Anthropology of Korean Society.* (23-38), Tokyo: Kobun-do.

Maruyama, Koichi. 1994. "Regeneration of Identity in Remote Islands: Concerning Movement of Making Hero in Geomun Island", *Bulletin of the Research Institute of Comparative Education and Culture* 45.

Maruyama, Koichi. 1997. "Vector of Rural Culture From the Perspective of Cultural Dynamics: A Case Study of Korea", *Bulletin of the Research Institute of Comparative Education and Culture* 49: 1-15.

Masaoka, Nobuhiro. 1997. "Funeral Ceremonies and Kinship in Jeju Island of Korea", Komoto Mitsugi, Yagi Tohru, eds., *Series Comparative Family (9) Family and Rites of the Dead.* Waseda-daigaku-shuppan-bu.

Masaoka, Nobuhiro. 1998. "Folkloric Background of Rites of Visiting Deity: A Case Study of Jeju Island (Discussion No.773)", *Japanese Folklore* 216).

Masaoka, Nobuhiro. 2000. "Possibility of Comparative Folklore Studies: A Case Study of Rites of Visiting Deity in Jeju Island and Okinawa", *Bukkyo University Research Institute Bulletin* (Extra Issue).

Masuda, Shozo. 1984. "Current Situation and Problems of Regional Promotion", in *Japan-Korea Joint Research Report Vol. 2 Hupo-ri, Pyeonghae-up, North Gyeongsang Province.* (246-268), Kobe: Joint Seminar of Fishing Community and Economy of Japan and Korea Office.

Masuda, Shozo. 1986. "Plan, Current Situation and Problems of Regional Promotion", in *Japan-Korea Joint Research Report Vol4 Wando-gun, South Jeolla Province, Korea.* (225-247), Kobe: Joint Seminar of Fishing Community and Economy of Japan and Korea Office.

Masuda, Shozo ed. 1991. *A Comparative Study of Fishing Village of Japan and Korea: Focusing on Society, Economy, and Culture.* Kyoto: Kohrosha.

Matsubara, Takatoshi. 1983. "Korean Genealogy and Ancestral Tradition Vol. 1" Shien, 120: 151-186.

Matsubara, Takatoshi. 1983. "Korean Genealogy and Ancestral Tradition Vol. 2", *Shien* 121: 93-145.

Matsubara, Takatoshi. 1985. "An Analysis of Stories: Communication Between Specters and Men", *Eureka* 17(2): 50-59.

Matsubara, Takatoshi. 1985. "Continuing Ethnic Entertainment: Festivals in the Rift of Ordinary", *Asahi Weekly Hyakka* 83 (World Geography 77 China, East Asia: Korea) 194-196.

Matsubara, Takatoshi. 1987. "View of Geneology in Choson Geneology and Its Changing Process", in Japan-Korea Society ed., *Treatises of The First Korean Studies International Seminar.* (76-81), Heilongjiang Korean Publishing.

Matsubara, Takatoshi. 1990. "Mechanism of Formation of Legends in Choson: Focusing on the Tale of Drifting Prince in Ryukyu", *Chosen-gakuho* 137.

Matsubara, Takatoshi. 1990. "Tales of Communication Between Man and Animals in Korea", *Journal of Oral Literature Studies* 13.

Matsubara, Takatoshi. 1992. "Heung-bu-jeon seen from Comparative Tale Study", Shirakawa Yutaka, Narisawa Mawaru eds., *Choson Literature Treatises in Honor of Dr. Ohtani Morishige's 60th Birthday.* Sugiyama-shoten.

Matsubara, Takatoshi. 1992. "Epitaph of King Gwanggaeto From the Perspective of Mythology", *Chosen-gakuho* 145.

Matsubara, Takatoshi. 1994. Translation with Notes "Articles From Korea in Chinese Novels", Lee Neungu, Matsubara Takatoshi trans. *Journal of*

Language Culture 5.

Matsubara, Takatoshi. 1995. *Prospect of Comparative Mythology.* Matsubara Takatoshi, Matsumura Kauzo, Seido-sha, 1995.12.

Matsubara, Takatoshi. 1996. "About Hong Seokmo Who Wrote 'Dongguk Almanac'", *Journal of Language Culture* 7.

Matsubara, Takatoshi. 1997. "The Frontiers of Choson Mythology: Focusing on the Myth of Dangun" (Special Issue: How to Read the Wrold Myths), *Eureka* 29(2).

Matsubara, Takatoshi. 1997. (Matsubara Takatoshi, Cho Jingyon) "A history of Izuhara Korean Language School in Tsusima and Choryang Korean Language School in Pusan: a Study in Methods of Korean Language Education in the Early Meiji Era", *Journal of Language Culture* (8).

Matsubara, Takatoshi. 1998. (Kobayashi Shigeru, Matsubara Takatoshi, Rokutanda Yutaka), "Chronological Table of Drifting From Choson to Ryukyu and From Ryukyu to Chosen", *Rekidai Hoan Studies* (9).

Matsubara, Takatoshi. 1999. "Ancient Stories of Korea" (Special Issue Ancient Stories: Common Folk tales) (Japan and Korean Peninsula, China: Turbulent Asia), *A Study of Exposition and Materials of National Literature* 44(14) 649.

Matsubara, Takatoshi. 2001. "Data List of Korean Old Books Owned by Liaoning Province Library in China", Lianoning Province Library, *Journal of Language Culture* (14).

Matsuda, Hirokimi. 1978. "Traces of Yao-bikuni: For Comparative Folklore of Japan and Korea", *The Japanese Journal of Ethnology* 43(2): 213-219.

Matsudaira, Makoto. 1995. "(Eating Asian Festivals 3) 'Tip of Korean Insular Ceremonies", *Chikuma* 297: 36-37.

Matsudaira, Makoto. 2000. "Korean Peninsular: From the Perspective of Comparison of Food Culture", Akino Koji, Obata So, eds., *Asian Food Culture.* Kenpaku-sha.

Matsumae, Takeshi. 1970. "Ancient Koreans' Worship of Dragons and Snakes and Regality", *Chosen-gakuho* 57: 1-22.

Matsumae, Takeshi. 1973. "Japanese Myths and Korea", *Possibility of Japanese Myth.* (154-177), Tokyo: dento-to-gendai-sha.

Matsumae, Takeshi. 1976. "Yu Dongsik 'Korean Shamanism'", *Chosen-gakuho* 80: 271-274.

Matsumae, Takeshi. 1981. "A Study of Origin of Ancient Shinto: A Comparative Study of Japanese and Korean Old Customs", *Kokugakuin-zasshi* 82(11): 1-17.

Matsumae, Takeshi. 1982. "Japan and Korea in Myths and Ethnic Customs", *Chosen-gakuho* 102: 29-43.

Matsumae, Takeshi. 1985. "Tradition of Japan and Korea From the Perspective of Method of Telling Myths", *Eureka* 17(1): 215-219.

Matsumae, Takeshi. 1985. *Mystery of Japanese Myth*. Tokyo: Yamato-shobo.

Matsumoto, Seiichi. 1978. "About Dr. Akiba Takashi", Chiba-ken kyodo-shi kenkyu renraku kyogi-kai ed., *Boso-no-kyodo-shi* (5th Anniversary Special Issue) 147-148.

Matsumoto, Seiichi. 1980. "Folk Cultures in Japan and Korea: an Introduction of Comparative Studies on the Organization of Communal Rite", *A Viewpoint of Cultural Anthropology, Composite Work.* Tokyo: Sai-shobo.

Matsumoto, Seiichi. 1981. "Organization and Process of Communal Rite in a Korean Village", *Annual Journal of the Asia-Africa Cultural Research Institute* No.15.

Matsumoto, Seiichi. 1982. tr., Jang Ju-Keun, *Korean Local Belief.* Daiichi-shobo.

Matsumoto, Seiichi. 1984. "A Communal Rite and its Organization of an East Coast Village in Korea", in *Japan-Korea Joint Research Report Vol. 2, Hupo-ri, Pyeonghae-up, North Gyeongsang Province.* (232-245), Kobe: Joint Seminar of Fishing Community and Economy of Japan and Korea Office.

Matsumoto, Seiichi. 1984. "Reference with Korean 'Chayon pulak (village)'", *Annual Journal of the Asia-Africa Cultural Research Institute* No.18.

Matsumoto, Seiichi. 1985. "Korean Studies Report", *Annual Journal of the Asia-Africa Cultural Research Institute* 19: 121-128.

Matsumoto, Seiichi. 1985. "Traces of Dr. Kim Hyeon-jun", *Hakusan Sociological Review* 3: 19-22.

Matsumoto, Seiichi. 1985. "Village Festival in Korea: the Case of a Fishery Village in Cholla-namdo", *Education and Medical Science* Vol.33 No.8.

Matsumoto, Seiichi. 1986. (A Bibliographical Introduction and Translation) "Han Sangbok, 'Rites and Belief of Residents in Korean Mountain Villages: A Case Study of Amyongsan 2-ri and Bongsan-ri, Pyeongchang-gun, Gangwon Province'", *Toyo-daigaku-shakai-gakubu-kiyo* 23(2): 141-164.

Matsumoto, Seiichi. 1986. "(Book Review): *'A Study of Choson Folk Culture: Concerning the Basic Culture and the Origin'* by Yoda Chihoko", *Gendai-korea* 259: 66-67.

Matsumoto, Seiichi. 1986. "Korean Family Trend", *Mother and Child Wellbeing around the World* 21: 6-9.

Matsumoto, Seiichi. 1986. "Korean Finger Calendar", *Minpaku-tsushin* 33: 2-4.

Matsumoto, Seiichi. 1986. "Korean University News", *Annual Journal of the Asia-Africa Cultural Research Institute* 20: 173-178.

Matsumoto, Seiichi. 1987. "A Note on Korean Family Size", *Annals of Family Studies* 12: 85-94.

Matsumoto, Seiichi. 1987. "Japanese National Moral Theory and the Government-General of Korea: As a Note of Study History of Choson Folk Customs", *Toyo University Special Research Report* 1986, 224-230.

Matsumoto, Seiichi. 1987. "Phases of Festivals Ⅱ Korea, 1. Ancestral Rites (Great Festival of Ancestral Shrine) 2. Regional Festivals (Kangreung Tano Festival)", Takahashi Toichi, Haga Masaaki, Matsumoto Seiichi, *Cultural Anthropology Note,* 103-112, Tokyo: Sai-shobo.

Matsumoto, Seiichi. 1987. "Pre-census Registration and Retirement of the Headship of a Family in Korea", *The Han* 107: 137-175.

Matsumoto, Seiichi. 1988. "Before the Theory of Conquering Korea", *Toyo University Special Study Report* 1987, 200-213.

Matsumoto, Seiichi. 1988. "Trends in Korean Research in Japanese Cultural Anthropology and Folklore Studies 1960-1980 with a Bibliography of Korean Studies by Japanese", *The Bulletin of Faculty of Sociology, Toyo University* 25(2): 37-76.

Matsumoto, Seiichi. 1989. *Advance into Korea before the Opening the Country: Focusing on Suo Uma-shima Island.* Toyo University Special Research Report 1988, 260-266.

Matsumoto, Seiichi. 1990. "(The 11th Conference for International Anthropology and Folklore) Koeranist Group Report", *The Japanese Journal of Ethnology* 54: 4-507.

Matsumoto, Seiichi. 1990. "An Inquiry of Family Studies on Cheju Island: the Difference in Size of Household Between the East and the West", in Takeda Akira, ed., *Progress and Problems of Folklore.* (251-272), Tokyo: Kokusho-kanko-kai.

Matsumoto, Seiichi. 1990. "On the Boundary of 'Tong-li (local community)' in Korea", Sugiyama Koichi, Sakurai Tetsuo eds., *Cultural Anthropology of Korean Society.* 56: 71, Tokyo: Kobun-do.

Matsumoto, Seiichi. 1990. "Regional Feature of Aged People Problems and Yangban Aged People Group in North Gyeongsang Province", *Annual Journal of the Asia-Africa Cultural Research Institute* 24: 108-115.

Matsumoto, Seiichi. 1991. "Marginal People in Kyushu: Kumamoto Spirits, View of Choson", *Special Study Report of Toyo University* 1990, 114-119.

Matsumoto, Seiichi. 1992. "Japanese Social Anthropological Studies on Korea.", *Cahiers d'Extreme-Asie (Far East Asian Studies Bulletin)* Vol.6, 1991-1992, France National Far East Gakuin Kyoto Branch, Research Institute for Hohingirin.

Matsumoto, Seiichi. 1996. "Village and Family in Korea", *Village and Family in East Asia*, 〈A Record of Symposium〉 22-24, 61-65, Kyoto: The Research Institute of Bukkyo University.

Matsumoto, Seiichi. 1998. "(Book Review) *Patriarchal System of East Asia: A Comparative Sociology of Gender* by Sechiyama Kaku", *Japanese Journal of Family Sociology* 10: 2: 149-151.

Matsumoto, Seiichi. 1998. "(Book Review): Kendall, Laurel. *Getting Married in Korea: Of Gender, Morality, and Modernity*", *Asian Folklore Studies* LVI: 2: 420-421, Nansan University.

Matsumoto, Seiichi. 1998. "Modernization and Cultural Traits of Fishing Community of Korean East Coast: A Case Study of Chukpyeon, Ulchin-gun, North Gyeongsang Province", *Annual Journal of the Asia-Africa Cultural Research Institute* 32: 11-72.

Matsumoto, Seiichi. 1999. "Age and Local Community in Japan and Korea", *The Bulletin of Faculty of Sociology, Toyo University* 36-2: 39-67.

Matsumoto, Seiichi. 2000. "Korean Epitaphs in Montreal", *Annual Journal of the Asia-Africa Cultural Research Institute* 34: 59-80.

Matsumoto, Seiichi. 2001. "Korean Church in Montreal (1)", *Annual Journal of the Asia-Africa Cultural Research Institute* (35).

Matsumoto, Seiichi. 2002. "Korean Church in Montreal (2)", *Annual Journal of the Asia-Africa Cultural Research Institute* (36).

Mikami, Tsugio. 1946. "An Investigation Report of Hanin: in Search for Remains of Kokuryo", *The Japanese Journal of Ethnology* 11(1): 81-104.

Min, Che. 1994. "Korean Alter", *Ritual Culture* 10.

Miura, Kunio. 2000. "A Glance of Korean Taoism Studies", *Asia Yugaku* 16.

Miura, Yoshiyuki. 1991. "A Study of East Asian Culture of Chopsticks: Origin and Development Two Chopsticks for Meal", *Comparative Folk Studies* 3.

Miyahara, Toichi. 1966. "Experience in Jeju Island", *Journal of Japanese Folklore Society* 44: 59-62.

Miyajima, Hiroshi. 1994. "Formation Korean Yangban Society", in Mizoguchi Yuzo, Hamashita Takeshi, Hiraishi Naoaki, Miyajima Hiroshi eds., *Society and Nation. (Thinking in Asia 4)* (131-166), Tokyo: Tokyo-daigaku-shuppan-kyoku.

Miyajima, Hiroshi. 1995. *Yangban.* Tokyo: Chuo-koron.

Miyara, Takahiro. 1982. "A Comparative Study of Clan System in Korea and Ryukyu", in Emori Itsuo, Choe Yonggi eds., *A Study of the Institution of the Same Blood of Yangban.* (357-417), Tokyo: Daiichi-shobo.

Mori, Masao. 1998. "View of History and Modern Times of Korea", Ogo Kin'ichi, Kaji Akira, Sasaki Kokan, Higa Masao, Miyamoto Masaru, eds., *Society and Symbol: Anthropological Approach.*(Treatises in Honor of Prof. Muratake Seiichi's 70th Birthday), Iwata-shoin.

Morieda, Takashi and Asakura, Toshio. 1986. *Food is in Korea.* Tokyo: Kobun-do.

Morita, Yoshio. 1991. "The End of Japanese Rule and Cultural Change in Korea", *Gakushuin-daigaku-toyo-bunka-kenkyu-jo-knkyu-hokoku* 26.

Motomura, Hiroshi. 1983. With Hong Sanguk, "A Comparative Study of Relationship of Parent and Child in Japan and Korea: Focusing on Parents' View and Attitude of Rearing and Children's Psychological Social Feature",

Osaka Municipal University Department of Life Science Bulletin 31(Separate Volume 5): 345-362.

Motomura, Hiroshi. 1985. With Hong Sanguk, "Family Change in Korea: A Comparative Study of Farming Family and Urban Family", *Osaka Municipal University Department of Life Science Bulletin* 33(Separate Volume 5): 245-258.

Mun, Hyo-Suk. 1996. "Women in Korean Society", in Seki Keiko, Kimoto Kimiko eds., *Reading the World From Gender.* (231-259), Tokyo: Akashi-shoten.

Mun, Kyeong-Su. 1991. "Korean Society and Civil Culture", *Asian and African Studies* 31(4).

Mun, Ok-Pyo. 1999. "(Book Review), Shima Mutsuhiko, Asakura Toshio, eds., *Changing Korean Society: From the Field of Research of Anthropology in the 1970's~80's*", *Minpaku-tsushin* 83: 33-39.

Murakami, Sachiko. 1999. "Korean Puppet Play and Puppet Dance of Hachiman-kohyo Shrine and Koyo Shrine", *Chosen-gakuho* 171.

Muratake, Seiichi. 1966. With Izumi Seiichi "Korea", in Japanese Society of Ethnology, ed., *Reflction and Prospect of Japanese Ethnology.* (258-265), Tokyo: Minzokugaku Shinkokai.

Muratake, Seiichi. 1973. *Social Anthropology of Family.* Tokyo: Kobun-do.

Muratake, Seiichi. 1977. "A Statue of Akiba Takashi Seen From the Last Pupil", *Annual Report of Social Anthropology* 3: 179-195.

Muratake, Seiichi. 1987. "Akiba Takashi", *Cultural Anthropology Dictionary.* Tokyo: Kobun-do.

Naito, Kanji. 1979. "Families of Goto Retto Islands and Jeju Island: Formative Foundation of the Succession of the Last born", in Editting Committee for Treatises in Honor of Prof. Yamaoka Eiichi's 70th Birthday, ed., *Issues of Regional Sociology: Treatises in Honor of Prof. Yamaoka Eiichi's 70th Birthday.* 1: 26, Kyoto: Koyo-shobo.

Nakadate, Ko. 1986. "A Note on Breeding Industry of Wando", *Japan-Korea Joint Research Report Vol. 4 Wando-gun, South Jeolla Province, Korea.* (70-82), Kobe: Joint Seminar of Fishing Community and Economy of Japan and Korea Office.

Nakagawa, Yuri. 1999. "Korean Christianity and Village Church", *Mirai* 389.

Nakagawa, Yuri. 2001. "On the Concept of the Jip ('House') in Korea", *Humanities Annual Report* (31).

Nakajima, Mineo. 1992. *A Comparative Study of East Asia.* Tokyo: Nihon-gakujutsu-shinko-kai.

Nakajima, Tomoko. 1997. "Education of Zainichi Koreans in Japanese School", Kobayashi Tetsuya, Ebuchi Kazuhiro eds., *A Comparative Study of Multicultural Education: Cultural Assimilation and Diversifier in Education.* Kyushu-daigaku-shuppan-kai.

Nakamura, Akira. 1983. "Origin of Silla Monarchy and Shamanism", *Review of Law and Political Sciences* 80(3, 4): 1-56.

Nakamura, Keisuke. 2000. "Change of Family Relations in Korean Society: Focusing on a Hearing Survey", Otemon University Research Society of Asian Culture ed., *Asia Which Accepts Multi-Culture.* Izumi-shobo.

Nakamura, Shunsaku. 1999. "Information and Image of Confucian Society", Aoki Tamotsu, Kajiwara Kageaki eds., *Culture of Information Society (1) Information and Asia, Image.* Tokyo-daigaku-shuppan-kai.

Nakamura, Teruko. 1984. "Traveling Entertainment Group of Korea: Namsa-dang", *Kikan-minzokugaku* 8(4): 110-118.

Nakamura, Yae. 2001. "Cremation and Idea of Filial Piety in Modern Korean Society", *Asian Social Culture Studies* (2).

Nakane, Chie. 1973. "A Comparative Study of Consanguinity of Okinawa, Mainland Japan, China, Korea", Japanese Society of Ethnology, ed., *An Ethnological Study of Okinawa: Ethnic Society and the Picture of the World.* Tokyo: Minzokugaku Shinkokai.

Nakane, Chie. 1973. "A Sketch of Korea", Nakane Chie ed., *Family and Rites in Korean Villages.* Tokyo: Tokyo-daigaku-shuppan-kyoku.

Nakane, Chie. 1975. "Korea: Giving Its Social Anthropological Position", *Chosen-gakuho* 75: 1-10.

Nakane, Chie. 1975. "Social Anthropology and East Asia East Asia", *The Japanese Journal of Ethnology* 39(4): 344-349.

Nakane, Chie. 1978. "Differences of Human Relations of Korea and Japan: A Comment on '*Social Characters of Koreans*' by Choe Jaeseok", *Social Structure of Japan.*

Nakane, Chie. 1979. *An Analysis of Social Structure: Focusing on Asia*, (NHK University Lecture), Tokyo: NHK Publishing.

Nakane, Chie. 1987. *Social Anthropology: A Study of Asian Societies.* Tokyo: Tokyo-daigaku-shuppan-kyoku.

Nakano, Yoshio. 1982. "Customs for Ceremonial Occasion of Former Choson", *Journal of Kyoto Sangyo University Law Society* 16(3): 79-86.

Nakano, Yoshio. 1984. "Annual Events of Former Choson: Miscellanies on Japanese Legal History 5", *Journal of Kyoto Sangyo University Law Society* 17(4): 29-38.

Naoe, Hiroji. 1976. "China, Taiwan, Korea" Wakamori Taro ed., Journal of Japanese Folklore Lecture 5 The Method of Folklore, Tokyo: Asakura-shoten.

Naoe, Hiroji. 1987. *A Comparative Study of Folk Belief: The Way to Comparative Folklore.* Tokyo: Yoshikawa Kobunkan.

Narisawa, Masaru. 1979. "A Note on Korean Folk Customs: Grass Tomb and Exorcism", *Han* 8(3, 4): 155-158.

Narisawa, Masaru. 1983. "About Change of Tale of Child Burial in Korea", *Chosen-gakuho* 109: 57-76.

Nie Lili. 2000. "Korean People in Social Development of Modern China", Maruyama Koichi ed., *A Cultural Anthropological Study of Chinese Nationalism and Changing Process of Minority Ethnic Culture.* Report for Grants-in-Aid for Scientific Research, Ministry of Education, Culture, Sports, Science and Technology.

Nikaido, Yuko. 2000. "Adapting Process of Zainichi Koreans: From Life History of a Family", *Journal of Municipal University Sociology* (1).

Nikaido, Yuko. 2001. "Ethnic Relations and Urban Community: A Case Study of Zainichi Korean Community and Japanese Community", *Journal of Municipal University Sociology* (2).

Nikkan Gyoson Syakai/Keizai Kyoudou Kenkyuukai. 1984. *Japan-Korea Joint Research Report Vol. 2: Hupo-ri, Pyeonghae-up, North Gyeongsang Province, Korea,* Kobe: Joint Seminar of Fishing Community and Economy of Japan and Korea Office.

Nikkan Gyoson Syakai/Keizai Kyoudou Kenkyuukai. 1986. *Japan-Korea Joint Research Report Vol. 4: Wando-gun, South Jeolla Province, Korea*, Kobe:

Joint Seminar of Fishing Community and Economy of Japan and Korea Office.

Nikkan Gyoson Syakai/Keizai Kyoudou Kenkyuukai. 1988. *Japan-Korea Joint Research Report Vol. 6: Chungmu City, South Gyeongsang Province, Korea and Peripheral Fishing Villages,* Kobe: Joint Seminar of Fishing Community and Economy of Japan and Korea Office.

Nishimura, Mieko. 1983. "Folk Customs of Seonyudo Island: Focusing on Grass Tomb", *Toho Gakuen College Bulletin* 208-231.

Nishimura, Mieko. 1984. "Korean Grass Tomb: Review in Research Journal", *Minzokugaku-hyoron* 24: 56-71.

Nishimura, Mieko. 1985. "Folk Customs Concerning Korean Grass Tomb", *Nihon-minzokugaku* 161: 32-49.

Niwa, Izumi. 1988. "Korean Shaman: A Case Study of Sobosal", *Shkaigaku-journal* 27(1).

Niwa, Izumi. 1989. "Korean Shamanism and Women (Special Issue: Religion and Women)", *Shukyo-kenkyu* 63(1).

Niwa, Izumi. 1990. "Korean Musok and Shamanism: Concerning Use of the Concept of Shamanism", *Shkaigaku-journal* 29(1).

Niwa, Izumi. 1994. "About a New Religious Group in Shin-donai of Mt. Gyeryong in Korea: A Case Study of the Headquarter of Jeongdogyo", *Journal of West Japan Religious Science* 16.

Niwa, Izumi. 1995. "Between Shaman and the Founder of a Religion", *Tokyo University of Foreign Studies Treatises* 51.

Niwa, Izumi. 1996. "Miyake Hitoshi, Suzuki Masataka eds., Shamanism and Folk Customs of East Asia", *Shukyo-kenkyu* 70(1).

Niwa, Izumi. 1996. Akizuki Nozomi, Niwa Izumi, *Korean Encyclopedia.* Taishukan-shoten.

Niwa, Izumi. 1999. "Korea (Special Issue: New Year's Day of Asia: Festivals of New Year and Races)", *Gekkan-shinika* 10(1).

Niwa, Izumi. 1999. "Why Are There Many Christians in Korea? A Comparative Study of Japanese and Korean Religion", *Soubun* 410.

Niwa, Izumi. 2001. "Patriotism to Kim Kyosin, a Christian of Non-Churchism", *Journal of West Japan Religious Science* (23).

Niwa, Izumi. 2001. "Walking in Korea (7) Belief of Jeonggamrok in the New Town of Mt. Gyeryong", *Asia Yugaku* (31).

No, T'ae-Ton. 1992. "A Logical Study of Formative Process of Korean People", *Chosen-gakuho* 142: 1-12.

No, Pu-Cha. 1992. "A Sociological Study of Union of Consanguinity in Modern Korean Cities: A Case Study of Royal Family Meeting of Seoul", *Nagoya University Sociology Treatises* 13: 155-182.

No, Pu-Cha. 1994. "A Study of Social Bond of the Group of the Same Surname and the Same Family Origin From the Perspective of Substructure", *Nagoya University Sociology Treatises* 15.

No, Pu-Cha. 1997. "Entire Structure of Organizations of the Same Surname in Korean Cities: A Case Study of Daedong-jongyak-won of Jeonjoo-Lee in Seoul", *Sociology* 41(3): 37-54.

No, Pu-Cha. 1997. "The Meaning of Union of the Same Surname in Korean Cities", *Japanese Sociology Review* 48(1): 47-61.

No, Pu-Cha. 2000. "Formation and Change of Union of the Same Surname According to Korean Urbanization", Yoshihara Kazuo, Suzuki Masataka, Suenari Michio eds., *Reconstruction of Blood Relation: Paternal Origin and Union of the Same Surname in East Asia.* Fukyo-sha.

No, Pu-Cha. 2000. "Korea", Nakata Minoru, *World's Inhabitant Structure: A International Comparative Study of Asia and Western Countries.* Jichitai-kenkyu-sha.

Noguchi, Takashi ed. 1976. *Emigration and Cultural Change : A Case Study of Hapcheon in Korea.* Tokyo: Nihon-gakujutsu-shinko-kai.

Nomura, Shin'ichi. 1982. "A Study of Place for Masque in Korea", *Journal of Art and Literature Studies* 43: 1-26.

Nomura, Shin'ichi. 1984. "Yangju Byeolsandae-nori", *The Japanese Journal of Ethnology* 49(2): 189-194.

Nomura, Shin'ichi. 1985. *Masque and Traveling Entertainer: Korean Folk Entertainment.* Tokyo: Arina-shobo.

Nomura, Shin'ichi. 1986. "Masque, Bugbear, Music of Peasants [Expansion of Music of Peasants and Honam Music of Peasants]", Ito Abito, Ohmura Masuo, Kajimura Hideki, Takeda Yukio eds., *A Dictionary for*

Understanding of Choson. Tokyo: Heibon-sha.

Nomura, Shin'ichi. 1987. "Tonchinkan and Dongmunseodap: Based on Abusive Language of Korean", *Journal of Language Life* 428.

Nomura, Shin'ichi. 1987. *Korean Folk Play: The World of Play and Shamanism.* Tokyo: Heibon-sha.

Nomura, Shin'ichi. 1992. "An Introduction to Choson Culture From the Perspective of Everyday Language", *Journal of Art and Literature Studies* 60.

Nomura, Shin'ichi. 1993. "An Introduction to Korean Culture From the Perspective of Everyday Language 2", *Journal of Art and Literature Studies* 62.

Nomura, Shin'ichi. 1993. "Cosmology of Chunhyangjeon", *Journal of Art and Literature Studies* 64.

Nomura, Shin'ichi. 1994. "Korean Entertainment of Beginning and End of the Year (From the Perspective of Asia: A Direction of Folk Entertainment Studies 〈〔Folk Entertainment〕 Society 10th Anniversary Symposium〉)", *Journal of Falk Entertainment Studies* 20.

Nomura, Shin'ichi. 1994. "Phases of Events of Expulsion of Devil and Masque", Miyake Hitoshi, Suzuki Masataka eds., *Shamanism and Folk Customs of East Asia.* Tokyo: Keiso-shobo, 268: 291.

Nomura, Shin'ichi. 1995. "Asia of Shamanism and Entertainer", *Chuo-koron Shinsho.* Chuo-koron.

Nomura, Shin'ichi. 1996. "Deity Exorcism: Drama of Deity and Man (1)", *Keio University Hiyoshi Bulletin: Language, Culture, Communication* 16: 51-82.

Nomura, Shin'ichi. 1996. "Deity Exorcism: Drama of Deity and Man (2)" *Keio University Hiyoshi Bulletin: Language, Culture, Communication* 17: 42-79.

Nomura, Shin'ichi. 1997. "Artistry of Ssitkim-kut", *Journal of Folk Entertainment Studies* 25: 18-41.

Nomura, Shin'ichi. 1997. "Deity Exorcism: Drama of Deity and Man (3)", (Original Text: Mun Museong) *Keio University Hiyoshi Bulletin: Language, Culture, Communication* 18: 68-137.

Nomura, Shin'ichi. 1997. "Donipuli-rites of Opening Jars", *Keio University Hiyoshi Bulletin: Language, Culture, Communication* 19: 116-140.

Nomura, Shin'ichi. 1999. "Artistry of Kut of Jeju Island", Suzuki Masataka, Nomura Shin'ichi eds., *A Study of Mask and Shamanism: Japan and Korea.*

Daiichi-shobo.

Nomura, Shin'ichi. 1999. "The First Masque: Revival of Possessions", Suzuki Masataka, Nomura Shinichi eds., *A Study of Mask and Shamanism: Japan and Korea.* Daiichi-shobo.

Nomura, Shin'ichi. 1999. Suzuki Masataka, Nomura Shinichi, *A Study of Mask and Shamanism.* Daiichi-shobo.

Nomura, Shin'ichi. 1999. tr., Hwang Jeokin, "Personal View of Korean Agriculture and Farming Organic Law: 'Study Forum' of Law Paper [1998.9.3]", *Investigation Report of Agricultural Administration* 514.

Nomura, Shin'ichi. 2000. "Visible Folk Customs, Invisible Folk Customs (Special Issue: Rural Culture: Jeju Province)", *Gekkan-kankoku-bunka* 252, 2000.11.

Nomura, Shin'ichi. 2000. Hoshino Hiroshi, Nomura Shinichi, *Asia of Singing, Dancing, Prayer.* Yugaku Series 10, Bensey-shuppan, 2000.11.

Nomura, Shin'ichi. 2001. "From the Perspective of Goddess Belief China Sea (Special Issue: Women's Rites and Goddess Belief Around East Asia Sea)", *Keio University Hiyoshi Bulletin: Language Culture, Communication* (26).

Nomura, Shin'ichi. 2001. "Special Issue: Murayama Chijun's Choson Folk Customs", *Nature and Culture* 66.

Nomura, Shin'ichi. 2002. "Forgotten Entertainment History. Introduction (2) From the Perspective of Entertainment Space in the Same Period History", *Chosen-bunka-kenkyu* (9).

Nomura, Shin'ichi. 2002. "Lee Neunghwa [Choson Shamanism] Note Vol. 2", *Keio University Hiyoshi Bulletin: Language, Culture, Communication* (29).

Nomura, Shin'ichi. 2002. "Lee Neunghwa [Choson Shamanism] Note Vol. 1", *Keio University Hiyoshi Bulletin: Language, Culture, Communication* (28).

Nomura, Shin'ichi. 2002. "Mass for Dead Soul in Korean Cultural History", *Keio University Hiyoshi Bulletin: Language, Culture, Communication* (28).

Nomura, Yoshifumi. 1981. *Korean House: Climate, Space Design.* Kyoto-Gakugei Publishing.

Nozaki, Mitsuhiko. 1982. "Private Library Specialized in Korea in Kansai (Report) (Special Issue: Expansion and Deepening of Library Service)(People

Isolated From Library Service)" *Library Journal* 34(1).

Nozaki, Mitsuhiko. 1986. "Choson's Development of 〈Kojinsaihotan〉: Focusing on Heosaeng-byeoljeon", *Chosen-gakuho* 121.

Nozaki, Mitsuhiko. 1986. tr., "Seon Jaeyeong, Life and Literature of Seok Jugeom", *Chosen-gakuho* 119, 120.

Nozaki, Mitsuhiko. 1990. tr., Cha Juhwan, *Choson Taoism*. Jimbun-shoin.

Nozaki, Mitsuhiko. 1992. "Geomancy of Modern Korea", *Journal of Humanities Sutdies* 44(1).

Nozaki, Mitsuhiko. 1993. Wei Shishong, *Chinese Classical Litearture and Choson.* Kenbun Publishing.

Nozaki, Mitsuhiko. 1994. "Yongjaechonghwa: About Vision and Story of Choson Court Rank in the 15th Century", *Journal of Humanities Sutdies* 46(8).

Nozaki, Mitsuhiko. 1994. *Korean Geomancers: Now Reviving Yongmaek.* Kyoto: Jimbun-shoin.

Nozaki, Mitsuhiko. 1995. "Immortality Myth and Thought: A Study of Sanhaegyeong, Pobakja, Yeolseonjeon, Sinseonjeon/Jeong Jaeseo (1994) 〔Original Text Korean〕", *Oriental Religion* 85.

Nozaki, Mitsuhiko. 1996. "About Formation of Choson Leaping Theory", *Journal of Humanities Sutdies* 48(1).

Nozaki, Mitsuhiko. 1996. "Choson Story(4) Miracle Monks: Haedong Buddhism Geniuses Legend", *Gekkan-shinika* 7(7).

Nozaki, Mitsuhiko. 1996. "Choson Story(5) Genealogy of Minor Official Literature-interests in Subculture", *Gekkan-shinika* 7(8).

Nozaki, Mitsuhiko. 1996. "Choson Story(6) Kim Siseup, Hoin, Im Geojeong: Spirit of Resistance and Rebellion", *Gekkan-shinika* 7(9).

Nozaki, Mitsuhiko. 1996. "Choson Story(7) Novels of War: Overcoming of Wound", *Gekkan-shinika* 7(10).

Nozaki, Mitsuhiko. 1996. "Choson Story(8) The World of Unofficial Historical Story: Kaleidoscope of Choson Society", *Gekkan-shinika* 7(11).

Nozaki, Mitsuhiko. 1996. "Choson Story(9) Positive School, The Age of Pak Jiwon: Confucianism is not Polished", *Gekkan-shinika* 7(12).

Nozaki, Mitsuhiko. 1997. "Choson Story(10) Pansori: Sounds of All Creation", *Gekkan-shinika* 8(1).

Nozaki, Mitsuhiko. 1997. "Choson Story(11) Choson Women's Image: Women in Korea", *Gekkan-shinika* 8(2).

Nozaki, Mitsuhiko. 1997. "Choson Story(12) 〈Last Issue〉 Complete Works of Choson Stories", *Gekkan-shinika* 8(3).

Nozaki, Mitsuhiko. 1997. "Korean Flowers (Special Issue: Cultural History of Flowers: Asian Flowers and People)", *Gekkan-shinika* 8(9).

Nozaki, Mitsuhiko. 1997. "Position of Dangun-Conflict of Peculiarity and Imported Things (Special Issue: Discovery of Traditoinal Culture in Modern Choson)", *Chosen-shi-kenkyu-kai-ronbun-shu* 35.

Nozaki, Mitsuhiko. 1997. Nozaki Mitsuhiko trans. "Data. Testimony of People: Learning From Asian Hearts", *Journal of Liberated Education* 27(14).

Nozaki, Mitsuhiko. 1998. "The End of the Century: Korean Geomancy (Special Issue: Asian Geomancy, Japanese Physiognomy of a House)(The Present of Asian Geomancy)" *Architecture Journal* 113(1417).

Nozaki, Mitsuhiko. 1998. *Choson Story* (Asia Books 2), Taishukan-shoten.

Nozaki, Mitsuhiko. 1999. "An Introduction to 'Chinese Literatures Studies in Korea'", *Toyo-gakuho* 217.

Nozaki, Mitsuhiko. 1999. "Eros of Choson: Deviated sex (Special Issue: Orchestrated Eros)", *Asia Yugaku* 8.

Nozaki, Mitsuhiko. 2000. (ed.,tr. and n.) Kim Gyeongjin ed., *Choengguyadam* (Toyo Bunko), Heibon-sha.

Nozaki, Mitsuhiko. 2000. "An Essay on P'an-soo: About Fortune-Telling, Curse, Pray for Rain of Choson Blind Monks", *Journal of Humanities Studies* 52(4 Separate Volume).

Nozaki, Mitsuhiko. 2000. "Chinese Literatures in Korea: Concerning Estrangement between Expression and Means (Special Issue Chinese Literatures of Asian Cultural Area)" *Asia Yugaku* (12).

Nozaki, Mitsuhiko. 2000. "Koreanization of Taoism", *Asia Yugaku* 16.

Nozaki, Mitsuhiko. 2001. "Overseas Scientific Trend, A Report of Korea Taoism Culture Society International Scientific Meeting", *Journal of Oriental Religions* (97).

Nozaki, Mitsuhiko. 2001. "Strange Stories of Choson Dynasty The World of Unofficial Historical Story(1) An Introduction", *Gekkan-kankoku-bunka*

257.

Nozaki, Mitsuhiko. 2001. "Strange Stories of Choson Dynasty The World of Unofficial Historical Story(2) Minor Official Literatures in the Early Choson Dynasty(1)", *Gekkan-kankoku-bunka* 258.

Nozaki, Mitsuhiko. 2001. "Strange Stories of Choson Dynasty The World of Unofficial Historical Story(3) Minor Official Literatures in the Early Choson Dynasty(2)", *Gekkan-kankoku-bunka* 259.

Nozaki, Mitsuhiko. 2001. "Strange Stories of Choson Dynasty The World of Unofficial Historical Story(4) Minor Official Literatures in the Early Choson Dynasty(3) The World of Yongjaechonghwa Vol. 1", *Gekkan-kankoku-bunka* 260.

Nozaki, Mitsuhiko. 2001. "Strange Stories of Choson Dynasty The World of Unofficial Historical Story(5) Minor Official Literatures in the Early Choson Dynasty(4) The World of Yongjaechonghwa (2-1)", *Gekkan-kankoku-bunka* 261.

Nozaki, Mitsuhiko. 2001. "Strange Stories of Choson Dynasty The World of Unofficial Historical Story(6) Minor Official Literatures in the Early Choson Dynasty(5) The World of Yongjaechonghwa (2-2)", *Gekkan-kankoku-bunka* 262.

Nozaki, Mitsuhiko. 2001. "Strange Stories of Choson Dynasty The World of Unofficial Historical Story(7) Minor Official Literatures in the Early Choson Dynasty(6) The World of Yongjaechonghwa (3-1)", *Gekkan-kankoku-bunka* 263.

Nozaki, Mitsuhiko. 2001. "Strange Stories of Choson Dynasty The World of Unofficial Historical Story(8) Minor Official Literatures in the Early Choson Dynasty(7)" The World of Yongjaechonghwa (3-2)", *Gekkan-kankoku-bunka* 264.

Nozaki, Mitsuhiko. 2001. "Strange Stories of Choson Dynasty The World of Unofficial Historical Story(9) Minor Official Literatures in the Early Choson Dynasty(8)" The World of Yongjaechonghwa (3-3)", *Gekkan-kankoku-bunka* 265.

Nozaki, Mitsuhiko. 2001. Seo Yeongsu et al., *Comic, Stories of Korean History 1.* Kokushokankokai, 2001.11.

Nozaki, Mitsuhiko. 2001. Seo Yeongsu et al., *Comic, Stories of Korean History 2*. Kokushokankokai, 2001.11.

Nozaki, Mitsuhiko. 2001. Seo Yeongsu et al., *Comic, Stories of Korean History 3*. Kokushokankokai, 2001.11.

Nozaki, Mitsuhiko. 2001. Yusa Noboru, Nozaki Mitsuhiko, Masuo Shinichiro. Yuzankaku eds., *Taoism of Asian Countries (Lecture Taoisu Vol. 6)*. Tokyo: Yuzan-kaku.

Nozaki, Mitsuhiko. 2002. "Image of Strangers in Korea", Publishing Committee of Choson Literatures Treatises in Honor of Dr. Ohtani Morishige's 70th Birthday, *Korean Literatures Treatises.* Hakutei-sha.

Nozaki, Mitsuhiko. 2002. "For Understanding of 'Friend'", *Book Story* 8(3) 82

Nozaki, Mitsuhiko. 2002. "Strange Stories of Choson Dynasty The World of Unofficial Historical Story (10) Choson Geniuses Stories (1)", *Gekkan-kankoku-bunka* 269.

Nozaki, Mitsuhiko. 2002. "Strange Stories of Choson Dynasty The World of Unofficial Historical Story (11) Choson Geniuses Stories (2)", *Gekkan-kankoku-bunka* 270.

Nozaki, Mitsuhiko. 2002. "Strange Stories of Choson Dynasty The World of Unofficial Historical Story (12) Choson Geniuses Stories (3)", *Gekkan-kankoku-bunka* 271.

Nozaki, Mitsuhiko. 2002. "Strange Stories of Choson Dynasty The World of Unofficial Historical Story (13) Choson Geniuses Stories (4)", *Gekkan-kankoku-bunka* 272.

Nozaki, Mitsuhiko. 2002. "Strange Stories of Choson Dynasty The World of Unofficial Historical Story (14) Choson Geniuses Stories (5)", *Gekkan-kankoku-bunka* 273.

Nozaki, Mitsuhiko. 2002. "Strange Stories of Choson Dynasty The World of Unofficial Historical Story (15) Choson Technique Stories (1)", *Gekkan-kankoku-bunka* 274.

Nozaki, Mitsuhiko. 2002. "Strange Stories of Choson Dynasty The World of Unofficial Historical Story (16) Choson Technique Stories (2)", *Gekkan-kankoku-bunka* 275.

Nozaki, Mitsuhiko. 2002. "Strange Stories of Choson Dynasty The World of

Unofficial Historical Story (17) Choson Technique Stories (3)", *Gekkan-kankoku-bunka* 276.

Nozaki, Mitsuhiko. 2002. "Strange Stories of Choson Dynasty The World of Unofficial Historical Story (18, Last Issue) Modern Geniuses", *Gekkan-kankoku-bunka* 277.

Nozaki, Mitsuhiko. 2003. "Direction of Autogenous Geomancy (Special Issue: History of Geomancy and the Present)", *Asia Yugaku* (47).

O, Chi-Eun. 1994. "Rites of Ancestor Worship and Women's Role: A Case Study of Korean Catholic Community", *Annual Report of Kyoto Sociology* 2: 19-37.

O, Chi-Eun. 1994. "Women's Position in Korean Catholic Community: A Case Study of Cheonho-dong, North Jeolla Province", *Sociology* 39(2): 37-54.

O, Mee-Hee. 1997. "A Study of Fawning of Modern Koreans and Japanese", *Politics Studies Treatises* 5.

Obayashi, Taryo. 1972. (Interview with Kim Yanggi) "Ancient Basic Culture of Japan and Korea: An Attempt of Intellectual Interchange in Asia", *Asia Review* (Mar).: 132-141.

Obayashi, Taryo. 1973. *Myth of Rice Farming.* Tokyo: Kobun-do.

Obayashi, Taryo. 1977. "What is the Relations Between Japanese Myths and Korean Myths?", *A Study of Exposition and Materials of National Literature* 22(11): 25-28.

Obayashi, Taryo. 1977. *Queendom of Queen Himiko: Tattoo, Poncho, and Himiko.* Tokyo: Chuo-koron.

Obayashi, Taryo. 1984. *Regality Myths of East Asia: Japan, Korea, Ryukyu.* Tokyo: Kobun-do.

Obayashi, Taryo. 1987. "Family and Kinship Group of Visiting People", in Obayashi Taryo ed., *Nihon-no-kodai 11 Uchi and Ie.* Tokyo: Chuo-koron, (259-282).

Obayashi, Taryo. 1993. "Wet Rice Culture of East Asia: Events of New Year's Day", *Gekkan-shinika* 4(8).

Ogasawara, Shin. 1976. "Korean Funeral Rites: A Case Study of Naegok-ri, South Gyeongsang Province", *Otani-gakuho* 55(4): 34-46.

Ogasawara, Shin. 1993. "Korean Funeral Ceremony", *Seiron* Mar. 216-220.

Ogasawara, Shin and Manabe, Yuko. 1986. "Korean Society and Shamanism: Modernization and Change of Shamanism", *Nara Educational University Bulletin* 35(1): 77-99.

Ogasawara, Shin and Manabe, Yuko. 1990. "The Function of Shamanic Ceremonies for Group Unity of Community: Pungeo Festival of Sorae Port in Korea", *SOSHIOROJIKUSU* 35(2): 143-158.

Ogawa, Haruhisa. 1997. *People of Korean Cultural History.* Kaden-sha.

Ogawa, Toru. 1957. "Village Life and Articles of Everyday Use in a South Korean Village: An Investigation Report of Tal-ri, Ulsan-up, South Gyeongsang Province in 1936", *The Japanese Journal of Ethnology* 21(4): 259-269.

Ohata, Hiroshi. 1986. "Social Movement Theory in Editorial of the Dong-a Ilbo in the 1920's", *Journal of Newspaper Studies* 35.

Ohata, Hiroshi. 1989. "Communication Strategy of Choson Independent Movement: Focusing on An Changho in the 1920's", *Tokyo University Research Institute for Newspaper Bulletin* 39.

Ohata, Hiroshi. 1994. "Trend of Civil Social Theory in Korea: Comments on 'Nation and Civil Society of Korea'", *Shiso* 844.

Ohata, Hiroshi. 1996. "Features of Civil Movement in Incheon, Korea: New Social Movements of Korea", Ryutsu Keizai University Edit Committee for Commemorative Treatises of the 30th Anniversary, ed., *Commemorative Treatises for the 30th Anniversary Department of Sociology Part.*

Ohno, Yuji. 1993. "Buddhist Temple and Shamanism in Zainichi Korean Community", *An Overall Study of Religious and Ethnicity of Zainichi Korean Community.* (53-61), Report of Grants-in-Aid for Scientific Research (Representative-Iida Takafumi).

Ohno, Yuji. 1995. "From Village Rites to Important Intangible Cultural Asset A Case Study of Eunsan Byeolsin Festival", *Chosen-gakuho* 157.

Ohno, Yuji. 1996. "Revival of Traditional Culture and Ever Since", *Seikyu-gakujutsu-ronshu* Vo.8, (Kankoku-bunka-kenkyu-shinko-zaidan).

Ohno, Yuji. 1997. "Buddhism", *Let's Know More About Korea 1*, 1: 01-107, Kobun-do.

Ohno, Yuji. 1998. " 'The Second Home' Mikawashima, Arakaw-ku: A Case Study of Konae-ri (Special Issue: The World of Jeju Island)", *Geography* 43(5).

Ohno, Yuji. 1998. "Symbol of Baekjae Culture in Development of Tourism", *Study Report,* Vol.6, Institute for the Culture of Travel.

Ohno, Yuji. 1999. "Phase of Moving and Settlement in Arakawa, Tokyo", *Report of Grants-in-Aid for Scientific Research* (Representative: Ito Abito).

Ohno, Yuji. 2000. "A Sketch of a Korean Buddhist Temple: A Case Study of A-gun", Sakurai Tokutaro ed., *Shamanism and Its Circumstance.* Daiichi-shobo.

Okada, Hiroki. 1997. "Dead People in Modern Korean Society (Workshop (3) Continuance and Change of Folk Religions in East Asia", *Religion and Society* (Extra Issue: 94-98).

Okada, Hiroki. 1997. "Series 〈World Peoples and Fiber〉 (10) Rhetoric of White and Primary Colors: Chima and Jeogori as Korean Tradition", *Journal of Textiles Consumption Science* 38(6): 284-294.

Okada, Hiroki. 1998. "Controlled Folk Religion: Focusing on Practice Related to Death in Modern Korean Society", *Koshien University Bulletin C,* (Volume of the Department of Human Culture, 2).

Okada, Hiroki. 1999. "Silent Majority: An Essay on Past of Korean Buddhism", Mio Yuko, Honda Hiroshi eds., *Cultural Multi-Centricity in East Asia.* Tokyo University of Foreign Studies Research Institute for Asian and African Language Culture.

Okada, Hiroki. 1999. Asakura Toshio, Okada Hiroki, "Talk: Change of Food Culture(1)", *Shoku-seikatsu-kekyu* 20(2) 111.

Okada, Hiroki. 1999. Asakura Toshio, Okada Hiroki, "Talk: Change of Food Culture(2)", *Shoku-seikatsu-kekyu* 20(3) 112.

Okada, Hiroki. 2001. "Reconsideration of Aged People's Folklore (Life, Aging, Death: Japanese View of Life-inner Eye, Outside Eye)(Aged People)", *Kokuritsu-rekishi-minzoku-hakubutsukan-kenkyu-hokoku* 91.

Okada, Hiroki. 2001. *Yangban.* Tokyo: Fukyo-sha.

Okada, Kozi. 1976. "Suzuki Mitsuo, Structure of Marebito : A Comparative Folklore Studies in East Asia", *Kokugakuin-zasshi* 77(2): 60-62.

Okinawa Kenritsu Geijutsu Daigaku Ryukan Densyou Bunka Chosadan. 1991. *A Study of Korean Traditional Culture: For Comparison with Okinawa.*

Naha: Okinawa-kenritsu-geijutsu-daigaku-ryu-kan-densho-bunka-chosa-dan.

Okuma, Yoko. 1993. "A Study of Gye in Korea: A Case Study of Seonchang, South Gyeongsang Province", *Hakusan-jinrui-gaku* 2.

Okuma, Yoko. 1995. "About Formation of Gye in Korea: A Case Study of Villages and Cities", *Toyo-daigaku-daigakuin-kiyo* 31: 59-72.

Okuma, Yoko. 1998. "Male University Students in Korean Society", Shimizu Hiroaki, Haga Masaaki and Matsumoto Seiichi eds., *Anthroplogy of Sex and Age.* Tokyo: Iwata-shoin.

Okuyama, Noriko. 1996. "Korean Blood Relationship and its Response to Industrialization", *Treatises of Department of Sociology* (Rikkyo University Graduate School) 3.

Oshitani, Daizo. 1977. "Korean People and White Robe", *Kaigai-jijo* 25(10): 37-44.

Ota, Simpei. 2002. "〈Neoliberalism〉: Process of Vice Practice and Its Influence Seen in A Korean Church", *Annual Report of Human Science* (23) (Separate Volume 1).

Otani, Michiyori. 1990. "Formation of Omok and the Method of Yut-nori: A Logical Analysis of the Method of Omok", *Gakuen Treatises* 67.

Otani, Michiyori. 1991. "Formation of Omok and the Method of Yut-nori: A Logical Analysis of the Method of Omok Vol.2", *Gakuen Treatises* 68.

Otani, Michiyori. 1992. "The Meaning of Korean-Style Karuta 'Tujeon': Origin and Spread of Gambling Game Vol. 1", *Gakuen Treatises* 71.

Otani, Michiyori. 1992. "The Meaning of Korean-Style Karuta 'Tujeon': Origin and Spread of Gambling Game Vol. 2", *Gakuen Treatises* 74.

Pak, Kye-Hong. 1982. *Village Festival of Korea.* Tokyo: Kokusho-kanko-kai.

Park, Jeon-Yull. 1989. *Structure of 'Begging and Performing in Front of Doors': A Comparative Study of Korea and Japan From the Perspective of Folklore.* Tokyo: Kobun-do.

Park, Jeon-Yull. 2000. "Itinerants in Korean Society", Choe Kil-Sung, Hinata Kazumasa eds., *Myth, Religion, Shamanism: An Attempt of Comparison of Japanese and Korean Culture.* Fukyo-sha.

Saeki Arikiyo Sensei Koki-kinenkai ed. 1995. *Japanese Ancient Tradition and*

East Asia. Yoshikawa Kobunkan.

Saiki, Kyoko. 1999. Naito Seichu, Imamura Minoru, Saiki Kyoko, *Gangwon Province of Korea and Tottori Province.* Fuji-shoten, 1999.1.

Saiki, Kyoko. 2000. "Creativity in Picture Books of Korean Old Tale: Structure and Expression of 〈White dog From Dark Country〉", *Tottori Women's College Research Bulletin* (42).

Saiki, Kyoko. 2000. "Problems of Succession of Ethnicity for Zainichi Koreans", *Northeast Asia-bunka-kenkyu* 11.

Saiki, Kyoko. 2001. "A Study of a Korean Picture Book 'Puppy's Dung'", *Northeast Asia-bunka-kenkyu* (13).

Saiki, Kyoko. 2002. "Reconsideration of Situation of Korean Picture Books", *Northeast Asia-bunka-kenkyu* (15).

Saiki, Takahito. 1999. Saiki Takahito, Shibuya Shizuaki, "Daedongyeojido and Environmental Unit (Art Engineering Society Autumn Conference in 1999)", *Art Engineering Journal* 21.

Sakai, Izuru. 1986. "Social Structure and Function of Korean Farm Village: A Case Study of Wando-up and Doam-ri in South Jeolla Province", in Joint Research Group for Fishing Community of Japan and Korea, *Japan-Korea Joint Research Report Vol. 4: Wando-gun, South Jeolla Province, Korea.* (142-155), Kobe: Economy Joint Seminar of Fishing Community of Japan and Korea Office.

Sakai, Shunji. 1984. With Kozawa Yasunori, "A Comparative Investigation Report on Korean and Japanese Coastal Fishing Villages", in Joint research Group for Fishing Community of Japan and Korea, *Japan-Korea Joint Research Report Vol. 2: Hupo-ri, Pyeonghae-up, North Gyeongsang Province, Korea.* (70-83), Kobe: Economy Joint Seminar of Fishing Community of Japan and Korea Office.

Sakai, Shunji. 1986. "A Comparative Study of World's Fishing Villages: From the Investigation of two Korean Fishing Villages", *Baeksan Sociology Sutdies* 1: 44-46.

Sakai, Shunji. 1986. "Social Structure and Life Structure of Naejeong-ri, Sinji-myeon", in Joint Research Group for Fishing Community of Japan and Korea, *Japan-Korea Joint Research Report Vol. 4: Wando-gun, South*

Jeolla Province, Korea. (121-141), Kobe: Economy Joint Seminar of Fishing Community of Japan and Korea Office.

Sakai, Shunji. 1988. "A Comparative Study of Collectivity of Japanese and Korean Fishing Vilalges", in Joint Research Group for Fishing Community of Japan and Korea, *Japan-Korea Joint Research Report Vol. 6: Chungmu-si, South Gyeongsang Province, Korea and Its Peripheral Fishing Villages.* (169-189), Kobe: Economy Joint Seminar of Fishing Community of Japan and Korea Office.

Sakai, Shunji. 1992. "Trend of Overseas Studies: Korea", *Sonraku-shakai-kenkyu* 28: 260-267.

Sakai, Shunji. 1998. "A Case Study of Modernization of Korean Fishing Village: A Case of Geumeum-sa-ri, Hupo-up, Uljin-gun, North Gyeongsang Province", *Chukyo Gakuin University Research Bulletin* 6(1): 65-78.

Sakai, Toshiki. 1997. *Korea, Choson and Education of Modern History: From the Perspective of Coexistence.* Otsuki-shoten.

Sakamoto, Ikko. 1983. "Feature of Adolescent Period in Korean Traditional Society from the Perspective of Rites of Passage", *Kyushu University Research Institution for Comparative Educational Culture Bulletin* 34: 49-66.

Sakamoto, Ikko. 1984. "An Essay on New Cultural Analysis of Settlement of Korean Christianity", *Kyushu University Department of Education Research Institution for Comparative Educational Culture Bulletin* 35: 73-89.

Sakamoto, Ikko. 1992. "An Aspect of Korean Rearing Customs: Focusing on Background and Change of Son Preference", *Comparative Folk Studies* 5.

Sakamoto, Shin'ichi. 1997. "Studies on Korean Family Register in Japan: Before Defeat of War", *Seikyu-gakujutsu-ronshu* 10: 231-293.

Sakamoto, Shinnosuke. 2000. "Hozumi Nobushige and Origin of Japanese Anthropology: Focusing on Ie, Family Register and the Theory of Registration Development", *The Japanese Journal of Ethnology* 64(4): 505-520.

Sakurai, Shoko. 1979. "Playing Song of Children in Jeju Island", *Oriental Music Studies* 44: 27-49.

Sakurai, Tetsuo. 1976. "An Attempt of Musical Anthropology 1: Folk Music of Jeju Island", *Music Studies* 21: 101-115.

Sakurai, Tetsuo. 1978. "Music Instruments of Korean Peninsula", *Gekkan-minpaku* 2(5): 12-13.

Sakurai, Tetsuo. 1980. "Formation of Songs in Jeju Island: From Sound to Music", *Research Report of Kokuritsu-minzokugaku-hakubutsukan* 13(4): 787-806.

Sakurai, Tetsuo. 1981. "An Introduction to Asian Music: Music of East Asia, Korean Peninsula", Fuji Tomoaki ed., *An Introduction to Asian Music.* (Extra Issue: Commentary), Tokyo: Japan Columbia.

Sakurai, Tetsuo. 1982. "Working Song in Jeju Island", in Umesao Tadao, Fujii Tomoaki eds., *World Travel: Ethnic Life 5 Creation, Rites.* (90-98), Tokyo: Japan Travel Bureau Foundation Publishing Office.

Sakurai, Tetsuo. 1983. "Bow Instruments of Asia" *Gekkan-minpaku* 7(11): 12-13.

Sakurai, Tetsuo. 1983. "Entertainment, Jangu, Mask", *Kokuritsu-minzokugaku-hakubutsukan General Guide Addition 3.* Tokyo: Ethnology Shinkokai.

Sakurai, Tetsuo. 1983. "Folk House of Seoneup-ri, Jeju Island", *Kokuritsu-minzokugaku-hakubutsukan General Guide Addition 6.* Tokyo: Ethnology Shinkokai.

Sakurai, Tetsuo. 1983. "Public Museum in Jeju Island: Jeju University Folk Museum", *Gekkan-minpaku* 7(4): 14.

Sakurai, Tetsuo. 1983. "Similarity and the Other Cultures: Korean National Central Museum", *Gekkan-minpaku* 7(6): 14.

Sakurai, Tetsuo. 1983. "Spring of Jeju Island", *Minpaku-tsushin* 21: 55-56.

Sakurai, Tetsuo. 1984. "Jeju Island's Woman Diver", *Kikan-minzokugaku* 27: 18-25.

Sakurai, Tetsuo. 1984. "Korean Sound Culture", *Kokuritsu-minzokugaku-hakubutsukan News Letter* 35.

Sakurai, Tetsuo. 1984. "Tradition and Fashion: Korean Long Skirt and Women's Sitting Posture", *TOKK* 10: 20-21.

Sakurai, Tetsuo. 1985. "Jeju Island: Climate, Environment, Children's Play", Iwata Keiji, Matsubara Masatake, Kurita Yasuyuki eds., *The World of Children: From 39 Field Notes.* Tokyo: Kumon Publishing.

Sakurai, Tetsuo. 1985. "Lamentation and Jeong: Korean Funeral Ceremony",

Kikan-minzokugaku 32: 94-101.

Sakurai, Tetsuo. 1985. "Play and Songs of Children: A Case Study of Jeju Island", *Minpaku-tsushin* 29: 44-65.

Sakurai, Tetsuo. 1985. "Q & A About Differences Between Japanese and Korean Court Music", *Gekkan-minpaku* 9(9): 29.

Sakurai, Tetsuo. 1986. "Culture of Korean Peninsula", Kokuritsu-minzokugaku-hakubutsukan ed., *Kokuritsu-minzokugaku-hakubutsukan Exhibition Guide 135.* Osaka: Senri-bunka-zaidan.

Sakurai, Tetsuo. 1986. "Modern Change of Folk Music of Jeju Island: An Attempt of Musical Anthropology Vol. 2", *Music Studies* 32(2): 116-134.

Sakurai, Tetsuo. 1986. "Music of Peasants and Masque in Korean Peninsula", *Gekkan-minpaku* 10(9): 8-9.

Sakurai, Tetsuo. 1986. "Play of Modern Korean Children", *Children and Family* 22(10): 12-17.

Sakurai, Tetsuo. 1986. "Sound of Shamanic Rites: A Case Study of Jeju Island of Korea", *Research Report of Kokuritsu-minzokugaku-hakubutsukan* 10(3): 551-573.

Sakurai, Tetsuo. 1986. "The World of Sound: Structure of Sound Culture in Korea", Editting Committee ed., *Sounds of Ethnic Peoples: Treatises in Memory of Prof. Koizumi Fumio.* (413-434), Tokyo: Ongaku-no-tomo-sha.

Sakurai, Tetsuo. 1986. "World Festivals 11: Korea, Kangreung Festival", *Voice* 11: Gravure 19-22.

Sakurai, Tetsuo. 1987. "Kayageum", *Gekkan-minpaku* 11(6): Back Cover.

Sakurai, Tetsuo. 1988. "Formation of Songs in Jeju Island: From Sound to Music", *Study Report of Kokuritsu-minzokugaku-hakubutsukan* 13(4).

Sakurai, Tetsuo. 1989. "Sound Structure of Jeju Island", Matsubara Masatake ed., *What is Anthropology?* Tokyo: NHK Publishing.

Sakurai, Tetsuo. 1989. *A Study of 'Sound': Ethnography of Sound and Music in Korean Village*. Tokyo: Kobun-do.

Sakurai, Tetsuo. 1990. "Development of Sound", in Sugiyama Koichi, Sakurai Tetsuo eds., *Cultural Anthropology of Korean Society.* (141-158), Tokyo: Kobun-do.

Sakurai, Tetsuo. 1990. Sugiyama Koichi, Sakurai Tetsuo, *Cultural Anthropology of Korean Society*. Kobun-do.

Sakurai, Tetsuo. 1992. *Sound of Deities*. Maruzen (CD Book).

Sakurai, Tetsuo. 1994. "Korean Popular Entertainment, Music of Peasants", *Nature and Culture* 45.

Sakurai, Tetsuo. 1994. "Travel and Entertainment: Why Do Entertainers Travel", *Treatises of Kumamoto University Department of Literatures* 44.

Sakurai, Tetsuo. 1996. "Transmission, Acceptance, Selected Musical Instruments and Sound in Korean and Japanese History", Sakurai Tetsuo, Yamaguchi Osamu eds., *The Present and Future of Sound.*. Kobun-do.

Sakurai, Tokutaro. 1973. Discussion with Naoe Hiroharu, Takeda Akira, Sato Nobuyuki, Choe Inhak, Tanikawa Kenichi, "Yanagida Folklore and Korea", *Kikan-yanagida-kunio-kenkyu* 2: 2-43.

Sakurai, Tokutaro. 1974. "Patronal Shaman and Shamanism: Korean Shamanism", *Kikan-dorumen* 3: 22-27.

Sakurai, Tokutaro. 1975. "Marriage of Departed Souls: A Comparative Study of Japan and Korea", *The Sankei Shimbun* Nov.17.

Sakurai, Tokutaro. 1975. "Thinking of Reality of Ethnic Culture: Returning from the Scientific Investigation in Korea", *The Komei Shimbun* Oct.18.

Sakurai, Tokutaro. 1976. "Comments" (to Choe Kil-sung, "Departed Soul Festival in Korean Shamanism"), *Kikan-jinruigaku* 7(3): 74-77.

Sakurai, Tokutaro. 1976. "Issues of Comparative Folklore: Nokutsurimu and Mabuigumi (Putting Souls in) in Korea and Okinawa", Commemorative Committee for Mr. Shibata Minoru's 70th Birthday, ed., *Japanese Cultural History Treatises.* (409-442), Suita: Commemorative Committee for Mr.Shibata Minoru's 70th Birthday.

Sakurai, Tokutaro. 1976. "Itako and Mudang: Japanese and Korean Shamanism", *The Kumamoto Daily News*, Aug.19.

Sakurai, Tokutaro. 1976. "Possessed Shaman of Korea", *Pareruga* 297: 6-7.

Sakurai, Tokutaro. 1976. "Washing Soul and Possessing Soul: A Comparative Study of Japanese and Korean Shamanism", *Tenbou* 209: 87-105.

Sakurai, Tokutaro. 1976. "Yamamiya of Japan and Dangsan of Korea", in Tokugawa Muneyoshi ed., *Deity and Shrine.* (113-117), Jingushicho General Administration Division.

Sakurai, Tokutaro. 1977. "Customs of New Year's Day's Morning in Korea: A Comparative Study with Japanese Events of New Year's Day", *Customs* 16(2): 87-98.

Sakurai, Tokutaro. 1979. "Beginning of Comparative Folklore: The 4th Asian Folklore Conference", *The Asahi Shimbun* Oct.6.

Sakurai, Tokutaro. 1980. "Introduction: Opening for Comparative Folklore", Choe Kil-sung, *Korean Festival and Shamanism*. i-v, Tokyo: Daiichi-shobo.

Sakurai, Tokutaro. 1980. "Korean Shamanism and Marriage of Souls: A Comparative Folklore Study of Marital Customs in the Other World 4", in Chiba Tokuji ed., *The Theory of Japanese Folk Customs.* (419-442), Tokyo: Kobun-do.

Sakurai, Tokutaro. 1980. "Shamanism of Two Peoples Vo.3: A Comparative Study of Rites of Departed Soul", *Gekkan-kankoku-bunka* 2(11): 4-9.

Sakurai, Tokutaro. 1980. "Shamanism of Two Peoples Vol. 1: Korea and Japan", *Gekkan-kankoku-bunka* 2(9): 9-14.

Sakurai, Tokutaro. 1980. "Shamanism of Two Peoples Vol. 2: Korea and Japan", *Gekkan-kankoku-bunka* 2(10): 39-44.

Sakurai, Tokutaro. 1980. "Square of Festivals 13: Korean Village Festival", *The Sankei Shimbun* July 28.

Sakurai, Tokutaro. 1984. "Introduction-shamanism of Neighboring Countries", Choe Kil-sung (tr. By Fukudome Noriaki), *Korean Shaman.* Tokyo: Kokubunsha.

Sakurai, Tokutaro. 1986. "Problems Concerning Marriage of Souls", *Gekkan-kankoku-bunka* 8(8): 4-12.

Sakurai, Tokutaro. 1986. "Problems Concerning Marriage of Souls", *Korean Cultural Center News Letter.*

Sakurai, Tokutaro. 1987. "(Interview With Esaka Teruya) Searching for Origin of Ancient Culture of Japan and Korea: A Contact Point of Archeology and Folklore", *Gekkan-kankoku-bunka* 9(7): 4-12.

Sakurai, Tokutaro. 1987. *A Folk Religion of East Asia* (Works of Sakurai Tokutaro Vo.7) Tokyo: Yoshikawa Kobunkan.

Sasaki, Michio. 1996. "Food and Culture of Korea", *Mugunghwa Series* : 4, Mugunghwahwe.

Sasaki, Michio. 2002. *Korean Food Culture.* Akashi-shoten.

Sasaki, Noriko. 1994. "Current Situation and Problems of Korean Consumption Cooperative Association Based on Changing Social Situation", *The 3rd Treatises of Life Cooperative Studies Fund*, Seikatsu-sogo-kenkyujo.

Sasaki, Noriko. 1996. "A Study of Industrialization and Korean Blood Relationship", *Treatises of Rikkyo University Graduate School Department of Sociology* Vol. 3.

Sasaki, Noriko. 2000. "Change of Modern Family", in Kobayashi Takayuki ed., *Changing Modern Korean Society.* (25-43), Kyoto: Sekai-shiso-sha.

Sasaki, Shiro(1951-). 1982. "A Study of House with Inside Lavatory in Korea", *Fukushima Engineering College Bulletin* 18(1).

Sasaki, Shiro(1951-). 1984. "Korean Houses in the Middle of Charyeong Mountains", *Journal of Physical Geography* 93(4).

Sasaki, Shiro(1951-). 1988. "My Study Experiences in Korea (Special Issue Students Interchange in Korea)", *Geography* 33(12).

Sasaki, Shiro(1951-). 1989. tr., (Jang, Bo-Woong), *Korean Houses.* Kokon-shoin.

Sasaki, Shiro(1951-). 1994. "A Preparatory Study on Formation of Another House of Same Premise in Jeju Island of Korea", *Journal of Historical Geography* 36(5) 171.

Sasaki, Shiro(1951-). 1994. "Changing Trend of Flat Structure of Korean Modern Residence", *Study Report of Utsunomiya University Department of Liberal Arts,* Vol. 1 28.

Sasaki, Shiro(1951-). 1994. "Features of Wooden Floor Room of Korean House and Its Distribution", *Journal of Physical Geography* 103(6).

Sasaki, Shiro(1951-). 1999. "Customs and Life Tradition In the North of Korean Peninsula (Special Issue Basics of North Korea)", *Geography* 44(4) (521).

Sasaki, Shiro(1951-). 2002. "Village and Scenery of Life, Seoul, Memory of City", *Area Development News* (276).

Sasaki, Shiro(1957-). 2000. "Korean People (Special Issue Encyclopedia of Chinese Minority Peoples 55 Ethnic Groups, Their History and Life)", *Gekkan-shinika* 11(1) (119).

Sasaki, Mamoru. 2000. "Problems of Studying Korean People in China", Maruyama Koichi ed., *A Cultural Anthropological Study of Chinese*

Nationalism and Changing Process of Minor Ethnic Culture. Study Report for Research Fund of Ministry of Education, Culture, Sports, Science and Technology.

Sato, Kensho. 1999. "Incantation of Bodhisattva, Religious Character: A Case Study of Seoul and Jindo", Sasaki Kokan ed., *A Cultural Anthropological Study of Structural Change of Shamanism Culture in East Asia.* Study Report for Scientific Research Funding 1996-1998.

Sato, Kensho. 2000. "A Memorandum about Korean Shaman", Komazawa University, *Culture* 19.

Sato, Kensho. 2002. "A Study of Korean Shaman: Focusing on Characters of Interchange Between Deity and Man", *Science of Religion Treatises* 21.

Sato, Nobuyuki. 1972. "House and Family of Jeju Island", *Urban Residence* 7210: 77-82.

Sato, Nobuyuki. 1973. "Ancestor Worship in Jeju Island", *Journal of Religion Studies* 46(3): 113-114.

Sato, Nobuyuki. 1973. "Family and Relatives of Jeju Island: A Case Study of O Village", *Asia-bunka-kenkyu* 7: 1-49.

Sato, Nobuyuki. 1973. "Family of Jeju Island: A Case Study of O village", *Toyo-bunka* 53: 109-145.

Sato, Nobuyuki. 1973. "From Jeju Island : Korean Situation and Realization in Korea", *Kikan-jinruigaku* 4(3):148-172.

Sato, Nobuyuki. 1974. "Submerged Area of Andong Dam, Korea", *Asahi Asia Review* 5(2): 134-135.

Sato, Nobuyuki. 1975. "Mountain Village Society in the Upper Reach of Nakdong River in Korea", *Asia-keizai* 16(3): 78-88.

Sato, Nobuyuki. 1976. "Matrimonimonial Relation of Jeju Island", in South Island Studies Society ed., *South Islands: Its History and Culture.* (219-231), Tokyo: Kokusho-kanko-kai.

Sato, Nobuyuki. 1977. "Structure of Priests of Rite for Near Generation Ancestors in Korea", *Kikan-jinruigaku* 8(1): 123-140.

Sato, Nobuyuki. 1977. "We and Others", in Katakura Motoko, Sato Nobuyuki, Aoyanagi Kiyotaka, *Cultural Anthropology: Nomadism, Farming, Cities.* (203-208), Tokyo: Yachiyo-shuppan.

Sawai, Keiichi. 1996. "A Comparative Study of Japanese and Korean Confucianism (Japanese Association for Comparative Philosophy, Korea-Japan Joint Scietntific Conference)", *Studies in Comparative Philosophy* 22.

Sawai, Keiichi. 1997. "A Comparative Study of Confucian Practice in Japan and Korea", *Hikaku-shiso-kenkyu* 23 (Extra Issue).

Sechiyama, Kaku. 1990. "Housewives and Women's Working in Korea and Taiwan: Direction of Women's Social Entry", *Asia-keizai* 31(12): 22-40.

Sechiyama, Kaku. 1996. "A Thought in a Corner of Pyeongyang (Special Issue Future of Humanity: From the Perspective of Asian Cities", *CEL* 37.

Sechiyama, Kaku. 1996. *East Asian Patriarchy: A Comparative Social Sociology of Gender.* Tokyo: Keiso-shobo.

Sechiyama, Kaku. 1997. "East Asia Edition 'For the Theory of Ie Society': Possibility of Cultural Comparison of Family (Special Issue Culture and Family)", *Kazoku-shakaigaku-kenkyu* 9.

Sekine, Hideyuki. 1997. "A Study of Continuance of Ethics as a Subject in Korea and Japan from the Perspective of Environment and Requirement", *Komin Education Studies* 5.

Sekine, Hideyuki. 1998. "Personal Morals and Public Morals of Adolescents in Japan and Korea", *Komin-kyoiku-kenkyu* 6.

Sekine, Hideyuki. 1998.(Umai Masayuki, Jo Bubaek, Sekine Hideyuki et al.) *An Investigation of Japanese Popular Culture in Korea.* Study Report of Shizuoka University Department of Education Humanities, Sociology Part 49.

Seo, Dae-Suk. 1997. Kumaki Tsutomu trans. "Relationship Between Heaven Deity and Water Deity Reflected in Korean National Foundation Myth", *Chosen-gakuho* 162.

Seo, Jeon-Beom. 1980. *Korean Shamanism.* Kyoto-dohosha Publishing.

Seo, Yeon-Ho. 1999. "A Study of Succession Process of Masque and Dolls in the 20th Century", SuzukiMasataka, Nomura Shin'ichi eds., *A Study of Masks and Shamanism: Japan and Korea.* Daiichi-shobo.

Shigematsu, Mayumi. 1976. "Life in Korea as an Asian Dispatched Student", *Kosei-hodo* 156: 44-48.

Shigematsu, Mayumi. 1978. "Taboo: A Religious Anthropological Study", *Shiron*

32.

Shigematsu, Mayumi. 1980. "Women's Social Relations Seen in Kut: A Case Study of Shamanism of Yangju-gun, Gyeonggi Province, Korea", *The Japanese Journal of Ethnology* 45(2): 93-110.

Shigematsu, Mayumi. 1981. "Ancestors and Souls in Jinogwi Kut: A Case Study of K-dong, Yangju-gun, Gyeongi Province, Korea", *Research Report of Kokuritsu-minzokugaku-hakubutsukan* 6(2): 256-282.

Shigematsu, Mayumi. 1981. "In the Valley of Study", *Minpaku-tsushin* 14: 42-44.

Shigematsu, Mayumi. 1981. "Jesu Kut: A Case Study of a Merchant in Seoul of Korea", *Kikan-jinruigaku* 12(2): 143-165.

Shigematsu, Mayumi. 1982. "Korean Women", in Ayabe Tsuneo ed., *Women's Cultural Anthropology.* (197-223), Tokyo: Kobun-do.

Shigematsu, Mayumi. 1983. "Eating Habits", *Kokuritsu-minzokugaku-hakubutsukan General Guide Addition 5,* Tokyo: Minzokugaku Shinkokai.

Shigematsu, Mayumi. 1984. "Tomb and Ancestors and Blood Relationship", *Gekkan-minpaku* 8(6): 15-17.

Shigematsu, Mayumi. 1984. Book Review "Lee Kwang-kyu, *Zainichi Koreans: Focusing on their Life Situation*", *Minpaku-tsushin* 24: 31-33.

Shigematsu, Mayumi. 1985. "Q & A About Korean Shamanism", *Gekkan minpaku* 9(6): 23-24.

Shigematsu, Mayumi. 1992. tr., Choe Kil-sung, *Korean Ancestor Worship.* Ochanomizu-shobo.

Shigematsu, Mayumi. 1993. "Korean Ancestor Worship: A Comparative Study with Japan", Muratake Seiichi, Ogo Kinichi eds., *Japan From the Perspective of Social Anthropology: Treatises in Memory of Dr. Gamo Masao.* Tokyo: Kawade-shobo Shinsha.

Shigematsu, Mayumi. 1995. "Shamanism and Buddhism in Korean Village: A Case Study of K village in Yangju-gun, Gyeonggi Province, Korea", *Minpaku-tsushin* 70: 81-93.

Shigematsu, Mayumi. 1996. "Changing Shamanism: A Memoirs of Villages in Gyeonggi Province, Korea", *Minpaku-tsushin* 74: 114-118.

Shigematsu, Mayumi. 1998. "Shamanism in Villages in the Late 1970's", in Shima Mutsuhiko, Asakura Toshio eds., *Changing Korean Society: From the*

Field Research of Anthropology in the 1970's～80's. (117-146), Tokyo: Daiichi-shobo.

Shigematsu, Mayumi. 1999. "Current Situation of Shamanism in A Korean Village: A Case Study of Yangju-gun, Gyeonggi Province", *Minpaku-tsushin* 84.

Shigematsu, Mayumi. 2000. "Shamanic Ceremonies in Korean Peninsula", *Gekkan-minpaku* 24: 12.

Shima, Mutsuhiko. 1976. "An Analysis of Chib-an: A Case Study of South Jeolla Province in Korea", *The Japanese Journal of Ethnology* 41(1): 75-90.

Shima, Mutsuhiko. 1977. (Book Review) Lee Kwang-kyu "*An Analysis into Family Structure of Korea*", *The Japanese Journal of Ethnology* 41(4): 399-402.

Shima, Mutsuhiko. 1977. tr. With Ito, Choe Jaeseok, *Social Character of Koreans.* Gakusei-sha.

Shima, Mutsuhiko. 1978. "An Essay on Korean Clan and Local Bond", *The Japanese Journal of Ethnology* 43(1): 1-17.

Shima, Mutsuhiko. 1979. "Korean People", in Obayashi Taryo ed., *Peoples of the Earth 13: East Asia Japan, China, Korea.* (64-77), 140, Tokyo: Heibon-sha.

Shima, Mutsuhiko. 1979. "Productional Relations in Korean Villages", *Chiiki-bunka-kenkyu* 5: 27-47.

Shima, Mutsuhiko. 1979. *Kinship and Economic Organization in a Korea Village.* Ph. D. dissertation, University of Toronto.

Shima, Mutsuhiko. 1979. "Productional Relations in Korean Villages", *Journal of Regional Culture Studies* 5: 27-47.

Shima, Mutsuhiko. 1979. tr. With Ito, Choe Jaeseok., *Studies of Korean Farming Community.* Gakusei-sha.

Shima, Mutsuhiko. 1980. "An Analysis of Korean Family: Focusing on Adopted Child and Branch Family", *Hiroshima-daigaku-Asia-kenkyu* 2: 39-52, 66.

Shima, Mutsuhiko. 1981. tr. With Ito, (Kim Taekkyu) *A Study of Korean Village of Consanguinity.* Gakusei-sha.

Shima, Mutsuhiko. 1983. "Cultivation of Commercial Crops and Farm Village: A Case Study of Seongju-gun, North Gyeongsang Province, Korea", *Hiroshima-daigaku-Asia-kenkyu* 3: 55-67.

Shima, Mutsuhiko. 1984. "Korean Villages: Dongne and Maul", *Japan Folk Culture System Vol. 8 Village and Village Folk, Monthly* 7: 12-14.

Shima, Mutsuhiko. 1985. "Genealogy and Family Organization", Commemorative Committee for Mr. Kikuchi Keijiro's 60th Birthday ed., *Hitakami-no-kuni,* (399-415), Kitakami: Commemorative Committee for Mr. Kikuchi Keijiro's 60th Birthday.

Shima, Mutsuhiko. 1985. "Local Community", Ito Abito ed., *Let's Know More About Korea.* (71-98), Tokyo: Kobun-do.

Shima, Mutsuhiko. 1985. *Korean Village Situation: Description of the Life of People Living in the Confucian Country.* Tokyo: PHP Research Institute.

Shima, Mutsuhiko. 1986. "Child-Rearing, Birth Deity, Floor Stove, 60th Birthday, Home, Children, House, Childbirth, Funeral, Rites of Ancestor Worship, Rites of Passage, Tomb, Aged People" in Ito Abito, Ohmura Masuo, Kajimura Hideki, Takeda Yukio eds., *Dictionary to Know Korea.* Tokyo: Heibon-sha.

Shima, Mutsuhiko. 1987. "Choson Race", *Cultural Anthropology Dictionary* 482-483.

Shima, Mutsuhiko. 1987. "Clan System and Family Organization", in Ito, Sekimoto, Funabiki eds., *Modern Social Anthropology 1: Kinship and Social Structure.* Tokyo: Tokyo-daigaku-shuppan-kai.

Shima, Mutsuhiko. 1990. "Genealogy: Historical Anthropological Prospect", in Sugiyama Koichi, Sakurai Tetsuo eds., *Cultural Anthropology of Korean Society.* (39-54), Tokyo: Kobun-do.

Shima, Mutsuhiko. 1990. "Gye and Village Society", in Abe, Ito, Ogiwara eds., *The World of Races Vol. 2: Social Unity and Movement.* (76-92), Tokyo: Shogakukan.

Shima, Mutsuhiko. 1990. "In Quest for Social Recognition: A Retrospective View on the Development of Korean Lineage Organization", *Harvard Journal of Asiatic Studies* 50(1): 87-129.

Shima, Mutsuhiko. 1992. "Change of Family Structure in the Late Choson Dynasty Seen in Family Register of Daegu: Focusing on Children Living Together with Parents", *Chosen-gakuho* 144: 51-88.

Shima, Mutsuhiko. 1992. "Korean Society: Formation and Change of Tradition",

Minpaku-tsushin 56: 35-40.

Shima, Mutsuhiko. 1992. "Korean Genealogy: Some Demographic Simulations", *Contacts Between Cultures: Proceedings of the 33rd International Congress of Asian and North African Studies* 4: 155-158, Lewiston: The Edwin Mellen Press.

Shima, Mutsuhiko. 1994. "Change of Choson Society Seen in Relative System: Focusing on an Examination of Genealogy", in Mizoguchi Yuzo, Hamashita Takeshi, Hiraishi Naoaki, Miyajima Hiroshi eds., *Long-Term Social Change (Thinking in Asia 6)* (131-162), Tokyo: Tokyo-daigaku-shuppan-kyoku.

Shima, Mutsuhiko. 1994. "Korea: Between Tradition and Modern Times", in Chugoku-shinbunsha ed., *Talking about Asia.* (33-54), Hiroshima: Chugoku-shinbunsha.

Shima, Mutsuhiko. 1995. "The World of Genealogy", *Gekkan-kankoku-bunka* 17(7): 2-7.

Shima, Mutsuhiko. 1996. "Movement of Village Structure in the Late Choson Dynasty: An Analysis of Family Registers of Daegu", *Toyo-bunka* 76: 201-226.

Shima, Mutsuhiko. 1996. "Reading Daedonggyechaek", *Chosen-bunka-kenkyu* 3: 95-110.

Shima, Mutsuhiko. 1997. "Korean Society: Filedwork during a High Economic Growth Period", *Minpaku-tsushin* 76: 69-74.

Shima, Mutsuhiko. 1997. "The Structure of Genealogy", in Funabiki Takeo ed., *Personal Social Views (Iwanamikoza Cultural Anthropology 4).* (97-127), Tokyo: Iwanami-shoten.

Shima, Mutsuhiko. 1998. "Retrieving the Past with Genealogies", in Shima, Mutsuhiko and Roger L. Janelli, eds., *The Anthropology of Korea: East Asian Perspectives (Senri Ethnological Studies 49).* (37-61), Osaka: National Museum of Ethnology.

Shima, Mutsuhiko. 1998. "Changing Korean Society and Anthropological Studies", Shima Mutsuhiko, Asakura Toshio eds., *Changing Korean Society: From the Field of Research of Anthropology in the 1970's~80's.* Tokyo: Daiichi-shobo.

Shima, Mutsuhiko. 1998. "Farming Customs in Naju-gun in the Middle of the 1970's: Just Before a Huge Change", in Shima Mutsuhiko, Asakura Toshio eds., *Changing Korean Society: From the Field of Research of Anthropology in the 1970's~80's.* (87-115), Tokyo: Daiichi-shobo.

Shima, Mutsuhiko. 1999. "Name of Koreans: Coexisting Names and Appelation", in Ueno Kazuo, Mori Kenji eds., *Names and Society: Family History of Naming (Series Comparative Family Vol. 2-3).* (230-251), Tokyo: Waseda- daigaku-shuppan-bu.

Shima, Mutsuhiko. 1999. Fujita Mariko, Shima Mutsuhiko, Takatani Michio, "An Analysis of International Interchange and Generational Interchange seen in Foundation of Village: A Social Anthropological Approach", *Study Report of Matsuda Fund Healthy Education of Adolescents 12.*

Shima, Mutsuhiko. 2000. "Relative Unity of Korea From the Perspective of Historical Anthropology", in Yoshihara Kazuo et al. eds., *Reconstruction of Blood Relation.* (167-184), Tokyo: Fukyo-sha.

Shima, Mutsuhiko. 2000. "Suenari Michio ed., Perspective of Central and Peripheral Anthropological Field", *The Japanese Journal of Ethnology* 64(4).

Shima, Mutsuhiko and Asakura Toshio eds. 1998. *Changing Korean Society: From the Field of Research of Anthropology in the 1970's~80's.* Tokyo: Daiichi-shobo.

Shima, Mutsuhiko and Roger L. Janelli, eds. 1998. *The Anthropology of Korea: East Asian Perspectives* (Senri Ethnological Studies 49), Osaka: Kokuritsu-minzokugaku-hakubutsukan.

Shimamoto, Midori. 2001. "Change of Korean Corporate Organizations and Management Information", 〔Japan International Secretary Society〕 The 9th Research Symposium, *Annual Bulletin of Japanese International Secretary Society* (8).

Shimamoto, Midori. 2001. "Korean Traditional Society and Business Activity", *Tohogakushi* 30(2).

Shimamura, Yasunori. 1999. "Words of the Minute in Korea in the 1970's", *Kokuritsu-rekishi-minzoku-hakubutsukan-kenkyu-hokoku* 82.

Shimamura, Yasunori. 2000. "Ethnography of Boundary City: Zainichi Koreans in Shimonoseki", *Rekihaku* 103.

Shimamura, Yasunori. 2000. "Korean Modern Folk tale: A Comparative Study of Japan and Korea", *Bukkyo-daigaku-sogo-kenkyujo-kiyo* (Extra Issue).

Shimamura, Yasunori. 2001. "Ethnography of Zainichi Koreans (Life, Aging, Death: View of Life of Japanese-inner Eye, Outer Eye)", *Kokuritsu-rekishi-minzoku-hakubutsukan-kenkyu-hokoku* 91.

Shimamura, Yasunori. 2002. "Occupation and Environment of Zainichi Koreans: A Case Study of Bottari Business", *Mingu-monthly* 35(1), 409.

Shimizu, Hiroaki. 2000. "Composition and Structure of Family with Aged People: A Comparative Study of Japan, Korea, America, Germany", *Shakaigaku-kiyou* 138, (Nihon Daigaku).

Shimono, Toshimi. 1989. "A Study of East Asian Funeral and Grave System: Korean Grass Tomb and Aerial Sepulchre of Okinawa etc.", *Hayato-bunka,* 22: 1-24.

Shimura, Tetsuo. 1990. "Immoral Namsadangpae: Korean Wandering Entertainment Group", *Ethnic Music Series1: Music as Function.* Tokyo: Tokyo-shoseki.

Shin, Jang-Ho. 1999. "Zainichi Korean Shamanism: Jaesu-shamanic Rites (Focusing on Jaesu-kut)", *Asia-bunka-kenkyu* (International Asian Society) 6.

Shinbo, Jun'ichiro. 1977. "Current Situation of Slash-and-Burn Cultivators in Korea", *Takasaki-keizai-daigaku-ronshu* 19(4): 109-136.

Shinozaki, Masami. 1992. "A Comparative Study of Family Senses in Family Change of Modern Korea and Japan: An Investigation of Seoul and Fukuoka", *Social Analysis-shakaigaku-kenkyu-nenpo* 20: 95-125.

Shinozaki, Masami. 1993. "An Approach to Family Senses of Modern Korea: Focusing on an Investigation of Seoul", *Family Sociology Studies* 5: 23-30.

Shinozaki, Masami. 1995. "Changing Forms and Anomie of Rural Families in Modern Korea: A Case study at Dojang-ri, Mangyeon-myeon, Gimje-gun, Jeollabuk-do", *Shakai-kankei-kenkyu* 1(2): 47-69.

Shoya, Reiko & Nakayama, Toru. 1997. *Aged Zainichi Koreans: Problems of Elderly Welfare for Zainichi Koreans in Osaka.* Ochanomizu-shobo.

Shu, Tassei. 1991. *An Exploration of East Asian Food Culture.* Tokyo: Sansei-do.

Smith, H. 1994. "Korean Folk Song and Folk Music: Its Destiny of Decline and Revival", *Koreana* 7(3).

Sofue, Takao. 1981. "The 5th Taniguchi Symposium Family System and Human Relations of China, Korea, Japan: Religion and Family in East Asia", *Gekkan-minpaku* 5(10): 18-19.

Sofue, Takao. 1983. "An Introduction of East Asia", *Kokuritsu-minzokugaku-hakubutsukan General Guide Addition 1,* Tokyo: minzokugaku Shinkokai

Sofue, Takao. 1983. "Displayed Koreans' Lives: Onyang Museum of Korea", *Gekkan-minpaku* 7(3): 14.

Sofue, Takao. 1983. "Korean Culture, Clothing Life", *Kokuritsu-minzokugaku-hakubutsukan General Guide Addition 4,* Tokyo: Minzokugaku Shinkokai.

Sofue, Takao. 1983. "Korean Culture, Folk Belief, and Confucianism", *Kokuritsu-minzokugaku-hakubutsukan General Guide Addition,* Tokyo: Minzokugaku Shinkokai.

Sofue, Takao. 1983. "Visual Folk Culture: National Folk Museum of Korea", *Gekkan-minpaku* 7(2): 14.

Sofue, Takao. 1990. "Awareness and Behavior of Koreans", in Sugiyama Koichi, Sakurai Tetsuo eds., *Cultural Anthropology of Korean Society.* (124-141), Tokyo: Kobun-do.

Suenari, Michio. 1974. (Book Review) "*A Korean Village: Between Farm and Sea* by Vincent S. R. Brandt", *The Japanese Journal of Ethnology* 39(1): 102-104.

Suenari, Michio. 1975. "Grave Rites of Jinseong-Lee in Andong, Korea", *Tokyo-daigaku-kyoyo-gakubu-kyoyo-gakka Bulletin* 7: 57-69.

Suenari, Michio. 1979. "Dozoku", in Hara Tadahiko, Suenari Michio, Shimizu Akitoshi, *Nakama (Folk Series 9)* (99-252), Tokyo: Kobun-do.

Suenari, Michio. 1982. "Cultural Conflict Between Similar Cultures: A Case Study of Japanese and Korean Society", in Obayashi Taryo ed., *A General Theory of Cultural Conflict.* (219-240), Tokyo:Gannan-do-shoten.

Suenari, Michio. 1982. "Village and Rites of Dongpo: An Investigation Report of Korean Fishing Village", *Seishin-joshi-daigaku-ronso* 59: 123-218.

Suenari, Michio. 1984. "Korean Social Organization: Focusing Its Variations", (Kokuritsu-minzokugaku-hakubutsukan Special Study Symposium: Comparative Studies of Origin of Japanese Ethnic Culture) *Social Organization: Ie, Mura, Uji Program*, (21-38).

Suenari, Michio. 1984. "Occupation and Cooperation of Dongpo: An Investigation Report Korean Fishing Village", *Seishin-joshi-daigaku-ronso* 63: 85-158.

Suenari, Michio. 1984. "Perception of Age and Rites of Passage: A Preliminary Comparative Study of East Asian Societies", in Ayabe Tsuneo ed., *Rites of Passage and a World View.* (105-114).

Suenari, Michio. 1985. "Human Relations", in Ito Abito ed., *Let's Know More About Korea.* (99-132), Tokyo: Kobun-do.

Suenari, Michio. 1985. "Age Stratified System", *Ningen-kagaku* 37: 1-19.

Suenari, Michio. 1985. "News from Sarang-bang", *Cultural Anthropology* 1: 270-276.

Suenari, Michio. 1985. "Rites of Ancestor Worship of Dongpo: An Investigation Report of Korean Fishing Village", *Seishin-joshi-daigaku-ronso* 65: 5-96.

Suenari, Michio. 1986. "Korean Social Organization: Focusing Its Variations", in Takemura Takuji ed., *Formation and Development of Japanese Folk Society: Origin of Ie, Mura, Uji.* (101-123), Tokyo: Yamakawa-shuppan.

Suenari, Michio. 1987. "〈Yangbanization〉 of Korean Society", in Ito, Sekimoto, Funabiki eds. *Modern Social Anthropology 1: Kinship and Social Structure.* (45-79), Tokyo: University of Tokyo Press.

Suenari, Michio. 1987. "Bongwan", *Cultural Anthropology Dictionary*, (711-712), Tokyo: Kobun-do.

Suenari, Michio. 1988. "Rites of Tablet of Korea and Taiwan", in Ishikawa Toshio et al. eds., *Living People and Dead People-rites of Ancestor Worship.* (17-46), Tokyo: Sansei-do.

Suenari, Michio. 1990. "A Comparative Study of Lineage of Korea and Han Chinese", in Sugiyama Koichi, Sakurai Tetsuo eds., *Cultural Anthropology of Korean Society.* (103-122), Tokyo: Kobun-do.

Suenari, Michio. 1992. "Different Nature of Funeral of Three East Asian Societies", in Mizoguchi Yuzo et al. eds., *History and Future of Cultural Area of Chinese Character.* (177-189).

Suenari, Michio. 1992. Anthropology of One's Own Society in East Asia", in Chiao Chien and Nakane Chie eds., *Homebound-Studies in East Asian Society.* (59-79), Hong Kong.

Suenari, Michio. 1997. ed., *Current Situation of East Asia* (Asia-kenkyu-hokoku-series No.1), Fukyo-sha.

Suenari, Michio. 1998. "Entry into Korea and Ever Since", in Shima Mutsuhiko, Asakura Toshio eds., *Changing Korean Society: From the Field of Research of Anthropology in the 1970's～80's.* (17-38), Tokyo: Daiichi-shobo.

Suenari, Michio. 1998. "Unilateral Kindred: A Reconsideration in East Asian Society", in Shima Mutsuhiko and Roger L. Janelli, eds., *The Anthropology of Korea: East Asian Perspectives* (Senri Ethnological Studies 49), (139-155), Osaka: Kokuritsu-minzokugaku-hakubutsukan.

Suenari, Michio. 2000. Yoshihara Kazuo, Suzuki Masataka, Suenari Michio eds., *Reconstruction of Blood Relation.* Fukyo-sha.

Suenari, Michio and Lee, Kwang-Kyu. 1973. "An Investigation Report of Baekin and Jungpo in North Gyeongsang Province: Focusing on Family and Kinship", *Toyo-bunka* 53.

Suenari, Michio and Lee, Kwang-Kyu. 1973. "An Investigation Report of Baekin and Jungpo in North Gyeongsang Province: Focusing on Family and Kinship", Nakane Chie ed., *Family and Rites in Korean Farming Villages.* University of Tokyo Press.

Sugiyama, Koichi. 1979. "A Glance on Korean Villages: Aspects of Society and Religion", *Tohoku-daigaku-nihon-bunka kenkyu-jo-kenkyu-hokoku* 15: 109-127.

Sugiyama, Koichi. 1981. "A Sketch of Farming Rites in a Korean Southern Village", *Tohoku-daigaku-nihon-bunka-kenkyu-jo-kenkyu-hokoku* 17: 79-101.

Sugiyama, Koichi. 1982. "Funeral Rites in a Korean Southern Village", Tohoku-indogaku-shukyo-gakkai, *Treatises Vol. 9.*

Sugiyama, Koichi. 1986. "Korean Peninsula", Nihon-minzokugaku Society ed., *Nihon-no-minzokugaku 1964-1983*, (188-192), Tokyo: Kobun-do.

Sugiyama, Koichi. 1987. (Book Review) "*A Study of Korean Folk Culture: Focusing on Korean Basic Culture and Its Origin* by Yoda Chihoko", *Minpaku-tsushin* 37: 19-21.

Sugiyama, Koichi. 1987. "Spirits of Grain", *Cultural Anthropology Dictionary,* (276-277), Tokyo: Kobun-do.

Sugiyama, Koichi. 1988. "View of Farming Deity in East Asia", *Nihon-bunka-*

kenkyu-jo-kenkyu-hokoku 24.

Sugiyama, Koichi. 1990. "Haengsang-gye: A Record of Gye", in Sugiyama Koichi, Sakurai Tetsuo eds., *Cultural Anthropology of Korean Society.* (87-102), Tokyo: Kobun-do.

Sugiyama, Koichi. 1990. "Rites of the Dead and Haengsang-gye in a Korean Southern Village", *Tohoku-daigaku-nihon-bunka-kenkyu-jo-kenkyu-hokoku* 26: 259-275.

Sugiyama, Koichi. 1991. "Gye of Householders and Housewives in Dong Community", *Tohoku-daigaku-nihon-bunka-kenkyu-jo-kenkyu-hokoku* 27: 57-69.

Sugiyama, Koichi. 1993. "Respect-for-the-Aged Gye in a Korean Southern Village", *Kagaku-kenkyu-hi-hokoku.*

Sugiyama, Koichi and Sakurai, Tetsuo eds. 1990. *Cultural Anthropology of Korean Society.* Tokyo: Kobun-do.

Sumi, Toyo. 1987. "A Comparative Study of Ancient Family of Choson", in Obayashi Taryo ed., *Japanese Ancient Times 11 Home and House.* (283-312), Tokyo: Chuo-koron.

Suwa, Haruo. 1973. "A Letter From a Student Majoring in Cultural Anthropology: A Problem Concerning Korea", *Kan* 2(1): 63-72.

Suzuki, Eitaro. 1953. "Gye and Pumasi of Korea", *The Japanese Journal of Ethnology* 27(3): 22-28.

Suzuki, Eitaro. 1973. *Collection of Suzuki Etaro's Works V: A Study of Korean Village Society.* Tokyo: Mirai-sha.

Suzuki, Fumiko. 1991. "Ritual Life of a Korean Fishing Village: Focusing on View of Ancestral Spirits", *Konan-daigaku-kiyo* (Literature Part) 83: 27-61.

Suzuki, Fumiko. 1992. (Book Review) Morita Saburou, Suzuki Fumiko, "Masuda Shozo ed., *A Comparative Study of Japanese and Korean Fishing Villages: Focusing on Society, Economy, and Culture* (including Comments of the Original Writer)", *Sociology* 37(2).

Suzuki, Fumiko. 1992. "The World of Korean Stories", *Kokoro-no-kagaku* 46.

Suzuki, Fumiko. 1995. "A Preliminary Study of View of Uncleanness of Childbirth in Korea", *Sanyo-minzoku-kenkyu* 1: 55-73.

Suzuki, Fumiko. 1995. No Sango, Suzuki Fumiko trans. "Spirit of Seonbi in

Korean Traditional Thought", *Shimane-daigaku-kyouiku-gakubu-Bulletin* (Humanities, Social Science) 29.

Suzuki, Fumiko. 1998. "The Era of Relative Poverty: Remote Island Society in the Late 1980's", in Shima Mutsuhiko, Asakura Toshio eds., *Changing Korean Society: From the Field of Research of Anthropology in the 1970's ~80's.* (223-260), Tokyo: Daiichi-shobo.

Suzuki, Fumiko. 2001. "A Walk in Korea (6) Change of the Times Seen in Remote Islands of West Sea: From the World of Belief", *Asia-yugaku* 30.

Suzuki, Fumiko. 2001. "Kinship From the Perspective of Women: Focusing on an Analysis of Women's Network in Korean Depopulating Fishing Villages", *Shimane-daigaku-kyouiku-gakubu-Bulletin* (Humanities, Social Science 35).

Suzuki, Masataka. 1999. *A Study of Masks and Shamanism: Japan and Korea.* Daiichi-shobo.

Suzuki, Masataka and Nomura, Shin'ichi. 1999. "Kagura of Japan and Gut of Korea: An Essay for Comparative Studies", Suzuki Masataka, Nomura Shinichi eds., *A Study of Masks and Shamanism: Japan and Korea.* Daiichi-shobo.

Suzuki, Mitsuo. 1972. "Korean Diary: A Memorandum for the Theory of Choson Society and Culture", *Kikan-jinruigaku* 3(1): 161-185.

Suzuki, Mitsuo. 1972. "Summer of 1972 in Korea: Some Sketches", *Shin-seiryoku* 17(10): 15-23.

Suzuki, Mitsuo. 1972. "The Perspective of the Theory of National Formation in the Ancient Korean Peninsula: Focusing on 'An Introduction to Ancient Korean History' by Inoue Hideo", *Chosen-gakuho* 97: 71-86.

Suzuki, Mitsuo. 1973. "Appearance of Male Shaman in Taiwanese Festivals: Position of Shamanism in Regard to Popular Taoism", *Bungaku* 41(5): 82-590.

Suzuki, Mitsuo. 1973. "Namwon and Unbong: Korean Folk Travel (2)", *Shin-seiryoku* 18(5): 58-68.

Suzuki, Mitsuo. 1973. "Theory of Korean Folk Customs: A Comparative Study of Japan and Korea as an Aspect of the Comparative Theory of

Modernization", in Kamishima Jiro ed., *Features of Japanese Modernization.* (111-138), Tokyo: Asia-bunka-kenkyu-jo.

Suzuki, Mitsuo. 1974. "A Study of Korean Studies: Based on International Journal of Korean Studies", *Chosen-gakuho* 72: 83-94.

Suzuki, Mitsuo. 1974. *Structure of Marebito: An East Asian Comparative Folklore Study.* Tokyo: Sanichi-shobo.

Suzuki, Mitsuo. 1975. "A Story of a Japanese Teacher in the Colonial Choson", *Nihonjin-dangi*, (Jun.).

Suzuki, Mitsuo. 1976. "Cemetery of National Forces and Chungryeol-sa: Souls of the War Dead and Ceremonies in East Asia", *Shin-seiryoku,* (Mar.) 7-15.

Suzuki, Mitsuo. 1976. "Facial Features and Manners of East Asians: Based on Travel Experience in Gimpo and Taipei", *Nikka-geppou* 113: 4, 114: 2-3.

Suzuki, Mitsuo. 1977. *An Experience Report of Hwaryeo Island: A Political Anthropological Note of East Asia.* Tokyo: Shisaku-sha.

Suzuki, Mitsuo. 1982. "Structure and Perspective of Comparison in Comparative Folklore", *Shiso* 693: 109-136.

Suzuki, Mitsuo. 1984. "Seat for the Aged: From the Perspective of political Anthropology", *Gendai-korea* 244: 52-63.

Suzuki, Mitsuo. 1985. "A Village Where Kind Sisters Live: Children's Records of Studying Abroad", *Gendai-korea* 257: 66-71.

Suzuki, Mitsuo. 1985. "Problematic of Korean Popular and National Culture: Background Factors of Folk Cultural Festivals" *Kyusyu-jinrui-gakkai-kaiho* 13: 36-46.

Suzuki, Mitsuo. 1985. "Social and Cultural Character of Korea: From the Perspective of Comparative Folklore", *Bungaku-kaishi* 36: 51-73, (Yamaguchi-daigaku).

Suzuki, Mitsuo. 1986. "A Village Where Kind Sisters Live: Children's Records of Studying in Seoul", *Gendai-korea* 258: 72-77, 260: 68-73, 262: 66-71, 263: 60-67, 266: 64-71.

Suzuki, Mitsuo. 1987. "Festival of Nationalism: Political Anthropological Observation of Korean Folk Cultural Festivals", *Han* 107: 84-136.

Suzuki, Mitsuo. 1988. "Folklore of Nationalism: An Aspect of Korean Studies in America", *The Japanese Journal of Ethnology* 53(1): 86-90.

Suzuki, Mitsuo. 1996. "Only New Religions Are Publicly Expressed Among Korean Public Culture: An Introduction to New Theory of Korean Religions", *Peace and Religion* 15: 111-119.

Takahashi, Toichi et. als. 1990. Takahashi Toichi, Shimizu Hiroaki, Kim Yong-T'aek and Matsumoto Seiichi, "Korean Local Community and the Position of the Aged People: Focusing on Tradition and Modernization", *Annual Journal of the Asia-Africa Cultural Research Institute* 25: 79-122.

Takahashi, Toichi et. als. 1998. (Takahashi Toichi, Matsumoto Seiichi, Okuma Yoko, Kim Mi-Young, Ozawa Yasunori, Usami Takanori and Suzuki Nobuaki), "Modernization and Cultural Traits in Korean East coastal Fishing Villages: A Case Study of Jukbyeon, Uljin-gun, North Gyeongsang Province", *Annual Journal of the Asia-Africa Cultural Research Institute* 32: 11-72.

Takasaki, Soji. 1996. *Korean People in China: History, Life, Culture, Ethnical Education*. Tokyo: Akashi-shoten.

Takeda, Akira. 1980. "About 〈Retirement〉 in Korean Family", Editing Committee for Treatises in Honor of Dr. Kokubu Naoichi's 70th Birthday ed., *Japanese Ethnic Culture and Its Periphery: Treatises in Honor of Dr. Kokubu Naoichi's 70th Birthday: (History, People Part)*. (607-629), Shimonoseki: Shin-nippon-kyoiku-tosho.

Takeda, Akira. 1980. "Korean Family: Focusing on Difference of Men and Women", *Psychology* 5: 4-9.

Takeda, Akira. 1983. Geese of Tree: Korean People and Family, Tokyo-Science-sha.

Takeda, Akira. 1984. "Division of Rites of Ancestor Worship in Korea", *Minzokugaku-hyoron* 24: 32-55.

Takeda, Akira. 1984. "Marriage After Death", *Gekkan-kankoku-bunka* 6(5): 2-3.

Takeda, Akira. 1985. (Book Review) "Im Donggwon (Kumagai Osamu, Yoda Chihoko trans.) *Korean Folk Customs and Tradition*", *Nihon-minzokugaku* 161.

Takeda, Akira. 1986. (Interview with Kim Yanggi) "New View of Marriage and Family of Korea Based on Data: Academic Career, Occupation,

Regional Difference, View of Family, Friendship, Leisure", *Kikan-arutoman* 14: 3-11.

Takeda, Akira. 1986. "Comparative Folklore of Marriage After Death", *Mikawa-minzoku* 1: 1-19.

Takeda, Akira. 1986. (Book Review), "Yoda Chihoko, *A Study of Choson Folk Culture*", *Nihon-minzokugaku* 165.

Takeda, Akira. 1987. "Marriage of Departed Souls in East Asia: Focusing on Korean Customs", *Ibaraki-daigaku-Kyoyo-bu-Bulletin* 19: 13-39.

Takeda, Akira. 1988. "Marriage After Death in Jindo Island, Korea", *Minzokugaku-ronso* (Sagami-minzoku-gakkai) 7: 1-23.

Takeda, Akira. 1988. tr. With Im Donggwon, *Kankoku-no-minzoku-taikei Vol. 1,* Kokusho-kanko-kai.

Takeda, Akira. 1988. tr. With Im Donggwon, *Kankoku-no-minzoku-taikei Vol. 2.* Kokusho-kanko-kai.

Takeda, Akira. 1989. tr. With Im Donggwon, *Kankoku-no-minzoku-taikei Vol. 3.* Kokusho-kanko-kai.

Takeda, Akira. 1990. "A Korean Rite of Offering the First Product of the Year", Kinki-daigaku-minzokugaku-kenkyu-jo ed., *Folk Culture 2.*

Takeda, Akira. 1990. "Aged in Korean Family", *Series-kazoku-shi 5: A Comparative Family History of Aged People.* Tokyo: Sansei-do.

Takeda, Akira. 1990. "Ancestral Pots of Korea", in Takeda Akira ed., *Progress and Problems of Folklore.* (291-329), Tokyo: Kokusho-kanko-kai.

Takeda, Akira. 1990. ed., *Progress and Problems of Folklore.* Tokyo: Kokusho-kanko-kai.

Takeda, Akira. 1990. *Rites of Ancestral Spirits and Marriage of Departed Souls: An Attempt of Comparative Folklore of Japan and Korea.* Tokyo: Jimbun-shoin.

Takeda, Akira. 1990. tr. With Im Donggwon, *Kankoku-no-minzoku-taikei Vol. 4.* Kokusho-kanko-kai.

Takeda, Akira. 1991. "Ancestral Rituals Around East China Sea: Focusing on Rituals of Tablet", *Kikan-shizen-to-bunka* 34.

Takeda, Akira. 1992. tr. With Im Donggwon, *Kankoku-no-minzoku-taikei Vol. 5.* Tokyo: Kokusho-kanko-kai.

Takeda, Akira. 1993. "Marriage of Departed Souls in Jindo, Korea", Matsuzaki Kenzo ed., *Marriage of Departed Souls of East Asia.* Tokyo: Iwata-shoten.

Takeda, Akira. 1995. *Comparative Folklore of Ancestor Worship: Ancestor Worship and Society in Japan and Korea.* Tokyo: Yoshikawa-kobun-kan.

Takeda, Akira. 1996. "Confrontation Between Law and Folk Customs: Focusing on Korean Laws Concerning Family RItes", *Nihon-minzokugaku* 207: 93-135.

Takeda, Akira. 2000. "Korean Festivals and Japanese Festivals", *Nihongo-nihon-bungaku* 10.

Takeda, Akira. 2000. "Soka-daigaku-tainin-kinen-ronbun: Expecting the Development of Comparative Folklore: Reminiscence of 10 Years of Soka University", *Nihongo-nihon-bungaku* 10.

Takeda, Akira. 2000. *A Comparative Study of Japanese and Korean Rites of Ancestor Worship.* Daiichi-shobo (Academic series new Asia : 35).

Takeda, Yuka. 2000. "Inner Structure of Traditional Mutual Aid Organization in Korean Cities: A Case Study of Gye of Seoul", *Soshioroji* (Research Group of Sociology) 45(2).

Takizawa, Hideki. 1988. *Shift of Korean Society.* Tokyo: Ochanomizu-shobo.

Takizawa, Hideki. 1990. "Stratum Structure and Regional Character in Korean Society: An Essay for an Regional Structural Analysis of Labor Market", *Konan-keizaigaku-ronshu* 31(2): 91-141.

Takizawa, Hideki. 1991. "Viewpoint of Analysis of Korean Modern Society", *Konan-keizaigaku-ronshu* 32(3): 189-203.

Takizawa, Hideki. 1992. *Economic Growth and Social Structure of Korea.* Tokyo: Ochanomizu-shobo.

Takizawa, Kenji. 1996. "Kinship Relations of Zainichi Koreans From the Perspective of Shamanism: A Case Study of Korean Temple and Daikoji Temple on the West Side of Mt. Sigi-san", *Toyo daigaku-daigakuin-Bulletin* 32.

Taniura, Takao. 1980. "Development of Policy on Villages in Korea", *Asia-keizai* 21(10): 4-21.

Taniura, Takao. 1992. ed., *Chiiki-kenkyu-series: Korean Peninsula.* Tokyo: Asia-bunka-kenkyu-jo.

The University Museum, University of Tokyo, ed. 1991. *The World Carved on Dry Plates: Asia Which Torii Ryuzo Saw.* Tokyo: Tokyo-daigaku-sogo-kenkyu-shiryo-kan (Publishing: Tokyo-daigaku-shuppan-kyoku).

Toguchi, Fumiko. 1991. "Korean Folk Costume: A Comparison with Ryukyu", Okinawa-kenritsu-geijutsu-daigaku-Ryu-kan-densho-bunka-chosa-dan, *A Study of Korean Traditional Culture: For the Comparison with Okinawa.* 19:142, Naha: Okinawa-kenritsu-geijutsu-daigaku-Ryu-kan-densho-bunka-chosa-dan.

Tokui, Ken. 1975. "An Experience Report of Slash-and burn Cultivators", *Kikan-dorumen* 6: 135-140.

Tokui, Ken. 1977. "A Record of a Visit to Hwajeon Folks", *Chiri* 22(7): 74-83, 22(8): 60-66.

Tokui, Ken. 1983. "A Record of a Visit to People Who Collect Ginsengs", *Chiri* 28(12): 113-121.

Tokui, Ken. 1991. "Slash-and-burn Cultivators of Korea", *Kikan-shizen-to-bunka* 34.

Torigoe, Hiroyuki. 1998. "Possibility of Residents Autonomy in Korea", *Kwansei-gakuin-daigaku-shakai-gakubu-kiyo* 81: 175-184.

Tosa, Masaki. 1988. "The Present of Possession: Description and the Cultural Meaning of Shamanic Rites in Jindo Island, Korea", *The Japanese Journal of Ethnology* 53(4): 374-398.

Tosa, Masaki. 1993. "Rites and Emotions", *Osaka-daigaku-ningen-kagakubu-kiyo* 19.

Tosa, Masaki. 1998. "Anti-Asian Paradigm of Korea", Aoki Tamotsu, Saeki Keishi eds., *What Is Asian Appraisal?.* TBS Britannica.

Tosa, Masaki. 1998. *Internet and Religion* (Series Internet Society). Iwanami-shoten.

Tosa, Masaki. 1999. "Information and Image of Colony: Focusing on the Dispute over 'Ugly Koreans'", Aoki Tamotsu, Kajiwara Kageaki eds., *Joho-shakai-no-bunka (1) Information, Asia and Image.* Tokyo-daigaku-shuppan-kyoku.

Tosa, Masaki. 2001. "Why is eating dogs bad? : Globalization of Korean Society and Direction of Taboo of Eating Dogs" (Special Issue: Destiny of Taboo Concerning Food), *Vesta* (43).

Toyofuku, Youichi. 1984. "Actual Conditions of Self-Government Gye of Fishing Villages", in Joint Research Group for Fishing Community in Japan and Korea, ed., *Japan-Korea Joint Research Report Vol. 2: Hupo-ri, Pyeonghae-up, North Gyeongsang Province, Korea.* (115-127), Kobe: Joint Seminar on Fishing Community of Japan and Korea Office.

Toyofuku, Youichi. 1986. "Autonomy of Village in Korean Fishing Villages", in Joint Research Group for Fishing Community in Japan and Korea, ed., *Japan-Korea Joint Research Report Vol. 4: Wando-gun, South Jeolla Province, Korea.* (198-207), Kobe: Joint Seminar on Fishing Community of Japan and Korea Office.

Tsuha, Takashi. 1985. "Succession Customs of the East of Jeju Island", *Journal of Comparative Folklore Society* 3: 2-5.

Tsuha, Takashi. 1987. trans. "Choe Jaeseok, Kinship Group of Korea and Ryukyu: Focusing on Similarities and the Diffusion", *Ryudai-shigaku* 15.

Tsuha, Takashi. 1989. "Family of Jeju Island From the Perspective of Succession and Inheritance", *Chiiki-bunka-kenkyu* 4: 99-104.

Tsuha, Takashi. 1990. "Marriage Contract of Jeju Island", in Sugiyama Koichi, Sakurai Tetsuo eds., *Kankoku-shakai-no-bunka-jinruigaku.* (72-86), Tokyo: Kobun-do.

Tsuha, Takashi. 1991. "Succession Customs of Jeju Island: A Case Study of the Eastern Village on the Side of Mountain", in Okinawa-kenritsu-geijutsu-daigaku-Ryu-kan-densho-bunka-chosa-dan, *Kankoku-densho-bunka-no-kenkyu: For the Comparison with Okinawa.* (75-86), Naha: Okinawa-kenritsu-geijutsu-daigaku-Ryu-kan-densho-bunka-chosa-dan.

Tsuha, Takashi. 1993. "Succession Customs of the East of Jeju Island", *Okinawa Folk Studies* 13.

Tsuha, Takashi. 1999. Han Sangbok, Tsuha Takashi et al., "Lecture: Epistemology of Studies of Natural Culture", *Okinawa Folk Studies* (19).

Tsuha, Takashi. 1999. *Hangeul and Chili Powder.* Border Ink.

Tsuha, Takashi. 2000. "(Book Review and Introduction) Suzuki Masataka, Nomura Shinichi eds., *A Study of Masks and Shamanism: Japan and Korea*", *Shukyo-kenkyu* 74(2) (325).

Tsuha, Takashi. 2002. "Women and Ancestor Worship Rituals: Sharing Rituals in Jeju Island", Commemorative Treatises Publishing, *Folk Customs and History of Ryukyu and Asia.* Yoju-shorin.

Tsuji, Ryozo. 1982. "Change of Slash-and-burn agriculture of Korea", *Chiri* 27(3): 143-48.

Tsuji, Ryozo. 1985. "A Study of Processing and Storing of Acorns in Korea", *Kikan-jinruigaku* 16(4): 117-150.

Tsuji, Ryozo. 1985. "Distribution of Muk in Markets of Daegu, Korea", *Jinbun-chiri* 37(4): 86-96.

Tsuji, Ryozo. 1985. "Trend of Korean Geography Society (1)", *Chiri* 30(1): 48-58.

Tsuji, Ryozo. 1985. "Trend of Korean Geography Society (2)", *Chiri* 30(2): 100-107.

Tsuji, Ryozo. 1985. trans. "Yang Bogyeong, An Introduction to Studies of Geography Books of the Choson Era", *Chosen-gakuho* 116: 1-18.

Tsuji, Ryozo. 1986. "Acorn Muk in Jeju Island of Korea", *Gekkan-kankoku-bunka* 8(11): 26-29.

Tsuji, Ryozo. 1987. "Contents of 'Wild Food Plants of Korea' and Its Value as Data", *Chosen-gakuho* 123: 153-177.

Tsuruzono, Hiroshi. 1995. "Studies of Korean History and Cultural Anthropology: A Note Concerning Studies of Foreign History and Understanding the Other Cultures", *Kanazawa-daigaku-kyoyo-bu-ronshu* 32(2): 61-70.

Uchida, Ruriko. 1978. "A Record of Korean Travel", *Onsei-gakkai-kaiho* 158: 20-21, 15.

Uchida, Ruriko. 1978. *A Study of Rice Planting Music.* Tokyo: Yuzankaku-shuppan.

Uemura, Yukio. 1989. "Shamanic Rites and Music of Zainichi Koreans", *Toyo-ongaku-kenkyu* 54.

Uemura, Yukio. 1993. "The Beginning of Korean Modern Musical History: Resarch Trend of the Late 1980's", *Toyo-ongaku-kenkyu* 57.

Uemura, Yukio. 1995. "A Study of Military Music System of the Early Choson Era: Chwirachi and Taebyeongso", *Tokyo: geijutsu-daigaku-ongaku-gakubu-Bulletin* 21.

Uemura, Yukio. 1996. Tsuge Genichi, Uemura Yukio, *History of Asian Music.* Ongaku-no-tomo-sha.

Uemura, Yukio. 1997. "Based on an Investigation of Court Music in the Colonial Korea: Political Context of 'An Investigation of Korean Court Music' by Tanabe Hisao (Special Issue: Discovery of Traditional Culture in Modern Korea)", *Chosen-kenkyu-kai-ronbun-shu* 35.

Uemura, Yukio. 1998. *An Exploration of Korean Music* (Book for The First Encounter with Music). Ongaku-no-tomo-sha.

Uemura, Yukio. 1999. Yamaguchi Osamu, Kato Tomiko, Yamaguchi Akiko eds., Takahashi Mitsunori dir., "Asian Music and Culture", *Oriental Music Studies* 64.

Uemura, Yukio. 2002. "Learning Korean Culture From Hyeongeum", *Fujin-no-tomo* 96(6).

Uezu, Hitoshi. 1986. "Folk Articles of Jeju Island", *Okinawa-minzoku-kenkyu* 6.

Uezu, Hitoshi. 1991. "Korean Folk Articles: A Comparative Study with Folk Articles of Okinawa" Okinawa-kenritsu-geijutsu-daigaku-ryu-kan-densho-bunka-chosa-dan, *Kankoku-densho-bunka-no-kenkyu: For the Comparison with Okinawa.,* (145-166), Naha: Okinawa-kenritsu-geijutsu-daigaku-ryu-kan-densho-bunka-chosa-dan.

Ukiba, Masachika. 1992. "Modernization and Change of Korean Village Society: From the Perspective of the Theory of Moral Economy", *Nihon-gakuho* (Osaka-daigaku) 11: 1-24.

Usami, Takanori. 1993. "Structure of Ethnic Wrestling of Korean People in China: Focusing on Rules and Technique System", *Hakusan Jinruigaku* 2.

Wada, Shohei. 1994. "Marriage of the Dead: Korean Marriage After Death", *Kikan-minzokugaku* 69: 74-79.

Wakamatsu, Minoru. 1975. *Korean Proverbs.* (Detailed Explanation of 263 proverbs), Tokyo: Koma-book-trading.

Wakamatsu, Minoru. 1982. *Ceremonial Occasions of Korea*. Tokyo: Koma-book-trading.

Wakamori, Tamio. 1986. "An Investigation Report of Korean Village Society: Acceptance of Christianity and Folk Customs in Daejang, Daechang-ri, Juksan-myeon, Kimje-gun, North Jeolla Province", *Toho-gakuen-daigaku-kiyo* 5: 67-77.

Wakamori, Tamio. 1990. "An Investigation Report of Korean Village Society Vol. 2: Acceptance of Christianity and Folk Customs in Daejang, Daechang-ri, Juksan-myeon, Kimje-gun, North Jeolla Province", *Toho-*

gakuen-daigaku-kiyo 8: 69-83.

Wakamori, Taro. 1975. "(Interview with Choi In-Hak) Korea-Japan Relationship From the Ethnic Perspective", *Asia-koron* 4(12): 89-95.

Wakamori, Taro. 1975. "Similarity of Korean and Japanese Folk Customs: Ethnic Life History and Its Tradition", *Asia-koron* 4(12): 90-93.

Watanabe, Hiroshi. 1991. "Confucianist, Seonbi, Yangban: Existing Style of Confucian Refined People", Umesao Tadao, Kurita Yasuyuki eds., *Chishiki-to-Kyoyo-no-Bunmeigaku*. Tokyo: Chuo-koron.

Watanabe, Yoshio. 1990. "Geomancy, Ancestor, Descent: Prospect of Geomancy of East Asia by Conversation Style", in Takeda Akira ed., *Progress and Problems of Folklore.* (359-387), Tokyo: Kokusho-kanko-kai.

Watanabe, Yoshio. 1996. "Geomantic Senses of East Asia: A Memorandum for Understanding the Trend and Differences From Graphs", *Tokyo-toritsu-daigaku-jinbun-gakuho* 271: 1-57.

Yagi, Saichi. 1975. "Korean Funerals and Funeral Institutions", *Hiroshima-minzoku* 4: 23-29.

Yagi, Saichi. 1978. "Family Characters of Korean Villages: A Case Study of Naegok-ri", *Hiroshima-hogaku* 2(2, 3): 173-198.

Yagi, Saichi, and Hirata, Junji, and Ogasawara, Shin. 1976. "Village Structure and Cultural Change: A Case Study of Naegok-ri", in Noguchi Takashi ed., *Emigration and Cultural Change: A Case Study of Hapcheon, Korea.* (65-147), Tokyo: Nihon-gakujutsu-shinko-kai.

Yamamoto, Kahori. 1996. "Life History of Japanese Wives in Korea", Tani Tomio ed., *For the People Who Learn Life History.* Sekai-shiso-sha.

Yamamoto, Kahori. 1998. "A Study of Ethnic Community in Aichi Province (1): A Case Study of Group Residence of Zainichi Koreans in Shinkawa-cho", *Aichi-kenritsu-daigaku-bungakubu-ronshu-shakai-fukushi-gakka-hen* 47.

Yamamoto, Kahori. 1999. "Earthquake of Zainichi Koreans", Iwasaki Nobuhiko et al. eds., *Hanshin-awaji-daijishin-no-shakaigaku* Vol. 3 Showa-do.

Yamamoto, Kahori. 1999. Yamada Masahiro, Okita Kayoko, Yamamoto Kahori, "Change of Region and Family, and Attitude on Support of Aged Parents", *Shakai-fukushi-kenkyu* 1(1).

Yamamoto, Kahori. 2000. "Women in Confucian Norms: A Study of Korean Women's Social Position", in Kobayashi Takayuki ed., *Changing Modern Family Society.* (44-65), Kyoto: Sekai-shiso-sha.

Yamanaka, Miyuki. 1978. "Relations Between Aged Parent and Children in Korean Urban Families", *Soshioroji* 23(2): 75-87.

Yamanaka, Miyuki. 1982. "A Record of Yeongjeol-hon of Korea", *Kagoshima-keizai-daigaku-shakai-gakubu-ronshu* 1: 63-73.

Yamanaka, Miyuki. 1983. trans., Kim Jongtaek, "Koreans' Traditional View of Women: Based on Proverbs", *Kagoshima-keizai-daigaku-shakai-gakubu-ronshu* 1(3): 87-104.

Yamanaka, Miyuki. 1985. "Selection of Spouse and View of Marriage of Korean Women in Villages: Findings of Andong-gun, North Gyeongsang Province", *Soshioroji* 30(2), 131-150.

Yamanaka, Miyuki. 1987. "Current Situation of Elderly Welfare in Korea: Focusing on Economic Life for the Aged in Regard of Social Security and Family Support", *Kagoshima-keizai-daigaku-shakai-gakubu-ronshu* 5(3, 4): 57-76.

Yamanaka, Miyuki. 1995. "Privatization Process From the Perspective of Change of Relationship Between Wife and Sisters-in-law in Korea", *Ryukoku-daigaku-shakai-gakubu-kiyo* 6: 87-97.

Yamanaka, Miyuki. 1996. "Korean Society and Family Change", in Nonoyama Hisaya, Sodei Takako, Shinozaki Masami eds., *What is Happening to Family Now?: Focusing on Paradigm Shift of Family Sociology.* (221-240), Kyoto: Minerva-shobo.

Yamane, Mari. 1995. "Network of Husband and Wife in Urban Families of Modern Korea : Bonds of Relative Group and Support Network", *Aichi-kyoiku-daigaku-kaseigaku-kyoshitsu-kiyo* 26: 123-130.

Yamane, Mari and Onode, Setsuko. 1992. *A Comparative Study Report of Korean and Japanese Family Relations.* Kobe: Hyogo-ken-katei-mondai-kenkyu-jo.

Yamawaki, Keizo. 2000. "An Essay of Classified Composition of Identity of Zainichi Koreans", *Meiji-daigaku-shakai-kagaku-kenkyu-jo-kiyo* 38: 2.

Yang, Ae-Soon. 1999. "Cosmology of the First Generation of Zainichi Koreans and Village Society: Belief System and Behavioral Style of Confucian

Family", *Ritsumeikan-sangyo-shakai-ronshu* 35-2.

Yang, Ae-Soon. 2000. "Rites and Zainichi Korean Community: Focusing on Alternation of Generations and Secularization", *Ritsumeikan-sangyo-shakai-ronshu* 36: 2.

Yano, Ken'ichi. 1998. "Change of Korean Language in Kazakhstan", *Kumamoto-gakuen-daigaku-bungaku-gengogaku-ronshu* 5(2).

Yano, Ken'ichi. 2001. Yano Kenichi trans. Dmitry V. Myong, "Political and Economic Situation of Kazakhstan and Koreans", *Kaigai-jijo-kenkyu* 28(2) 56.

Yano, Takao. 2000. Im Jaegyu, Yano Takao, "Irrigation Custom in Tribal Villages: A Case Study of a Lineage Village in Dangjin-gun, South Chungcheong Province, Korea", *Waseda-daigaku-ningen-kagaku-kenkyu* 13(1).

Yano, Takao. 2001. Yano Takao, Im Jaegyu, "Funeral Tradition of Korea and Its Change: A Case Study of Dangjin-gun, South Chungcheong Province (Special Issue: Cultural Tradition and Change: Focusing on Funeral System and Graveyard System)", *Human Science* 14(1).

Yasuda, Hiromi. 1990. "Oppression of Women in Korean Traditional Society and Shamanism: As a Correspondence to Life Stage of Women", *Sokietasu* 17.

Yasuda, Hiromi. 1991. "Brief History of Studies on Korean Shamanism", in Ogo Kin'ichi, Takakuwa Fumiko, Yamauchi Kenji eds., *East Asian Cultural Anthropology.* Tokyo: Yachiyo-shuppan.

Yasuda, Hiromi. 1991. "The Present of Korean Shamanism Studies: Domestic and Overseas Research Trend From the Year of 1970 and Prospect", *Meiji-daigaku-daigakuin-kiyo Politics and Economics Part* 28: 197-212.

Yasuda, Hiromi. 1997. "Korean Women: Another Side of Confucian Norms, the World of Shamanism", Ayabe Tsuneo ed., *Ethnography of Women (1) Asia Part.* Tokyo: Kobun-do.

Yasuda, Hiromi. 1999. "Change of Korean Shamanism and the Peripheral Cultures", in Sasaki Kokan ed., *A Cultural Anthropological Study of Structure and Change of Shamanism Culture in East Asia.* Study Report for Scientific Research Fund of 1996-1998.

Yasuda, Hiromi. 2000. "A Study of Characters of Marriage of Departed Souls in Korea", in Sakurai Tokutaro ed., *Shamanism and Its Circumstance.* Tokyo: Daiichi-shobo.

Yatazawa, Noriko. 1993. "Korean Family: Family of Dozoku Village", in Kameyama Keiichi ed., *An Investigation Report of Korean Villages.* Toyota: Toyota- tanki-daigaku.

Yatazawa, Noriko. 1995. "Korean Family 3: Change of Family in Fishing Villages and Elderly Welfare", *Toyota-senmon-daigaku-kiyo* 5: 10-24.

Yoda, Chihoko. 1966. "Rites of Rice Farming in Korea: Focusing on the Types", *The Japanese Journal of Ethnology* 31(2): 107-137.

Yoda, Chihoko. 1967. (Book Review) "'*Korean Entertainment*' '*Korean Masks* Ⅰ, Ⅱ, Ⅲ' Kim Yanggi", *The Japanese Journal of Ethnology* 32(3): 245.

Yoda, Chihoko. 1968. (Book Review) "Jang, Ju-Keun, Choe Kil-sung, *An Investigation Report of Folk Data 'Shamanism of Gyeonggi Province* (Shaman of Yangju-gun, Jo Yeongja Part)'", *The Japanese Journal of Ethnology* 33(1): 95-98.

Yoda, Chihoko. 1969. "A Study of Forms of Acceptance of Chinese Culture in Korea: Seen in Annual Events", *Chosen-gakuho* 52: 93-131.

Yoda, Chihoko. 1971. (Book Review) "Lee Duhyeon, '*Korean Masks*'", *The Japanese Journal of Ethnology* 36(2): 187-191.

Yoda, Chihoko. 1971. (Book Review) "*An Investigation Report of Korean Folk Customs (South Jeolla Province)* Korea Cultural Anthropology Society ed.", *The Japanese Journal of Ethnology* 36(1): 74-77.

Yoda, Chihoko. 1972. "Japanese Myths and Korean Myths (Special Issue: The World of Japanese Myths)(Descent of Japanese Myth)", *Kokubungaku-kaishaku-to-kansho* 37(1).

Yoda, Chihoko. 1975. "Korean Belief of Mountain Deity(1): Mountain Deity of Hunting Folk and Hunting Culture of Korea" *Chosen-gakuho* 75: 25-76.

Yoda, Chihoko. 1977. (Book Review) "'*Korean Falk Belief*' '*Korean Local Belief*' Jang Jugeun", *The Japanese Journal of Ethnology* 41(4): 396-399.

Yoda, Chihoko. 1977. "Japanese Myths and Korean Myths", in Ito Seiji, Obayashi Taryo eds., *Nihon: shinwa-kenkyu Ⅰ.* (172-178), Tokyo: Gakusei-sha.

Yoda, Chihoko. 1978. tr., Kim Yeolgyu, *A Study of Korean Folk Tradition and*

Folktales. Gakusei-sha.

Yoda, Chihoko. 1980. "Korean Female Shaman", *Kikan-yukyu* 2: 90-103.

Yoda, Chihoko. 1980. "Korean Funeral System and View of Another World", Editing Committee for Treatises in Honor of Dr. Kokubu Naoichi's 70th Birthday ed., *Japanese Ethnic Culture and Its Periphery: Treatises in Honor of Dr. Kokubu Naoichi's 70th Birthday (History, Race Part).* (533-586), Shimonoseki: Shin-nippon-kyoiku-tosho.

Yoda, Chihoko. 1981. "Cultural Meaning of Shamanism: Focusing on Korean Shamanism", *Dento-to-gendai* 71: 119-134.

Yoda, Chihoko. 1982. "Structure of Korean Tales of Visits to Foreign Countries", *Kosho-bungei-kenkyu* 5: 47-57.

Yoda, Chihoko. 1983. "(Book Review), Park Gyuhong's *Korean Village Festivals*", *Nihon-minzokugaku* 147: 61-66.

Yoda, Chihoko. 1984. "Mediums and Priests in Japanese and Korean Shamanism: Focusing on Personnel Organization of Matsuriba of Deities", *Koriyama-joshi-daigaku-kiyo* 20: 119-134.

Yoda, Chihoko. 1984. (tr. With Kumagai Osamu, Im Donggwon), *Korean Folk Customs and Tradition.* Ofu-sha.

Yoda, Chihoko. 1985. "Korean Shaman Myths and Japanese Middle Age Myths: Focusing on Kami-no-ko-kaiko-gata-nikko-kanjo-setsuwa". *Eureka* 17(1): 198-207.

Yoda, Chihoko. 1985. *A Study of Korean Folk Culture: Focusing on Basic Culture of Korea and Its Origin.* Tokyo: Ruri-shobo.

Yoda, Chihoko. 1986. "Mt. Geumseong; Bear; Mt. Odae; Sipjangsaeng; (with Choe Kilsung) Shamanism; Chusoek National Holiday; New Year's Day; Myth; Mt. Sokri; Seonang-dang; The Seventh Day of the Seventh Month of the Lunar Calendar; Tano; Jangseung; Annual Events; Farming Rites; Festival; Folk tales; Mineral Water", Ito Abito, Ohmura Masuo, Kajimura Hideki, Takeda Yukio eds., *Dictionary for Understanding Korea.* Tokyo: Heibon-sha.

Yoda, Chihoko. 1986. With Murakami Yoshio, "(Book Review) Kumagai Osamu '*East Asian Folk Customs and Rites*'", *Chosen-gakuho* 121: 161-163.

Yoda, Chihoko. 1987. "Rites and Belief of Ancient Korea", in Obayashi Taryo ed., *Nihon-no-kodai 13 Universe in Hearts.* (333-360), Tokyo: Chuo-koron.

Yoda, Chihoko. 1987. "Akamatsu Chijo/ Im Donggwon/ Mishina Shoei/ Murayama Chijun", *Bunka-jinruigaku-jiten.* Tokyo: Kobun-do.

Yoda, Chihoko. 1987. "Queens of Ancient East Asia From the Perspective of Cultural Anthropology: Focusing on Queens of Ancient Korea and Kingship, Dual System of Sacred and Secular", *Soritsu-40-shunen-kinen-ronbun-shu.* (77-111), Koriyama: Koriyama-kaisei-gakuen.

Yoda, Chihoko. 1989. "Competition of Deities: The Myth of the Creation of Korea and Its Structure", *East Asian Myths of the Creation.* (124-167), Tokyo: Kobun-do.

Yoda, Chihoko. 1990. (Book Review) "Araki Hiroyuki, Nomura Junichi, Fukuda Akira, Miyata Noboru and Watanabe Shogo eds., *Japanese Myths Collection* (Separate Volume 1) Study Part.", *Kokugakuin-zasshi* 91(4).

Yoda, Chihoko. 1990. "Heavenly Beings of Korea: Setter of Order", in Takeda Akira ed., *Progress and Problems of Folklore.* (477-505), Tokyo: Kokusho-kanko-kai.

Yoda, Chihoko. 1990. "Korean Food Culture and Women: Rising in the World and Gaining Fame of Housewives, Confucianism, Redistribution of Wealth", in Sugiyama Koichi, Sakurai Tetsuo eds., *Kankoku-shakai-no-bunka-jinruigaku.* Tokyo: Kobun-do.

Yoda, Chihoko. 1990. "Structure of Choson Myths of Regality: Flower Theft, Foreign Kings, Assignment of Nation", *Kokugakuin-zasshi* 91(6): 54-97.

Yoda, Chihoko. 1991. "A Study of the Origin of Pickled Mussels: Food Culture Delivered by Balhaesa", *Kokugakuin-daigaku-nihon-bunka-kenkyu-jo-ho* 165.

Yoda, Chihoko. 1991. "Cultural Historical Meaning of Korean Tigers, Mountain Deity and Symbol of Power", *Kokugakuin-daigaku-kiyo* 29: 33-56.

Yoda, Chihoko. 1991. "Shaman", in Uematsu Akashi ed., *Folk Customs and Rites of the Rim of China Sea 2: Rites of Deities.* (337-368), Tokyo: Gaifu-sha.

Yoda, Chihoko. 1991. *A Study of Korean Myths and Folklore.* Ruri-shobo.

Yoda, Chihoko. 1992. "Belief of Dragons and Snakes of Choson: Regality and Water Deity, Symbol of Wealth and Spirits", Asia-minzoku-zokei-bunka-kenkyu-jo ed., *Asian Dragons and Snakes-shape and Symbol.* Tokyo: Yuzankaku-shuppan.

Yoda, Chihoko. 1992. "Influence of Food Culture of Ancient Korea Toward Japan", *Kokugakuin-daigaku-nihon-bunka-kenkyusyo-kiyo* 69: 57-102.

Yoda, Chihoko. 1993. "Myths of Koguryo and Japan", in Ueda Masaaki ed., *Rites and Tradition of Deities.* Doho-sha-shuppan 1993.6.

Yoda, Chihoko. 1994. Yoda Chihoko and Nakanishi Masaki tr., *Collection of Kim Deok-sun's Old Tales: Legends of Korean in China.* MIyai-shoten.

Yoda, Chihoko. 1996. "Confectionery and Koryo teacups", in Publishing Committee of Treatises in Honor of Mr. Kaneko Kazushige's 70th Birthday, *Ethnic Plastic Culture of Asia*. Chozokan.

Yoda, Chihoko. 1996. "Choson Myths of Metal: Focusing on Northern Myths", in Yu Muwon ed., *Anthropology of People, Things, Language: Treatises in Honor of Dr. Kokubu Naoichi's 88th Birthday.* (440-456), Tokyo: Keiyu-sha.

Yoda, Chihoko. 2001. "Korean Belief of Dragon: Regality and the Water Deity, Symbol of Wealth(Special Issue: Dragons)", *Asia-yugaku* 28.

Yokota, Ken'ichi. 1972. "Demise of Dr. Mishina Shoei", *The Japanese Journal of Ethnology* 37(1): 66-67.

Yokoyama, Minoru. 1986. "Awareness of Korean and Japanese Teenagers: An Analysis Based on David Riesman's Hypothesis", *Kokusai-hogaku* 23(4): 81-130.

Yoo, Dong-Sik. 1975. *Korean Shamanism.* Tokyo: Gakusei-sha.

Yoo, Kyung-Mi. 2002. "About the Origin of Yut Game", *Gekkan-kankoku-bunka* 266.

Yoo, Si-Jung. 1976. Hayashi Takeshi ed., "Formation and Change of Korean Cities during the Colonial Period: Focusing on the Early Stage of the Colonial Period", *Urbanization of Developing Countries.* (111-146), Tokyo: Asia-bunka-kenkyu-jo.

Yoo, Si-Jung. 1979. "Change of Local Communities and Problems Following Korean Industrialization: Focusing on Gumi (2)", *Asia-keizai* 20(4): 27-47.

Yoo, Si-Jung. 1979. "Change of Local Communities and Problems Following Korean Industrialization: Focusing on Gumi (1)", *Asia-keizai* 20(2): 27-41.

Yoo, Young-Tae. 1999. "Exorcism for Living People: Distance and Idea of Exorcism of Jindossikim", in Suzuki Masataka, Nomura Shinichi eds., *A Study of Masks and Shamanism: Japan and Korea*. Daiichi-shobo.

Yoon, Kwang-Bong. 1998. "The Theory of Progress of Masque: Based on Original Aspects of Entertainments of the Three States", *Gengo-bunka-kenkyu,* 24.

Yoon, Kwang-Bong. 2001. "Phases of Theme of Korean Masque: Focusing on Masque of Sandae", *Gengo-bunka-kenkyu* 27.

Yoon, Kwang-Bong. 2002. "Phases of Development of Korean Plays: Focusing on Korean Theatrical Poems", *Asia-shakai-bunka-kenkyu* 3.

Yoshida, Hajime. 2000. "Transfer of Japanese Liquor to Taiwan, Choson and China", Umesao Tadao, Yoshida Shuji eds., *Liquor and Japanese Civilization*. Kobun-do.

Yoshida, Mitsuo. 1977. "About 'Hanwon' and 'Koryogi': Focusing on Its Author and thc Writtcn Ycar", *Chosen-gakuh*o 85.

Yoshida, Mitsuo. 1979. "Local-Government of the Early Choson Dynasty: Focusing on an Examination of Character of the List of Surnames of Sejong-sillok-jiriji", *Shakai-keizai-shigaku* 44(5).

Yoshida, Mitsuo. 1980. "About Kang, Implements of Water Transport of the Koryo Dynasty", *Shakai-keizai-shigaku* 46(4).

Yoshida, Mitsuo. 1981. "Choson's Togwan System in the 15th Century: A Phase of Local Governing System of the Early Choson Era (Special Issue: Problems of the History of Choson Dynasty)", *Chosen-shi-kenkyu-kai-ronbun-shu* 18.

Yoshida, Mitsuo. 1984. "Structure of Disaster of the End of the Choson Dynasty and An Example of Rescue in Disaster: Seongdangchang in 1875 Recorded in Johaengillok", *Chosen-gakuho* 113.

Yoshida, Mitsuo. 1985. "About Mijeon, American Merchant Union of Seoul in the Late Choson Era: Focusing on the Period Around Sinhae-tonggong, in 1791 (Special Issue: Merchants and Craftsmen of Middle and Modern Times)", *Shicho* 17.

Yoshida, Mitsuo. 1986. "Shipwrecks of Chungcheong Province in the 19th Century: Based on 190 Cases of Shipwrecks", *Chosen-gakuho* 121.

Yoshida, Mitsuo. 1988. "Reconsideration of Studies of Gaeseong Account Books", *Chosen-shi-kenkyu-kai-ronbun-shu* 25.

Yoshida, Mitsuo. 1989. "Mourning of Demise of Mr. Tagawa Kozo (Including a Chronological Table and a List of Works)", *Toyo-gakuho* 70(3, 4).

Yoshida, Mitsuo. 1990. Han Sangil, Yoshida Mitsuo trans. "Trend and Problems of Studies of Japanese Modern Political History in Korea (Special Issue: Trend of Studies of Japanese History: Prospect From Outside)", *Rekishigaku-kenkyu* 607.

Yoshida, Mitsuo. 1991. "An Attempt of Quantitative Analysis Concerning Shipping Phases of Transport Ships for Tax Grain of the Choson Dynasty in the 19th Century: A Case Study of Gyeongsang Province, Jeolla Province, and Chungcheong Province (Including a List of Cases of Transport Ships for Tax Grain)", *Kaiji-shi-kenkyu* 48.

Yoshida, Mitsuo. 1992. "Urban Space of Hanseong: An Introduction to the Theory of Modern Seoul (Special Issue: An Approach to the Theory of Choson Cities)", *Chosen-shi-kenkyu-kai-ronbun-shu* 30.

Yoshida, Mitsuo. 1993. "People and Houses of Seoul in the Early 20th Century Seen in Family Registers: An Basic Analysis of Hanseong-bu's Family Registers Possessed by Kyoto University", *Chosen-gakuho* 147.

Yoshida, Mitsuo. 1997. Kim Dongcheol, Yoshida Mitsuo trans. "Change of Banyeok System and Formation of Magye in the 18th Century", *Nenpo-toshishi-kenkyu* 5.

Yoshida, Mitsuo. 1999. "Castle Towns and Imperial Capitals of Modern Choson (Special Issue: Capitality)", *Nenpo-toshi-shi-kenkyu* 7.

Yoshida, Mitsuo. 1999. "Changing Perceptions of Choson: A Dilemma of Researchers of Choson History)", *Dai-kokai* 30.

Yoshida, Mitsuo. 1999. "Historical Value of the Records of Gaeseong Account Books Possessed by Kobe University", *Chosen-bunka-kenky*u 6.

Yoshida, Mitsuo. 2000. "Tribal Unity of Noble Families in Modern Choson and Eup Space: A Case Study of Andong-Gwon in Danseong, Gyeongsang Province", *Toyoshi-kenkyu* 58(4).

Yoshida, Mitsuo. 2000. *History and Society of Korea.* Hoso-daigaku-kyoiku-shinko-kai, (Materials of Hoso University).

Yoshida, Mitsuo. 2001. "A Walk in Korea (5) Noble Family of Andong", *Asia Yugaku* (29).

Yoshida, Mitsuo. 2002. "History of Seoul (Special Issue 2: Town of Living History)", *Gekkan-shinika* 13(7) 149.

Yosihara, Kazuo, Suzuki, Masataka and Suenari, Michio eds. 2000. *Reconstruction of Blood Relation: Paternal Descent and the Union of the Same Surname.* Tokyo: Fukyo-sha.

APPENDIX II

Bibliography: Japanese Studies on Korea

(Korean translation)

Compiled by Seiichi Matsumoto

Toyo University of Japan

Akada, Mitsuo. 赤田光男. 1975.「朝鮮의 墓地와 祖先祭祀」森浩一(編)『墓地: 日本古代文化의 探求』197-217, 京都: 世界思想社.

Akamatsu, Chijo and Akiba, Takashi. 赤松智城・秋葉隆. 1937.『朝鮮巫俗의 研究』大阪: 大阪屋號書店.

Akiba, Takashi. 秋葉隆. 1932.「濟州島에 있어서의 蛇鬼의 信仰: 遮歸文化圈의 試圖」『青丘學叢』7: 100-110.

Akiba, Takashi. 秋葉隆. 1949.「巫와 火: 朝鮮샤머니즘에 있어서의 聖火의 行事」『民族學研究』14(1): 13-16.

Akiba, Takashi. 秋葉隆. 1950.『朝鮮巫俗의 現地研究』丹波: 養德社.

Akiba, Takashi. 秋葉隆. 1954.『朝鮮民俗誌』東京: 六三書院.

Amino, Husako. 網野房子. 1997.「韓國－巫女의 宗教的世界: 全羅南道珍島의 調查로부터」『民族學研究』62(3): 273-293.

Amino, Husako. 網野房子. 1997.「韓國－巫女의 神觀念: 天然痘의 神〈손님〉을 중심으로」『東京都立大學 人文學報』280: 43-66.

Amino, Husako. 網野房子. 1998.「韓國－巫女의 生命觀을 둘러싼 覺書: 全羅南道珍島調查 노트로부터」『東京都立大學 人文學報』290: 139-155.

Amino, Husako. 網野房子. 1998.「檀那場과 단골무당」大胡欽一・加治明・佐々木宏幹・比嘉政夫・宮本勝(編)『社會와 象徵－人類學的어프로치 村武精一教授古稀記念論文集』岩田書院.

Amino, Husako. 網野房子. 1999.「〈異者〉로서의 단골」三尾裕子・本田洋(編)

『東아시아에 있어서의 文化의 多中心性』東京外國語大學아시아・아프리카言語文化硏究所.

Amino, Husako. 網野房子. 1999.「濟州島의 宗教的職能者 신방을 둘러싼 覺書－金寧現地調査로부터」『現文硏』(專修大學)75.

An, Byeong-Kon. 安秉坤. 1993.「韓國에 있어서의 伝統的家族硏究의 現狀」『社會學評論』44(1): 46-53.

An, Byeong-Kon. 安秉坤. 1995.「韓國伝統家族에 있어서의 分居的直系家族의 類型化의 試図: 日本의 家(이에)에 있어서의 〈潛在的直系家族〉과의 比較를 중심으로」『關西學院大學社會學部紀要』72: 153-163.

Ando, Kunihiro. 安藤邦廣. 1989.「온돌과 마루: 韓國民家의 構造」『季刊民族學』49: 59-71.

Aono, Masaaki. 青野正明. 1990.「植民地期朝鮮에 있어서의 農村再編成政策의 자리매김－農村振興運動期를 중심으로」『朝鮮學報』(通号 136).

Aono, Masaaki. 青野正明. 1991.「朝鮮農村의 '中堅人物'－京畿道驪州郡의 경우」『朝鮮學報』(通号 141).

Aono, Masaaki. 青野正明. 1995.「朝鮮總督府의 對民衆宗教政策－1930年代를 중심으로」『聖和大學論集 人文學系』(通号 23).

Aono, Masaaki. 青野正明. 1996.「近代朝鮮에 있어서의 天道教의 〈地上天國〉」『聖和大學論集 人文學系』(通号 24).

Aono, Masaaki. 青野正明. 1996.「朝鮮總督府의 神社政策－1930年代를 중심으로」『朝鮮學報』(通号160) [1996.7].

Aono, Masaaki. 青野正明. 1997.「朝鮮總督府의 對巫俗政策」『聖和大學論集 人文學系』(通号 25).

Aono, Masaaki. 青野正明. 1999.「近代朝鮮에 있어서의 民衆宗教・金剛道의 〈新都〉 建設」『聖和大學論集 人文學系』(通号 27) [1999.12].

Aono, Masaaki. 青野正明. 2001.『朝鮮農村의 民族宗教－植民地期의 天道教・金剛大道를 중심으로』社會評論社.

Aoyagi, Kiyotaka. 青柳清孝. 1973.「全羅南道光山郡大村面A部落에 있어서의 世帶構成과 住居의 構成: 中間報告」『아시아文化硏究』7: 51-60.

Aoyagi, Yuko. 青柳優子. 1989.「現代韓國에 있어서의 女性의 位置와 家族法改正運動」『女性學年報』10: 42-46.

Aoyagi, Yuko. 青柳優子. 1999.『韓國語와 日本語로 배우는 韓國의 社會와 女性』釜山: 滿守出版社.

Aruga, Kizaemon. 有賀喜左衛門. 1973.「鈴木榮太郎의 朝鮮研究」『未來』83: 2-11.

Asakawa, Shigeo & Sakata, Shohei. 淺川滋男・坂田昌平. 1997.「온돌과 丸屋根의 家－中國黑龍江省瀑布村의 朝鮮族住居」『季刊民族學』81.

Asakura, Toshio. 朝倉敏夫. 1981.「全羅南道都草島調査予備報告(1): 특히 婚姻에 대하여」『明治大學大學院紀要』18: 78-87.

Asakura, Toshio. 朝倉敏夫. 1982.「全羅南道都草島調査予備報告(2): 葬礼에 대하여」『明治大學大學院紀要』19: 49-61.

Asakura, Toshio. 朝倉敏夫. 1983.「全羅南道都草島一農村의 家族」『社會人類學年報』9: 153-166.

Asakura, Toshio. 朝倉敏夫. 1983.「全羅南道都草島調査予備報告(3): 契에 대하여」『明治大學大學院紀要』20: 17-31.

Asakura, Toshio. 朝倉敏夫. 1984.「全羅南道都草島調査予備報告(4): "Chib-an" 選擧에 보는 農村社會의 一面」『明治大學大學院紀要』21: 19-31.

Asakura, Toshio. 朝倉敏夫. 1985.「韓國一農村의 社會的性格: 契를 通하여」『朝鮮史研究會會報』81: 11-14.

Asakura, Toshio. 朝倉敏夫. 1986.「勞働慣行」『基礎한글』2(4): 46-47.

Asakura, Toshio. 朝倉敏夫. 1986.『食은 韓國에 있다』(森枝卓士, 朝倉敏夫) 弘文堂, [1986.4].

Asakura, Toshio. 朝倉敏夫. 1987.「韓國社會考: 地域性에 관한 覺書」『Field』2: 41-50.

Asakura, Toshio. 朝倉敏夫. 1987.「韓國民俗學의 現狀」『民俗學評論』27: 11-20.

Asakura, Toshio. 朝倉敏夫. 1988.「現代韓國社會와 女性: 서울・아파트 団地에 있어서의 主婦의 네트워크부터」『民博通信』42: 63-67.

Asakura, Toshio. 朝倉敏夫. 1989.「韓國의 位牌祭祀」渡邊欣雄(編)『環中國海의 民族과 文化 3 祖先祭祀』121-143, 東京: 凱風社.

Asakura, Toshio. 朝倉敏夫. 1989.「韓國의 祖先祭祀와 社會組織」渡邊欣雄(編)『環中國海의 民族과 文化 3 祖先祭祀』41-64, 東京: 凱風社.

Asakura, Toshio. 朝倉敏夫. 1989.「韓國祖先祭祀의 変化－都市아파트 団地居住者를 중심으로」『國立民族學博物館研究報告』13(4): 741-786.

Asakura, Toshio. 朝倉敏夫. 1990.「韓國의 風水研究: 그 回顧와 展望」竹田旦(篇)『民俗學의 進展과 課題』331-357, 東京: 國書刊行會.

Asakura, Toshio. 朝倉敏夫. 1990.「韓國社會의 地域性」杉山晃一・櫻井哲男(編)

『韓國社會의 文化人類學』 東京: 弘文堂.

Asakura, Toshio. 朝倉敏夫. 1992. 「移動하는 韓國人」『Field』 2: 41-50.

Asakura, Toshio. 朝倉敏夫. 1992. 「現代韓國社會에 있어서의 〈伝統文化〉의 研究의 現狀과 展望」『國立民族學博物館研究報告』 17(4): 809-850.

Asakura, Toshio. 朝倉敏夫. 1992. 「現代韓國社會의 歲時風俗」『月刊시니카』 3(4): 62-67.

Asakura, Toshio. 朝倉敏夫. 1994. 「韓國의 家族과 아이 키우기」『教育과 医學』 42(7).

Asakura, Toshio. 朝倉敏夫. 1994. 『日本의 燒肉 韓國의 刺身: 食文化가 "-nized" 될 때』 (人間選書 178) 東京: 農山漁村文化協會.

Asakura, Toshio. 朝倉敏夫. 1998. "Aspects of Yangbanization" in Mutsuhiko, Shima and Roger L. Janelli, eds., *The Anthropology of Korea: East Asian Perspectives* (Senri Ethnological Studies 49: 191-211) Osaka: National Museum of Ethnology.

Asakura, Toshio. 朝倉敏夫. 1998. 「韓國의 飮酒文化에 대한 覺書」 石毛直道(編) 『論集 酒와 飮酒의 文化史』 平凡社.

Asakura, Toshio. 朝倉敏夫. 1998. 「日本化한 朝鮮半島의 食－燒肉을 중심으로」 石毛直道(監) 『日本의 食事文化』 味의 素食의 文化센터.

Asakura, Toshio. 朝倉敏夫. 1998. 「変貌 시작하는 島의 農村: 80年代, 南西部島嶼部農村의 家族生活과 그 変化」 嶋陸奧彦・朝倉敏夫(編) 『変貌하는 韓國社會: 1970～80年代의 人類學調查의 現場으로부터』 147-184, 東京: 第一書房.

Asakura, Toshio. 朝倉敏夫. 1998. 『変貌하는 韓國社會』 (嶋陸奧彦, 朝倉敏夫) 第一書房, [1998.6]. － (Academic series new Asia ; 26).

Asakura, Toshio. 朝倉敏夫. 1999. 「韓國文化人類學會參加報告」『民博通信』 83: 88-93.

Asakura, Toshio. 朝倉敏夫. 1999. 「韓國의 藥食同源 (特集 不老不死라는 欲望)」 『아시아遊學』 (通号 2) [1999.3].

Asakura, Toshio. 朝倉敏夫. 2000. 『韓國을 알다 Q&A115』 44頁, 吹田: 千里文化財团.

Asakura, Toshio. 朝倉敏夫. 2000. 「韓國의 日本食」『Vesta』 (味의素 食의文化센터) 37.

Asakura, Toshio. 朝倉敏夫. 2000. 「兩班의 食生活－그 研究方法의 模索」『青丘

學術論集』(韓國文化研究振興財団) 16.

Asakura, Toshio. 朝倉敏夫. 2000.「韓國을 알다 Q&A115」『季刊民族學』24(2) (通号 92) [2000.4].

Asakura, Toshio. 朝倉敏夫. 2000.「韓國의 日本食 (特集 國境를 넘은 日本食)」『Vesta』(通号 39) [2000.8].

Asakura, Toshio. ed. 朝倉敏夫(編). 2000.『日本에 있어서의 韓國文化의 表象』國立民族學博物館, [2000.7]. (國立民族學博物館調査報告書 14).

Asakura, Toshio. 朝倉敏夫. 2001.「無煙 roaster에서 숯불까지－燒き肉(불고기)엔 不況없다」(朝倉 敏夫 ; 吳 善花 ; 宮塚 利雄)『諸君』33(2) [2001.2].

Asakura, Toshio. 朝倉敏夫. 2002.『2002年서울 스타일』(朝倉敏夫, 佐藤浩司) 千里文化財団, [2002.3].

Asakura, Toshio. 朝倉敏夫. 2002.「서울의 삶을 '있는 그대로' 朝倉敏夫선생에 묻다: 2002年서울 스타일展 (메이킹・업・2002年서울 스타일)」『季刊民族學』26(2) (通号 100) [2002.春].

Asakura, Toshio. 朝倉敏夫. 2002.「市場의 社會史」鄭勝謨[他]. 法政大學出版局,『韓國의 學術과 文化 ; 11』.

Asakura, Toshio. 朝倉敏夫. 2003.「韓國－漢字語에 보는 中國大伝統의 継承様式 (特集 食의 名言・名句伝承과 創造)」『Vesta』(49) [2003.Win.].

Asakura, Toshio and Okada. 朝倉敏夫・岡田浩樹. 1999.「對談 食文化의 変容(1)」『食生活研究』20(2): 21-29.

Asakura, Toshio and Okada. 朝倉敏夫・岡田浩樹. 1999.「對談 食文化의 変容(2)」『食生活研究』20(3): 19-25.

Asanuma, Masashi. 淺沼政誌. 1995.「韓國에 있어서의 祖先祭祀의 構造: 除去芋錢의 祖先祭祀를 중심으로」『古代文化研究』55.

Asaoka, Koji. 朝岡康二. 1991.「韓國의 伝承技術: 鍛冶와 그 製品」沖縄縣立芸術大學琉韓伝承文化調査団『韓國伝承文化의 研究: 沖縄와의 比較를 지향하여』89-116, 那覇: 沖縄縣立芸術大學琉韓伝承文化調査団.

Chang, Chu-Keun. 張籌根. 1973.『韓國의 民間信仰: 濟州島의 巫俗과 巫歌』東京: 金花舍.

Chang, Chu-Keun. 張籌根. 1982.『韓國의 鄕土信仰』(松本誠一譯)東京: 第一書房.

Cheong, Chin-Seong. 鄭鎮星. 1991.「韓國과 日本의 家族構造의 比較研究: 日本의 核家族化鈍化과 女性勞働의 關係를 중심으로」『社會科學研究』42(4):

121-144.

Cheong, Ki-Hwan. 鄭起煥. 1993.「韓國에 있어서의 農家人口의 流失과 家族意識構造의 変化」『村落社會硏究』80.

Cheong, Seung-Mo. 鄭勝模. 1994.「서울의 市場」『코리아나』7(3).

Cheong, Tae-Kyun. 鄭大均. 1978.「池上町 "朝鮮人部落"의 社會關係－上－」『朝鮮硏究』(通号 185) [1978.12].

Cheong, Tae-Kyun. 鄭大均. 1979.「外國人居住者論－上－」(鄭 大均 ; Wetherall, William)『朝鮮硏究』(通号 196) [1979.12].

Cheong, Tae-Kyun. 鄭大均. 1979.「다시 岐路에 서는 在日朝鮮人問題－1－'自由에의 逃走'인가－새로운 在日朝鮮人論에의 視角 〈特集〉」『朝鮮硏究』(通号 189) [1979.5].

Cheong, Tae-Kyun. 鄭大均. 1979.「池上町 "朝鮮人部落"의 社會關係－下－」『朝鮮硏究』(通号 186) [1979.1].

Cheong, Tae-Kyun. 鄭大均. 1980.「外國人居住者論－下－」(鄭 大均 ; Wetherall, William)『朝鮮硏究』(通号 202) [1980.8].

Cheong, Tae-Kyun. 鄭大均. 1981.「日系 아메리카人의 收容体驗(投稿)」(Don Nakanishi ; 鄭 大均)『思想의 科學』第6次. (通号 126) [1981.1].

Cheong, Tae-Kyun. 鄭大均. 1984.「日本에의 〈誘引〉과 〈反發〉－韓國日語日文科生의 對日關心과 그 分析」『海外事情』32(2) [1984.2].

Cheong, Tae-Kyun. 鄭大均. 1985.「軍政期南朝鮮의 〈日本文化〉」『海外事情』33(2) [1985.2].

Cheong, Tae-Kyun. 鄭大均. 1985.「두 사람 같이 짓는 釜山 소식－1－釜山의 繪」『現代코리아』(通号 251) [1985.5].

Cheong, Tae-Kyun. 鄭大均. 1985.「두 사람 같이 짓는 釜山 소식－2－韓國이라는 迷路」『現代코리아』(通号 255) [1985.10].

Cheong, Tae-Kyun. 鄭大均. 1985.「두 사람 같이 짓는 釜山 소식－4－父祖達의 故鄕」『現代코리아』(通号 257) [1985.12].

Cheong, Tae-Kyun. 鄭大均. 1986.「韓國이라는 鏡」川村湊, 鄭大均.『東洋書院』[1986.6].

Cheong, Tae-Kyun. 鄭大均. 1986.「在日朝鮮人의 同化냐 異化냐」『現代코리아』(通号 263) [1986.7].

Cheong, Tae-Kyun. 鄭大均. 1987.「近景의 祖國 (海外日本人의 想像力－北아메리카로부터)」『思想의 科學』第7次. (通号 93) [1987.9].

Cheong, Tae-Kyun. 鄭大均. 1987.「父祖들의 故鄕－在日韓國人의 韓國体驗」『海外事情』35(2) [1987.2].

Cheong, Tae-Kyun. 鄭大均. 1988.「文化主義的 韓國論을 물리치다」『中央公論』103(11) [1988.11].

Cheong, Tae-Kyun. 鄭大均. 1989.「日本論과 韓國論의 不幸한 連帶」『中央公論』104(5) [1989.5].

Cheong, Tae-Kyun. 鄭大均. 1990.「'在日'의 神話」『諸君』22(10) [1990.10].

Cheong, Tae-Kyun. 鄭大均. 1991.「韓國・日本文化는 왜 터부시되는가」『諸君』23(5) [1991.5].

Cheong, Tae-Kyun. 鄭大均. 1991.「韓國의 '反日'이 변할 날은 언젠가?」『中央公論』106(2) [1991.2].

Cheong, Tae-Kyun. 鄭大均. 1992.「Los Angeles暴動・韓國의 報道(焦点・論点)」『現代코리아』(通号 322) [1992.6].

Cheong, Tae-Kyun. 鄭大均. 1992.「日韓의 parallelism」三交社, 1992.9.

Cheong, Tae-Kyun. 鄭大均. 1993.「韓國내셔널리즘의 性格 (내셔널리즘) (내셔널리즘의 視点)」『思想』(通号 823) [1993.1].

Cheong, Tae-Kyun. 鄭大均. 1994.「韓國社會의『反日』構造－日本文化에 對한 兩面的인 反応의 背景」『世界週報』75(13) [1994.4.5].

Cheong, Tae-Kyun. 鄭大均. 1995.「韓國의 이미지」中央公論社, [1995.10]. (中公新書).

Cheong, Tae-Kyun. 鄭大均. 1995.「韓國을 不幸하게 하는 進步派라는 日本人(戰後檢証－5－아시아의 日本의 体驗〈特集〉)」『思想의 科學』第8次. (通号 33) [1995.10].

Cheong, Tae-Kyun. 鄭大均. 1996.「'在日'의 民族疲勞－國籍條項에 대한 少數意見」『中央公論』111(10) [1996.9].

Cheong, Tae-Kyun. 鄭大均. 1997.「왜 日本國籍을 요구하지 않는 것인가 (特集 在日韓國・朝鮮人과 國籍)」(鄭 大均 ; 西岡 力)『現代코리아』(通号 375) [1997.10].

Cheong, Tae-Kyun. 鄭大均. 1997.「韓國人知識人의 本音鼎談－우려 되는 韓國의 反日感情」(崔 吉城 ; 吳 善花 ; 鄭 大均)『正論』(通号 295) [1997.3].

Cheong, Tae-Kyun. 鄭大均. 1997.「韓國의 反日主義에 대하여」栗原彬(編)『講座差別의 社會學(3)現代世界의 差別構造』弘文堂.

Cheong, Tae-Kyun. 鄭大均. 1998.「台湾人과 韓國人의 本音對談 在日의 心, 共

生의 心」(金 美齢 ; 鄭 大均)『正論』(通号 306) [1998.2].
Cheong, Tae-Kyun. 鄭大均. 1998.「日本의 이미지」中央公論社, 1998.10. (中公新書).
Cheong, Tae-Kyun. 鄭大均. 1998.「'倭色'의 領域－韓國에 있어서의 日本文化受容의 方法과 過程」五十嵐曉郎(編)『変貌하는 아시아와 日本－아시아에 浸透하는 日本의 파퓰러(popular) 컬처』世織書房.
Cheong, Tae-Kyun. 鄭大均. 2000.「韓國人을 그만두고 日本國民이 되자－在日의 견딜 수 없는 경지에 대하여」『正論』(通号 336) [2000.8].
Cheong, Tae-Kyun. 鄭大均. 2000.「對談 韓國의 美人・日本의 美人: 文化의 차이를 이해하면... (特集 변하는 아시아・변하지 않는 日本)」(鄭 大均 ; 吳善花)『Voice』(通号 271) [2000.7].
Cheong, Tae-Kyun. 鄭大均. 2001.「永住外國人參政權 在日韓國人은 特權階級인가 (어리둥절하고 있으면 악법이 거침없이 통해버린다)」『諸君』33(4) [2001.4].
Cheong, Tae-Kyun. 鄭大均. 2001.「韓國: 日韓의 지나가지 않는 過去」『世界週報』82(26) (通号 4006) [2001.7.10].
Cheong, Tae-Kyun. 鄭大均. 2001.「在日韓國人의 終焉」『文藝春秋』2001.4. (文春新書).
Cheong, Tae-Kyun. 鄭大均. 2002.「韓國내서널리즘의 不幸」『小學館』2002.4. (小學館文庫).
Cheong, Tae-Kyun. 鄭大均. 2002.「変化하는 在日의 이미지 (特集 歷史 속의 '在日'－'在日'의 意味를 東아시아의 過去・現在・未來속에서 생각한다) － ('在日'에 대한 눈의 표정(눈길))」『環』11 [2002.Aut.].
Cheong, Tae-Kyun. 鄭大均. 2003.「討論 日韓歷史認識의 共有는 可能인가」(藤岡 信勝 ; 鄭 大均 ; 勝岡 寬次 他)『諸君』35(1) [2003.1].
Cheong, Tae-Seong. 鄭大聲. 1977.『朝鮮食品學』講談社, [1977.5].
Cheong, Tae-Seong. 鄭大聲. 1979.『朝鮮食物誌: 日本과의 관계를 살핀다』238頁, 東京: 柴田書店.
Cheong, Tae-Seong. 鄭大聲. 1979.『朝鮮食物誌』柴田書店, [1979.1].
Cheong, Tae-Seong. 鄭大聲. 1981.「朝鮮料理의 만드는 방법」全鎭植, 鄭大聲. 農山漁村文化協會, 1981.8.
Cheong, Tae-Seong. 鄭大聲. 1982.『朝鮮의 料理書』平凡社, [1982.12]. (東洋文庫 ; 416).

Cheong, Tae-Seong. 鄭大聲. 1983.『粥譜』全鎭植, 鄭大聲. 柴田書店, [1983.1].

Cheong, Tae-Seong. 鄭大聲. 1984.『朝鮮의 음식』東京: 築地書館.

Cheong, Tae-Seong. 鄭大聲. 1985.『朝鮮料理全集. 1』(全鎭植, 鄭大聲). 柴田書店, [1985.4].

Cheong, Tae-Seong. 鄭大聲. 1985.『朝鮮料理全集. 3』(全鎭植, 鄭大聲) 柴田書店, [1985.9].

Cheong, Tae-Seong. 鄭大聲. 1985.『朝鮮料理全集. 4』(全鎭植, 鄭大聲) 柴田書店, [1985.9].

Cheong, Tae-Seong. 鄭大聲. 1985.『論集東아시아의 食事文化』(石毛直道) 平凡社, [1985.8].

Cheong, Tae-Seong. 鄭大聲. 1986.『朝鮮料理全集. 2』(全鎭植, 鄭大聲) 柴田書店, [1986.6].

Cheong, Tae-Seong. 鄭大聲. 1986.『朝鮮料理全集. 5』(全鎭植, 鄭大聲) 柴田書店, [1986.4].

Cheong, Tae-Seong. 鄭大聲. 1986.『朝鮮料理全集. 6』(全鎭植, 鄭大聲) 柴田書店, [1986.8].

Cheong, Tae-Seong. 鄭大聲. 1987.『朝鮮의 酒』219頁, 東京: 築地書館.

Cheong, Tae-Seong. 鄭大聲. 1992.『食文化를 통해 본 日本과 朝鮮』東京: 講談社.

Cheong, Tae-Seong. 鄭大聲. 1992.『東아시아에 있어서의 社會와 文化』(創立20周年記念論文集發刊部會) 大阪経濟法科大學出版部, [1992.11].

Cheong, Tae-Seong. 鄭大聲. 1995.『食文化入門』(石毛直道, 鄭大聲) 講談社, [1995.4].

Cheong, Tae-Seong. 鄭大聲. 1998.「朝鮮半島의 酒文化－須須許理에 대하여」石毛直道(編)『論集 酒과 飮酒의 文化史』平凡社.

Cheong, Tae-Seong. 鄭大聲. 1998.『朝鮮半島의 食과 酒: 儒教文化가 육성한 民族의 伝統』(中公新書1443), 193頁, 東京: 中央公論社.

Cheong, Tae-Seong. 鄭大聲. 1998.『韓國家庭料理入門』(金日麗, 鄭大聲) 農山漁村文化協會, [1998.10].

Cheong, Tae-Seong. 鄭大聲. 1998.「韓民族의 强精」『앞으로21』2(8) [1998.8].

Cheong, Tae-Seong. 鄭大聲. 1998.「民族과 酒」『앞으로21』2(10) [1998.10].

Cheong, Tae-Seong. 鄭大聲. 1999.『韓國料理文化史』(李盛雨[他]) － 平凡社,

[1999.6].

Cheong, Tae-Seong. 鄭大聲. 2000.「朝鮮半島의 食思想－儒教의 倫理가 낳은 食文化」福井勝義・秋道智彌・田中耕司(編)『講座 人間과 環境(六) 食의 倫理를 묻는다－몸과 環境의 調和』昭和堂.

Cheong, Tae-Seong. 鄭大聲. 2000.「朝鮮通信使接待의 記錄에 보는 '朝鮮人好物'에 관한 硏究(1)」(鄭大聲 ; 日比 喜子)『生活文化史』(通号 37) [2000.3].

Cheong, Tae-Seong. 鄭大聲. 2001.「인터뷰 鄭大聲氏 김치는 日本의 食文化에 定着할 것인가 (特集 發酵되는 辛味文化)」『食의 科學』(279) [2001.5].

Cheong, Tae-Seong. 鄭大聲. 2001.「김치는 日本의 食文化에 定着할 것인가(後編) 인터뷰 鄭大聲氏 (特集 發酵되는 辛味文化)」『食의 科學』(280) [2001.6].

Cheong, Tae-Seong. 鄭大聲. 2001.「燒肉을 좋아합니까?」『新潮社』2001.7. －(新潮選書).

Cheong, Tae-Seong. 鄭大聲. 2001.「朝鮮通信使接待의 記錄에 보는 '朝鮮人好物'에 관한 硏究(그 2)」(澤 麻衣子 ; 日比 喜子 ; 鄭 大聲)『生活文化史』(40) [2001.9].

Cheong, Tae-Seong. 鄭大聲. 2001.「朝鮮半島의 菓子, 그 特徵 (特集 外來食文化와 和菓了)」『和菓子』(8) [2001.4].

Cheong, Tae-Seong. 鄭大聲. 2001.「日本과 朝鮮半島의 食文化의 比較硏究(2)若者의 辛味에 對하는 嗜好性日本과 韓國의 場合」(日比 喜子 ; 澤 麻衣子 ; 鄭 大聲 他)『人間文化』9 [2001.1].

Cheong, Tae-Seong. 鄭大聲. 2002.『헬씨(healthy) 김치』祥伝社, [2002.5].

Cheong, Tae-Seong. 鄭大聲. 2002.「伝統酒막걸리의 만드는 방법과 그 文化」『日本醸造協會誌』97(4) [2002.4].

Cheong, Tae-Seong. 鄭大聲. 2002.「日本의 食文化와 '在日' (特集 歷史속의 '在日'－'在日'의 意味를 東아시아의 過去・現在・未來속에서 생각한다) － ('在日'의 生活現場)」『環』11 [2002.Aut.].

Cho, Kyeong-Tal. 趙景達. 1994.「東學에 있어서의 正統과 異端」溝口雄三・濱下武志・平石直昭・宮嶋博史(編)『주변으로부터의 歷史』(아시아에서 생각한다3), 55-98, 東京: 東京大學出版會.

Ch'oe, Chae-Seok. 崔在錫. 1953.「韓國農村에 있어서의 親族의 範囲」『民族學硏究』27(3): 541-551.

Ch'oe, Chae-Yul. 崔在律. 1988.「韓國의 契에 대하여」『아시아・아프리카文化研究所研究年報』23: 181-190.

Ch'oe, Chong-Min. 崔鍾敏. 1994.「國樂에 종사하는 사람들」『코리아나』7(3):

Ch'oe, In-Hak. 崔仁鶴. 1976.『韓國昔話의 研究』東京: 弘文堂.

Ch'oe, In-Hak. 崔仁鶴. 1977.『朝鮮伝説集』東京: 日本放送出版協會.

Ch'oe, Kil-Seong. 崔吉城. 1973.「韓國샤머니즘에 있어서의『入巫過程』」『民族學研究』38(2): 108-119.

Ch'oe, Kil-Seong. 崔吉城. 1976.「韓國巫俗의 死靈祭」『季刊人類學』7(3): 54-74.

Ch'oe, Kil-Seong. 崔吉城. 1976.「韓國巫俗에 있어서의 死靈祭와 靈魂觀－捨姫公主神話의 構造分析」『朝鮮學報』(通号 78) [1976.1].

Ch'oe, Kil-Seong. 崔吉城. 1977.「韓國巫業集団에 있어서의 血緣・姻戚關係: 東海岸地域의 단골을 중심으로」『東京大學東洋文化研究所紀要』71: 263-295.

Ch'oe, Kil-Seong. 崔吉城. 1977.『韓國民俗學概說』(李杜鉉, 張籌根, 李光奎[他]) 學生社, [1977.4].

Ch'oe, Kil-Seong. 崔吉城. 1977.「韓國巫業集団에 있어서의 血緣・婚姻關係 東海岸地域의 단골을 중심으로」『東洋文化研究所紀要』(通号 71) [1977.3].

Ch'oe, Kil-Seong. 崔吉城. 1978.「韓國단골巫의 액션・그룹의 分析」『民族學研究』42(4) [1978.3].

Ch'oe, Kil-Seong. 崔吉城. 1980.『韓國의 축제와 巫俗』東京: 第一書房.

Ch'oe, Kil-Seong. 崔吉城. 1984.「死後結婚祭」『民話의 手帖(日本民話의 會)』22: 125-127.

Ch'oe, Kil-Seong. 崔吉城. 1984.『韓國의 샤머니즘: 社會人類學的研究』東京: 弘文堂.

Ch'oe, Kil-Seong. 崔吉城. 1984.『韓國의 샤먼』(崔吉城[他]) 國文社, 1984.7.

Ch'oe, Kil-Seong. 崔吉城. 1987.「沖繩오니리神信仰一考」『日本民俗學』(通号 169) [1987.2].

Ch'oe, Kil-Seong. 崔吉城. 1988.「韓國에 있어서의 日本民俗研究의 回顧와 展望」『日本民俗學』(通号 175) [1988.8].

Ch'oe, Kil-Seong. 崔吉城. 1989.「축제는 神々의 퍼포먼스－芸能을 둘러싼 日本과 東아시아」梅棹忠夫監修, 守屋毅(編)『民族學研究』54(1) [1989.6].

Ch'oe, Kil-Seong. 崔吉城. 1989.「韓國에 있어서의 人類學的日本研究 (밖에서 본 日本〈特集〉〔含 코멘트・応答〕)」『民族學研究』54(3) [1989.12].

Ch'oe, Kil-Seong. 崔吉城. 1990.「韓國에 있어서의 日本文化研究의 動向」『季刊 코리아나』 3(3).

Ch'oe, Kil-Seong. 崔吉城. 1990.「波市考」竹田旦篇『民俗學의 進展과 課題』 459-476, 東京: 國書刊行會.

Ch'oe, Kil-Seong. 崔吉城. 1991.「韓國의 村축제」植松明石(編)『環中國海의 民俗과 祭祀2 神々의 祭祀』27-37, 東京: 凱風社.

Ch'oe, Kil-Seong. 崔吉城. 1991.「巨文島 [日帝時代에 식민지화된 韓國南島]」『季刊自然과 文化』 34.

Ch'oe, Kil-Seong. 崔吉城. 1992.「韓國에 있어서의 日本文化의 受容과 葛藤」『思想』 817: 167-176.

Ch'oe, Kil-Seong. 崔吉城. 1992.「韓國의 基督教와 샤머니즘의 關係」『日韓文化 포럼 韓國文化와 日本文化』 40-43.

Ch'oe, Kil-Seong. 崔吉城. 1992.「나라양보 신화와 王權의 論理〔含 解說「韓國에 있어서의 日本文化의 研究」〕(脫神話하는「古事記」〈特集〉)」(魯 成煥 著 ; 崔 吉城 解說)『現代思想』20(4) [1992.4].

Ch'oe, Kil-Seong. 崔吉城. 1992.「韓國의 祖先崇拜」(崔吉城[他]) 御茶의 水書房, [1992.12].

Ch'oe, Kil-Seong. 崔吉城. 1993.「沖縄의 '노로'와 韓國의 단골」『日中文化研究』 5: 46-54.

Ch'oe, Kil-Seong. 崔吉城. 1993.「韓國 샤머니즘의 변모: 샤머니즘의 故鄕再訪」『春秋』 345.

Ch'oe, Kil-Seong. 崔吉城. 1993.「韓國의 宗教와 社會制度」『韓國』 124-135 ; 146-155.

Ch'oe, Kil-Seong. 崔吉城. 1993.「韓國社會에 있어서의 飮酒・飮茶의 意味」『日本民俗學』 195: 98-109.

Ch'oe, Kil-Seong. 崔吉城. 1993.「韓國巫俗의 死靈祭」松崎憲三(編)『東아시아의 死靈結婚』 293-317, 東京: 岩田書店.

Ch'oe, Kil-Seong. 崔吉城. 1993.「植民地에 의한 文化変容」『韓國』 305-315.

Ch'oe, Kil-Seong. 崔吉城. 1993.『神々의 祭祀와 伝承』(上田正昭), 同朋舍出版, 1993.6.

Ch'oe, Kil-Seong. 崔吉城. 1994.「韓國의 샤머니즘에 있어서의 女性」宮家準・鈴木正崇(編)『東아시아의 샤머니즘과 民俗』 東京: 勁草書房.

Ch'oe, Kil-Seong. 崔吉城. 1994.「韓國의 喫茶店 〈茶房〉의 文化人類學」『國際研

究 (中部大學國際地域硏究所)』 10: 199-213.

Ch'oe, Kil-Seong. 崔吉城. 1994.「韓國女性에 있어서의 近代化와 宗教 宮家準」鈴木正崇(編)『東아시아의 샤머니즘과 民俗』182-196, 東京: 頸草書房.

Ch'oe, Kil-Seong. 崔吉城. 1994.「巨文島의 民俗誌序說」『日本植民地와 文化変容: 韓國・巨文島』83-104, 東京: 御茶의 水書房.

Ch'oe, Kil-Seong. 崔吉城. 1994.「在日韓國그리스도教의 普遍性과 民族性」『國際硏究』10, 中部大學國際地域硏究所.

Ch'oe, Kil-Seong. 崔吉城. 1994.「日本植民地時代의 民俗學・人類學」『日本植民地와 文化変容: 韓國・巨文島』3-32, 東京: 御茶의 水書房.

Ch'oe, Kil-Seong. 崔吉城. 1994.『恨의 人類學』(眞鍋祐子譯)467頁, 東京: 平河出版社.

Ch'oe, Kil-Seong. 崔吉城. 1994.『日本植民地와 文化変容: 韓國・巨文島』東京: 御茶의 水書房.

Ch'oe, Kil-Seong. 崔吉城. 1995.「韓國에 있어서의 천벌 信仰」『아시아의 靈魂觀』35-62, 雄山閣.

Ch'oe, Kil-Seong. 崔吉城. 1995.「日本文化의 変容과 葛藤」(重点領域硏究「情報化社會와 人間」1991年度第5群심포지엄「文化変容의 現在」) (第3세션 아시아의 情報文化네트워크) (報告 崔 吉城)『東京大學社會情報硏究所紀要』(通号 48).

Ch'oe, Kil-Seong. 崔吉城. 1996.「베트남과 韓國」『日中文化硏究』(中國長江文明과 日本・베트남) 2: 55-65, 勉誠社.

Ch'oe, Kil-Seong. 崔吉城. 1996.「韓國의 내셔널리즘과 宗教」『내셔널리즘과 宗教』世界思想社.

Ch'oe, Kil-Seong. 崔吉城. 1996.「韓國의 祖先崇拜: 영혼이 머무는 位牌와 샤머니즘」『靈魂을 둘러싼 日本의 深層』(梅原猛・中西進編) 35-50, 角川書店.

Ch'oe, Kil-Seong. 崔吉城. 1996.「韓國稻作文化에 있어서의 餠」『아시아稻作文化와 日本』138-162, 雄山閣.

Ch'oe, Kil-Seong. 崔吉城. 1996.「韓國現代社會에 있어서의 賣春」『日中文化硏究』9: 84-94, 勉誠社.

Ch'oe, Kil-Seong. 崔吉城. 1996.「東아시아의 曆」『아우로라』(Kansai Forum 21) 2: 122-129.

Ch'oe, Kil-Seong. 崔吉城. 1996.『韓國民俗에의 招待』302頁, 東京: 風響社.

Ch'oe, Kil-Seong. 崔吉城. 1996.「座談會 環東지나海文化圈」(特集 環東지나海의 比較文化) (諏訪 春雄 ; 川村 湊 ; 崔 吉城 他)『日中文化硏究』(通号 9) [1996.5].

Ch'oe, Kil-Seong. 崔吉城. 1997.「새마을運動과 農村振興運動」『國立歷史民俗博物館硏究報告』70: 161-183.

Ch'oe, Kil-Seong. 崔吉城. 1997.「韓國의 儒教와 巫俗에 있어서의 喪과 死穢」孝本貢・八木透(編)『시리즈比較家族 (9) 家族과 死者祭祀』早稻田大學出版部.

Ch'oe, Kil-Seong. 崔吉城. 1997.「日韓의 文化侵略・文化摩擦」青木保 이외 (編)『異文化의 共存』(岩波講座文化人類學8) 85-104, 東京: 岩波書店.

Ch'oe, Kil-Seong. 崔吉城. 1998. "Belief in Malevolent Spirits", Shima, Mutsuhiko and Janelli, Roger L. eds., *The Anthropology of Korea: East Asian Perspectives* (Senri Ethnological Studies 49), 95-109, Osaka: National Museum of Ethnology.

Ch'oe, Kil-Seong. 崔吉城. 1998.「韓國: 植民地와 日本의 이미지」『情報社會의 文化』東大出版會.

Ch'oe, Kil-Seong. 崔吉城. 1998.「韓國社會에 있어서의 축제와 내셔널리즘」『東아시아의 神과 축제』213-257, 雄山閣.

Ch'oe, Kil-Seong. 崔吉城. 1998.「韓國人의 意識과 차별」『基礎文化를 통하여 본 韓國人의 想像体系』民俗院(韓國) 423-437.

Ch'oe, Kil-Seong. 崔吉城. 1998.「韓國人의 貞操觀」『아시아의 性』勉誠社.

Ch'oe, Kil-Seong. 崔吉城. 1998.「韓國人의 貞操觀」『韓國人類學의 成果와 展望』集文堂.

Ch'oe, Kil-Seong. 崔吉城. 1998.「韓國側에서 본 韓日民俗文化의 交流」『民俗音樂硏究』28-30, 日本民俗音樂學會.

Ch'oe, Kil-Seong. 崔吉城. 1998.「在日韓國・朝鮮人에 있어서의 結婚差別과 民族的아이덴디티」『近代日本文化論』岩波書店.

Ch'oe, Kil-Seong. 崔吉城. 1998.「儒教文化圈에 있어서의 伝統的 価値觀과 近代化」青木 保・佐伯啓思(編)『아시아的 価値는 무엇인가』TBS브리테니커, 129-143.

Ch'oe, Kil-Seong. 崔吉城. 1998.「中國・朝鮮族의 漢族과의 結婚과 民族的아이덴디티」『比較家族史學』13, 比較家族史學會.

Ch'oe, Kil-Seong. 崔吉城. 1998.「朝鮮戰爭과 韓國社會의 変化」嶋陸奧彦・朝倉

敏夫(編)『変貌하는 韓國社會: 1970～80年代의 人類學調査의 현장에서』 305-332, 東京: 第一書房.

Ch'oe, Kil-Seong. 崔吉城. 1998.「東아시아에 있어서의 文化와 開發」『日本學年報』日本研究學會(韓國) 8: 5-21.

Ch'oe, Kil-Seong. 崔吉城. 1999.「샤머니즘의 比較」『比較民俗學과 比較文化』民俗院.

Ch'oe, Kil-Seong. 崔吉城. 1999.「韓國－植民地와 日本의 이미지」青木保・梶原景昭(編)『情報社會의 文化(1) 情報化와 아시아・이미지』東京大學出版會.

Ch'oe, Kil-Seong. 崔吉城. 1999.「韓國人의 貞操觀」諏訪春雄『아시아의 性』勉誠出版.

Ch'oe, Kil-Seong. 崔吉城. 1999.「韓國人의 名前에 관한 人類學的研究」上野和男・森謙二(編)『이름과 社會－명명하기의 家族史』早稲田大學出版部.

Ch'oe, Kil-Seong. 崔吉城. 1999.「在日라는 存在: 儒教의 祖先祭祀와 아이덴디티」『講座日本民俗學』10, 雄山閣.

Ch'oe, Kil-Seong. 崔吉城. 1999.「在日韓國・朝鮮人에 있어서의 結婚差別과 民族的아이덴디티」青木保이외 (編)『近代日本文化論(11) 愛와 苦難』岩波書店.

Ch'oe, Kil-Seong. 崔吉城. 1999.「東北아시아의 샤머니즘의 比較」『比較文化研究』5, 서울大學.

Ch'oe, Kil-Seong. 崔吉城. 1999.「日本의 水子供養과 東아시아의 男兒選好」『比較民俗學』16.

Ch'oe, Kil-Seong. 崔吉城. 1999.『새롭게 쓴 韓國巫俗』아시아文化社: 서울.

Ch'oe, Kil-Seong. 崔吉城. 1999.「朝鮮總督府廳舍의 破壞와 '風水' 내셔널리즘」『日本民俗學』(通号 218) [1999.5].

Ch'oe, Kil-Seong. 崔吉城. 2000.「序論－東아시아에 있어서의 文化의 比較」崔吉城・日向一雅(編)『神話・宗教・巫俗－日韓比較文化의 試図』風響社.

Ch'oe, Kil-Seong. 崔吉城. 2000.「中國에 있어서의 法輪功과 迷信打破」『아우로라』19, 21世紀의 關西를 생각하는會.

Ch'oe, Kil-Seong. 崔吉城. 2000.「朝鮮半島의 南北分斷과 敵對双方의 觀光化」『아시아社會文化研究』廣島大學國際協力研究科아시아文化講座.

Ch'oe, Kil-Seong. 崔吉城. 2000.「日帝植民地時代와 朝鮮民俗學」中生勝美(編)『植民地人類學의 展望』風響社.

Ch'oe, Kil-Seong. 崔吉城. 2001.「서울에 사는 風水・샤머니즘・그리스도教 (特集 서울 六百年의 歷史와 未來의 共存)」『아시아遊學』(34) [2001.12].

Ch'oe, Kil-Seong. 崔吉城. 2001.『神話・宗教・巫俗』(崔吉城, 日向一雅) 風響社, [2000.1].

Ch'oe, Kil-Seong. 崔吉城. 2001.「船王(船城隍)信仰」(特集 韓國의 海洋文化)『月刊韓國文化』(通号 261) [2001.8].

Ch'oe, Kil-Seong. 崔吉城. 2001.「朝鮮戰爭에 있어서의 國連軍의 性暴行과 賣春」『아시아社會文化研究』(2) [2001.3].

Ch'oe, Kil-Seong. 崔吉城. 2002.『'親日'과 '反日'의 文化人類學』明石書店, 2002.8. (明石라이브러리 ; 40).

Ch'oe, Kil-Seong. 崔吉城. 2002.「韓國의 正月」(特集 아시아의 正月)『아시아遊學』(46) [2002.12].

Ch'oe, Kil-Seong. 崔吉城・日向一雅(編) 2000『神話・宗教・巫俗－日韓比較文化의 試図』風響社.

Ch'oe, Kil-Seong and Fukudome, Noriaki. 崔吉城・福留範昭. 1983.「濟州島加波島의 家族과 祭儀」『崔正如博士頌壽記念民俗語文論叢』457-491, 啓明大學校出版部.

Ch'oe, Yun. 崔潤. 1992.「韓國中小都市에 있어서의 貧困家族의 調查研究」『龍谷大學社會學論集』.

Choi, Baek. 崔柏. 1979.「韓國에 있어서의 五家統制에 대하여」『民族學研究』44(2): 160-167.

Choi, Baek. 崔柏. 1987.「祖先崇拝와 韓國의 社會시스템: 특히 安東郡川前洞・義城金氏의 事例를 중심으로」『아시아・아프리카文化研究所研究年報』22: 58-82.

Choi, Cyang-Jo. 崔 昌祚. 1997. 金在浩・澁谷鎮明(譯),『한국의 풍수사상(風水思想)』, 人文書院.

Choi, In-Tag. 崔 仁宅. 1989.「양묘제(兩墓制)와 사자제례－토바시(鳥羽市) 스가시마(菅島)의 사례를 중심으로 (밖에서 본 일본 〈特集〉〔코멘트포함・응답〕)」『民族學研究』54(3), [1989.12].

Choi, In-Tag. 崔 仁宅. 1996. 崔 仁宅・石川 浩之・森 雅文(他),「아마미(奄美)・오키나와(沖縄)는 어떻게 이야기할 수 있을까 (특집「류쿠」연구를 중심으로)」『民族學研究』61(3), [1996.12].

Choi, In-Tag. 崔 仁宅. 1998. 梅田博之(監)・松原孝俊(編),「전통사회」『한국 핸

드북－언어와 문화』, 東方書店.

Choi, In-Tag. 崔 仁宅. 1999.「韓國어촌사회의 조사노트－제례의례의 변모를 보다」『宮崎公立大學人文學部紀要』6-1.

Choi, In-Tag. 崔 仁宅. 2002.『류큐(琉球)ㆍ아시아의 민속과 역사』, 記念論集刊行會.榕樹書林, [2002.7].

Choi, Jang-Jib. 崔 章集. 1997.『현대한국의 정치변동－근대화와 민주주의의 역사적 조건』, 木鐸社.

Chu, Nam-Ch'eol. 周南哲. 1994.「서울의 伝統的住宅」『코리아나』7(3).

De Vos, George A. and Sofue, Takao ed. De Vos, George A. and Sofue, Takao ed. 1984. *Religion and Family in East Asia* (Senri Ethnological Studies 11). Osaka: National Museum of Ethnology.

De Vos, George A. and Sofue, Takao ed. De Vos, George A. and Sofue, Takao ed. 1986. *Religion and Family in East Asia*. Berkeley, Los Angels and London: University of California Press.

Deguchi, Akiko. 出口晶子. 1987.「韓國東岸의 筏船떼배」『民博通信』35: 39-48.

Deguchi, Akiko. 出口晶子. 1987.「濟州島의 떼배」『季刊民族學』42: 72-79.

Deguchi, Akiko. 出口晶子. 1987.「刳船의 發達諸形態의 分類와 地域類型: 日本과 그 隣接地域을 중심으로」『國立民族學博物館研究報告』12(2): 449-497.

Deguchi, Akiko. 出口晶子. 1996.「韓國의 在來型構造船」『青丘學術論集』9: 97-142.

Ejima, Shusaku. 江嶋修作. 1976.「韓國農村에 있어서의 親族構造分析의 一問題: '同族' 概念使用의 問題를 중심으로」『廣島修大論集 人文編』16(2): 87-112.

Ejima, Shusaku and Maruyama, Koichi. 江嶋修作ㆍ丸山孝一 1976「移民과 社會構造: 金陽里의 場合」野口隆(編)『移民과 文化変容: 韓國陜川地域의 事例研究』149-234, 東京: 日本學術振興會.

Emori, Itsuo. 江守五夫. 1982.「婚姻慣行」江守五夫ㆍ崔龍基(編)『韓國兩班同族制의 研究』206-232, 東京: 第一書房.

Emori, Itsuo. 江守五夫. 1982.「序章」江守五夫ㆍ崔龍基(編)『韓國兩班同族制의 研究』1-37, 東京: 第一書房.

Emori, Itsuo. 江守五夫. 1982.「日本의 婚姻成立儀礼의 史的変遷과 民俗: 韓國과의 對比에 있어서」『千葉史學』1: 93-117.

Emori, Itsuo. 江守五夫. 1982.「兩班支配의 構造와 歷史的変遷」江守五夫・崔龍基(編)『韓國兩班同族制의 硏究』118-148, 東京: 第一書房.

Emori, Itsuo and Ch'oe, Yong-Ki, eds. 江守五夫・崔龍基(編). 1982.『韓國兩班同族制의 硏究』東京: 第一書房.

Endo, Koichi. 遠藤興一. 1997.「植民地社會事業의 基礎動向에 대하여－朝鮮總督府施政年報(明治43～昭和16年)硏究序說」『明治學院論叢』592.

Fijita, Akiyoshi. 藤田明良. 2001.「島嶼에서 본 朝鮮半島와 他地域의 交流－濟州島를 중심으로」(藤田 明良; 李 善愛; 河原 典史)『青丘學術論集』19 [2001.11].

Fuchigami, Kyoko. 渕上恭子. 1991.「韓國그리스도教會의 信仰治療: 現代샤머니즘社會에 있어서의 그리스도教會」『케이오기쥬크대학(慶応義塾大學)大學院社會學硏究科紀要』31: 1-8.

Fuchigami, Kyoko. 渕上恭子. 1992. "Faith Healing in Korean Christianity: The Christian Church in Korea and Shamanism", *Nanzan Bulletin* 16: 33-59.

Fuchigami, Kyoko. 渕上恭子. 1993.「'祈禱院'에 보이는 民族史와 民俗宗教: 韓國그리스도教의 프론티어」『宗教硏究』296: 105-130.

Fuchigami, Kyoko. 渕上恭子. 1994.「韓國그리스도教와 샤머니즘: 〈神憑의 能力〉을 둘러싼 祈禱院과 韓國教會」宮家準・鈴木正崇(編)『東아시아의 샤머니즘과 民俗』232-253, 東京: 頸草書房.

Fuchigami, Kyoko. 渕上恭子. 1996.「現代韓國의 〈壇君〉과 〈하나님〉」『宗教硏究』307: 287-288.

Fuchigami, Kyoko. 渕上恭子. 1997.「韓國의 〈水子靈〉: 現代韓國의 마리아 信仰」『宗教硏究』311: 294-295.

Fuchigami, Kyoko. 渕上恭子. 1997.「韓國仏教의 〈水子供養〉」『平和와 宗教』16: 98-103.

Fuchigami, Kyoko. 渕上恭子. 1999.「哭의 女俗: 朝鮮의 民俗宗教에 있어서의 儀禮의 情動」宮家準(編)『民俗宗教의 地平』275-286, 東京: 春秋社.

Fujii, Takashi. 藤井隆至. 1975.「柳田國男의 아시아意識」『아시아経濟』16(3): 68-77.

Fukudome, Noriaki. 福留範昭. 1984.「韓國의 샤머니즘」崔吉城(著)『宗教硏究』58(2): 246-250.

Fukudome, Noriaki. 福留範昭. 1986.「韓國東海岸 S洞에 있어서의 祖先祭祀」『西日本宗教學雜誌』8: 105-117.

Fukudome, Noriaki. 福留範昭. 1986.「秋夕」『基礎한글』2(5): 48-49.

Fukudome, Noriaki. 福留範昭. 1987.「韓國의 家祭와 祖先」『山陰民俗』49: 1-9.

Fukudome, Noriaki. 福留範昭. 1987.「正月」『基礎한글』2(10): 42-43.

Fukudome, Noriaki. 福留範昭. 1991.「韓國의 샤머니즘과 治療儀禮」『教育과 医學』39(4).

Fukuoka, Yasunori. 福岡安則・金明秀. 1997.『在日韓國人青年의 生活과 意識』東京大學出版會.

Furuno, Kiyoto. 古野清人. 1976.「宗教人類學上에서 본 朝鮮」『朝鮮學報』79: 1-11.

Fuse, Tetsuji. 布施鐵治. 1973.「書評『村落構造와 親族組織』」『未來』81: 60-64.

Gamo, Masao. 蒲生正男. 1966.「社會人類學: 日本에 있어서의 그 成立과 展開」日本民族學會(編)『日本民族學의 回顧과 展望』27-49, 東京: 民族學振興會.

Gibo, Eijiro. 宜保榮治郎. 1986.「韓國의 줄다리기: 全羅北道扶安邑內蔘里의 場合」『沖縄民俗研究』6.

Goda, Hiroko. 合田博子. 1998.「高麗時代의 親族關係와 系譜意識의 形成－kindred과 出自集団을 둘러싼 一考察」『姫路人間學研究』1(1) [1998.3].

Goda, Hiroko. 合田博子. 1998.「『新羅本紀』에 보는 親族關係와 系譜意識－葛文王과 骨品制를 중심으로」大胡欽一・加治明・佐々木宏幹・比嘉政夫・宮本勝(編)『社會와 象徵－人類學的아프러치 村武精一教授古稀記念論文集』岩田書院.

Gotoda, Yuko. 後藤田遊子. 1994.「서울의 純福音教會: 1970年代의 急成長과 그 背景」『北陸學院短期大學紀要』26: 201-217.

Gotoda, Yuko. 後藤田遊子. 1995.「韓國의 中學校英語教科書에 있어서의 民族・文化意識」『北陸學院短期大學紀要』27: 195-210.

Hagiwara, Hidesaburo. 萩原秀三郎. 1978.「韓國의 巫俗」『季刊民族學』4: 110-113.

Hagiwara, Hidesaburo and Ch'oe, In-Hak. 萩原秀三郎・崔仁鶴. 1974.『韓國의 民俗』東京: 第一法規出版.

Hamamoto, Mariko. 浜本まり子. 1996.「在日朝鮮人－在日朝鮮人의 아이덴디티의 問題」青木保이외 (編)『岩波講座文化人類學7 移動의 民族誌』岩波書店.

Han, Kyeong-Ki. 韓景旭. 1994.「朝鮮族의 名節: 中國吉林省S縣의 事例를 중심으로」『民族學研究』59(2): 161-169.

Han, Kyeong-Ki. 韓景旭. 1995.「中國『內地朝鮮族』의 에스니시티: 若者三世의 事例를 중심으로」『民族學硏究』60(3): 249-259.

Han, Kyoung-Uk. 韓 景旭. 1994.「조선족의 〈명예와 지조〉-중국吉林省S촌의 사례를 중심으로」『民族學硏究59(2)』[1994.9].

Han, Kyoung-Uk. 韓 景旭. 1995.「중국 〈내지(內地) 조선족〉의 에스니시티-젊은이 3세의 사례를 중심으로」『民族學硏究60(3)』[1995.12].

Han, Kyoung-Uk. 韓 景旭. 1997.「중국조선족의 마을생활-吉林省星火村의 조사보고」『國立民族學博物館硏究報告21(3)』.

Han, Kyoung-Uk. 韓 景旭. 1999.「국경을 넘는 북한 여성들-2명의 북한여성 인터뷰」『西南學院大學國際文化論集. 14(1)』[1999.9].

Han, Kyoung-Uk. 韓 景旭. 2000.「자료 북한보고」『西南學院大學國際文化論集 14(2)』[2000.2]

Han, Kyoung-Uk. 韓 景旭. 2000.「중국조선족의 집」『西南學院大學國際文化論集15(1)』[2000.9]

Han, Kyoung-Uk. 韓 景旭. 2001.『한국계 중국인: 조선족』中國書店, [2001.12].

Han, Kyoung-Uk. 韓 景旭. 2001.「중국민족정책론」『西南學院大學國際文化論集 15(2)』[2001.2].

Han, Kyoung-Uk. 韓 景旭. 2002. 中野 卓・韓 景旭 (譯),「산서성(山西省)日俘武裝遺留的陰謀与我的体驗 (上)」『西南學院大學國際文化論集17(1)』[2002.7].

Han, Meong-Hwi. 1994.「國樂의 特異性: 韓國音樂의 루츠와 分類」『코리아나』 7(3).

Han, Seung-Mi. 韓 承美. 2000.「근대의 消費-세계화, 일본화, 그리고 한국에 있어서의 문화적 아이덴티티를 둘러싼 정치」『The Journal of Pacific Asia』(아시아태평양연구회 6).

Han, Tong-Kwi ed. 韓東龜(編). 1973.『韓國의 冠婚葬祭: 民俗學上에서 본 지금 옛날』東京: 國書刊行會.

Harajiri, Hideki. 原尻英樹. 1993.「韓國朴政權以後의 移民政策에 관한 韓國內의 資料 및 그 硏究動向에 대하여」『調査와 硏究』24(1) [1993.3].

Harajiri, Hideki. 原尻英樹. 1996.『半島와 列島의 각국』(原尻英樹, 六反田豊) 新幹社, [1996.9].

Harajiri, Hideki. 原尻英樹. 1996.「兵庫縣伊丹市에 있어서의 異文化(國際)理解敎育實踐을 위한 文化人類學的・社會學的基礎硏究」(原尻 英樹 ; 倉石一郎 ; 金 明美)『硏究助成論文集』(通号 32).

Harajiri, Hideki. 原尻英樹. 1997. 「生野의 子供들」『호르몬文化』 (通号 7) [1997.2].

Harajiri, Hideki. 原尻英樹. 1998. 『在日 코리언』講談社, 1998.7. (講談社現代新書).

Harajiri, Hideki. 原尻英樹. 1998. 「濟州島人의 네트워크 커뮤니티 - (特集 濟州島世界)」『地理』 43(5) [1998.5].

Harajiri, Hideki. 原尻英樹. 1998. 「濟州島世界의 지금 옛날 (特集 濟州島世界)」『地理』 43(5) [1998.5].

Harajiri, Hideki. 原尻英樹. 1998. 「書評: 福岡安則・金明秀『在日韓國人青年의 生活과 意識』」『코리언・마이너리티研究』 (1) [1998.1].

Harajiri, Hideki. 原尻英樹. 1998. 『世界의 民族』 放送大學教育振興會, 1998.3. (放送大學教材).

Harajiri, Hideki. 原尻英樹. 2000. 「戰後日本 〈在日外國人〉의 虛像과 實像 - 〈朝日新聞〉에 보는 코리언系 〈外國人勞働者〉 (特集 石原知事批判)」『世界』 (680) [2000.10].

Harajiri, Hideki. 原尻英樹. 2001. 「書評: 前山隆著『에스니시티와 브라질 日系人』」『民族學硏究』 66(1).

Harajiri, Hideki. 原尻英樹. 1986. 「在日朝鮮人의 에스니시티 -: 筑豊A地區의 事例에서」『民族學硏究』 51(3): 275-289.

Harajiri, Hideki. 原尻英樹. 1989. 『在日朝鮮人의 生活世界』 東京: 弘文堂.

Harajiri, Hideki. 原尻英樹. 1997. 『日本定住코리언의 日常과 生活 - 文化人類學的아프러치』 明石書店.

Harajiri, Hideki. 原尻英樹. 1998. 「地域社會와 學校教育 - 日米코리언 town의 比較」 江淵一公(編) 『Transculturalism의 硏究』 明石書店.

Harajiri, Hideki. 原尻英樹. 2000. 「괭당・父系・〈地緣〉 - 〈民族〉의 再構築 프로세스」 吉原和男・鈴木正崇・末成道男(編) 『〈血緣〉의 再構築 - 東아시아에 있어서의 父系出自와 同姓結合』 風響社.

Harajiri, Hideki. 原尻英樹. 2000. 「코리언・타운의 比較硏究 - 새로운 에스니시티論으로 향하여」 五十嵐武士(編) 『아메리카의 多民族体制 - 〈民族〉의 創出』 東京大學出版會.

Harajiri, Hideki. 原尻英樹. 2000. 『코리언타운의 民族誌 - 하와이・ＬＡ・生野』 筑摩書房.

Hatanaka, Sachiko and Harayama, Akira eds. 畑中幸子, 原山煌(編) 1991. 『東北

아시아의 歷史와 社會』.

Hattori, Shiro. 服部四郎. 1948.「日本語와 琉球語 朝鮮語 알타이語와의 親族關係」『民族學硏究』13(2): 109-131.

Hattori, Tamio. 服部民夫. 1973.「書評: 鈴木榮太郎著 〈朝鮮農村社會의 硏究〉」『아시아経濟』14(10): 92-96.

Hattori, Tamio. 服部民夫. 1974.「鈴木榮太郎著作集Ⅴ 〈朝鮮農村社會의 硏究〉 刊行에 있는 問題点에 대하여」『未來』89: 48-56.

Hattori, Tamio. 服部民夫. 1975.「日本・朝鮮에 있어서의 同族概念의 比較史論: 養子와 相續을 중심으로」『아시아経濟』16(2): 60-72.

Hattori, Tamio. 服部民夫. 1976.「韓國과 日本의 家族에 대한 一視角: 崔在錫著 〈韓國農村社會硏究〉」『아시아経濟』17(3): 77-83.

Hattori, Tamio. 服部民夫. 1976.「李光奎著 〈韓國家族의 構造分析〉(1975)」『아시아經濟』17(10) [1976.10].

Hattori, Tamio. 服部民夫. 1977.「書評: 李光奎 〈韓國家族의構造分析〉 1975」『民族學硏究』41(4): 395-397.

Hattori, Tamio. 服部民夫. 1978.『韓國家族의 構造分析 / 李光奎[他]』國書刊行會, [1978.2].

Hattori, Tamio. 服部民夫. 1978.「韓國・財閥오너의 経營意識－調査結果報告(韓國経濟의 現況〈特集〉)」(服部 民夫 ; 宇山 博)『아시아経濟』19(7) [1978.7].

Hattori, Tamio. 服部民夫. 1978.「朝鮮時代後期의 養子收養에 관한 硏究: 東萊鄭氏族譜의 分析」『韓國學報』11: 111-154.

Hattori, Tamio. 服部民夫. 1979.「韓國的 経營은 무엇인가－日本的 経營과의 比較에 있어서의 試論 (日本企業을 위한 韓國最新리포트)」『中央公論経營問題』18(6) [1979.12].

Hattori, Tamio. 服部民夫. 1979.「書評: 金泳謨(著) 〈朝鮮支配層硏究〉 1977」『아시아経濟』20(8): 114-116.

Hattori, Tamio. 服部民夫. 1980.「朝鮮後期에 있어서의 名門兩班의 婚姻關係: sub-lineage連合의 形成과 그 意味」『아시아経濟』21(6): 22-56.

Hattori, Tamio. 服部民夫. 1980. (書評)「森谷正規著 〈日本・中國・韓國産業技術比較〉: 〈比較技術論〉에서의 接近」『아시아経濟』21(10): 116-121.

Hattori, Tamio. 服部民夫. 1980.「韓國은 어디까지 왔는가: 70年代의 國民生活水準」『코리아評論』22(217): 11-24.

Hattori, Tamio. 服部民夫. 1982.「韓國<財閥>의 株式所有에 대하여」『社會科學同志社大學人文科學研究所紀要』30: 122-169.

Hattori, Tamio. 服部民夫. 1982.「韓國에 있어서의 business elite의 形成」『日本勞働協會雜誌』24(2): 77-90.

Hattori, Tamio. 服部民夫. 1982.「韓國의 経營風土: 그 特性과 課題」『國際経濟』19(9): 96-99.

Hattori, Tamio. 服部民夫. 1983.「아, 兩班意識: 尹學準氏 〈온돌夜話〉를 읽고」『朝鮮研究』230: 40-45.

Hattori, Tamio. 服部民夫. 1984.「書評: 〈韓國企業의 経營的特質〉 吳鍾錫(著)」『아시아経濟』25(1): 103-105.

Hattori, Tamio. 服部民夫. 1984.「現代韓國企業의 所有와 経營: 〈財閥〉系企業을 중심으로」『아시아経濟』25(5/6): 132-150.

Hattori, Tamio. 服部民夫. 1984.「韓國의 企業－日本과 어디가 다른 것인가〔含資料〕」(鼎談 鳥羽 欽一郎 ; 鼎談 服部 民夫 ; 鼎談 玉城 素)『現代코리아』(通号 241) [1984.6].

Hattori, Tamio. 服部民夫. 1984.「韓國上場企業의 株主構成: 1981-1982年」『아시아経濟』25(7): 70-80.

Hattori, Tamio. 服部民夫. 1985.「韓國의 経濟開發에 있어서의 財閥의 役割〔含코멘트〕」(現代國際経濟의 課題－國際金融問題と市場解放問題〔國際経濟學會第43回研究報告全國大會〕) (自由論題)『國際経濟』(通号 36).

Hattori, Tamio. 服部民夫. 1985.「政治・経濟」부분, 伊藤亞人(編)『더욱 알고싶은 韓國』(233-260), 東京: 弘文堂.

Hattori, Tamio. 服部民夫. 1986.「大韓民國 (日本에 있어서의 發展途上地域研究 1978～85－地域篇〔含 文獻list〕) － (東아시아)」(櫻井 浩 ; 服部 民夫)『아시아経濟』27(9・10) [1986.10].

Hattori, Tamio. 服部民夫. 1986.「婚姻」『基礎한글』1(5): 54-55.

Hattori, Tamio. 服部民夫. 1987.「韓國政治 elite 研究資料」(服部民夫, 鐸木昌之),『東京大學東洋文化研究所附屬東洋學文獻center』[1987.3]. － (東洋學文獻center 叢刊 ; 第52輯).

Hattori, Tamio. 服部民夫. 1987.『發展의 構図』아시아経濟研究所, [1987.3]. (아시아工業化시리즈 ; 2).

Hattori, Tamio ed. 服部民夫(編). 1987.『韓國의 工業化: 發展의 構図』東京: 아시아経濟出版會.

Hattori, Tamio. 服部民夫. 1988.『韓國의 経營發展』文眞堂, [1988.9].

Hattori, Tamio. 服部民夫. 1991.「네트워크 論의 試図(Ⅰ): 朝鮮朝時代에 있어서의 人間關係와 權力」『아시아経濟』32(6): 59-82.

Hattori, Tamio. 服部民夫. 1991.「네트워크 論의 試図(Ⅱ): 朝鮮朝後期安東金氏의 結婚關係(上)」『아시아経濟』32(9): 64-92.

Hattori, Tamio. 服部民夫. 1991.「네트워크 論의 試図(Ⅲ): 朝鮮朝後期安東金氏의 結婚關係(下)」『아시아経濟』32(10): 45-103.

Hattori, Tamio. 服部民夫. 1992.『韓國: 네트워크와 政治文化』東京: 東京大學出版會.

Hattori, Tamio. 服部民夫. 1992.「東아시아의 財閥은 지금－1－韓國－高度成長을 實現한 家族支配가 限界로－先進國化와 世代交代로 変貌한다」『世界週報』73(31) [1992.8.11].

Hattori, Tamio. 服部民夫. 1992.『東아시아의 國家와 社會. 4』(猪口孝), 東京大學出版會, [1992.12].

Hattori, Tamio. 服部民夫. 1993.「朝鮮社會의 하나의 見方－人間關係에서의 接近 (朝鮮近現代史에 있어서의 連續과 轉換〈特集〉)」『朝鮮史研究會論文集』(通号 31) [1993.10].

Hattori, Tamio. 服部民夫. 1994.「韓國 '財閥'의 所有와 経營・再論」『東京経大學會誌』(通号 188) [1994.9].

Hattori, Tamio. 服部民夫. 1995.「日韓経濟關係의 30年－上－(日韓關係의 現住所〈特集〉)」『現代코리아』(通号 357) [1995.12].

Hattori, Tamio. 服部民夫. 1996.『韓國・台湾의 發展메커니즘』(服部民夫, 佐藤幸人), 아시아経濟研究所, [1996.3]. － (研究双書 ; no.464).

Hattori, Tamio. 服部民夫. 1997. "Sociological findings from South Korea", *International Journal of Japanese Sociology* 6:1: 51-59.

Hattori, Tamio. 服部民夫. 1999.「財閥解体과 経營의 継續－日本에 있어서의 財閥解体의 經驗」『評論・社會科學』(通号 59) [1999.3].

Hattori, Tamio. 服部民夫. 2000.「経濟發展과 同姓結合－韓國社會를 중심으로」吉原和男・鈴木正崇・末成道男(編)『〈血緣〉의 再構築－東아시아에 있어서의 父系出自와 同姓結合』風響社.

Hattori, Tamio. 服部民夫. 2001.『韓國経濟의 解剖』(松本厚治, 服部民夫), 文眞堂, [2001.7].

Hattori, Tamio. 服部民夫. 2001.「韓國社會研究의 意義와 課題 (特集 現代아시

아에서 日本을 본다)」『社會學雜誌』(通号 18).

Hattori, Tamio. 服部民夫. 2001.「日韓大企業集団의 形成과 変容 (韓國의 経濟危機에의 制度的아프러치)」(企業集団의 發展에 관한 日韓比較)『NIRA政策研究』14(9) (通号 165).

Hattori, Tamio. 服部民夫. 2002.『아시아中間層의 生成과 特質』(服部民夫, 船津鶴代, 鳥居高), 日本貿易振興會아시아経濟研究所, [2002.2]. (研究双書 ; no.521).

Hattori, Tamio and Omichi, Yasunori 服部民夫・大道康則 1985.『韓國의 企業: 人과 経營』東京: 日本経濟新聞社.

Hattori, Tamio and Uyama, Hiroshi. 服部民夫・宇山博. 1978.「韓國・財閥오너의 経營意識: 調査結果報告」『아시아経濟』19(7): 69-81.

Hayashi, Fumiki. 林史樹. 1994.「韓國民俗行事의 "変容"」『現代코리아』339: 2-3.

Hayashi, Fumiki. 林史樹. 1997.「韓國서커스에 있어서의 "家族": 移動集団의 構造와 戰略」『同志社社會學研究』(同志社大學社會學研究學會)創刊号: 51-65.

Hayashi, Fumiki. 林史樹. 1998.「韓國서커스의 성장과정: 移動芸能集団의 흐름의 속에서」『季刊民族學』83: 104-109.

Hayashi, Fumiki. 林史樹. 1999.「朝鮮・韓國市場研究文獻一覽」朝倉敏夫(監修), 村山智順(著)『朝鮮場市의 研究』253-273, 東京: 國書刊行會.

Hayashi, Fumiki. 林史樹. 1999.「韓國에 있어서의 旅商人의 生活戰略과 그 変化」旅의 文化研究所(編)『旅의 文化研究所研究報告』8: 127-138.

Hayashi, Fumiki. 林史樹. 1999.「朝鮮・韓國의 市場研究略史」朝倉敏夫(監修), 村山智順(著)『朝鮮場市의 研究』235-252, 東京: 國書刊行會.

Hayashi, Fumiki. 林史樹. 2000.「"旅"와 "旅를 하는 生活"」『마호라』(旅의 文化研究所) 24: 40-41.

Hayashi, Humiki. 林史樹. 2002.『市場의 社會史』(鄭勝謨[他]). 法政大學出版局, [2002.6]. (韓國의 學術과 文化 ; 11).

Hayashi, Humiki. 林史樹. 2002. (資料와 通信)「美州韓人移民100周年記念國際學術大會에 參加하여」『民族學研究』67(2).

Heo, Kwang-Mo. 許 光茂. 2000.「전전(戰前) 교토(京都)의 도시하층사회와 조선인의 유입」『코리언・마이너리티연구4』.

Hidemura, Kenji. 秀村研二. 1987.「서울의 地下鐵」『基礎한글』2(10): 64-67.

Hidemura, Kenji. 秀村研二. 1987.「韓國의 擬制的親族關係覺書」成城大學大學院日本常民文化專攻院生學生會議『常民文化』10: 55-67.

Hidemura, Kenji. 秀村研二. 1987.「漁村」『基礎한글』2(12): 56-57.

Hidemura, Kenji. 秀村研二. 1990.「韓國社會에 보는 그리스도教와 伝統文化」『社會科學journal』28(2): 147-170.

Hidemura, Kenji. 秀村研二. 1992.「教會와 女性: 韓國그리스도教의 一斷面」『明星大學研究紀要』28: 13-20.

Hidemura, Kenji. 秀村研二. 1994.「그리스도教속의 샤머니즘」『韓國文化』8月号: 8-12.

Hidemura, Kenji. 秀村研二. 1995.「韓國그리스도教의 現在와 그 理解」『社會人類學年報』21: 79-100.

Hidemura, Kenji. 秀村研二. 1995.「現代韓國社會에 있어서의 그리스도教」田辺繁治(編)『東아시아에 있어서의 宗教의 再生: 宗教的経験의 politicus』389-402, 京都: 京都大學學術出版局.

Hidemura, Kenji. 秀村研二. 1996.「韓國의 그리스도教: 1945年까지를 중심으로」原尻秀樹, 六反田豊(編)『半島와 列島의 각국: 日朝比較交流史入門』131-156, 東京: 新幹社.

Hidemura, Kenji. 秀村研二. 1998. "Social Change and Christianity in Modern South Korean Society", Shima, Mutsuhiko and Roger L. Janelli eds., *The Anthropology of Korea: East Asian Perspectives (Senri Ethnological Studies 49)*, 111-127, Osaka: National Museum of Ethnology.

Hidemura, Kenji. 秀村研二. 1998.「〈兩班〉이라고 말하지 않는 사람들: 80年代중간의 韓國東海岸漁村의 調査에서」嶋陸奥彦・朝倉敏夫(編)『変貌하는韓國社會: 1970~80年代의 人類學調査의 현장에서』185-222, 東京: 第一書房.

Hidemura, Kenji. 秀村研二. 1998.「儒教와 巫俗의 사이－韓國社會에 있어서의 그리스도教」(1998年度워크숍報告書) (워크숍(2)東아시아에 있어서의 그리스도教의 受容)『宗教와 社會』(通号 別冊).

Hidemura, kenji. 秀村研二. 1999.「牧師와 教會－韓國그리스도教의 獨自性」三尾裕子・本田 洋(編)『東아시아에 있어서의 文化의 多中心性』東京外國語大學아시아・아프리카言語文化研究所.

Hidemura, Kenji. 秀村研二. 1999.「受容하는 그리스도教에서 宣教하는 그리스도教로－韓國그리스도教의 展開」『朝鮮文化研究』(通号 6).

Hidemura, kenji. 秀村硏二. 2000.「朝鮮의 社會文化」「朝鮮의 宗教文化」吉田光男(編)『朝鮮의 歷史와 社會』放送大學教育振興會.

Hidemura, Kenji. 秀村硏二. 2000.「特集2 歷史의 향기 나는 마을 · 서울」(桑野榮治 ; 月脚 達彦 ; 秀村 硏二 他)『月刊시니까』13(7) (通号 149) [2002.6].

Hidemura, Kenji. 秀村硏二. 2001.「韓國을 걷는다 (1)에 향한 마을에서」『아시아遊學』(24) [2001.2].

Higa, Masao. 比嘉政夫. 1996.「環東지나海地域의 社會組織의 比較民俗論 - 韓國과 沖縄의 〈門中〉의 構造와 生成」『日中文化硏究』9.

Higa, Masao. 比嘉政夫. 1991.「韓國의 門中과 沖縄의 門中: 比較硏究序說」沖縄縣立芸術大學琉韓伝承文化調査団『韓國伝承文化의 硏究: 沖縄와의 比較』51-58, 那覇: 沖縄縣立芸術大學琉韓伝承文化調査団.

Higaki, Ko. 檜垣巧. 1984.「厚浦里의 儒教的体質과 日韓兩國의 祖先崇拝」日韓漁村社會 · 経濟共同硏究會『日韓合同學術調査報告 第2輯: 韓國慶尙北道平海邑厚浦里』159-189, 神戶: 日韓漁村社會 · 経濟共同硏究會事務局.

Higaki, Ko. 檜垣巧. 1984.「日本과 韓國의 祖先崇拝」『密教文化』145: 1-33.

Higaki, Ko. 檜垣巧. 1986.「全羅南道莞島郡莞島邑長佐里에 있어서의 祖先崇拝의 調査硏究」日韓漁村社會 · 経濟共同硏究會『日韓合同學術調査報告 第4輯: 韓國全羅南道莞島郡』163-185, 神戶: 日韓漁村社會 · 経濟共同硏究會事務局.

Higuchi, Atsushi. 樋口淳. 1990.「韓國의 村과 지난 이야기」(樋口 淳 ; 南 富鎭 ; 金 美榮)『專修大學社會科學硏究所月報』(通号 318) [1990.1].

Higuchi, Atsushi. 樋口淳. 1993.「祖先祭祀와 韓國社會」(R.Janelli, 任敦姬[他]) 第一書房,『Academic Series New Asia』12.

Higuchi, Atsushi. 樋口淳. 2001.「韓國에 있어서의 〈兄弟投金〉說話의 硏究를 중심으로」『專修人文論集』(通号 69) [2001.11].

Higuchi, Setsuo. 樋口節夫. 1986.「韓國의 都市시스템과 서울의 変容」『地理』31(12): 18-25.

Hinata, Kazumasa. 日向一雅. 1992.「'二河白道'와 韓國巫俗儀礼 - 迎講 · 淨土庭園 · 謠曲 '舟橋'를 媒介로서」『明治大學人文科學硏究所紀要』(通号 32).

Hinata, Kazumasa. 日向一雅. 1993.「'二河白道'와 韓國巫俗儀礼 - 2」『明治大學人文科學硏究所紀要』(通号 34).

Hinata, Kazumasa. 日向一雅. 1994. 「'二河白道'와 韓國의 死靈祭의 巫俗」『學術月報』 47(12) [1994.12].

Hioki, Koichiro. 日置弘一郎. 1983. (吳鐘錫과 共著) 「組織行動의 文化的差異: 日韓比較의 試図로부터」『組織科學』 17(1): 37-47.

Hiraki, Makoto. 平木實. 1982. 「『續三綱行實図』와 教化教育 (景印『續三綱行實図』)」 平木實 解題『朝鮮學報』 (通号 105) [1982.10].

Hiraki, Makoto. 平木實. 1986. 「韓國에 있어서의 天神(祭天)信仰에 대하여: 親神・神의 翻譯語と關連して」『天理大學學報』 151.

Hiraki, Makoto. 平木實. 1986. 「明治期에 있어서의 天理教의 朝鮮・韓國伝教史」『朝鮮學報』 (通号 119・120) [1986.7].

Hiraki, Makoto. 平木實. 1987. 『朝鮮社會文化史研究』 東京: 國書刊行會.

Hiraki, Makoto. 平木實. 1990. 「朝鮮朝中宗・明宗代의 旱魃을 둘러싼 天譴意識과 그 社會」『朝鮮學報』 (通号 134) [1990.1].

Hiraki, Makoto. 平木實. 1991. 「朝鮮半島에 있어서의 王權에 대하여: 朝鮮王朝를 중심으로」 松原正毅編『王權의 位相』 東京: 弘文堂.

Hiraki, Makoto. 平木實. 1991. 「朝鮮史의 展開에 있어서의 王權－朝鮮王朝時代를 중심으로」『朝鮮學報』 (通号 138) [1991.1].

Hiraki, Makoto. 平木實. 1995. 「朝鮮後期에 있어서의 圜丘壇祭祀에 대하여 (1)」『朝鮮學報』 (通号 157) [1995.10].

Hiraki, Makoto. 平木實. 1998. 「漢字文化圈에 있어서의 한글文化의 展開」『外國語教育』 (通号 24).

Hiraki, Makoto. 平木實. 1999. 「『鄉飮酒禮儀節』 解題 (資料 影印『鄉飮酒禮儀節』)」『朝鮮學報』 (通号 172) [1999.7].

Hiraki, Makoto. 平木實. 1999. 「朝鮮後期의 社會変動과 鄉村社會史研究」 (金仁杰 ; 平木 實 譯)『朝鮮學報』 (通号 170) [1999.1].

Hiraki, Makoto. 平木實. 1999. 「朝鮮時代의 鄉村에 있어서의 儒教的教化의 一側面－鄉飮酒儀礼・鄉射儀礼에 대하여」『天理大學學報』 50(2) (通号 190) [1999.2].

Hiraki, Makoto. 平木實. 2000. 「朝鮮後期에 있어서의 圜丘壇祭祀에 대하여 (2) 〈圜丘壇〉에서 〈南壇〉에의 名称変更」『朝鮮學報』 (176・177) [2000.10].

Hiraki, Makoto. 平木實. 2001. 「朝鮮社會文化史研究 2」『阿吽社』 [2001.12]. 民博は 1957.

Hirasawa, Yutaka. 平澤豊. 1984. 「日・韓水産業協同組合의 性格의 比較研究」

日韓漁村社會・経濟共同硏究會『日韓合同學術調査報告 第2輯: 韓國慶尙北道平海邑厚浦里』 141-158, 神戸: 日韓漁村社會・経濟共同硏究會事務局.

Hirasawa, Yutaka. 平澤豊. 1986.「莞島郡의 김・미역 養殖의 漁場利用」日韓漁村社會・経濟共同硏究會『日韓合同學術調査報告 第4輯: 韓國全羅南道莞島郡』37-42, 神戸: 日韓漁村社會・経濟共同硏究會事務局.

Hirata, Junji. 平田順治. 1984.「韓國漁業村落의 社會民俗의 動態: 慶尙北道蔚珍郡平海面金音3里의 事例」日韓漁村社會・経濟共同硏究會『日韓合同學術調査報告 第2輯: 韓國慶尙北道平海邑厚浦里』208-231, 神戸: 日韓漁村社會・経濟共同硏究會事務局.

Hirata, Junji. 平田順治. 1986.「韓國漁業的村落의 社會民俗의 動態: 全羅南道莞島郡莞島邑長佐里의 事例」日韓漁村社會・経濟共同硏究會『日韓合同學術調査報告 第4輯: 韓國全羅南道莞島郡』208-224, 神戸: 日韓漁村社會・経濟共同硏究會事務局.

Honda, Hiroshi. 本田洋. 1989.「農村의 経濟發展과 女性의 地位－日本과 韓國의 比較 (外에서 본 日本〈特集〉〔含 코멘트・応答〕)」(文 玉杓 著 ; 本田 洋 譯)『民族學硏究』54(3) [1989.12].

Honda, Hiroshi. 本田洋. 1993.「墓를 媒介로 한 祖先의 〈追慕〉: 韓國南西部一農村의 事例로부터」『民族學硏究』58(2): 142-169.

Honda, Hiroshi. 本田洋. 1994.「韓國家族論의 現在: 全羅南道南原郡一山間農村의 事例로부터」『朝鮮學報』152: 109-166.

Honda, Hiroshi. 本田洋. 1995.「鄕土芸能은 누구의 것?: 現代韓國農村에 있어서의 民俗伝承의 一側面」『朝鮮文化硏究』2: 141-172.

Honda, Hiroshi. 本田洋. 1995.「更定儒道의 成立과 展開: 韓國의 土着主義的宗教運動과 民族文化의 創造」『東京大學教養學部教養學科紀要』27: 1-22.

Honda, Hiroshi. 本田洋. 1996. (書評)「崔吉城『韓國民俗에의 招待』」『民族學硏究』61(2): 342.

Honda, Hiroshi. 本田洋. 1996. (書評)「伊藤亞人『아시아讀本韓國』」『民族學硏究』61(2): 340-341.

Honda, Hiroshi. 本田洋. 1996.「南原地方에 있어서의 〈鄕土文化〉의 現在: 둘의 鄕土文化祭의 事例로부터」『靑丘學術論集』8: 116-130.

Honda, Hiroshi. 本田洋. 1996.「日韓人流의 推移와 코리언 newcomers의 性格」『靑丘學術論集』8: 246-283.

Honda, Hiroshi. 本田洋. 1998.「小農社會의 終焉과 韓國農村의 現在: 南原地域의 fieldwork(1989年～)」嶋陸奧彦・朝倉敏夫(編)『変貌하는 韓國社會: 1970～80年代의 人類學調査의 현장에서』261-304, 東京: 第一書房.

Honda, Hiroshi. 本田洋. 1999.「儒教規範의 實踐과 評価－韓國南西部南原地域에 있어서의 鄕校表彰의 事例로부터」三尾裕子・本田 洋(編)『東아시아에 있어서의 文化의 多中心性』東京外國語大學아시아・아프리카言語文化研究所.

Honda, Hiroshi. 本田洋. 1999.「韓國의 地方邑에 있어서의 〈鄕紳〉集団과 文化伝統－植民地期南原邑의 都市化와 在地勢力의 動向」『아시아・아프리카言語文化研究』(通号 58) [1999.9].

Honda, Hiroshi. 本田洋. 1999.『東아시아에 있어서의 文化의 多中心性』(三尾裕子, 本田洋) 東京外國語大學아시아・아프리카言語文化研究所, [1999.11].

Honda, Hiroshi. 本田洋. 2001.『東아시아에 있어서의 文化의 多中心性』(三尾裕子, 本田洋) 風響社, [2001.5]. － (아시아研究報告시리즈 : no.3).

Honda, Hiroshi. 本田洋. 2002. 書評 岡田浩樹(著)「兩班－変容하는 韓國社會의 文化人類學的研究」『民族學研究』67(3).

Honda, Hiroshi. 本田洋. 2003.「韓國의 村과 町 (特集 韓國의 深層)」『地理』48(3) (通号 571) [2003.3].

Honda, Yasuji. 本田安次. 1978.「韓國의 축제와 神座」『芸能』20(8): 31-33.

Honda, Yasuji. 本田安次. 1982.「韓國의 芸能」『아시아公論』11(2): 60-75.

Hong, Hyeon-Su. 洪 賢秀. 1994.「韓國의 國民學校 現行教科書에 나타난 〈男女有別〉: 夫婦의 會話에 보는 待遇表現」『오차노미즈女子大學 女性文化研究센터年報』8: 63-77.

Hong, Hyeon-Su. 洪 賢秀. 1996.「韓國의 國民學校教科書에 나타난 〈男女有別〉」『오차노미즈女子大學 人間文化研究年報』19: 178-187.

Hong, Hyeon-Su. 洪 賢秀. 2001.「젊은이를 둘러싼 가족상황－교육열과 모자관계(母子關係)를 중심으로: 특집 한국젊은이의 사정(事情)」『月刊韓國文化』(通号 263), [2001.10].

Hori, Ichiro. 堀一郎. 1970.「韓國의 宗教事情」『未來』50: 2-10.

Hwan, Lucy. 黃縷詩. 1999.「巫堂 굿의 演劇的要素」鈴木正崇・野村伸一(編)『仮面과 巫俗의 研究－日本과 韓國』第一書房.

Hwang, Eun-Cha. 黃恩子. 1995.「韓國에 있어서의 女性學의 動向」『아시아女性研究』4: 83-87.

Hwang, Hye-Seong and Ishige, Naomichi. 黃慧性・石毛直道. 1988.『韓國의 食』東京: 平凡社.

Hwang, P'ae-Kang. 黃 *江. 1991.『韓國의 神話・伝說』東京: 東方書店.

Hyon, Yong-Chun. 玄容駿. 1972.「濟州島의 巫俗: 그 儀祀形式으로 보이는 信仰複合」『民族學硏究』36(4): 269-279.

Hyon, Yong-Chun. 玄容駿. 1975.「濟州島의 신방」『에토노스』3.

Hyon, Yong-Chun. 玄容駿. 1977.「濟州島의 喪祭: K村의 事例를 중심으로」『民族學硏究』42(3): 249-266.

Hyon, Yong-Chun. 玄容駿. 1985.『濟州島巫俗의 硏究』東京: 第一書房.

Hyon, Yong-Chun. 玄容駿. 1990.「濟州島에 있어서의 巫歌神話의 機能」阿部・伊藤・荻原(編)『民族의 世界(上)儀祀와 伝承의 民族誌』563-533, 東京: 小學館.

Hyon, Yong-Chun. 玄容駿. 1991.「濟州島의 神々과 축제」『自然과 文化』34.

Ichikawa, Shigeru. 市川繁. 2001.「耽羅神話의 変遷」(심포지엄報告 歷史學과 神話)『史滴』(通号 23) [2001.12].

Ide, Hirotake. 井出弘毅. 2000.「日本籍코리언의 아이덴디티에 관한 考察-<出自>를 둘러싼 이야기로부터」『東洋大學大學院紀要』37 (社會學硏究科).

Iida, Takafumi. 飯田剛史. 1986.「生駒山地의 朝鮮寺・概說」『富山大學日本海経濟硏究所硏究年報』(通号 12).

Iida, Takafumi. 飯田剛史. 1989.「在日韓國・朝鮮人社會에 있어서의 仏教 및 民俗宗教寺院의 諸形態」『富山大學日本海経濟硏究所硏究年報』(通号 15).

Iida, Takafumi. 飯田剛史. 1994.「ある在日巫俗寺院의 開創儀礼와 社會的 네트워크」『富大経濟論集』39(3) [1994.03].

Iida, Takafumi. 飯田剛史. 2002.「在日코리언의 宗教와 축제」『世界思想社』[2002.2].

Iida, Takafumi. 飯田剛史. 2002.「在日코리언의 宗教-文化創造의 過程 (特集 歷史속의 '在日'-'在日'의 意味를 東아시아의 過去・現在・未來속에서 생각한다)-('在日'의 生活現場)」『環』11 [2002.Aut.].

Iida, Takafumi. 飯田剛史. 2002.「在日코리언의 文化創造와 伝統 (特集 海外同胞와 그 文化)」『月刊韓國文化』(通号 274) [2002.9].

Iida, Takahumi. 飯田剛史. 2000.「宗教的伝統과 그리스도教의 發展-韓日比較의 視点에서」小林孝行(編)『変貌하는 現代韓國社會』世界思想社.

Ijichi, Noriko 伊地知紀子. 1997.「살아 있는 역사・선택된 언어: 濟州島와 大阪

에서의 필드 워크로부터」『人文論叢(大阪市立大學文學研究科)』25: 29-44.

Ijichi, Noriko. 伊地知紀子. 2000.「日常의 生活實踐誌: 韓國近現代와 濟州島의 経驗에서」小林孝行(編)『変貌하는 現代韓國社會』188-211, 京都: 世界思想社.

Im, Tong-Kwon. 任東權. 1990.「分与의 民俗」竹田旦(編)『民俗學의 進展과 課題』東京: 國書刊行會.

Im, Tong-Kwon. 任東權. 1994.「韓國의 村축제와 伝統思想」『코리아나』7(1).

Imamura, Minoru. 今村實. 1998.「韓國・江原道에 있어서의 婚姻制度」『鳥取女子短大 北東아시아文化研究』8: 45-69.

Imamura, Minoru. 今村實. 1998.「鳥取縣에서 본 韓國・江原道의 正月行事」『鳥取女子短大 北東아시아文化研究』7: 29-51.

Inaba, Tsugio. 稻葉継雄. 1982.「韓國의 地名에 보는 儒教의 影響」『地名의 世界: 地理』臨時增刊号: 162-163.

Inaba, Tugio 稲葉継雄. 1998.「韓國・北朝鮮에서 본 日韓・日朝關係史－高校歴史教科書의 分析을 통하여」江淵一公(編)『Transculturalism의 研究』明石書店.

Inaduki, Tadasi. 稻月正. 1997.「地域社會와 民族關係－日本人과 在日韓國・朝鮮人과의『結合－分離』志向」奥田道大(編)『都市社會學研究叢書(7)都市에스니시티의 社會學－民族／文化／共生의 意味를 묻는다』Mincrva書房.

Inafuku, Mikiko. 稻福みき子. 1991.「韓國의 샤먼的職能者의 成巫過程에 대하여」沖縄縣立芸術大學琉韓伝承文化調査団『韓國伝承文化의 研究: 沖縄와 의 比較를 목표로 해』23-34, 那覇: 沖縄縣立芸術大學琉韓伝承文化調査団.

Ishige, Naomichi and Ruddle, Kenneth. 石毛直道・ケネス・ラドル. 1987.「(아시아의 市場) 韓國의 定期市〈場市〉」『季刊民族學』39: 102-113.

Ishige, Naomichi ed. 石毛直道編. 1981.『東아시아의 食의 文化』東京: 平凡社.

Itagaki, Ryuta. 板垣龍太. 2000.「韓國 朝鮮半島의 民族主義와 權力의 言說－比較史的問題提起 (特集 脫冷戰과 東아시아)」(林 志弦 ; 板垣 龍太 譯)『現代思想』28(7) [2000.6].

Itagaki, Ryuta. 板垣龍太. 2001.「〈光州〉二〇年後－歷史의 記憶과 人間의 記憶(戰後東아시아와 아메리카의 存在－〈post colonial狀況〉을 東아시아에서 생각한다)－(post colonial狀況과 東아시아)」(文 富軾 ; 板垣 龍太 譯)

『現代思想』 29(9) (臨增) [2001.7].

Itagaki, Ryuta. 板垣龍太. 2001. 「國家暴力과 性의 政治學－濟州4・3虐殺을 중심으로 (特集=人種 panic과 移民의 記憶)－(國家의 記憶)」 (金 成禮 ; 板垣 龍太 譯) 『TRACES』 (通号 2) [2001.8].

Itagaki, Ryuta. 板垣龍太. 2001. 「世界化와 아메리카認識－아메리카覇權主義와 民族主義를 넘어서 (戰後東아시아와 아메리카의 存在－〈postcolonial狀況〉을 東아시아에서 생각한다) (東아시아와 아메리카의 存在)」 (權 赫範 ; 板垣 龍太 譯) 『現代思想』 29(9) (臨增) [2001.7].

Itagaki, Ryuta. 板垣龍太. 2002. 「植民地下의 普通學校와 地域社會－慶北尙州의 一學校를 중심으로」 『朝鮮史硏究會論文集』 (40) [2002.10].

Itagaki, Ryuta. 板垣龍太. 1999. 「植民地期朝鮮에 있어서의 識字調査」 『아시아・아프리카言語文化硏究』 58.

Itagaki, Ryuta. 板垣龍太. 2000. 「農村振興運動에 있어서의 官僚制와 村落: 그 文書主義에 주목하여」 『朝鮮學報』 175.

Itaya, Toru. 板谷徹. 1984. 「韓國巫俗의 芸能性: 東海岸地域의 場合」 『芸能史硏究』 86: 1-41.

Ito, Abito.(Itoh, Abito) 伊藤亞人. 1973. 「韓國農村社會의 一面: 全羅南道珍島에서」 『東洋文化』 53: 147-159.

Ito, Abito. 伊藤亞人. 1973. 「韓國農村의 家族과 祭儀」 『中根千枝』. 東京大學出版會, 1973.

Ito, Abito. 伊藤亞人. 1977. (佐藤信行 「韓國에 있어서의 忌祭의 祭官構成에 대하여」에 對한) 「코멘트」 『季刊人類學』 8(1): 141-142.

Ito, Abito. 伊藤亞人. 1977. 「韓國村落社會에 있어서의 契: 全羅南道珍島農村의 事例」 『東洋文化硏究所紀要』 71: 167-230.

Ito, Abito. 伊藤亞人. 1977. 「契시스템에 보이는 ch'inhan-sai의 分析: 韓國全羅南道珍島에 있어서의 村落構造의 一考察」 『民族學硏究』 41(4): 281-299.

Ito, Abito. 伊藤亞人. 1977. 「코멘트 (韓國에 있어서의 忌祭의 祭官構成에 대하여)」 『季刊人類學』 8(1) [1977.3].

Ito, Abito. 伊藤亞人. 1977. 『韓國人의 社會的性格』 崔在錫[他] 學生社, [1977.12].

Ito, Abito. 伊藤亞人. 1978. 「家族構成(과) 住居空間」 『新羅伽倻文化』 9・10: 165-176.

Ito, Abito. 伊藤亞人. 1978. 「日本의 축제와 都市化」 『아시아公論』 7(9): 120-122.

Ito, Abito. 伊藤亞人. 1979.『韓國農村社會硏究』(崔在錫[他]) 學生社, [1979.6].

Ito, Abito. 伊藤亞人. 1980.「一宗家의 推移에 보는 兩班의 家庭」『月刊韓國文化』 2(9): 27-31.

Ito, Abito. 伊藤亞人. 1980.「兩班의 伝統과 常民: 韓國社會의 文化人類學的硏究」『中央公論』95(4): 312-319.

Ito, Abito. 伊藤亞人. 1981.『韓國同族村落의 硏究』(金宅圭[他]) 學生社, 1981.4.

Ito, Abito. 伊藤亞人. 1982.「朝鮮半島」祖父江孝男(監修)・星埜平和編集代表『社會科를 위한 文化人類學(上)』134-159, 東京: 東京法令出版.

Ito, Abito. 伊藤亞人. 1982.「甕과 主婦: 韓國農村의 女性의 〈領分〉」『季刊民族學』24: 26-35.

Ito, Abito. 伊藤亞人. 1983. "Jar for Ancestor Spirits: Social Implication of Household in Rural Korea", *East Asian Cultural Studies* 22(1-4): 187-202.

Ito, Abito. 伊藤亞人. 1983.「儒教祭祀의 社會的脈絡: 韓國全羅南道珍島農村의 一事例를 통하여」江淵一公・伊藤亞人(編)『儀礼와 象徵: 文化人類學的考察』415-442, 福岡: 九州大學出版會.

Ito, Abito. 伊藤亞人. 1984.「韓國近代化와 伝統의 再認識」國學院大學日本文化硏究所(編)『아시아文化의 再發見: 比較國學을 지향하며』112-119, 東京: 弘文堂.

Ito, Abito. 伊藤亞人. 1984.「伝統的 医療行動에 對한 一考察」『宜民李杜鉉博士回甲紀念論文集』469-482, 서울: 學硏社.

Ito, Abito. 伊藤亞人. 1985.「서울과 韓國의 都市: 巨大化하는 首都와 地方都市의 成長」『週刊朝日百科』483 (世界의 地理77 中國・東아시아－大韓民國): 177-181.

Ito, Abito. 伊藤亞人. 1985.「甕과 主婦」『韓國文化人類學』17: 235-244.

Ito, Abito ed. 伊藤亞人(編). 1985.『더욱 알고 싶은 韓國』東京: 弘文堂.

Ito, Abito. 伊藤亞人. 1985.『음식물』(東京大學出版會) 1985.6. (東京大學公開講座 ; 41).

Ito, Abito. 伊藤亞人. 1986.「韓國伝統社會에 있어서의 女性」聖心女子大學그리스도教文化硏究所(編)『女性과 文明』134-158, 東京: 春秋社.

Ito, Abito. 伊藤亞人. 1986.「契」『基礎한글』1(11): 52-53.

Ito, Abito. 伊藤亞人. 1986.「正統性과 土着性: 朝鮮民俗文化와 現代韓國에 있어서의 syncretism의 様相」『文化人類學』3: 131-147, 京都: Academia 書店.

Ito, Abito. 伊藤亞人. 1986.「朝鮮半島」日本民族學會(編)『日本의 民族學 1964-1983』186-188, 東京: 弘文堂.

Ito, Abito. 伊藤亞人. 1987.「韓國의 親族組織에 있어서의 集団과 非集団」伊藤・關本・船曳(編)『現代의 社會人類學1 親族과 社會의 構造』163-186, 東京: 東京大學出版會.

Ito, Abito. 伊藤亞人. 1987.「金宅圭/ 張籌根/ 李光奎/ 李杜鉉」『文化人類學事典』東京: 弘文堂.

Ito, Abito. 伊藤亞人. 1987.「요사코이축제, 中國・韓國의 축제와의 比較 (都市의 축제 都市人類學的考察〈심포지엄〉) (코멘트)」『季刊人類學』18(3).

Ito, Abito. 伊藤亞人. 1987.「文化人類學에서 본 韓國論－韓國의 人間關係」『現代코리아』(通号 275) [1987.10].

Ito, Abito. 伊藤亞人. 1989.『古代의 日本과 韓國』9. 學生社, [1989.8].

Ito, Abito. 伊藤亞人. 1990.「韓國에 있어서의 祖先과 歷史認識」阿部・伊藤・荻原(編)『民族의 世界(下)社會의 統合과 動態』196-217, 東京: 小學館.

Ito, Abito. 伊藤亞人. 1991. "Religion and Social Integration in Korea", Umesao, T., Hardacre, H. & Nakamaki, H. eds. *Senri Ethnological Studies 29*, 87-95, Osaka: National Museum of Ethnology.

Ito, Abito. 伊藤亞人. 1991.「韓國에 있어서의 親族体系와 歷史認識」『思想』808: 139-151.

Ito, Abito. 伊藤亞人. 1991.「朝鮮의 族譜」『日本姓氏家系總覽(歷史讀本特別增刊)』448-451, 東京: 新人物往來社.

Ito, Abito. 伊藤亞人. 1992. "Style and Approach of Japanese Studies in Korea", Befu, Harumi and Joseph Kreiner eds., *Othernesses of Japan: Historical and Cultural Influences on Japan Studies in Ten Countries*. (319-326), Deutschen Institute für Japanstudien der Philipp-Franz-von-Siebold-Stiftung.

Ito, Abito. 伊藤亞人. 1992. "The Perception of History in Korea and Japan", Chian, Jiao ed., *Home Bound: The Study of East Asian Societies* (Symposium in Honour of Professor Fei Hsiao-tung's 80th Birthday), 167-177, Hong Kong: University of Hong Kong Press.

Ito, Abito. 伊藤亞人. 1992.「家庭의 守護神」『青丘』15: 92-99.

Ito, Abito. 伊藤亞人. 1992.「書堂」『青丘』14: 117-123.

Ito, Abito. 伊藤亞人. 1992.「家船」『漂海民－家船과 糸滿』(日本民俗文化資料集成) 第3卷 / 谷川健一, 三一書房.

Ito, Abito. 伊藤亞人. 1993.「韓國에 있어서의 巡祀와 祖先」『시니까』 9: 26-27.

Ito, Abito. 伊藤亞人. 1993.「現代에 있어서의 mesianism」『現代와 Toynbee』 82: 6-9.

Ito, Abito. 伊藤亞人. 1993.「朝鮮에 있어서의 宗教와 社會統合」梅棹忠夫・中牧弘允(編)『宗教의 比較文明學』191-216, 東京: 春秋社.

Ito, Abito. 伊藤亞人. 1993.「珍島의 民間信仰: 매귀와 방법」『青丘』17: 88-93.

Ito, Abito. 伊藤亞人. 1993.「珍島의 民間信仰: 山을 중심으로」『青丘』 16: 98-105.

Ito, Abito. 伊藤亞人. 1993.「東아시아의 國家와 社會(4) 韓國－네트워크와 政治文化」服部民夫『아시아経濟』34(10) [1993.10].

Ito, Abito. 伊藤亞人. 1993.「東아시아의 社會와 儒教: 韓國의 民族誌에 의한 展望」 溝口雄三・濱下武志・平石直昭・宮嶋博史(編) 『交錯하는 아시아』(아시아에서 생각한다1) 53-76, 東京: 東京大學出版會.

Ito, Abito. 伊藤亞人. 1993. "Coordination and Brokerage: Leadership in Community Development in Rural Korea." *International Conference on Korean Studies in East Asian Anthropology 1993*. National Musium of Ethnology.

Ito, Abito. 伊藤亞人. 1993. "Community development and cultural tradition in Korea." *East Asian Regional Conference 1993*. Japan Society for International Development.

Ito, Abito. 伊藤亞人. 1994.「韓國民間信仰에 있어서의 道教의 伝統」『朝鮮文化研究』 1: 179-191.

Ito, Abito. 伊藤亞人. 1994.「珍島農村에 있어서의 土器」『青丘』19: 140-147.

Ito, Abito. 伊藤亞人. 1994.「讀経師」『青丘』20: 98-108.

Ito, Abito. 伊藤亞人. 1995.「집과 家族」『韓國文化』17: 19-24.

Ito, Abito. 伊藤亞人. 1995.「韓國農村에 있어서의 土器의 利用」吉田集而編『生活技術의 人類學』168-184, 東京: 平凡社.

Ito, Abito. 伊藤亞人. 1995.「契(1) 村의 公共的인 契」『青丘』23: 102-109.

Ito, Abito. 伊藤亞人. 1995.「契(2) 任意參加의 契」『青丘』24: 150-157.

Ito, Abito. 伊藤亞人. 1995.「現代韓國文化의 根」『CREO』第1号: 42-47.

Ito, Abito. 伊藤亞人. 1995.「人類學에서 본 朝鮮學의 展望」『朝鮮學報』156: 1-12.

Ito, Abito. 伊藤亞人. 1995.「珍島의 正月行事」『青丘』21: 84-91.

Ito, Abito. 伊藤亞人. 1995.「風水地理」『青丘』22: 92-99.

Ito, Abito. 伊藤亞人. 1995.「文化人類學에서 본 朝鮮學의 展望」『朝鮮學報』(通号 156) [1995.7].

Ito, Abito. 伊藤亞人. 1996.「韓國・朝鮮」Josef Kreiner(編)『日本民族學』238-251, 東京: 新曜社.

Ito, Abito. 伊藤亞人. 1996.「韓國의 山과 文化」『韓國文化』(特集・韓國의 山과 文化) [1996.7]: 2-7.

Ito, Abito. 伊藤亞人. 1996.「새마을運動과 民俗文化」『青丘』(青丘文化社) 24: 128-135.

Ito, Abito. 伊藤亞人. 1996.「朝鮮의 宗教와 民間信仰」『朝鮮의 歷史와 文化』東京: 放送大學教育振興會.

Ito, Abito. 伊藤亞人. 1996.「朝鮮의 民俗과 現代生活」『朝鮮의 歷史와 文化』東京: 放送大學教育振興會.

Ito, Abito. 伊藤亞人. 1996.『아시아讀本 韓國』東京: 河出書房新社.

Ito, Abito. 伊藤亞人. 1996.「韓國」『河出書房新社』[1996.7]. (생활을 알게된 아시아讀本).

Ito, Abito. 伊藤亞人. 1997.「韓國의 空間認識에 있어서의 中心性과 周緣性」末成道男(編)『東아시아의 現在: 人類學的研究의 試図』55-73, 東京: 風響社.

Ito, Abito. 伊藤亞人. 1997.「日本社會와 韓國社會에 있어서의 '物'」現代日本學會(編)『21世紀韓日關係』243-257.

Ito, Abito. 伊藤亞人. 1997.『더욱 알고 싶은 韓國』第2版. 弘文堂, 1997.12.

Ito, Abito. 伊藤亞人. 1998. "Coordination and Brokerage: Leadership in Community Development in Rural Korea", Shima, Mutsuhiko and Roger L. Janelli eds., *The Anthropology of Korea: East Asian Perspectives* (Senri Ethnological Studies 49), 157-169, Osaka: National Museum of Ethnology.

Ito, Abito. 伊藤亞人. 1998.「珍島에 있어서의 農村生活과 그 変化」嶋陸奧彦・朝倉敏夫(編)『変貌하는 韓國社會: 1970~80年代의 人類學調査의 현장에서』39-86東京: 第一書房.

Ito, Abito. 伊藤亞人. 1999.「韓國의 宗教文化의 歷史와 現在」『大航海』30: 83-89.

Ito, Abito. 伊藤亞人. 1999.『韓國珍島의 民俗紀行』東京: 青丘文化社.

Ito, Abito. 伊藤亞人. 1999.「講演記錄 韓國的發展과 韓國的限界－그 文化・社會的背景」『日韓経濟協會協會報』(通号 326) [1999.1].

Ito, Abito. 伊藤亞人. 2000.「父系血緣原理의 現代的脈絡－韓國社會를 중심으로」吉原和男・鈴木正崇・末成道男(編)『〈血緣〉의 再構築－東아시아에 있어서의 父系出自와 同姓結合』風響社.

Ito, Abito. 伊藤亞人. 2000. 『朝鮮을 아는 事典』 (新訂增補). 平凡社, [2000.11].

Ito, Abito. 伊藤亞人. 2000.「文化人類學(2) 朝鮮・韓國研究의 狀況과 展望 (21世紀를 향한 東方學의 展望)」『東方學』(100) [2000.9].

Ito, Abito. 伊藤亞人. 2002. 『韓日社會組織의 比較』 (伊藤亞人, 韓敬九) 慶應義塾大學出版會 [2002.2]. (日韓共同研究叢書 : 5).

Ito, Abito. 伊藤亞人. 2003.「〈씻김굿〉에 보는 日韓交流 (特集 아시아속의 日韓交流) (日韓의 共同作業・共通課題의 解決)」『國際交流』25(2) (通号 98).

Ito, Abito. 伊藤亞人. 2000.「朝鮮・韓國研究의 狀況과 展望」『東方學』100.

Ito, Abito. 伊藤亞人・大村益男・梶村秀樹・武田幸男(監修) 1986.『朝鮮을 아는 事典』東京: 平凡社.

Ito, Kaichi. 伊藤嘉一. 1980.「感覺의 차이에 기초한 國際比較文化研究 2 日本과 韓國의 比較」『東京學芸大學紀要 第2部門 人文科學』31: 15-25.

Ito, Yoshihide. 伊藤好英. 2000.「日韓의 〈축제〉의 比較－이자이호・江陵端午祭・恩山別神祭」崔吉城・日向一雅(編)『神話・宗教・巫俗－日韓比較文化의 試図』風響社.

Iwamoto, Michiya. 岩本通弥. 2001. 『都市와 境界의 民俗』 (筑波大學民俗學研究室) 吉川弘文館, [2001.12].

Iwamoto, Michiya. 岩本通弥. 1993.「〈親子心中〉을 둘러싼 象徵的시스템 의 日韓比較(1): 神話的인 〈이야기〉로서의 〈自殺事件〉의 民俗學的分析」『國立歷史民俗學博物館研究報告』54: 73-144.

Iwamoto, Michiya. 岩本通弥. 1997.「都域의 象徵性과 王權의 祭祀: 朝鮮의 事例를 중심으로」『國立民族學博物館研究報告』74: 135-148.

Izumi, Seiichi. 泉靖一. 1965.「韓國感傷旅行」『日本』12月号.

Izumi, Seiichi. 泉靖一. 1966.「韓國의 國學」『図書』198(2月号): 32-36.

Izumi, Seiichi. 泉靖一. 1966.『濟州島』東京: 東京大學東洋文化研究所.

Izumi, Seiichi. 泉靖一. 1968.「韓國샤머니즘의 世界: 韓國의 巫俗을 중심으로」『世界』267: 224-231.

Izumi, Seiichi. 泉靖一. 1969.「〈巫党來歷〉 考」『東洋文化』46・47: 55-74.

Izumi, Seiichi. 泉靖一. 1970. (金石範과 對談)「고향 濟州島」『世界』293: 245-256.

Izumi, Seiichi. 泉靖一. 1970. (張籌根「古代的儀禮와 神話의 一形態」에 對하는) 「解說」『文學』38(11): 159.

Izumi, Seiichi. 泉靖一. 1970.「旧植民地帝國大學考」『中央公論』1月号.

Izumi, Seiichi. 泉靖一. 1970.「朝鮮의 샤머니즘」『朝鮮學報』56: 1-12.

Izumi, Seiichi. 泉靖一. 1970.『文化속의 人間』東京: 文芸春秋社.

Izumi, Seiichi. 泉靖一. 1971.『아득히 멀리 떨어진 산들』東京: 新潮社.

Izumi, Seiichi. 泉靖一. 1971.『泉靖一著作集6 文化人類學에 무엇을 요구할 것인가』397頁, 東京: 讀賣新聞社.

Izumi, Seiichi. 泉靖一. 1972.『泉靖一著作集7 文化人類學의 眼』465頁, 東京: 讀賣新聞社.

Izumi, Seiichi. 泉靖一. 1972.『泉靖一著作集5 文化人類學・思索의 旅』385頁, 東京: 讀賣新聞社.

Izumi, Seiichi. 泉靖一. 1972.『泉靖一著作集1 fieldwork의 記錄(1)』東京: 讀賣新聞社.

Jeon, Kyoung-Uk. 田 耕旭. 1999.「한국가면극과 의례의 관련양상」鈴木正崇・野村伸一(編),『가면과 무속의 연구－일본과 한국』第一書房.

Jeong, A-Young. 鄭 雅英. 2000.『중국조선족(中國朝鮮族)의 민족관계(民族關係)』, 아시아 정치경제학회(政経學會).

Jeong, Yoon-Suk. 鄭 潤錫. 2000.「국경을 초월하는 일본문화와 한국의 젊은이－한국 젊은이의 문화에 보이는 者－韓國의 若者文化에 보는 일본화를 단서로」『원생론집(院生論集)』(中京大學大學院社會科學研究科) 2.

Ji, Young-Im. 池 映任. 2001.「(書評)신화・종교・무속 한일비교문화의 시도」崔吉城・日向一雅(編)『國際協力研究誌』7(2), 風響社.

Ji, Young-Im. 池 映任. 2002.「현대 한국에 있어서의 '국립묘지'의 형성－안장(安葬)의 대상자(對象者)를 중심으로」『아시아社會文化研究』(3), [2002.3].

Jin, Dae-Chul. 陳 大哲. 1996.「재일교포의 선조제례에 있어서의 문화변천－이상적 제례와 현대 제례의 사례」『民族學研究』60(4), [1996.3].

Jin, Dae-Chul. 陳 大哲. 1999.「韓國전후50年에 있어서의 전통문화로의 회귀－한국전통가면극의 재현과 가면극의 민중문화운동으로의 재창출(前編)」『院生論集』(中京大學大學院社會學研究科) (通号 1), [1999.3].

Jin, Dae-Chul. 陳 大哲. 2000.「한국전후 50년에 있어서의 전통문화로의 회귀－전통가면극의 제한과 가면극의 민중문화운동에 향한 재창출(後編)」『院

生論集』(中京大學大學院社會學研究科) (通号 2), [2000.3].

Jodo, Takuya. 淨土卓也. 1992.『朝鮮人의 强制連行과 徵用』東京: 社會評論社.

Kabumoto, Chizuru 株本千鶴. 1996.「現代韓國人의 <죽는 법>: hospice movement를 중심으로」『東아시아地域研究』3: 47-60.

Kabumoto, Chizuru 株本千鶴. 1997.「仏教社會福祉에 관한 日韓의 比較研究: 韓國・曹溪宗의 仏教福祉活動을 중심으로」『日本仏教社會福祉學會年報』27: 85-105.

Kabumoto, Chizuru 株本千鶴. 1998.「仏教社會福祉에 관한 日韓의 比較研究: 仏教系 老人福祉施設 利用者의 生活實態를 중심으로」『日本仏教社會福祉學會年報』29: 79-105.

Kabumoto, Chizuru 株本千鶴. 1998.「韓國型福祉社會의 仮構와 現實」仁科健一, 舘野(Akira)(編)『新韓國讀本8 韓國의 福祉－希望과 現實』123-133, 社會評論社.

Kabumoto, Chizuru 株本千鶴. 1998.「韓國에 있어서의 老人福祉政策: 1980年代末까지」『社會事業研究所年報』34: 1-17.

Kabumoto, Chizuru 株本千鶴. 1999.「韓國의 hospice運動」『NHK社會福祉seminar』12, 2月号: 140-145.

Kabumoto, Chizuru 株本千鶴. 1999.「韓國型社會福祉시스템의 實態와 指向性」『月刊福祉』4月号: 38-41.

Kabumoto, Chizuru 株本千鶴. 2000. (翻譯)「韓國社會福祉士의 現況과 課題」(李英芬著)『人文學報』310: 55-86.

Kabumoto, Chizuru 株本千鶴. 2000.「韓國에 있어서의 老齡手当制度와 敬老年金制度의 形成過程에 대하여」『人文學報』310: 25-53.

Kabumoto, Chizuru 株本千鶴. 2000.「失業・貧困・欠食: 韓國에 있어서의 欠食兒童의 再發見」『母子研究』20: 61-80.

Kabumoto, Chizuru 株本千鶴. 2000.「老人home利用者의 life history」『現代社會와 家族政策』(副田義也, 樽川典子編) 163-193, Minerva書房.

Kabumoto, Chizuru 株本千鶴. 2000.「社會保険制度」石坂浩一, 舘野(Akira)(編)『現代韓國을 아는 55章』64-67, 明石書店.

Kabumoto, Chizuru 株本千鶴. 2000.「障害者의 社會進出」石坂浩一, 舘野(Akira)(編)『現代韓國을 아는 55章』72-75, 明石書店.

Kabumoto, Chizuru 株本千鶴. 2000.「祖先祭祀와 死生觀」石坂浩一, 舘野(Akira)(編)『現代韓國을 아는 55章』146-149, 明石書店.

Kabumoto, Chizuru 株本千鶴. 2000.「老後의 保障」石坂浩一, 舘野(Akira)(編)『現代韓國을 아는 55章』68-71, 明石書店.

Kabumoto, Chizuru 株本千鶴. 2000.「韓國의 hospice運動」Carl Becker (編)『生과 死의 care를 생각한다』184-204, 法藏館.

Kabumoto, Chizuru 株本千鶴. 2001. (翻譯)「諸外國의 專門職制度 韓國」(李英芬著), Soeda Akemi, 古川孝順(編)『社會福祉士・精神保健福祉士・care manager가 되기 위해서』140-143, 誠信書房.

Kamata, Shigeo ed. 鎌田茂雄(編) 1980.『朝鮮仏教의 寺와 歷史』東京: 大法輪閣.

Kamata, Shigeo ed. 鎌田茂雄(編) 1991.『講座: 仏教의 受容과 変容5 韓國編』東京: 佼成出版社.

Kameyama, Keiichi 龜山慶一. 1977.「日韓漁勞民俗의 比較를 중심으로」『日本民俗學』109: 1-17.

Kameyama, Keiichi 龜山慶一. 1978.「韓國漁民의 信仰: 특히 船 제사의 神에 대하여」『生江義男先生還曆記念歷史論集』289-308.

Kameyama, Keiichi. 龜山慶一. 1983.「韓國의 漁船에서 제사 지내는 神의 性格에 대하여: 日本과의 比較」『史潮』14: 69-80.

Kameyama, Keiichi. 龜山慶一. 1984.「韓國의 漁撈民俗調査의 中에서」『民俗學評論』24: 72-83.

Kameyama, Keiichi. 龜山慶一. 1985.「韓國의 漁船에서 제사 지내는 神의 地域性」『桐朋學園大學短期大學部紀要』4: 37-68.

Kameyama, Keiichi. 龜山慶一. 1986.『漁民文化의 民俗研究』東京: 弘文堂.

Kameyama, Keiichi. 龜山慶一. 1991.「漁民信仰의 比較試論」沖縄縣立芸術大學琉韓伝承文化調査団『韓國伝承文化의 研究: 沖縄와의 比較를 목표로 해』那覇: 沖縄縣立芸術大學琉韓伝承文化調査団.

Kameyama, Keiichi. 龜山慶一. 1991.「日韓에 있어서의 船에서 제사 지내는 神의 比較」『季刊自然과 文化』34.

Kamiya, Niji. 神谷丹治. 1997.『韓國의 작은 村에서 - 가까운 옛날의 記憶』凱風社.

Kanai, Tenbi. 金井典美. 1972.「扶余郊外(恩山)의 別神祭: 韓國의 御柱祭」『季刊人類學』3(3): 118-132.

Kanda, Yoriko. 神田より子. 1994.「濟州島의 샤먼과 女들」『月刊韓國文化』719.

Kanda, Yoriko. 神田より子. 1994.「濟州島의 巫俗儀礼와 儒教式儀礼: 三多의 島의 男과 女」 家準・鈴木正崇(編) 『東아시아의 샤머니즘과 民俗』 197-231, 東京: 頸草書房.

Kanda, Yoriko. 神田より子. 1994.「濟州島의 巫俗儀礼와 女들」『東横學園大學短期大學女性文化研究所紀要』 19(1).

Kaneko, Erika. 金子エリカ. 1963.「韓國訪問記」『民族學研究』27(3): 605-606.

Kang, Myoung-Gu. 姜 明求. 1997.「韓國에 있어서의 노동자문화의 형성－계급적 조건의 통찰과 편입」 栗原彬(編),『강좌 차별의 사회학(3)현대세계의 차별구조』, 弘文堂.

Kang, Sin-Hang. 姜信沆. 1991.「王權과 訓民正音의 創製」『朝鮮學報』 138: 19-44.

Kasamoto(Miyajima), Mika. 笠本(宮島)美花. 1998.「延辺을 舞台로 하는 朝鮮民族의 transnational教育・學術交流」『環日本海研究』(4).

Kasamoto(Miyajima), Mika. 笠本(宮島)美花. 1998.「東아시아의 에스니크・transnational・actor 華人과 朝鮮民族의 transnational活動에 注目하며(國際的行爲主体의 再檢討)」『季刊國際政治』(通号 119) [1998.10].

Kasamoto(Miyajima), Mika. 笠本(宮島)美花. 2001.「延辺朝鮮族研究者의 統一研究－方秀玉「南北朝鮮關係의 展開와 在中同胞의 役割」, 方秀玉「中國朝鮮族과의 協力關係와 南北統一」을 중심으로」『笠本美花/社會科學研究科紀要』別冊. 7.

Katayama, Takahiro. 片山隆裕. 1985.「gender의 相對性: 韓國儒教를 둘러싼 文化人類學的考察」『九州大學比較教育文化研究施設紀要』36: 21-40.

Katayama, Takahiro. 片山隆裕. 1985.「韓國의 社會変化와 家族文化의 展開: 第2次世界大戰 以後를 중심으로」『戰後 아시아諸國의 教育政策의 変容過程과 그 社會文化的 基盤에 관한 總合的 比較研究』19-26, 九州大學教育學部.

Katayama, Takahiro. 片山隆裕. 1990.「韓國에 있어서의 女性과 儒教」杉山晃一・櫻井哲男(編)『韓國社會의 文化人類學』159-172, 東京: 弘文堂.

Kato, Koichi. 加藤光一. 1993.「東北庄內地方의 農家・韓國全羅北道의 農家: 現代家族経營危機의 日韓比較」『村落社會研究』29: 43-76.

Kato, Kyuzo. 加藤九祚. 1979.「壇君神話에 대한 excursion的 覺書」『學術月報』32(7): 32-36.

Kato, Takashi. 加藤 敬. 1985.「노래 부르고, 춤추는 샤먼」『季刊民族學』9(4)

[1985.10].

Kato, Takashi. 加藤 敬. 1987. 「소놀이굿 – 되 살아 난다 "소 놀이"의 축제」『季刊民族學』11(4).

Kato, Takashi. 加藤 敬. 1989. 「용등 할망의 축제」『季刊民族學』13(1).

Kato, Takashi. 加藤 敬. 1990. 「韓國의 家具裝飾」(加藤敬[他]) – 平河出版社, [1990.12]. (아시아民俗寫眞叢書).

Kato, Takashi. 加藤敬. 1987. 「할머니들의 神: 江陵端午祭 見聞記」『季刊民族學』39: 6-26.

Kato, Takashi. 加藤敬. 1990. 『万神: 韓國의 샤머니즘』東京: 平河出版社.

Kato, Takashi. 加藤敬. 1993. 『巫神과 의 饗宴: 韓의 國・巫祭記』東京: 平河出版社.

Kato, Yasushi. 加藤泰. 1979. 「濟州島 2개 神話의 構造分析」『民族學研究』44(1): 83-90.

Katsuki, Yoichiro. 香月洋一郎. 1996. 「韓國・慶尙北道의 筏船」『民具 monthly』29(3): 6340-6342.

Katsuki, Yoichiro. 香月洋一郎. 1997. 「慶尙北道羅北의 筏船과 미역漁 – 韓國漁業調査노트(1)」『歷史과 民俗』14.

Kawa, Kaoru. 河かおる. 1998. 「植民地期朝鮮에 있어서의 同友會 – 植民地下내셔널리즘에 대한 一考察」『朝鮮史研究會論文集』(通号 36) [1998.10].

Kawa, Kaoru. 河かおる. 2001. 「學習院大學東洋文化研究所所藏・友邦文庫錄音記錄에 대하여」『Archivist』(52) [2001.8].

Kawa, Kaoru. 河かおる. 2001. 「總力戰下의 朝鮮女性 (特集「帝國」・植民地의 女性)」『歷史評論』(612) [2001.4].

Kawagoe, Michiko. 川越道子. 2000. 「〈在日의 経驗〉 – 표명되는 呼称과 経驗을 중심으로」『코리언・마이너리티研究』4.

Kawahara, Norihumi. 河原典史. 2001. 「島嶼에서 본 朝鮮半島와 他地域의 交流 – 濟州島를 중심으로」(藤田 明良 ; 李 善愛 ; 河原 典史)『青丘學術論集』19 [2001.11].

Kawakami, Shinji. 川上新二. 1998. 「現代韓國社會에 있어서의 巫俗儀礼의 一考察 – 全羅南道珍島의 事例에서」『國際地域學研究』(1) [1998.3].

Kawakami, Shinji. 川上新二. 2002. 「中國延辺朝鮮族의 職能者에 관한 一考察 – 朝鮮巫俗과 의 關連을 중심으로」『宗教學論集』21.

Kawakami, Shinji. 川上新二. 1996. 「中國延辺朝鮮族에 있어서의 治療師」『宗教

研究』 307: 291-292.

Kawakami, Shinji. 川上新二. 1997.「韓國에 있어서의 巫俗과 仏教: 보살이라고 불리는 職能者를 중심으로」『宗教研究』 311: 293-294.

Kawakami, Shinji. 川上新二. 1997.「韓國의 降神巫 보살과 祖先과의 關係: 서울과 全羅南道珍島와의 比較」『國學院大學 紀要』 35: 31-35.

Kawakami, Shinji. 川上新二. 1998.「韓國의 巫俗儀礼에 있어서 제사 지내지는 祖先: 全羅南道珍島의 事例에서」『駒澤宗教學研究會 宗教學論集』 20: 81-96.

Kawakami, Shinji. 川上新二. 1999.「降臨하는 神靈를 통하여본 韓國降臨神巫의 類型分類에 관한 一考察－보살, 점쟁이 등으로 칭해지는 職能者를 중심으로」三尾裕子・本田 洋(編)『東아시아에 있어서의 文化의 多中心性』東京外國語大學아시아・아프리카言語文化研究所.

Kawamori, Hiroshi. 川森博司. 1991.「來訪者를 둘러싼 說話－日韓比較의 視点에서」『國立歷史民俗博物館研究報告』(通号 35) [1991.11].

Kawamori, Hiroshi. 川森博司. 1994.「韓國口承說話의 分類体系－比較研究의 視点에서」『日本民俗學』(通号 199) [1994.8].

Kawamori, Hiroshi. 川森博司. 2000.『日本昔話의 構造와 이야기꾼』大阪大學出版會, [2000.2].

Kawamori, Hiroshi. 川森博司. 1993.「異類婚姻譚의 類型分析: 日韓比較의 視点에서」『國立歷史民俗博物館研究報告』50: 385-406.

Kawamori, Hiroshi. 川森博司. 1996.「比較의 視点으로서의 〈風水〉: 東아시아에 있어서의 死者의 埋葬을 중심으로 (死者儀礼와 死의 觀念: 近隣諸國의 死者儀礼와 死의 觀念)」『國立歷史民俗博物館研究報告』68: 187-201.

Kawamura, Minato. 川村湊. 1983.『異樣의 領域』國文社, [1983.3].

Kawamura, Minato. 川村湊. 1986.「魂의 구전씨족・黃晰暎」『群像』41(4) [1986.4].

Kawamura, Minato. 川村湊. 1988.「列島와 半島의 社會史」(網野善彦, 川村湊) 作品社, [1988.8]. (〈現在〉와의 對話 ; 8).

Kawamura, Minato. 川村湊. 1989.『아시아라는 鏡』思潮社, [1989.5]. (〈昭和〉의 critic).

Kawamura, Minato. 川村湊. 1989.「言靈과 他界－9－王仁의 暗号」『群像』44(8) [1989.8].

Kawamura, Minato. 川村湊. 1992.「Mother아시아의 旅人」『人文書院』[1992.10].

Kawamura, Minato. 川村湊. 1993.「差別・風水・陰陽－中上健次와 서울 (中上

健次〈特集〉)」『Eureka』 25(3) [1993.3].

Kawamura, Minato. 川村湊. 1994.『아시아稻作民의 民俗과 芸能』(諏訪春雄, 川村湊) 雄山閣出版, [1994.7].

Kawamura, Minato. 川村湊. 1994.「왜 〈西便制〉는 유행한 것인가－韓國文化의 一側面 (韓國의 現代詩〈特集〉)」『現代詩手帖』 37(9) [1994.9].

Kawamura, Minato. 川村湊. 1995.『아시아의 靈魂觀』(諏訪春雄, 川村湊) 雄山閣出版, [1995.10].

Kawamura, Minato. 川村湊. 1995.『아시아 山民 海民의 民俗과 芸能』(諏訪春雄, 川村湊) 雄山閣出版, [1995.6].

Kawamura, Minato. 川村湊. 1995.『海를 건넌 日本語』 青土社, [1995.3].

Kawamura, Minato. 川村湊. 1996.『〈大東亞民俗學〉의 虛實』講談社, [1996.7]. (講談社選書 metier ; 80)

Kawamura, Minato. 川村湊. 1996.『아시아稻作文化와 日本』(諏訪春雄, 川村湊) 雄山閣出版, [1996.6].

Kawamura, Minato. 川村湊. 1996.「環東지나海의 女神信仰 (特集 環東지나海의 比較文化)」『日中文化研究』 (通号 9) [1996.5].

Kawamura, Minato. 川村湊. 1996.「座談會: 環東지나海文化圈 (特集 環東지나海의 比較文化)」(諏訪 春雄 ; 川村 湊 ; 崔 吉城 他)『日中文化研究』(通号 9) [1996.5].

Kawamura, Minato. 川村湊. 1997.『방문하는 神々』(諏訪春雄, 川村湊) 雄山閣出版, [1997.9].

Kawamura, Minato. 川村湊. 1998.「post colonialism의 〈修學旅行〉 大江志乃夫『日本植民地探訪』」『波』 32(7) [1998.7].

Kawamura, Minato. 川村湊. 1999.「移民과 棄民－移民文學論序說 (特集 新世紀에의 課題集－未來에의 strategy) (歷史, 國家, native)」『國文學 解釋과 教材의 研究』 44(12) (通号 647) [1999.10].

Kawamura, Minato. 川村湊. 1999.「坂口安吾의 古代史와 朝鮮半島 (坂口安吾와 日本文化) (歷史・文化・社會)」『國文學解釋과 鑑賞』 64(別冊) [1999.9].

Kawamura, Minato. 川村湊. 1999.『태어나면 거기가 고향－在日朝鮮人文學(論)』 平凡社, [1999.9]. (平凡社選書 ; 195).

Kawamura, Minato. 川村湊. 2000.『서울都市이야기』平凡社, [2000.4]. (平凡社新書).

Kawamura, Minato. 川村湊. 2000.「作文속의 大日本帝國」『岩波書店』[2000.2].

Kawamura, Minato. 川村湊. 2000.「샤먼으로 걸어가기: 韓國의 샤먼과의 만남(特集 巫女가 있는 風景)」『東北學』(通号 2) [2000.4].

Kawamura, Minato. 川村湊. 2001.「〈濁音〉의 破壞力－韓國(語)에서 본 日本(語)(特集 말의 最前線)」『國文學 解釋과 敎材의 硏究』46(12) (通号 675) [2001.10].

Kawamura, Minato. 川村湊. 2001.『妓生』作品社, [2001.9].

Kawamura, Minato. 川村湊. 2002.「서울－風水都市에서 未來都市에 (特集 文明의 劇場・首都－ㅗ 變遷과 未來) －(世界의 首都)」『Civil cngincering consultant』(通号 214) [2002.1].

Kawamura, Minato. 川村湊. 2002.『韓國』作品社, [2002.5]. (思想讀本 ; 6).

Kawamura, Minato. 川村湊. 1984.「蔚山의 〈지노귀굿〉」『群像』39(11): 268-272.

Kawamura, Minato. 川村湊. 1985.「日本古典에 나타난 樹木信仰」『比較民俗學會會報』3: 19-21.

Kawamura, Minato. 川村湊. 1985.「傀儡子와 社堂碑: 韓日比較芸能에 관한 一試論」比較民俗學會『比較民俗學』1: 79-88.

Kawamura, Minato. 川村湊. 1986. (鄭大均과 共著)『韓國이라는 鏡: 戰後世代가 본 韓國』東京: 東洋書院.

Kawamura, Minato. 川村湊. 1986.「市場」『基礎한글』1(9): 54-55.

Kawamura, Minato. 川村湊. 1986.「伝統芸能」『基礎한글』1(8): 56-57.

Kawamura, Minato. 川村湊. 1986.『나의 釜山』名古屋: 風媒社.

Kawamura, Minato. 川村湊. 1996.「〈作文〉의 帝國－近代日本의 文化帝國主義의 一樣相」酒井直樹(編)『Nationality의 脫構築』柏書房.

Kawamura, Minato. 川村湊. 1999.「妓生의 図像學」諏訪春雄『아시아의 性』勉誠出版.

Kawase, Takaya. 川瀨貴也. 1996.「〈國家〉 觀과 〈近代文明〉 觀－天道教幹部 〈民族代表〉에 대하여」『東京大學宗教學年報』(通号 14).

Kawase, Takaya. 川瀨貴也. 1998.「第6回日韓宗教硏究者交流심포지엄報告 (近代)東아시아에 있어서의 '民族'과 宗教－使命感을 중심으로」『東京大學宗教學年報』(通号 16).

Kawase, Takaya. 川瀨貴也. 1998.「東學과 그 가르침」『宗教硏究』72(3) [1998.12].

Kawase, Takaya. 川瀨貴也. 2001.「書評 眞鍋祐子(著)『烈士의 誕生－韓國의 民衆運動에 있어서의 恨의 力學』」『宗教와 社會』(7).

Kawase, Takaya. 川瀨貴也. 2001.「植民地期朝鮮에 있어서의 日本그리스도教의 植民地伝道」『思想史研究』(1) [2001.3].

Kawase, Takaya. 川瀨貴也. 2002.「植民地朝鮮에 있어서의 日本仏教와 宗教政策－淨土眞宗을 중심으로」『國學院大學日本文化研究所紀要』89 [2002.3].

Kawashima, Fujiya. 川島藤也. 1976.「文化柳氏에 볼 수 있는 氏族의 移動과 그 性格」『朝鮮學報』70: 43-74.

Kayanuma, Noriko. 萱沼紀子. 1999.「星축제의 행방－日韓北斗七星信仰의 比較研究」『作新學院女子短期大學紀要』(23) [1999.12].

Kayanuma, Noriko. 萱沼紀子. 2000.「아시아를 이야기하는 北辰信仰－日韓北斗七星信仰의 比較研究」『아시아遊學』(13) [2000.2].

Kayanuma, Noriko. 萱沼紀子. 2000.「아시아를 이야기하는 北辰信仰－日韓北斗七星信仰의 比較研究(2)」『아시아遊學』(18) [2000.7].

Kigana, Setsuko. 木鎌節子. 1990.「韓國에 있어서의 天主教의 土着化: 江原道横城郡横城天主教會의 事例」『常民文化』13: 1-10.

Kim, Byoung-Chul. 金 柄徹. 1996.「어민세대민족 재고－선적생활민족의 육지와의 교섭의 분석을 중심으로」『民族學研究. 61(1)』, [1996.6].

Kim, Byoung-Chul. 金 柄徹. 1997.「왜와 〈以船爲家〉」『超域文化科學紀要. (通号 2)』.

Kim, Byoung-Chul. 金 柄徹. 1999. 金柄徹[他],『日本의 어민세대』, 富士제록스小林節太郎記念基金, [1999.10].

Kim, Byoung-Chul. 金 柄徹. 2000.「어민의 신체기법－전통적 '기술'과 첨단 테크놀로지의 병용」『民族學研究』65(2).

Kim, Byoung-Chul. 金 柄徹. 2000.「제국주의와 어민의 이동－히로시마현(廣島縣)토시마(豊島)어민의 〈조선해〉 출어에 관한 역사인류학적 고찰(1)」『亞細亞大學國際關係紀要』9(1・2), [2000.2].

Kim, Byoung-Chul. 金 柄徹. 2000.「제국주의와 어민의 이동－히로시마현(廣島縣)토시마(豊島)어민의 〈조선해(朝鮮海)〉 출어에 관한 역사인류학적 고찰(2)」『亞細亞大學國際關係紀要』10(1), [2000.10].

Kim, Byoung-Chul. 金 柄徹. 2001.「〈근대적 선적생활〉의 출현에 관한 역사인류학적 고찰(1)」『아시아研究所紀要』(28).

Kim, Byoung-Chul. 金 柄徹. 2001.「근대국가와 어민」『亞細亞大學國際關係紀要』11(1), [2001.12].

Kim, Byoung-Chul. 金 柄徹. 2000.「제국주의와 어민의 이동－히로시마현(廣

島縣)토시마(豊島)어민의 〈조선해〉 출어에 관한 역사인류학적 고찰(1)」『亞細亞大學國際關係紀要』 9(1・2)(合併号).

Kim, Byoung-Chul. 金 柄徹. 2000. 「제국주의와 어민의 이동－히로시마현(廣島縣)토시마(豊島)어민의 〈조선해〉 출어에 관한 역사인류학적 고찰(2)」『亞細亞大學國際關係紀要』 10(1).

Kim, Ch'eol. 金哲. 1865. 『韓國의 人口와 經濟』 東京: 岩波書店.

Kim, Chun-Hwa. 金俊華. 1997. 「中國朝鮮族에 있어서의 民族文化의 再構築: 〈祭祀〉와 〈婚禮〉의 事例를 중심으로」『九州大學教育學部比較教育文化研究施設紀要』 49: 39-47.

Kim, Eung-Yeo. 金應烈. 1977. 「韓國에 있어서의 農村家族과 自生的利益集団」『家族研究年報』 3: 43-54.

Kim, Eun-Mi and Motomura, Hiroshi. 金恩美・本村汎. 1992. 「韓國에 있어서의 〈女性의 就勞活動〉에 對하는 既婚男女의 態度研究: 屬性要因 및 〈家族志向性〉과의 關連으로」『家族研究年報』 17: 27-40.

Kim, Hak-Hyoun. 金 學鉉. 1999. 「〈공생〉의 길을 걷는 재일교포」 宮本 勝・淸水芳見(編), 『文化人類學講義－文化와 政策을 考える』 八千代出版.

Kim, Hwan. 金 渙 2000. 『韓國歲時記』 明石書店.

Kim, Ik-Ki, Park Kyeong-Suk and Kojima, Hiroshi. 金益基・朴京淑・小島宏. 1998. 「現代의 韓國과 日本에 있어서의 老親의 地理的네트워크」『人口問題研究』 54(4): 63-84.

Kim, Joon-Hwa. 金 俊華. 1998. 江淵一公(編), 「재일교포의 아이덴디티에 관한 일고찰－〈실태조사〉와 〈관계론〉에의 방법론적 전환에 대해」『트랜스문화주의(トランスカルチャリズム)의 研究』 明石書店.

Kim, Ki-Ho. 金基虎. 1997. 「韓國의 都市保存의 課題와 展望: 韓屋保存地區嘉會洞의 事例」『都市問題』 88(11).

Kim, Mi-Ran. 金美蘭. 1993. 「韓國에 있어서의 女子高等教育의 擴大와 文化: 女性에 있어서의 學歷과 〈賢母良妻〉」『東京大學教育學部紀要』 33: 55-66.

Kim, Mi-Suk. 金美淑. 1991. 「韓國의 既婚女性勞働力과 女性勞働政策: 1980年以後의 母性保護政策과 託兒政策을 중심으로」『社會科學研究』 47(2): 285-304.

Kim, Mi-Yeong. 金美榮. 1991. 「韓國의 主婦權: 安東地域의 안방물림을 중심으로」 沖縄縣立芸術大學琉韓伝承文化調査団 『韓國伝承文化의 研究: 沖縄와의 比較을 목표로 해』 59-74, 那覇: 沖縄縣立芸術大學琉韓伝承文化調

査団.

Kim, Mi-Yeong. 金美榮. 1993.「韓國慶尙南仙倉의 父系親族」『白山人類學』2.

Kim, Mi-Yeong. 金美榮. 1993.「婚姻時의 互助事例에서본 이웃(近隣關係): 韓國慶尙南道仙倉의 事例에서」『民族學研究』57(4): 437-455.

Kim, Myoung-Mi. 金 明美. 1996. 原尻 英樹・倉石 一郎・金 明美,「효고현(兵庫縣) 이타미시(伊丹市)에 있어서의 異文化(국제)이해교육실천을 위한 문화인류학적・사회학적 기초연구」『研究助成論文集』(通号32).

Kim, Myoung-Mi. 金 明美. 1998. 吉野耕作,「(書評)文化내셔널리즘의 사회학－현대 일본의 아이덴티티의 방향」『코리언・마이너리티研究』(1) [1998.1].

Kim, Myoung-Mi. 金 明美. 1998. 李青若,「(書評)재일교포3세의 마음의 집」『코리언・마이너리티研究』(1) [1998.1].

Kim, Myoung-Mi. 金 明美. 1999.「Ryang, Sonia. North Koreans in Japan: Language, Ideology, and Identity〔和文〕」『코리언・마이너리티研究』(2) [1999.6].

Kim, Myoung-Mi. 金 明美. 2000.「日本에 있어서의 에스니시티論의 재검토: 경계론을 중심으로」『民族學研究』65(1) [2000.6].

Kim, Myoung-Mi. 金 明美. 2001.「타라마지마(多良間島)의 앞바다에서 난파한 네덜란드상선 팬보세호의 역사적 증거」『日蘭學會會誌』26(1) (通号 48), [2001.10].

Kim, Myoung-Mi. 金 明美. 2002. 原尻英樹(著)「(書評)코리언타운의 민족지－하와이・LA・이쿠노」『民族學研究』. 67(2).

Kim, Myoung-Mi. 金 明美. 2000.「日本에 있어서의 에스니시티론의 재검토－경계론을 중심으로」『民族學研究』65(1).

Kim, P'a-Mang. 金巴望. 1994.「賓儀로서의 茶礼」『野村美術館研究紀要』3: 12-28.

Kim, Pong-Chin. 金鳳珍. 1994.「朝貢体系와 朝鮮의 近代國家形成」溝口雄三・濱下武志・平石直昭・宮嶋博史(編)『社會와 國家』(아시아에서 생각한다 4) 213-238, 東京: 東京大學出版會.

Kim, Sang-Bo. 金 尙寶. 1998. 石毛直道(編),「東아시아에 있어서의 의례적 향연－비교고찰」『論集 술과 음주의 문화사』, 平凡社.

Kim, Sang-Kyu. 金相圭. 1993.「東아시아에 있어서의 親族集団의 諸概念」『社會學雜誌』(神戸大學社會學研究室).

Kim, Taek-Kyu. 金宅圭. 1963.「韓國文化人類學會의 活動狀況」『民族學研究』

27(4): 664-665.

Kim, Taek-Kyu. 金宅圭. 1990.「東아시아諸地域의 族体系에 대하여: 族体系의 理念과 實態에서 본 連續과 変容에 관한 比較試論」『朝鮮學報』 134: 1-46.

Kim, Taek-Kyu. 金宅圭. 2000.『日韓民俗文化比較論』九州大學出版會.

Kim, Tae-Kon. 金泰坤. 1990.「新年祭의 原義」(坂倉正康譯) 竹田旦(編)『民俗學의 進展과 課題』441-457, 東京: 國書刊行會.

Kim, Tae-Kon. 金泰坤. 1991.「韓國에 있어서의 神觀念과 世界觀」植松明石(編)『環中國海의 民俗과 祭祀 2 神々의 祭祀』423-441, 東京: 凱風社.

Kim, Tae-Kon. 金泰坤. 1994.「韓國샤머니즘에 있어서의 神觀念과 祭儀의 象徵的原義」(淵上恭子譯) 宮家準・鈴木正崇(編)『東아시아의 샤머니즘과 民俗』東京: 勁草書房.

Kim, Tae-Kon, Chi, Ch'un-Sang and Hyon, Yong-Chun. 金泰坤・池春相・玄容駿. 1977.『靈을 부르다: 韓國의 샤먼』東京: 國書刊行會.

Kim, Tae-Young. 金 泰泳. 1999.『아이덴티티・정책을 넘어－재일교포의 에스니시티』世界思想社.

Kim, Yang-Gi. 金 兩基. 1999.『日本의 文化 韓國의 풍습』明石書店.

Kim, Yang-Gi. 金兩基. 1991.「巫俗儀礼와 音樂」藤井知昭(編)『民族音樂叢書 5 儀礼와 音樂 II 民間信仰編』東京: 東京書籍.

Kimura, Kan. 木村幹. 2000.『조선/ 한국 내셔널리즘과 '작은 나라' 의식』Minerva書房.

Kimura, Mitsuhiko 木村光彦. 1997.「제국의 단절과 연속－북한의 경우」『인문학보(人文學報)』79.

Kishi, Shodo. 岸昭道. 1999.「韓國낙동江流域 農村生活文化의 研究－葬制와 相續에 關해서 그 1」『岐阜女子大學紀要』(通号 28).

Kishi, Shodo. 岸昭道. 2000.「韓國낙동江流域 農村生活文化의 研究(그 2)各流域의 農家相續의 意識調查」『岐阜女子大學紀要』(通号 29).

Kishi, Shodo. 岸昭道. 2001.「韓國낙동江流域 農村生活文化의 研究(그 3)各流域의 農家相續의 意識調查」『岐阜女子大學紀要』(30).

Kishi, Shodo. 岸昭道. 2001.「訪韓學術研究者論文集. 第1卷」日韓文化交流基金. 日韓文化交流基金, [2001.3].

Kishi, Shodo. 岸昭道. 2002.「韓國낙동江流域 農村生活文化의 研究(그 4)倭館地區의 農家相續의 意識調查」『岐阜女子大學紀要』(31).

Kishibe, Kumi. 岸部くみ. 1976. 「朝鮮民話의 知恵」『코리아評論』 18(173): 42-46.

Kitami, Toshio. 北見敏夫. 1986. 「日・韓比較民俗學에의 一試論」『月山任東權博士 頌壽紀念論文集 民俗學篇』 서울: 集文堂.

Kitami, Toshio. 北見敏夫. 1986. 「濟州島 [潛女]」 伊藤亞人・大村益男・梶村秀樹・武田幸男(監修) 『朝鮮을 아는 事典』 東京: 平凡社.

Ko, Kwang-Min. 高光敏. 1991. 「濟州島一部地域에 있어서의 信仰圈과 行政圈」 沖縄縣立芸術大學琉韓伝承文化調査団 『韓國伝承文化의 硏究: 沖縄와의 比較를 목표로 해』 35-46, 那覇: 沖縄縣立芸術大學琉韓伝承文化調査団.

Ko, Sa-Myoung. 高 史明. 1998. 「<삶의 의미>와 그 후」 在日朝鮮人研究會(編) 『코리언・마이너리티연구(1)』, 新幹社.

Ko, Sun-Hwi. 高 鮮徽. 1997. 奧田道大(編), 「제주도(濟州島)에서 요코하마(横浜)로－1980년대 일본으로의 정착시도」 『都市社會學硏究叢書(7) 도시(都市) 에스니시티의 社會學－민족/문화/공생의 의미를 묻는다』 Minerva 書房.

Ko, Yon-Ui 高 演義. 1998. 『<民族>이라는 존재－제 3세계로서의 재일교포』 社會評論社.

Kobayashi, Kazumi 小林和美. 1999. 「韓國村落悉皆調査의 手法과 経緯－大邱廣域市近郊農村調査의 記録－」 『大阪教育大學紀要 第Ⅱ部門』 第48巻 第1号, 27～49頁, 1999年(平成11) 8月.

Kobayashi, Kazumi. 小林和美. 1999. 「와리깡에 대한 사회학적 이해」 『일본어문학』 第7輯, 411～432頁, 1999年(平成11) 8月.

Kobayashi, Kazumi. 小林和美. 1999. 『韓國村落社會의 基層構造와 変化－大邱廣域市近郊農村에 있어서의 世帶調査票調査集計結果－』, A4版・92頁, 1999年(平成11) 6月.

Kobayashi, Kazumi. 小林和美. 2000. 「韓國都市近郊農村에 있어서의 人口移動과 就業構造－大邱廣域市Ｂ里에 있어서의 世帶調査票調査結果로－」 『日韓村落構造의 比較研究(平成9～11年度文部省科學硏究費補助金(國際學術硏究)硏究成果報告書)』, 61～75頁(日本語), 111～125頁(韓國語), 2000年(平成12) 3月.

Kobayashi, Kazumi. 小林和美. 2000. 「韓國農村에 있어서의 教育問題와 人口移動－大邱廣域市近郊農村의 事例－」 『大阪教育大學紀要 第Ⅱ部門』 第48巻 第2号, 75～88頁, 2000年(平成11) 1月.

Kobayashi, Kazumi. 小林和美. 2000. 李昌基「韓國의 '집'과 '마을'」『日韓村落構造의 比較研究(平成9～11年度文部省科學研究費補助金(國際學術研究)研究成果報告書)』, 17～31頁, 2000年(平成12) 3月.

Kobayashi, Kazumi. 小林和美. 2000. 李昌基「韓國同族集団의 構成原理－形成要因을 중심으로」神戶大學社會學研究會『社會學雜誌』第17号, 102～116頁, 2000年(平成12年) 3月.

Kobayashi, Kazumi. 小林和美. 2001.「韓國大都市近郊農村에 있어서의 若年層의 就學流出 大邱廣域市S集落의 事例」『村落社會研究』(日本村落研究學會)第8卷 第1号, 12～23頁, 2001年(平成13年) 9月.

Kobayashi, Takayuki. 小林孝行. 2000.『変貌하는 現代韓國社會』京都: 世界思想社.

Kobayashi, Takayuki. 小林孝行(編). 2000.『変貌하는 現代韓國社會』世界思想社.

Kobayashi, Yuriko. 小林由里子. 1987.『韓國의 家族』東京: 日本總合研究所.

Kodama, Toshihiko. 小玉敏彥. 1988.「韓國重工業의 史的展開－韓國政府의 自動車工業育成政策을 중심으로」『千葉商大論叢』26(3) [1988.12].

Kodama, Toshihiko. 小玉敏彥. 1991.「韓國에 있어서의 勞働組合關連法의 変遷에 대하여－1」『千葉商大論叢』29(2) [1991.9].

Kodama, Toshihiko. 小玉敏彥. 1991.「韓國에 있어서의 勞働組合關連法의 変遷에 대하여－2」『千葉商大論叢』29(3) [1991.12].

Kodama, Toshihiko. 小玉敏彥. 1991.「韓國의 家族法改正을 중심으로」『Jurist』(通号 988) [1991.10.15].

Kodama, Toshihiko. 小玉敏彥. 1993.「企業間關係의 日韓比較－日本型企業group과 韓國型企業group」(麻生 幸 ; 小玉 敏彥)『千葉商大論叢』31(1) [1993.6].

Kodama, Toshihiko. 小玉敏彥. 1995.「韓國工業化와 企業集団」『小玉敏彥』學文社, [1995.9].

Kodama, Toshihiko. 小玉敏彥. 1991.「韓國의 家族法改正을 중심으로」『Jurist』988: 80-82.

Koguma, Eiji. 小熊英二. 1996.「有色의 植民帝國－1920年前後의 日系移民排斥과 朝鮮統治論」酒井直樹(編)『Nationality의 脫構築』柏書房.

Koguma, Eiji. 小熊英二. 1998.「朝鮮출생의 日本人－朝鮮人衆議院議員 朴春琴」在日朝鮮人研究會(編)『코리언・마이너리티研究(1)』新幹社.

Koguma, Eiji. 小熊英二. 1998.『〈日本人〉의 境界－沖縄・Ainu・台湾・朝鮮 植民地支配에서 復歸運動까지』新曜社.

Kono, Michihiro. 河野通博. 1991.『世界地誌seminar I 新訂東아시아』東京: 大明堂.

Kozawa, Yasunori. 小澤康則. 1984.「韓國과 日本의 沿岸漁村比較調査report」1984年 6月 『日韓合同學術調査報告』 第二輯日韓漁村社會・経濟共同研究會.

Kozawa, Yasunori. 小澤康則. 1987.「在日韓國人一世와 二・三世의 比較硏究」『論文集』第20集 1987年 韓國外國語大學校.

Kozawa, Yasunori. 小澤康則. 1990.「韓國의 口頭伝承에 있어서의 禁止事項」『論文集』第23集 1990年 韓國外國語大學校.

Kozawa, Yasunori. 小澤康則. 1992.「日本과 韓國에 있어서의 俗信의 比較硏究 -動物의 事例를 중심으로」『論文集』第25集 1992年 韓國外國語大學校.

Kozawa, Yasunori. 小澤康則. 1992.「日本과 韓國에 있어서의 植物俗信語의 比較硏究」『日本文化硏究』第7号 韓國外國語大學校日本文化硏究所.

Kozawa, Yasunori. 小澤康則. 1996.「東石見의 俗信語-口承文化素描」『研究年報』第30号 東洋大學아시아・아프리카文化硏究所.

Kozawa, Yasunori. 小澤康則. 1996.「韓國禁忌語의 制裁表現에 관한 統計的分析」『論文集』第29集 韓國外國語大學校.

Kozawa, Yasunori. 小澤康則. 1997.「韓國新聞의 投書欄에서 보는 日本」『研究年報』31号 東洋大學아시아・아프리카文化硏究所.

Kozawa, Yasunori. 小澤康則. 1997.「日本島根縣의 俗信語」『民俗硏究』第7 1997年 安東大學校民俗學硏究所.

Kozawa, Yasunori. 小澤康則. 1998.「韓國의 禁忌語 -東海岸의 事例-」『研究年報』第32号 1998年 東洋大學아시아・아프리카文化硏究所.

Kozawa, Yasunori. 小澤康則. 1998.「氣候에 관한 俗信語의 韓・日比較 竹辺調査와 五十猛調査를 중심으로」『民俗硏究』第8輯 1998年 安東大學校民俗學硏究所.

Kozawa, Yasunori. 小澤康則. 1998.「講義評価에 보는 學生意識 -日本語會話授業에 期待하는 것」『日本硏究』12号 1998年 韓國外國語大學校日本文化硏究所.

Kozawa, Yasunori. 小澤康則. 1998.「竹辺青年會와 씨름同友會」(共同)『研究年報』第32号 1998年 東洋大學아시아・아프리카文化硏究所.

Kozawa, Yasunori. 小澤康則. 1998.『性과 年齡의 人類學』清水浩昭, 芳賀正明, 松本誠一. 岩田書院, [1998.7].

Kozawa, Yasunori. 小澤康則. 1999.「韓國 매스컴에 있어서의 天皇呼称論爭」『研究年報』第33号 1999年 東洋大學아시아・아프리카文化研究所.

Kozawa, Yasunori. 小澤康則. 2000.「漢字併用論爭에 보는 韓國」『研究年報』第34号 2000年 東洋大學아시아・아프리카文化研究所.

Kozawa, Yasunori. 小澤康則. 2000.「〈社會変動과 文化変動의 社會人類學的研究－韓國社會의 國際化에 관한 協同研究〉의 調査 (調査・研究活動－2000年度)」(松本誠一 ; 小澤康則)『아시아・아프리카文化研究所研究年報』(35).

Kumagai, Osamu. 熊谷治. 1972.「朝鮮半島에 있어서의 農耕儀礼로서의 綱引」『朝鮮學報』64: 1-13.

Kumagai, Osamu. 熊谷治. 1975.「朝鮮半島에 있어서의 火祭: 그 性格과 系譜」『季刊dolmen』7.

Kumagai, Osamu. 熊谷治. 1975.「洞祭: 그 本質 및 性格에 대하여」『朝鮮學報』74: 97-110.

Kumagai, Osamu. 熊谷治. 1978.「朝鮮半島에 있어서의 떠다니는 섬에 관한 伝說」『朝鮮學報』87: 101-111.

Kumagai, Osamu. 熊谷治. 1979.「朝鮮半島에 있어서의 팥에 관한 儀礼・習俗」『朝鮮學報』92: 1-15.

Kumagai, Osamu. 熊谷治. 1980.「『三國遺事』에 보이는 護法龍」國分直一博士古稀記念論集編纂委員會(編)『日本民族文化와 그 周辺: 國分直一博士古稀記念論集: (歷史・民族篇)』519-532, 下關: 新日本教育図書.

Kumagai, Osamu. 熊谷治. 1981.「朝鮮半島에 있어서의 匏瓜」『朝鮮學報』101: 29-38.

Kumagai, Osamu. 熊谷治. 1984.『東아시아의 民俗과 祭儀』東京: 雄山閣.

Kumakura, Isao. 熊倉功夫. 1976.「煎茶史序考: 日本과 朝鮮」『風俗』14(3): 1-19.

Kumekawa, Emiko. 粂川惠美子. 1975.「朝鮮의 民族衣裝에 대하여 1」『武藏野女子大學紀要』10: 109-123.

Kuramochi, Kazuo. 倉持和雄. 1993.「80年代後半韓國에 있어서의 農村人口의 流出과 農村家族構造의 変化에 관한 實証的考察: 忠南道四箇村落의 事例研究의 分析」『아시아研究』39(3): 1-34.

Kurata, Masahiko. 藏田雅彦. 2000.「아시아의 民族共生과 在日韓朝鮮人」橋內武이외 (編)『多文化共生社會에의 展望』日本評論社.

Kurita, Eiji. 栗田英二. 1991.「植民地下朝鮮의 神社와 神祠에 대하여」『西日本

宗教學雜誌』(通号 13).

Kurokawa, Kozo. 黑川幸三. 1979.「臼田甚五郎・崔仁鶴(編)『東北아시아民族說話의 比較研究』를 읽어」『國學院雜誌』80(4): 55-58.

Kusano, Taeko. 草野妙子. 1984.「韓國伝統音樂의 魅力을 살핀다」『現代코리아』242: 48-56.

Kusano, Taeko. 草野妙子. 1984.『아리랑의 歌: 韓國伝統音樂의 魅力을 살핀다』東京: 白水社.

Kusano, Taeko. 草野妙子. 1986.「아리랑/ 音樂/ 樂學軌範/ 樂器/ 伽倻琴/ 歌謠曲/ 奚琴/ 玄琴/ 國樂/ 散調/ 杖鼓/ 打令/ 도라지/ 舞踊/ 鳳仙花/ 民謠」伊藤亞人・大村益男・梶村秀樹・武田幸男(監修)『朝鮮을 아는 事典』東京: 平凡社.

Lee, Byoung-Nam. 李 炳男. 1998. 大胡欽一(編),「韓國고대에 있어서의 샤머니즘에 관한 일고찰－소도신앙(蘇塗信仰)을 중심으로」『아시아세계－그 구조와 원래의 의미를 중심으로(상)』, 八千代出版.

Lee, Chak-Yeon. 李 * 然. 1993.「歷史觀・歷史意識」溝口雄三・濱下武志・平石直昭・宮嶋博史(編)『交錯하는 아시아』(아시아에서 생각한다1) 159-188, 東京: 東京大學出版會.

Lee, Chang-Gi. 李 昌基. 2000.「韓國동족집단의 구성원리」『사회학잡지』17.

Lee, Cyung-Ja. 李 充子. 2000.「韓國의 식사방법」秋野晃司・小幡壯(編)『아시아의 식문화(食文化)』建帛社.

Lee, Doo-Hyun. 李 杜鉉. 2000.「강신무당(降神巫堂)의 鐵乞粒－동북아시아의 샤머니즘과 한국무속과 비교연구서설」崔吉城・日向一雅(編)『신화・종교・무속－한일비교문화의 시도』風響社.

Lee, Ho-San. 李 鎬山. 1999.「韓國의 샤머니즘－다큐멘터리 작품에 의한 고찰」『아시아文化研究』6, 國際아시아學會.

Lee, Hui-Yeong. 李熙永. 1966.「高麗朝歷代妃・嬪의 継承에 관한 一試論: 同姓不婚制의 形成過程에 있어서의 一現象의 究明」『民族學研究』31(1): 28-37.

Lee, In-Ja. 李 仁子. 1994.「묘(墓) 이야기 (<특집>여자는 종교에서 무엇을 갈망하는가)－(삶속의 종교감각)」『사상의 과학 第8次』(通号 20), [1994.9].

Lee, In-Ja. 李 仁子. 1994.「나와 일본어(모국어가 아닌 일본어<특집>)」『사상의 과학 第8次』(通号 15), [1994.4].

Lee, In-Ja. 李 仁子. 1996.「異문화에 있어서의 이주자의 아이덴티티표현의 중층성－재일교포의 묘(墓)를 중심으로」『民族學研究』61(3), [1996.12].

Lee, In-Ja. 李 仁子. 1999.「이주하는 〈삶(生)〉, 귀향하는 〈죽음(死)〉－어느 제주도출신 재일교포의 귀향송장의 사례」新谷尙紀(編)『강좌: 인간과 환경(9) 사후의 환경』昭和堂.

Lee, Jin-Young. 李 鎭榮. 1993. 渡辺欣雄,「민속지식론의 과제－오키나와(沖縄)의 지식인류학」『民族學研究』57(4) [1993.3].

Lee, Jin-Young. 李 鎭榮. 1993.「오키나와(沖縄)의 친족어휘의 사회문화적인 의미에 관한 예비적 고찰」『民族學研究』58(1) [1993.6].

Lee, Jin-Young. 李 鎭榮. 1999.『방일학숙연구자논문집. 제1권』한일문화교류기금, 한일문화교류기금, [1999.3].

Lee, Jin-Young. 李 鎭榮. 2000.「족보(族譜)와 역사인식－베트남과 한국」베트남사회문화연구회(編)『베트남의 社會와 文化』(2) 風響社.

Lee, Jin-Young. 李 鎭榮. 2002. 記念論集刊行會,『류큐(琉球·아시아의 민속과 역사』榕樹書林, 2002.7.

Lee, Kwang-Kyu. 李光圭. 1982.「韓國의 老人問題」『民族學研究』46(4): 410-421.

Lee, Kwang-Kyu. 李光圭. 1986.「韓國에 있어서의 農村家族의 変貌의 樣相」『커뮤니티』76: 29-53.

Lee, Kyeong-Sin. 李敬信. 1992.「韓國의 青少年의 學校給食에서 본 健康과 榮養狀態」『保險의 科學』34(21).

Lee, Kyeong-Won. 李景媛. 1997.『性別役割分業의 現況(意識과 實態 및 規定要因)에 관한 韓日比較研究: 韓國·春川市와 日本·奈良市에 있어서의 調査에서』調査報告書.

Lee, Man-Kap. 李萬甲. 1971.「戰後에 있어서의 韓國家族의 変化」『社會學評論』85: 82-90.

Lee, Peom-Chik. 李範稷. 1991.「朝鮮王朝에 있어서의 王權과 五礼」(淺井良純譯)『朝鮮學報』138: 45-52.

Lee, Sang-Ho. 李相鎬. 1997.「續·韓國의 전통적 소규모 뱀장어어업」『월간 민구(月刊民具)』29-11.

Lee, Sang-Jin. 李尙珍. 2001.「淺川巧의「조선관(朝鮮觀)」－식민지시대에 있어서의 그 업적을 중심으로」『人間文化論叢』4.

Lee, Sang-Ki. 李相禧. 1991.「韓·日關係40年(1945-1985): 韓國의 社會, 文化的変化」『季刊코리아나』4(3).

Lee, Seung-hyun. 李勝鉉. 2000.「書評 한국종교연구회편『한국종교문화사강의』」

『東京大學宗教學年報』(通号 18).

Lee, Sun-E. 李 善愛. 1996. 李 相高・李 善愛 (譯),「韓國의 전통적 소규모 뱀장어어업(1)」『民具 Monthly(マンスリー)』29(7) [1996.10].

Lee, Sun-E. 李 善愛. 1996. 李 相高・李 善愛 (譯),「韓國의 전통적 소규모 뱅장어어업(2)」『民具 Monthly(マンスリー)』29(8) [1996.11].

Lee, Sun-E. 李 善愛. 1997. 李 相高・李 善愛 (譯),「속・한국의 전통적 소규모 뱀장어어업」『民具 Monthly(マンスリー)』29(11) [1997.2].

Lee, Sun-E. 李 善愛. 1998.「염직(染織)의 전통기법을 배운다－전통적 염색의 기법을 찾아서(8) 濟州島의 감즙염색(柿澁染め)」『纖維製品消費科學』39(1) [1998.1].

Lee, Sun-E. 李 善愛. 1999.「한국의 출산문화」『宮崎公立大學人文學部紀要』7(1).

Lee, Sun-E. 李 善愛. 1999.「생식・출산・육아의 모노그래프－異문화속에서의 아기(5) 한국의 출산문화의 현재」『프리네이탈・케아(Prenatal care)』18(10) (通号 229), [1999.10].

Lee, Sun-E. 李 善愛. 2000.「바위가 많은 물가주변(磯)자원의 이용과 식문화에 관한 사례연구(1) 휴가나다(日向灘)연안을 중심으로」『宮崎公立大學人文學部紀要』8(1).

Lee, Sun-E. 李 善愛. 2001. 李善愛,『바다를 넘는 제주도의 해녀』明石書店, [2001.2].

Lee, Sun-E. 李 善愛. 2001.「어민의 생활－해녀의 삶을 중심으로 (特集 韓國의 海洋文化)」『月刊韓國文化』(通号 261) [2001.8].

Lee, Sun-E. 李 善愛. 2001. 藤田 明良・李 善愛・河原 典史,「섬에서 본 한반도와 타지역의 교류－제주도를 중심으로」『青丘學術論集』19 [2001.11].

Lee, Sun-E. 李 善愛. 2001.「비일상적 자원이용을 위한 전략: 휴가나다(日向灘) 대합바둑돌의 사례」『宮崎公立大學人文學部紀要』9(1).

Lee, Sun-E. 李 善愛. 2002.「휴가나다(日向灘)남부연안의 바위가 많은 물가주변(磯)자원이용에 관한 사례연구－울산과의 비교」『日本研究』25 [2002.4].

Lee, Sung-Woo. 李 盛雨. 1998.「한반도의 식문화(食文化)」石毛直道(監)・吉田集而(編)『강좌 식문화(1) 인류의 식문화』, 맛의 素食의 문화센터.

Lee, Sung-Woo. 李 盛雨. 1999. 鄭大聲・佐々木直子(譯),『한국요리문화사』, 平凡社.

Lee, To-Hyeon. 李杜鉉. 1981.「韓國의 野外仮面劇」『季刊民族學』15: 104-113.

Lee, To-Hyeon. 李杜鉉. 1990.『朝鮮芸能史』東京: 東京大學出版會.

Lee, Wol-Sun. 李月順. 1986.「韓國에 있어서의 女性의 現況과 展望:『女性白書』를 중심으로」『人間科學社會學・心理學硏究(關西大學大學院社會學硏究科院生協議會)』26: 59-74.

Lee, Young-Joo. 李 英珠. 2001.「혼인규칙에서 본 황실의 〈순혈통성〉-근대일본의 〈집안〉과 〈혈연〉」『日本民俗學』(通号 225) [2001.2].

Lee, Young-Sook. イ・ヨンスク. 1998. 佐伯 胖(編),「민족차별과 교육-스테레오타입과 〈중간존재〉」『이와테강좌(岩波講座) 현대의 교육-위기와 개혁(5) 공생교육』岩波書店.

Mabuchi, Kazuo. 馬淵和夫. 1982.「朝鮮半島의 古代地名」『地名의 世界: 地理』臨時增刊号: 160-161.

Makino, Nobuo. 牧野暢男. 1998.「社會變動下의 韓國의 女子大學: 動向과 現狀」『人間硏究』34: 57-68.

Makino, Tatsumi. 牧野巽. 1973.「朝鮮의 自然村을 중심으로 하여」『(鈴木榮太郎著作集Ⅴ) 朝鮮農村社會의 硏究』499-526, 東京: 未來社.

Manabe, Yuko. 眞鍋祐子. 1990.「韓國의 巫者을 눌러싼 社會關係: 都市化社會에서 사는 〈恨〉의 論理」『比較民俗學硏究』1.

Manabe, Yuko. 眞鍋祐子. 1990.「커뮤니티의 集团統一性에 對하는 巫祭의 機能-韓國・蘇來浦口의 豊漁祭」(眞鍋 祐子; 小笠原 眞)『소시오로기』35(2) [1990.10].

Manabe, Yuko. 眞鍋祐子. 1991.「韓國巫俗에 있어서의 死: 〈恨〉을 중심으로」『比較民俗學』3: 193-201.

Manabe, Yuko. 眞鍋祐子. 1994.「〈烈士〉의 誕生: 韓國運動圈의 死生觀을 중심으로」『SOSHIOROJI』39(2): 19-36.

Manabe, Yuko. 眞鍋祐子. 1994.「샤머니즘의 思想과 民衆運動」『月刊韓國文化』16(8): 13-18.

Manabe, Yuko. 眞鍋祐子. 1994.『恨의 人類學』崔吉城[他]. 平河出版社, [1994.8].

Manabe, Yuko. 眞鍋祐子. 1996.「干拓事業에 따른 伝統社會의 変動에 대하여: 忠淸南道瑞山郡浮石面倉里」『靑丘學術論集』8: 149-161.

Manabe, Yuko. 眞鍋祐子. 1996.「韓國의 民衆運動에 있어서의 殉教者神話의 形成: 全泰壹의 生과 死를 중심으로」『宗教과 社會』2: 46-67.

Manabe, Yuko. 眞鍋祐子. 1996.「韓國民衆運動속의 〈光州〉(1)」『月刊百科』408: 8-11.

Manabe, Yuko. 眞鍋祐子. 1996.「韓國民衆運動속의 〈光州〉(2): 〈民主聖地〉 光

州의 今」『月刊百科』409: 12-15.

Manabe, Yuko. 眞鍋祐子. 1996.『campus에 보는 異文化: 韓國살기의 素描』東京: 平河出版社.

Manabe, Yuko. 眞鍋祐子. 1997.「韓國・反日文化의 〈놀이〉와 〈진심〉」『三色旗』595: 24-29.

Manabe, Yuko. 眞鍋祐子. 1997.「韓國民衆運動속의 〈光州〉(3): 光州에 모이는 사람들」『月刊百科』411: 10-13.

Manabe, Yuko. 眞鍋祐子. 1997.「韓國民衆運動속의 〈光州〉(4): 民衆世界와 ideology의 사이」『月刊百科』417: 17-20.

Manabe, Yuko. 眞鍋祐子. 1997.『烈士의 誕生: 韓國의 民衆運動에 있어서의 恨의 力學』東京: 平河出版社.

Manabe, Yuko. 眞鍋祐子. 1998.「Simmel의 宗教社會學에서 본 韓國民衆運動의 理念: 民衆神學의 形成과 展開를 중심으로」『Simmel 研究會會報』4: 10-17.

Manabe, Yuko. 眞鍋祐子. 2000.「日本人學者들은 왜 韓國巫俗을 研究하는가: 自己內省에서 post modern의 民俗學으로 (創立25周年記念特集 地域研究25年: 地域研究의 新世代)」『筑波大學地域研究』18: 141-155.

Manabe, Yuko. 眞鍋祐子. 2000.『광주사건으로 읽는 현대 한국』東京: 平凡社.

Manabe, Yuko. 眞鍋祐子. 2001. 2000年度심포지엄「宗教의 〈臨界〉 混沌한 現代宗教에의 研究視座(관점, 견지)」記錄 (岩井 洋 ; 樫尾 直樹 ; 眞鍋 祐子 他)『宗教와 社會』(7).

Manabe, Yuko. 眞鍋祐子. 2001.「現代韓國의 〈巡礼〉와 民族主義－光州事件(1980年)以後 (生・老・死:日本人의 人生觀－內에서의 眼, 外에서의 眼)(死)」『國立歷史民俗博物館研究報告』91 [2001.3].

Maruyama, Koichi. 丸山孝一. 1978.「居住空間의 社會性: 韓國民家의 予備的調査報告」『九州人類學會報』6: 49-55.

Maruyama, Koichi. 丸山孝一. 1979.「韓國儒教의 保守와 革新에 관한 覺書: 특히 親族構造의 分析을 통하여」『廣大아시아研究』1: 25-37.

Maruyama, Koichi. 丸山孝一. 1979.「性의 社會的展開: 韓國社會의 경우」綾部恒雄(編)『人間의 一生: 文化人類學的探求』95-98, 京都: Academia出版會.

Maruyama, Koichi. 丸山孝一. 1980.「韓國社會에 있어서의 National아이덴디티의 形成」『九州大學教育學部比較教育文化研究施設紀要』31: 65-80.

Maruyama, Koichi. 丸山孝一. 1982.「儒教社會에 있어서의 헤어짐・자식과의

생이별」『教育과 医學』30(3): 45-51.

Maruyama, Koichi. 丸山孝一. 1982.「日系 및 韓國系移民社會에 있어서의 文化의 持續性과 変容過程」綾部恒雄(編)『아메리카民族文化의 研究』201-248, 東京: 弘文堂.

Maruyama, Koichi. 丸山孝一. 1982.「文化의 周辺性에 대하여: 韓國全羅南道巨文島의 事例에서」『九州大學教育學部比較教育文化研究施設紀要』33: 39-54.

Maruyama, Koichi. 丸山孝一. 1982.「離島文化의 求心性과 遠心性: 韓國巨文島의 事例를 중심으로 본 내셔널・아이덴디티」權藤与志夫(編)『發展途上國에 있어서의 내셔널・아이덴디티의 教育에 관한 比較研究』(昭和56年度科學研究費總合(A)報告) 26-31.

Maruyama, Koichi. 丸山孝一. 1983.「韓國社會에 있어서의 內와 外의 展開」江淵一公・伊藤亞人(編)『儀礼와 象徵: 文化人類學的考察』443-466, 福岡: 九州大學出版會.

Maruyama, Koichi. 丸山孝一. 1983.「都市의 中의 마이너리티: 在日朝鮮人의 戰後生活과 文化」廣島市(編)『廣島新史 都市民俗文化編』301-390, 廣島: 廣島市.

Maruyama, Koichi. 丸山孝一. 1985.「教育에 있어서의 中央文化의 遠心性과 求心性: 韓國全羅南道巨文島의 事例研究에서」弘中和彦(編)『戰後아시아諸國의 教育政策의 変容過程과 그 社會的文化的基盤에 관한 總合的比較研究』37-52.

Maruyama, Koichi. 丸山孝一. 1985.「教育에 있어서의 文化的多元主義와 meritocracy(그 2) 韓國系米人의 場合」『九州大學比較教育文化研究施設紀要』36: 1-19.

Maruyama, Koichi. 丸山孝一. 1986.「周緣文化의 持續性에 대하여: 특히 韓國島嶼社會의 사례를 중심으로」『九州大學教育學部比較教育文化研究施設紀要』37: 15-23.

Maruyama, Koichi. 丸山孝一. 1987.「韓國離島社會에 있어서의 儒教의 展開에 관한 一考察」『九州大學教育學部比較教育文化研究施設紀要』38: 35-46.

Maruyama, Koichi. 丸山孝一. 1990.「離島研究의 一視座: 巨文島의 사례」杉山晃一・櫻井哲男(編)『韓國社會의 文化人類學』23-38, 東京: 弘文堂.

Maruyama, Koichi. 丸山孝一. 1994.「離島에 있어서의 아이덴디티의 再形成－巨文島에 있어서의 英雄만들기 運動을 중심으로」『九州大學比較教育文化研究施設紀要』(通号 45) [1994.3].

Maruyama, Koichi. 丸山孝一. 1997.「文化動態論에서 본 地方文化의 vector: 韓國의 事例를 중심으로」『九州大學教育學部比較教育文化研究施設紀要』49: 1-15.

Masaoka, Nobuhiro. 政岡伸洋. 1998.「來訪神儀礼의 民俗學的背景－韓國濟州島의 事例에서(談話會 第773回)」『日本民俗學』(通号 216) [1998.10].

Masaoka, Nobuhiro. 政岡伸洋. 2000.「比較民俗研究의 可能性－韓國濟州島와 沖縄의 來訪神儀礼의 事例에서」『仏教大學總合研究所紀要』(通号 別冊) [2000.3].

Masaoka, Nobuhiro. 正岡伸洋. 1997.「韓國濟州島에 있어서의 葬送儀礼와 親族」孝本貢・八木透(編)『시리즈 比較家族(9) 家族과 死者祭祀』早稲田大學出版部.

Masuda, Shozo. 益田庄三. 1984.「地域振興의 現狀과 課題」日韓漁村社會・経済共同研究會『日韓合同學術調査報告 第2輯: 韓國慶尚北道平海邑厚浦里』246-268, 神戸: 日韓漁村社會・経済共同研究會事務局.

Masuda, Shozo. 益田庄三. 1986.「地域振興의 計畫・現狀・課題」日韓漁村社會・経済共同研究會『日韓合同學術調査報告 第4輯: 韓國全羅南道莞島郡』225-247, 神戸: 日韓漁村社會・経済共同研究會事務局.

Masuda, Shozo ed. 益田庄三(編). 1991.『日韓漁村의 比較研究: 社會・経済・文化를 중심으로』京都: 行路社.

Matsubara, Takatoshi. 松原孝俊. 1983.「朝鮮族譜와 始祖伝承(上)」『史淵』120: 151-186.

Matsubara, Takatoshi. 松原孝俊. 1983.「朝鮮族譜와 始祖伝承(中)」『史淵』121: 93-145.

Matsubara, Takatoshi. 松原孝俊. 1985.「계속되는 民俗芸能: 日常의 갈라진 곳으로서의 祝祭」『週刊朝日百科』483 (世界의 地理77中國・東아시아－大韓民國－): 194-196.

Matsubara, Takatoshi. 松原孝俊. 1985.「物語의 分析: 妖怪도깨비와 人間의 communication」『Eureka』17(2): 50-59.

Matsubara, Takatoshi. 松原孝俊. 1986.「姓・本貫・族譜」『基礎한글』1(8): 33-35.

Matsubara, Takatoshi. 松原孝俊. 1987.「朝鮮族譜에 나타난 系譜親과 그 変質過程」日本 KOREA學會(編)『第一次 KOREA學 國際交流세미나論文集』76-81, 黑龍江朝鮮民族出版社.

Matsubara, Takatoshi. 松原孝俊. 1990.「朝鮮에 있어서의 〈人間과 動物의 交涉〉譚」『口承文芸研究』13.

Matsubara, Takatoshi. 松原孝俊. 1990.「朝鮮에 있어서의 伝說生成의 mechanism에 대하여 主에 琉球王子漂着譚을 중심으로」『朝鮮學報』(通号 137) [1990.10].

Matsubara, Takatoshi. 松原孝俊. 1992.「神話學에서 본 〈廣開土王碑文〉」『朝鮮學報』(通号 145) [1992.10].

Matsubara, Takatoshi. 松原孝俊. 1992.『大谷森繁博士還暦記念朝鮮文學論叢』白川豊, 成澤勝. 杉山書店, [1992.2].

Matsubara, Takatoshi. 松原孝俊. 1994. 譯注「中國小說類의 韓來記事」(李 能雨 著 ; 松原 孝俊 譯(編))『言語文化論究』(通号 5).

Matsubara, Takatoshi. 松原孝俊. 1995.「日本古代의 伝承과 東아시아」『佐伯有清先生古稀記念會』吉川弘文館, [1995.3].

Matsubara, Takatoshi. 松原孝俊. 1995.『比較神話學의 展望』松原孝俊, 松村一男. 青土社, [1995.12].

Matsubara, Takatoshi. 松原孝俊. 1995.「姜南周의 詩的世界〔韓文〕」『言語文化論究』(通号 6).

Matsubara, Takatoshi. 松原孝俊. 1996.「『東國歲時記』의 著者洪錫謨에 대하여」『言語文化論究』(通号 7).

Matsubara, Takatoshi. 松原孝俊. 1997.「雨森芳洲와 對馬藩 〈韓語司〉에서의 教育評価方法에 대하여」(松原 孝俊 ; 趙 眞〔エイ〕)『言語科學』(通号 32).

Matsubara, Takatoshi. 松原孝俊. 1997.「嚴原語學所와 釜山草梁語學所의 沿革－明治初期의 朝鮮語教育을 중심으로」(松原 孝俊 ; 趙 眞〔エイ〕)『言語文化論究』(通号 8).

Matsubara, Takatoshi. 松原孝俊. 1997.「朝鮮神話研究의 最前線－檀君神話를 중심으로 하여 (特集 世界의 神話를 어떻게 읽을 것인가)」『Eureka』29(2) [1997.2].

Matsubara, Takatoshi. 松原孝俊. 1998.「朝鮮에서 琉球에, 琉球에서 朝鮮에 의 漂流年表」(小林 茂 ; 松原 孝俊 ; 六反田 豊)『歷代宝案研究』(通号 9) [1998.3].

Matsubara, Takatoshi. 松原孝俊. 1999.「韓國의 옛 이야기 (特集 昔話－通底하는 folk tales) (日本과 朝鮮半島・中國－激動의 아시아에서)」『國文學 解釋과 教材의 研究』44(14) (通号 649) [1999.12].

Matsubara, Takatoshi. 松原孝俊. 2001.「資料紹介 中國遼寧省立図書館藏朝鮮古籍書目」中國遼寧省立図書館特藏部『言語文化論究』(14).

Matsuda, Hirokimi. 松田博公. 1978.「八百比丘尼의 足跡: 日朝比較民俗學를 위하여」『民族學研究』43(2): 213-219.

Matsudaira, Makoto. 松平誠. 1995.「(아시아의 祭를 먹는다 3) 韓國의 島의 축의」『Chikuma』297: 36-37.

Matsudaira, Makoto. 松平誠. 2000.「朝鮮半島－食文化比較의 視点에서」秋野晃司・小幡壮(編)『아시아의 食文化』建帛社.

Matsumae, Takeshi. 松前健. 1970.「古代韓族의 龍蛇崇拜와 王權」『朝鮮學報』57: 1-22.

Matsumae, Takeshi. 松前健. 1973.「日本神話와 朝鮮」『日本神話의 可能性』154-177, 東京: 伝統と現代社.

Matsumae, Takeshi. 松前健. 1976.「柳東植著『朝鮮의 샤머니즘』」『朝鮮學報』80: 271-274.

Matsumae, Takeshi. 松前健. 1981.「古神道의 源流에 對한 一考察: 日本과 朝鮮의 古俗의 比較」『國學院雜誌』82(11): 1-17.

Matsumae, Takeshi. 松前健. 1982.「神話와 民俗에 있어서의 日本과 朝鮮」『朝鮮學報』102: 29-43.

Matsumae, Takeshi. 松前健. 1985.「神話이야기의 方式에서 본 日本과 韓國의 伝承」『Eureka』17(1): 215-219.

Matsumae, Takeshi. 松前健. 1985.『日本神話의 謎』269頁, 東京: 大和書房.

Matsumoto, Seiichi. Matsumoto, S. 1999.「Age and Local Community in Japan and Korea」『東洋大學社會學部紀要』36-2: 39-67.

Matsumoto, Seiichi. 松本誠一. 1995.「神話・天領・近代化－山陰・東石見의 漁村과 山村」(高橋 統一 ; 松本 誠一 ; 宇佐美 隆憲 他)『아시아・아프리카文化研究所研究年報』(通号 30).

Matsumoto, Seiichi. 松本誠一. 1998.「性과 年齡의 人類學」清水浩昭, 芳賀正明, 松本誠一(編)『岩田書院』[1998.7].

Matsumoto, Seiichi. 松本誠一. 2001.「Montreal의 韓人教會(1)」『아시아・아프리카文化研究所研究年報』(35).

Matsumoto, Seiichi. 松本誠一. 2002.「Montreal의 韓人教會(2)」『아시아・아프리카文化研究所研究年報』(36).

Matsumoto, Seiichi. 松本誠一. 1978.「秋葉隆博士에 대하여」千葉縣鄉土史研究

連絡協議會(編)『房總의 鄉土史』五周年特集号: 147-148.

Matsumoto, Seiichi. 松本誠一. 1980.「日韓兩國의 民俗文化: 宮座와 堂祭組織의 比較序說」高橋他(編)『文化人類學의 視角: 伝統과 現代』187-211, 東京: 犀書房.

Matsumoto, Seiichi. 松本誠一. 1981.「湖南堂山祭의 祭祀組織과 変化: 全羅南道長城郡長城邑Y里의 事例, 화주(化主)와 当家를 중심으로」『東洋大學아시아・아프리카文化研究所研究年報』15: 69-88.

Matsumoto, Seiichi. 松本誠一. 1982. (翻譯)張籌根著『韓國의 鄉土信仰』225, 第一書房.

Matsumoto, Seiichi. 松本誠一. 1984.「韓國의 〈自然部落〉에 대하여」『東洋大學아시아・아프리카文化研究所研究年報』18: 29-44.

Matsumoto, Seiichi. 松本誠一. 1984.「東海岸狗岩의 골맥이 洞神祭와 洞組織」日韓漁村社會・経濟共同研究會『日韓合同學術調査報告 第2輯: 韓國慶尙北道平海邑厚浦里』232-245, 神戶: 日韓漁村社會・経濟共同研究會事務局.

Matsumoto, Seiichi. 松本誠一. 1985.「韓國의 村축제: 全羅南道漁村의 事例」『教育과 医學』33(8): 65-70.

Matsumoto, Seiichi. 松本誠一. 1985.「韓國研究消息」『東洋大學아시아・아프리카文化研究所研究年報』19: 121-128.

Matsumoto, Seiichi. 松本誠一. 1985.「金賢準博士의 足跡」『白山社會學會會報』3: 19-22.

Matsumoto, Seiichi. 松本誠一. 1986. (解題와 譯)「韓相福著 〈韓國山村住民의 儀式과 信仰: 江原道平昌郡岩龍山二里 및 鳳山里의 事例〉」『東洋大學社會學部紀要』23(2): 141-164.

Matsumoto, Seiichi. 松本誠一. 1986.「韓國의 家族의 動向」『世界의 兒童과 母性: 海外福祉情報』21: 6-9.

Matsumoto, Seiichi. 松本誠一. 1986.「韓國의 指暦」『民博通信』33: 2-4.

Matsumoto, Seiichi. 松本誠一. 1986.「韓國大學消息」『東洋大學아시아・아프리카文化研究所研究年報』20: 173-178.

Matsumoto, Seiichi. 松本誠一. 1986.「書評 依田千百子著『朝鮮民俗文化의 研究: 朝鮮의 基層文化와 그 源流를 중심으로』」『現代코리아』259: 66-67.

Matsumoto, Seiichi. 松本誠一. 1987.「韓國의 〈小家族〉에 대하여」『家族研究年報』12: 85-94.

Matsumoto, Seiichi. 松本誠一. 1987.「축제의 諸相 Ⅱ韓國 1.祖先의 제사 (宗廟大祭) 2.地域의 축제 (江陵端午祭)」高橋統一・芳賀正明・松本誠一『文化人類學노트』103-112, 東京: 犀書房.

Matsumoto, Seiichi. 松本誠一. 1987.「民籍調査와〈隱居〉」『韓』107: 137-175.

Matsumoto, Seiichi. 松本誠一. 1987.「國民道德論과 朝鮮總督府－朝鮮民俗研究史노트로서」『東洋大學昭和61年度特別研究報告書』224-230.

Matsumoto, Seiichi. 松本誠一. 1988.「日本에 있어서의 文化人類學的韓國調査의 展開1960-1980 付・韓國研究者別著述目錄 日本人: 文化人類學・民俗學編1965-1987」『東洋大學社會學部紀要』25(2): 37-76.

Matsumoto, Seiichi. 松本誠一. 1988.「征韓論의前」『東洋大學昭和62年度特別研究報告書』200-213.

Matsumoto, Seiichi. 松本誠一. 1989.「開國以前의 朝鮮進出－周防馬島를 중심으로」『東洋大學昭和63年度 特別研究報告書』260-266.

Matsumoto, Seiichi. 松本誠一. 1990. (第11回國際人類學・民族學會議)「코리아ニスト部會報告」『民族學研究』54-4: 507.

Matsumoto, Seiichi. 松本誠一. 1990.「慶尙北道의 老人問題에 관한 地域特性과 兩班老人會」『東洋大學아시아・아프리카文化研究所 研究年報』24: 108-115.

Matsumoto, Seiichi. 松本誠一. 1990.「濟州島家族論의 檢討: 世帶規模의 東西差」竹田旦篇『民俗學의 進展과 課題』251-272, 東京: 國書刊行會.

Matsumoto, Seiichi. 松本誠一. 1990.「洞里의 境界」杉山晃一・櫻井哲男(編)『韓國社會의 文化人類學』56-71, 東京: 弘文堂.

Matsumoto, Seiichi. 松本誠一. 1991.「九州의 辺境人－熊本spirits・朝鮮觀」『東洋大學1990年度 特別研究報告書』114-119.

Matsumoto, Seiichi. 松本誠一. 1991. 秦恩淑譯「濟州島家族의 檢討－世帶規模의 東西差」(韓國語)『耽羅文化』11: 169-190, 濟州大學校.

Matsumoto, Seiichi. 松本誠一. 1991.「朝鮮半島問題에 맞춰」『philos東洋』5: 24-25.

Matsumoto, Seiichi. 松本誠一. 1992.「Japanese Social Anthropological Studies on Korea」『*Cahiers d'Extreme-Asie*(極東아시아研究紀要)』France國立極東學院京都支部・法寶義林研究所.

Matsumoto, Seiichi. 松本誠一. 1993.「眞理의 言葉－한글」『Satia』11.

Matsumoto, Seiichi. 松本誠一. 1993.「父母子女關係의 変化에 대하여 －韓日親

族과 家族의 予備的考察(韓國語)」『第1期博物館大學市民講座(韓國語)』353-367, 濟州市・濟州大學校博物館.

Matsumoto, Seiichi. 松本誠一. 1996.「韓國・朝鮮의 祖先祭祀」『事典 家族』570, 弘文堂.

Matsumoto, Seiichi. 松本誠一. 1996.「韓國의 村落과 家族」『東아시아의 村落과 家族 〈심포지엄의 記錄〉』22-24, 61-65, 京都: 佛教大學總合研究所.

Matsumoto, Seiichi. 松本誠一. 1997.「『海禁』時代의 山陰地域漂着民에 관한 小考(韓國語)」『民俗研究』7: 3-12, 安東大學校民俗學研究所.

Matsumoto, Seiichi. 松本誠一. 1998.「(書評)Kendall, Laurel. *Getting Married in Korea: Of Gen-der, Morality, and Modernity*」*Asian Folklore Studies*, LVI-2: 420-421, 南山大學.

Matsumoto, Seiichi. 松本誠一. 1998.「韓國東海岸・漁村社會의 近代化와 文化伝統－慶尙北道蔚珍郡竹辺의 事例」『東洋大學아시아・아프리카文化研究所 研究年報』32: 11-72(14-20, 26-33을 分担執筆).

Matsumoto, Seiichi. 松本誠一. 1998.「(書評)瀬地山角『東아시아의 家父長制 - gender의 比較社會學』」『家族社會學研究』10-2: 149-151.

Matsumoto, Seiichi. 松本誠一. 2000.「Montreal의 韓人墓碑銘」『東洋大學아시아・아프리카文化研究所 研究年報』34: 59-80.

Mikami, Tsugio. 三上次男. 1946.「桓仁調查行記: 高句麗의 遺跡을 묻어」『民族學研究』11(1): 81-104.

Min, Che. 閔濟. 1994.「韓國의 祭壇」『儀礼文化』10.

Miura, Kunio. 三浦國雄. 2000.「韓國의 道教研究瞥見」『아시아遊學』16.

Miura, Yoshiyuki. 三浦良幸. 1991.「東아시아의 箸文化考: 食事用二本箸의 起源과 展開」『比較民俗研究』3.

Miyahara, Toichi. 宮原兎一. 1966.「濟州島의 見聞」『日本民俗學會會報』44: 59-62.

Miyajima, Hiroshi. 宮嶋博史. 1994.「朝鮮兩班社會의 形成」溝口雄三・濱下武志・平石直昭・宮嶋博史(編) 『社會와 國家』 (아시아에서 생각한다 4) 131- 166, 東京: 東京大學出版會.

Miyajima, Hiroshi. 宮嶋博史. 1995.『兩班』東京: 中央公論社.

Miyao, Shigeyoshi. 宮尾滋良. 1994.『아시아演劇人類學의 世界』東京: 親書館.

Miyao, Shigeyoshi. 宮尾滋良. 1994.『宇宙를 비추는 身体: 아시아의 舞踊』東京: 親書館.

Miyara, Takahiro. 宮良高弘. 1982.「韓・琉門中制度의 比較」江守五夫・崔龍基(編)『韓國兩班同族制의 硏究』357-417, 東京: 第一書房.

Mori, Masao. 森雅雄. 1998.「史觀과 朝鮮의 近代」大胡欽一・加治明・佐々木宏幹・比嘉政夫・宮本勝(編)『社會과 象徵－人類學的 접근: 村武精一教授古稀記念論文集』岩田書院.

Morieda, Takashi and Asakura, Toshio. 森枝卓士・朝倉敏夫. 1986.『食은 韓國에 있다』東京: 弘文堂.

Morita, Yoshio. 森田芳夫. 1991.「朝鮮에 있어서의 日本統治의 終末과 文化面의 推移」『學習院大學東洋文化硏究所硏究報告』26.

Motomura, Hiroshi. 本村汎. 1983. (洪上旭과 共著)「日・韓兩國의 親子關係를 둘러싼 比較硏究: 親의 養育觀・養育態度와 子의 心理的社會特性을 중심으로」『大阪市立大學生活科學部紀要』31(分冊5): 345-362.

Motomura, Hiroshi. 本村汎. 1985. (洪上旭과 共著)「韓國에 보는 家族変動: 農村家族과 都市家族의 比較를 통하여」『大阪市立大學生活科學部紀要』33(分冊5): 245-258.

Mun, Hyo-Suk. 文孝淑. 1996.「韓國社會의 女性」關啓子・木本喜美子(編)『gender에서 世界를 읽는다』231-259, 東京: 明石書店.

Mun, Kyeong-Su. 文京洙. 1991.「韓國社會와 市民文化」『아시아・아프리카硏究』31(4).

Mun, Ok-Pyo. 文玉杓. 1999. (書評)「嶋陸奥彦・朝倉敏夫(編)『変貌하는 韓國社會: 1970~80年代의 人類學調査의 현장에서』」『民博通信』83: 33-39.

Mun, Ok-Seok. 文玉*. 1991.「日帝의 植民地 文化政策: 〈同化主義〉의 虛構」『季刊코리아나』4(2).

Murakami, Sachiko. 村上祥子. 1999.「꼭두각시놀이와 하치만코효신사(八幡古表神社)・코요신사(古要神社)의 쿠구츠시춤(傀儡子舞)」『朝鮮學報』(通号 171), [1999.4].

Muratake, Seiichi. 村武精一. 1966. (泉靖一과 連名)「朝鮮」日本民族學會(編)『日本民族學의 回顧와 展望』258-265, 東京: 民族學振興會.

Muratake, Seiichi. 村武精一. 1973.『家族의 社會人類學』東京: 弘文堂.

Muratake, Seiichi. 村武精一. 1977.「末弟子에서 본〈秋葉隆〉像」『社會人類學年報』3: 179-195.

Muratake, Seiichi. 村武精一. 1987.「秋葉隆」『文化人類學事典』東京: 弘文堂.

Naito, Kanji. 內藤完爾. 1979.「五島列島와 濟州島의 家族: 末子相續形成의 基盤」

山岡榮市教授古稀記念論文集編集委員會(編)『地域社會學의 諸問題: 山岡榮一教授古希記念論文集』1-26, 京都: 晃洋書房.

Nakadate, Ko. 中楯興. 1986.「莞島의 養殖業에 관한 노트」日韓漁村社會・經濟共同研究會『日韓合同學術調査報告 第4輯: 韓國全羅南道莞島郡』70-82, 神戶: 日韓漁村社會・経濟共同研究會事務局.

Nakagawa, Yuri. 仲川裕里. 1999.「韓國의 그리스도敎와 農村의 敎會」『未來』(通号 389) [1999.2].

Nakagawa, Yuri. 仲川裕里. 2001.「On the Concept of the Jip('House') in Korea」『人文科學年報』(31).

Nakajima, Mineo. 中嶋嶺雄. 1992.『東아시아比較研究』東京: 日本學術振興會.

Nakajima, Tomoko. 中島智子. 1997.「日本의 學校에 있어서의 在日朝鮮人教育」小林哲也・江淵一公(編)『多文化教育의 比較研究－教育에 있어서의 文化的同化와 多樣化』九州大學出版會.

Nakamura, Akira. 中村哲. 1983.「新羅王制起源과 샤머니즘」『法學志林』80(3・4): 1-56.

Nakamura, Keisuke. 中村啓佑. 2000.「韓國社會에 있어서의 家族關係의 変化－Hearing Survey를 중심으로」追手門大學아시아文化研究會(編)『多文化를 受容하는 아시아』和泉書房.

Nakamura, Shunsaku. 中村春作. 1999.「情報化와 儒教社會의 이미지」青木保・梶原景昭(編)『情報社會의 文化(1) 情報化와 아시아・이미지』東京大學出版會.

Nakamura, Teruko. 中村輝子. 1984.「韓國의 放浪芸一座: 男寺党」『季刊民族學』8(4): 110-118.

Nakamura, Yae. 中村八重. 2001.「現代韓國社會에 있어서의 火葬과 〈孝〉의 理念」『아시아社會文化研究』(2) [2001.3].

Nakane, Chie. 中根千枝. 1973.「沖縄・本土・中國・朝鮮의 同族・門中의 比較」日本民族學會(編)『沖縄의 民族學的研究: 民族社會와 世界像』東京: 民族學振興會.

Nakane, Chie. 中根千枝. 1973.「韓國素描」中根千枝(編)『韓國農村의 家族과 祭儀』東京: 東京大學出版會.

Nakane, Chie. 中根千枝. 1975.「韓國: 그 社會人類學的 위치」『朝鮮學報』75: 1-10.

Nakane, Chie. 中根千枝. 1975.「社會人類學과 東아시아」『民族學研究』39(4):

344-349.

Nakane, Chie. 中根千枝. 1978.「韓日兩國의 人間關係의 相違에 대하여: 崔在錫著『韓國人의 社會的性格』을 읽고」『日本의 社會構造』.

Nakane, Chie. 中根千枝. 1979.『社會構造의 分析: 아시아를 중심으로』(NHK大學講座) 111頁, 東京: 日本放送出版協會.

Nakane, Chie. 中根千枝. 1987.『社會人類學: 아시아諸社會의 考察』東京: 東京大學出版會.

Nakane, Chie ed. 中根千枝(編). 1973.『韓國農村의 家族과 祭儀』東京: 東京大學出版會.

Nakano, Yoshio. 中埜喜雄. 1982.「旧朝鮮의 冠婚葬祭習俗」『產大法學』16(3): 79-86.

Nakano, Yoshio. 中埜喜雄. 1984.「旧朝鮮의 年中行事: 日本法制史掌篇: 5」『產大法學』17(4): 29-38.

Naoe, Hiroji. 直江廣治. 1976.「中國・台湾・韓國」和歌森太郎(編)『日本民俗學講座5 民俗學의 方法』東京: 朝倉書店.

Naoe, Hiroji. 直江廣治. 1987.『民間信仰의 比較研究－比較民俗學에의 道』東京: 吉川弘文館.

Narisawa, Masaru. 成澤勝. 1979.「韓國民俗노트: 草墳 및 굿」『韓』8(3・4): 155-158.

Narisawa, Masaru. 成澤勝. 1983.「埋兒說話의 朝鮮的変容相에 대하여」『朝鮮學報』109: 57-76.

Nie Lili. 聶 莉莉. 2000. 丸山孝一(編),「현대 중국의 사회발전중에서 중국조선족」『중국내셔널리즘과 소수민족문화의 변용과정에 관한 문화인류학적 연구』, 文部省科學研究費補助金(基礎研究) 研究成果報告書.

Nikaido, Yuko. 二階堂裕子. 2000.「在日韓國人의 適応過程－어떤 一家의 life history에서」『市大社會學』(1).

Nikaido, Yuko. 二階堂裕子. 2001.「민족관계와 도시커뮤니티－재일교포사회와 일본인사회의 사례」『市大社會學』(2).

Nikkan Gyoson Syakai/Keizai Kyoudou Kenkyuukai. 日韓漁村社會・経濟共同研究會. 1984.『日韓合同學術調查報告 第2輯: 韓國慶尙北道平海邑厚浦里』神戶: 日韓漁村社會・経濟共同研究會事務局.

Nikkan Gyoson Syakai/Keizai Kyoudou Kenkyuukai. 日韓漁村社會・経濟共同研究會. 1986.『日韓合同學術調查報告 第4輯: 韓國全羅南道莞島郡』神戶:

日韓漁村社會・経濟共同硏究會事務局.

Nikkan Gyoson Syakai/Keizai Kyoudou Kenkyuukai. 日韓漁村社會・経濟共同硏究會. 1988. 『日韓合同學術調査報告 第6輯: 韓國慶尙南道忠武市와 그 周辺漁村』 神戶: 日韓漁村社會・経濟共同硏究會事務局.

Nishimura, Mieko. 西村美惠子. 1983. 「仙遊島의 民俗: 草墳을 중심으로」 『桐朋學園大學短期大學部紀要』 208-231.

Nishimura, Mieko. 西村美惠子. 1984. 「韓國의 草墳: 硏究誌에서 의 再檢討」 『民族學評論』 24: 56-71.

Nishimura, Mieko. 西村美惠子. 1985. 「韓國의 草墳을 둘러싼 民俗」 『日本民俗學』 161: 32-49.

Niwa, Izumi. 丹羽泉. 1988. 「韓國의 무당－Sobosal의 事例」 『社會科學 journal』 27(1) [1988.10].

Niwa, Izumi. 丹羽泉. 1989. 「韓國巫俗과 女性 (宗教와 女性〈特集〉)」 『宗教硏究』 63(1) [1989.6].

Niwa, Izumi. 丹羽泉. 1990. 「韓國巫俗과 샤머니즘－샤머니즘概念의 使用을 중심으로」 『社會科學 Journal』 29(1) [1990.10].

Niwa, Izumi. 丹羽泉. 1993. 「巫俗儀禮에 나타나는 動態論的인 視角」 『朝鮮學報』 (通号 149) [1993.10].

Niwa, Izumi. 丹羽泉. 1994. 「韓國鷄龍山新都內地域에 있어서의 新宗教教団에 대하여 正道教總本部의 事例를 통하여」 『西日本宗教學雜誌』 (通号 16).

Niwa, Izumi. 丹羽泉. 1995. 「〈무당〉과 〈教祖〉의 間」 『東京外國語大學論集』 (通号 51).

Niwa, Izumi. 丹羽泉. 1996. 『韓國百科』 秋月望, 丹羽泉. 大修館書店, [1996.7].

Niwa, Izumi. 丹羽泉. 1996. 「宮家準・鈴木正崇(編) 『東아시아의 샤머니즘과 民俗』」 『宗教硏究』 70(1) [1996.6].

Niwa, Izumi. 丹羽泉. 1999. 「왜 韓國에는 크리스천이 많은 것인가?－日韓宗教比較考」 『創文』 (通号 410) [1999.6].

Niwa, Izumi. 丹羽泉. 1999. 「韓國 (特集 아시아의 설날－新年의 축제와 民族)」 『月刊시니까』 10(1) [1999.1].

Niwa, Izumi. 丹羽泉. 1999. 「東京外國語大學에 있어서의 專攻語教育과 進級要件－教育目標와의 關連에서 (特集 大學에 있어서의 curriculum改革 等에 대하여)」 『大學과 學生』 (通号 407) [1999.2].

Niwa, Izumi. 丹羽泉. 2001. 「韓國을 歩く(7)鷄龍山新都內와 鄭鑑錄信仰」 『아시

아遊學』(31) [2001.9].

Niwa, Izumi. 丹羽泉. 2001.「無教會主義그리스도者 金教臣에 있어서의 〈愛國〉」『西日本宗教學雜誌』(23).

No, T'ae-Ton. 盧泰敦. 1992.「韓國民族의 形成過程에 관한 理論的考察」『朝鮮學報』142: 1-12.

No, Pu-Cha. 魯富子. 1992.「現代韓國의 都市에 있어서의 同族結合의 社會學的研究: 서울市의 宗親會의 事例」『日本社會學會報告』13: 155-182.

No, Pu-Cha. 魯富子. 1992.「現代韓國의 都市에 있어서의 同族結合의 社會學的研究: 서울市의 宗親會를 중심으로」『名古屋大學社會學論集』13: 155-182.

No, Pu-Cha. 魯富子. 1994.「下部組織에서 본 同姓同本集団의 結合의 一考察」『名古屋大學社會學論集』15.

No, Pu-Cha. 魯富子. 1997.「韓國의 都市에 있어서의 同姓結合이 意味하는 것: 非西洋社會의 都市化에 있어서의 〈歸屬的 機能組織〉의 生成과 変容」『社會學評論』48(1): 47-61.

No, Pu-Cha. 魯富子. 1997.「韓國의 都市에 있어서의 同姓組織의 全体構造: 서울市의 〈全州李氏大同宗約院〉을 事例로 하여」『SOSHIOROJI』41(3): 37-54.

No, Pu-Cha. 魯富子. 2000.「韓國」中田 實『世界의 住民組織－아시아와 歐米의 國際比較』自治体研究社.

No, Pu-Cha. 魯富子. 2000.「韓國의 都市化의 展開에 따르는 同姓結合의 生成과 変容」吉原和男・鈴木正崇・末成道男(編)『〈血緣〉의 再構築－東아시아에 있어서의 父系出自와 同姓結合』風響社.

Noguchi, Takashi ed. 野口隆編. 1976.『移民과 文化変容: 韓國陜川地域의 事例研究』東京: 日本學術振興會.

Nomura, Shinichi. 野村伸一. 1982.「韓國의 仮面戱의 場의 考察」『문예연구(芸文研究)』43: 1-26.

Nomura, Shinichi. 野村伸一. 1984.「楊州別山台戱에 대해」『民族學研究』49(2): 189-194.

Nomura, Shinichi. 野村伸一. 1985.『가면놀이(仮面戱)와 방랑예능인(放浪芸人): 韓國의 民俗芸能』, 東京: ありな書房.

Nomura, Shinichi. 野村伸一. 1986.「仮面劇/ 도깨비/ 農樂 [農樂의 확대와 호남농악(湖南農樂)]」伊藤亞人・大村益男・梶村秀樹・武田幸男(監修)『朝鮮을 이해하는 事典』, 東京: 平凡社.

Nomura, Shinichi. 野村伸一. 1987.『韓國의 民俗戱: 놀이와 巫의 世界로』, 東京: 平凡社.

Nomura, Shinichi. 野村伸一. 1994.「악귀를 쫓는 행사(儺)와 仮面劇의 諸相」宮家準・鈴木正崇(編)『東아시아의 샤머니즘과 民俗』, 東京: 頸草書房, 268-291.

Nomura, Shinichi. 野村伸一. 1996.「신굿: 신과 인간의 드라마(1)」『케이오기쥬크대학(慶應義塾大學)日吉紀要 言語・文化・커뮤니케이션』, 16: 51-82.

Nomura, Shinichi. 野村伸一. 1996.「신굿: 신과 인간의 드라마(2)」『케이오기쥬크대학(慶應義塾大學)日吉紀要 言語・文化・커뮤니케이션』, 17: 42-79.

Nomura, Shinichi. 野村伸一. 1997.「씻김굿의 芸能性」『民俗芸能研究』, 25: 18-41.

Nomura, Shinichi. 野村伸一. 1997.「돈이풀이: 단지(甕)를 푸는 의례」『케이오기쥬크대학(慶應義塾大學)日吉紀要 言語・文化・커뮤니케이션』, 19: 116-140.

Nomura, Shinichi. 野村伸一. 1997.「신굿: 신과 인간의 드라마(3)」(原文: 文武秉),『케이오기쥬크대학(慶應義塾大學)日吉紀要 言語・文化・커뮤니케이션』, 18: 68-137.

Nomura, Shinichi. 野村伸一. 1999.「濟州島의 굿의 芸術性」鈴木正崇・野村伸一(編)『仮面과 巫俗의 研究: 日本과 中國』, 東京: 第一書房, 203-244.

Nomura, Shinichi. 野村伸一. 1999.「동아시아해: 배(船)의 往來」宮家準(編)『民俗宗教의 地平』, 東京: 春秋社, 251-274.

Nomura, Shin'ichi. 野村伸一. 1987.「뚱딴지(頓珍漢)와 동문서답(東問西答)－朝鮮語의 욕설(辱說)을 기초로」『言語生活』(通号 428), [1987.7].

Nomura, Shin'ichi. 野村伸一. 1992.「日常語에서 본 朝鮮文化叙說」『예문연구(芸文研究)』(通号 60).

Nomura, Shin'ichi. 野村伸一. 1993.「春香伝의 우주론」『예문연구(芸文研究)』(通号 64).

Nomura, Shin'ichi. 野村伸一. 1993.「日常語에서 본 朝鮮文化－서설(叙說)2－」『예문연구(芸文研究)』(通号 62).

Nomura, Shin'ichi. 野村伸一. 1994.「朝鮮의 年末年始의 芸能 (아시아의 視点에서－民俗芸能研究의 하나의 方向<〔民俗芸能〕學會設立10周年記念심포지엄>)」『民俗芸能研究.』(通号 20), [1994.11].

Nomura, Shin'ichi. 野村伸一. 1995.「巫와 芸能者의 아시아」『中公新書』, 中央公論社, [1995.11].

Nomura, Shin'ichi. 野村伸一. 1999. 鈴木正崇・野村伸一,『仮面과 巫俗의 研究』, 第一書房, [1999.5].

Nomura, Shin'ichi. 野村伸一. 1999. 黃 迪仁・野村 伸一(譯),「韓國의 〈農業・農村基本法(案)〉에 대한 管見」1998年9月3日付け『法律新聞』「研究論壇」에서,『農政調査時報』(通号 514), [1999.7].

Nomura, Shin'ichi. 野村伸一. 2000.「보이는 民俗, 보이지 않는 民俗 (特集 地方文化－濟州道)」『月刊韓國文化』(通号 252), [2000.11].

Nomura, Shin'ichi. 野村伸一. 2000. 星野紘・野村伸一,「노래(歌)・춤(踊り)・기도(祈り)의 아시아」『遊學叢書 ; 10』, 勉誠出版, [2000.11].

Nomura, Shin'ichi. 野村伸一. 2001.「동아시아해 周辺의 女神信仰라는 視点 (特集 東아시아해 周辺의 女性祭祀와 女神信仰)」『케이오기쥬크대학(慶応義塾大學)日吉紀要 言語・文化・커뮤니케이션(26)』.

Nomura, Shin'ichi. 野村伸一. 2001.「特集 村山智順가 본 朝鮮民俗」『自然과 文化』(通号 66).

Nomura, Shin'ichi. 野村伸一. 2002.「朝鮮文化史에 있어서의 死者靈의 공양(供養)」『케이오기쥬크대학(慶応義塾大學)日吉紀要 言語・文化・커뮤니케이션』(28).

Nomura, Shin'ichi. 野村伸一. 2002.「잊혀진 芸能史, 序說(2)同時代史의 芸能空間라는 視点에서」『朝鮮文化研究』(9).

Nomura, Shin'ichi. 野村伸一. 2002.「李能和[朝鮮의 巫俗]註(下)」『케이오기쥬크대학(慶応義塾大學) 日吉紀要 言語・文化・커뮤니케이션』(29).

Nomura, Shin'ichi. 野村伸一. 2002.「李能和[朝鮮의 巫俗]註(上)」『케이오기쥬크대학(慶応義塾大學) 日吉紀要 言語・文化・커뮤니케이션』(28).

Nomura, Shin'ichi. 野村伸一. 1999. 鈴木正崇・野村伸一(編),「최초의 가면놀이(仮面戯)－소유물의 소생」『仮面과 巫俗의 研究－日本과 韓國』, 第一書房.

Nomura, Shin'ichi. 野村伸一. 1999. 鈴木正崇・野村伸一(編),「濟州島의 굿의 芸能性」『仮面과 巫俗의 研究－日本과 韓國』, 第一書房.

Nomura, Takafumi 野村孝文. 1981.『朝鮮의 民家: 風土・空間・意匠』, 京都: 學芸出版社.

Nozaki, Mitsuhiko. 野崎充彦. 1982.「關西에 있어서의 朝鮮關係專門의 私設図書館에 대하여 (報告) (図書館서비스의 확대와 심화〈特集〉)－(図書館서비스에서 소외되는 사람들)」『図書館界』34(1), [1982.5].

Nozaki, Mitsuhiko. 野崎充彦. 1986. 薛在英(著)・野崎充彦(譯),「석주검(石洲檢)

의 生涯와 文學」『朝鮮學報』(通号 119・120), [1986.7].

Nozaki, Mitsuhiko. 野崎充彦. 1986.「〈胡人採宝譚〉의 朝鮮的 展開－〈허생별전(許生別伝)〉을 중심으로」『朝鮮學報』(通号 121), [1986.10].

Nozaki, Mitsuhiko. 野崎充彦. 1990.『朝鮮의 道教』車柱環[他], 人文書院, [1990.6].

Nozaki, Mitsuhiko. 野崎充彦. 1992.「現代韓國의 風水說」『人文研究』44(1).

Nozaki, Mitsuhiko. 野崎充彦. 1992. 白川豊, 成澤勝.杉,『大谷森繁博士 환갑기념 朝鮮文學論叢』, 山書店, [1992.2].

Nozaki, Mitsuhiko. 野崎充彦. 1993. 韋旭昇[他],『中國古典文學과 朝鮮』, 研文出版, [1999.3].

Nozaki, Mitsuhiko. 野崎充彦. 1994.「〈용재총화(慵齋叢話)〉－15世紀朝鮮士大夫의 시야(視野)와 이야기에 대하여」『人文研究』46(8).

Nozaki, Mitsuhiko. 野崎充彦. 1994.『韓國의 風水師들－지금 소생하는 龍脈』, 京都: 人文書院.

Nozaki, Mitsuhiko. 野崎充彦. 1995. 鄭在書(1994),「不死의 神話와 思想－山海経・抱朴子・列仙伝・神仙伝에 대한 研究」〔原文한글文字〕,『東方宗教』(通号 85), [1995.5].

Nozaki, Mitsuhiko. 野崎充彦. 1996.「朝鮮斷脈說의 形成에 대하여」『人文研究』48(1).

Nozaki, Mitsuhiko. 野崎充彦. 1996.「朝鮮의 이야기(4)奇跡의 僧들－海東仏教異人伝」『月刊しにか』7(7), [1996.7].

Nozaki, Mitsuhiko. 野崎充彦. 1996.「朝鮮의 이야기(5)패관(稗官)文學의 系譜－서브컬쳐로의 관심」『月刊しにか』7(8), [1996.8].

Nozaki, Mitsuhiko. 野崎充彦. 1996.「朝鮮의 이야기(6)金時習・許〔인〕・林巨正－抵抗과 反逆의 精神」『月刊しにか』7(9), [1996.9].

Nozaki, Mitsuhiko. 野崎充彦. 1996.「朝鮮의 이야기(7)軍談小説－상처(傷痕)의 克服」『月刊しにか』7(10), [1996.10].

Nozaki, Mitsuhiko. 野崎充彦. 1996.「朝鮮의 이야기(8)야담(野談)의 世界－李朝社會의 万華鏡」『月刊しにか』7(11), [1996.11].

Nozaki, Mitsuhiko. 野崎充彦. 1996.「朝鮮의 이야기(9)實學派・朴趾源의 時代－〈儒〉냐, 세련되지 않아(クサイのう)」『月刊しにか』7(12), [1996.12].

Nozaki, Mitsuhiko. 野崎充彦. 1997.「朝鮮의 이야기(10)판소리－삼라만상(森羅万象)의 소리」『月刊しにか』8(1), [1997.1].

Nozaki, Mitsuhiko. 野崎充彦. 1997.「朝鮮의 이야기(11)朝鮮의 女性像－위먼 인

코리아」『月刊しにか』8(2), [1997.2].

Nozaki, Mitsuhiko. 野崎充彦. 1997.「朝鮮의 이야기(12)〈最終回〉朝鮮의 이야기 전집」『月刊しにか』8(3), [1997.3].

Nozaki, Mitsuhiko. 野崎充彦. 1997. 山田 宗睦・狩俣 惠一・野崎 充彦(他),「【컬럼】 아시아의 꽃 기행 (特集 花의 文化史－아시아의 꽃과 사람들)」『月刊しにか』8(9), [1997.9].

Nozaki, Mitsuhiko. 野崎充彦. 1997.「檀君의 位相－固有와 外來의 상극(相克) (特集 近代朝鮮에 있어서의 伝統文化의 "發見")」『朝鮮史硏究會論文集』(通号 35), [1997.10].

Nozaki, Mitsuhiko. 野崎充彦. 1997. 野崎 充彦(譯),「資料・人間의 証言－아시아의 心으로부터 배우다」『解放教育』27(14), [1997.12].

Nozaki, Mitsuhiko. 野崎充彦. 1998.「世紀末: 韓國의 風水思想 (特集 아시아의 風水・日本의 家相) (아시아의 風水論의 現在)」『建築雜誌』113 (通号 1417), [1998.1].

Nozaki, Mitsuhiko. 野崎充彦. 1998.『朝鮮이야기』, 大修館書店, 1998.6.(あじあブックス ; 2).

Nozaki, Mitsuhiko. 野崎充彦. 1999.「紹介〈韓國漢文學硏究〉」『東方』(通号 217), [1999.3].

Nozaki, Mitsuhiko. 野崎充彦. 1999.「朝鮮의 에로스・일탈하는 性(特集 교향(交響)하는 에로스)」『아시아 놀면서 배우기(遊學)』(通号 8), [1999.9].

Nozaki, Mitsuhiko. 野崎充彦. 2000.「핀스試論－朝鮮盲僧의 占卜・呪詛・祈雨에 대해서」『人文硏究52(4分冊)』.

Nozaki, Mitsuhiko. 野崎充彦. 2000.「朝鮮의 漢文學－表現과 手段의 괴리(乖離)를 중심으로 (特集 아시아文化圈의 中國文學)」『아시아 놀면서 배우기』(12), [2000.1].

Nozaki, Mitsuhiko. 野崎充彦. 2000.〔金敬鎭〕[他],『청구야담(靑邱野談)』, 平凡社, [2000.5](東洋文庫).

Nozaki, Mitsuhiko. 野崎充彦. 2000.「도교(道教)의 朝鮮化에 대하여」『아시아 놀면서 배우기(遊學)』16.

Nozaki, Mitsuhiko. 野崎充彦. 2001.「조선왕조기담집(朝鮮王朝奇譚集) 야담(野談)의 世界(1)序論을 대신해」『月刊韓國文化』(通号 257), [2001.4].

Nozaki, Mitsuhiko. 野崎充彦. 2001.「해외학술동향(海外學界動向)〈韓國道教文化學會 國際學術大會〉報告記」『동방종교(東方宗教)』(97), [2001.5].

Nozaki, Mitsuhiko. 野崎充彦. 2001.「조선왕조기담집(朝鮮王朝奇譚集) 야담(野談)의 世界(2)朝鮮王朝前期의 패관(稗官)文學(1)」『月刊韓國文化』(通号 258), [2001.5].

Nozaki, Mitsuhiko. 野崎充彦. 2001.「조선왕조기담집(朝鮮王朝奇譚集) 야담(野談)의 世界(3)朝鮮王朝前期의 패관(稗官)文學(2)」『月刊韓國文化』(通号 259), [2001.6].

Nozaki, Mitsuhiko. 野崎充彦. 2001.「조선왕조기담집(朝鮮王朝奇譚集) 야담(野談)의 世界(4)朝鮮王朝前期의 패관(稗官)文學(3)『용재총화(慵齋叢話)』의 世界(上)」『月刊韓國文化』(通号 260), [2001.7].

Nozaki, Mitsuhiko. 野崎充彦. 2001.「조선왕조기담집(朝鮮王朝奇譚集) 야담(野談)의 世界(5)朝鮮王朝前期의 패관(稗官)文學(4)『용재총화(慵齋叢話)』의 世界(中－1)」『月刊韓國文化』(通号 261), [2001.8].

Nozaki, Mitsuhiko. 野崎充彦. 2001.「조선왕조기담집(朝鮮王朝奇譚集) 야담(野談)의 世界(6)朝鮮王朝前期의 패관(稗官)文學(5)『용재총화(慵齋叢話)』의 世界(中－2)」『月刊韓國文化』(通号 262), [2001.9].

Nozaki, Mitsuhiko. 野崎充彦. 2001.「조선왕조기담집(朝鮮王朝奇譚集) 야담(野談)의 世界(7)朝鮮王朝前期의 패관(稗官)文學(6)『용재총화(慵齋叢話)』의 世界(下－1)」『月刊韓國文化』(通号 263), [2001.10].

Nozaki, Mitsuhiko. 野崎充彦. 2001. 遊佐昇, 野崎充彦, 増尾伸一郎.雄山閣,『아시아 諸地域과 道教』, [2001.10](講座道教 ; 第6卷).

Nozaki, Mitsuhiko. 野崎充彦. 2001. 徐永洙[他],『만화 이야기韓國史. 1』, 國書刊行會, [2001.11].

Nozaki, Mitsuhiko. 野崎充彦. 2001. 徐永洙[他],『만화 이야기韓國史. 2』, 國書刊行會, [2001.11].

Nozaki, Mitsuhiko. 野崎充彦. 2001. 徐永洙[他],『만화 이야기韓國史. 3』, 國書刊行會, [2001.11].

Nozaki, Mitsuhiko. 野崎充彦. 2001.「조선왕조기담집(朝鮮王朝奇譚集) 야담(野談)의 世界(8)朝鮮王朝前期의 패관(稗官)文學(7)『용재총화(慵齋叢話)』의 世界(下－2)」『月刊韓國文化』(通号 264), [2001.11].

Nozaki, Mitsuhiko. 野崎充彦. 2001.「조선왕조기담집(朝鮮王朝奇譚集) 야담(野談)의 世界(9)朝鮮王朝前期의 패관(稗官)文學(8)『용재총화(慵齋叢話)』의 世界(下－3)」『月刊韓國文化』(通号 265), [2001.12].

Nozaki, Mitsuhiko. 野崎充彦. 2002.「『友에 친구』를 해독하기 위해」『책이야기』

8(3) (通号 82), [2002.3].

Nozaki, Mitsuhiko. 野崎充彦. 2002.『조선문학논총(朝鮮文學論叢)』, 大谷森繁博士古稀記念朝鮮文學論叢刊行委員會, 白帝社, [2002.3].

Nozaki, Mitsuhiko. 野崎充彦. 2002.「조선왕조기담집(朝鮮王朝奇譚集) 야담(野談)의 世界(10)朝鮮의 異人譚(1)」『月刊韓國文化』(通号 269), [2002.4].

Nozaki, Mitsuhiko. 野崎充彦. 2002.「조선왕조기담집(朝鮮王朝奇譚集) 야담(野談)의 世界(11)朝鮮의 異人譚(2)」『月刊韓國文化』(通号 270), [2002.5].

Nozaki, Mitsuhiko. 野崎充彦. 2002.「조선왕조기담집(朝鮮王朝奇譚集) 야담(野談)의 世界(12)朝鮮의 異人譚(3)」『月刊韓國文化』(通号 271), [2002.6].

Nozaki, Mitsuhiko. 野崎充彦. 2002.「조선왕조기담집(朝鮮王朝奇譚集) 야담(野談)의 世界(13)朝鮮의 異人譚(4)」『月刊韓國文化』(通号 272), [2002.7].

Nozaki, Mitsuhiko. 野崎充彦. 2002.「조선왕조기담집(朝鮮王朝奇譚集) 야담(野談)의 世界(14)朝鮮의 異人譚(5)」『月刊韓國文化』(通号 273), [2002.8].

Nozaki, Mitsuhiko. 野崎充彦. 2002.「조선왕조기담집(朝鮮王朝奇譚集) 야담(野談)의 世界(15)朝鮮의 方術譚(1)」『月刊韓國文化』(通号 274), [2002.9].

Nozaki, Mitsuhiko. 野崎充彦. 2002.「조선왕조기담집(朝鮮王朝奇譚集) 야담(野談)의 世界(16)朝鮮의 方術譚(2)」『月刊韓國文化』(通号 275), [2002.10].

Nozaki, Mitsuhiko. 野崎充彦. 2002.「조선왕조기담집(朝鮮王朝奇譚集) 야담(野談)의 世界(17)朝鮮의 方術譚(3)」『月刊韓國文化』(通号 276), [2002.11].

Nozaki, Mitsuhiko. 野崎充彦. 2002.「조선왕조기담집(朝鮮王朝奇譚集) 야담(野談)의 世界(18・最終回)現代에 사는 이방인(異人)들」『月刊韓國文化』(通号 277), [2002.12].

Nozaki, Mitsuhiko. 野崎充彦. 2003.「자생풍수(自生風水)의 방향 特集 風水의 歷史와 現代」『아시아 놀면서 배우기(遊學)』(47), [2003.1].

O Mee-Hee. 吳 美喜. 1997.「현대 한국인과 일본인의 〈승낙(甘え)〉에 관한 일고찰」『政治學研究論集』5.

O, Chi-Eun. 吳知恩. 1994.「韓國의 카톨릭 〈교우촌(教友村)〉 共同体에 있어서의 女性의 地位: 전라북도(全羅北道) 천호동(天呼洞)에서의 사례연구(事例研究)」『SOSHIOROJI』39(2): 37-54.

O, Chi-Eun. 吳知恩. 1994.「조상숭배의례(祖先崇拝儀礼)와 女性의 역할(役割): 韓國의 한 카톨릭 〈교우촌(教友村)〉을 사례로서」『京都社會學年報』2: 19-37.

Obayashi, Taryo. 大林太良. 1972. (金兩基와 對談)「日韓의 고대기층문화(古代

基層文化): 아시아의 지적 교류의 시도」『아시아 리뷰』3月号: 132-141.
Obayashi, Taryo. 大林太良. 1973.『벼농사의 神話』, 東京: 弘文堂.
Obayashi, Taryo. 大林太良. 1977.「日本神話와 朝鮮神話는 어떠한 關係에 있는가」『國文學 解釋과 教材의 硏究』22(11): 25-28.
Obayashi, Taryo. 大林太良 1977『邪馬台國: 문신(入墨)과 본쵸(ポンチョ)와 히미코(卑弥呼)』, 東京: 中央公論社.
Obayashi, Taryo. 大林太良. 1984.『東아시아의 왕권신화(王權神話): 日本・朝鮮・류큐(琉球)』, 東京: 弘文堂.
Obayashi, Taryo. 大林太良. 1987. 大林太良(編),「도래인(渡來人)의 家族과 親族集団」『日本의 古代11 우지(ウヂ)와 이에』, 東京: 中央公論社, 259-282.
Obayashi, Taryo. 大林太良. 1993.「東아시아의 수전문화(水稻文化): 正月行事」『月刊시니카』4(8).
Ogasawara, Shin. 小笠原眞. 1976.「韓國의 장송의례(葬送儀礼): 경상남도 내곡리(慶尙南道內谷里)의 사례」『大谷學報』55(4): 34-46.
Ogasawara, Shin. 小笠原眞. 1993.「韓國의 장례(葬礼)」『正論』3月号: 216-220.
Ogasawara, Shin and Manabe, Yuko. 小笠原眞・眞鍋祐子. 1986.「韓國社會와 무속(巫俗): 近代化와 巫俗의 変容」『奈良教育大學紀要』35(1): 77-99.
Ogasawara, Shin and Manabe, Yuko. 小笠原眞・眞鍋祐子. 1990.「커뮤니티의 집단통일성(集団統一性)에 대한 무속제례(巫祭)의 기능: 韓國・소래포구(蘇來浦口)의 풍어제(豊漁祭)」『SOSHIOROJIKUSU』35(2): 143-158.
Ogawa, Haruhisa. 小川晴久. 1997.『朝鮮文化史의 사람들』花伝社.
Ogawa, Toru. 小川徹. 1957.「南朝鮮의 한 農村에 있어서의 村落生活과 民具에 대하여: 1936年 경상남도(慶尙南道) 울산읍(蔚山邑) 달리(達里)조사 개인보고」『민족학연구(民族學硏究)』21(4): 259-269.
Ohata, Hiroshi. 大畑裕嗣. 1986.「1920年代의 〈東亞日報〉 社說에 있어서의 社會運動論」『新聞學評論』(通号 35), [1986.3].
Ohata, Hiroshi. 大畑裕嗣. 1986. 大畑 裕嗣・三上 俊治,「關東大震災下의 '朝鮮人' 報道와 論調－上」『東京大學新聞硏究所紀要』(通号 35).
Ohata, Hiroshi. 大畑裕嗣. 1986. 三上 俊治・大畑 裕嗣,「關東大震災下의 '朝鮮人' 報道의 分析」『東洋大學社會學硏究所年報』(通号 18).
Ohata, Hiroshi. 大畑裕嗣. 1987. 大畑 裕嗣・三上 俊治,「關東大震災下의 '朝鮮人' 報道와 論調－下－」『東京大學新聞硏究所紀要』(通号 36), [1987.3].
Ohata, Hiroshi. 大畑裕嗣. 1989.「朝鮮獨立運動의 커뮤니케이션戰略－1920年代

의 안창호(安昌浩)와 신채호(申采浩)를 중심으로」『東京大學新聞研究所紀要』(通号 39).

Ohata, Hiroshi. 大畑裕嗣. 1990.『高度情報社會의 커뮤니케이션』, 東京大學新聞研究所, [1990.3].

Ohata, Hiroshi. 大畑裕嗣. 1994.「韓國에 있어서의 市民社會論의 動向－〈韓國의 國家와 市民社會〉를 읽는다」『思想』(通号 844) [1994.10].

Ohata, Hiroshi. 大畑裕嗣. 1996.『創立三十周年記念論文集. 社會學部篇』流通経濟大學創立三十周年記念論文集編集委員會. 流通経濟大學出版會, [1996.3].

Ohata, ~Hiroshi. 大畑裕嗣. 1997.「〈民主化〉의 運命을 짊어질 수 있는가－90年代韓國新聞界의 斷面(韓國)(亞州言論)」『新聞研究』(通号 551), [1997.6].

Ohata, Hiroshi. 大畑裕嗣. 1989.「韓國 〈民族言論〉의 어제와 내일: 〈東亞日報〉」『東京大學新聞研究所新聞資料센터뉴스』 8: 4-6.

Ohata, Hiroshi. 大畑裕嗣. 1996.「韓國・仁川의 市民運動의 特徵: 韓國의 〈새로운 社會運動〉」流通経濟大學創立 三十周年記念論文集編集委員會(編)『創立三十周年記念論文集 社會學部篇』.

Ohno, Yuji. 大野祐二. 1995.「촌락제사(村落祭祀)에서 중요무형문화재(重要無形文化財)로－韓國・은산별신제(恩山別神祭)의 事例」『朝鮮學報』(通号 157), [1995.10].

Ohno, Yuji. 大野祐二. 1998.「제2의 故鄕 〈아라카와구(荒川區) 미카와시마(三河島)〉－고내리(高內里)에서의 사람들의 事例 (特集 濟州島世界)」『地理』 43(5), [1998.05].

Ohno, Yuji. 大野祐二. 2000.「韓國의 한 仏教寺院의 素描－A郡의 事例에서」櫻井德太郎(編)『샤머니즘과 그 周辺』, 第一書房.

Ohno, Yuji. 大野祐二. 1993.「在日韓國・朝鮮人社會에 있어서의 仏教寺院과 샤머니즘」『在日韓國・朝鮮人社會의 宗教들과 에스니시티－에 관한 종합적 연구』53-61,『科研費研究成果報告書(研究代表者: 飯田剛史)』.

Ohno, Yuji. 大野祐二. 1995.「村落祭祀에서 無形文化財로」『朝鮮學報』157号, 朝鮮學會.

Ohno, Yuji. 大野祐二. 1996.「伝統文化의 再生과 그 後」『青丘學術論集』第8集, 韓國文化研究振興財団.

Ohno, Yuji. 大野祐二. 1997.「불교(仏教)」『더욱 알고 싶은 韓國1』1:01-107, 弘文堂.

Ohno, Yuji. 大野祐二. 1998.「觀光開發에 있어서의 〈百濟文化〉의 表象」『研究

報告』 第6号, 旅의 文化研究所.

Ohno, Yuji. 大野祐二. 1998.「第二의 故鄕 〈미카와시마(三河島)〉」『月刊地理』 43巻5号, 古今書院.

Ohno, Yuji. 大野祐二. 1999.「東京 아라카와(荒川)로의 移住와 정착화樣相」『科研費研究成果報告』(研究代表者: 伊藤亞人).

Ohno, Yuji. 大野祐二. 2000.「韓國 한 仏教寺院의 채색(素描)」『샤머니즘과 그 주변(周辺)』, 第一書房.

Okada, Hiroki. 岡田浩樹. 1998.「操作되는 〈民俗宗教〉-現代韓國社會의 죽음(死)을 둘러싼 實踐을 중심으로」 人間文化學部(編) 『甲子園大學紀要C』(通号 2).

Okada, Hiroki. 岡田浩樹. 1999. 朝倉 敏夫・岡田 浩樹,「對談 食文化의 変容(1)」『食生活研究』. 20(2) (通号 111), [1999.8].

Okada, Hiroki. 岡田浩樹. 1999. 朝倉 敏夫・岡田 浩樹,「對談 食文化의 変容(2)」『食生活研究』. 20(3) (通号 112), [1999.10].

Okada, Hiroki. 岡田浩樹. 2001.「〈老人의 民俗學〉再考 (生・老・死:日本人의 人生觀-안쪽의 눈, 바깥쪽의 눈)-(노인)」『國立歷史民俗博物館研究報告』 91, [2001.3].

Okada, Hiroki. 岡田浩樹. 2001.『양반(兩班)』, 風響社, [2001.2].

Okada, Hiroki. 岡田浩樹. 1997.「시리즈 〈世界의 民族과 纖維〉(10)白과 原色의 수사학: 韓民族의 伝統으로서의 치마와 저고리」『纖維製品消費科學』 38(6): 284-294.

Okada, Hiroki. 岡田浩樹. 1997.「現代韓國社會에 있어서의 死者(워크숍 (3)東아시아世界에 있어서의 民俗宗教의 持續과 変容)」『宗教과 社會』 別冊: 94-98.

Okada, Hiroki. 岡田浩樹. 1999.「沈默하는 多數派-韓國仏教의 〈過去〉에 관한 試論」三尾裕子・本田 洋(編)『東아시아에 있어서의 文化의 多中心性』東京外國語大學아시아・아프리카言語文化研究所.

Okada, Kozo. 1976. 鈴木滿男(著)「〈손님(マレビト)의 構造: 東아시아比較民俗學研究〉」『國學院雜誌』 77(2): 60-62.

Okinawa Kenritsu Geijutsu Daigaku Ryukan Densyou Bunka Chosadan. 沖縄縣立芸術大學琉韓伝承文化調査団 1991.『韓國伝承文化의 研究: 오키나와(沖縄)와의 比較를 목표로서』, 那覇: 沖縄縣立芸術大學琉韓伝承文化調査団.

Okuma, Yoko. 奥間葉子. 1993. 「韓國에 있어서의 契의 一考察 경상남도(慶尙南道) 선창(仙倉)의 事例를 중심으로」『白山人類學』 2.

Okuma, Yoko. 奥間葉子. 1995. 「韓國에 있어서의 契의 結成에 대하여: 農村과 都市에 있어서의 事例를 중심으로」『東洋大學大學院紀要』 31: 59-72.

Okuyama, Noriko. 奥山則子. 1996. 「韓國의 〈血族主義〉의 産業化의 對応에 관한 研究」『社會學研究科論集』 (立教大學大學院) 3.

Omine, Jissei and Tasato, Osamu. 大嶺實清・田里修. 1991. 沖縄縣立芸術大學琉韓伝承文化調査団, 「韓國의 도자기(陶磁器): 韓國의 분청사기(粉青抄器)와 류큐(琉球)의 도기(陶器)」『韓國伝承文化의 研究: 오키나와(沖縄)와의 比較를 중심으로』 167-185, 那覇: 沖縄縣立芸術大學琉韓伝承文化調査団.

Oshitani, Daizo. 押谷大藏. 1977. 「朝鮮民族과 白衣」『海外事情』 25(10): 37-44.

Ota, Simpei. 太田心平. 2002. 「〈新自由主義〉: 韓國의 어느 교회에서 본 악덕행위의 過程과 그 影響」『年報人間科學(23)』 (分冊1).

Otani, Michiyori. 大谷通順. 1990. 「오목(五木)의 형상과 카리우치(樗蒲)의 방법에 대하여-〈오목의 방법〉의 합리적 해석」『學園論集』 (通号 67), [1990.12].

Otani, Michiyori. 大谷通順. 1991. 「오목(五木)의 형상과 카리우치(樗蒲)의 방법에 대하여-〈오목의 방법〉의 합리적 해석(하)」『學園論集』 (通号 68), [1991.3].

Otani, Michiyori. 大谷通順. 1992. 「한국식 카루타 〈투전〉이 가지는 의미-어느 도박법의 기원과 전파(상)」『學園論集』 (通号 71), [1992.3].

Otani, Michiyori. 大谷通順. 1992. 「한국식 카루타 〈투전〉이 가지는 의미-어느 도박법의 기원과 전파(중)」『學園論集』 (通号 74), [1992.12].

Pak, Kye-Hong. 朴桂弘. 1982. 『韓國의 村축제』, 東京: 國書刊行會.

Park, Jeon-youl. 朴 銓烈. 2000. 「韓國사회에 있어서의 예능인」 崔吉城・日向一雅(編) 『신화・종교・무속-한일비교문화의 시도』, 風響社.

Park, Jeon-youl. 朴銓烈. 1989. 『「門첨부」의 構造: 韓日比較民俗學의 視点에서』, 東京: 弘文堂.

Saiki Kyoko. 齋木恭子. 1999. 內藤正中, 今村實, 齊木恭子, 『韓國 江原道와 도토리현(鳥取縣)』, 富士書店, [1999.1].

Saiki Kyoko. 齋木恭子. 2000. 「韓國옛날이야기 그림책에 있어서의 창조성-〈어둠의 나라에서 온 백구(むく犬)〉의 構造와 表現」『鳥取女子短期大學

研究紀要(42)』.

Saiki Kyoko. 齋木恭子. 2000.「在日韓國・朝鮮人에 의한 民族性継承의 課題」『北東아시아文化研究(通号 11)』, [2000.3].

Saiki Kyoko. 齋木恭子. 2001.「韓國그림책『강아지 똥』에 관한 一考察」『北東아시아文化研究』(13), [2001.3].

Saiki Kyoko. 齋木恭子. 2002.「韓國그림책 事情再考」『北東아시아文化研究』(15), [2002.3].

Saiki Takahito. 齋木崇人. 1999. 齊木 崇人・澁谷 鎭明,「『내동여지도(大東輿地図)』와 環境單位 (芸術工學會1999年秋期大會(韓國大會)号)」『芸術工學會誌』(通号 21), [1999.11].

Sakai, Izuru. 酒井出. 1986.「韓國農村의 社會構造와 機能: 전라남도(全羅南道) 완도읍(莞島邑) 도암리(道岩里)의 事例」日韓漁村社會・経濟共同研究會『한일합동학습조사보고(日韓合同學術調查報告) 第4輯: 韓國全羅南道莞島郡』142-155, 神戸: 日韓漁村社會・経濟共同研究會事務局.

Sakai, Shunji. 酒井俊二. 1984.「韓國과 日本의 沿岸漁村比較調查레포트」日韓漁村社會・経濟共同研究會(小澤康則과 共著)『日韓合同學術調查報告 第2輯: 韓國慶尙北道平海邑厚浦里』70-83, 神戸: 日韓漁村社會・経濟共同研究會事務局.

Sakai, Shunji. 酒井俊二. 1986.「漁村의 국세비교화화. 韓國 두 漁村의 調查에서」『白山社會學研究』1: 44-46.

Sakai, Shunji. 酒井俊二. 1986.「신지면(薪智面) 내정리(內井里)의 社會構造와 住民의 生活構造」日韓漁村社會・経濟共同研究會『日韓合同學術調查報告 第4輯: 韓國 전라남도(全羅南道) 완도군(莞島郡)』121-141, 神戸: 日韓漁村社會・経濟共同研究會事務局.

Sakai, Shunji. 酒井俊二. 1988.「日韓漁村의 集団性에 관한 比較考察」日韓漁村社會・経濟共同研究會『日韓合同學術調查報告 第6輯: 韓國 경상남도(慶尙南道) 충무시(忠武市)와 그 周辺 漁村』169-189, 神戸: 日韓漁村社會・経濟共同研究會事務局.

Sakai, Shunji. 酒井俊二. 1992.「外國研究의 動向: 韓國」『村落社會研究』28: 260-267.

Sakai, Shunji. 酒井俊二. 1998.「韓國漁村의 近代化에 관한 事例考察: 韓國 경상북도(慶尙北道) 울진군(蔚珍郡) 후포읍(厚浦邑) 금음사리(金音四里)의 事例」『中京學院大學研究紀要』6(1): 65-78.

Sakai, Toshiki. 坂井俊樹. 1997.『韓國・朝鮮과 近現代史教育－共生・共存의 視点에서』, 大月書店.

Sakamoto, Kazumitsu. 坂元一光. 1983.「통과의례(通過儀礼)에서 본 韓國伝統社會의 青少年期의 特質」『九州大學比較教育文化研究施設紀要』34: 49-66.

Sakamoto, Kazumitsu. 坂元一光. 1984.「韓國 기독교의 토착화(土着化)에 있어서의 문화적 〈新解釋〉 試論」『九州大學教育學部比較教育文化研究施設紀要』35: 73-89.

Sakamoto, Kazumitsu. 坂元一光. 1992.「韓國産育民俗의 한 側面: 남아선호(男兒選好)의 背景과 変容을 중심으로」『比較民俗研究』5.

Sakamoto, Shin'ichi. 坂本眞一. 1997.「敗戰前日本國에 있어서의 조선호적(朝鮮戸籍)의 研究」『青丘學術論集』10: 231-293.

Sakamoto, Shinnosuke. 坂元新之輔. 2000.「호즈미 노부시게(穗積陳重)와 日本人類學의 起源:『집(家)』/ 호적(戸籍)과 그의 登錄進化論을 중심으로」『民族學研究』64(4): 505-520.

Sakurai, Shoko. 櫻井笙子. 1979.「濟州島 아이들의 놀이노래」『東洋音樂研究』44: 27-49.

Sakurai, Tetsuo. 櫻井哲男. 1988.「濟州島에 있어서의 歌의 形成－音에서 音樂으로」『國立民族學博物館研究報告』13(4).

Sakurai, Tetsuo. 櫻井哲男. 1990. 杉山晃一・櫻井哲男,『韓國社會의 文化人類學』, 弘文堂, [1990.11].

Sakurai, Tetsuo. 櫻井哲男. 1992.『신들의 音像』, 丸善, [1992.2](CD북).

Sakurai, Tetsuo. 櫻井哲男. 1976.「音樂人類學의 試図: 1 濟州島의 民俗音樂」『音樂學』21: 101-115.

Sakurai, Tetsuo. 櫻井哲男. 1978.「朝鮮半島의 樂器」『月刊Minpaku』2(5): 12-13.

Sakurai, Tetsuo. 櫻井哲男. 1980.「濟州島에 있어서의 歌의 形成: 音에서 音樂으로」『國立民族學博物館研究報告』13(4): 787-806.

Sakurai, Tetsuo. 櫻井哲男. 1981.「아시아音樂의 概觀: 東아시아의 音樂・韓國(朝鮮半島)」藤井知昭(監修)『아시아音樂入門別冊解說書』東京: 日本코롬비아(コロムビア).

Sakurai, Tetsuo. 櫻井哲男. 1982.「濟州島에 흐르는 노동가(仕事歌)」梅棹忠夫監修・藤井知昭責任(編集)『世界旅行: 民族의 삶5 창조・제사』90-98, 東京: 日本交通公社出版事業局.

Sakurai, Tetsuo. 櫻井哲男. 1983.「아시아의 궁주악기(弓奏樂器)」『月刊Minpaku』

7(11): 12-13.

Sakurai, Tetsuo. 櫻井哲男. 1983.「예능(芸能)/장고(杖鼓)/가면(仮面)」『國立民族學博物館總合案內追錄』3, 東京: 民族學振興會.

Sakurai, Tetsuo. 櫻井哲男. 1983.「濟州島(城邑里)의 民家」『國立民族學博物館總合案內追錄』6, 東京: 民族學振興會.

Sakurai, Tetsuo. 櫻井哲男. 1983.「濟州島의 봄(春)」『民博通信』21: 55-56.

Sakurai, Tetsuo. 櫻井哲男. 1983.「島內唯一의 公的博物館: 濟州大學校付屬民俗博物館」『月刊 Minpaku』7(4): 14.

Sakurai, Tetsuo. 櫻井哲男. 1983.「類似性과 異文化: 韓國國立中央博物館」『月刊 Minpaku』7(6): 14.

Sakurai, Tetsuo. 櫻井哲男. 1984.「韓國의 音의 文化」『國立民族學博物館友會 뉴스』35.

Sakurai, Tetsuo. 櫻井哲男. 1984.「濟州島의 海女」『季刊民族學』27: 18-25.

Sakurai, Tetsuo. 櫻井哲男. 1984.「伝統과 패션: 韓國의 롱스커트와 여성이 앉는 자세」『TOKK』10: 20-21.

Sakurai, Tetsuo. 櫻井哲男. 1985.「Q & A 日韓의 아악(雅樂)의 차이에 대해서」『月刊Minpaku』9(9): 29.

Sakurai, Tetsuo. 櫻井哲男. 1985.「濟州島: 風土・環境・아이들의 놀이」岩田慶治・松原正毅・栗田靖之(編)『아이들의 世界: 39冊의 필드 노드에시』東京: 쿠몬出版.

Sakurai, Tetsuo. 櫻井哲男. 1985.「아이들의 놀이와 노래: 韓國(濟州島)의 事例를 중심으로」『民博通信』29: 44-65.

Sakurai, Tetsuo. 櫻井哲男. 1985.「哭과 情: 韓國의 장의(葬儀)」『季刊民族學』32: 94-101.

Sakurai, Tetsuo. 櫻井哲男. 1986.「소리의 世界: 韓國에 있어서의 音의 文化의 構造」編集委員會『諸民族의 音: 小泉文夫先生追悼論文集』413-434, 東京: 音樂之友社.

Sakurai, Tetsuo. 櫻井哲男. 1986.「現代韓國의 아이들의 놀이」『아이들과 家庭』22(10): 12-17.

Sakurai, Tetsuo. 櫻井哲男. 1986.「濟州島民俗音樂의 現代的変容: 續・音樂人類學의 試図」『音樂學』32(2): 116-134.

Sakurai, Tetsuo. 櫻井哲男. 1986.「世界의 축제 11: 韓國・강릉제(江陵祭)」『Voice』11: 그라비어 19-22.

Sakurai, Tetsuo. 櫻井哲男. 1986. 「朝鮮半島의 農樂과 仮面劇」『月刊Minpaku』 10(9): 8-9.

Sakurai, Tetsuo. 櫻井哲男. 1986. 「朝鮮半島의 文化」 國立民族學博物館(編) 『國立民族學博物館展示案內』 135, 大阪: 千里文化財団.

Sakurai, Tetsuo. 櫻井哲男. 1986. 「무속의례(巫俗儀礼)의 소리(音): 韓國濟州島의 事例에서」『國立民族學博物館研究報告』 10(3): 551-573.

Sakurai, Tetsuo. 櫻井哲男. 1987. 「伽耶琴(가야금)」『月刊Minpaku』 11(6): 표지 뒷면.

Sakurai, Tetsuo. 櫻井哲男. 1989. 「濟州島에 있어서의 音의 体系」 松原正毅(編) 『人類學이란 무엇인가』 東京: 日本放送出版協會.

Sakurai, Tetsuo. 櫻井哲男. 1989. 『「소리」의 硏究: 韓國農村에 있어서의 音과 音樂의 民族誌』 東京: 弘文堂.

Sakurai, Tetsuo. 櫻井哲男. 1990. 「소리의 展開」 杉山晃一・櫻井哲男(編) 『韓國社會의 文化人類學』 141-158, 東京: 弘文堂.

Sakurai, Tetsuo. 櫻井哲男. 1992. 「소리의 展開: 濟州島民俗音樂槪說」 玄容駿博士華甲記念論叢出版委員會(編) 『濟州島言語民俗論叢(玄容駿博士華甲記念論叢)』 濟州文化社.

Sakurai, Tetsuo. 櫻井哲男. 1994. 「韓國의 民衆芸能・農樂」『自然과 文化』 45.

Sakurai, Tetsuo. 櫻井哲男. 1994. 「여행과 예(芸): 예능인은 왜 여행을 하는가」『熊本大學文學部論叢』 44.

Sakurai, Tetsuo. 櫻井哲男. 1996. 「전래, 수용, 도태－朝鮮半島・日本의 歷史속에서 選擇된 樂器과 音」 櫻井哲男・山口修(編) 『音의 지금과 옛날』 弘文堂.

Sakurai, Tokutaro. 櫻井德太郎. 1973. 直江廣治・竹田旦・佐藤信行・崔仁鶴・谷川健一와의 座談會, 「야나기다(柳田)民俗學과 朝鮮」『季刊 야나기다 쿠니오 연구(柳田國男硏究)』 2: 2-43.

Sakurai, Tokutaro. 櫻井德太郎. 1974. 「단골=무당과 巫俗: 朝鮮의 샤머니즘」『季刊Dolmen』 3: 22-27.

Sakurai, Tokutaro. 櫻井德太郎. 1975. 「死靈의 結婚: 日韓民族의 比較」『산케이(サンケイ)新聞』 11月17日.

Sakurai, Tokutaro. 櫻井德太郎. 1975. 「民族文化의 실상을 생각하다: 韓國學術調査로 돌아가」『公明新聞』 10月18日.

Sakurai, Tokutaro. 櫻井德太郎. 1976. 「崔吉城 「韓國巫俗의 死靈祭」에 대한 코

멘트」『季刊人類學』 7(3): 74-77.

Sakurai, Tokutaro. 櫻井德太郎. 1976.「이타코(イタコ)와 무당: 일본과 조선의 샤머니즘」『쿠마모토매일신문(熊本日々新聞)』 8月19日.

Sakurai, Tokutaro. 櫻井德太郎. 1976.「韓國의 빙령(憑靈) 샤먼」『파렐가(ぱれるが)』 297: 6-7.

Sakurai, Tokutaro. 櫻井德太郎. 1976.「洗靈과 憑靈: 日韓巫俗의 比較試論」『展望』 209: 87-105.

Sakurai, Tokutaro. 櫻井德太郎. 1976.「日本의 야마미야(山宮)와 韓國의 당산(堂山)」 德川宗敬(監修)『신(神)과 사(社)』 113-117, 神宮司廳總務課.

Sakurai, Tokutaro. 櫻井德太郎. 1976.「比較民俗論의 課題: ノクツリム와 マブイグミ」 柴田實先生古稀記念會(編)『日本文化史論叢』 409-442, 吹田: 柴田實先生古稀記念會.

Sakurai, Tokutaro. 櫻井德太郎. 1977.「韓國의 설날아침의 풍속: 日本의 正月行事와의 比較」『風俗』 16(2): 87-98.

Sakurai, Tokutaro. 櫻井德太郎. 1979.「比較民俗學에의 胎動: 第4回아시아民俗學大會에서」『朝日新聞』 10月6日.

Sakurai, Tokutaro. 櫻井德太郎. 1980.「〈축제의 광장13〉 韓國의 村축제」『산케이(サンケイ)新聞』 7月28日.

Sakurai, Tokutaro. 櫻井德太郎. 1980.「韓國의 巫俗과 魂魄婚姻: 冥界婚姻習俗의 比較民俗學的考察(四)」 千葉德爾(編)『日本民俗風土論』 419-442, 東京: 弘文堂.

Sakurai, Tokutaro. 櫻井德太郎. 1980.「序: 比較民俗學에의 포석」 崔吉城『朝鮮의 축제와 巫俗』 i－v, 東京: 第一書房.

Sakurai, Tokutaro. 櫻井德太郎. 1980.「두 민족의 샤머니즘(下): 死靈巫儀의 比較」『月刊韓國文化』 2(11): 4-9.

Sakurai, Tokutaro. 櫻井德太郎. 1980.「두 민족의 샤머니즘(上): 韓國과 日本」『月刊韓國文化』 2(9): 9-14.

Sakurai, Tokutaro. 櫻井德太郎. 1980.「두 민족의 샤머니즘(中): 韓國과 日本」『月刊韓國文化』 2(10): 39-44.

Sakurai, Tokutaro. 櫻井德太郎. 1984.「序: 인접국가의 샤머니즘」 崔吉城(著)・福留範昭(譯)『韓國의 샤먼』, 東京: 國文社.

Sakurai, Tokutaro. 櫻井德太郎. 1986.「靈界의 結婚을 둘러싼 諸問題」『月刊韓國文化』 8(8): 4-12.

Sakurai, Tokutaro. 櫻井德太郎. 1986.「靈界의 婚姻을 둘러싼 問題」『韓國文化院友의 모임 뉴스』.

Sakurai, Tokutaro. 櫻井德太郎. 1987.「(江坂輝弥과 對談)古代日韓文化의 源流를 찾다: 考古學과 民俗學의 接点」『月刊韓國文化』 9(7): 4-12.

Sakurai, Tokutaro. 櫻井德太郎. 1987.『東아시아의 民俗宗教(櫻井德太郎著作集第7卷)』, 東京: 吉川弘文館.

Sasaki, mamoru. 佐々木衛. 2000.「中國朝鮮族研究의 課題」丸山孝一(編)『中國내셔널리즘과 少數民族文化의 変容過程에 관한 文化人類學的研究』, 文部省科學研究費補助金(基礎研究) 研究成果報告書.

Sasaki, Michio. 佐々木道雄. 1996.「朝鮮의 食과 文化」『무궁화叢書 ; 4』, 무궁화회, [1996.4].

Sasaki, Michio. 佐々木道雄. 2002.『韓國의 食文化』, 明石書店, [2002.10].

Sasaki, Noriko. 佐々木典子. 1994.「激変하는 社會狀況을 背景으로 한 韓國의 消費生活協同組合의 現狀과 課題」『第3回生活協同研究奬勵助成研究論文集』, 生活總合研究所.

Sasaki, Noriko. 佐々木典子. 1996.「韓國의 血族主義의 產業化의 對応에 관한 研究」『立教大學大學院社會學研究科論集』 第3号.

Sasaki, Noriko. 佐々木典子. 2000.「現代家族의 変動」小林孝行(編)『変貌하는 現代韓國社會』 25-43, 京都: 世界思想社.

Sasaki, Shiro. 佐々木史郎(1951-). 1982.「韓國의 내구(內廐)式 民家小考」『福島工業高等專門學校紀要』 18(1).

Sasaki, Shiro. 佐々木史郎(1951-). 1984.「韓國 차령산맥(車嶺山脈) 中部地域의 民家」『地學雜誌』 93(4).

Sasaki, Shiro. 佐々木史郎(1951-). 1988.「韓國留學의 体驗에서 (아시아의 留學生交流〈特集〉)」『地理』 33(12), [1988.12].

Sasaki, Shiro. 佐々木史郎(1951-). 1989. 張保雄[他],『韓國의 民家』, 古今書院, [1989.1].

Sasaki, Shiro. 佐々木史郎(1951-). 1994.「韓國의 現代住居에 있어서의 平面構成의 変化傾向」『宇都宮大學教養部研究報告』 第1部. (通号 28), [1994.9].

Sasaki, Shiro. 佐々木史郎(1951-). 1994.「韓國濟州島의 건물마다 용마루가 떨어져 있는 형식(別棟型)의 民家成立에 관한 추찰적 研究」『歷史地理學』 36(5) (通号 171), [1994.12].

Sasaki, Shiro. 佐々木史郎(1951-). 1994.「韓國民家에 있어서의 판자집(板間)의

性格과 그 地方性」『地學雜誌』103(6), [1994.12].

Sasaki, Shiro. 佐々木史郎(1951-). 1999.「朝鮮半島北部地方의 風土와 衣食住伝統 (特集 北朝鮮의 基礎知識)」『地理』44(4) (通号 521), [1999.4].

Sasaki, Shiro. 佐々木史郎(1951-). 2002.「삶이 키우는 마을과 경관 서울, 도시(마을)의 기억」『地域開發뉴스』(276).

Sasaki, Shiro. 佐々木史郎(1957-). 2000.「朝鮮族(特集 中國少數民族百科－55民族・그 歷史와 삶」『月刊시니까』11(1) (通号 119), [2000.1].

Sato, Nobuyuki. 佐藤信行. 1972.「濟州島의 家와 家族」『都市住宅』7210: 77-82.

Sato, Nobuyuki. 佐藤信行. 1973.「濟州島에서: 韓國의 사정과 韓國에서 깨달은 부분」『季刊人類學』4(3): 148-172.

Sato, Nobuyuki. 佐藤信行. 1973.「濟州島의 家族: O村의 事例에서」『東洋文化』53: 109-145.

Sato, Nobuyuki. 佐藤信行. 1973.「濟州島의 家族과 親族: O村의 事例」『아시아文化研究』7: 1-49.

Sato, Nobuyuki. 佐藤信行. 1973.「濟州島의 조상숭배(祖先崇拜)」『崇拜研究』46(3): 113-114.

Sato, Nobuyuki. 佐藤信行. 1974.「韓國・安東댐 수몰지구에서」『朝日아시아 리뷰』5(2): 134-135.

Sato, Nobuyuki. 佐藤信行. 1975.「韓國 洛東江上流의 山村社會」『아시아経濟』16(3): 78-88.

Sato, Nobuyuki. 佐藤信行. 1976.「濟州島의 〈사돈〉」南島史學會(編)『南島: 그 歷史와 文化』219-231, 東京: 國書刊行會.

Sato, Nobuyuki. 佐藤信行. 1977.「우리와 남」片倉もとこ・佐藤信行・青柳清孝『文化人類學: 遊牧・農耕・都市』203-208, 東京: 八千代出版.

Sato, Nobuyuki. 佐藤信行. 1977.「韓國에 있어서의 忌祭의 제관(祭官)構成에 대하여」『季刊人類學』8(1): 123-140.

Sato, Noriaki. 佐藤憲昭. 2002.「韓國의 샤먼에 관한 一考察－神人交流의 特色을 중심으로」『宗教學論集』21.

Sato, Noriaki. 佐藤憲昭. 1999.「보살의 주술(呪術)・宗教的 性格에 대하여－韓國의 서울市와 진도(珍島)의 事例에서」佐々木宏幹(編)『東아시아에 있어서의 샤머니즘文化의 構造와 変容에 관한 文化人類學的研究』, 1996～1998年度科學研究費補助金研究成果報告書.

Sato, Noriaki. 佐藤憲昭. 2000.「韓國의 샤먼에 관한 覺書」『駒澤大學 文化』一九.

Sawai, Keiichi. 澤井啓一. 1996.「日本과 韓國에 있어서의 儒教의 比較研究에 향하여 (〔比較思想學會〕 韓日合同學術大會)」『比較思想研究』(通号 22), [1996.3].

Sawai, Keiichi. 澤井啓一. 1997.「日・韓의 儒教的 실행의 比較에 대하여」『比較思想研究』(通号 23別冊) [1997.3].

Sawai, Keiichi. 澤井啓一. 2000.「韓國에 있어서의「日本思想」研究의 現狀에 대하여(特集 韓國의 日本研究)」『季刊日本思想史』(56).

Sechiyama, Kaku. 瀬地山 角. 1996.「평양(平壤)의 길목에서의 사색(特集 人間의 未來－아시아의 視点과 〈아시아的 都市〉」『CEL』(通号 37) [1996.6].

Sechiyama, Kaku. 瀬地山 角. 1997.「東아시아版 〈이에社會論〉을 향하여－家族의 文化比較의 可能性 (特集 文化와 家族)」『家族社會學研究』(通号 9).

Sechiyama, Kaku. 瀬地山角. 1990.「韓國・台湾의 主婦와 女子勞働: 女性의 社會進出의 방향을 차지하다」『아시아経濟』31(12): 22-40.

Sechiyama, Kaku. 瀬地山角. 1996.『東아시아의 家父長制: gender의 比較社會學』, 東京: 勁草書房.

Sekine, Hideyuki. 關根英行. 1997.「〈環境〉 및 〈要求〉의 觀点에서 본 日・韓의 道德教科目의 存續에 관한 一考察」『公民教育研究』(通号 5).

Sekine, Hideyuki. 關根英行. 1998.「韓國에 있어서의 日本의 大衆文化에 대한 調查研究」馬居 政幸・曹 夫伯・關根 英行 他『静岡大學教育學部研究報告 人文・社會科學篇』(通号 49).

Sekine, Hideyuki. 關根英行. 1998.「青少年의 個人道德과 公共道德의 日・韓比較」『公民教育研究』(通号 6).

Seo, Dae-Suk. 徐 大錫. 1997.「韓國의 建國神話에 반영된 천신(天神)과 수신(水神)과의 관계」熊木勉(譯)『조선학보(朝鮮學報)』162.

Seo, Jeon-Beom. 徐廷範. 1980.『韓國의 샤머니즘』, 京都: 同朋舍出版.

Seo, Yeon-Ho. 徐 淵昊. 1999.「20世紀의 가면극(仮面劇)과 인형의 예능전승과정연구」鈴木正崇・野村伸一(編)『가면(仮面)과 무속(巫俗)의 연구－일본과 한국』第一書房.

Shigematsu, Mayumi. 重松眞由美. 1978.「금기－宗教人類學的考察」『史論(通号 32)』.

Shigematsu, Mayumi. 重松眞由美. 1992. 崔吉城[他],『韓國의 조상숭배(祖先崇拜)』, 御茶の水書房, [1992.12].

Shigematsu, Mayumi. 重松眞由美. 1976.「아시아派遣留學生으로서 韓國에 살고」『厚生補導』156: 44-48.

Shigematsu, Mayumi. 重松眞由美. 1980.「새신(賽神)에게 보이는 女性의 社會關係: 韓國 京畿道 楊州郡에 있어서의 巫俗의 一考察」『民族學研究』45(2): 93-110.

Shigematsu, Mayumi. 重松眞由美. 1981.「지노귀굿(チノギ賽神)에 있어서의 조상(祖上)과 신령(神靈): 韓國京畿道楊州郡K洞의 事例」『國立民族學博物館研究報告』6(2): 256-282.

Shigematsu, Mayumi. 重松眞由美. 1981.「研究의 골(谷間)에서」『民博通信』14: 42-44.

Shigematsu, Mayumi. 重松眞由美. 1981.「財數賽神(제수굿): 韓國서울의 商家에 있어서의 事例를 중심으로」『季刊人類學』12(2): 143-165.

Shigematsu, Mayumi. 重松眞由美. 1982. 綾部恒雄(編),「韓國의 女」『女의 文化人類學』197-223, 東京: 弘文堂.

Shigematsu, Mayumi. 重松眞由美. 1983.「제수굿: 서울商家에 있어서의 事例를 중심으로」『韓國文化人類學』15: 93-108.

Shigematsu, Mayumi. 重松眞由美. 1983.「食生活」『國立民族學博物館總合案內追錄』5, 東京: 民族學振興會.

Shigematsu, Mayumi. 重松眞由美. 1984. 李光奎(著)「(書評)『在日韓國人: 生活實態를 中心으로』」『民博通信』24: 31-33.

Shigematsu, Mayumi. 重松眞由美. 1984.「墓와 조상(祖先)과 血緣」『月刊Minpaku』8(6): 15-17.

Shigematsu, Mayumi. 重松眞由美. 1985.「Q & A 韓國의 巫俗(샤머니즘)에 대하여」『月刊 Minpaku』9(6): 23-24.

Shigematsu, Mayumi. 重松眞由美. 1993.「韓國의 조상숭배(祖先崇拜): 日本과의 比較」村武精一・大胡欽一(編)『社會人類學에서 본 日本: 蒲生正男教授追悼論文集』東京: 河出書房新社.

Shigematsu, Mayumi. 重松眞由美. 1995.「韓國農村社會에 있어서의 巫俗과 仏教: 韓國 京畿道 楊州郡 K村의 事例」『民博通信』70: 81-93.

Shigematsu, Mayumi. 重松眞由美. 1996.「변해가는 巫俗－韓國京畿道의 農村견문록」『民博通信』74: 114-118.

Shigematsu, Mayumi. 重松眞由美. 1998.「70年代末의 農村에 있어서의 巫俗」嶋陸奥彦・朝倉敏夫(編)『変貌하는 韓國社會: 1970~80年代의 人類學調査의 현장에서』117-146, 東京: 第一書房.

Shigematsu, Mayumi. 重松眞由美. 1999.「韓國農村社會에 있어서의 巫俗의 現狀－京畿道 楊州郡의 事例」『民博通信』84.

Shigematsu, Mayumi. 重松眞由美. 2000.「朝鮮半島의 巫俗儀礼」『月刊 Minpaku』24-12.

Shima, Mutsuhiko. 嶋陸奥彦. 1977. 崔在錫[他],『韓國人의 社會的性格』學生社, 1977.12.

Shima, Mutsuhiko. 嶋陸奥彦. 1979. 崔在錫[他],『韓國農村社會研究』學生社, 1979.6.

Shima, Mutsuhiko. 嶋陸奥彦. 1981. 金宅圭[他],『韓國同族村落의 研究』學生社, 1981.4.

Shima, Mutsuhiko. 嶋陸奥彦. 1996.「大洞契冊을 읽는다」『朝鮮文化研究』3.

Shima, Mutsuhiko. 嶋陸奥彦. 1998. 嶋陸奥彦・朝倉敏夫,『変貌하는 韓國社會』第一書房, 1998.6.(Academic series new Asia ; 26).

Shima, Mutsuhiko. 嶋陸奥彦. 1999. 藤田 眞理子・嶋陸奥彦・高谷 紀夫,「『마을설립』에서 보는 國際交流 및 世代間交流의 네트워크 分析: 社會人類學에서의 접근」『마츠다(マツダ)財団研究報告書 青少年健全育成關係』(通号 12) [1999.4].

Shima, Mutsuhiko. 嶋陸奥彦. 2000.「中原과 周辺－人類學的 field에서의 視点」末成道男(編)『民族學研究』64(4) [2000.3].

Shima, Mutsuhiko. 嶋陸奥彦. 1975.「커뮤니티研究에 대한 展望」『文化人類學』7: 157-158, 韓國文化人類學會.

Shima, Mutsuhiko. 嶋陸奥彦. 1976.「집안(Chib-an)의 分析: 韓國 全羅南道에 있어서의 事例檢討」『民族學研究』41(1): 75-90.

Shima, Mutsuhiko. 嶋陸奥彦. 1977. (書評)「李光奎『韓國家族의 構造分析』」『民族學研究』41(4): 399-402.

Shima, Mutsuhiko. 嶋陸奥彦. 1978.「韓國의 門中과 地緣性에 관한 試論」『民族學研究』43(1): 1-17.

Shima, Mutsuhiko. 嶋陸奥彦. 1979. *Kinship and Economic Organization in a Korea Village*. Ph. D. dissertation, University of Toronto.

Shima, Mutsuhiko. 嶋陸奥彦. 1979.「韓國農村에 있어서의 生産關係」『地域文化

研究』 5: 27-47.

Shima, Mutsuhiko. 嶋陸奧彦. 1979.「朝鮮사람들」大林太良(監修)『世界의 民族 13 東아시아 日本・中國・朝鮮』64-77, 140, 東京: 平凡社.

Shima, Mutsuhiko. 嶋陸奧彦. 1980.「韓國의『家』의 分析: 養子와 分家를 중심으로」『廣大아시아研究』2: 39-52, 66.

Shima, Mutsuhiko. 嶋陸奧彦. 1983.「換金作物栽培와 農村: 韓國 慶北 星州郡의 事例에서」『廣大아시아研究』3: 55-67.

Shima, Mutsuhiko. 嶋陸奧彦. 1983.「韓國農村村落構造研究노트」『韓國文化人類學』15: 177-191.

Shima, Mutsuhiko. 嶋陸奧彦. 1984.「韓國의 촌: 동네와 마을」『日本民俗文化大系 第8卷 촌(村)과 촌사람(村人)』月報7: 12-14.

Shima, Mutsuhiko. 嶋陸奧彦. 1985.「마을: 촌社會」『基礎한글』1(1): 64-65.

Shima, Mutsuhiko. 嶋陸奧彦. 1985.「집(家)」『基礎한글』1(2): 54-55.

Shima, Mutsuhiko. 嶋陸奧彦. 1985.「葬儀」『基礎한글』1(3): 54-55.

Shima, Mutsuhiko. 嶋陸奧彦. 1985.「族譜와 門中組織」菊池啓治郎學兄還曆記念委員會(編)『日高見國』399-415, 北上: 菊池啓治郎學兄 환갑기념회.

Shima, Mutsuhiko. 嶋陸奧彦. 1985.「地域社會」伊藤亞人(編)『더욱 알고 싶은 韓國』71-98, 東京: 弘文堂.

Shima, Mutsuhiko. 嶋陸奧彦. 1985.『韓國農村事情: 〈유교〉의 나라에 사는 사람들의 生活誌』東京: PHP研究所.

Shima, Mutsuhiko. 嶋陸奧彦. 1986.「育兒/ 産神/ 온돌/ 환갑/ 故鄕/ 아이들/ 住居/ 出産/ 장례식/ 祖先祭祀/ 通過儀禮/ 墓/ 老人」伊藤亞人・大村益男・梶村秀樹・武田幸男(監修)『朝鮮을 아는 事典』, 東京: 平凡社.

Shima, Mutsuhiko. 嶋陸奧彦. 1987.「氏族制度와 문중조직(門中組織)」伊藤・關本・船曳(編)『現代의 社會人類學1 親族과 社會의 構造』東京: 東京大學出版會.

Shima, Mutsuhiko. 嶋陸奧彦. 1987.「朝鮮族」『文化人類學事典』482-483.

Shima, Mutsuhiko. 嶋陸奧彦. 1988. "Computer Analysis of Genealogies: An Interim Report", *Korean Studies, Its Tasks & Perspectives: Papers of the 5th International Conference on Korean Studies* 2: 639-654, Academy of Korean Studies.

Shima, Mutsuhiko. 嶋陸奧彦. 1989.「大邱戶籍試掘: 方法論的 試図」斗山金宅圭博士華甲記念論文集刊行委員會(編)『文化人類學論叢』199-211.

Shima, Mutsuhiko. 嶋陸奥彦. 1990. "In Quest for Social Recognition: A Retrospective View on the Development of Korean Lineage Organization", *Harvard Journal of Asiatic Studies* 50(1): 87-129

Shima, Mutsuhiko. 嶋陸奥彦. 1990.「계와 村사회」阿部・伊藤・荻原(編)『民族의 世界(下) 社會의 統合과 動態』76-92, 東京: 小學館.

Shima, Mutsuhiko. 嶋陸奥彦. 1990.「族譜: 歷史人類學的展望」杉山晃一・櫻井哲男(編)『韓國社會의 文化人類學的研究』39-54, 東京: 弘文堂.

Shima, Mutsuhiko. 嶋陸奥彦. 1992. "Korean Genealogy: Some Demographic Simulations", *Contacts Between Cultures: Contacts Between Cultures: Proceedings of the 33rd International Congress of Asian and North African Studies* 4:155-158, Lewiston: The Edwin Mellen Press.

Shima, Mutsuhiko. 嶋陸奥彦. 1992.「韓國社會: 伝統의 形成과 그 변형」『民博通信』56: 35-40.

Shima, Mutsuhiko. 嶋陸奥彦. 1992.「大邱戶籍에 보이는 朝鮮後期의 家族構造의 変化: 부모와 동거하는 자식을 중심으로」『朝鮮學報』144: 51-88.

Shima, Mutsuhiko. 嶋陸奥彦. 1994.「韓國: 伝統과 現代 사이」中國新聞社(編)『아시아를 語る』33-54, 廣島: 中國新聞社.

Shima, Mutsuhiko. 嶋陸奥彦. 1994.「親族制度에서 본 朝鮮社會의 変動: 族譜의 檢討를 중심으로」溝口雄三・濱下武志・平石直昭・宮嶋博史(編)『長期社會変動』(아시아에서 생각한다 6)131-162, 東京: 東京大學出版會.

Shima, Mutsuhiko. 嶋陸奥彦. 1995.「族譜의 世界」『月刊韓國文化』17(7): 2-7.

Shima, Mutsuhiko. 嶋陸奥彦. 1996.「大洞契冊을 읽는다」『朝鮮文化研究』3: 95-110.

Shima, Mutsuhiko. 嶋陸奥彦. 1996.「朝鮮時代後期의 村落構成의 動態: 大丘戶籍의 分析」『東洋文化』76: 201-226.

Shima, Mutsuhiko. 嶋陸奥彦. 1997.「韓國社會: 高度経濟成長下의 fieldwork」『民博通信』76: 69-74.

Shima, Mutsuhiko. 嶋陸奥彦. 1997.「韓國社會: 高度経濟成長下의 fieldwork」『民博通信』76.

Shima, Mutsuhiko. 嶋陸奥彦. 1997.「族譜의 구조」船曳建夫(編)『個로 하는 社會展望』(岩波講座文化人類學4)97-127, 東京: 岩波書店.

Shima, Mutsuhiko. 嶋陸奥彦. 1998. "Retrieving the Past with Genealogies", Shima, Mutsuhiko and Janelli, Roger L. eds., *The Anthropology of Korea:*

East Asian Perspectives (Senri Ethnological Studies 49) 37-63, Osaka: National Museum of Ethnology.

Shima, Mutsuhiko. 嶋陸奥彦. 1998.「韓國農村에 있어서의 世帶의 長期的 流動性과 그 의미」『韓國文化人類學』31(2): 293-301.

Shima, Mutsuhiko. 嶋陸奥彦. 1998.「70年代中期 羅州郡農村의 農業慣行: 큰 変化의 直前」嶋陸奥彦・朝倉敏夫(編)『変貌하는 韓國社會: 1970～80年代의 人類學調査의 현장에서』87-115, 東京: 第一書房.

Shima, Mutsuhiko. 嶋陸奥彦. 1998.「変貌하는 韓國社會와 人類學調査」嶋陸奥彦・朝倉敏夫(編)『変貌하는 韓國社會: 1970～80年代의 人類學調査의 현장에서』, 東京: 第一書房.

Shima, Mutsuhiko. 嶋陸奥彦. 1999.「韓國人의 名前: 併存하는 複數의 名前과 호칭」上野和男・森謙二(編)『이름과 사회: 작명의 가족사』(시리즈比較家族第Ⅱ期3) 230-251, 東京: 早稲田大學出版部.

Shima, Mutsuhiko. 嶋陸奥彦. 2000. 吉原和男他(編),「歴史人類學에서 본 韓國의 親族結合」『〈血縁〉의 再構築』167-184, 東京: 風響社.

Shima, Mutsuhiko and Asakura Toshio eds. 嶋陸奥彦, 朝倉敏夫(編). 1998.『変貌하는 韓國社會: 1970～1980年代의 人類學調査의 현장에서』東京: 第一書房.

Shima, Mutsuhiko and Janelli, Roger L. eds. 嶋陸奥彦, R. L. ジャネリ(編). 1998. *The Anthropology of Korea: East Asian Perspectives* (Senri Ethnological Studies 49), Osaka: National Museum of Ethnology.

Shima, Mutsuhiko and Janelli, Roger L. 嶋陸奥彦, R. L. ジャネリ(編). 1998. "Introduction", Shima, Mutsuhiko and Janelli, Roger L. eds., *The Anthropology of Korea: East Asian Perspectives* (Senri Ethnological Studies 49), 1-5, Osaka: National Museum of Ethnology.

Shimamoto, Midori. 島本みどり. 2001.「韓國의 伝統社會와 企業活動」『東邦學誌』30(2) [2001.12].

Shimamoto, Midori. 島本みどり. 2001.「韓國企業의 組織変容과 経營情報 (特集 組織의 変容과 秘書의 情報管理(〔日本國際秘書學會〕第9回硏究大會심포지엄))」『日本國際秘書學會硏究年報』(8).

Shimamura, Yasunori. 島村恭則. 1999.「70年代韓國에 있어서의 유행어」『國立歴史民俗博物館硏究報告』(通号 82) [1999.3].

Shimamura, Yasunori. 島村恭則. 2000.「韓國의 現代民話－日韓比較의 視点에서」

『仏教大學總合研究所紀要』(通号 別冊) [2000.3].

Shimamura, Yasunori. 島村恭則. 2001.「〈在日朝鮮人〉의 民俗誌 (生・老・死:日本人의 人生觀－안과 바깥에서의 눈)－(人生)」『國立歷史民俗博物館研究報告』91 [2001.3].

Shimamura, Yasunori. 島村恭則. 2002.「在日朝鮮半島系住民의 生業과 環境－보따리장사의 事例를 중심으로」『月刊民具』35(1) (通号 409), [2002.4].

Shimamura, Ysunori. 島村恭則. 2000.「境界都市의 民俗誌－시모세키(下關)의『在日코리언』들」『歷博』103.

Shimizu, Hiroaki. 清水浩昭. 2000.「高齢者家族의 構成과 構造－日本・韓國・아메리카・독일과의 比較研究」『社會學論叢』(日本大學)一三八.

Shimono, Toshimi. 下野敏見. 1989.「東아시아 장례식 및 묘제도 小考: 韓國의 草墳과 류큐(琉球)의 風葬, 他」『隼人文化』22: 1-24.

Shimura, Tetsuo. 志村哲男. 1990.「背德의 男寺党牌: 韓國의 放浪芸能集団」『民族音樂叢書1 職能으서의 音樂』, 東京: 東京書籍.

Shin, Jang-Ho. 申 長鎬. 1999.「재일 한국샤머니즘－재수무의(財數巫儀)(제숙의 사례를 중심으로(1)」『아시아文化研究』(通号 6), [1999.6].

Shin, Jang-Ho. 申 長鎬. 1999.「재일 한국샤머니즘－재수무의(財數巫儀)(제숙의 사례를 중심으로)」『아시아文化研究』(國際아시아學會)6.

Shinbo, Jun'ichiro. 眞保潤一郎. 1977.「韓國에 있어서의 화전민(火田民)의 現況에 대하여」『高崎経濟大學論集』19(4):109-136.

Shinozaki, Masami. 篠崎正美. 1992.「現代韓國과 日本의 家族変動에 있어서의 家族意識의 比較研究: 서울・후쿠오카(福岡)調查에서」『社會分析: 社會學研究年報』20: 95-125.

Shinozaki, Masami. 篠崎正美. 1993.「現代韓國의 家族意識에의 接近: 서울調查를 중심으로」『家族社會學研究』5: 23-30.

Shoya, Reiko & Nakayama, Toru. 庄谷怜子・中山徹. 1997.『高齢재일교포－오사카(大阪)에 있어서의「재일교포(在日)」의 生活構造와 高齢福祉의 課題』御茶の水書房.

Shu, Tatsusei. 周達生. 1991.『東아시아의 食文化探檢』東京: 三省堂.

Smith, H. ハワード スミス. 1994.「韓國의 민요와 민속음악: 그 衰退와 復活의 運命」『코리아나』7(3).

Sofue, Takao. 祖父江孝男. 1981.「第5回 타니구치(谷口)심포지엄 中國・韓國・日本의 家族制度와 대인관계: 東아시아에 있어서의 宗教와 家族」『月刊

Minpaku』 5(10): 18-19.

Sofue, Takao. 祖父江孝男. 1983. 「朝鮮半島의 文化 · 衣生活」『國立民族學博物館總合案內追錄』 4, 東京: 民族學振興會.

Sofue, Takao. 祖父江孝男. 1983. 「朝鮮半島의 文化 · 民間信仰과 儒敎」『國立民族學博物館總合案內追錄』 2, 東京: 民族學振興會.

Sofue, Takao. 祖父江孝男. 1983. 「展示된 韓國人의 生活: 韓國, 溫陽博物館」『月刊 Minpaku』 7(3): 14.

Sofue, Takao. 祖父江孝男. 1983. 「東아시아槪說」『國立民族學博物館總合案內追錄』 1, 東京: 民族學振興會.

Sofue, Takao. 祖父江孝男. 1983. 「눈으로 理解하는 民俗文化: 韓國國立民俗博物館」『月刊 Minpaku』 7(2): 14.

Sofue, Takao. 祖父江孝男. 1990. 「韓國人의 意識과 行動」 杉山晃一 · 櫻井哲男(編) 『韓國社會의 文化人類學』 124-141, 東京: 弘文堂.

Suenari, Michio. 末成道男. 1973. 『韓國農村의 家族과 祭儀』, 中根千枝.東京大學出版會.

Suenari, Michio. 末成道男. 1973. 「慶尙北道百忍 · 中浦兩部落調査予報－특히 家族 · 親族에 대하여(韓國農村調査(特集))」 李光奎 · 末成道男 『東洋文化(通号 53)』, [1973.3.].

Suenari, Michio. 末成道男. 1983. 江淵一公 · 伊藤亞人, 『儀礼와 象徵』, 九州大學出版會, [1983.5].

Suenari, Michio. 末成道男. 1988. 瀧本孝雄 · 鈴木乙史, 『講座人間關係의 心理 5』, 브레인出版, [1988.4].

Suenari, Michio. 末成道男. 1992. 『아시아의 文化와 社會』, 東京大學東洋文化研究所.汲古書院, [1992.3].

Suenari, Michio. 末成道男. 1997. 「東아시아의 現在」『아시아研究報告시리즈 ; no.1』, 風響社, [1997.5].

Suenari, Michio. 末成道男. 1998. 淸水浩昭 · 芳賀正明 · 松本誠一, 『性과 年齡의 人類學』, 岩田書院, [1998.7].

Suenari, Michio. 末成道男. 2000. 吉原和男 · 鈴木正崇 · 末成道男, 『〈血緣〉의 再構築』, 風響社, [2000.11].

Suenari, Michio. 末成道男. 1974. (書評)「Vincent S. R. Brandt, *A Korean Village: Between Farm And Sea*」『民族學研究』 39(1): 102-104.

Suenari, Michio. 末成道男. 1975. 「韓國安東地方에 있어서의 眞城李氏의 墓祀에

대하여」『東京大學教養學部教養學科紀要』 7: 57-69.

Suenari, Michio. 末成道男. 1979.「同族」原忠彦・末成道男・清水昭俊『仲間(ふぉるく叢書9) 99-252』, 東京: 弘文堂.

Suenari, Michio. 末成道男. 1980.「韓日相互理解를 위해」『日本學誌』 1.

Suenari, Michio. 末成道男. 1982.「東浦의 마을과 제례: 韓國漁村調査報告」『聖心女子大學論叢』 59: 123-218.

Suenari, Michio. 末成道男. 1982.「類似文化間에 있어서의 文化摩擦: 日韓兩社會의 事例에서」 大林太良(編)『文化摩擦의 一般理論』 219-240, 東京: 巖南堂書店.

Suenari, Michio. 末成道男. 1983.「Age Stratified System in Korea」『韓國文化人類學』 15: 195-304.

Suenari, Michio. 末成道男. 1984.「韓國의 社會組織: 그 변화를 중심으로」『國立民族學博物館特別研究 日本民族文化의 源流의 比較研究심포지엄Ⅴ「社會組織: 집(이에)・마을(무라)・성씨(우지)」프로그램』 21-38.

Suenari, Michio. 末成道男. 1984.「東浦의 生業과 協同: 韓國漁村調査報告」『聖心女子大學論叢』 63: 85-158.

Suenari, Michio. 末成道男. 1984.「年齡認識과 通過儀礼: 東아시아社會比較에의 予備的 考察」 綾部恒雄(編)『通過儀礼과 世界觀』 105-114.

Suenari, Michio. 末成道男. 1985.「사랑방(舍廊房)」『文化人類學』 1: 270-276.

Suenari, Michio. 末成道男. 1985.「親族」『基礎한글』 1(3): 58-59.

Suenari, Michio. 末成道男. 1985.「人間關係」 伊藤亞人(編)『더욱 알고 싶은 韓國』 99-132, 東京: 弘文堂.

Suenari, Michio. 末成道男. 1985.「東浦의 조상제사(祖先祭祀): 韓國漁村調査報告」『聖心女子大學論叢』 65: 5-96.

Suenari, Michio. 末成道男. 1985.「年齡」『基礎한글』 1(4): 56-57.

Suenari, Michio. 末成道男. 1985.「年齡意識의 韓・日比較: 年齡層序制를 중심으로」『比較民俗學』 1: 39-56.

Suenari, Michio. 末成道男. 1985.「年齡層序制」『人間科學』 37: 1-19.

Suenari, Michio. 末成道男. 1986. "Continuity and Change of Ancestor Worship in East Asia: A Comparative Study of Memorial Tablet", in Sang-Bok Han ed., *Asian Peoples and Their Cultures: Continuity and Change* (16-184), Seoul: Seoul National University Press.

Suenari, Michio. 末成道男. 1986.「韓國의 社會組織: 그 변화를 중심으로」 竹村

卓二(編)『日本民俗社會의 形成과 發展: 집(이에)·마을(무라)·성씨(우지)의 源流을 찾다』 101-123, 東京: 山川出版.

Suenari, Michio. 末成道男. 1987.「韓國社會의 <양반(兩班)>化」伊藤·關本·船曳(編)『現代의 社會人類學1 親族과 社會의 構造』45-79, 東京: 東京大學出版會.

Suenari, Michio. 末成道男. 1987.「本貫」『文化人類學事典』711-712, 東京: 弘文堂.

Suenari, Michio. 末成道男. 1988.「韓國과 대만(台湾)의 위패제사(位牌祭祀)」石川利夫 이외 (編)『生者과 死者: 조상제사(祖先祭祀)』17-46, 東京: 三省堂.

Suenari, Michio. 末成道男. 1990.「韓國과 中國漢族의 대소혈통의 比較」杉山晃一·櫻井哲男(編)『韓國社會의 文化人類學』103-122, 東京: 弘文堂.

Suenari, Michio. 末成道男. 1992. "Anthropology of One's Own Society in East Asia", Chiao Chien and Nakane Chie eds., *Homebound: Studies in East Asian Society* 59-79, Hong Kong.

Suenari, Michio. 末成道男. 1992.「東아시아三社會의 葬礼에서 보이는 異質性」溝口雄三他(編)『漢字文化圈의 歷史와 未來』177-189.

Suenari, Michio. 末成道男. 1998. "Unilateral Kindred: A Reconsideration in East Asian Society", in Shima, Mutsuhiko and Janclli, Roger L. eds., *The Anthropology of Korea: East Asian Perspectives* (Senri Ethnological Studies 49), 139-155, Osaka: National Museum of Ethnology.

Suenari, Michio. 末成道男. 1998.「韓國입국과 그 후」嶋陸奥彦·朝倉敏夫(編)『変貌하는 韓國社會: 1970~80年代의 人類學調查의 현장에서』17-38, 東京: 第一書房.

Suenari, Michio and Lee, Kwang-Kyu. 末成道男·李光奎. 1973.「慶尙北道百忍·中浦兩部落調查予報: 특히 家族·親族에 대하여」『東洋文化』53: 41-78.

Sugiyama, Koichi. 杉山晃一. 1988.「東아시아의 農耕神觀」『日本文化研究所研究報告(通号 24)』[1988.3].

Sugiyama, Koichi. 杉山晃一. 1979.「韓國農村瞥見: 社會와 宗教의 諸側面」『東北大學日本文化研究所研究報告』15: 109-127.

Sugiyama, Koichi. 杉山晃一. 1981.「韓國南部 한 水田村에 있어서의 農耕儀礼素描」『東北大學日本文化研究所研究報告』17: 79-101.

Sugiyama, Koichi. 杉山晃一. 1982. 東北인도학宗教學會, 「韓國南部 한 農村에 있어서의 葬送儀礼에 대하여」『論集』9号.

Sugiyama, Koichi. 杉山晃一. 1986. 「朝鮮半島」日本民族學會(編)『日本의 民族學 1964-1983』188-192, 東京: 弘文堂.

Sugiyama, Koichi. 杉山晃一. 1987. 依田千百子(著), 「(書評)朝鮮民俗文化의 研究: 朝鮮의 基層文化와 그 源流를 중심으로」『民博通信』37: 19-21.

Sugiyama, Koichi. 杉山晃一. 1987. 「穀靈」『文化人類學事典』276-277, 東京: 弘文堂.

Sugiyama, Koichi. 杉山晃一. 1990. 「韓國南部 한 農村에 있어서의 死者儀礼와 行喪契」『東北大學日本文化研究所研究報告』26: 259-275.

Sugiyama, Koichi. 杉山晃一. 1990. 「行喪契: 契의 記錄에서」杉山晃一・櫻井哲男(編)『韓國社會의 文化人類學』87-102, 東京: 弘文堂.

Sugiyama, Koichi. 杉山晃一. 1991. 「洞社會에 있어서의 世帶主의 계와 主婦의 계(契)」『東北大學日本文化研究所研究報告』27: 57-69.

Sugiyama, Koichi. 杉山晃一. 1993. 「韓國南部 한 農村에 있어서의 敬老契에 대하여」『科學研究費報告』.

Sugiyama, Koichi and Sakurai, Tetsuo eds. 杉山晃一・櫻井哲男(編). 1990.『韓國社會의 文化人類學』東京: 弘文堂.

Sumi, Toyo. 鷲見等曜. 1987. 「朝鮮古代家族과의 比較」大林太良(編)『日本의 古代 11 Home과 House』283-312, 東京: 中央公論社.

Suwa, Haruo. 諏訪春生. 1973. 「어느 文化人類學專攻學生의 手紙: 韓國을 테마로 한 고민」『韓』(1): 63-72.

Suzuki, Eitaro. 鈴木榮太郎. 1953. 「朝鮮의 계와 품앗이」『民族學研究』27(3): 22-28.

Suzuki, Eitaro. 鈴木榮太郎. 1973. 『鈴木榮太郎著作集Ⅴ 朝鮮農村社會의 研究』東京: 未來社.

Suzuki, Fumiko. 鈴木文子. 1989. 「韓國에 있어서의 出産의 不淨觀에 관한 予備的 一考察」斗山金宅圭博士華甲記念論文集刊行委員會(編)『文化人類學論叢』.

Suzuki, Fumiko. 鈴木文子. 1991. 「韓國에 있어서의 한 漁村의 儀礼生活: 그 祖靈觀을 중심으로」『甲南大學紀要(文學編)』83: 27-61.

Suzuki, Fumiko. 鈴木文子. 1992. 「韓國이야기의 世界」『마음의 科學』46.

Suzuki, Fumiko. 鈴木文子. 1995. 「韓國에 있어서의 出産의 不淨觀에 관한 予備

的一考察」『山陽民俗研究』 1: 55-73.

Suzuki, Fumiko. 鈴木文子. 1998.「相對的貧困感의 時代: 80年代末의 離島社會」嶋陸奥彦・朝倉敏夫(編)『変貌하는 韓國社會: 1970～80年代의 人類學調査의 현장에서』223-260, 東京: 第一書房.

Suzuki, Humiko. 鈴木文子. 1992. 益田庄三(編著)〔含 原著者코멘트〕・森田 三郎・鈴木 文子,「日韓漁村의 比較研究－社會・経済・文化를 중심으로」『SOSHIOROJI. 37(2)』 [1992.10].

Suzuki, Humiko. 鈴木文子. 1995. 盧 相〔고〕・鈴木文子 (譯),「韓國伝統思想에 있어서의 선비精神」『島根大學教育學部紀要 人文・社會科學(通号 29)』, [1995.12].

Suzuki, Humiko. 鈴木文子. 2001.「韓國를걷다(6) 西海(서해)의 離島에 보는 時代変化－信仰의 世界를 단서로」『아시아 遊學』 30 [2001.8].

Suzuki, Humiko. 鈴木文子. 2001.「女性에서 본 親族－韓國漁村의 人口減少化에 있어서의 女性의 네트워크 分析을 중심으로」『島根大學教育學部紀要 人文・社會科學』 35 [2001.12].

Suzuki, Masataka. 鈴木正崇・野村伸一(編). 1999.『仮面과 巫俗의 研究－日本과 韓國』, 第一書房.

Suzuki, Masataka and Nomura, Shin'ichi. 鈴木正崇. 1999. 鈴木正崇・野村伸一(編),「日本의 神樂과 韓國의 굿－比較研究를 위한 試論」『仮面과 巫俗의 研究－日本과 韓國』 第一書房.

Suzuki, Mitsuo. 鈴木満男. 1972.「韓國1972年夏: 몇 가지의 素描」『新勢力』 17(10): 15-23.

Suzuki, Mitsuo. 鈴木満男. 1972.「韓國日記: 朝鮮社會・文化論을 위한 覺書」『季刊人類學』 3(1): 61-185.

Suzuki, Mitsuo. 鈴木満男. 1972.「古代朝鮮半島에 있어서의 國家形成論의 視角: 井上秀雄著『古代朝鮮史序說』을 중심으로」『朝鮮學報』 97: 71-86.

Suzuki, Mitsuo. 鈴木満男. 1973.「台湾의 祭祀에 있어서의 男性巫者의 登場: 民間道教에 對한 巫術의 位相」『文學』 41(5): 82-590.

Suzuki, Mitsuo. 鈴木満男. 1973.「朝鮮民俗論: 比較近代化論의 한 側面으로서의 日韓의 比較」神島二郎(編)『日本近代化의 特質』 111-138, 東京: 아시아 経済研究所.

Suzuki, Mitsuo. 鈴木満男. 1973.「南原과 雲峰: 韓國民俗紀行(2)」『新勢力』 18(5): 58-68.

Suzuki, Mitsuo. 鈴木滿男. 1974. 「〈韓國學〉研究: *International Journal of Korean Studies*를 중심으로」『朝鮮學報』72: 83-94.

Suzuki, Mitsuo. 鈴木滿男. 1974. 『손님(マレビト)의 構造: 東아시아比較民俗學研究』東京: 三一書房.

Suzuki, Mitsuo. 鈴木滿男. 1975. 「殖民地朝鮮의 어느 日本人教師의 이야기」『日本人談義』6月号.

Suzuki, Mitsuo. 鈴木滿男. 1976. 「國軍墓地와 충렬사(忠烈祠): 東아시아에 있어서의 戰死者의 靈와 祭祀」『新勢力』3月号: 7-15.

Suzuki, Mitsuo. 鈴木滿男. 1976. 「東아시아인의 얼굴생김새와 物腰: 金浦・台北間의 여행経驗에서」『日華月報』113: 4, 114: 2-3.

Suzuki, Mitsuo. 鈴木滿男. 1977. 『華麗島見聞記: 東아시아 政治人類學노트』251頁, 東京: 思索社.

Suzuki, Mitsuo. 鈴木滿男. 1981. 韓國法史學會, 「現代韓國思想에 있어서의 〈民俗〉의 意味」『法史學研究』6: 167-195.

Suzuki, Mitsuo. 鈴木滿男. 1982. 「比較民俗學에 있어서의 〈比較〉의 構造와 視界」『思想』693: 109-136.

Suzuki, Mitsuo. 鈴木滿男. 1984. 「敬老席: 政治人類學의 視角에서」『現代코리아』244: 52-63.

Suzuki, Mitsuo. 鈴木滿男. 1985. 「자상한 언니들이 있는 마을: 아이들의 서울 유학기」『現代코리아』257: 66-71.

Suzuki, Mitsuo. 鈴木滿男. 1985. 「韓國의 社會・文化的特質: 比較民俗學의 視角에서」『文學會誌』36: 51-73, 山口大學.

Suzuki, Mitsuo. 鈴木滿男. 1985. 「韓國의 民衆/ 國民文化의 Problematik: 鄕土文化祭의 背景요소」『九州人類學會會報』13: 36-46.

Suzuki, Mitsuo. 鈴木滿男. 1986. 「자상한 언니들이 있는 마을: 아이들의 서울 유학기」『現代코리아』258: 72-77, 260: 68-73, 262: 66-71, 263: 60-67, 266: 64-71.

Suzuki, Mitsuo. 鈴木滿男. 1987. 「내셔널리즘의 祝祭: 韓國의 民俗文化祭에 대한 政治人類學的 관찰」『韓』(Han)107: 84-136.

Suzuki, Mitsuo. 鈴木滿男. 1987. 「자상한 언니들이 있는 마을: 아이들의 서울 유학기」『現代코리아』268: 68-75, 271: 58-64.

Suzuki, Mitsuo. 鈴木滿男. 1988. 「내셔널리즘의 Folklore: 아메리카에 있어서의 韓國研究의 一側面」『民族學研究』53(1): 86-90.

Suzuki, Mitsuo. 鈴木滿男. 1996.「코리아의 民衆文化는 단지 신종교만 공적으로 표현되고 있다: 韓國新宗敎論·序說」『平和와 宗敎』 15: 111-119.

Takahashi, Shigehiro. 高橋重宏. 1983. (渡辺治 共著)「韓國民間社會福祉의 한 측면」長谷川仏教文化研究所(編)『仏教와 社會事業와 敎育』 373-393, 東京: 長谷川仏教文化研究所.

Takahashi, Shigehiro. 高橋重宏. 1983.「田內千鶴子와 목포 공생원」『아이들과 가정』 19(10): 18-23.

Takahashi, Toichi. 高橋統一. 1977.「年齢集団」增田義郎(編)『日本人의 社會』(講座比較文化6)41-65, 東京: 研究社出版.

Takahashi, Toichi. 高橋統一. 1987.「家族과 親族」高橋統一·芳賀正明·松本誠一『文化人類學노트』 37-45, 東京: 犀書房.

Takahashi, Toichi, Matsumoto, Seiichi, Okuma, Yoko, Kim, Mi-Yeon, Ozawa, Yasunori, Usami, Takanori and Suzuki, Nobuaki. 高橋統一, 松本誠一, 奥間葉子, 金美榮, 小澤康則, 宇佐見隆憲, 鈴木信昭. 1998.「韓國東海岸·漁村社會의 近代化와 文化伝統: 경상북도(慶尙北道) 울진군(蔚珍郡) 죽변(竹辺)의 事例」『아시아·아프리카文化研究所研究年報』 32: 11-72.

Takahashi, Toichi, Shimizu, Hiroaki, Kim, Yong-T'aek and Matsumoto, Seiichi. 高橋統一·清水浩昭·金龍澤·松本誠一. 1990.「韓國의 地域社會와 老人의 地位: 伝統과 近代化를 중심으로」『東洋大學아시아·아프리카文化研究所研究年報』 25: 79-122.

Takasaki, Soji. 高崎宗司. 1996.『中國朝鮮族: 歷史·生活·文化·民族敎育』, 東京: 明石書店.

Takasaki, Soji. 高崎宗司. 1996.『中國朝鮮族: 歷史·生活·文化·民族敎育』, 明石書店.

Takeda, Akira. 竹田旦. 1985. 任東權(著)·熊谷治·依田千百子(譯),「韓國의 民俗과 伝承」『日本民俗學』(通号 161), [1985.09].

Takeda, Akira. 竹田旦. 1986. 依田千百子,「朝鮮民俗文化의 研究」『日本民俗學』(通号 165), [1986.05].

Takeda, Akira. 竹田旦. 1988. 竹田旦,『韓國의 民俗大系. 第1卷』任東權.國書刊行會, 1988.10.

Takeda, Akira. 竹田旦. 1988. 竹田旦,『韓國의 民俗大系. 第2卷』任東權.國書刊行會, 1988.2.

Takeda, Akira. 竹田旦. 1989. 竹田旦,『韓國의 民俗大系. 第3卷』任東權.國書刊

行會, 1989.10.

Takeda, Akira. 竹田旦. 1990. 竹田旦,『韓國의 民俗大系. 第4卷』任東權.國書刊行會, 1990.10.

Takeda, Akira. 竹田旦. 1992. 竹田旦,『韓國의 民俗大系. 第5卷』任東權.國書刊行會, 1992.7.

Takeda, Akira. 竹田旦. 2000.「韓國의『祝祭』と日本의『축제』」『日本語日本文學』(通号 10), [2000.3].

Takeda, Akira. 竹田旦. 2000.「創価大學退任記念論文 比較民俗學의 進展을 중심으로－創価大學10年의 回顧」『日本語日本文學』(通号 10), [2000.3].

Takeda, Akira. 竹田旦. 2000.『日韓祖先祭祀의 比較研究』第一書房, [2000.11] (Academic series new Asia; 35).

Takeda, Akira. 竹田旦. 1978.「韓國의 家族을 둘러싼 斷面(1): 男과 女」『파렐가(ぱれるが)』309: 10-11.

Takeda, Akira. 竹田旦. 1978.「韓國의 家族을 둘러싼 斷面(2): 夫와 妻」『파렐가(ぱれるが)』310: 6-8.

Takeda, Akira. 竹田旦. 1978.「韓國의 家族을 둘러싼 斷面(3): 兄弟의 이름」『파렐가(ぱれるが)』311: 5-7.

Takeda, Akira. 竹田旦. 1978.「韓國의 家族을 둘러싼 斷面(4): 一族의 連帶」『파렐가(ぱれるが)』12: 8-10.

Takeda, Akira. 竹田旦. 1978.「韓國의 家族을 둘러싼 斷面(5): 主婦權」『파렐가(ぱれるが)』313: 5-7.

Takeda, Akira. 竹田旦. 1978.「韓國의 家族을 둘러싼 斷面(6): 隱居」『파렐가(ぱれるが)』314: 14-16.

Takeda, Akira. 竹田旦. 1978.「韓國의 家族을 둘러싼 斷面(7): 家의 神」『파렐가(ぱれるが)』316: 10-12.

Takeda, Akira. 竹田旦. 1978.「韓國의 家族을 둘러싼 斷面(8): 死後結婚(1)」『파렐가(ぱれるが)』317: 9-11.

Takeda, Akira. 竹田旦. 1978.「韓國의 家族을 둘러싼 斷面(9): 死後結婚(2)」『파렐가(ぱれるが)』318: 6-8.

Takeda, Akira. 竹田旦. 1979.「韓國의 家族을 둘러싼 斷面(10): 正月을 맞이하다」『파렐가(ぱれるが)』319: 2-4.

Takeda, Akira. 竹田旦. 1979.「韓國의 家族을 둘러싼 斷面(11): 養子(1)」『파렐가(ぱれるが)』320: 11-13.

Takeda, Akira. 竹田旦. 1979.「韓國의 家族을 둘러싼 斷面(12): 養子(2)」『파렐가(ぱれるが)』321: 6-8.

Takeda, Akira. 竹田旦. 1979.「韓國의 家族을 둘러싼 斷面(13): 族譜」『파렐가(ぱれるが)』323: 10-12.

Takeda, Akira. 竹田旦. 1979.「韓國의 家族을 둘러싼 斷面(14): 結婚式」『파렐가(ぱれるが)』324: 8-11.

Takeda, Akira. 竹田旦. 1979.「韓國의 家族을 둘러싼 斷面(15): 나무의 기러기(雁)」『파렐가(ぱれるが)』325: 7-9.

Takeda, Akira. 竹田旦. 1979.「韓國의 家族을 둘러싼 斷面(16): 궁합(合い性)」『파렐가(ぱれるが)』326: 10-12.

Takeda, Akira. 竹田旦. 1979.「韓國의 家族을 둘러싼 斷面(17): 중매인(仲人)과 친정」『파렐가(ぱれるが)』327: 2-7.

Takeda, Akira. 竹田旦. 1979.「韓國의 家族을 둘러싼 斷面(18): 祈子」『파렐가(ぱれるが)』328: 12-14.

Takeda, Akira. 竹田旦. 1979.「韓國語 "(친구)"의 受容에 대하여: 九州北部島嶼에 있어서의 〈同輩集団〉의 構造分析試論」『湖南文化研究』10・11合併号: 271-290.

Takeda, Akira. 竹田旦. 1980.「韓國의 家族: 男과 女의 差를 중심으로」『사이코로지』5: 4-9.

Takeda, Akira. 竹田旦. 1980.「韓國家族에 있어서의 〈隱居〉에 대하여」國分直一博士古稀記念論集編纂委員會(編)『日本民族文化와 그 周辺: 國分直一博士古稀記念論集: (歷史・民族篇)』607-629, 下關: 新日本教育図書.

Takeda, Akira. 竹田旦. 1983.『나무의 기러기(雁)－韓國의 사람과 家』東京: 사이언스社.

Takeda, Akira. 竹田旦. 1984.「韓國에 있어서의 祖先祭祀의 分割에 대하여」『民俗學評論』24: 32-55

Takeda, Akira. 竹田旦. 1984.「死後結婚」『月刊韓國文化』6(5): 2-3.

Takeda, Akira. 竹田旦. 1986. (金兩基와 對談)「데이터에 보는 韓國의 새로운 結婚觀・家庭觀: 學歷・職種・地域差・家庭觀・友人關係・余暇活動에 대하여」『季刊アルトマン』14: 3-11.

Takeda, Akira. 竹田旦. 1986.「死後結婚의 比較民俗學的研究」月山任東權博士頌壽紀念論文集刊行委員會(編)『月山任東權博士頌壽紀念論文集 民俗學篇』245-277, 서울: 集文堂.

Takeda, Akira. 竹田旦. 1986.「死後結婚의 比較民俗學」『三河民俗』1: 1-19.

Takeda, Akira. 竹田旦. 1987.「東아시아에 있어서의 死靈結婚: 韓國의 習俗을 중심으로」『茨城大學教養部紀要』19: 13-39.

Takeda, Akira. 竹田旦. 1988.「韓國・珍島에 있어서의 死靈結婚」『民俗學論叢(相模民俗學會)』7: 1-23.

Takeda, Akira. 竹田旦. 1990.「韓國에 있어서의 햇것을 바치는 의식(初穗儀礼)」近畿大學民俗學硏究所(編)『民俗文化』2.

Takeda, Akira. 竹田旦. 1990.「韓國의 〈제기(祖先壺)〉에 대하여」竹田旦(篇)『民俗學의 進展과 課題』291-329, 東京: 國書刊行會.

Takeda, Akira. 竹田旦. 1990.「韓國家族에 있어서의 老人」『시리즈家族史 5 노인의 比較家族史』, 東京: 三省堂.

Takeda, Akira. 竹田旦. 1990.『祖靈祭祀와 死靈結婚: 日韓比較民俗學의 試図』, 東京: 人文書院.

Takeda, Akira. 竹田旦. 1991.「東아시아海에 걸친 祖先의 축제 [특히 位牌의 축제에 대하여]」『季刊自然과 文化』34.

Takeda, Akira. 竹田旦. 1993.「韓國珍島에 있어서의 死靈結婚」松崎憲三(編)『東아시아의 死靈結婚』, 東京: 岩田書店.

Takeda, Akira. 竹田旦. 1993.「東아시아에 있어서의 死靈結婚: 韓國의 習俗을 중심으로」松崎憲三(編)『東아시아의 死靈結婚』211-260, 東京: 岩田書店.

Takeda, Akira. 竹田旦. 1995.『祖先崇拜의 比較民俗學: 日韓兩國에 있어서의 祖先祭祀와 社會』, 東京: 吉川弘文館.

Takeda, Akira. 竹田旦. 1996.「法과 民俗의 對立: 韓國의 家庭儀礼에 관한 法令을 중심으로」『日本民俗學』207: 93-135.

Takeda, Akira ed. 竹田旦編. 1990.『民俗學의 進展과 課題』, 東京: 國書刊行會.

Takeda, Yuka. 武田祐佳. 2000.「韓國의 都市에 있어서의『伝統的』相互扶助組織의 內部構造－서울市의 契의 事例에서」『SOSHIOROJI』(社會學硏究會) 45(2).

Takizawa, Hideki. 瀧澤秀樹. 1988.『韓國社會의 轉換』, 東京: 御茶노水書房.

Takizawa, Hideki. 瀧澤秀樹. 1990.「韓國社會의 階層構造와 地域的 特質: 勞働力市場의 地帶構造的 分析을 위한 試論」『甲南経濟學論集』31(2): 91-141.

Takizawa, Hideki. 瀧澤秀樹. 1991.「韓國現代社會分析의 視点」『甲南経濟學論

集』 32(3): 189-203.

Takizawa, Hideki. 瀧澤秀樹. 1992.『韓國의 経濟發展과 社會構造』東京: 御茶노水書房.

Takizawa, Kenji. 瀧澤健次. 1996.「巫俗信仰에서 본 在日코리언의 親族關係－信貴山西麓의 朝鮮寺・大興寺의 事例를 중심으로」『東洋大學大學院紀要』 32.

Taniura, Takao. 谷浦孝雄. 1980.「韓國에 있어서의 農村政策의 展開」『아시아経濟』 21(10): 4-21.

Taniura, Takao ed. 谷浦孝雄(編). 1992.『地域研究시리즈 朝鮮半島』東京: 아시아経濟研究所.

The University Museum, University of Tokyo, ed. 東京大學總合研究資料館特別展示實行委員會(編). 1991.『乾板에 새겨진 世界: 鳥居龍藏가 본 아시아』東京: 東京大學總合研究資料館(發賣: 東京大學出版會).

Toguchi, Fumiko. 渡口文子. 1991.「韓國의 民族衣裝: 琉裝와의 比較」沖縄縣立芸術大學琉韓伝承文化調査団『韓國伝承文化의 研究: 沖縄와의 比較를 목표로서』 119-142, 那覇: 沖縄縣立芸術大學琉韓伝承文化調査団Tokui, Ken. 德井賢. 1975.「火田民見聞記」『季刊 Dolmen』 6: 135-140.

Tokui, Ken. 德井賢. 1977.「火田民방문기」『地理』 22(7): 74-83, 22(8): 60-66.

Tokui, Ken. 德井賢. 1983.「高麗人參採取人 방문기」『地理』 28(12): 113-121.

Tokui, Ken. 德井賢. 1991.「朝鮮半島의 火田民」『季刊自然과 文化』 34.

Torigoe, Hiroyuki. 鳥越皓之. 1998.「韓國에 있어서의 住民自治의 可能性」『關西學院大學社會學部紀要』 81: 175-184.

Tosa, Masaki. 土佐昌樹. 1993.「儀禮와 情動」『大阪大學人間科學部紀要』(通号19).

Tosa, Masaki. 土佐昌樹. 1998.『인터넷과 宗教』, 岩波書店, 1998.11, (「叢書」internet社會).

Tosa, Masaki. 土佐昌樹. 2001.『왜 개를 먹어야 하는가－韓國社會의 세계화와 개고기 금식(犬食タブー)의 방향(特集 食을 둘러싼 금기의 運命)』Vesta. (43), [2001.夏].

Tosa, Masaki. 土佐昌樹. 1988.「憑依의 現在: 韓國 珍島에 있어서의 巫俗儀禮의 記述과 文化的意義」『民族學研究』 53(4): 374-398.

Tosa, Masaki. 土佐昌樹. 1998.「韓國의 反아시아的 패러다임」青木 保・佐伯啓思(編)『「아시아적 평가」란 무엇인가』 TBS브리테니커.

Tosa, Masaki. 土佐昌樹. 1999.「情報化와 植民地이미지－〈추한(醜い) 韓國人〉騷動을 중심으로」青木 保・梶原景昭(編)『情報社會의 文化(1) 情報化와 아시아・이미지』東京大學出版會.

Toyofuku, Youichi. 豊福陽一. 1984.「漁村契의 自治的實態」日韓漁村社會・経濟共同硏究會『日韓合同學術調査報告 第2輯: 韓國 慶尙北道 平海邑 厚浦里』115-127, 神戸: 日韓漁村社會・経濟共同硏究會事務局.

Toyofuku, Youichi. 豊福陽一. 1986.「韓國漁村에 있어서의 마을의 自治」日韓漁村社會・経濟共同硏究會『日韓合同學術調査報告 第4輯: 韓國全羅南道 莞島郡』198-207, 神戸: 日韓漁村社會・経濟共同硏究會事務局.

Tsuha, Takashi. 津波高志. 1987. 崔在錫 (著)・津波高志 (譯),「韓國의 친족집단과 류큐(琉球)의 친족집단－유사점(類似点)과 전파를 중심으로」『琉大史學』(通号 15), [1987.10].

Tsuha, Takashi. 津波高志. 1999.『한글과 고추가루(唐辛子)』보더 잉크(ボーダーインク), [1999.9].

Tsuha, Takashi. 津波高志. 1999. 韓相福・津波高志(他),「강연 자문화연구의 인식론」『沖縄民俗硏究』(19), [1999.3].

Tsuha, Takashi. 津波高志. 2000. 鈴木正崇・野村伸一(編),「(서평과 소개)가면과 무속의 연구－일본과 한국」『宗教硏究』74(2) (通号 325), [2000.9].

Tsuha, Takashi. 津波高志. 2002. 記念論集刊行會,『류큐(琉球)・아시아의 민속과 역사』榕樹書林, [2002.7].

Tsuha, Takashi. 津波高志. 1985.「濟州島東部地域의 相續慣行」『比較民俗學會會報』3: 2-5.

Tsuha, Takashi. 津波高志. 1989.「상속과 계승에서 본 제주도의 가족」『지역문화연구(地域文化硏究)』4: 99-104.

Tsuha, Takashi. 津波高志. 1990.「제주도의 通婚圈」杉山晃一・櫻井哲男(編)『한국사회의 문화인류학』72-86, 東京: 弘文堂.

Tsuha, Takashi. 津波高志. 1991. 沖縄縣立芸術大學琉韓伝承文化調査団,「제주도에 있어서의 상속관행: 동부 중산촌의 한 사례를 중심으로」『한국전승문화의 연구: 오키나와(沖縄)와의 비교를 목표로서』75-86, 那覇: 沖縄縣立芸術大學琉韓伝承文化調査団.

Tsuha, Takashi. 津波高志. 1993.「제주도 동부에 있어서의 상속관행」『沖縄民俗硏究』13.

Tsuji, Ryozo. 辻稜三. 1982.「한국의 화전의 변모에 대해서」『지리(地理)』27(3):

143-48.

Tsuji, Ryozo. 辻稜三. 1985. 楊普景(著), (번역)「조선시대의 지리서에 관한 연구서설」『조선학보(朝鮮學報)』 116: 1-18.

Tsuji, Ryozo. 辻稜三. 1985.「한국에 있어서의 도토리(ドングリ)의 가공과 저장에 관한 연구」『계간인류학(季刊人類學)』 16(4): 117-150.

Tsuji, Ryozo. 辻稜三. 1985.「한국 대구시의 시장에 있어서의 묵 (도토리가공식품)의 유통」『인문지리(人文地理)』 37(4): 86-96.

Tsuji, Ryozo. 辻稜三. 1985.「한국지리학회의 동향(1)」『지리(地理)』 30(1): 48-58.

Tsuji, Ryozo. 辻稜三. 1985.「한국지리학회의 동향(2)」『지리(地理)』 30(2): 100-107.

Tsuji, Ryozo. 辻稜三. 1986.「한국제주도의 도토리묵(ドングリドーフ)」『월간한국문화(月刊韓國文化)』 8(11): 26-29.

Tsuji, Ryozo. 辻稜三. 1987.「<조선산 야생식용식물>의 내용과 그 자료적 가치」『조선학보(朝鮮學報)』 123: 153-177.

Tsuruzono, Hiroshi. 鶴園裕. 1995.「조선사연구와 문화인류학: 외국사연구와 이문화이해를 둘러싼 노트」『金澤大學教養部論集』 32(2): 61-70.

Uchida, Ruriko. 內田るり子. 1978.「한국기행」『음성학회회보(音聲學會會報)』 158: 20-21, 15.

Uchida, Ruriko. 內田るり子. 1978.『모내기논(田植ばやし)연구』, 東京: 雄山閣出版.

Ueda, Chiak. 上田千秋. 1987.「아시아 각국의 노인복지」山下袈裟男・上田千秋(編)『개설 노인복지』 246-255, 京都: Minerva書房.

Uemura, Yukio. 植村幸生. 1989.「재일교포의 무속의례와 음악」『東洋音樂硏究』(通号 54), [1989.8].

Uemura, Yukio. 植村幸生. 1993.「한국근대음악사로의 태동－80년대후반의 연구동향에서」『東洋音樂硏究』 (通号 57), [1993.8].

Uemura, Yukio. 植村幸生. 1995.「조선전기 군악제도(軍樂制度)의 일고찰－취라치(吹螺赤)와 태평소(大平簫)」『東京芸術大學音樂學部紀要』 (通号 21).

Uemura, Yukio. 植村幸生. 1996. 柘植元一・植村幸生,『아시아음악사』, 音樂之友社, [1996.10].

Uemura, Yukio. 植村幸生. 1997.「식민지기 조선에 있어서의 궁정음악의 조사를 중심으로－田辺尙雄「조선아악조사(朝鮮雅樂調査)」의 정치적 문맥(政

治的文脈)(특집 근대조선에 있어서의 전통문화의 “발견”)」『朝鮮研究會論文集』(通号 35), [1997.10].

Uemura, Yukio. 植村幸生. 1998.『한국음악탐험』, 音樂之友社, 1998.11, (처음 음악과 만나는 책).

Uemura, Yukio. 植村幸生. 1999. 山口修・加藤富美子・山口明子 制作監修・高橋光則構成(演出), 「아시아의 음악과 문화」『東洋音樂研究』(通号 64), [1999.8].

Uemura, Yukio. 植村幸生. 2000. 植村幸生・塚原康子・寺内直子 他, 「동아시아에 있어서의 국민국가형성과 궁정음악의 변화(日本音樂學會第50回全國大會總覽)(Colloquium)」『音樂學』45(3), [2000.6].

Uemura, Yukio. 植村幸生. 2002.『현금(玄琴)에 한국문화를 배우다』, 婦人之友. 96(6), [2002.6].

Uezu, Hitoshi. 上江州均. 1986.「제주도의 민속도구(濟州島의 民具)」『오키나와 민속연구(沖縄民俗研究)』6.

Uezu, Hitoshi. 上江州均. 1991. 오키나와현립 예술대학(沖縄縣立芸術大學) 류한전승문화조사단(琉韓伝承文化調査団), 「한국의 민속도구: 오키나와민속도구(沖縄民具)와의 비교」『한국전승문화의 연구: 오키나와(沖縄)와의 비교를 목표로서』145-166, 나하(那覇): 오키나와현립예술대학(沖縄縣立芸術大學) 류한전승문화조사단(琉韓伝承文化調査団).

Ukiba, Masachika. 浮葉正親. 1992.「근대화와 한국(조선)농촌사회의 변용: 〈모럴・이코노미〉 론의 시점에서」『일본학보(日本學報)(오오사카대학(大阪大學))』11: 1-24.

Ukiba, Masachika. 浮葉正親. 2001.「한국의 도시에 있어서의 샤머니즘문화의 변용－광주시의 사례를 중심으로」『沙平裵俊鎬教授華甲紀念論叢』887-907.

Usami, Takanori. 宇佐美隆憲. 1993.「중국조선족의 민족씨름의 구조: 규칙과 기술의 체계를 중심으로」『白山人類學』2.

Wada, Shohei. 和田正平. 1994.「명혼(冥婚): 한국의 사후결혼」『계간민속학』69: 74-79.

Wakamatsu, Minoru. 若松實編. 1982.『한국의 관혼상제』, 東京: 高麗書林.

Wakamatsu, Minoru. 若松實編譯. 1975.『한국 속담(상세해석)』263頁, 東京: 高麗書林.

Wakamori, Tamio. 和歌森民男. 1986.「한국농촌사회조사개보: 전라북도 김제군 죽산면 대창리 대장에 있어서의 기독교의 수용과 민속」『桐朋學園大學

短期大學部紀要』 5: 67-77.

Wakamori, Tamio. 和歌森民男. 1990.「한국농촌사회조사개보(속): 전라북도 김제군 죽산면 대창리 대장에 있어서의 기독교의 수용과 민속」『桐朋學園大學短期大學部紀要』 8: 69-83.

Wakamori, Taro. 和歌森太郎. 1975.「(최인학과의 대담)민족적 시각으로 바라본 한일관계」『아시아공론』 4(12): 89-95.

Wakamori, Taro. 和歌森太郎. 1975.「한・일민속의 유연성(類緣性): 민족의 생활사와 그 전승」『아시아공론』 4(12): 90-93.

Watanabe, Hiroshi. 渡辺浩. 1991.「유학자・선비・양반: 유학적 〈교양인〉의 존재형태」梅棹忠夫・栗田靖之(編)『지식과 교양의 문명학』, 東京: 中央公論社.

Watanabe, Toshio and Kajiwara, Hirokazu. 渡辺利夫・梶原弘和. 1980.「한국농업의 신전개」『아시아경제』 21(3): 71-79.

Watanabe, Yoshio. 渡辺欣雄. 1990.「풍수(風水)・선조(祖先)・출자(出自): 대화형식에 의한 동아시아 풍수론의 전망」竹田旦編『민속학의 진전과 과제』 359-387, 東京: 國書刊行會.

Watanabe, Yoshio. 渡辺欣雄. 1996.「동아시아의 풍수의식: 그래프에 의한 경향과 차이를 알기 위한 각서」『東京都立大學 人文學報』 271: 1-57.

Yagi, Saichi. 八木佐市. 1975.「한국의 상례(喪礼)・장례제도(葬制)」『히로시마민속(廣島民俗)』 4: 23-29.

Yagi, Saichi. 八木佐市. 1978.「한국농촌의 가족주의적 성격: 내곡리의 실태를 중심으로」『히로시마법학(廣島法學)』 2(2・3): 173-198.

Yagi, Saichi, and Hirata, Junji, and Ogasawara, Shin. 八木佐市・平田順治・小笠原眞. 1976.「촌락구조와 문화변용: 내곡리의 경우」野口隆(編)『이민과 문화변용: 한국 대야성(陜川)지역의 사례연구』 65-147, 東京: 日本學術振興會.

Yamamoto, Hanako. 山本華子. 2000.「쉽게 배우는 한국문화 태극기・애국가편」『月刊韓國文化』 (通号 252), [2000.11].

Yamamoto, Hanako. 山本華子. 2000.「쉽게 배우는 한국문화－추석(秋夕)편」『月刊韓國文化』 (通号 251), [2000.10].

Yamamoto, Hanako. 山本華子. 2001.「쉽게 배우는 한국문화 사물놀이편」『月刊韓國文化』 (通号 255), [2001.2].

Yamamoto, Hanako. 山本華子. 2002.「이왕직(李王職)의 아악부(雅樂部)에 관한 연구－<직원록>과 청취조사를 중심으로」『青丘學術論集』20, [2002.3].

Yamamoto, Kahori. 山本かほり. 1996. 谷富夫(編),「재한일본인처의 생활사」『life history를 배우는 사람을 위해서』, 世界思想社.

Yamamoto, Kahori. 山本かほり. 1998.「아이치현(愛知縣)에 있어서의 에스니크 커뮤니티의 연구(1) 新川町의 재일교포집단주거지역을 사례로서」『愛知縣立大學文學部論集. 社會福祉學科編』(通号 47).

Yamamoto, Kahori. 山本かほり. 1999.「재일교포의 지진」岩崎信彦他(編)『한신(阪神)・아와지(淡路)대지진의 사회학』第3巻, 昭和堂.

Yamamoto, Kahori. 山本かほり. 1999. 山田正浩・沖田佳代子・山本かほり,「한국에 있어서의 지역・가족의 변화와 노친부양의식」『社會福祉研究1(1)』, [1999.7].

Yamamoto, Kahori. 山本かほり. 2000.「유교규범속의 여성: 한국여성의 사회적 지위에 관한 고찰」小林孝行(編)『변모하는 현대가족사회』44-65, 京都: 世界思想社.

Yamanaka, Miyuki. 山中美由紀. 1978.「한국도시가족의 노친자관계 (老親子關係)」『SOSHIOROJI』23(2): 75-87.

Yamanaka, Miyuki山中美由紀. 1982.「한국의 영절혼(Yon'jul-hon)에 관한 기록」『鹿兒島経濟大學社會學部論集』1: 63-73.

Yamanaka, Miyuki. 山中美由紀. 1983. 金宗澤(著),「(번역)한국인의 전통적인 여성관: 속언(俗諺)・속담을 통해」『鹿兒島経濟大學社會學部論集』1(3): 87-104.

Yamanaka, Miyuki. 山中美由紀. 1985.「한국농촌여성의 배우자선택과 결혼관: 경상북도 안동군의 조사결과에서」『SOSHIOROJI』30(2), 131-150.

Yamanaka, Miyuki. 山中美由紀. 1987.「한국에 있어서의 노인복지현황: 사회보장과 가족부양에서 본 노후경제생활을 중심으로」『鹿兒島経濟大學社會學部論集』5(3, 4): 57-76.

Yamanaka, Miyuki. 山中美由紀. 1995.「한국에 있어서의 며느리・시누이관계의 변화에서 본 私事化과정」『龍谷大學社會學部紀要』6: 87-97.

Yamanaka, Miyuki. 山中美由紀. 1996.「한국사회와 가족변동」野々山久也・袖井孝子・篠崎正美(編)『지금 가족에게 무엇이 일어나고 있는가: 가족사회학의 패러다임전환을 중심으로』221-240, 京都: Minerva書房.

Yamane, Mari. 山根眞理. 1995.「현대한국의 도시가족에 있어서의 남편과 아내

의 네트워크: 친족집단의 유대(絆)와 지원네트워크」『愛知教育大學家政學教室紀要』26: 123-130.

Yamane, Mari and Onode, Setsuko. 山根眞理・斧出節子. 1992.『대한민국과 일본의 가족관계에 관한 비교연구보고서』, 兵庫: 兵庫縣家庭問題研究所.

Yamawaki, Keizo. 山脇啓造. 2000.「재일코리언의 아이덴티티 분류편성에 관한 시론」『明治大學社會科學研究所紀要』38-2.

Yang, Ae-Soon. 梁 愛舜. 1999.「재일교포1세의 우주론과 향촌사회－『유교적 가족』의 신념체계와 행동양식」『立命館産業社會論集』35-2.

Yang, Ae-Soon. 梁 愛舜. 2000.「제사와 재일교포사회－세대교체와 세속화를 중심으로」『立命館産業社會論集』36-2.

Yano, Ken'ichi. 矢野謙一. 1997.「단음절 의성어, 의태어의 주요부와 공감각」『熊本學園大學文學・言語學論集』4(2), [1997.12].

Yano, Ken'ichi. 矢野謙一. 1997.「조선어의 의성어, 의태어－단음절어의 음형태와 음교체」『朝鮮學報』(通号 164), [1997.7].

Yano, Ken'ichi. 矢野謙一. 1998.「카자흐스탄에 있어서의 조선어의 변용」『熊本學園大學文學・言語學論集』5(2), [1998.12].

Yano, Ken'ichi. 矢野謙一. 2000.「조선어용언의 활용에 있어서의 음운현상과 음운규칙」『海外事情研究』28(1) (通号 55), [2000.9].

Yano, Ken'ichi. 矢野謙一. 2001. 矢野 謙一 (譯)・Dmitry V. Myong,「번역 카자흐스탄의 정치경제적 상황과 고려인」『海外事情研究』28(2) (通号 56), [2001.2].

Yano, Takao. 矢野敬生. 2000. 林 在圭・矢野 敬生,「종족(宗族)마을에 있어서의 수리(水利)관행－한국 충청남도 당진군 종족마을의 사례」『早稲田大學人間科學研究』13(1).

Yano, Takao. 矢野敬生. 2001. 矢野 敬生・林 在圭,「한국에 있어서의 장례제도의 전통과 그 변용－충청남도(忠淸南道) 당진군(唐津郡)의 사례 (특집・문화의 전통과 변용－장례제(葬制)・묘지제(墓制)를 중심으로)」『휴먼사이언스(ヒューマンサイエンス)』14(1), [2001.11].

Yano, Yuriko. 矢野百合子. 1987.「李陸史考－그 생애와 시」『學苑』(通号 569), [1987.5].

Yano, Yuriko. 矢野百合子. 1996.「聖德山觀音寺연기설화(緣起說話)의 형성과 변용」『朝鮮學報』(通号 158), [1996.1].

Yasuda, Hiromi. 安田ひろみ. 1990.「한국전통사회의 여성에 있어서의 〈억압〉과 샤머니즘: 여성의 라이프 스테이지로의 대응으로서」『소키에타스』 17.

Yasuda, Hiromi. 安田ひろみ. 1991.「한국샤머니즘연구의 현재: 1970년이후의 내외연구동향과 전망」『메이지대학(明治大學)대학원기요(大學院紀要)정치경제학편』 28: 197-212.

Yasuda, Hiromi. 安田ひろみ. 1991.「한국샤머니즘연구소사」大胡欽一・高桑史子・山内健治(編)『동아시아의 문화인류학』, 東京: 八千代出版.

Yasuda, Hiromi. 安田ひろみ. 1997.「한국의 여성: 유교적 규범의 뒷면, 무당의 세계에서」綾部恒雄(編)『여성의 민족지1 아시아편』39-64, 東京: 弘文堂.

Yatazawa, Noriko. 谷田澤典子. 1993.「한국의 가족: 동족촌(同族村)의 가족」龜山慶一(編)『한국농촌조사보고서』, 豊田市: 豊田短期大學.

Yatazawa, Noriko. 谷田澤典子. 1995.「한국의 가족3: 어촌가족의 변동과 고령자복지」『도요타전문대학기요』 5: 10-24.

Yazawa, Shujiro. 矢澤修次郎. 1987.「아시아의 〈근대화〉의 방향」『Up』 16(11): 25-30.

Yoda, Chihoko. 依田千百子. 1972.「일본신화와 조선신화(일본신화의 세계(특집))-(일본신화의 출자와 그 계통)」『國文學解釋과 鑑賞』 37(1), [1972.1].

Yoda, Chihoko. 依田千百子. 1978. 金烈圭[他],『한국민간전승과 민화의 연구』, 學生社, [1978.12].

Yoda, Chihoko. 依田千百子. 1984. 任東權[他],『한국의 민속과 전승』, 櫻楓社, [1984.11].

Yoda, Chihoko. 依田千百子. 1990. 荒木博之・野村純一・福田晃, 宮田登・渡辺昭五(編),「일본전설대계(별권1)연구편」『國學院雜誌』 91(4), [1990.4].

Yoda, Chihoko. 依田千百子. 1991. 依田千百子,『조선신화전승의 연구』, 瑠璃書房, [1991.9].

Yoda, Chihoko. 依田千百子. 1993.『신의 제례와 전승』, 上田正昭.同朋舍出版, [1993.6].

Yoda, Chihoko. 依田千百子. 1994. 依田千百子・中西正樹,『김덕순 옛날이야기집』, 三弥井書店, [1994.6].

Yoda, Chihoko. 依田千百子. 1996. 〈金子量重선생 고희기념논집〉간행위원회,『아시아의 민족조형문화』 徵藏館, [1996.1].

Yoda, Chihoko. 依田千百子. 2001. 依田 千百子,『한국의 용(龍)신앙－왕권과 수신(水神), 부(富)의 심볼 (특집 드래곤・나가・용)』.

Yoda, Chihoko. 依田千百子. 1966.「조선의 벼농사의례: 그 累型을 중심으로」『민속학연구』31(2): 107-137.

Yoda, Chihoko. 依田千百子. 1967. (서평)「김양기『조선의 예능』『조선의 가면 Ⅰ, Ⅱ, Ⅲ』」『민속학연구』32(3): 245.

Yoda, Chihoko. 依田千百子. 1968. (서평)「張籌根・崔吉城, 민속자료조사보고서『경기도지역 무속(양주군 무녀 조영자편)』」『민족학연구(民族學研究)』33(1): 95-98.

Yoda, Chihoko. 依田千百子. 1969.「연중행사에서 본 조선에 있어서의 중국문화 수용형식에 대한 일고찰」『조선학보(朝鮮學報)』52: 93-131.

Yoda, Chihoko. 依田千百子. 1971. (서평)「한국문화인류학회편『한국민속종합조사보고서(전남)』」『민족학연구』36(1): 74-77.

Yoda, Chihoko. 依田千百子. 1971.「이두현『한국가면극』」『민족학연구』36(2): 187-191.

Yoda, Chihoko. 依田千百子. 1975.「조선의 산신(山神)신앙(1): 수렵민의 산신(山神) 및 조선의 수렵민문화」『조선학보(朝鮮學報)』75: 25-76.

Yoda, Chihoko. 依田千百子. 1977. (서평)「張籌根『한국의 민간신앙』『한국의 향토신앙』」『민족학연구(民族學研究)』41(4): 396-399.

Yoda, Chihoko. 依田千百子. 1977.「추석고찰(秋夕考)」『白初 洪淳昶博士 환갑기념사학논총』267-290, 서울: 螢雪出版社.

Yoda, Chihoko. 依田千百子. 1977.「일본신화와 조선신화」伊藤清司・大林太良(編)『일본신화연구Ⅰ』172-178, 東京: 學生社.

Yoda, Chihoko. 依田千百子. 1980.「한국의 무녀」『季刊 유구(悠久)』2: 90-103.

Yoda, Chihoko. 依田千百子. 1980.「조선의 장례제도와 타계관」國分直一博士古稀記念論集編纂委員會(編)『일본민족문화와 그 주변: 國分直一博士古稀記念論集: (歷史・民族篇)』533-586, 下關: 新日本教育図書.

Yoda, Chihoko. 依田千百子. 1981.「한국의 무녀」『한일관계연구소기요』10・11: 183-197.

Yoda, Chihoko. 依田千百子. 1981.「무속의 문화적 의미: 조선샤머니즘을 중심으로」『전통과 현대』71: 119-134.

Yoda, Chihoko. 依田千百子. 1982.「한국의 異鄕訪問譚의 구조」『구승문예연구』5: 47-57.

Yoda, Chihoko. 依田千百子. 1983. 朴桂弘(著), 「(서평) 『한국의 마을축제』」 『한국민속학』 17: 137-145.

Yoda, Chihoko. 依田千百子. 1983. 朴桂弘(著), 「(서평) 『한국의 마을축제』」 『일본민속학』 147: 61-66.

Yoda, Chihoko. 依田千百子. 1984. 「한국문화의 이중성에 관한 일고찰: 여성 · 제례 · 샤머니즘을 중심으로」 『宜民李杜鉉博士回甲紀念論文集』 483-515, 서울: 學硏社.

Yoda, Chihoko. 依田千百子. 1984. 「일본과 한국의 샤머니즘에 있어서의 영매(靈媒)와 사제(司祭): 신(神)의 축제장(まつり場)의 인적 구성을 중심으로」 『郡山女子大學紀要』 20: 119-134.

Yoda, Chihoko. 依田千百子. 1985. 「한국의 식문화에 관한 문화인류학적 문제」 斗山金宅圭博士華甲記念論文集刊行委員會(編) 『문화인류학논총』.

Yoda, Chihoko. 依田千百子. 1985. 「조선의 무속신화와 일본의 중세신화: 신의 子邂逅型日光 감정설화를 중심으로」 『Eureka』 17(1): 198-207.

Yoda, Chihoko. 依田千百子. 1985. 『조선민속문화의 연구: 조선의 기층문화와 그 원류를 중심으로』, 東京: 瑠璃書房.

Yoda, Chihoko. 依田千百子. 1986. 熊谷治(著) · 村上四男共(著)(서평) 「『동아시아의 민속과 제례』」 『조선학보』 121: 161-163.

Yoda, Chihoko. 依田千百子. 1986. 「금성산(錦城山)/곰/오대산(五台山)/십장생(十長生)/(崔吉城과 共著)샤머니즘/추석(秋夕)/축제일(祝祭日)/정월(正月)/신화(神話)/속리산(俗離山)/서낭당/칠월칠석(七夕)/단오(端午)/장승/연중행사(年中行事)/농경의례(農耕儀禮)/축제/민화(民話)/약수(藥水)」 伊藤亞人 · 大村益男 · 梶村秀樹 · 武田幸男(監修) 『조선을 이해하는 사전』, 東京: 平凡社.

Yoda, Chihoko. 依田千百子. 1986. 「조선의 연중행사」 『기초한글』 1(9): 31-33.

Yoda, Chihoko. 依田千百子. 1986. 「요괴(도깨비)한국의 민속우주」 『한국민속학』.

Yoda, Chihoko. 依田千百子. 1987. 「고대조선의 제례와 신앙」 大林太良(編) 『일본의 고대13 마음속의 우주』 333-360, 東京: 中央公論社.

Yoda, Chihoko. 依田千百子. 1987. 赤松智城 · 任東權 · 三品彰英 · 村山智順, 『문화인류학사전』, 東京: 弘文堂.

Yoda, Chihoko. 依田千百子. 1987. 「문화인류학에서 본 고대 동아시아의 여왕(제): 고대조선의 여왕과 왕권의 聖과 俗의 二分구조를 중심으로」 『創立四十周年記念論文集』 77-111, 郡山: 郡山開成學園

Yoda, Chihoko. 依田千百子. 1989.「신의 경쟁: 조선의 創世신화와 그 구조」『동아시아의 創世신화』124-167, 東京: 弘文堂.

Yoda, Chihoko. 依田千百子. 1990.「한국의 식문화와 여성: 주부의 입신양명(揚名)・유교・부(富)의 재분배」杉山晃一・櫻井哲男(編)『한국사회의 문화인류학』, 東京: 弘文堂.

Yoda, Chihoko. 依田千百子. 1990.「조선의 왕권신화의 구조: 꽃도둑질(花盜み)・외래왕(外來王)・국토위양(國讓り)」『國學院雜誌』91(6): 54-97.

Yoda, Chihoko. 依田千百子. 1990.「조선의 천인(天人)들: 질서의 설정자」竹田旦(編)『민속학의 진전과 과제』477-505, 東京: 國書刊行會.

Yoda, Chihoko. 依田千百子. 1991.「홍합젓갈(いずし)원류고찰: 발해사(渤海使)가 전한 식문화」『국학원대학일본문화연구소보고(國學院大學日本文化研究所報)』165.

Yoda, Chihoko. 依田千百子. 1991.「무당」植松明石(編)『중국주변해(環中國海)의 민속과 제례2 신의 제례』337-368, 東京: 凱風社.

Yoda, Chihoko. 依田千百子. 1991.「조선의 호랑이의 문화사적 의미 산신(山神)과 권력(權力)의 상징」『국학원대학 기요(紀要)』29: 33-56.

Yoda, Chihoko. 依田千百子. 1992.「고대에 있어서의 조선의 식문화의 일본으로의 영향」『국학원대학 일본문화연구 기요(紀要)』69: 57-102.

Yoda, Chihoko. 依田千百子. 1992.「조선의 용과 뱀의 신앙: 왕권과 수신(水神), 부(富)와 영혼의 상징」아시아민속조형문화연구소편(民俗造形文化研究所編)『아시아의 용과 뱀: 조형과 상징』, 東京: 雄山閣出版.

Yoda, Chihoko. 依田千百子. 1996.「조선의 금속전승: 북방계를 중심으로」劉茂源(編)『사람・물건・언어의 인류학: 國分直一박사 미수기념논집』440-456, 東京: 慶友社.

Yokota, Ken'ichi. 横田健一. 1972.「미시나 쇼에이(三品彰英)박사의 서거」『민족학연구』37(1): 66-67.

Yokota, Nobuko. 横田伸子. 1994.「1980년대 한국에 있어서의 노동시장구조의 변화－제조업 생산직 남자노동자를 중심으로」『아시아經濟』35(10), [1994.10].

Yokota, Nobuko. 横田伸子. 1995. 李根 (著)・横田伸子 (譯)「환황해(環黃海)경제권과 한・중・일 경제협력 (환황해(環黃海)지역경제교류의 발전과 산구(山口)〈특집〉)」『東亞經濟研究』55(2), [1995.8].

Yokota, Nobuko. 横田伸子. 1996. 金大煥 (著)・横田伸子 (譯)「민영화와 노동문

제 (특집 한국노사관계의 현황과 전망－한일교류심포지엄)」『大原社會問題研究所雜誌』(通号 457), [1996.12].

Yokota, Nobuko. 横田伸子. 1997.「한국의 〈도시하층민〉과 노동시장 (특집 아시아의 노동문제 (2))」『大原社會問題研究所雜誌』(通号 464), [1997.7].

Yokota, Nobuko. 横田伸子. 2000.「1987년 이후의 한국노동시장의 구조변화와 노사관계－제조업 남자생산노동자를 중심으로」『東亞経済研究』58(3), [2000.1].

Yokota, Nobuko. 横田伸子. 2000. 尹辰浩 (著)・横田伸子 (譯),「한국노사관계의 현황과 전망 (특집 환황해(環黃海)지역경제의 신전개를 중심으로: 21세기의 과제－제7회 동아시아 국제심포지엄보고)」『東亞経済研究』59(1), [2000.6].

Yokota, Nobuko. 横田伸子. 2001.「한국의 개발체제와 새마을운동－1970년대를 중심으로」『東亞経済研究』59(4), [2001.3].

Yokota, Nobuko. 横田伸子. 2001.「민주화과정에 있어서의 한국노동시장의 구조변화와 노사관계－제조업 남자생산노동자를 중심으로 (経済危機와 産業再編)」『韓國経済研究』1(2), [2001.3].

Yokota, Nobuko. 横田伸子. 2002.「한국/새마을운동과 농촌여성 (특집 발전도상국의 여성노동과 사회정책)」『아지研월드・트렌드』8(9) (通号 84), [2002.9].

Yokota, Nobuko. 横田伸子. 2002.「한국의 여성노동과 노동운동 (특집 제10회 동아시아 국제심포지엄－동아시아의 사회개발과 일본)－(발표자의 보고)」『東亞経済研究』61(1), [2002.6].

Yokota, Nobuko. 横田伸子. 2002.「연재자료 후발공업국에 있어서의 여성노동과 사회정책(4)한국」『아시아経済』43(11), [2002.11].

Yokoyama, Minoru. 横山實. 1986.「한국과 일본의 청소년의식: 데이빗 리스먼의 가설을 이용한 분석」『國際法學』23(4): 81-130.

Yoo, Kyung-Mi. 劉 卿美. 2002.「특별기고 윷놀이의 유래에 관하여」『月刊韓國文化』(通号 266), [2002.1].

Yoo, Young-Tae. 劉 永大. 1999.「살아 있는 사람을 위한 굿－진도 씨김굿의 거리와 이념」鈴木正崇・野村伸一(編)『가면(仮面)과 무속(巫俗)의 연구－일본과 한국』第一書房.

Yoon, Kwang-Bong. 尹 光鳳. 1998.「민속극(民俗劇)의 진행론－삼국예능의 원초적인 측면에서」『言語文化研究』(通号 24).

Yoon, Kwang-Bong. 尹 光鳳. 2001. 「韓國가면극(仮面劇)의 주제양상(1) – 야마다이극(山台劇)을 중심으로」『언어문화연구』 27.

Yoon, Kwang-Bong. 尹 光鳳. 2002. 「韓國연극의 전개양상 – 韓國 연극시(演戯詩)를 중심으로」『아시아 사회문화연구(3)』, [2002.3].

Yoshida, Hajime. 吉田元. 2000. 「일본 술 제조 기술의 대만, 조선, 중국으로의 이전」 梅棹忠夫 · 吉田集而(編) 『술(酒)과 日本文明』, 弘文堂.

Yoshida, Mitsuo. 吉田光男. 1977. 「『한림원(翰苑)』 註所引 『고려기(高麗記)』에 대해 – 특히 필자와 작성연차」『朝鮮學報』 (通号 85), [1977.10].

Yoshida, Mitsuo. 吉田光男. 1979. 「이조(李朝)초기의 지방지배에 대해 – 『세종실록(世宗實錄)』지리지 성씨조(姓氏條)의 성격검토를 중심으로」『社會経濟史學』 44(5), [1979.3].

Yoshida, Mitsuo. 吉田光男. 1980. 「고려시대(高麗時代)의 수운기구 〈강(江)〉에 대하여」『社會経濟史學』 46(4), [1980.11].

Yoshida, Mitsuo. 吉田光男. 1981. 「15세기 조선의 토관제(土官制) – 이조초기 지방지배체제의 단면 (이조사(李朝史)의 문제〈특집〉)」『朝鮮史研究會論文集』 (通号 18), [1981.3].

Yoshida, Mitsuo. 吉田光男. 1984. 「이조(李朝)말기의 조난구조와 조난작업의 일례 – 「조행일록(漕行日錄)」에서의 1875年의 성당창(聖堂倉)」『朝鮮學報』 (通号 113), [1984.10].

Yoshida, Mitsuo. 吉田光男. 1985. 「이조(李朝)후기 서울의 미상인조합(米商人組合) 〈미전(米廛)〉에 대하여 – 1791年의 신해통공(辛亥通共)전후를 중심으로 (중 · 근세의 상인과 직인(職人)〈특집〉)」『史潮』 (通号 17) [1985.7].

Yoshida, Mitsuo. 吉田光男. 1986. 「19세기 충청도의 해난(海難) – 조운선(漕運船)의 조난 사례를 통하여」『朝鮮學報』 (通号 121), [1986.10].

Yoshida, Mitsuo. 吉田光男. 1988. 「개성부기(開城簿記)연구의 재검토」『朝鮮史研究會論文集』 (通号 25), [1988.3].

Yoshida, Mitsuo. 吉田光男. 1989. 「다가와 코조(田川孝三)선생의 서거를 애도하다〔연표포함 · 저작목록〕」『東洋學報』 70(3 · 4), [1989.3].

Yoshida, Mitsuo. 吉田光男. 1990. 韓 相一 (著) · 吉田光男 (譯), 「한국에 있어서의 근현대일본정치사연구의 동향과 과제 (일본사연구의 동향 – 밖에서 본 시선〈특집〉)」『歴史學研究』 (通号 607), [1990.6].

Yoshida, Mitsuo. 吉田光男. 1991. 「19세기조선에 있어서의 세곡수송선(稅穀輸送船)의 운항양상에 관한 정량분석의 시도 – 경상(慶尙) · 전라(全羅) · 충청도(忠淸道)의 경우〔含 稅穀輸送船事例一覽〕」『海事史硏究』(通号 48), [1991.6].

Yoshida, Mitsuo. 吉田光男. 1992.「한성(漢城)의 도시공간 - 근세 서울론 서설(조선도시론으로의 접근〈특집〉)」『朝鮮史硏究會論文集』(通号 30) [1992.10].

Yoshida, Mitsuo. 吉田光男. 1993.「호적(戶籍)에서 본 20세기 초 서울의 〈사람〉과 〈집〉 - 교토대학(京都大學)소장「한성부호적(漢城府戶籍)」의 기초적 분석」『朝鮮學報』(通号 147), [1993.4].

Yoshida, Mitsuo. 吉田光男. 1997. 金 東哲 (著)・吉田光男 (譯),「18세기 서울에 있어서의 방역제(坊役)의 변동과 마계(馬契)의 성립」『年報都市史硏究』(通号 5).

Yoshida, Mitsuo. 吉田光男. 1999.「고베대학(神戶大學)소장 〈개성부기장부〉의 사료적 가치」『朝鮮文化硏究』(通号 6).

Yoshida, Mitsuo. 吉田光男. 1999.「조선 근세의 왕도(王都)와 제도(帝都) (특집 수도성(首都性))」『年報都市史硏究』(通号 7).

Yoshida, Mitsuo. 吉田光男. 1999.「변화하는 조선인식 - 조선사 연구자의 딜레마 (특집 조선 - 역사적 현재)」『大航海』(通号 30), [1999.10].

Yoshida, Mitsuo. 吉田光男. 2000. 吉田光男,『조선의 역사와 사회』, 방송대학교육진흥회(放送大學敎育振興會), [2000.3](放送大學敎材).

Yoshida, Mitsuo. 吉田光男. 2000.「조선근세사족(朝鮮近世士族)의 족적(族的) 결합과「읍(邑)」공간 - 경상도(慶尙道) 단성(丹城)의 안동권씨(安東權氏)의 경우」『東洋史硏究』58(4), [2000.3].

Yoshida, Mitsuo. 吉田光男. 2001.「한국을 걷다(5) 안동(安東)의 사족(士族)」『아시아 놀면서 배우기(遊學)』(29), [2001.7].

Yoshida, Mitsuo. 吉田光男. 2002.「서울의 역사 (특집2 역사가 숨쉬는 마을・서울)」『月刊시니카』13(7) (通号 149), [2002.6].

Yosihara, Kazuo & Suzuki, Masataka. 吉原和男・鈴木正崇・末成道男(編). 2000.『〈혈연〉의 재구축 - 동아시아에 있어서의 부계출자와 동성결합』風響社.

Ysuda, Hiromi. 安田ひろみ. 1997.「한국의 여성 - 유교적 규범의 뒷면, 무당의 세계에서」綾部恒雄(編)『여자의 민족지(1) 아시아편』弘文堂.

Ysuda, Hiromi. 安田ひろみ. 1999.「한국샤머니즘의 변용과 주변문화」佐々木宏幹(編)『동아시아에 있어서의 샤머니즘문화의 구조와 변용에 관한 문화

인류학적 연구』 平成8～10年度科學研究費補助金研究成果報告書.

Ysuda, Hiromi. 安田ひろみ. 2000.「한국의 망령(亡靈)결혼의 성격에 관한 고찰」 櫻井德太郎(編)『샤머니즘과 그 주변』 第一書房.

Yu, Si-Jung. 柳時中. 1976.「식민지시대의 한국도시의 형성과 변용: 식민지초기를 중심으로」 林武(編)『발전도상국의 도시화』 111-146, 東京: 아시아經濟研究所.

Yu, Si-Jung. 柳時中. 1979.「한국의 산업화에 따른 지역사회의 변화와 문제: 구미(龜尾)지역을 중심으로(1)」『아시아經濟』 20(2): 27-41.

Yu, Si-Jung. 柳時中. 1979.「한국의 산업화에 따른 지역사회의 변화와 문제: 구미(龜尾)지역을 중심으로(2)」『아시아經濟』 20(4): 27-47.

Yu, Tong-Sik. 柳東植. 1975.『조선의 샤머니즘』 東京: 學生社.

Index

L

M

N

O

P

■ Contributors to this volume

Hyup Choi is Professor Emeritus in the Department of Anthropology at Chonnam National University. He studied anthropology at Seoul National University and received Ph.D. in anthropology from the University of Kentucky. He was Visiting Scholar at Harvard-Yenching Institute, and Fulbright Senior Research Fellow at the University of California, Berkeley and Smithsonian Institution. He has authored books such as *Agricultural Change in America*(1981), *Bushmen and Levi-Strauss*(1996), *Multi-ethnic Society, Minorities, Korean-American*(2011), *Panja-chon Diary*(2012).

Kyung-soo Chun is Professor of Anthropology at Seoul National University. He received his Ph.D. from the University of Minnesota and was Visiting Professor at National Museum of Ethnology of Japan as well as at the University of Auckland of New Zealand and Yunnan University of China. He has written numerous books and papers including *Reciprocity and Korean Society*(1984), *Dung is Resource: An Anthropologist Looks at Environment*(1992), *Vietnam Diary*(1993), *One Hundred Years of Korean Anthropology*(1999).

Abito Itoh is a graduate of The University of Tokyo receiving B.A. and M.A. in Cultural Anthropology. He served as Professor in the Department of Cultural Anthropology, Faculty of Liberal Arts and Sciences at The University of Tokyo. At present, he is Professor Emeritus. His speciality is the cultural anthropology of Korea and Japan. He was Senior Visiting Associate at School of Oriental and African Studies, University of London and Visiting Professor in the Department of Anthropology at Seoul National University. He is author of "Jar for Ancestor Spirits: Social Implications of Household in Rural Korea." in Nakane and Yanagawa, eds., *Ritual and Society*, Vol. XXII(Tokyo, 1983), and "Kinship and the consciousness of history in Korea." in Abe, Ito, and Hagiwara, eds. *Minzoku bunka no sekai*(Tokyo, 1990).

Hiroshi Honda is Professor of Korean Studies, Graduate School of Humanities and Sociology, The University of Tokyo. He graduated from Tokyo University majoring in cultural anthropology and sociology. He received Ph.D. in Cultural Anthropology from the same university. He was Visiting Scholar, Institute of Cross-Cultural Studies, Seoul National University, and Institute of Social and Cultural Anthropology, The University of Oxford. His publication on Korea includes: "Localism and Community in a Korean Rural Society", in Abito Ito and Kyung-gu Han eds., *Cross-cultural Study on Korean and Japanese Social Organizations*(2002), and *Cultural Multi-Centrality in East Asia* (co-edited with Yuko Mio),(2001).

Toshio Asakura is Professor & Director of Research Center for Cultural Resources at National Museum of Ethnology in Osaka, Japan. He studied anthropology at Musashi University and obtained Ph.D. in anthropology from Meiji University. He had conducted extensive fieldwork in Korea and published numerous books such as *Food in Korea*(1986), *Japan's Yakiniku and Korea's Sahimi*(1994), *Let's Know about Korea Q&A 115*(2000), *Representation of Korean Culture in Japan*(2000), *Korea in Globalization; Dynamic Intertwining of the Domestic and the Overseas*(2007).

Seiichi Matsumoto is Professor, Faculty of Sociology, Toyo (東洋) University of Japan. He taught at Kyung-Hee University in Korea, and was Associate Member at Joint Studies of National Museum of Ethnology of Japan. He has published extensively on Korea. Some of his works include: "Aged People and Community in Korea: Concerning the Cultural Traits and Modernization, Composite Work", *Annual Journal of the Asia-Africa Cultural Research Institute*, No.24.(1990) "Japanese Social Anthropological Studies on Korea", *Cahiers d'Extreme-Asie*, Vol.6, 1991-1992., "Age and Local Community in Japan and Korea", *The Bulletin of Faculty of Sociology*, Toyo University, No.36-2.(1999).